PRINCIPLES OF CANADIAN INCOME TAX LAW

Second Edition

by

PETER W. HOGG
Professor of Law, Osgoode Hall Law School
York University, Toronto

and

JOANNE E. MAGEE
Associate Professor of Taxation,
Atkinson College
York University, Toronto

CARSWELL

Canadian Cataloguing in Publication Data

Hogg, Peter W.
    Principles of Canadian income tax law

2nd ed.
Includes index.
ISBN 0-459-57524-4

1. Income tax – Law and legislation – Canada.
I. Magee, Joanne E.   II. Title.

KE5759.H634 1997   343.7105'2   C97-931444-5
KF6370.ZA2H6 1997

CARSWELL
Thomson Professional Publishing

One Corporate Plaza   Customer Service:
2075 Kennedy Road   Toronto: 1-416-609-3800
Scarborough, Ontario   Elsewhere in Canada/U.S.: 1-800-387-5164
M1T 3V4   Fax: 1-416-298-5094

PREFACE

This is the second edition of *Principles of Canadian Income Tax Law*. The first edition was published in 1995, and the usual pace of change in the world of income tax has necessitated a revision of the text.

The book originated as a set of lecture notes prepared by Professor Hogg for his course in Income Tax Law at the Osgoode Hall Law School of York University. The notes were handed out to students, and were revised from time to time. In order to help convert the notes into a book, Professor Hogg enlisted the aid of Professor Magee, who teaches income tax to accounting students at Atkinson College of York University. She joined the project in 1994, and participated in an extensive rewriting. The final version of the first edition was the joint product of both of us, and that is true of the second edition as well.

The book covers personal income tax, with single chapters on corporations, partnerships, and trusts. The book is designed for law students doing their first course in income tax law. It should also be useful for lawyers who need a refresher in the basic principles of personal income tax. We hope as well that it will be useful to courts, especially when they have to deal with fundamental issues, and we have been delighted that the first edition has been cited in several decisions of the Supreme Court of Canada.

As the title indicates, the emphasis of the book is on the principles of income tax law. That means the ideas of the income tax system, the policies that underlie the system, and the major features of the system. Income tax law is portrayed as a rational system. There is a reason for everything, and we always try and explain what that reason is. The law is never portrayed as a set of purposeless technicalities. The approach is not merely descriptive. Alternative ideas and policies are examined, and the provisions of the Act and the case law are evaluated critically in light of our conceptions of sound tax policy.

The book is progressive. The early chapters assume an intelligent reader who has no knowledge of tax concepts or accounting concepts, and little of commercial matters. As ideas are explained and information provided, the chapters become more demanding. The book is intended to be an aid to learning rather than a reference work. However, the detailed table of contents, the table of cases and the index should make it easy for the non-continuous reader to find what he or she is looking for.

PREFACE

We have tried to avoid the complex abstractions with which the Income Tax Act is replete. Our language is as simple, concrete and non-technical as our capability and the nature of the subject permitted. Obviously, a lot of detail is unavoidable, but the minutiae of the subject are avoided or, where they are necessary for accuracy, are relegated to footnotes. Difficult numerical examples are avoided, although simple numerical examples are used from time to time to explain a concept. The book is designed to be easy to read.

We both have the good fortune to be employed by York University, which provides an environment that both encourages and facilitates the writing of a book such as this one. Over the years, several outstanding law students have helped Professor Hogg develop the student notes that have now grown into this book. They are Elaine Franklin, LL.B. 1983, David Steele, LL.B. 1990, Kathryn Moore, LL.B. 1990, Randy Graham, LL.B. 1995 and Eliza Erskine, LL.B. 1996. In preparing the second edition, we have been helped by the reviews of the first edition that were published in the Canadian Bar Review (by Warren Grover) and the Canadian Tax Journal (by Brian Arnold), and by comments on the first edition by Bob Beam, Neil Brooks, Warren Grover, Alan Macnaughton, Lisa Phillips, Lee St. Aubin and David Spiro. We also had help with the research, writing and proofreading from Ted Cook, LL.B. 1997 and Allison Bushell, LL.B. 1998. Deanna Jubas, who is Professor Hogg's secretary, helped construct tables, and looked after the copying and assembly of the manuscript. The editing, printing and production of the book went smoothly thanks to Steven Webb, Catherine Leek, Leanne Scagnetti and Lisa Carreiro of Carswell.

Professor Hogg's spouse, Frances Hogg, was supportive, as she has been through many other similar projects; his children, having left home, no longer have to put up with him. Professor Magee thanks Professor Hogg for giving her the opportunity to work with him on the book. She also acknowledges the tremendous support which she has received from colleagues, friends and family throughout her career, particularly from her parents, Bruce and Dorothy Magee. Her deepest thanks go to her spouse, Douglas Hartkorn, for his wise counsel over the years, and to their four young daughters, for their continuing patience.

Income tax law goes out of date with distressing rapidity. We have not confined ourselves to the rules that have been enacted by Parliament, but have also examined a number of proposed rules that have not been enacted at the time of writing. We believe that the second edition is accurate up to June 30, 1997.

Toronto   Peter W. Hogg
June 30, 1997   Joanne E. Magee

Summary of Chapters

For detailed table of contents, see page vii.

Contents

CONTENTS

CONTENTS

CONTENTS

CONTENTS

CONTENTS

CONTENTS

CONTENTS

CONTENTS

CONTENTS

CONTENTS

CONTENTS

CONTENTS

CONTENTS

Table of Cases

References are to sections, not pages.

TABLE OF CASES

References are to sections, not pages.

TABLE OF CASES

References are to sections, not pages.

TABLE OF CASES

References are to sections, not pages.

TABLE OF CASES

References are to sections, not pages.

TABLE OF CASES

References are to sections, not pages.

References are to sections, not pages.

TABLE OF CASES

References are to sections, not pages.

TABLE OF CASES

References are to sections, not pages.

TABLE OF CASES

References are to sections, not pages.

TABLE OF CASES

References are to sections, not pages.

TABLE OF CASES

References are to sections, not pages.

TABLE OF CASES

References are to sections, not pages.

TABLE OF CASES

References are to sections, not pages.

1

Sources

1.1   Income Tax Act

Canadian federal income tax is imposed by the Income Tax Act,[1] which was enacted in 1971,[2] and came into force at the beginning of 1972. The Act is the principal primary source of the law.[3] The Act is amended so frequently that the only way to use it is in the form of the consolidations that are produced by commercial publishers after each set of significant amendments.[4]

---

[1] R.S.C. 1985 (5th Supp.), c. 1. Unlike other revised statutes, the Income Tax Act retains the section numbers used in the 1971 version of the Act.

[2] S.C. 1970-71-72, c. 63 (Royal Assent December 23, 1971) enacted the substance of the Act, although it did not wholly repeal the previous Act.

[3] Sherman, *Income Tax Research: A Practical Guide* (Carswell) is an excellent account of the sources of Canadian income tax law.

[4] Consolidations of the Income Tax Act, with helpful annotations, are produced by each of the two major tax publishers, namely, Carswell and CCH. These volumes also include the Income Tax Application Rules, the Income Tax Regulations and the tax treaties with the United States and the United Kingdom. Where the text of pending amendments to the Act or regulations is available, this is also generally included.

The Income Tax Act is generally subject to the same rules of statutory interpretation as other statutes.[5] It is more complex and detailed than most other statutes, but this is only a matter of degree. The style of drafting that is usual today is very specific and detailed, and is rarely reduced to broad general principles. Most of the rules of statutory interpretation have been developed by the courts, and they are set out in texts on statutory interpretation.[6] Some of the rules have been enacted into statutory form by the Interpretation Act.[7] For example, it is the Interpretation Act that stipulates that every statute "shall be given such fair, large and liberal construction and interpretation as best ensures the attainment of its objects" (s. 11); that definitions in a statute apply to all provisions of the statute unless a contrary intention appears (s. 15); that definitions in a statute also apply to regulations made under the authority of that statute (s. 16); and that when a time-limit or due date falls on a holiday, the deadline is extended to the following working day (s. 26).

The Income Tax Act relies implicitly on the general law, especially the law of contract and property. For example, the person who is liable to pay tax on income is normally the person who has the legal right to receive the income; the existence and nature of that right will depend upon the law of the province in which the income is payable. Whether a person is an employee, independent contractor, partner, agent, beneficiary of a trust or shareholder of a corporation will usually have an effect on tax liability and will turn on concepts contained in the general law, usually provincial law. A tax problem often contains issues of federal income tax law combined with issues of provincial law.

Each province also has an income tax act, and provincial income taxes are a significant impost, typically adding more than 50 per cent to an individual's tax bill. However, the federal government has entered into tax collection agreements with most provinces.[8] Under these agreements, the federal government collects the provincial tax, and, in return, the provinces agree to accept the rules of the federal Act for the measurement of income (these rules are commonly referred to as the federal "tax base"). All that each agreeing province needs to do is to set the rate of tax for its residents. Therefore, provincial income tax acts are mostly short and simple (and uninformative). With respect to the personal income tax (payable by individuals), all provinces except Quebec have entered into tax collection agreements. With respect to the corporate income tax (payable by corporations), the system is less uniform, but all provinces except Quebec, Ontario and Alberta have entered into tax collection agreements. A province that

---

[5] The interpretation of the Income Tax Act is discussed in ch. 22, Avoidance, under heading 22.3, "Role of courts", below.

[6] Côté, *The Interpretation of Legislation in Canada* (Yvon Blais, 2nd ed., 1991); Sullivan, *Driedger on the Construction of Statutes* (Butterworths, 3rd ed., 1994).

[7] R.S.C. 1985, c. I-21.

[8] The tax collection agreements are described in more detail in ch. 5, Rates, under heading 5.1, "Federal sharing of tax room", below.

has not entered into a tax collection agreement needs to define its own tax base and provide for the collection of the provincial tax by the provincial government.

1.2   Income tax application rules

A second primary source of income tax law is the Income Tax Application Rules, 1971[9] (ITARs), which were enacted in 1971, along with the present Act. They consist of transitional rules, which were needed to shift from the old Act to the new one. As time passes, the ITARs steadily lose their significance, but some of the rules are still relevant. For example, the ITARs have to be used in order to calculate a capital gain on the disposition of property that was acquired before 1972 (which was the year when capital gains first became taxable).

1.3   Income tax regulations

A third primary source of income tax law is the Income Tax Regulations, which have been made under authority conferred by s. 221 of the Act. Section 221 provides, among other things, that the Governor in Council may make regulations "prescribing anything that, by this Act, is to be prescribed or is to be determined or regulated by regulation". The Act makes frequent reference to "prescribed forms", "prescribed amounts", and so on. The word "prescribed" is the signal to look for a regulation. The sections of the Income Tax Act in the commercial consolidations are annotated with references to any applicable regulation, and the full text of the Income Tax Regulations is consolidated and published in the commercial consolidations.[10]

The Income Tax Regulations contain much of the detail of income tax law. As regulations, they are made by cabinet (the Governor in Council). Since they do not have to be enacted by Parliament, they can be changed much more easily than the Act. However, they have the same force of law as the Act itself.

1.4   Tax treaties

A fourth primary source of income tax law is the tax treaty. Canada has entered into a tax treaty (or convention) with each of more than 50 countries, tax haven countries being the major exceptions. The most important treaty is that with the United States; the current treaty was signed in 1980 and came into effect in 1984. Under Canadian constitutional law, a treaty does not have the force of law unless and until it is implemented by legislation. After each treaty has been ratified by both countries, the Canadian Parliament implements the treaty by enacting a short statute which provides that the treaty has the force of

---

[9] R.S.C. 1985 (5th Supp.), c. 2.

[10] Note 4, above.

law in Canada; the full text of the treaty is appended to the statute as a schedule.[11]

The purpose of each tax treaty is to avoid double taxation and to make some other provisions with respect to taxpayers who have income or residential ties in both treaty countries.[12] Each treaty makes some changes to the Income Tax Act in its application to taxpayers covered by the treaty. For that reason, each implementing statute gives the treaty primacy over the Act by providing that in the event of inconsistency between the treaty and any other law the terms of the treaty are to prevail.

1.5   Tax cases

A fifth primary source of income tax law is cases. The procedure by which disputes between Revenue Canada and taxpayers enter the court system is discussed in the next chapter.[13] The decisions of the courts in tax cases are reported in two series of law reports: Canada Tax Cases (C.T.C.), published by Carswell,[14] and Dominion Tax Cases (D.T.C.), published by CCH.[15] These two series of reports cover not only the Supreme Court of Canada and the Federal Court of Canada (and its predecessor, the Exchequer Court of Canada, 1917-1971), but also the Tax Court of Canada (and its predecessors, the Tax Review Board 1972-1983, the Tax Appeal Board, 1958-1971, and the Income Tax Appeals Board, 1949-1958).[16] In tax writing, it is customary to cite these two series of reports, even when the case is reported in a more official series, such as the Supreme Court Reports (S.C.R.) or the Federal Court Reports (F.C.).

Many of the provisions of the Act have never been the subject of any judicial decision. However, there are topics upon which the Act is silent or incomplete or unclear and which have given rise to many judicial decisions. The most frequently litigated issues include:

---

[11] E.g., Canada-United States Tax Convention Act, 1984, S.C. 1984, c. 20.

[12] The tax treaties are discussed in more detail in ch. 8, Residence, under heading 8.5(c), "Tax treaties", below.

[13] Chapter 2, Process, under headings 2.5, "Collection procedure", and 2.6, "Criminal prosecutions", below.

[14] Until 1971, De Boo (which later became part of Carswell) also published Tax Appeal Board Cases (Tax A.B.C.), which was a separate series of reports of decisions of the Income Tax Appeals Board (1949-1958) and the Tax Appeal Board (1958-1971). In 1971, the decisions of the Tax Review Board, which replaced the Tax Appeal Board in that year, were included in the C.T.C. series. In 1983, when the Tax Court of Canada replaced the Tax Review Board, the decisions of the Tax Court of Canada were also included in the C.T.C. series.

[15] Note the peculiar form of citation of the Dominion Tax Cases. Although each volume is numbered, the number is not used in the citation. Each volume is identified by the last two numbers of the year. Thus, volume 47 for 1993 is cited as 93 D.T.C.

[16] For a list of the tax reports from the United States, the United Kingdom, Australia and New Zealand, see Sherman, note 3, above, Part V.

- whether a person is a resident of Canada;
- whether income is from employment or from a business;
- whether a profit on the sale of property is a capital gain or income from a business;
- whether certain types of expenses are deductible from income;
- whether losses from farming or from unprofitable ventures are fully deductible from other income; and
- whether generally accepted accounting principles apply to the computation of income from a business.

1.6 Revenue Canada publications

The Department of National Revenue (Revenue Canada), which is responsible for the collection of income tax, issues the forms and guides that are necessary to prepare an income tax return. The Department also issues information circulars, interpretation bulletins and advance tax rulings, which cumulatively constitute an extensive and valuable commentary on the law. Aside from some of the forms, which are prescribed by regulation, these publications do not have the force of law, but they are exceptionally reliable secondary sources of the law. These and other Revenue Canada publications are described in more detail in the next chapter.[17]

1.7 Private publications

The need to keep abreast of a rapidly-changing, complex body of law is met by a variety of private publications.[18] The most important are the multi-volume, looseleaf services, of which there are several examples. The two most popular services are published by Carswell (formerly De Boo), *Canada Tax Service* (14 volumes) and CCH, *Canadian Tax Reporter* (ten volumes), and take the form of a commentary on each provision of the Act. These services are updated frequently — weekly in some cases.[19] They also contain information circulars, interpretation bulletins, published advance tax rulings and other government publications. Other commercial services, such as CCH's *Window on Canadian Tax*, focus on Revenue Canada's pronouncements and practices in administering the Act.

---

[17] Chapter 2, Process, under heading 2.3, "Department of National Revenue", below.

[18] There is excellent bibliographic information in Sherman, note 3, above.

[19] There are also several electronic tax services available on compact disk, such as those published by Carswell and CCH. The Canadian Institute of Chartered Accountants also publishes an electronic tax service on compact disk as part of their Virtual Professional Library. These electronic services are generally updated on a monthly basis.

Moving from the looseleaf services to bound books, the Canadian literature on tax is vast. There are casebooks designed for law students,[20] textbooks designed for law students (and practitioners),[21] textbooks designed for accounting students (and practitioners)[22] and books on tax policy.[23] As well, many books have been written to assist in the preparation of tax returns, and there are many monographs on specialized aspects of income tax law and policy.[24] The speed with which the law changes makes any bound text unreliable. Most texts are frequently revised, some of them annually, but the date of the edition should always be noted before a book is consulted.

The Canadian Tax Foundation is an independent tax research organization, which publishes a great deal of material, including many specialized monographs. Its regular publications include the *Canadian Tax Journal*, which is published every two months, and the *Conference Report*, which is the record of the proceedings of the Foundation's annual national tax conference.[25] Some tax writing appears in non-tax journals, but the great bulk of Canadian writing on tax appears in the *Canadian Tax Journal* and in the records of the Canadian Tax Foundation's conferences. The contributors are by no means only lawyers. Accountants and economists do much of the writing. The different perspectives of lawyers, accountants and economists make for a rich, interdisciplinary literature, especially on issues of policy.

---

[20] E.g., Arnold, Edgar, Li and Sandler, *Materials on Canadian Income Tax* (Carswell); Arnold, McNair and Young, *Taxation of Corporations and Shareholders* (Carswell); Cullity, Brown and Rajan, *Taxation and Estate Planning* (Carswell). [Dates and editions have been omitted, because they change so frequently.]

[21] E.g., Harris, *Canadian Income Taxation* (Butterworths); Krishna, *The Fundamentals of Canadian Income Tax* (Carswell); Rand and Stitt, *Understanding the Income Tax Act* (Carswell); Sherman, *Basic Income Tax Law*, (Law Society of Upper Canada) (transcript of computer-assisted instruction course); Sherman, *Income Tax Research: A Practical Guide* (Carswell). [Dates and editions have been omitted, because they change so frequently.]

[22] E.g., Beam and Laiken, *Introduction to Federal Income Taxation in Canada* (CCH); Buckwold, *Canadian Income Taxation: Planning and Decision Making* (McGraw-Hill Ryerson); Byrd, Chen and Jacobs, *Canadian Tax Principles* (Prentice-Hall); Denhamer, *Taxation in Canada* (Irwin); Hoey and Zimmerman, *Tax Principles to Remember* (Can. Institute of Chartered Accountants); Huot, *Understanding Income Tax* (Carswell); Thornton, *Managerial Tax Planning: A Canadian Perspective* (Wiley). [Most of these books are revised annually.]

[23] E.g., Boadway and Kitchen, *Canadian Tax Policy* (Can. Tax Foundation, 2nd ed., 1984); Salyzyn, *Canadian Income Tax Policy* (CCH, 4th ed., 1990); Brooks (ed.), *The Quest for Tax Reform* (Carswell, 1988); Ontario Fair Tax Commission, *Fair Taxation in a Changing World* (U. Toronto Press, 1993).

[24] For a critical account of the academic writing, see Brooks, "Future Directions in Canadian Tax Law Scholarship" (1985) 23 *Osgoode Hall L.J.* 441.

[25] The Canadian Tax Foundation also holds a Corporate Management Tax Conference as well as several regional conferences each year and publishes a monthly feature called "Canadian Tax Highlights". The Foundation has an excellent library in Toronto which is open to the general public. The Foundation also has a website, http://www.ctf.ca.

2

Process

2.1   Departmental responsibilities for taxation

There are three federal government departments involved in the income tax process: the Department of Finance, which is responsible for tax policy, the Department of National Revenue (Revenue Canada), which is responsible for tax collection, and the Department of Justice, which is responsible for tax litigation.

2.2   Department of Finance

(a)   Tax policy

The Department of Finance is responsible for tax policy, which includes amendments to the Income Tax Act. Amendments are formulated in the Department of Finance, and introduced into Parliament by the Minister of Finance. These amendments are not necessarily announced in the Minister's annual budget. Recent practice has been for the Minister to introduce a separate technical bill at least once a year dealing with technical deficiencies in the Act and areas of perceived abuse. Press releases sometimes announce changes to the Act when a single area is being targeted and there is a need for immediate action. Sometimes these technical changes are significant changes of policy, but, for the most part, they deal with particular fact situations and small numbers of taxpayers. It is usually the budget that is the source of major policy initiatives and substantive changes to the Act.[1]

(b)   Budget

The Minister of Finance presents a budget to Parliament each year, usually in February. The budget provides an estimate of the government's revenues and expenditures for the next financial year, which starts on April 1. Because of the significance of income taxes for the revenue side, the budget usually proposes a set of changes to the Income Tax Act. These proposals, along with the rest of the budget, are held in strict secrecy until the date of the Minister's presentation of the budget to Parliament. The reason for secrecy is to prevent taxpayers from anticipating the changes and taking avoidance measures or otherwise profiting from the proposals. When the budget is presented, the changes in the Income Tax Act are normally proposed to be effective from the date of the budget, so that taxpayers have no incentive to take avoidance measures during the hiatus between the date of the budget and the date of the enactment of implementing legislation. Then, when the legislation is enacted, most of the changes are made retroactive to the date of the budget.

---

[1] Much of the material published by the Department of Finance can be obtained without charge and is also available on the Internet at the Department's website, http://www.fin.gc.ca.

(c)   Legislative process

A "notice of ways and means motion to amend the Income Tax Act" is prepared by the Department of Finance. It lists and describes all of the amendments to the Act that have been proposed. The notice of ways and means motion is followed by legislation in draft form and, since 1983, the Department of Finance has followed the practice of issuing "explanatory notes" or "technical notes" to accompany the draft legislation. This material is helpful in explaining the purpose of amendments that are often exceedingly difficult (even for tax professionals) to understand on their own. The purpose of issuing the legislation initially in draft form is to provide an opportunity for the tax community to comment on the legislation, and commentary is in fact received and does in fact lead to changes in the legislation.

Eventually, a bill amending the Act is introduced into the House of Commons by the Minister of Finance. That bill then follows the normal legislative process, which includes scrutiny by standing committees of both the House of Commons and the Senate, and in due course the bill is enacted into law. As mentioned earlier, the amending Act will usually make many of its provisions retroactive to the date when the changes were first publicly announced in the budget (or elsewhere).[2] The time elapsed from the date of the budget (or other announcement) to the date of enactment is sometimes more than a year, in which case the tax proposals of one budget will not be implemented by the time of the next budget, 12 months later. When amendments that are proposed to be retroactive to the date of the budget have not been enacted by the time that the income tax return forms have to be printed, the proposed changes are simply incorporated into the forms on the (normally safe) assumption that the changes will eventually be enacted and will be retroactive. The taxpayer is, of course, not legally bound to comply with amendments that have not been enacted by the time that he or she files a return, but compliance is the course of prudence that is followed by nearly all taxpayers.

(d)   Regulations

Income Tax Regulations are also prepared by officials in the Department of Finance. They are made by the cabinet (the Governor in Council), under the authority conferred by s. 221 of the Income Tax Act. They generally deal with matters of detail, and are not usually announced in the budget. Sometimes,

---

[2] Occasionally, an amendment is made retroactive to a date prior to the announcement date, e.g., proposed s. 10(1.01), which was announced on December 20, 1995 as the legislative response to *Friesen v. Can.* [1995] 2 C.T.C. 369, 95 D.T.C. 5551 (S.C.C.) and proposed amendment to s. 227, which was announced on April 7, 1997 as the legislative response to *Royal Bank of Can.* v. *Sparrow Electric Corp.*, [1997] 1 S.C.R. 411, 97 D.T.C. 5089 (S.C.C.). Although it is generally accepted that it is unfair to apply a new law to transactions that were complete by the time of the announcement of the law, Parliament probably has the authority to do so: *Huet v. Can.* [1995] 1 C.T.C. 367, 95 D.T.C. 5008 (F.C.T.D.).

however, new regulations are issued in advance in draft form to provide an opportunity for public comment.

(e)   Provinces

Each province follows a budget process essentially similar to the federal process. In the budget, the Minister of Finance (or Treasurer) of the province will propose changes to provincial taxes, including the income tax. However, as explained above,[3] in those provinces that have entered into income tax collection agreements with the federal government, the Minister of Finance is mainly confined to proposing the rate of provincial income tax: the province has agreed to accept the federal Act on other aspects of tax policy.

2.3   Department of National Revenue

(a)   Tax collection

The Department of National Revenue (known as Revenue Canada)[4] is responsible for the administration of the Income Tax Act. This involves the collection of tax through the system of tax returns, assessments, source deductions, refunds, audits and enforcement. The Act itself always describes its administrator as "the Minister", which is defined as the Minister of National Revenue (s. 248(1)), but, in practice, of course, nearly all of the Minister's functions are performed by officials in the Department.

(b)   Organization

The Department of National Revenue has its headquarters in Ottawa. The headquarters develops policies for the department in all its areas of activity; it issues information circulars, interpretation bulletins and advance tax rulings (to be described shortly); and it deals with some individual files that are in the appeal process.

The Department has several taxation centres, which are controlled by six regional offices. Taxpayers send their returns, not to the headquarters in Ottawa, but to the nearest taxation centre. The taxation centres process the returns and issue notices of assessment; when the process is complete, the taxation centres store the files.

There are more than 30 tax service offices (district offices), also controlled by the six regional offices. The tax service offices are responsible for dealing with the public. They issue forms and other publications, and they answer telephone and over-the-counter enquiries from taxpayers. The tax service

---

[3] Chapter 1, Sources, under heading 1.1, "Income Tax Act", above. The tax collection agreements are described in more detail in ch. 5, Rates, under heading 5.1, "Federal sharing of tax room", below.

[4] The full name is Revenue Canada–Customs, Excise and Taxation.

offices also handle enforcement activities, such as auditing, collections, special investigations and the initiation of prosecutions.

(c) Information Circulars

Revenue Canada issues Information Circulars (ICs), which are designed to provide information on tax matters to the general public. They are couched in non-technical language, and they cover the Department's organization and procedures, and other information that is useful to lay people.[5] The first information circular, issued in 1970, announced the Department's programme of issuing information circulars and interpretation bulletins.[6] The circulars are available from Revenue Canada's tax service offices (district offices) or by subscription. They are also available on the Internet at Revenue Canada's website (http://www.rc.gc.ca), and they are reproduced in the commercial tax services.

(d) Interpretation Bulletins

Revenue Canada also issues Interpretation Bulletins (ITs) which explain the Department's interpretations of many of the provisions of the Act. Unlike information circulars, which are directed to the general public, interpretation bulletins are directed to lawyers, accountants and other specialists, and they deal with much complex and difficult law. Both publications were inaugurated in 1970,[7] and several hundred circulars and bulletins have been issued, constituting an exceedingly valuable account of much taxation law and practice. Like the information circulars, the interpretation bulletins may be obtained from Revenue Canada's tax service offices (district offices) or by subscription. They are also available on the Internet at Revenue Canada's website (http://www.rc.gc.ca), and they are reproduced in the commercial tax services.

Needless to say, the policy of the Department is to assess in accordance with the legal opinions expressed in its interpretation bulletins. The interpretation bulletins are kept up to date with amendments to the Act or judicial decisions by the issuance of revised versions, and many bulletins have been revised several times. Sometimes, the Department will change its collective mind about the correct interpretation of a provision, and that will usually prompt the issue of a new or revised bulletin, which will include a date upon which the new

---

[5] A notable exception is Information Circular 88-2, "General anti-avoidance rule" (1988), which explains Revenue Canada's policy with respect to the general anti-avoidance rule (GAAR) (s. 245). This is a detailed commentary on the law that is primarily addressed to tax specialists.

[6] Information Circular 70-1, "Information Circulars and Interpretation Bulletins" (1970).

[7] *Ibid.*

interpretation is to become effective.[8] In practice, the taxpayer is usually safe in relying upon a legal opinion in an interpretation bulletin as being an accurate and up-to-date account of the Department's view of the law. However, the interpretation bulletins are not like regulations, which are authorized by the Act, and which accordingly have the force of law. The Act is silent about interpretation bulletins (and information circulars) and it is clear that they do not have the force of law. The courts have looked at the bulletins as a persuasive aid to interpretation,[9] but the courts are not bound by the Department's opinions, and do not always follow them.[10]

Even the Department itself is not bound to follow its own interpretation bulletins, although it nearly always does so. It is well established that the doctrine of estoppel does not preclude the department from issuing an assessment that is inconsistent with a previously published statement, or with a previous assessment, even when the taxpayer has relied upon the Department's opinions as to the legal position.[11] In the rare case where the Department departs from its own interpretation bulletin in assessing a return, the court will uphold the assessment if it concludes that the assessment is correct in law, notwithstanding the inconsistent interpretation bulletin.[12] In *Stickel* v. *M.N.R.* (1973),[13] the Minister had assessed the taxpayer on a basis that contradicted the applicable interpretation bulletin, upon which the taxpayer had relied. The Federal Court - Trial Division rejected the taxpayer's argument that the Crown was estopped, and upheld the assessment.[14] On appeal, the Federal Court of Canada reversed, not on the ground of estoppel, but on the ground that the interpretation bulletin, not the assessment, was the correct interpretation of the law.[15]

---

[8] Sometimes changes in Revenue Canada's interpretations are announced at a public conference (such as the Canadian Tax Foundation's annual conference) or in Revenue Canada's Income Tax Technical News, which is published on an ad hoc basis. Interpretations published in Income Tax Technical News carry the same weight as those in the Interpretation Bulletins: Information Circular 70-6R3, "Advance Income Tax Rulings" (1996), para. 27. Like information circulars and interpretation bulletins, Income Tax Technical News may be obtained from Revenue Canada's tax service offices or by subscription. It is also available on the internet at Revenue Canada's website (http://www.rc.gc.ca), and is reproduced in the commercial tax services.

[9] E.g., *Nowegijick* v. *The Queen*, [1983] C.T.C. 20, 24, 83 D.T.C. 5041, 5044 (S.C.C.).

[10] E.g., *Southside Car Market* v. *The Queen*, [1982] C.T.C. 214, 82 D.T.C. 6179 (F.C.T.D.).

[11] *Liberty & Co.* v. *C.I.R.* (1924), 12 T.C. 630, 639; *Woon* v. *M.N.R.*, [1950] C.T.C. 263, 4 D.T.C. 871 (Ex. Ct.); *M.N.R.* v. *Inland Industries*, [1972] C.T.C. 27, 72 D.T.C. 6013 (S.C.C.); *Gibbon* v. *The Queen*, [1977] C.T.C. 334, 77 D.T.C. 5193 (F.C.T.D.).

[12] E.g., *74712 Alberta* v. *The Queen*, [1994] 2 C.T.C. 191, 94 D.T.C. 6392 (F.C.T.D.).

[13] [1973] C.T.C. 202, 73 D.T.C. 5178 (F.C.A.); affd. [1974] C.T.C. 416, 74 D.T.C. 6268 (S.C.C.).

[14] [1972] C.T.C. 210, 72 D.T.C. 6178 (F.C.T.D.).

[15] See generally Quigley, "Estoppel against the Crown: Selected Problems in the Tax Context", LL.M. thesis, McGill University, 1982, ch. 7, parts (ii), (iii).

(e) Advance Income Tax Rulings

In addition to information circulars and interpretation bulletins, Revenue Canada also issues Advance Income Tax Rulings. An advance income tax ruling is issued at the request of a taxpayer, who pays a fee for the service, and the ruling will explain to the taxpayer how the Department will assess a transaction that is contemplated by the taxpayer.[16] In that way, the taxpayer obtains a secure opinion as the precise tax consequences of a proposed transaction. If the tax consequences are sufficiently unfavourable, the transaction might be able to be abandoned; sometimes, a restructuring is possible to avoid some of the bad consequences. In any event, it is always helpful to be aware of the tax consequences before a transaction is consummated.

The formal procedure of issuing advance income tax rulings was started in 1970, although informal rulings were sometimes given before then. In *Woon* v. *M.N.R.* (1950),[17] the taxpayer had obtained an informal ruling as to the tax consequence of a dividend-stripping scheme. In reliance on the ruling, the taxpayer carried out the scheme, but the Minister assessed him for a tax liability far in excess of that stipulated in the ruling. The Court held that the assessment was correct in law, and that the Minister could not be estopped by the earlier ruling from applying the law correctly.

At the inception of the formal advance income tax ruling programme in 1970, the Department announced that an advance income tax ruling "will be regarded as binding on the Department",[18] and there seem to have been no instances where the Department has not followed a ruling.[19] However, in the unlikely event that the Department did decide to assess a taxpayer in violation of a ruling, the *Woon* case probably states the legal position: the Department would not be estopped by its ruling. It would be desirable for the Act to recognize the advance income tax rulings programme, and to provide that the rulings are binding.

The Department releases all of the advance income tax rulings in "severed form", that is, with names and other details omitted to preserve the anonymity of the taxpayer.[20] These rulings are reproduced in the commercial tax services and are available in electronic form on Revenue Canada's Legislation Access

[16] The details of the Department's policy respecting advance rulings, including the procedure for obtaining rulings, are set out in Information Circular 70-6R3, "Advance Income Tax Rulings" (1996).

[17] [1950] C.T.C. 263, 4 D.T.C. 871 (Ex. Ct.).

[18] Information Circular 70-6R3, para. 6.

[19] Some special situations are contemplated by Information Circular 70-6R3, paras. 10-14, such as misrepresentation of the applicable facts or amendment of the applicable law.

[20] The policy with respect to publication is described in Information Circular 70-6R3, paras. 16(m), 21, 24-25 and Appendix A.

Database (LAD), which is available for public viewing in the tax services offices. Taxpayers have to exercise caution in relying on published rulings, even if the facts of a particular ruling appear to be identical to a taxpayer's situation. It must be remembered that material facts may have been severed from the published version. Also, the Department's view of the law may have changed since the ruling was given.[21]

2.4   Department of Justice

The Department of Justice is responsible for providing legal advice to other departments of the government, and for conducting litigation on behalf of the government. Lawyers providing legal services within the Department of Finance or the Department of National Revenue will generally be employees of the Department of Justice, not the Department in which they are physically located. Litigation in the Tax Court, Federal Court and Supreme Court of Canada on behalf of the Department of National Revenue is conducted by counsel in the Tax Law section of the Department of Justice, which is located in the head office and each of the regional offices of the Department of Justice. Prosecutions of tax evaders in the provincial courts are conducted by criminal prosecutions counsel in the head or regional offices of the Department of Justice or by private lawyers employed as agents by the Department of Justice.

2.5   Collection procedure

(a)   Tax return

We have already noticed that the collection of tax is the responsibility of the Department of National Revenue (Revenue Canada). The process of collection is started by the filing of a return by the taxpayer. The Act, by s. 150(1), requires that every individual who is liable to pay tax in a particular taxation year must file a tax return for that year. In most cases, the obligation to file a return applies only if the individual has received enough income to become liable to pay tax.[22] However, the Minister has the power, under s. 150(2), to

---

[21] Revenue Canada will also provide, at a taxpayer's request, a written "technical interpretation", explaining how the Department would assess a contemplated transaction: see Information Circular 70-6R3, paras. 22-23, 28-31. This is an alternative to an advance ruling. A technical interpretation differs from an advance ruling in that it can be requested without identifying the taxpayer, no fee is charged by the Department, and the Department does not undertake to be bound by its interpretation. Technical interpretations are not published by the Department, but the commercial tax services publish many of the more important technical interpretations (which they obtain under the Access to Information Act).

[22] Subsection 150(1) also requires taxpayers who do not owe tax but who have disposed of capital property during the year or who have capital gains to file a return. This requirement was introduced in 1985 at the same time as the lifetime capital gains exemption (s. 110.6). The purpose of the change was to enable Revenue Canada to keep track of a taxpayer's capital gains even in situations where no tax was owing because of the claiming of the exemption. Since 1994, the

demand the filing of a return by an individual who is not liable to pay tax. Corporations are required to file returns whether or not they are liable to pay tax (s. 150(1)). The Act sets the deadlines by which filing must be accomplished. In the case of individuals, the general rule is that the return for a particular taxation year must be filed by April 30 of the next year (s. 150(1)(d)).[23]

The return is in a form prescribed by the Minister. It not only requires the reporting of all relevant income and expenses with supporting documentation, it also requires the taxpayer to estimate the amount of tax payable (s. 151), and payment of the tax must accompany the filing of the return (s. 156.1(4)).

The return is filed by mailing it to the taxation centre for the region in which the taxpayer lives. It is also possible to file electronically (E-file) (s. 150.1), and each year several million returns are in fact E-filed.

(b) Payment

We have noticed that payment of unpaid tax must accompany an individual's income tax return. We shall see later that an assessment by the Minister also generates an obligation to pay the unpaid part of the amount assessed. The Act and regulations also contain rules for the withholding of tax at source from employment income (and some other types of income), and for the payment of tax by instalments during the taxation year. The rules regarding withholding and payment are closely linked to the concept of the "taxation year", which is the topic of chapter 6, below. Accordingly, detailed discussion of payment of tax is put off until that chapter.

(c) Assessment

The Minister is required by s. 152(1) to assess the tax payable by the taxpayer. This task must be accomplished "with all due dispatch" (s. 152(1)).[24]

---

lifetime exemption has applied only to farming property and small business corporation shares. There seems no point in reporting other capital gains if the taxpayer is not liable to pay any tax. However, the requirement has not been repealed.

[23] The concept of the taxation year is examined in ch. 6, Taxation Year, below. The position of individuals, corporations and trusts with respect to filing deadlines is more fully explained there.

[24] The courts have given a flexible meaning to the phrase "with all due dispatch", defining it as meaning no more than a reasonable period in all the circumstances. With this definition, the courts have accepted as valid assessments issued after quite lengthy delays: e.g., *Hutterian Brethren Church of Wilson* v. *R.*, [1979] C.T.C. 1, 79 D.T.C. 5042 (F.C.T.D.) (15 months); *Lipsey* v. *M.N.R.*, [1984] C.T.C. 675, 84 D.T.C. 6192 (F.C.T.D.) (2 years); *Weih* v. *M.N.R.*, [1988] 2 C.T.C. 2013, 88 D.T.C. 1379 (T.C.C.) (15 months). However, the limits of tolerance were exceeded by a six-year delay in *J. Stollar Construction* v. *M.N.R.*, [1989] 1 C.T.C. 2171, 89 D.T.C. 134 (T.C.C.); in that case the court vacated the assessment. An assessment will not be vacated for failure to assess with all due dispatch unless the taxpayer goes through the objection and appeal process described under headings 2.5(g) and 2.5(h), below: *The Queen* v. *Ginsberg*, [1996] 3 C.T.C. 63, 96 D.T.C. 6372 (F.C.A.).

When the return is received at the taxation centre (whether by mail or electronically) the process of assessment takes place. The return is checked by officials at the taxation centre to see that the arithmetic is correct, that all required documentation has been supplied, and that the return is, on its face, otherwise in order. This process may involve obtaining more information from the taxpayer, and may result in additions to or subtractions from the income reported by the taxpayer. When the process is complete, the taxation centre issues a notice of assessment which is mailed to the taxpayer demanding payment of any tax still owing. That tax must be paid "forthwith" (s. 158). If tax has been overpaid, a refund cheque is mailed to the taxpayer.[25]

The assessment will include interest on overdue taxes (ss. 152, 161). The "prescribed rate" of interest is set quarterly, and consists of the average yield on 90-day treasury bills sold in the first month of the previous quarter, rounded up to the nearest percentage point, plus four percentage points (reg. 4301). The prescribed rate of interest that is paid by the Department on refunds of overpaid taxes is the same treasury-bill rate plus two (instead of four) percentage points (reg. 4301).

(d)   Examination

Because the review of tax returns by the taxation centre is only a limited one, a more thorough examination of some returns is conducted by the taxation centre after the notices of assessment have been issued. That examination takes place within the centre and involves cross-checking the information provided by related taxpayers, for example, employers and employees, companies and shareholders, lenders and borrowers, and the like.

(e)   Audit

A small number of returns are selected for "audit" by the district offices. The audit programme is mainly directed at those categories of taxpayers who are most likely to have under-reported their income. Wage and salary earners, who comprise about 80 per cent of the taxpaying population, are rarely audited. Their taxes are deducted at source and their income is readily cross-checked against information in returns filed by employers. Taxpayers who have sources of income other than salary or wages, such as self-employed individuals, corporations and trusts, are the most likely candidates for audit, but less than 5 per cent of the returns in these categories are in fact audited each year. An audit

---

[25] The notification by the Minister that no tax is payable is sometimes described as a "nil assessment". It is not, however, technically, an "assessment", and this carries the important consequence that no objection can be made and no appeal can be brought from any of the Minister's determinations: *Okalta Oils* v. *M.N.R.*, [1955] C.T.C. 271, 55 D.T.C. 1176 (S.C.C.); *R.* v. *Garry Bowl*, [1974] C.T.C. 457, 74 D.T.C. 6401 (F.C.A.).

usually occurs at the taxpayer's place of business, where the Department's auditor will inspect the books and records kept by the taxpayer.

The power of the auditor to inspect the books and records of the taxpayer is contained in s. 231.1(1), which also permits the auditor to enter business premises without a warrant and requires the owner or manager of the premises to provide "all reasonable assistance" and to answer "all proper questions". Entry to a dwelling-house without the consent of the occupant requires a warrant issued by a judge (s. 231.1(3)). Section 231.2 empowers the Minister to demand information or documents from the taxpayer and from others.

When the audit is complete, the Department may reassess the taxpayer in light of the auditor's findings. Most audits do result in an upward adjustment of the taxpayer's tax liability.

(f) Reassessment

An examination or audit, which has been conducted after the original assessment, may lead the Minister to reassess the taxpayer. A taxpayer may also seek reassessment. For example, after receiving the notice of assessment, the taxpayer may discover that he or she omitted some reportable item, in which case he or she should write to the taxation centre seeking an adjustment of the tax payable. Another example is where a taxpayer in a later year incurs a loss that under the Act's loss carryover rules can be carried back and deducted from the income of an earlier year. In that case, the taxpayer should file the prescribed form to claim the loss carryback, which of course involves the reassessment of the tax for the earlier year.

The Act confers on the Minister the power to reassess a return that has already been assessed, but imposes limits on the power. The rules are established by s. 152(4). The general rule for individual taxpayers is that a reassessment must be made within three years of the date of mailing of the original assessment (or notification that no tax is payable). This time limit may be waived by the taxpayer by filing a prescribed form of waiver within the normal reassessment period, in which case the Minister can reassess at any time. The taxpayer might wish to file a waiver in order to obtain time to produce more information, for example. If the taxpayer fails to file a waiver within the normal period of reassessment for a given taxation year, the Minister is powerless to reassess the taxpayer's return for that year once the normal reassessment period of three years has elapsed.[26] Where no waiver has been filed, it is only in cases of misrepresentation or fraud that the Minister can reassess beyond the prescribed period.[27]

---

[26] *The Queen* v. *Canadian Marconi Co.*, [1991] 2 C.T.C. 352, 91 D.T.C. 5626 (F.C.A.).

[27] The Minister does, however, have power to refund an overpayment of tax after the expiry of the three-year deadline (s. 164(1.5)).

A reassessment will, of course, include interest on overdue taxes (ss. 152, 161). It will also include the civil penalties provided by ss. 162 and 163[28] if the Minister concludes that a breach of the Act has been committed by the taxpayer.

(g)   Objection

A taxpayer who disagrees with a notice of assessment should initially contact the nearest district office of Revenue Canada for an explanation. Many disputes of a minor nature are resolved informally by the district office without recourse to the formal process of objection.

The formal means of initiating an appeal from an assessment (or reassessment) is by serving a notice of objection on the Minister. The deadline is the later of one year after the filing-due date (which for most individuals is April 30 following the relevant taxation year) and 90 days from the mailing of the notice of assessment (s. 165(1)). The Minister has a discretion to extend the deadline (s. 166.2(1)). There is no prescribed form of notice of objection, but the Act provides that the taxpayer must set out in the form "the reasons for the objection and all relevant facts" (s. 165(1)). The notice of objection is served by mailing it or delivering it to the chief of appeals in a district office or a taxation centre (s. 165(2)). The taxpayer will be contacted and given an opportunity to make representations during this process. At the end of the process, the Minister will decide whether to confirm or vary or vacate the assessment, and will notify the taxpayer of the decision.

(h)   Appeal

If the taxpayer is unhappy with the Minister's decision on the notice of objection, the taxpayer has a right of appeal. All appeals lie to the Tax Court of Canada, which is a federal court established for the purpose of hearing tax appeals. (The Court replaced the Tax Review Board in 1983, which in turn replaced the Tax Appeal Board in 1971.) Taxpayers have 90 days from the day of mailing of the notification of the Minister's decision on the notice of objection to appeal to the Tax Court of Canada.

There are two alternative procedures for appeals heard by the Tax Court of Canada.[29] The first is an "informal procedure", which can be elected by the taxpayer for cases where the amount of federal tax and penalties in issue is no more than $12,000, or the amount of loss in issue is no more than $24,000, or where only interest is in issue. Under the informal procedure, the taxpayer may appear in person or be represented by an agent who need not be a lawyer; no special form of pleadings or other formalities is required; the Court is not bound by technical rules of evidence; costs may not be awarded against the taxpayer;

---

[28] See description under heading 2.6(b), "Civil penalties", below.

[29] See McMechan and Bourgard, *Tax Court Practice* (Carswell, 1995).

and (unless there are exceptional circumstances) judgment must be rendered within 60 days. However, the decision of the Court under the informal procedure is final: there is no further right of appeal.[30]

The other procedure for an appeal to the Tax Court of Canada is the "general procedure". This procedure is to be used for cases where the amount of federal tax and penalties in issue is more than $12,000 or the amount of loss in issue is more than $24,000. The general procedure also applies in cases where the amount of tax or loss in issue is less than the prescribed amounts but the taxpayer has not elected for the informal procedure. Under the general procedure, a taxpayer may not be represented by a non-lawyer; the proceedings are more formal; costs may be awarded against the taxpayer; and there is no time-limit on the rendering of judgment. The decision of the Court under the general procedure is subject to appeal to the Federal Court of Appeal, and from there (with leave) to the Supreme Court of Canada.

The foregoing appeal procedures apply only to those cases that originate as an objection by a taxpayer to an assessment. Prosecutions of taxpayers who are alleged to have evaded tax in violation of the penal provisions of the Act are a different matter entirely. Neither the Tax Court nor the Federal Court has jurisdiction over criminal matters. Prosecutions occur in the courts of the provinces in accordance with the procedure laid down by the Criminal Code. Prosecutions are discussed later in this chapter.

(i)   Burden of proof

When the taxpayer appeals to the Tax Court of Canada, there is a trial in which both sides adduce evidence on issues of fact and make submissions on issues of law. It has been held by the Supreme Court of Canada in *Johnston* v. *M.N.R.* (1948)[31] that the burden of proof lies on the taxpayer to establish that the factual findings[32] upon which the Minister based the assessment were wrong. In that case, the Minister's position that the taxpayer did not support his wife was sustained on the ground that the taxpayer had not discharged the onus of proving that he did support his wife. A variety of reasons have been suggested for imposing the burden of proof on the taxpayer. One is the text of what is now s. 152(8) of the Act, which provides, rather cryptically, that an assessment is "deemed to be valid and binding notwithstanding any error, defect or omission in the assessment". A second reason is that the taxpayer is the appellant, who ought to affirmatively establish the propositions upon which he or she relies. A

---

[30] The Court's decision is, however, subject to judicial review by the Federal Court of Appeal under s. 28 of the Federal Court Act, which permits review of the decisions of federal tribunals for breach of the rules of natural justice, error of law, or perverse error of fact.

[31] [1948] C.T.C. 195, 48 D.T.C. 1182 (S.C.C.).

[32] The doctrine is sometimes expressed with reference to the Minister's rulings of law as well as his or her findings of fact, but there can be no burden of proof on issues of law.

third reason, perhaps the most persuasive one, is that the taxpayer has the best access to the facts.

The taxpayer's burden of proof does not require the taxpayer to rebut every imaginable set of facts that would justify the Minister's assessment. The Court in *Johnston* made clear that the Minister was under a duty to disclose to the taxpayer the findings upon which the assessment was based, and it was only those findings that the taxpayer came under a duty to rebut. The standard of proof that must be satisfied by the taxpayer is of course the civil standard of the balance of probability.

Section 163 of the Act imposes penalties on taxpayers in two cases. One is the repeated failure by a taxpayer to report income, and the other is the knowing or negligent making of a false statement or omission in a return. These are civil penalties, usually equal to 25 per cent of the understatement of tax liability. If the Minister considers that s. 163 of the Act is applicable to a taxpayer, the assessment will include the penalty stipulated by the section. If the taxpayer appeals the imposition of the penalty to the Tax Court of Canada, the normal burden of proof is reversed by s. 163(3), which provides that "the burden of establishing the facts justifying the assessment of the penalty is on the Minister". This special burden is confined to the facts that justify the imposition of a penalty under s. 163. The burden of establishing that the underlying assessment of tax is wrong remains with the taxpayer.[33]

Another provision that imposes a special burden of proof on the Minister is s. 152(4), which is the section that permits the Minister to reassess a taxpayer outside the usual three-year time-limit. This power arises where the taxpayer has been guilty of misrepresentation or fraud. The section does not say anything express about the onus of proof in such a case. However, it has been held that where a taxpayer appeals from a reassessment that has been issued outside the three-year limit in reliance on this power, the onus of proving the misrepresentation or fraud that is the pre-condition of the power of reassessment rests on the Minister.[34]

Where a taxpayer is prosecuted for a criminal offence under s. 238 or 239 of the Act, the prosecution is conducted in the provincial court system under the rules of criminal procedure of the Criminal Code. In a prosecution, it is the normal criminal rules as to the burden of proof that apply. Therefore, the burden of proving all elements of the offence charged rests on the Crown, and the standard of proof is proof beyond a reasonable doubt.[35]

---

[33] *De Graaf* v. *The Queen*, [1985] 1 C.T.C. 374, 85 D.T.C. 5280 (F.C.T.D.).

[34] *M.N.R.* v. *Taylor*, [1961] C.T.C. 211, 61 D.T.C. 1139 (Ex. Ct.).

[35] *Medicine Hat Greenhouses* v. *The Queen*, [1981] C.T.C. 141, 81 D.T.C. 5100 (Alta. C.A.).

(j)   Settlement

Revenue Canada is willing in certain circumstances to settle a dispute with a taxpayer, and many such settlements are in fact made. Typically, of course, each side gives up some part of what had originally been claimed in return for a similar compromise by the other side.

It is essential that both sides be bound by a settlement agreement. In *Smerchanski* v. *M.N.R.* (1976),[36] the Supreme Court of Canada held that a taxpayer, who had agreed to waive a right of appeal from an assessment as part of a settlement agreement, could not later change his mind and exercise that right of appeal. But, in *Cohen* v. *The Queen* (1980),[37] the Federal Court of Appeal held that a settlement agreement, under which the Minister agreed to assess a taxpayer's profit as a capital gain while the taxpayer agreed not to object to other assessments, could not bind the Minister. "The Minister has a statutory duty to assess the amount of tax payable on the facts as he finds them in accordance with the law as he understands it"; it followed that an agreement by the Minister to assess otherwise than in accordance with law would be "illegal".[38] The Court accordingly upheld the Minister's assessment, even though it did not comply with the agreement, and even though the taxpayer had complied with his part of the agreement.

The effect of the *Smerchanski* and *Cohen* cases is that the taxpayer is bound by a settlement agreement, but the Minister is not. Of course, a settlement of litigation that was implemented by a formal entry of judgment would then have the force of a court judgment, which is binding on both parties. However, in *Galway* v. *M.N.R.* (1974),[39] the Federal Court of Appeal refused an application for a consent judgment to implement the terms of a settlement agreement between the Minister and a taxpayer. According to the Court, the Minister has no power to assess in accordance with a "compromise settlement", and the Court should not sanctify an ultra vires act. The Minister's duty is to assess in accordance with the law, and the only kind of settlement that the Court would be prepared to implement by a consent judgment would be one in which the parties were agreed on the application of the law to the facts.[40]

---

[36] [1976] C.T.C. 488, 76 D.T.C. 6247 (S.C.C.).

[37] [1980] C.T.C. 318, 80 D.T.C. 6250 (F.C.A.).

[38] *Id.*, 319; 6251.

[39] [1974] C.T.C. 454, 74 D.T.C. 6355 (F.C.A.).

[40] As Smith, "Reassessments, Waivers, Amended Returns, and Refunds" [1988] Corp. Management Tax Conf. 8:1, 8:14, points out, some compromises are possible within this doctrine. An issue of valuation could be compromised because value is a matter of opinion. Where there are several issues of law in dispute, a compromise could be achieved by the Minister accepting the taxpayer's position on some issues, while maintaining his or her own position on others. What cannot be compromised is a single issue to which there can only be one answer, e.g., is a particular profit a capital gain or ordinary income? In that case, the Minister cannot make a compromise settlement

The attitude of the Federal Court of Appeal in *Cohen* and *Galway* is far too rigid and doctrinaire. If the Minister were really unable to make compromise settlements, he or she would be denied an essential tool of enforcement. The Minister must husband the Department's limited resources, and it is not realistic to require the Minister to insist on every last legal point, and to litigate every dispute to the bitter end. Most disputes about tax are simply disputes about money which are inherently capable of resolution by compromise. Presumably, the Minister would agree to a compromise settlement only on the basis that it offered a better net recovery than would probably be achieved by continuance of the litigation. It seems foolish to require the Minister to incur the unnecessary costs of avoidable litigation in the name of an abstract statutory duty to apply the law.[41] It seems obvious that the Act should be amended to give the Minister express authority to settle cases.[42]

(k)   Remission order

Generally speaking, liability to income tax does not depend upon administrative discretion.[43] There is, however, one exception to this proposition, and that is the power to make a remission order, which is conferred by s. 23 of the federal Financial Administration Act.[44] Subsection 23(2) provides that:

> 23(2) The Governor in Council, on the recommendation of the Treasury Board, whenever he considers it in the public interest, may remit any tax, fee or penalty.

This power cannot be used to impose any new liability on a taxpayer; it can only be used to forgive a liability imposed by the Income Tax Act (or any other taxing statute). This power is exercised sparingly, in order to relieve against

---

of the "split-the-difference" kind.

[41] Compare the ruling in *Optical Recording Laboratories* v. *Canada*, [1990] 2 C.T.C. 524, 90 D.T.C. 6647 (F.C.A.), where it was held that the Minister did have the power to negotiate postponed-payment arrangements with a taxpayer who was unable to pay in full. This power stemmed from the Minister's authority over "the management of taxes".

[42] Smith, note 40, above, points out (at p. 8:14) that in the United States the Internal Revenue Service is given express authority to settle cases: Internal Revenue Code, ss. 7121, 7122, and regulations thereunder. In the United Kingdom, there is similar authority: Taxes Management Act 1970 (U.K.), c. 9, s. 54.

[43] The "fairness package", which was a set of amendments (S.C. 1990, c. 49) enacted in 1991, provides discretionary relief from some cases of taxpayer hardship. The three-year limitation on refunding overpayments of tax can be extended (s. 164(1.5)). There is a power to waive or cancel penalties or interest (s. 220(3.1)). There is also a power to allow a taxpayer to revoke, amend or late-file a number of elections in the Act. The provisions involved and the Department's guidelines for the exercise of the discretions are set out in Information Circulars 92-1, "Guidelines for accepting late, amended or revoked elections" (1992), 92-2, "Guidelines for the cancellation and waiver of interest and penalties" (1992), and 92-3, "Guidelines for refunds beyond the normal three year period" (1992). None of the discretions enacted in the fairness package directly authorize any change in the liability to pay tax.

[44] R.S.C. 1985, c. F-11.

cases of hardship. For example, complex provisions of the Act may have unexpectedly produced double taxation, or a taxpayer may have been misled by Revenue Canada, or a taxpayer may have fallen ill and lost the financial capacity to meet a tax liability.

By the terms of the Financial Administration Act, the power of remission is exercised by the Governor in Council on the recommendation of the Treasury Board. In practice, however, most remissions of income tax are determined by the Department of National Revenue. Requests for remission orders are considered, first, by a district office and, secondly, by a remission committee at the headquarters of the Department. If the remission committee were to recommend in favour of a remission order, the Minister of National Revenue would normally recommend to the Treasury Board that the order be made, and the order would normally be made.

Like other orders in council, remission orders are published in Part II of the *Canada Gazette*. They are also required to be reported to the House of Commons in the *Public Accounts*,[45] and they are also reported by the commercial tax services. The Department of National Revenue has published the guidelines developed by its remission committee to identify cases worthy of remission.[46] There is, therefore, a reasonable information base upon which a tax professional may determine whether or not it is worthwhile to apply for a remission order to correct a particular perceived injustice.

(l) Confidentiality

Section 241 of the Income Tax Act prohibits the use or release of "taxpayer information" by an "official". "Taxpayer information" is defined in s. 241(10) as including information of any kind relating to one or more taxpayers that was "obtained by or on behalf of the Minister for the purposes of this Act". The prohibition applies only to an "official", who is defined as a person "in the service" of the Crown or a person formerly in the service of the Crown. No provision of the Income Tax Act attempts to protect taxpayer information that is in the hands of persons who are not civil servants. For example, there is no protection for the taxpayer's own copy of his or her tax return.

Subsections (3) through (5) of s. 241 create more than 30 exceptions to the prohibition on the release or use of taxpayer information. Subsection 241(3) provides that the prohibition does not apply in respect of "criminal proceedings" or "legal proceedings relating to the administration or enforcement of this Act". Accordingly, income tax returns may be subpoenaed, and officials are free to

---

[45] *Id.*, s. 17(8).

[46] Sherman and Sherman, "Income Tax Remission Orders" (1986) 34 *Can. Tax J.* 801, set out the guidelines and analyze the orders that have been made.

testify or otherwise release taxpayer information in such proceedings.[47] Subsection 241(3.1) provides that officials may release taxpayer information to the appropriate persons in situations where an individual is in imminent danger. Subsection 241(4) provides for the use of taxpayer information in a variety of circumstances, such as where the information is required in formulating government policy, or where the information is needed for the enforcement or administration of various federal or provincial laws. Subsection 241(5) allows the release of taxpayer information where the taxpayer concerned has given his or her consent.[48]

2.6 Criminal prosecutions

(a) Sections 238, 239

The Income Tax Act, by ss. 238 and 239, makes tax evasion a criminal offence.[49] Section 238 makes it an offence to fail to file a tax return or to break various other provisions of the Act. The offences under s. 238 are ones of strict liability, that is to say, there is no requirement of mens rea (a guilty mind), although a taxpayer may be exculpated by proving that he or she acted with due diligence.[50] Section 239 makes it an offence to falsify records, or to evade compliance or payment in other ways. The offences under s. 239 are ones of which mens rea is an essential ingredient.[51]

(b) Civil penalties

Sections 162 and 163 of the Act provide civil penalties for a variety of delinquent acts and omissions, including (for example) the late filing of a tax return, the failure to file a return, the repeated failure to file a return, the failure to provide information on a prescribed form, the failure to report an item of income, and the making of a false statement or omission in a return.

The acts and omissions that are the subject of civil penalties under ss. 162 and 163 may also be the subject of criminal penalties under ss. 238 and 239. The civil penalties are imposed on taxpayers by the Minister as part of the assessment

---

[47] The phrase "legal proceedings relating to the administration or enforcement of this Act" has received a broad interpretation by the courts. In *Slattery (Trustee of)* v. *Slattery*, [1993] 2 C.T.C. 243, 93 D.T.C. 5443 (S.C.C.), the Supreme Court of Canada held that in a bankruptcy initiated by the Minister of National Revenue, proceedings by the trustee in bankruptcy for the recovery of assets were proceedings concerning the administration of the Income Tax Act within the meaning of s. 241(3).

[48] See Green, "The Confidentiality of Income Tax Returns" (1972) 20 *Can. Tax J.* 568; Toope and Young, "The Confidentiality of Tax Returns Under Canadian Law" (1982) 27 *McGill L.J.* 479.

[49] See generally Innes, *Tax Evasion in Canada* (1987).

[50] *Id.*, 13.

[51] *Id.*, 101-125.

process, and so when a criminal charge is laid against a taxpayer under ss. 238 and 239, the taxpayer has usually already been assessed for the applicable civil penalty. When this is the case, any punishment imposed on conviction for the criminal offence is in addition to the civil penalty (ss. 238(1), 239(1)). (The criminal court would of course take the civil penalty into account in fixing the punishment.) The decision to prosecute in such a case involves a judgment by the Departments of National Revenue and Justice that the civil penalty is an inadequate punishment for the taxpayer's conduct. In the unusual case where the taxpayer has not been assessed for a civil penalty at the time when the criminal charge is laid, then the punishment imposed on conviction for the criminal offence is the exclusive sanction, and no civil penalty can be imposed for the same conduct (ss. 238(3), 239(3)).

(c) Investigatory powers

The special investigations division of each district office of the Department of National Revenue investigates suspected cases of tax evasion, and when it obtains evidence prepares the case for prosecution. The Act provides officials of the Department with investigatory powers.[52] In the earlier discussion of audits, we noticed the power conferred by s. 231.1 to enter business premises without a warrant, and to enter a dwelling-house with a warrant, in order to inspect the books and records of a taxpayer. We also noticed the power conferred by s. 231.2 to demand documents or information. These powers are available to an investigator as well as to an auditor. Where material has not been surrendered voluntarily or cannot be found, s. 231.3 empowers a judge to issue a search warrant authorizing the investigator to search premises for evidence and seize the evidence. Where all these measures have apparently not yielded full information, s. 231.4 authorizes an "inquiry" to be held by a "hearing officer", who is appointed by the Tax Court of Canada, and who has the power to compel the attendance of witnesses and the giving of testimony under oath.

(d) Prosecution

Where evidence is obtained that the Department of National Revenue considers is sufficient to justify the preferring of a criminal charge, the case is handed over to the Department of Justice for prosecution. Prosecutions are conducted in the provincial court system under the criminal procedure stipulated by the Criminal Code.[53]

---

[52] *Id.*, ch. 2.

[53] *Id.*, ch. 3.

3

History

3.1   Confederation

At the time of confederation in 1867, the most important sources of governmental revenue were the "indirect" taxes of customs and excise, which accounted for 80 per cent of the revenues of the uniting provinces. By s. 122 of the British North America Act, "the customs and excise laws of each province" were transferred to the new federal government. By s. 91(3), the new federal government was given the power to raise money "by any mode or system of taxation", which authorized the imposition of any new taxes, direct or indirect.

The provinces, by s. 92(2), were confined to "direct" taxation and, by s. 92(9), licence fees.

The courts have adopted, as their definition of direct and indirect taxes, the language of John Stuart Mill in 1848 as follows:[1]

> A direct tax is one which is demanded from the very person who it is intended or desired should pay it. Indirect taxes are those which are demanded from one person in the expectation and intention that he shall indemnify himself at the expense of another.

An income tax is an example of a direct tax, because the taxpayer is normally unable to pass on the burden of the tax to anyone else. A customs or excise tax, on the other hand, is indirect, because, although it is paid by the importer or manufacturer, the tax will normally be passed on as part of the price that the importer or manufacturer charges for the taxed goods.[2]

3.2 Provincial income taxes

Excluded from the lucrative indirect taxes, the provinces gradually developed various forms of direct taxation. Property taxes, corporation taxes (on the basis of place of business, paid-up capital, etc.) and inheritance taxes began to be levied by the turn of the century. Income taxes (being direct) were available, but the provinces initially shied away from income taxes because of their unpopularity. British Columbia and Prince Edward Island were the only provinces to levy income taxes in the half century after confederation. Between 1923 and 1939, five more provinces followed their example, and the remaining three waited until 1962. All provinces now levy income taxes.

3.3 Federal income tax

The federal government first imposed an income tax in 1917, during World War I. The tax was supposed to be a temporary wartime measure, because it was accepted that the field of direct taxation should be left to the provinces. Although there was a lowering of federal rates after the war, the tax was never repealed.

3.4 Federal-provincial agreements

(a) Tax rental agreements

At the beginning of World War II, the federal government and seven provinces were each levying their own income taxes. In 1941, the provinces agreed to abandon their income taxes and leave the federal government alone in

---

[1] *Bank of Toronto* v. *Lambe* (1887), 12 App. Cas. 575.

[2] On the distinction between direct and indirect taxes, and the constitutional position generally, see Hogg, *Constitutional Law of Canada* (3rd ed., 1992), chs. 6, 30. The most detailed account is LaForest, *The Allocation of Taxing Powers under the Canadian Constitution* (2nd ed., 1981).

the field. The provinces were compensated for the lost revenue by grants from the federal government. This arrangement was intended to last only for the duration of the war, but after the war (in 1947) the federal government persuaded all provinces except Ontario and Quebec to enter into "tax rental agreements", under which the agreeing provinces would continue to refrain from enacting their own income taxes in return for grants ("rent") from the federal government. In 1952, on the renewal of the five-year agreements, Ontario joined the system, so that only Quebec was then levying a provincial income tax.

(b)   Tax collection agreements

The tax rental agreements ended in 1962 and were replaced by the "tax collection agreements". Under these agreements, the provinces imposed their own income taxes at their own rates. However, it was agreed that, if a province levied its tax as a percentage of the federal tax (so that the federal Income Tax Act became the basis of the provincial tax), the federal government would collect the provincial tax free of charge. In this way, taxpayers would only have to satisfy a single set of (federally-enacted) rules for the computation of their taxable income, and would only have to file a single return. In 1962, all provinces except Ontario and Quebec signed collection agreements covering both personal and corporate income taxes; Ontario signed a collection agreement for its personal income tax, but collected its own corporate income tax; Quebec collected its own personal and corporate income taxes. Alberta has since opted out of the corporate tax collection system, but remains within the personal tax collection system. The tax collection agreements have been renewed every five years. At the time of writing, all provinces except Quebec have agreements with respect to personal income taxes, and all provinces except Quebec, Ontario and Alberta have agreements with respect to corporate income taxes.

3.5   Tax reform of 1971

(a)   Carter Commission report

The effect of the tax collection agreements is to make the federal Income Tax Act extremely important, because it defines the tax base of not only the federal income taxes but most of the provincial income taxes as well. Since its genesis in 1917, the federal Act has been frequently amended, and it was substantially revised in 1945 and 1952. But in 1962 there was widespread agreement that a further revision was necessary. In that year, the federal government established a Royal Commission on Taxation under the chairmanship of Kenneth LeM. Carter, a chartered accountant who practised in Toronto. The Commission reported in 1966 with a six-volume document which constitutes perhaps the most thorough, lucid and brilliant analysis of income tax policy that has ever been produced. The Carter Report provided a comprehensive study of

Canada's income tax system, and a design for a radically different system of tax.[3]

The Carter Report was acclaimed by tax experts all over the world, and will continue for a long time to be a major contribution to the literature of taxation.[4] The general philosophy of the report was that all gains in wealth should be taxed — "a buck is a buck is a buck" — and this led the Commission to recommend the inclusion in income of capital gains, gifts, inheritances and windfalls. These and other proposals attracted strong opposition. The opposition came not only from those who would have had to pay more tax, but also from those who would have benefitted from the general lowering of tax rates that would have been a consequence of the broadening of the tax base.

The federal government moved slowly in implementing the recommendations of the report. A government white paper was issued in 1969 which accepted some of the report's recommendations, including the full taxation of capital gains.[5] A Senate Committee reported on the white paper,[6] and so did a House of Commons committee.[7] Both committees thought that even the white paper had reformed too much of the old system. In June 1971, the government introduced its final proposals for tax reform. These became the Income Tax Act which was enacted in 1971 to take effect (for the most part) in 1972. That Act, revised by frequent amendments since 1972, continues in force today.

The end result of the process of tax reform was a far cry from the Carter Report. However, the 1971 legislation made three basic changes in the Income Tax Act: (1) it broadened the tax base, (2) it restructured the rates of tax, and (3) it altered the taxation of corporations and shareholders so as to partially "integrate" the corporate and personal income taxes.

(b)   Base broadening

So far as the tax base was concerned,[8] the principal reform was the inclusion of one-half of capital gains in income. Some other receipts which had previously not been taxable were also added to income; these included adult training allowances, research grants and scholarships and, most important in

---

[3] *Report of the Royal Commission on Taxation* (Carter Report) (1966), 6 volumes. The Report is admirably summarized in vol. 1, pp. 1-49. The Commission also published 30 studies on aspects of tax policy, which are listed in vol. 1, p. 131.

[4] Despite the importance of the Commission's report, it was not even published by the Canadian government, and exists in mimeo form only.

[5] Benson, *Proposals for Tax Reform* (1969).

[6] *Report on the White Paper Proposals for Tax Reform presented to the Senate of Canada* (1970).

[7] *Eighteenth Report of the Standing Committee on Finance, Trade and Economic Affairs respecting the White Paper on Tax Reform* (1970).

[8] See ch. 9, Tax Base, below.

terms of revenue, unemployment insurance benefits. At the same time there was some increase in deductions. Deductions from employment income were made more generous, including a general expense allowance of 3 per cent of employment income up to a maximum of $150 (this was repealed in 1988, see below). The limits of deductibility of pension plan and savings plan contributions and of charitable donations were increased. New deductions were established for capital losses, unemployment insurance premiums, child care expenses and moving expenses.

(c)   Rate structure

The rate structure[9] was altered by an increase in the personal and married exemptions (a tax-free bracket) and a reduction in tax rates at the top end of the scale. In other respects, tax rates rose slightly after reform. The increase in rates was required because the increases in exemptions and deductions more than offset the inclusion of one-half of capital gains and other increases in assessed income and had the effect of reducing the total amount of taxable income. Some increase in rates was therefore necessary to keep revenue constant. Only in the highest income bracket did taxable income rise after reform: in that bracket the inclusion of one-half of capital gains was the dominating factor.

(d)   Integration of corporate and personal taxes

In the corporate area,[10] the 1971 Act allowed a low rate of tax (approximately 25 per cent) on the investment income of private corporations and, within limits, on the active business income of Canadian-controlled private corporations. Dividends were to be taxed in the hands of shareholders by a gross-up-and-credit procedure which had the effect of giving the shareholder credit for at least some of the tax paid by the corporation, and in the case of income taxed at the low corporate rate, for all of the tax paid by the corporation.

3.6   Introduction of indexing

The years between the major tax reforms of 1971 and 1988 saw many alterations in the income tax structure. Perhaps the most important was the "indexing" of the system,[11] which became effective in 1974, and continues in force to the present. The effect of indexing is that the fixed-dollar deductions, credits and tax brackets expand automatically by the rate of inflation, so that increases in a taxpayer's income that match the rate of inflation are taxed at the same average rate as the previous year's income. In the years of high inflation that followed, indexing caused a major expansion of the exemptions, credits and

---

[9] See ch. 5, Rates, below.

[10] See ch. 19, Corporations and Shareholders, below.

[11] See ch. 5, Rates, under heading 5.3, "Indexing for inflation", below.

brackets. In 1986, the system was partially de-indexed. As a result of this change, only inflation above 3 per cent is now taken into account by the indexing provisions. This measure permits an upward creep in government revenues without the need to enact an increase in rates.   (bracket creep)

3.7   Tax reform of 1988

(a)   The 1987 white paper

In 1987, the government introduced a white paper into Parliament, which proposed many amendments to the Income Tax Act.[12] Most of these amendments were enacted in 1988. The major changes were (1) the "flattening" of the rate structure, (2) the broadening of the tax base, (3) the conversion of many deductions from income into credits against tax, and (4) the introduction of a new general anti-avoidance rule.

A second phase of tax reform, also contemplated by the 1987 white paper, resulted in the Goods and Services Tax (GST), which is a value-added sales tax. The GST was enacted in 1990, and came into force at the beginning of 1991.

(b)   Rate structure

The most obvious change implemented by the tax reform of 1988 was the restructuring of the rates at which tax is levied.[13] The number of tax brackets was reduced from ten to three, and the rates of federal tax were reduced. The rate structure following the 1988 reform was as follows:

(a)   17 per cent on taxable income not exceeding $27,500;

(b)   26 per cent on taxable income between $27,500 and $55,000; and

(c)   29 per cent on taxable income exceeding $55,000.

Subject to indexing for inflation, which has expanded the brackets somewhat, the rate structure of 1988 continues in force to the present. The 1988 rates were higher than the 1987 rates applicable to the bottom two of the ten 1987 brackets, but the conversion of personal deductions to credits against tax (see below) was designed to more than compensate for the increase. In other respects, the 1988 rates were lower, the top rate being lower by five percentage points. According to the white paper, the lower rates were designed to increase the incentives to work and save, and to bring Canada's rates of income tax into closer conformity with those of the United States.[14]

---

[12] Wilson, *Tax Reform 1987: Income Tax Reform* (1987), 3.

[13] See ch. 5, Rates, below.

[14] Wilson, note 12, above, 69-70.

(c)   Base broadening

Several changes in 1988 had the effect of broadening the base on which tax is levied.[15] The major one was an increase in the inclusion rate of capital gains from its former level of one-half to two-thirds for 1988 and 1989, and thereafter to three-quarters, which is its current level. This reform moves closer to Carter's recommendation of full inclusion, and improves the equity of the system. As well, the 1988 amendments included some restrictions on the deductibility of business expenses and the elimination of some deductions.

(d)   Deductions and credits

Before 1988, taxpayers were entitled to a number of personal deductions, for example, a basic personal exemption (to which everyone was entitled) and deductions for a dependent spouse and other dependants. There were also deductions for contributions to the Canada Pension Plan and Unemployment Insurance, for charitable contributions, tuition fees and a number of other expenses not directly related to the earning of income. The trouble with these provisions was that they all took the form of deductions from income, and under progressive rates of tax a deduction from income is more valuable to a high-income taxpayer (whose income is being taxed at higher rates) than it is to a low-income taxpayer (whose income is being taxed at lower rates). The 1988 amendments converted these deductions into credits against tax. The new credits yield the same reduction in tax to all taxpayers regardless of their level of income. This change from deductions to credits improves the equity of the system. It is more fully explained in the next chapter.[16]

(e)   General anti-avoidance rule

One of the more controversial reforms of 1988 was the introduction of a new general anti-avoidance rule (s. 245). This provision denies to taxpayers the tax benefits of any transactions that may reasonably be considered to be undertaken primarily for the purpose of avoiding the payment of tax. The provision was introduced to catch avoidance behaviour that escaped the many specific anti-avoidance provisions of the Act. It was (and remains) controversial, because of the vagueness of its language. The provision is discussed in greater detail in a later chapter.[17]

---

[15] See ch. 9, Tax Base, below.

[16] Chapter 4, Objectives, under heading 4.5, "Deductions and credits", below.

[17] Chapter 22, Avoidance, under heading 22.4, "General anti-avoidance rule", below.

4

Objectives

4.1   Revenue

The purpose of the income tax is to raise revenue to finance government spending. This is, of course, the purpose of every tax, but the income tax is the most important source of government revenue. In the 1996-97 fiscal year, federal income tax (on personal and corporate income) yielded 58 per cent of the federal government's revenue. The next most lucrative taxes are employment insurance premiums (unemployment insurance premiums before 1996), which yield 15 per cent of the revenue, the federal goods and services tax, which yields 12 per cent, and customs and excise duties, which yield 8 per cent.[1] Table 4-1 sets out the present and projected revenues of the Government of Canada from the various taxes. It can be seen that the role of income taxes has increased, and will continue to increase.

Table 4-1
Government of Canada Budgetary Revenues

	1995-96 (Actual) Billions	%	1996-97 (Forecast) Billions	%	1997-98 (Projection) Billions	%
Personal income tax	$60.2	46.2	$63.3	46.7	$66.5	48.3
Corporate income tax	16.0	12.3	15.8	11.7	16.2	11.8
Employment insurance premiums	18.5	14.2	19.6	14.5	19.3	14.0
Goods and Services tax	16.4	12.6	16.9	12.5	17.5	12.7
Customs and other excise taxes	10.3	7.9	10.1	7.5	10.2	7.4
Other revenues	9.1	7.0	9.8	7.2	8.2	6.0
Total budget revenues	130.3	100.0	135.5	100.0	137.8	100.0

Note: Totals may not add due to rounding
Source: Department of Finance, *The Budget Plan,* February 18, 1997, p. 61

The income tax is the most important source of revenue for the provinces as well. Provincial income taxes (on personal and corporate income) yield 30 per cent of all the provincial governments' revenues; this is followed by federal transfer payments, which yield 19 per cent, and the general retail sales tax, which yields 13 per cent.[2]

4.2　Other objectives

Given that the main purpose of the income tax is to raise revenue, the question arises what subsidiary objectives should be pursued by the tax system. The design of the system will be powerfully influenced by the choice of subsidiary objectives. The trouble is that the various possible objectives are not

---

[1] Department of Finance, *The Budget Plan* (1997), 61.

[2] Treff and Cook, *Finances of the Nation 1995* (Can. Tax Foundation, 1995), 5:6, 17:9.

all consistent with each other. A list of objectives that are often claimed for the income tax[3] is set out in Table 4-2, below.

<table>
<tr><td colspan="2" align="center">**Table 4-2**
Objectives of Income Tax</td></tr>
<tr><td>Revenue</td><td>The tax system must raise revenues for government.</td></tr>
<tr><td>Equity
(horizontal &
vertical)</td><td>Equity (or fairness) requires a fair sharing of the tax burden based on ability to pay. This calls for graduated rates that rise as income rises. This is a "progressive" system.</td></tr>
<tr><td>Neutrality</td><td>Neutrality requires a tax system that does not affect people's behaviour. Business or personal opportunities, rather than tax planning, should drive business or personal decisions.</td></tr>
<tr><td>Simplicity</td><td>Compliance by taxpayers and administration by government are both easier and less costly in a system that is simple and understandable.</td></tr>
<tr><td>Economic stabilization</td><td>A progressive tax system has a stabilizing effect on the economy, restraining expansions by moving taxpayers into higher tax brackets, and restraining contractions by moving taxpayers into lower tax brackets. By the same token, income tax revenues are subject to more severe fluctuations than revenues from other taxes.</td></tr>
<tr><td>Economic growth</td><td>The use of the tax system to promote economic growth has led to special incentives for small business, farming, manufacturing and processing, research and development, etc. These provisions contradict equity, neutrality and simplicity, and many economists doubt that they enhance economic growth.</td></tr>
<tr><td>International competitiveness</td><td>The mobility of capital and skilled labour suggests that tax rates (and other elements of the system) should be competitive with other countries, especially the United States.</td></tr>
<tr><td>Balance</td><td>Balance signifies that the government should not be overly reliant on one kind of tax. A balance must be achieved between personal and corporate income taxes and between income taxes and other taxes, such as payroll and sales taxes.</td></tr>
</table>

---

[3] See Brooks, "Future Directions in Canadian Tax Law Scholarship" (1985) 23 *Osgoode Hall L.J.* 441, 457-473, reviewing the literature on tax policy.

4.3   Equity

The Carter Commission took the view, which is still widely shared,[4] that equity (or fairness) should be the major subsidiary objective of the income tax system. The Commission distinguished between "horizontal equity", which requires that persons "in similar circumstances" bear the same taxes, and "vertical equity", which requires that persons in different circumstances bear "appropriately different" taxes.[5]

Phrases such as horizontal equity and vertical equity do not help to decide the policy questions of what circumstances should be recognized by the tax system as relevant, and what differences in taxation should flow from differences in the circumstances. Carter held, and again his view is widely shared, that both dimensions of equity required that tax be levied in accordance with "ability to pay". How does one measure ability to pay? John Stuart Mill, the 19th century philosopher and economist, said that the idea of ability to pay was to achieve "equality of sacrifice".[6] By this he meant that contributions to the expenses of government should be so apportioned that each person "shall feel neither more nor less inconvenience from his share of the payment than any other person experiences from his". Mill acknowledged that this standard could not be "completely realized", but he averred that "the first object in every political discussion should be to know what perfection is".

In practice, of course, it is very difficult to secure agreement on what counts as equality of sacrifice. The problem is not just that people differ greatly in wealth, but also that many other features of social and economic life arguably affect the amount of sacrifice that taxpayers must make. There is room for considerable difference of opinion as to how to design a tax system around the concept of equality of sacrifice (or ability to pay). For example, decisions have to be made about the rates of tax, about the tax base (what counts as "income"), about the tax unit (the individual or the family), and about the treatment of income received through intermediaries (such as corporations, partnerships and trusts). The Carter Commission took the view that the criterion of ability to pay required (1) that tax be levied at progressive rates;[7] (2) that tax be levied on a "comprehensive tax base" as opposed to the relatively narrow concept of "income";[8] (3) that tax be levied on families as opposed to individuals;[9] (4) that

---

[4] Fair Tax Commission (Ontario), *Fair Taxation in a Changing World* (U. Toronto Press, 1993), 44-68.

[5] *Report of the Royal Commission on Taxation* (Carter Report) (1966), vol. 1, pp. 4-5.

[6] Mill, *Principles of Political Economy* (Longmans, Green and Co., London, 1923), bk. 5, ch. 2, sec. 2.

[7] See ch. 5, Rates, below.

[8] See ch. 9, Tax Base, below.

[9] See ch. 7, Taxation Unit, below.

tax concessions to particular industries or activities be avoided;[10] and (5) that corporate and personal income tax on corporate profits be "integrated" to avoid "double taxation".[11] Each of these recommendations is examined in the appropriate place later in this book.

While the criterion of ability to pay is widely accepted as the measure of equity in a tax system, the opposition to Carter's recommendations showed that many people could not accept all the implications that Carter drew from that criterion. As explained in the previous chapter, the Act of 1971 accepted some of Carter's recommendations and rejected others, but the net effect of the reform was an improvement in the equity of the system. This pattern was continued with the tax reform of 1988, which also improved the equity of the system.

4.4   Neutrality

(a)   Definition

The government uses the tax system — as well as government borrowing and spending, monetary policy and foreign trade policy — as one of its tools of economic management. The use of changes in the mix of taxes and their rates to influence the general level of economic activity is relatively uncontroversial. What is much more controversial is the use of the tax system to provide incentives for particular kinds of activities by taxing those activities more lightly. For example, the tax system provides incentives for Canadian-owned small businesses, for pollution controls, for mining exploration and development, for manufacturing and processing businesses, for the motion picture industry, for Canadian newspapers and magazines, for capital gains, for scientific research, for political contributions, for charitable donations, for saving for retirement, for home-ownership and a host of other social or economic purposes which have no necessary relationship to the tax system, and which could be encouraged by other means, for example, by direct subsidies.

The Carter Commission argued, and many experts agree, that the tax system should be "neutral". What is meant by a neutral system is one that is "designed to bring about a minimum change in the allocation of resources within the private sector of the economy".[12] The reason that Carter gave for neutrality was that, "at least in the present state of knowledge, the allocation of resources in response to free market forces will in general give in the short run the best utilisation of resources, and in the long run the most satisfactory rate of increase in the output of the economy".[13] In a neutral tax system, people's work practices and business and investment decisions would be no different than they

---

[10] See heading 4.6, "Tax Expenditures", below.

[11] See ch. 19, Corporations and Shareholders, below.

[12] Carter Report, vol. 2, p. 8.

[13] *Ibid.*

would have been in a world without taxes. To the extent that behaviour is influenced by the tax system, there is tax-induced change in the allocation of society's resources; that is the effect of a tax system that is not neutral. Of course, a tax-induced change in behaviour may be a desirable change, but most tax-policy experts agree with Carter that the use of the tax system to accomplish social and economic goals is usually less effective and more expensive than the use of other policy instruments. This point is pursued in the later section of this chapter on tax expenditures.

(b)   Distinction between neutrality and equity

Neutrality is not synonymous with equity. A poll tax levied in the same amount on every individual would be the most neutral tax; nothing could be done to avoid it, and therefore it would not change anyone's behaviour. But such a tax would not be an equitable tax because it would not be related to ability to pay.

However, in a system that is generally related to ability to pay, the provisions that violate neutrality (tax concessions) tend also to violate equity by abandoning the criterion of ability to pay in favour of other policy objectives. For example, take the case of the taxpayer who makes political contributions, charitable donations and contributions to a registered retirement savings plan, and who obtains the credits and the deductions that the tax system provides for these expenditures. That taxpayer will pay less tax than a taxpayer with equal ability to pay whose consumption did not include the tax-favoured expenditures. The tax concessions violate equity, because they cause differences in the liability to pay tax that are unrelated to differences in the ability to pay tax.

(c)   Deliberate policies

Despite all the arguments in favour of neutrality, the government continues to use the tax system to pursue various social and economic policies, often using deductions from income or credits against tax as the means of providing the desired incentive. It is fair to note that even the Carter Commission did not always remain true to its goal of neutrality. For example, the Commission favoured a tax deduction for persons who saved for their retirement[14] and a fast write-off of capital costs for new small businesses.[15] But these recommendations were considered compromises between the goal of neutrality and other considerations deemed of equal value in the circumstances. Concessions to help particular industries or activities were not, in Carter's system, to be a normal, recurring use of the income tax.

---

[14] *Id.*, vol. 3, ch. 15.

[15] *Id.*, vol. 4, pp. 276-282.

The white paper preceding the tax reform of 1971,[16] while agreeing that the tax system should not interfere seriously with economic growth and productivity, pointed out that the tax laws had long been used to provide incentives to certain kinds of valuable business activities, and stated that "the government believes they should continue to be so used in a number of specific ways that are clearly understood and justified". Those who make a practice of listening to budget speeches, and of following the steady flow of amendments to the Income Tax Act, will appreciate that the goal of neutrality is in fact often compromised by the government in aid of other objectives.

(d)   Unintended effects

The discussion to this point has assumed that the various violations of neutrality in the Income Tax Act represent deliberate choices on the part of government. In most cases that is true, but in some cases the Income Tax Act influences behaviour in ways that are not intended by government. For example, the fact that fewer deductions are available from income from employment than are available from income from business has led taxpayers to order their affairs so as to receive business income rather than employment income; the fact that capital gains are only three-quarters taxable has led taxpayers to order their affairs so as to receive capital gains rather than ordinary income; similarly, the more generous tax treatment of incorporated businesses than unincorporated businesses has encouraged taxpayers to incorporate their businesses; and deductions for business-related travel and entertainment expenses have subsidized the restaurant, hotel, travel and entertainment industries. These kinds of incidental effects of the tax system cannot be defended, even by those who do not share the belief that a tax system should be neutral, because these effects have not been the subject of a deliberate policy decision.

4.5   Deductions and credits

(a)   Deductions

Where deductions from income are used by the tax system for purposes other than to measure income, the violation of equity is particularly acute. Because income tax is levied at progressive rates, and because a deduction will take money out of a taxpayer's highest tax bracket, a deduction increases in value as income increases. The top (combined federal-provincial) tax rate in Ontario for 1997 (including surtaxes) was 51.64 per cent, and it applied to a taxpayer's income above $63,490. A deduction of $100 saved $51.64 for a taxpayer who (after claiming the deduction) earned over $63,590 of taxable income in Ontario in 1997 (because the extra $100 of taxable income would have been taxed at 51.64 per cent). The same deduction saved $39.26 for a taxpayer

---

[16] *Proposals for Tax Reform* (1969), 7.

who earned $50,000, since he or she was in the 39.26 per cent bracket. The same deduction saved $25.67 for a taxpayer who earned $10,000.[17] It saved a person who did not earn sufficient income to be liable to tax exactly nothing. These examples will vary over the years with indexing, as well as changes in rates or brackets, but they demonstrate that in a system that levies tax at progressive rates a deduction is necessarily regressive, giving a greater benefit to the person with a high income than to the person with a low income.

The "upside-down" effect of tax deductions led the National Council on Welfare, in a well-publicized report in 1976,[18] to describe the panoply of tax concessions as a "hidden welfare system for the non-poor", and to argue that such a system could exist only because it did remain "hidden". It was in response to criticism of this kind that the Government of Canada began in 1979 to publicly identify, list and value all "tax expenditures"; the tax expenditure account exposes formerly hidden tax deductions to public scrutiny. This development is discussed later in this chapter. As for the upside-down effect, the tax reform of 1988 converted most of the more important deductions into tax credits, which have the same dollar value to taxpayers at all income levels. This development is discussed later in this chapter.

(b)   Credits

If the tax system is to be used to provide special incentives on non-tax policy grounds, a more equitable method is through fixed-dollar tax credits. A tax credit allows a deduction from the tax liability (as opposed to the income) of the taxpayer. A tax credit of $100 enables each taxpayer to deduct $100 from his or her tax. The benefit is the same in dollar terms for rich and poor alike.[19] It is however progressive in that it frees from tax a larger proportion of a lower income than of a higher income.

(c)   Conversion of deductions to credits

Before the tax reform of 1988, the Income Tax Act allowed many deductions that were not directly related to the measurement of income. There were "personal exemptions" (which took the form of deductions) for all taxpayers (the basic exemption), for those with a dependent spouse or other dependants, for those aged 65 and over, and for those with a disability. There were also deductions for pension income, tuition fees, sales tax, medical

---

[17] The applicable rates of tax are set out in the table in ch. 5, Rates, under heading 5.2(d), "Progressive rates", below.

[18] *The Hidden Welfare System* (Ottawa, 1976).

[19] The use of surtaxes by both the federal and provincial governments means that even fixed-dollar credits are worth somewhat more to high-income taxpayers than to low-income taxpayers. This is because surtaxes are levied, not on the taxpayer's income, but on the taxpayer's tax liability after non-refundable credits have been subtracted.

expenses, charitable contributions, Canada Pension Plan contributions and Unemployment Insurance premiums (now called Employment Insurance premiums). These deductions suffered from the drawback common to all deductions that they were more valuable to a high-income taxpayer than they were to a low-income taxpayer. In the 1988 amendments to the Act, these deductions were all converted into credits. The credits yield the same reduction in tax to all taxpayers regardless of their level of income.

The credits, which are to be found in ss. 118-118.9,[20] are set at 17 per cent[21] of the taxpayer's expenditure or (in the case of the former personal exemptions) 17 per cent of a figure stipulated by the Act.[22] Why 17 per cent? Because 17 per cent is the rate that is applicable to the lowest of the three tax brackets in s. 117 of the Act. This means that the credit has the same value as a deduction for a taxpayer in the lowest tax bracket, but (being a credit) it has no greater value for taxpayers in the higher brackets.

For example, a $100 contribution to the Canada Pension Plan yields a credit of $17 in federal tax, which yields a reduction in Ontario tax (at the 1997 rate of 48 per cent) of $8.16 for a total of $25.16. If the contribution gave rise to a deduction instead of a credit, the $100 contribution would be worth the same amount of $25.33 only to a taxpayer in the lowest (17 per cent) tax bracket; a taxpayer in the second (26 per cent) bracket would save $26 in federal tax and $12.48 in provincial tax for a total of $38.48; a taxpayer in the highest (29 per cent) bracket would save $29 in federal tax and $13.92 in provincial tax for a total of $42.92. (These figures omit the complications of surtaxes, which of course widen the differences between the rates.)

---

[20] The Act describes as "personal credits" the basic credit (s. 118(1)(c)), the married credit (s. 118(1)(a)), the equivalent-to-married credit (s. 118(1)(b)) and the credit for dependants (s. 118(1)(d)). There is also a credit for age over 65 (s. 118(2)), pension income (s. 118(3)), charitable contributions (s. 118.1), medical expenses (s. 118.2), mental or physical impairment (of taxpayer or dependant) (s. 118.3), tuition (s. 118.5(1)), education (s. 118.5(2)), Employment Insurance premiums and Canada Pension Plan contributions (s. 118.7), goods and services tax (s. 122.5) and the child tax benefit (s. 122.61). There is provision for the transfer of some unused credits (age, pension, mental or physical impairment, tuition and education) to a spouse (s. 118.8) or (in the case of the tuition and education credits) to a parent or grandparent (s. 118.9). Students have the option of carrying forward unused tuition and education credits to a future year.

[21] In one of those circumlocutions that make the Act unnecessarily difficult, s. 118 speaks only of "the appropriate percentage". One eventually discovers that this phrase is a defined term in s. 248, where it is defined as "the lowest percentage referred to in subsection 117(2) that is applicable in determining tax payable under Part I for the year".

[22] The credit for charitable contributions (s. 118.1) is more complicated: 17 per cent of the first $200 (lowered to $200 from $250 in 1994), and 29 per cent (the top federal rate) of the amount in excess of $200. In order to avoid a decline in charitable contributions, the credit for contributions over $200 has the same value (to all taxpayers) as a deduction has for a taxpayer in the top tax bracket.

The 1988 conversion of deductions to credits was an important gain in tax equity. It did not, however, contribute to the simplicity of the system. Deductions (however inequitable) are easy for taxpayers to understand and apply in filling in their tax returns. Taxpayers must be bemused by the 17 per cent calculation, the purpose of which would be obscure to all but the most sophisticated. This is another area where complexity is a price of progressivity. Under a flat-rate tax system, the value of deductions would not vary inversely with taxable income; the flat rate of tax would maintain the same tax value of a $100 deduction for taxpayers at all levels of income. There would be no need to convert deductions into credits and the ensuing complications would be avoided.

(d)   Refundable and income-tested credits

The tax credit does share one disadvantage with the deduction: it provides no help for those whose incomes are so low that they are outside the tax system altogether. The tax credit also does not confer a full benefit upon those whose tax liabilities are less than the amount of the credit. These regressive features can be eliminated by making the credit "refundable". The refundable feature requires Revenue Canada to make payments to individuals who qualify for the credit but who have insufficient income to employ (or fully employ) the credit as an offset to their tax liability. Another possible refinement of a tax credit is to make it subject to an income test. An income-tested (or "vanishing") credit declines and eventually vanishes as a taxpayer's income rises above a stipulated level. Both the refundable and the income-tested features steepen the progressivity of a tax credit.[23]

Most of the credits allowed by the Income Tax Act are neither refundable nor income-tested. There is one credit that is income-tested but not refundable, namely, the age credit allowed by s. 118(2) to persons over 65. There are three credits that are both refundable and income-tested. One such credit is the goods and services tax credit allowed by s. 122.5. This credit is refundable so that an individual whose tax liability is too low to absorb the credit will still benefit from it. The credit is subject to an income test: it starts to reduce when the net income of the family (taxpayer and cohabiting spouse) reaches a stipulated (indexed) threshold ($25,921 in 1997); the credit (which is calculated by a formula based on the size of the family) is reduced by 5 per cent of the family income (income of the taxfiler and cohabiting spouse) above the threshold, so that it eventually vanishes altogether.

The second credit that is both refundable and income-tested is the child tax benefit allowed by s. 122.61. The child tax benefit is a credit that is calculated by a formula that depends primarily upon the number and ages of the

---

[23] The difficulty with an income-tested credit is that it creates a spike in the overall progressivity of the tax system. At income levels where the credit is being reduced, the taxpayer's effective marginal rate is increased, sometimes to levels above those applicable to higher income levels.

taxfiler's children. The basic credit is income-tested in that it begins to vanish at the rate of 5 per cent (or 2.5 per cent where there is only one child) of family income when family income reaches a stipulated threshold. The threshold is the same as for the goods and services tax credit ($25,921 in 1997). Families with working parents receive an additional working income supplement which begins to vanish when family income is in excess of a stipulated amount ($20,921 in 1997). The federal budget of February 18, 1997 announced a combined federal-provincial Canada child tax benefit which will include an increased working income supplement. Discussions with the provinces and territories are to precede the introduction of the new system, which is supposed to start in the fall of 1997.

A third refundable and income-tested credit was also announced in the federal budget of Febuary 18, 1997. This is a medical expense credit for taxpayers eligible for the mental or physical impairment credit (s. 118.3) who have income from employment or business. Starting in 1997, the basic credit is the lesser of $5,000 and 25 per cent of the taxpayer's allowable medical expenses.

An innovative feature of both the goods and services tax credit and the child tax benefit is the timing of the payment of the "refunds". An ordinary tax refund is paid in one cheque, which is sent out several weeks or months after the filing of the tax return for the taxation year in which tax was over-paid or over-withheld; it is only then that the tax situation of a taxpayer has been finally assessed. Both the goods and services tax credit and the child tax benefit are calculated on the basis of earlier year's tax returns, and they are paid in advance in instalments. The goods and services tax credit is paid quarterly. The child tax benefit is paid monthly. The frequency of payment of the child tax benefit reflects the fact that it is really an income-support programme.[24] It could be expanded into a negative income tax, under which all taxfilers reporting incomes below a stipulated poverty line would receive regular payments from the government. This would be one way of designing a guaranteed annual income, which would replace a myriad of existing programmes, and which would ensure that no Canadian lacked the means to maintain an adequate standard of living.

4.6   Tax expenditures

(a)   Public scrutiny

Each tax concession, whether in the form of a deduction or a credit or a rate-reduction or an omission from income, has a cost to government, namely,

---

[24] The federal budget of March 6, 1996 proposed the creation of a seniors' benefit to start in 2001. The benefit would be refundable and income-tested, and would replace the Old Age Security payments and the tax credits for age over 65 (s. 118(2)) and pension income (s. 118(3)). This proposal is similar to what was done in 1992, when the child tax benefit was created using funds from other programmes for children.

the amount of revenue foregone by the concession. Its effect on government revenue is the same as if the tax system lacked that particular concession, and the government made a direct expenditure of the cost of the concession to those persons who would have benefited from it. The effect of a tax concession is thus no different from that of an expenditure. The analogy to an expenditure was emphasized by Professor Stanley S. Surrey of the Harvard Law School, who coined the term "tax expenditures" to describe tax preferences.[25] What Surrey publicized was the absence of public scrutiny of tax expenditures in comparison with direct expenditures. The United States Treasury moved to correct this situation in 1969 by preparing a "tax expenditure budget", which listed and estimated the cost of various tax concessions in the United States' tax system. This became an annual practice which, under the Congressional Budget Act of 1974, is now required by law. Some American states have also begun to develop tax expenditure budgets.

In Canada, until 1979, tax expenditures were immune from the annual scrutiny which is applied to direct expenditures. The cost of a tax expenditure did not appear in any budget, and once established it did not need to win annual approval from the Treasury Board, Cabinet or Parliament. Indeed, the cost of a particular tax concession was only estimated officially upon its first introduction, and then only for the first year of its operation. If this estimate were wrong, or if the cost increased dramatically, there was no regular procedure for discovering the new facts, let alone debating them: no further figures were ever provided. And, despite the Carter Commission's widely-accepted warning of the inefficiency of tax concessions, there was rarely any examination of the degree to which a tax concession was accomplishing its stated objectives, or of who was benefiting from it. This situation attracted criticism, and various unofficial analyses of tax expenditures began to appear and to receive publicity.[26]

In 1979, the Department of Finance issued a document entitled "Government of Canada Tax Expenditure Account" (1979), in which an attempt was made to identify all of the tax concessions in the Canadian income tax system, and to estimate the cost in foregone revenue of each concession. The tax expenditure account was divided into the same categories as are used for direct expenditures in the public accounts of Canada. The figures were preceded by an analysis of the concept of a tax expenditure and the criteria for identifying it and estimating its cost. The document did not provide estimates for some of the

---

[25] Surrey, *Pathways to Tax Reform: The Concept of Tax Expenditures* (Harvard U. Press, 1973) and Surrey and McDaniel, *Tax Expenditures* (Harvard U. Press, 1985) are the seminal works on the topic.

[26] National Council of Welfare, *The Hidden Welfare System* (Ottawa, 1976); *The Hidden Welfare System Revisited* (Ottawa, 1979); Perry, "Fiscal Figures" (1976) 24 *Can. Tax J.* 528; Kesselman, "Non-Business Deductions and Tax Expenditures in Canada: Aggregates and Distributions" (1977) 25 *Can. Tax J.* 160; Smith, *Tax Expenditures* (Can. Tax Foundation, 1979).

concessions, no attempt was made to estimate the total cost, and no attempt was made to show the distribution of benefits by income classes. However, the document did show that there was a very large number of concessions, that many were very costly, and that they had been growing in both numbers and cost. The document, true to its scholarly approach, even speculated that the existence of budgetary restraint policies in the 1970s had led to an increase in tax expenditures as a means of avoiding the restraint policies.[27] The message implicit in this last comment was picked up by the federal government, which instituted a new budgetary management system (known as the "envelope" system) under which tax expenditures as well as direct expenditures are taken into account in allocating spending limits ("expenditure envelopes") to each area of policy. In 1980, a second "Government of Canada Expenditure Account" reported this new system.

The budget introduced by Finance Minister MacEachen on November 12, 1981 was obviously influenced by the tax expenditure accounts of 1979 and 1980. That budget proposed to eliminate a number of tax preferences. This broadening of the tax base led to a parallel proposal to reduce rates of tax, so that the top marginal rate was to be reduced from approximately 62 per cent (including provincial tax) to approximately 50 per cent. This budget proved to be extremely controversial: the elimination of the tax preferences was vigorously attacked by various business groups. These attacks were so successful that many of the preferences were restored by the government. The lowering of rates, to which no one objected, but which made sense only as a complement to the elimination of the tax preferences, was not altered. The result was that the federal government endured much controversy, looked weak by backing down on many of its budget proposals, and, because of the lowering of rates, ended up with a system that raised less revenue. After this experience, the federal Liberal government lost interest in the removal of tax preferences. Later budgets did not touch any tax preferences and even introduced a few new ones. The government even stopped publishing the tax expenditure accounts: the publications of 1979 and 1980 were not repeated from 1981 to 1984.

In 1984, the Liberal government was defeated and a Progressive Conservative government took office. In 1985, the Department of Finance issued a document entitled "Account of the Cost of Selected Tax Measures", which was essentially an update of the accounts published in 1979 and 1980. Once again, tax expenditures, now described as "selective tax measures", were catalogued and costed. In 1988, in a different political climate, the Progressive Conservative government was able to do what had caused the Liberal government so much

---

[27] Department of Finance, *Government of Canada Tax Expenditure Account* (1979), 30.

grief. The tax reform of 1988 eliminated a number of tax preferences[28] and lowered rates. However, the government did not resume issuing tax expenditure accounts until 1992. Since then, accounts have appeared periodically.[29] It is to be hoped that the routine, annual accounting for tax expenditures, which has been achieved in the United States, is now a reality in Canada as well.

(b)   Difficulties of description

There are several difficulties in accounting for tax expenditures. The first is the difficulty of identifying them. How does one distinguish those deductions, credits or other provisions which really are preferences to particular kinds of income from those provisions which are necessary in order to define net income? The latter class of deductions, which include, for example, routine business expenses, are not tax expenditures. As the first (1979) Canadian tax expenditure account pointed out,[30] it is "necessary to define a benchmark tax structure, deviations from which are to be classified as tax expenditures". It is only after inventing a "benchmark tax structure" (which contains no tax preferences) that it is possible to determine whether a particular tax measure should be classified as a tax preference. The 1979 tax expenditure account[31] in cases of doubt decided to "err on the side of comprehensiveness". The 1993 tax expenditure account[32] reported doubtful items separately as "memorandum items". Needless to say, disagreement about the inclusion or exclusion of particular controversial items does not impair the usefulness of the bulk of a tax expenditure account.

A second problem concerns the treatment of tax provisions which seek to discourage an activity by taxing it more heavily, for example, the disallowance as a business expense of the cost of advertising in foreign media (s. 19.1). These "tax penalties" are departures from the "benchmark tax structure", and should probably be treated as "negative tax expenditures" since they offset some of the revenue lost through positive tax expenditures. The solution of the 1979 tax expenditure account,[33] which has been carried forward in later accounts, was to list such items ("memorandum items") separately from the tax expenditures,

---

[28] The inclusion rate for capital gains was raised from one-half to three-quarters; the dividend gross-up and credit was reduced from one-third to one-quarter; the standard employment expense deduction was repealed; restrictions were imposed on deductions for meals and entertainment, the home office and the use of an automobile; capital cost allowance rates were lowered; and a general anti-avoidance rule was introduced.

[29] E.g., Department of Finance, *Government of Canada Tax Expenditures* (1995).

[30] Department of Finance, *Government of Canada Tax Expenditure Account* (1979), 4.

[31] *Id.*, 5.

[32] Department of Finance, *Government of Canada, Personal and Corporate Tax Expenditures* (1993), 5.

[33] Department of Finance, *Government of Canada Tax Expenditure Account* (1979), 11.

but to provide the same information about their revenue impact as was provided for the tax expenditures.

A third problem is estimating the amount of each tax expenditure; the amount consists of the revenue foregone by the tax concession, or, in other words, the extra revenue that would be raised if the tax concession were removed. The tax expenditure accounts estimate the cost "by simulating the change in federal revenues as if that provision alone were eliminated, keeping all other provisions in place",[34] so that the revenue impact is measured by reference to the existing rather than the benchmark tax structure. In fact, of course, if a tax concession were removed, people would alter their behaviour, setting in train a series of changes with various effects on tax revenues. It is likely, therefore, that the full estimated cost of a tax expenditure would not actually be realized in additional tax revenue if the tax expenditure were to be eliminated.[35] In some cases, too, there is insufficient information about a tax expenditure to enable any estimate to be calculated.[36]

(c) Alternatives

Tax expenditure analysis treats tax expenditures as if they were direct expenditures. Looking at provisions of the Act in this way, it is not appropriate to criticize them as violating tax equity or tax neutrality or eroding the tax base. These tax- policy criteria would not be used to criticize a direct expenditure, and they should not be used to criticize a tax expenditure either. Tax expenditure analysis assumes a benchmark tax structure that is equitable, neutral and comprehensive; the tax expenditure is then analyzed on its merits as if it were a separate assistance programme. How much does it cost? Does it fulfil its objectives? Who benefits from it?

Under tax expenditure analysis, the question is whether a tax expenditure is appropriately designed to achieve its purpose in the most cost-effective way. The fact that the expenditure is delivered through the tax system does not necessarily condemn the programme. However, the general thrust of tax expenditure analysis is to discourage policy-makers from using the tax system as the policy instrument for programmes of social assistance. This is because a programme delivered through the tax system will usually exhibit some or all of the following flaws: (1) the upside-down effect of tax deductions and the failure of either deductions or credits (except refundable credits) to help those without any taxable income; (2) the difficulty of estimating the cost and effects of a tax

---

[34] *Id.*, 27.

[35] This point is regularly acknowledged in the Department of Finance's tax expenditure accounts.

[36] These items are usually reported nevertheless, with an indication that their cost is not available.

expenditure;[37] (3) the virtual impossibility of limiting the size of a tax expenditure by placing a "cap" on it; (4) the administrative problems caused by entrusting diverse social programmes to Revenue Canada instead of to more appropriate departments or agencies (whose budgets would reflect the cost); (5) the complexity which is introduced into the Income Tax Act and to the tax returns which individuals must prepare; and (6) the erosion of public confidence in the fairness of the income tax when it is known that so many groups are allowed concessions or "loopholes".[38]

These flaws in the design of tax-expenditure programmes are serious, but a balanced view would have to concede that direct-expenditure programmes have their disadvantages as well. They too are often not easy to control effectively. They require a costly bureaucracy to administer them. In many cases, direct expenditures are discretionary, in the sense that officials must pass judgment on the qualifications of applicants or even choose between qualified applicants. Discretion has its merit, since in principle it enables assistance to be directed to where it is most needed. But discretion carries with it the danger that the administrators will succumb to pressures from members of parliament and lobbyists of various kinds so that the administration will not be as fair as it ought to be. The provisions of the Income Tax Act typically involve little discretion on the part of officials: the rules are set down in black and white and are administered with total indifference to political pressures.[39] Indeed, it is possible that some form of guaranteed annual income, administered by Revenue Canada, through a "negative income tax" utilizing a refundable tax credit mechanism, could replace the host of diverse, overlapping and inconsistent income-support programmes which are now being administered by a wide variety of federal, provincial and municipal agencies.

---

[37] Examples of failures in the design of tax expenditures are the deductions for Multiple Unit Residential Buildings (MURBs), which were discontinued in 1981, and the Scientific Research Tax Credits (SRTCs), which were discontinued in 1993. Both programmes were extremely costly. The former led to the subsidization of the builders of luxury apartment buildings. The latter were successfully claimed by companies who did not actually do any scientific research.

[38] In the *1994 Report of the Auditor General*, vol. 16, ch. 32, p. 22, the Auditor General pointed out that, despite the development of tax expenditure accounts, the monitoring, evaluation and reporting was still inferior to that applied to direct expenditures. He commented: "It is difficult, if not impossible, for Parliament to hold the government accountable for this spending through the tax system when it does not have proper information".

[39] Needless to say, tax expenditures can be designed to be conditional upon the exercise of some official discretion, and direct expenditures can be made non-discretionary.

5

Rates

5.1   Federal sharing of tax room

The rates of tax imposed by the Income Tax Act are rates of federal income tax, but taxpayers must pay provincial income tax as well. As explained in chapter 3, History, above, most provinces have entered into tax collection agreements with the federal government. Under these agreements, the federal government collects the provincial income tax as well as the federal income tax, so that a taxpayer need only file one return for both federal and provincial purposes.

In the case of the personal income tax (which is levied on individuals), nine of the ten provinces have entered into tax collection agreements with the federal government. Only Quebec has no agreement, which means that Quebec collects its own personal income tax. Quebec residents are therefore obliged to file a provincial income tax return as well as a federal return.

In the case of the corporate income tax (which is levied on corporations), seven of the ten provinces have entered into tax collection agreements with the federal government. Quebec, Ontario and Alberta are the provinces that have no agreements, so that those three provinces collect their own corporate income tax. In those provinces, corporations must file two returns, whereas in the other seven provinces only one corporate return is required.

What does the federal government gain by offering to undertake for the provinces the most unpopular of all governmental functions, namely, the collection of taxes? The answer is: control of the provincial tax base. The tax collection agreements stipulate that the personal income tax levied by an agreeing province must be expressed as a percentage of the federal personal income tax, and that the province's corporate income tax must be expressed as a percentage of federally-defined corporate income. By virtue of these stipulations, it is the rules of the federal Income Tax Act with respect to the measurement of income that constitute the tax base of the agreeing province. In that way, federal taxing policies prevail in the agreeing provinces not only in respect of federal taxes but also in respect of provincial taxes.

In the case of the personal income tax, the provincial tax must take the form of a tax on tax rather than a tax on income.[1] In Ontario, for example, where the rate of provincial tax in 1997 is 48 per cent, a taxpayer first calculates his or her "basic federal tax" (from which federal tax credits have been deducted but federal surtaxes have not been added); the taxpayer then adds a further 48 per cent to the federal figure to produce the combined federal-provincial liability. If the basic federal tax was $100, then the provincial tax liability would be $48, and the combined federal-provincial liability (not including surtaxes) would be $148. In this system, Ontario (like the other agreeing provinces) is effectively bound not only by the federal rules respecting the measurement of income (the

---

[1] This is not the case with the corporate income tax, which is shared through an abatement procedure. After the corporation has calculated its basic federal tax, it deducts from the tax an abatement of 10 per cent of the corporation's taxable income earned in a province. The abatement is expressed as a percentage of corporate income, not federal tax. The abatement leaves room for each province to levy a corporate income tax which is expressed as a percentage of corporate income. Each province does levy a tax at a rate which is the same as or a few points above the abatement of 10 per cent. The corporate income tax is briefly described in ch. 19, Corporations and Shareholders, below.

tax base),[2] but also by the federal progression of rates and the federal tax credits.[3]

A province can escape from the federal Income Tax Act by not entering into a collection agreement with the federal government. As noted earlier, Quebec has not entered into a tax collection agreement with respect to either personal or corporate income tax, and Ontario and Alberta have not entered into agreements with respect to corporate income tax. These provinces retain the freedom to design the taxes they collect in ways that differ from the federal Income Tax Act.

5.2 Rates of personal income tax

(a) Federal and provincial rates

The rates of tax payable by an "individual" are set out in s. 117 of the Income Tax Act. The definition section (s. 248) defines an "individual" as a person other than a corporation. Thus, s. 117 is concerned only with tax on personal income and that is the topic of this chapter. (Corporate income, which is taxed at a flat rate, is the topic of a later chapter.)[4]

Subsection 117(2), which contains the rate schedule, provides as follows:

> 117(2) The tax payable under this Part by an individual on the individual's taxable income or taxable income earned in Canada, as the case may be, (in this subdivision referred to as the "amount taxable") for the 1988 and subsequent taxation years is
>
> (a) 17% of the amount taxable if the amount taxable does not exceed $27,500;
>
> (b) $4,675 plus 26% of the amount by which the amount taxable exceeds $27,500 if the amount taxable exceeds $27,500 and does not exceed $55,000; and
>
> (c) $11,825 plus 29% of the amount by which the amount taxable exceeds $55,000.

The dollar figures are subject to indexing for inflation, discussed later in this chapter.[5]

---

[2] The federal government has become more flexible in its collection arrangements. Several provinces allow credits against personal income tax for property and sales taxes paid by low-income taxpayers. The federal government has accommodated these credits in its tax forms, and collects the provincial tax.

[3] The provinces have found ways to make the progression steeper for provincial purposes: by allowing credits against provincial tax for low-income taxpayers (previous note) and by imposing a provincial surtax on high-income taxpayers. The collection agreements permit both these devices. The provinces would have more freedom if they were allowed to levy income taxes on federally-defined income (as they do in the case of corporate income) rather than on federal tax, but the change would lead to a more complicated tax return: see Department of Finance discussion paper, "Personal Income Tax Coordination — The Federal-Provincial Tax Collection Agreements" (Ottawa, June 25, 1991).

[4] Chapter 19, Corporations and Shareholders, below.

[5] Section 5.3, "Indexing for inflation", below.

The rate schedule of s. 117(2) gives the rates of federal tax. For the reasons explained previously, in order to obtain an individual's total combined federal and provincial tax rate the s. 117 rates have to be grossed-up by the rate of tax imposed by the province. When an individual computes his or her income tax he or she must multiply the federal tax by the rate of provincial tax to obtain the amount of provincial tax payable, and then total the federal tax figure and the provincial tax figure. Thus in Ontario, the top marginal rate of tax, which is levied on income in excess of $55,000 (subject to indexing) is not merely the 29 per cent imposed by s. 117(2)(c), but also the 13.92 per cent (29 x 48%) which is imposed by Ontario (in 1997), making a total of 42.92 per cent.

The rate schedule of s. 117(2) could be grossed up to show not only the federal tax rates, but the combined federal and provincial rates for Ontario. Since Ontario's tax (in 1997) is 48 per cent of the federal tax, the combined federal and provincial rate for Ontario is obtained by multiplying each federal rate by 148 per cent. If the rates are grossed up in this way, and if the brackets are indexed for inflation (see heading 5.4, "Indexing for inflation", below), the schedule would then appear as follows:

Tax Bracket 1988	Tax Bracket 1997 (indexed)	Federal Rate s. 117(2)	Ontario Rate 1997	Combined Rate 1997
(1) $0 — 27,500	$0 — 29,590	17%	48%	25.2%
(2) $27,501 — $55,000	$29,591 — $59,180	26%	48%	38.5%
(3) $55,001+	$59,181+	29%	48%	42.9%

(b)   Surtaxes

The rates described in the previous section are complicated by the existence of federal and provincial surtaxes. Section 180.1 of the Income Tax Act imposes a surtax of 3 per cent on each taxpayer's basic federal tax, and a further surtax of 5 per cent on basic federal tax over $12,500. The surtaxes are calculated on tax, not income. The taxpayer first determines the amount of his or her basic federal tax, and then calculates and adds the surtax (or surtaxes) to yield the full federal tax liability. These surtaxes were not built into the rate schedule, because they were supposed to be temporary; but the state of the federal deficit has discouraged successive federal governments from getting rid of them. The surtaxes should be incorporated into the rate schedule, which would cause a general raising of federal rates (the 3 per cent surtax on all basic federal tax) and the creation of a fourth federal tax bracket (the 5 per cent surtax on basic federal tax over $12,500). In that way, the actual rates of tax would be apparent.

The provinces have taken their cue from the federal government, and many provinces impose surtaxes on basic provincial tax. In Ontario in 1997, for example, the 48 per cent rate of provincial tax is a very misleading figure, because there is a surtax of 20 per cent on basic provincial tax in excess of $4,555 and a second surtax of 26 per cent (for a total of 46 per cent) on basic provincial tax in excess of $6,180. Ontario's flat rate of 48 per cent is really a three-bracket progression of (1) 48 per cent of basic federal tax, (2) 57.6 per cent (48 x 120%), and (3) 70.1 per cent (48 x 146%). The effect, of course, is to add a fifth and a sixth bracket to the combined rates of tax for Ontario residents. After taking into account the two federal surtaxes and the two provincial surtaxes, the top combined rate in Ontario in 1997 is 51.64 per cent, and it is reached at a taxable income of $59,700, which is the point at which all four surtaxes are applicable. (This assumes a taxpayer who has no tax credits; the threshold is higher if credits are taken into account.)

(c)   Marginal and average rates

It is important to note that the rates of tax which are applicable within each bracket of income are applicable only to that part of an individual's income which falls within that bracket. For example, an individual who earned $65,000 of taxable income in Ontario in 1997 falls within the 29 per cent top federal tax bracket. The rate of 29 per cent is known as the individual's *marginal rate*, because it is the rate that is levied at the margin, that is, on the last dollar of taxable income. But the marginal rate is not applied to the whole of the taxpayer's income. It is applied only to the income falling within the same bracket as the last dollar. In our example, the taxpayer's marginal rate will be applicable to that part of his or her income which exceeds $59,180 (the bottom of the top tax bracket after indexing), namely $5,820 ($65,000 - $59,180). The rest of the taxpayer's taxable income, namely the first $59,180, will be taxed at the rates applicable to lower income brackets (17 per cent on the first $29,590, and 26 per cent on the next $29,590). The result is that the taxpayer's *average rate* (or overall rate) of tax will be substantially less than his or her marginal rate. In this example, the federal tax payable by the taxpayer would be 29 per cent of $5,820 (which is $1,688), plus the tax payable on the lower brackets of income (which comes to $12,724), making a total of $14,412. This is 22.17 per cent of the taxpayer's total taxable income of $65,000 (14,412 / 65,000 x 100 / 1). The average rate of tax is therefore 22.17 per cent. The marginal rate, it will be recalled, was 29 per cent — nearly seven points higher.

In the foregoing example, only the federal tax calculation has been given. (The figure of $14,412 would in 1997 be reduced by federal tax credits and increased by a federal surtax; these complications can be ignored for present purposes.) The taxpayer would still have to calculate provincial tax, which in Ontario in 1997 is 48 per cent of basic federal tax. Working from a federal tax figure of $14,412, Ontario tax would be $6,918 ($14,412 x 48%), and the taxpayer's combined federal-provincial tax liability would be $21,330. This figure is 33 per cent of the taxpayer's taxable income of $65,000. The *average rate* of combined federal-provincial tax is therefore 33 per cent. The *marginal rate* of combined federal-provincial tax for a taxpayer in the top tax bracket, it will be recalled from the earlier chart, is 42.9 per cent.

The marginal rate is often more important than the average rate, because it is the marginal rate that governs a taxpayer's economic decisions. For example, a taxpayer who has a choice whether or not to work overtime at his or her employment would compare the value of the time as leisure with the after-tax earnings from the extra work. It would be the taxpayer's marginal rate that would determine the amount of after-tax earnings that the taxpayer would receive. Similarly, the value to the taxpayer of the deduction for contributing to a registered retirement savings plan (RRSP) would be determined by the marginal rate rather than the average rate.

It is worth pointing out here, although the point will recur, that income which is recognized for tax purposes does not include some of the annual accretions to a taxpayer's worth. For example, only three-quarters of most capital gains is recognized as income, and some capital gains (for example, on the sale of a principal residence) are not recognized at all. Windfalls such as gambling winnings are also not recognized. Obviously, a taxpayer whose economic worth has increased in ways which are not recognized by the Income Tax Act is really being taxed at a somewhat lower average rate than would be indicated by his or her income tax return.

(d)   Progressive rates

The tax rates are "progressive": the rates increase with increased income. Consider the following examples. (The figures are 1997 figures after indexing in a province (Ontario) that levies tax at a rate of 48 per cent; the basic personal tax credit and federal and provincial surtaxes are also included.)

taxable income 1997	tax liability 1997	marginal rate (combined)	average rate (combined)
$ 10,000	$ 909	25.7% includes surtax	9.1% includes surtax
$ 50,000	$ 13,951	39.3% includes surtax	27.9% includes surtax
$ 100,000	$ 38,643	51.6% includes surtax	38.6% includes surtax

It can be seen that, with progressive rates of tax, one income of $100,000 attracts much more tax than two incomes of $50,000, and very much more tax than ten incomes of $10,000. As income rises, not only does the amount of tax rise, but the rate of tax rises so that a greater proportion of the higher income is payable in tax.

A progressive tax, which is levied at "graduated" rates, may be contrasted with a proportionate tax, which is levied at a single "flat" rate. If the personal income tax were levied at a flat rate of, say, 20 per cent (an idea which has its advocates: see below), then every taxpayer would pay 20 per cent of his or her income in tax. The person earning $10,000 would pay $2,000, while the person earning $100,000 would pay $20,000. As income increased so would the amount of tax payable increase, but the increase in tax would be proportional to the increase in income; the rate would remain constant. Marginal and average rates of tax would be the same.

Canada's corporate income tax is an example of a proportionate tax. Corporate income is not taxed in accordance with a graduated rate schedule. Subject to many exceptions and qualifications, corporate income is taxed at a flat rate of 38 per cent. Corporations with differing income accordingly pay tax at the same rate, the amount of tax payable increasing only proportionately to increases in income.

The provincial personal income tax, which is levied at a basic flat rate (48 per cent in Ontario in 1997) is not an example of a proportionate tax. That is because the rate is applied to the amount of federal tax and the federal tax is levied at graduated rates. A tax which is a fixed percentage of a progressive tax is itself progressive.

A progressive tax and a proportionate tax may be contrasted with a "regressive" tax. A regressive tax is the opposite of a progressive tax. The rates of a regressive tax increase as income decreases. The clearest example would be a "poll tax", in which every adult person was required to pay a tax of, say, $1,000. The levy would constitute a higher proportion of a low income than of a high income. Its effective rate would therefore diminish as income rose.

Progressive, proportionate and regressive are terms that describe the *incidence* of a tax. But there are two kinds of incidence, legal and economic. The legal obligation to pay the tax in the first instance defines the tax's legal incidence, while the tax's economic incidence depends upon who ultimately bears the burden of the tax. Economic incidence measures how progressive a tax is after the reactions of the taxpayers have been factored in. Two studies in 1994 examined the economic incidence of taxes; one study covered the whole of

Canada, while the other focused on Ontario.[6] The studies found that the personal income tax is the only strongly progressive tax. The cost to a taxpayer of the personal income tax cannot usually be passed on to others, so that its progressive legal incidence is a reliable indicator of its economic incidence as well. Despite the magnitude of the personal income tax, the tax system as a whole is only progressive up to the level of middle-income taxpayers and is proportional above that level.

The real property tax, which is levied by local governments under provincial law, was found by the studies to be regressive. Taking into account its indirect impact on rents as well as its direct impact on homeowners, it constitutes a relatively heavier burden on low-income persons than on high-income persons.[7] In several provinces, including Ontario, a property tax credit is available against provincial income tax to low-income taxpayers, which is designed to redress the regressivity of the real property tax.

Sales taxes are generally regressive, because people with low incomes spend more of their income on goods and services, that is, they save less, than people with high incomes. Each of the provinces, except Alberta, imposes a retail sales tax on most goods at rates that vary from 6.5 per cent to 12 per cent.[8] The provinces mitigate the regressivity of their provincial sales taxes by two means. The first, employed by all provinces, is to exempt from tax certain basic necessities, such as food and drugs, which constitute a higher proportion of the expenditures of the poor than the rich. The second, employed by some provinces, is to provide a refundable sales tax credit against provincial income tax to low-income taxpayers. Despite these measures, the studies found that the provincial sales taxes were still slightly regressive.

The federal government levies the goods and services tax (GST) on most goods and services at the rate of 7 per cent. Unlike the provincial sales taxes, the GST tax covers services as well as goods, which is a progressive feature in that high-income taxpayers spend more of their income on services (airline tickets, hotel accommodations, theatre tickets and the like) than do low-income taxpayers. Like the provincial sales taxes, there are exemptions for certain basic necessities; and there is a refundable GST credit against federal income tax for low-income taxpayers. These features combine to make the GST significantly

[6] Vermaeten, Gillespie, Vermaeten, "Tax Incidence in Canada" (1994) 42 *Can. Tax J.* 348; Block and Shillington, "Incidence of Taxes in Ontario in 1991" in *Taxation and the Distribution of Income* (U. Toronto Press, 1994). Another study was published in the same year, but it examined the position of taxpayers after including the value of government expenditures and so is more properly considered a fiscal incidence study: Ruggeri, Van Wart, Howard, "The Redistributional Impact of Taxation in Canada" (1994) 42 *Can. Tax J.* 417.

[7] There is some dispute over the way in which property taxes are distributed: see Kitchen, *Property Taxation in Canada* (Can. Tax Foundation, 1992), ch. 3.

[8] Treff and Perry, *Finances of the Nation 1996* (Can. Tax Foundation, 1997), 5:4.

less regressive than the provincial sales taxes. However, the actual economic incidence of the GST was not measured in the 1994 studies.

The incidence of the corporate income tax depends upon whether the corporations pass the tax on to their shareholders (in the form of reduced dividends) or their employees (in the form of lower wages) or their consumers (in the form of higher prices for the corporation's goods or services). There is a consensus that corporate income tax is ultimately borne by individuals, but no consensus on which groups of individuals bear the tax. One of the studies assumed that the tax was born entirely by shareholders, while the other assumed that part of the tax was shifted back to employees and forward to consumers. Different assumptions yield different conclusions about the incidence of the tax. To the extent that corporations are successful in passing the tax on to consumers through higher prices for their products, the corporate income tax is, in effect, a sales tax without exemptions, which is a regressive tax.

(e)   **Justification for progressive rates**

The reason for progressive rates of tax is the idea of tax equity that liability to tax should depend upon ability to pay.[9] A person with a low income needs all or most of the income simply to survive. A person with a high income can provide for necessities and have a substantial amount left over. The taxpayer's ability to pay taxes is determined by the amount of income available for discretionary use. In general, the greater the total income, the higher is the fraction of that income which is available for discretionary use. The ability-to-pay principle dictates not merely that upper-income taxpayers should pay more dollars in tax than lower-income taxpayers, but that upper-income taxpayers should pay a greater *proportion* of their income in tax than lower-income taxpayers. This conclusion necessitates a progressive rate schedule.

The personal income tax is particularly adaptable to the graduated rates which make it progressive. That is because it is a "direct" tax, meaning one which cannot usually be shifted by the taxpayer to others. A direct tax can take account of the personal circumstances of each taxpayer, and in particular the total amount of the taxpayer's income, his or her family circumstances and other factors which bear on the taxpayer's ability to pay. An "indirect" tax is one which is levied on producers, importers or sellers in the expectation that they will pass it on to their customers in the form of higher prices for their products. An indirect tax cannot take account of the individual circumstances of the widely dispersed and unascertained class of people who will ultimately bear the tax, and so customs and excise duties and sales taxes tend to take the form of flat-rate charges on the value of each article or transaction which is taxed.

---

[9] On ability to pay as the criterion of equity, see ch. 4, Objectives, under heading 4.3, "Equity", above.

A subsidiary advantage of a progressive rate schedule is that it has a stabilizing effect on the economy. In a time of economic decline, tax receipts are reduced disproportionately to the decline in taxable incomes, thereby helping to sustain disposable income and bolster consumer expenditures. In a time of economic expansion, tax receipts increase more than proportionately to the increase in taxable incomes, thereby acting as a brake on consumer expenditures. In this way, the tax system tends to restrain contractions or expansions of economic activity.[10]

There has been considerable debate of the question whether a progressive rate structure provides a disincentive to work. On the one hand, it is reasonable to expect that the incentive to work would decline as the after-tax return from work declines, creating a preference for leisure. On the other hand, it is also reasonable to expect that the reduction in disposable income which is caused by the income tax creates an incentive to work longer and harder to make up some of the lost income. It is hard to know what the net effect of these competing pulls will be on any given individual. Of course, most individuals have little choice as to their hours of work and cannot give effect to their preferences anyway. For those who do control their hours of work many influences other than after-tax monetary returns affect their decisions to work, for example, job satisfaction, power and prestige. Empirical studies suggest that the income tax has little effect on the total supply of labour in the economy.[11]

There is also room for debate about whether a progressive rate structure provides a disincentive to enterprise (risk-taking). On the one hand, it is reasonable to expect that the incentive to take risks would decline when any profits have to be shared with Revenue Canada. On the other hand, since the tax system allows losses to be deducted, it is also reasonable to expect that the sharing of losses with Revenue Canada would increase the incentive to take risks.[12] As is the case with the propensity to work, the propensity to take risks seems to be pulled in opposite directions by a progressive tax structure. It seems likely that the income tax has little effect on the total amount of risk-taking in the economy.

---

[10] See *Report of the Royal Commission on Taxation* (Carter Report) (1966), vol. 3, p. 243; Krishna in Hansen, Krishna, Rendall (eds.), *Canadian Taxation* (1981), 10.

[11] See generally Krishna, previous note, 13-16; Salyzyn, *Canadian Income Tax Policy* (4th ed., 1990), 221-224; Goode, *The Individual Income Tax* (1976), ch. 4; Babey and others, "Effects of the personal income tax on work effort: a sample survey" (1978) 26 *Can. Tax J.* 582.

[12] Normally, the profits from a risk-taking enterprise would be income from business, and losses from business are deductible on the same basis that gains are includible. Of course, in a progressive rate structure, losses may be deductible at a lower rate than gains would be taxed. In the case of capital gains and losses, losses are deductible on a less favourable basis than gains are includible: see ch. 15, Capital Gains, under heading 15.13, "Capital losses", below. It is, therefore, possible that the disincentive effect exceeds the incentive effect.

Even if it can be said that a progressive income tax has little effect on the aggregate amount of work or risk-taking in the economy, it should not be assumed that it is entirely neutral.[13] Individual taxpayers may well have reduced or increased their efforts as the result of the rising rates of tax. Even if the reductions are roughly balanced by the increases, so that the aggregate of effort is unchanged, there is still some distortion in the allocation of resources. As well, a progressive income tax diverts effort into attempts to avoid paying the higher rates of tax. Income splitting is the most obvious direct consequence of progressive rates.[14] Efforts to receive tax-free forms of income, for example, fringe benefits,[15] or less heavily taxed forms of income, for example, capital gains,[16] are also stimulated by high marginal rates. It is probably fair to conclude that many forms of tax avoidance would be abandoned if all income were taxed at a single, relatively low, flat rate. However, this consideration is not sufficient, in the view of most tax theorists, to outweigh the case in equity for progressive rates.

(f)   Arguments for a flat rate

As discussed above, one alternative to a progressive system of taxation is a proportionate (or flat-rate) system.[17] Under the proportionate system, income from all sources would be taxed at a single, flat rate applicable to all taxpayers. Proponents of a flat rate usually rely on arguments based on neutrality, especially the disincentives to work and enterprise (discussed in the previous section) that are supposed to be created by progressive rates. The incentive to tax avoidance (also discussed in the previous section) is another argument against the progressive system. A flat-rate system would be somewhat simpler since complexities such as indexing, anti-income-splitting measures and the conversion of deductions to credits would not be needed in a flat-rate system. As for equity, the proponents of a flat-rate system would acknowledge the need for exemption of the lowest-income individuals, which of course makes the flat-rate system mildly progressive. Aside from this low-income exemption, the argument is that considerations based on ability to pay do not outweigh the advantages of a flat rate.

An argument for a flat rate can be framed in terms of fiscal accountability. According to this argument, the public (most of whom are not

---

[13] On neutrality, see ch. 4, Objectives, under heading 4.4, "Neutrality", above.

[14] See ch. 7, Taxation Unit, below.

[15] See ch. 10, Income from Employment, below.

[16] See ch. 15, Capital Gains, below.

[17] Kornhauser, "The Rhetoric of the Anti-Progressive Income Tax Movement" (1987) 86 *Mich. L. Rev.* 465, outlines the arguments for and against the proportionate and progressive systems of taxation.

rich) accedes to increased governmental spending on the assumption that someone else (the rich) will pay for it. If taxes were levied at a single flat rate, it would be obvious to everyone (so the argument goes) that increases in spending would cause increases in everyone's taxes. Therefore, there would be a greater sense of shared responsibility for the expenses of government, and politicians would be required to be more prudent in their spending decisions.

Another argument for a flat rate proceeds from an assumption that taxes are really the purchase by taxpayers of governmental services. Since the most expensive governmental services, such as defence, criminal justice, education, medical care and highways are provided to all citizens, regardless of income, in roughly similar quantities, it follows that high-income individuals should not have to pay at a higher rate than low-income individuals. This is the most radical argument for a flat rate, because it rejects the proposition that equity favours a system based on the taxpayer's ability to pay. On the contrary, since the benefit of governmental services is not correlated to ability to pay, it is inequitable to base taxes on ability to pay. The difficulty with this argument is that there is no agreement on how the benefits of governmental services are distributed. At one extreme, it could be argued that the rich receive less than their fair share, because of their ability to purchase private alternatives to many governmental services such as public education, public transit, public parks and facilities; and of course they have no need for the costly array of income-support programmes. At the other end of the political spectrum, it would be argued that the rich receive the enormous benefit of the protection of their wealth and power, and expenditures to the poor are really for the benefit of the rich — they are palliatives to forestall the revolution.

In the literature of tax policy, support for a flat rate has mostly been outside the mainstream. Since the early 1980s, however, the ascendancy of conservative politics has revived interest in the idea. This did not lead to the adoption of a flat rate in any of the English-speaking countries, but it did cause governments in the United States, the United Kingdom, Australia and New Zealand to move to flatter rate structures. Canada was not immune from these influences. The tax reform of 1988 in Canada reduced the number of tax brackets from ten to three, and reduced the top rate of federal tax from 34 per cent to 29 per cent. The effect was to reduce the progressivity of the rate schedule. However, much of the former progressivity has since been reclaimed with the increased use of surtaxes.

(g) History of progressivity

The Carter Report (1966),[18] with its emphasis on equity and on ability-to-pay as the criterion of equity, naturally came out strongly in favour of

---

[18] The Carter Report is more fully discussed in ch. 3, History, above.

progressive rates of income tax. The Report aimed to increase the progressiveness of the tax system. One measure to this end was the widening of the definition of income subject to tax (the "tax base") to include not only "ordinary" income but capital gains, gifts, inheritances, windfalls and nearly all other accretions to wealth from whatever source. The adoption of this "comprehensive tax base" would have had the result of exacting more tax from upper-income individuals, because they were the usual recipients of benefits in the form of capital gains, gifts and inheritances. Lower-income individuals tended to receive their revenue in the form of ordinary income from employment, which was fully taxed under the existing definition of income. The Carter proposal for a "comprehensive tax base" will be considered in more detail when we reach the topic of income.[19] It is relevant here, however, because it led the Carter Commission to recommend a general lowering of personal income tax rates, and a substantial lowering of the top rates that existed when Carter reported. In the Commission's view, the marginal rates at the upper end of the schedule were so high as to provide a disincentive to work, and an incentive to emigrate to the United States.[20] In addition, of course, high marginal rates, coupled with a relatively narrow definition of income, provided the incentive and opportunity for manifold schemes of tax avoidance and postponement.

When the Carter Commission reported in 1966, and on until 1971, the tax rates rose to a top marginal rate of 80 per cent, which was reached when taxable income exceeded $400,000. The Commission recommended that the top rate be reduced to 50 per cent, and that it be reached when taxable income exceeded $100,000. The rate of 50 per cent was selected for two reasons. First, the Commission thought that there would be "psychological merit in a rate structure that would limit the state's claim against a man's additional income to one-half".[21] Secondly, for reasons that will appear later, the Commission wanted the top marginal rate of personal income tax to be the same as the flat rate of corporate income tax. The Commission's recommendation involved a huge decrease in the tax rate for high incomes, and the proposed schedule imposed somewhat lower rates at all levels. The Commission's studies indicated however that because the proposed rates were to be applied to a wider base of income (the "comprehensive tax base" mentioned earlier), the proposed system would raise just as much revenue as the existing system *and* would be more progressive than the existing system.

The government did not accept the Commission's recommendation for a comprehensive tax base, and accordingly could not accept the Commission's rate schedules without a substantial loss of revenue. However, the new Act that was

---

[19] Chapter 9, Tax Base, below.

[20] Carter Report, vol. 3, p. 154.

[21] Carter Report, vol. 1, p. 20.

enacted in 1971 did widen the tax base by bringing one-half of capital gains into taxable income (subsequently raised to three-quarters), and it did lower the rates of tax at the upper levels of income. The top rate of federal tax became 47 per cent, which was reached at a taxable income of $60,000. When the federal rates were grossed-up by the provincial rate of tax, the top combined rate was well in excess of Carter's recommended 50 per cent: in Ontario it was 61 per cent, and it was higher in most other provinces.[22]

The tax reform of 1988 substantially altered the rate structure of the Act, reducing the total number of tax brackets from ten to three and reducing the top federal rate to 29 per cent. Taking into account Ontario's 1997 rate of provincial tax of 48 per cent, the top rate of tax paid by taxpayers in Ontario is now 42.9 per cent, finally below Carter's recommended top rate of tax. However, when the several federal and provincial surtaxes are taken into account, the top rate in Ontario still exceeds 50 per cent (51.64 per cent in 1997).[23]

5.3   Indexing for inflation

(a)   Effect of inflation

Without indexing, one of the characteristics of a progressive tax system is that when an individual's income rises his or her tax liability rises more than proportionately: the taxpayer becomes liable to pay more tax on the new dollars than the taxpayer was paying on the old dollars. This is obvious if the rise pushes the individual into a new tax bracket. But even if the rise does not push the individual into a new tax bracket, the increase in income will be taxed at the individual's marginal rate — and the marginal rate is always higher than the previous year's average rate. From the point of view of the individual taxpayer, a rise in before-tax income of 5 per cent produces a rise in after-tax income of somewhat less than 5 per cent. Where a rise in income is equal to the rate of inflation, the recipient's purchasing power will actually decline, because of the progressive increase in the related tax liability. From the point of view of the government, a rise in incomes of 5 per cent produces a rise in income tax revenues of more than 5 per cent. With a progressive rate structure, tax revenues are bound to grow at a faster rate than incomes. To the extent that the rise in incomes is due simply to inflation, there is a regular but surreptitious increase in the real rates of tax without the necessity of any amendment to the Income Tax Act.

The increase in the rate of tax which is caused by inflation is exacerbated if personal deductions from income or credits against tax are defined in

---

[22] There was a reduction in federal rates in 1977, but this was in part the consequence of new federal-provincial tax-sharing arrangements; provincial rates rose at the same time, and combined rates did not change much.

[23] See sec. 5.2(b), "Surtaxes", above.

fixed-dollar terms rather than as a percentage of income. The effect of inflation on income causes the fixed-dollar deductions or credits to become less valuable to the taxpayer. When income rises due to inflation, the fixed-dollar deductions or credits (which would remain unchanged without indexing) constitute a smaller percentage of the inflated income, effectively causing the average rate of tax paid by the taxpayer to rise.

If the tax system is to offset the increase in the rate of tax which is caused by inflation, then the tax brackets and all the fixed-dollar deductions and credits have to be adjusted (or "indexed") so that they will rise with the rate of inflation.[24]

(b)   Introduction of indexing

The Income Tax Act that was enacted in 1971 (like its predecessors) did not include any provision for the indexing of the system to adjust automatically for inflation. The probable reason for the omission was not only that indexing was a relatively novel and untried idea, but also that the Carter Commission had opposed the idea of automatic adjustments to take account of changes in the general level of prices. In the Commission's view, a system which only taxed increases in "real" purchasing power would not only be "extremely complex", but would also "irreparably damage the built-in stability of the system".[25] By "the built-in stability of the system" the Commission meant the tendency of a progressive rate structure to restrain expansions or contractions of economic activity by increasing or reducing tax payments more than proportionately.[26] It is worth noting that the Commission reported in 1966 when there had been a long period of mild inflation, averaging merely 1.5 per cent per annum from 1952 to 1965 and never rising above 3.2 per cent in one year (that was in 1957). The moderation of inflation in this period "may have contributed to the [Commission's] assessment that an inflationary offset in the income tax structure was not of paramount importance".[27]

What led to a change in attitude towards inflation indexing was the higher rates of inflation that were experienced in Canada (and nearly everywhere else as well) in the 1970s and 1980s. The acceleration of inflation made the inflation-induced increase in tax liabilities a much more serious problem than it appeared to be in the 1960s. In the federal budget of 1973, the Minister of Finance announced that an amendment to the Income Tax Act would be introduced which would offset the automatic increase in tax collections that was

---

[24] See Allan, Dodge, Poddar, "Indexing the Personal Income Tax: A Federal Perspective" (1974) 22 *Can. Tax J.* 355.

[25] Carter Report, vol. 2, p. 33

[26] Section 5.2(e), "Justification for progressive rates" above.

[27] Allan, Dodge, Poddar, note 24, above, 357.

generated by inflation. The amendment was enacted as a new s. 117.1 of the Act to take effect in 1974.

(c)   Operation of indexing

When it was introduced in 1974, s. 117.1 caused the tax system to be indexed by the annual change in the Consumer Price Index. Section 117.1 provided that each of the principal personal deductions (which had not then been converted into credits) and each of the tax brackets in the rate schedule would be increased for each taxation year by the same percentage as the Consumer Price Index had increased in the 12 months ending in the previous September. In the years of high inflation that followed, the results were dramatic. The basic personal deduction (or exemption) to which every individual taxpayer was entitled rose from $1,600 in 1973 to $4,140 in 1985 — a cumulative increase of 159 per cent. A similar increase took place in the other personal deductions and in the tax brackets.

Effective in 1986, s. 117.1 was amended so as to exclude from the indexing formula the first 3 per cent of the annual increase in the Consumer Price Index. This meant that if the rate of increase in the Consumer Price Index were 4.8 per cent (as it was for the 12-month period ending in September 1991), the adjustment for inflation would only be 1.8 per cent (as it was for 1992). If the rate of increase in the Consumer Price Index were less than 3 per cent (as it was for the 12-month period ending in September 1996), then no adjustment for inflation would take place. Inflation has been consistently below 3 per cent since the 12-month period ending September 1991 (when it was 4.8 per cent), so that no adjustments for inflation were made for the years 1993 to 1997.

Because the indexing factor for a taxation year is based on the movement of the Consumer Price Index for the 12-month period ending in the previous year, indexing always lags a year behind reality. Each year's indexing factor is based on the previous year's inflation. The selection of September as the cut-off time to calculate the rate for the next taxation year (which would start on January 1) was driven by the need to ascertain the indexing factor some time before the beginning of the year so as to give time for the printing and distribution of the source-deduction tables that are used by employers to calculate how much income tax they are supposed to deduct from their employees' pay. The system's reliance on the previous year's inflation may in fact be a virtue. It provides an answer to the Carter Commission's objection that indexing would "irreparably damage the built-in stability of the system".[28] The answer is that "by applying indexing with a lag, the taxpayers are compensated for past inflation, thereby

---

[28] Note 25, above.

preserving the current response of revenue flows to the current level of inflation".[29]

Prior to the partial de-indexing of 1986, the result of indexing was to raise automatically the amount of the fixed-dollar deductions and the tax brackets to correspond with the rate of inflation for the previous year ending in September. An increase in income that was exactly equal to that rate of inflation was therefore spread evenly over all the applicable deductions and all the applicable brackets. Instead of being taxed at the taxpayer's marginal rate, and thereby increasing the taxpayer's average rate, the increase in income was taxed at the same average rate as was applicable in the previous year. An increase in income that exceeded the rate of inflation would of course be taxed at the taxpayer's marginal rate, and might even push the taxpayer into a new tax bracket. Either way, the taxpayer's average rate of tax would be increased. But, since indexing would offset the increased rate on the part of the taxpayer's new income that was attributable to inflation, the increase in the taxpayer's rate of tax would be less than it would have been if the system were not indexed. The taxpayer whose income failed to keep pace with inflation would find his or her loss in purchasing power mitigated somewhat by the decline in his or her average rate of tax caused by the expansion of the credits and brackets.

Indexing, in its pure pre-1986 form, denies to government the accelerated increase in revenues which would otherwise be generated by inflation. In a fully indexed system, the personal income tax revenues continue to increase as incomes rise, but insofar as the rise corresponds to the rate of inflation the revenue increases proportionately instead of progressively. Indexing therefore forces the government to openly obtain statutory authority for increases in personal income taxes, instead of obtaining them automatically through inflation. The reason for the 1986 partial de-indexing of the system was no doubt a nostalgia by a debt-strapped government for the good old days before 1974 when tax revenues could be counted on to increase by more than the annual rate of inflation. By denying any adjustment for the first 3 per cent of the annual inflation rate, in a period of inflation the government can now count on a steady upward creep in its income tax collections. By the same token, taxpayers whose incomes increase at the rate of inflation experience a steady surreptitious rise in their average tax rate. For example, under full indexation, the top federal tax rate of 29 per cent would have applied to taxable incomes of over $71,883 in 1997, rather than the $59,180, which is the figure yielded by the present system of partial indexation.

These negative effects of the partial de-indexing of 1986 are less profound since the flattening of the rate structure that took place in 1988. In a pure flat-rate system, there would be no need for indexing. A gain in income caused

---

[29] Allan, Dodge, Poddar, note 24, above, 368.

by inflation (or anything else) would not be taxed at higher rates than the rest of the taxpayer's income. There would be only one rate, and there would be no difference between a taxpayer's average rate and the taxpayer's marginal rate. Therefore, the flatter the rate structure the less important is indexing. However, even after 1988, the degree of progression in the Canadian rate structure (especially when surtaxes are taken into account) could not plausibly be regarded as so gradual as to obviate the need for indexing.

It should perhaps be added, to avoid over-simplification, that inflation penetrates deeply into economic activity and distorts income in ways which are not offset by indexing the tax system. For example, inflation causes allowances for depreciation (capital cost allowances) to be inadequate to provide for replacement of depreciable property when it wears out or becomes obsolete; inflation causes rises in the value of inventory which has to be replenished at current price levels; inflation causes interest rates to rise to compensate the lender for the anticipated decline in the real value of the loaned money; and inflation creates illusory capital gains. Each of these consequences of inflation gives rise to higher taxable income without really increasing purchasing power at all. It is arguable that such gains should be entirely excluded from taxable income, because they do not add to the wealth of the recipient. Accountants have not been able to agree on accounting principles that would systematically account for the effects of inflation.[30] Inflation-adjusted accounts do not conform to generally accepted accounting principles and are not acceptable for tax purposes.

5.4   The alternative minimum tax

As we saw in chapter 4, Objectives, several provisions of the Income Tax Act create "tax preferences" which run counter to the objective of neutrality. Many violations of neutrality are unintentional, for example, the preferential treatment of capital gains has the unintended effect of encouraging people to earn income from dispositions of property. Other non-neutral provisions of the Act are deliberate attempts by the government to encourage behaviour that furthers government policy, for example, the availability of deductions or credits for money saved for retirement in a registered retirement savings plan or for funds spent on research and development or pollution control. One inevitable result of violations of neutrality is that taxpayers will attempt to employ these provisions to reduce their overall tax liability. As many of the Act's tax preferences are available only to wealthy individuals, higher-income taxpayers are sometimes able to avail themselves of sufficient tax preferences to reduce their tax liability to an extremely low figure. Indeed, it became apparent in the mid-1980s that tax preferences enabled a few wealthy individuals to escape the bite of tax

---

[30] The accounting literature is briefly reviewed in Arnold, *Timing and Income Taxation* (Can. Tax Foundation, Toronto, 1983), 46-51.

altogether. The ensuing public protest caused the enactment in 1986 of the alternative minimum tax (AMT).

Section 127.5 of the Income Tax Act creates the alternative minimum tax. It is "alternative", because taxpayers must calculate both the amount of their AMT and their "ordinary tax", and then pay whichever figure is greater. The rate of the AMT is 17 per cent (the rate applicable to the lowest tax bracket in s. 117), which combines with provincial tax to yield a combined rate of approximately 25 per cent. The AMT differs from ordinary income tax in that it is calculated on a broader tax base (one that excludes many tax preferences) than the ordinary income tax. However, if AMT is payable, the amount by which it exceeds the ordinary income tax is available as a credit against ordinary income tax in any of the following seven years. In most cases, therefore, the AMT will not be an additional tax liability, but rather an early payment of a future tax liability.

The political appeal of an AMT can be easily understood, but its tax policy rationale is less easy to fathom. If the tax preferences that are excluded from the AMT base are unfair, then surely the appropriate response is to repeal them. Since it is the policy of the government to retain the provisions, why should some taxpayers be precluded from using them? In any case, the AMT applies to few taxpayers and raises little revenue, so that it is of little practical importance.[31]

There are four steps involved in determining the amount of the alternative minimum tax. First, a taxpayer must re-calculate his or her taxable income based on the peculiar rules found in s. 127.52. This process basically involves the calculation of taxable income in the normal way, followed by the adding back into income of those deductions considered to be tax preferences. For example, a taxpayer who had taken a deduction from income due to registered retirement savings plan contributions would be required to add the amount of the deduction back into his or her taxable income for the purposes of the AMT. Once this "adjusted taxable income" has been calculated, the next step is that the taxpayer is allowed to deduct a "basic exemption" of $40,000 from the adjusted taxable income. The $40,000 exemption ensures that only upper-income taxpayers making extensive use of tax preferences will be subjected to the AMT. The third step in calculating the AMT is to apply the rate of 17 per cent to the figure determined by the previous calculations. Finally, taxpayers are permitted to deduct certain credits from the amount of tax thus far determined. However, many credits that would otherwise be available are not available for the purposes of the AMT, on the ground that they are tax preferences.

---

[31] Larin and Jacques, "Is the Alternative Minimum Tax a Paper Tiger?" (1994) 42 *Can. Tax J.* 442, studied the effect of the AMT on Quebec taxpayers in 1988 and answered their own question "yes".

   Having derived the amount of the AMT, the taxpayer must now compare
this figure to the ordinary tax otherwise payable, and pay the greater of the two
amounts. Only where the amount of the AMT exceeds the amount of tax
calculated in the ordinary way is the taxpayer obliged to pay the AMT. If the
taxpayer must pay the AMT rather than his or her ordinary tax, the amount by
which the AMT exceeds the ordinary tax may be carried forward for up to seven
years and used as a credit against tax in any year where ordinary tax payable
exceeds the AMT. For example, if in year 1 a taxpayer has calculated $30,000
of ordinary tax, and $36,000 of AMT, the taxpayer must pay the higher figure
of $36,000. However, the $6,000 difference between ordinary tax and AMT may
be carried forward for up to seven years. If in year 2 the taxpayer's ordinary tax
payable is $40,000 and his or her AMT is only $30,000, the $6,000 carried
forward from the previous year may be applied to reduce the tax liability for year
2 to $34,000.

The four steps for the calculation of AMT are summarized in Table 5-1, which follows.

**Table 5-1
Calculation of AMT**

	Taxable income
Step 1	+/−Adjustments (1)
	Adjusted taxable income
Step 2	($40,000 Exemption)
	Net
Step 3	× 17% Rate
	Minimum tax before minimum tax credits
Step 4	(Minimum tax credits) (2)
	Minimum tax (compare to basic federal tax and use the greater)
	Surtax (3)
	Provincial tax (3)
	Total tax

Notes

(1) The adjustments to taxable income are

    Add   Most RPP/RRSP deductions

              Losses due to capital cost allowance claimed on films and MURBS

              Losses due to resource deductions

              Non-taxable portion of a capital gain

              Stock option and home relocation loan deductions

              Losses from limited partnerships (and partnerships in which the taxpayer is a passive partner) after 1994

              Losses from tax shelters after 1994

              Interest and carrying charges on rental, leasing, film properties and resource-related deductions after 1994

    Deduct Non-allowable portion of an allowable capital loss or allowable business investment loss

              Dividend gross-up

(2) The credits exclude

              Credits transferred from others

              Pension and dividend tax credits

              Political tax credit

              Investment tax credit

(3) Surtaxes and provincial taxes are based on the greater of basic federal tax and minimum tax.

Source: Income Tax Act, Part I, Division E.1.

6

Taxation Year

6.1 Definition of taxation year

(a) Section 249

Income tax is calculated and paid annually, on the basis of a taxpayer's income for a "taxation year" (ss. 2, 3). The definition of a taxation year is to be found in s. 249 of the Act. Subsection 249(1) provides as follows:

> 249(1) For the purpose of this Act, a "taxation year" is
>
> (a) in the case of a corporation, a fiscal period, and
>
> (b) in the case of an individual, a calendar year,

and when a taxation year is referred to by reference to a calendar year, the reference is to the taxation year or years coinciding with, or ending in, that year.

The definition introduces the concept of a "fiscal period", which is the taxation year of a corporation. As will be explained, the concept of a fiscal period is also relevant to the taxation of individuals earning business income.

(b)   Corporations

"Fiscal period", as it applies to corporations, is defined in s. 249.1(1) as follows:

> . . . a "fiscal period" of a business or property of a person . . . means the period for which the person's . . . accounts in respect of the business or property are made up for purposes of assessment under this Act, but no fiscal period may end
>
> (a)   in the case of a corporation, more than 53 weeks after the period began, . . .

This definition permits a corporation to select its own fiscal period, and therefore its own taxation year.[1] A corporation could choose the calendar year, in which case its year-end would be December 31, but a corporation could select any other date as its year-end. For example, if a corporation selected March 31 as its year-end for tax purposes, its fiscal period, and therefore its taxation year, would run from April 1 to March 31. The privilege of selecting its own fiscal period enables a corporation to fit its tax-filing obligation into a convenient part of the annual business cycle. Normally, of course, a corporation will select the same year-end for tax purposes that it uses for general accounting purposes.

Once a corporation has established a fiscal period, it must continue to use the same period. The definition of fiscal period stipulates that no change in the fiscal period may be made without the consent of the Minister. The purpose of this requirement is to prevent a corporation from rearranging its fiscal period from time to time in order to reduce or postpone tax.[2] The Department has explained that requests for changes in fiscal periods "will be approved if they can be demonstrated to be prompted solely by sound business reasons other than obtaining tax benefits".[3] An example of a sound business reason would be a change of fiscal period to end when the corporation's inventory is at a seasonally low level, or when the corporation's business activity is in a seasonally slack

---

[1]   There is one limitation on the ability of a corporation to set its own fiscal period. Subparagraph 249.1(1)(b)(iii) requires a professional corporation (a corporation that carries on the practice of an accountant, dentist, lawyer, medical doctor, veterinarian or chiropractor: s. 248) that is a member of a partnership to adopt a year-end that coincides with the end of the calendar year, unless the business carried on by the corporation either is not carried on in Canada or is a "prescribed business" (no businesses have been prescribed).

[2]   The Minister will apply the general anti-avoidance rule (GAAR) (s. 245) when a corporation amalgamates with a shell company solely for the purpose of acquiring a new fiscal period for tax purposes: Information Circular 88-2, "General anti-avoidance rule" (1988), para. 21.

[3]   Interpretation Bulletin IT-179R, "Change of fiscal period" (1993), para. 2.

period. The reduction or postponement of tax is not regarded by the Minister as a sound business reason.[4]

Some corporations use a fiscal period that is not precisely the length of a calendar year. These are corporations that choose to end their fiscal period on the same day of the week each year, for example, Saturday. This is particularly convenient for a corporation that makes up an account of its operations at the end of every week. Because 52 weeks is one day less than a full year (365 days) and two days less than a leap year, the corporation will occasionally have to have a 53-week period to arrest the backward creep of its year-end. It is to sanction this practice that the definition of a fiscal period permits a corporation to have a 53-week fiscal period.[5]

(c) Individuals

Paragraph 249(1)(b) (set out earlier) provides that the taxation year of an individual is a "calendar year". Unlike a corporation, an individual has no choice as to the period for which income is to be reported for tax purposes: the period from January 1 to December 31 has to be the taxation year.

However, an individual is allowed by s. 11(1) to select a fiscal period other than the calendar year for the calculation of business income, but not other types of income. Such an individual would still use the calendar year as her taxation year, but in each calendar year would report the business income for the fiscal period ending in that calendar year. Before 1995, this privilege enabled an individual to postpone recognition of business income, with a consequent postponement of tax liability. For example, an individual who selected January 31 as the year-end for her business would report only the business income earned to January 31, 1993 in her income tax return for 1993; the business income earned from February 1, 1993 to December 31, 1993 did not have to be reported until calendar year 1994.

Starting in 1995, an individual is still permitted to use an off-calendar fiscal period for business income (s. 249.1(4)),[6] but is required to use a formula

---

[4] *Id.*, para. 3.

[5] The 53-week fiscal period can also produce the result that a corporation has no fiscal period ending in a particular calendar year. Subsection 249(3) precludes this result by deeming the year-end that occurs early in the next year to have occurred in the previous year.

[6] The use of the off-calendar year requires an election (s. 249.1(4)), which must be made in the taxpayer's return for the first taxation year (after 1994) in which the taxpayer carries on business. (The election may be revoked at any time, which would cause a shift to a December 31 year-end for subsequent taxation years (s. 249.1(6)).) A designation is available that allows the individual to report business income in the first taxation year (s. 34.1(2)) even though no business income needs to be reported in that year because no fiscal period for the business ended in that year. The designation will often cause the income earned in the first taxation year to be taxed at a lower rate than would be the case if the income were not reported until the next taxation year (when the first fiscal period ends). If no designation were made, the next taxation year would include the

set out in the Act to adjust the business income to a calendar-year basis. In general terms, the individual who uses a January 31 year-end, for example, is required to add 11 months of estimated business income (calculated according to the formula), so that the advantage of putting off the recognition of 11 months of business income is lost.[7] The intent is to permit individuals who operate businesses to adopt an off-calendar year-end, where that makes business sense, but not to allow the off-calendar year-end to be used as a tax-postponement measure.[8]

(d)   Partnerships

A partnership is, of course, not a legal entity separate from its members, and the Income Tax Act does not treat it as a separate taxpayer. Under s. 96, the income of a partnership is initially calculated at the partnership level, and then each partner separately reports his or her share of the income. Under s. 249.1, a partnership of corporations is permitted to use a fiscal period other than the calendar year. A partnership that has an individual or a professional corporation as a member is obliged to use the calendar year.[9] A partnership of individuals is allowed the election to use an off-calendar fiscal period.[10] As a practical matter, the decision to use an off-calendar fiscal period will be made at the partnership level, but the formal election to use the off-calendar fiscal period for tax purposes is made by each individual partner. The rules respecting that election and the calculation of income for tax purposes by the individual partner are the same rules that were described earlier under heading 6.1(d), "Individuals", above.

---

equivalent of more than 12 months of business income, because no s. 34.1(3) deduction would be available for income included in the previous year under s. 34.1(1) or s. 34.2(2): see next note.

[7] In the case of an individual with a business with a January 31 year-end, the individual's business income for 1997 would be computed by taking:

> Business income for fiscal period ending January 31, 1997 *plus* 334/365 × business income for fiscal period ending January 31, 1997 (s. 34.1(1)) *minus* 334/365 × business income for fiscal period ending January 31, 1996 (s. 34.1(3) deduction for s. 34.1(1) or (2) addition to income in 1996)

There is no s. 34.1(1) addition to income in a taxation year in which the taxpayer has died, ceased to carry on business, or become bankrupt (s. 34.1(8)).

[8] A transitional rule allows an individual with an off-calendar fiscal period that straddles December 31, 1994 (the end of the old system) to spread her business income for the remaining months of 1995 over a ten-year period (s. 249.1(6)). For example, an individual with a fiscal period ending on January 31, 1995 could spread her income for the stub period February 1, 1995 to December 31, 1995 over a ten-year period. Without this transitional rule, she would have had to report 23 months of business income in 1995.

[9] There is an exception for the partnership that carries on a business outside Canada or a "prescribed business" (none have been prescribed); they may use an off-calendar year.

[10] The election is only available if each member of the partnership is an individual and the partnership is not a member of another partnership: s. 249.1(4).

(e) Trusts

Because a trust is deemed to be an individual for tax purposes (s. 104(2)), it is subject to the same rules regarding the taxation year as an individual, except to the extent that the Act makes a different provision. No different provision has been made for inter vivos trusts, and their taxation year is therefore the calendar year (s. 249(1)(b)), but with the privilege of electing an off-calendar fiscal period for business income (s. 249.1(1)(b)). In the case of testamentary trusts, the Act provides that the taxation year is a fiscal period to be selected by the trustee (s. 104(23)). Testamentary trusts are expressly excluded from s. 249.1(1)(b), which means that they are allowed to use an off-calendar fiscal period as the taxation year for all of their income.

6.2 Filing of tax returns

Section 150 of the Act sets out the time-limits for the filing of returns for a taxation year. In the case of individuals, returns must generally be filed by April 30 of the year following the taxation year, which is the calendar year. The filing deadline is extended to June 15 for individuals reporting business income (and their spouses). The reason for the extended deadline is to accommodate the additional bookkeeping required by an individual using an off-calendar fiscal period. However, the deadline for paying any tax that is due remains April 30, which means that, in order to avoid interest charges, all calculations have to be done by April 30 anyway. The extension of the filing deadline is, therefore, not particularly helpful.

In the case of corporations, returns must be filed within six months of the end of the taxation year, which is their fiscal period. In the case of trusts, returns must be filed within 90 days of the end of the taxation year, which is the calendar year for an inter vivos trust and a fiscal period for a testamentary trust.

6.3 Payment of tax

(a) Withholding at source

We have already noted that individual taxpayers are obliged to pay any tax estimated to be due at the time of filing their returns, that is, by April 30 of the year following the taxation year (s. 156.1(4)). However, those taxpayers receiving income from employment (and some other sources) have their tax withheld at source: the tax is deducted by the employer from each pay cheque and remitted by the employer to Revenue Canada (s. 153(1)). For a taxpayer with little or no income other than tax-withheld employment income, there is unlikely to be any tax unpaid at the time of filing the return, and therefore there would be no obligation to pay anything by April 30. Indeed, there is no obligation even to file a return if there is no further tax payable (s. 150). However, a taxpayer in this situation should normally file a return, because the withholdings are often too high (for example, because they do not take account of all the deductions or credits to which the taxpayer is entitled), in which case the taxpayer will be entitled to a refund of the overpaid tax.[11]

(b)   Instalments

The general rule is that an individual who derives income from which tax has not been withheld at source (for example, income from business or property) must pay tax by quarterly instalments throughout the calendar year (s. 156), and then (if the instalments were insufficient) pay any balance on the "balance-due day" (s. 156.1(4)), which, for individual taxpayers, is defined as April 30 of the following year (s. 248(1)).

The general rule is subject to this exception: if the individual's total federal and provincial tax liability, apart from tax withheld at source, is less than $2,000, then no instalments need to be paid; any tax liability is not payable until April 30 of the following year (s. 156.1).[12] The exception is designed to cover the common case where an individual derives most of his or her income from employment, which is subject to withholding by the employer, and derives some additional income from investments (property) or business, which is not subject to withholding. Provided the additional income is not so great as to generate an additional tax liability of $2,000 or more, the individual need not pay instalments; the tax on the additional income need not be paid until April 30 of the following year.

The $2,000 exemption would also apply to a person who is self-employed or retired, and who has such a low total income that it attracts a combined federal-provincial tax liability of less than $2,000. That person would not have to pay tax by instalments, but could wait until April 30 of the following year.

Tax instalments are payable quarterly, approximately two weeks before the end of each quarter, on March 15, June 15, September 15 and December 15 of each year. The general requirement is that four equal payments be made, even though the taxpayer's income may not be received evenly throughout the year.[13]

The calculation of the amount of the instalment payments is complicated by the fact that the taxpayer will not know the precise amount of tax that is due until after the end of the year, because it is not until then that all relevant information is available to enable the taxpayer to file a return. The Act permits

---

[11] Low-income taxpayers should also file in order to establish their entitlement to the refundable GST credit and (if they have children) the child tax benefit: see ch. 4, Objectives, under heading 4.4, "Deductions and credits", above.

[12] More precisely, under s. 156.1, an individual is required to make instalment payments if the difference between total (federal and provincial) tax payable and tax withheld at source is greater than $2,000 in the current year *and* one of the previous two years.

[13] Farmers and fishermen do not pay quarterly instalments. They must pay a single instalment of two-thirds of their liability (provided it exceeds $2,000) on or before December 31, and the balance on or before April 30 of the following year: s. 155.

instalment payments to be calculated in one of three ways, at the option of the taxpayer.[14] The current-year option enables the taxpayer to use an estimate of the current year's tax liability as the basis for the calculation of instalments (s. 156(1)(a)(i)). The prior-year option enables the taxpayer to use the prior year's tax liability as the basis for the calculation of instalments in the current year (s. 156(1)(a)(ii)). The prior-year option creates some difficulty regarding the first and second instalments (payable in March and June), as the previous year's tax liability may not have been assessed by the time these instalments are due. The third method, the no-calculation option, relieves the taxpayer of the burden of estimating his or her tax liability for the current year or the prior year. Under this third option, Revenue Canada calculates the amount payable in each instalment through the application of a formula found in s. 156(1)(b). The first two quarterly instalments are each equal to one-quarter of the taxpayer's total tax liability two years prior to the current taxation year. The third and fourth instalments are calculated by subtracting the total amount paid in the first two instalments from the total tax liability of the taxpayer in the year immediately preceding the current year. Half of the figure obtained by this calculation will be payable in the September instalment, and the remainder will be payable in December. By basing the amounts payable in the first two instalments on the taxpayer's liability two years earlier, this method avoids the difficulty (encountered in the prior-year option) of estimating the prior year's tax liability before it has been assessed. Another benefit of the no-calculation option is that all calculations are performed by Revenue Canada. The Department simply informs the taxpayer of the amounts payable before the instalments fall due. Whichever method is used, if the instalments turn out to be insufficient, any balance due must be paid on the "balance-due day" (s. 156.1(4)), which is defined as April 30 for individuals (s. 248(1)).

Corporations are required to pay tax in 12 monthly instalments throughout the taxation year (fiscal period) calculated on the basis of an estimate of the current year's tax liability (s. 157(1)(a)). Any balance is due within two months of the end of the taxation year (s. 157(1)(b)).[15] A corporation has a period of six months from the end of the taxation year to file a return (s. 150(1)(a)), and so the return may not have been prepared by the time that the balance of tax liability is due. In that case, the corporation should make an estimate of the balance and pay that, because interest will accrue on tax unpaid after the due date. The obligation of corporations to pay instalments throughout the fiscal period means that corporations pay tax as they earn the related income.

---

[14] Planning for quarterly instalment payments is discussed by Carr and Yull, "Tax on the Instalment Plan", *CA Magazine*, August 1994, 35.

[15] The period is three months for a Canadian-controlled private corporation claiming the small business deduction that had taxable income of $200,000 or less in the preceding year: s. 157(1)(b).

(c)   Filing of return

In the income tax return, the taxpayer is obliged to estimate the amount of tax that is payable (s. 151). In the case of individual taxpayers, any tax that has not been paid through withholding at source or instalments is due on the "balance-due day" (s. 156.1(4)), which, for individuals, is defined as April 30 of the year following the taxation (calendar) year (s. 248(1)). This is also the deadline for the filing of a tax return for most individuals. In the case of individuals earning business income (and their spouses), and in the case of corporations, we have noticed that any unpaid balance of tax is due before their tax returns are due, but of course if the return later indicates that further tax is due, then the amount due should be paid to stop interest from accruing.

(d)   Assessment

When the Minister issues an assessment to a taxpayer (individual or corporation), and part of the amount assessed has not been paid through withholdings, instalments or other payments, then the taxpayer comes under an obligation to pay the unpaid part to Revenue Canada "forthwith" (s. 158). Note that all payments up to this point, with the important exception of withholdings at source, have been based on self-assessment by the taxpayer. This is the first official notification of tax liability. Needless to say, the same obligation of payment applies in the case of a reassessment.

(e)   Interest

Interest is payable at a prescribed rate on tax that is unpaid after it is due, including late or deficient instalments (s. 161). The prescribed rate is set quarterly and consists of the average yield of 90-day treasury bills in the first month of the previous quarter plus 4 per cent (reg. 4301). When a refund is due to the taxpayer, interest at the treasury-bill rate plus 2 per cent (not 4 per cent) is paid by the Minister (s. 164(3)).[16] In the case of individuals, the general rule is that refund interest is paid from 45 days after the later of (a) the "balance-due day" (April 30 of the following year) and (b) the date on which the return was filed. In the case of corporations, the general rule is that refund interest is paid from the later of (a) 120 days after the end of the corporation's taxation year and (b) the date on which the return was filed.

---

[16] There is an exception for "contra interest" which is interest on instalment overpayments owed by Revenue Canada that is not paid to the taxpayer, but is used to offset interest owed by the taxpayer for late or deficient payments. This would arise, for example, if the first quarter's instalment was early or excessive and a later quarter's instalment was late or deficient (or vice versa). Contra interest is credited to the taxpayer at the treasury-bill-plus-4-per-cent rate.

6.4   Income fluctuation

(a)   Impact on tax liability

When a taxpayer's income fluctuates from year to year, the progressive rate structure exacts a heavier total tax than it does from the same total amount of income earned in fairly even annual amounts. For example, taxpayer A, who earns $20,000 in year 1 and $70,000 in year 2, will find that her tax bill for the two years is more than $1,000 higher than taxpayer B, who earns $45,000 in year 1 and $45,000 in year 2. Yet both taxpayers have earned the same amount of income, namely, $90,000, in the two-year period.

From one point of view, the discrepancy in tax treatment arises from progressive rates of tax. Part of taxpayer A's high income in year 2 will be taxed at the top marginal rate, while none of taxpayer B's income rises into the top bracket. Certainly, if the income of the two taxpayers were taxed at a flat rate, then the amount of tax payable by each taxpayer would be the same. But, from another point of view, the discrepancy in tax treatment arises from the measurement of income in annual periods. Certainly, if income were measured in two-year periods, then the amount of tax payable by each taxpayer would be the same.[17]

(b)   Averaging

If it is agreed that it is unfair for a person with a fluctuating income to pay more tax than a person with a steady income, then a tax system that measures income on an annual basis and levies tax at progressive rates has to provide "averaging" techniques to provide relief for the taxpayer with the fluctuating income. "General averaging" is a device that widens the tax brackets or lowers the rates of tax on the peak income. "Block averaging" is a device that deems the fluctuating income to have been earned evenly over a period of years. "Forward averaging" enables a taxpayer to postpone receiving some of the peak income, either by depositing it with the government or by purchasing an income-averaging annuity, and to recognize the income for tax purposes only when it is received in a later year.

The Canadian Income Tax Act has employed all of the foregoing averaging techniques from time to time. However, the tax reform of 1988 abolished all forms of averaging. The rationale for this change was that the broader tax brackets and lower rates of tax that were introduced in 1988 would diminish the adverse impact of fluctuating income, and the Act would be simpler without such complexities.

---

[17] See Arnold, *Timing and Income Taxation* (Can. Tax Foundation, Toronto, 1983), ch. 2.

(c)   Loss carryovers

Since the tax reform of 1988, the only relief available to taxpayers with fluctuating income is provided by the Act's loss carryover rules. These rules form an exception to the annual measurement of income, because they enable a taxpayer who has incurred a loss in one year to carry the loss over to another year and deduct it against the income for that year. The policy reason for loss carryovers is much the same as the policy reason for averaging. There is no magic to the requirement that income be measured in watertight annual compartments, and there is force in the argument that only net income over a reasonable period of years should be taxed. There has never been any suggestion that the loss carryover rules should be repealed, and they were not touched by the 1988 tax reform. The topic of losses is discussed in a later chapter.[18]

6.5   Postponement of tax

It is easy to understand why taxpayers would want to reduce or avoid paying tax. It is less easy to understand why taxpayers would want to postpone paying tax. And yet, the Act provides more opportunities for postponement than it does for outright reduction, and taxpayers eagerly embrace those opportunities. We shall see that the advantage of the deduction of capital cost allowances (the Act's term for depreciation charges) that are higher than the actual decline in value of capital assets is that it causes a postponement of tax. We shall see that the various deferred income plans that are authorized by the Act, such as the registered retirement savings plan and the registered pension plan, permit taxpayers who contribute to such plans to postpone (not avoid) tax on the contributions. Other examples of tax postponement will be encountered as we move through this book. Why is tax postponement so attractive? If a payment of tax cannot be avoided, why not face up to the inevitable without delay?

The primary advantage to the taxpayer in postponing a liability to pay tax is that the taxpayer retains the use of money which would otherwise have to be paid to the government in tax. This is an obvious benefit to the taxpayer who needs extra cash, for example, for working capital in a business, and who would otherwise have to borrow the money at current interest rates. But even a taxpayer who has no special need of the money will benefit by having extra funds available for investment. Tax postponed is like an interest-free loan from the government to the taxpayer.

When a taxpayer succeeds in postponing tax, he or she takes advantage of what economists call the "time value" of money. The time value of money reflects the idea that a sum of money that is due to be received in the future is worth less than the same sum of money that is due to be received immediately. The assumption underlying the time value of money is that a sum of money on hand today could be invested at compound interest, which over a period of time would cause it to grow. The longer the period of compounding, and the higher

---

[18] Chapter 18, Losses, below.

the rate of interest, the more the sum will grow. A useful guide is the rule of 72: money invested at compound interest will double in the number of years obtained by dividing 72 by the after-tax rate of interest. Thus, a sum invested inside a registered retirement savings plan (where income is untaxed) at a rate of 7.2 per cent compound interest will double in ten years; a sum invested at 10 per cent compound interest will double in 7.2 years.

Another way of expressing the idea of the time value of money is by reference to the "present value" of a sum of money to be received in the future. Determining the present value of a future obligation is known as "discounting", and it is simply the reverse of compounding. The present value of a future obligation decreases as (1) the payment date extends further into the future, and (2) the discount rate increases. For example (recalling our rule of 72), the present value of $1,000 to be received in ten years' time is $500, using an after-tax discount rate of 7.2 per cent. If a discount rate of 15 per cent were used, instead of 7.2 per cent, the present value of the $1,000 to be received in ten years' time would shrink to $247. This is the same as saying that $247 invested at 15 per cent compound interest would grow to $1,000 in ten years. The practical consequence of the present value concept is that, when the applicable rate of return stands at 15 per cent, a rational person ought to be indifferent as between (1) paying (or receiving) $247 now, and (2) paying (or receiving) $1,000 in ten years' time.

From the standpoint of the taxpayer, the longer that an obligation to pay tax can legally be put off, the more the present value of the obligation shrinks. A very simple concrete example will illustrate the point. Suppose that T, who pays tax at a rate of 50 per cent, has received a sum of $1,000 that she can either (a) recognize as taxable income in the current year, or (b) not recognize until a future year. Assume that she invests the $1,000 income at 7.2 per cent. Consider alternatives (a) and (b) after ten years:

(a) If she pays tax immediately:

Income	$1,000
Less tax on $1,000	(500)
Available for investment	500
Interest over ten years	500
Less tax on interest	(250)
Net result of investment	$ 750

(b) If she postpones payment of tax for ten years:

Income	$1,000
Less tax	—
Available for investment	$1,000
Interest over ten years	1,000
Less tax on entire $2,000	(1,000)
Net result of investment	$1,000

The net result of the investment in example (b) (postponement) is $250 more than in example (a) — a difference of one-third. This substantial gain is entirely the result of the postponement of tax. Notice that in example (b), the postponement case, there is no actual saving of tax. On the contrary, the taxpayer pays one-third more tax, $1,000 instead of $750. But the net result is still more favourable to the taxpayer because the total taxable income is also one-third more. What has happened in example (b) is that the money which would otherwise have been paid in tax ($500) has also been earning income ($500 in all), and only half of that extra income ($250) is paid in tax by T (who pays tax at a rate of 50 per cent).

This example demonstrates that the advantages of tax postponement are so substantial that even if the taxpayer has moved into a higher tax bracket during the period of postponed liability (ten years in our example) she would still make more money by postponing tax. But a taxpayer with the means of deferring taxable income may be able to recognize that income in a year, or over a period of years, when his or her other income has fallen and taken the taxpayer down into a lower tax bracket. This is a great feature of the registered pension plans and registered retirement savings plans that are permitted by the Income Tax Act. Contributions to these plans are deductible from income (subject to certain limits) so that the contributor is in effect investing not only the money he or she would have been able to save after the payment of tax, but also the money he or she would have paid in tax. This means that the fund invested will grow very much larger than would a fund built up solely of the money saved from after-tax dollars. Moreover, the income of the fund is not taxed as it is earned. The money in the fund is taxed when it is paid to the taxpayer in his or her years of retirement. In retirement, other income has normally fallen off, and the pension receipts, swollen by their years of tax-sheltered growth, are accordingly taxed at lower rates than would have been applicable in the years when the contributions were actually earned.

Sometimes there are other advantages of tax postponement. Occasionally, something "turns up" which unexpectedly diminishes the taxpayer's liability. One way in which this may occur is that the law may change in the taxpayer's favour. For example, taxpayers who control companies in which profits have accumulated have in the past occasionally been relieved of part of the potential tax liability inherent in the retained earnings by a special temporary provision enabling retained earnings to be removed on payment of a flat tax of 15 per cent. Another way in which postponed tax liabilities may be reduced is where a taxpayer's personal circumstances change to his or her advantage. For example, the taxpayer may incur a business loss in a particular year which would make it advantageous to recognize some of the deferred income. Or a taxpayer may become a non-resident of Canada, and be able to recognize the deferred income at the low 15 per cent rate of withholding tax (where there is a tax treaty) that is applicable to much of the income of a non-resident.

In other words, the old adage that one should not put off until tomorrow what one can do today is one that only Revenue Canada can be expected to endorse. For the taxpayer, there are bound to be economic gains in tax postponement. And, occasionally, the predictable economic gains are further sweetened by an unpredictable windfall.

7

Taxation Unit

7.1   Individual as taxation unit

(a)   Introduction

Under Canada's Income Tax Act, one large income bears a heavier tax load than it would if split into two or more smaller incomes. For example, in 1997 in Ontario, an individual earning $100,000 would pay (combined federal and provincial) income tax of $38,186 (assuming the taxpayer claims only basic, CPP and EI credits). An individual earning $50,000 would pay tax of $13,507. Thus, two incomes of $50,000 would attract a tax liability of $27,014, which is $11,172 less than the tax liability of a single income of $100,000. There are two reasons for this result. First, under the Act's graduated rate structure, a substantial part of the income of $100,000 is taxed at higher rates than those applicable to the incomes of $50,000. As well, each taxpayer is entitled to a number of deductions and credits. The two incomes of $50,000 enjoy the benefit of two sets of deductions and credits, while the one income of $100,000 will benefit from only one set of deductions and credits.

The discrepancy in tax liability between one large income and two smaller incomes is the inevitable result of a progressive tax system. The higher income-earner has the ability to pay a higher proportion of his or her income in tax than the lower income-earner. Therefore, if ability-to-pay is the criterion of tax equity, the higher marginal and average rates of tax that the higher income-earner bears are fair. This rationale only holds true as long as the comparisons are between financially independent taxpayers. The fairness of the result may be questioned when families, rather than individuals, are used as the basis of comparison. Assume that family A has one income-earner with an income of $100,000, and family B has two income-earners each with an income of $50,000. Each family has a total income of $100,000, and (assuming that each family is otherwise similarly situated) would seem to have an equal ability to pay tax. Yet family A (with one income of $100,000) will pay far more tax than family B (with two incomes of $50,000). The credit for the dependent spouse (s. 118(1)(a)), which will be available to the income-earner in family A, and will not be available to either income-earner in family B, is worth $1,629 in 1997 to family A,[1] so that it only slightly offsets the great advantage of family B's income-split.

Under a flat-rate income tax system, there would be no difference between the tax liability of family A and family B. The tax reform of 1988 is sometimes described as a modified flat-rate system, because it lowered the top rates and broadened the brackets. But the figures given above are based on the

---

[1] The federal credit is worth $915 in 1997, rising in value to $1,629 for a taxpayer in Ontario as the result of the consequent reduction of provincial income tax (48%), provincial surtaxes (20% + 26%) and federal surtaxes (3% + 5%): $915 × (1.70 + .05 + .03) = $1,629. See ch. 5, Rates, under heading 5.2(b), "Surtaxes", above.

1988 rates (admittedly steepened by federal and provincial surtaxes), and they illustrate how progressive the system still is.[2]

(b) Carter Commission's recommendation

The Carter Commission, which reported in 1966, argued that it was inequitable that a family with one income-earner should pay more tax than a family with two (or more) income-earners and the same total income. In the Commission's view, the proper measure of ability to pay was the income of a family (spouses and children under 18) rather than the income of individuals within a family.[3] If the family were the taxpaying unit, then two families with the same total income would pay the same amount of tax regardless of how the income was split among individual members of each family. The Commission accordingly recommended that the family become the taxpaying unit. For adult individuals who were not living within a family, the individual would of course remain as the taxpaying unit.

The White Paper that was issued by the federal government after the Carter Report agreed that there was "logic in the argument that the family, or at least the husband and wife together, is the basic spending unit". However, the White Paper went on to say that "the Commission's proposed family unit tax would have imposed a "tax on marriage" — that is, a husband and wife each having an income would together pay more tax than two people with the same income who were not married". The government took the view that such a "tax on marriage" would be "unfair and undesirable", and decided against any change.[4] The Income Tax Act that was enacted in 1971 therefore continued to recognize the individual, and not the family, as the basic taxation unit in Canada.

7.2 Family as taxation unit

(a) Argument

The idea that the family should be treated as the taxation unit[5] depends

---

[2] See ch. 5, Rates, above.

[3] *Report of the Royal Commission on Taxation* (Carter Report) (1966), vol. 3, ch. 10.

[4] Benson, *Proposals for Tax Reform* (1969), 14.

[5] See generally Surrey, "Family Income and Federal Taxation" [1946] *Taxes* 980; Oldman and Temple, "Comparative Analysis of the Taxation of Married Persons" (1960) 12 *Stanford L. Rev.* 585; McIntyre and Oldman, "Taxation of the Family in a Comprehensive and Simplified Income Tax" (1977) 90 *Harv. L. Rev.* 1573; Dulude, "Joint Taxation of Spouses — A Feminist View" (1979) 1 *Can. Taxation* 8; McIntyre, "Individual Filing in the Personal Income Tax" (1980) 58 *N.J.L. Rev.* 469; Pahl, "Patterns of Money Management within Marriage" (1980) 9 *J. of Social Policy* 313; Rea, "Taxes, Transfers, and the Family" (1984) 34 *U.T.L.J.* 314; Dulude, "Taxation of the Spouses" (1985) 23 *Osgoode Hall L. J.* 67; Woodman, "The Family as a Unit of Taxation" and Lahey, "The Tax Unit in Income Tax Theory", both in *Pask* (ed.), *Women, the Law and the Economy* (1984), 273, 277; Maloney, "Women and the *Income Tax Act*" (1989) 3 *Can. J. Women*

upon three assumptions, each of which is controversial. The first assumption is that the family is the basic consumption unit in society. This assumption is undermined by high divorce rates and the prevalence of a variety of cohabitation arrangements. At the very least, difficult questions of definition would have to be resolved, and it would be hard to avoid investigations into the living arrangements of people who might be cohabiting in lieu of marriage or for convenience.

The second assumption is that taxation should be based on the benefit derived from income, rather than on legal title to income. Under a legal title test, even if the sole income-earner in a family did typically share the income with the other members of the family, the income-earner's legal title to the income gives him or her a degree of control over expenditure decisions which, it could be argued, makes it reasonable to treat him or her as the sole taxpayer in respect of the income. Under a benefit test, if sharing is typical, then it may be appropriate to share the tax burden by treating the family as the taxation unit. Oddly enough, this particular issue does not arise in other taxation contexts, and it is difficult to derive a principled answer to the question whether it is legal title or benefit that counts.

If the first two assumptions are accepted, the third assumption has to be considered, namely, that the benefit of family income is usually shared among the members of the family regardless of who actually earns the income. Intuitively, it seems obvious that sharing is prevalent and substantial in a family that shares the run of the house or apartment, eats the same food, is clothed to the same standard, and goes on vacations together. For most families, these consumption expenditures would absorb most of the income. On the other hand, there do not seem to be comprehensive empirical studies of the patterns of family expenditures, and those studies that do exist cast doubt on the prevalence of sharing.[6]

The final step in the argument for the family as the unit of taxation is to apply the criterion of ability-to-pay in light of the foregoing three assumptions. It follows from these assumptions (subject to a question about imputed income which is addressed next) that families with equal total income have an equal ability to pay and should pay an equal amount of tax. This can be accomplished by aggregating the income of both spouses (and perhaps children, as Carter recommended) and basing tax liability on the aggregate figure. In that way, the family would become the unit of taxation.

---

and the Law 182; Woolley, "Women and Taxation: A Survey" (working paper for Ontario Fair Tax Commission's Women and Taxation Working Group Report, 1991); Ontario Fair Tax Commission, "Women and Taxation Working Group Report" (1992); Ontario Fair Tax Commission, *Fair Taxation in a Changing World* (U. Toronto Press, 1993), ch. 14.

[6] See Pahl, note 5, above, 328; Dulude (1985), note 5, above, 94; Woolley, note 5, above, 13; Ontario Fair Tax Commission (1993), note 5, above, 269-270.

(b)   Household labour

A possible difference between the one-job family and the two-job family, each with the same total cash income, consists in the amount of "imputed income" derived by each family. Imputed income is the value of the benefit derived by a person from his or her own personal services (such as dressmaking, gardening, automobile maintenance or whatever else people do for themselves) or from the use of his or her own property (such as a house, a cottage, or an automobile). The concept of imputed income is discussed in a later chapter,[7] where it is explained that imputed income is untaxed.

It is arguable that the family with two spouses and only one job has greater taxable capacity because of the imputed income of the non-earning spouse, who usually increases the taxable capacity of the family by performing caregiving and other unpaid household services which the two-job family would have to purchase (or forego). The value of this work, like other forms of imputed income, is not directly recognized for tax purposes. The present higher tax on the one-job family could be defended as an indirect recognition of that family's higher imputed income from unpaid household services. But of course the present law is not based on any measurement of the imputed income of a housekeeping spouse and is therefore a very arbitrary recognition of imputed income. Should some attempt be made to measure the imputed income from unpaid household services and incorporate it into the tax base? The Carter Commission rejected this approach on the ground that it was unfair to single out and tax one form of imputed income while ignoring other forms of imputed income.[8] Of course, like other forms of imputed income, household labour is difficult to value, and it does not bring in any of the cash that would be needed to pay the tax.[9]

(c)   Rates of taxation

The adoption of the family as the taxation unit implies a decision that families with equal incomes should be treated alike, but it does not decide the question of how tax burdens should be allocated as between families and single individuals. The question remains whether the aggregated family income should

---

[7] Chapter 9, Tax Base, under heading 9.9, "Imputed income", below.

[8] Carter Report, vol. 3, 118.

[9] Another problem with the taxation of imputed income from household services is that most home-centred work is performed by women, so that the taxation of the imputed income would indirectly place a disproportionate burden on women. This has led to other proposals to reduce the bias in the tax system in favour of unpaid household work, as well as proposals to use the tax system to compensate for the economic disparities between men and women. For a discussion of a variety of proposals, see Lahey, note 5, above, 299-302; Maloney, note 5, above, 194-203; Ontario Fair Tax Commission, "Women and Taxation Working Group Report", note 5, above, 24-25; Ontario Fair Tax Commission (1993), note 5, above, 269-270.

be taxed at the same rates as are applicable to the income of a single individual, or at lower rates. There are two polar positions. At one pole (represented in some European systems), the aggregated income of the two spouses is taxed under a rate schedule which is applicable to single taxpayers as well; under this system, a married couple in which H earns $50,000 and W earns $40,000 would pay the same tax as a single individual earning $90,000. At the other pole (represented in the United States from 1948 until 1969), the aggregated income of the two spouses is taxed as if each spouse had earned exactly one-half of it; under this system, a married couple in which H earned $50,000 and W earned $40,000 would pay the same tax as two single individuals each earning $45,000; in other words, the married couple is given the benefit of a perfect income-split. The Carter Commission recommended a middle ground.[10] The Commission recommended that tax should be levied on the family under a rate schedule which would differ from the rate schedule applicable to a single individual; the two rate schedules should be so designed that a family would pay less tax than one single individual with the same income as the family, but more than two single individuals with the same total income as the family.

(d)   Disincentive to employment

Using the family as the tax unit would probably operate as a disincentive to a non-earning spouse entering the paid labour force. (It is, of course, hard to know to what extent people take into account tax considerations in making occupational choices, but it seems reasonable to assume that tax considerations have some influence.) Under the present system, under which the individual is the unit of taxation, when a non-earning spouse starts earning income, the new income is taxed as if it were the income of a single individual. The advantage of that income-split would be lost if the family became the unit of taxation: the new income would have to be added to the existing income and would not be taxed at the lower rates appropriate to a separate individual. The possible discouragement of married women from entering the paid labour force has formed the basis for some opposition to the idea of the family as a unit of taxation.[11]

7.3   Present recognition of family

While the individual continues to be the basic taxation unit in Canada, the Income Tax Act does recognize in various ways the interdependence of family members. First, there are the "attribution" rules, which attribute back to the donor (or lender) the income from property given (or lent) to a spouse or a

---

[10] Carter Report, vol. 3, ch. 10.

[11] See the articles by Dulude (both articles), Woodman and Lahey, note 5, above.

related minor (ss. 74.1-74.5); these are discussed in detail later in this chapter.[12] Second, there are the "rollover" rules, which exempt from recognition of capital gains and recapture of capital cost allowance dispositions of property between spouses (s. 73(1)) and some dispositions between parents and children (farm property and farm corporations (ss. 73(3), (4)). Third, the ability to designate a home as a principal residence (to obtain an exemption from capital gains) is lost if the homeowner's spouse or child under 18 has made a rival designation (s. 54(g)). (The capital gains rules are discussed in the chapter on capital gains.)[13] Fourth, there are tax credits for a dependent spouse and other dependants (s. 118(1)(a), (b), (d)). Fifth, there is the provision for the transfer from one spouse to another of the benefit of certain unused tax credits (s. 118.8), and for the transfer from a child to a parent of the disability credit (s. 118.3(2)) and the tuition credit and education credit (s. 118.9). Sixth, there is the provision allowing a deduction for a contribution to a registered retirement savings plan for the spouse of the taxpayer (s. 146(5.1)). The seventh and most recent additions to the list are the child tax benefit (s. 122.61) and the goods and services tax credit (s. 122.5); both these programmes are means-tested, depending on the combined income of the claimant and the claimant's spouse.

The use of family income as the test of eligibility for the child tax benefit and the goods and services tax credit is consistent with social security programmes which tend to use the same approach, denying benefits to the wife of the millionaire even if she has no income of her own. Louise Dulude, who opposes the use of the family as the unit of taxation, argues that the family unit is appropriate to programmes designed to ensure that the basic needs of the poor are met, because a family which requires all of the income just to meet its basic needs is by necessity a single economic unit.[14] And yet, it is not easy to see why (1) we should pool the shared consumption of poor families because that will reduce their entitlement to income support, but (2) we should not pool the shared consumption of more affluent families because that would increase their liability to pay tax.

Moreover, it is arguable that income support and income tax should as a matter of policy be treated as two sides of the same coin. The refundable credits provide a limited model for a negative income tax, under which any taxfiler reporting income below a stipulated "poverty line" would receive a payment from the government. A negative income tax is probably the simplest way of

---

[12] Section 7.5, "Attribution rules", below.

[13] Chapter 15, Capital Gains, under heading 15.15, "Rollovers", below.

[14] Dulude (1979), note 5, above, 10. The Ontario Fair Tax Commission report (1993), note 5, above, does not directly address this issue, but its Women and Taxation Working Group Report, note 5, above, 17, recommended that the unit for both purposes be the individual, except "when he or she is living with a spouse who is legally obligated to provide support". In the latter case, a benefit programme could test entitlement by reference to combined incomes.

implementing a guaranteed annual income, which would replace all existing welfare or income support programmes. If a negative income tax were implemented, the poverty line would probably be defined by reference to family income rather than individual income. But if family income becomes the basis for entitlement to tax "refunds" to the poor, it is going to be difficult to explain why it should not also be the basis for tax liability for everyone else.

7.4　Income splitting

Income splitting means dividing one large income into several smaller incomes. For the reasons discussed at the beginning of this chapter, in a progressive tax system an income split will reduce the total burden of taxation on the income.

High income-earners are not normally willing to divest themselves of any of their income, because, although the divestment would save some income tax, it would also reduce their disposable income and therefore their standard of living. However, when part of a high income can be diverted to a spouse or child (or to a corporation or trust owned by a spouse or child), the divested income will remain available to essentially the same persons or purposes that it would have been spent on anyway. In this way, the high income-earner is able to reduce his or her tax liability without suffering any real loss of command over goods and services.

If the family were the taxation unit, the incentive to split income among members of a family would disappear. Many jurisdictions remove the most obvious temptation to income-splitting by aggregating for tax purposes the incomes of spouses. The Carter Commission's recommended family unit went one step further by including children's income in the aggregation. Canada has rejected these approaches, but the Income Tax Act still attempts to combat tax avoidance through income-splitting within a family. This policy is pursued by the provisions of the Act known as the "attribution rules". These are the topic of the next section of this chapter.

7.5　Attribution rules

(a)　Description

The "attribution rules" of the Income Tax Act[15] change the general rule that the person who recognizes income for tax purposes is the person who is entitled to that income. When an attribution rule applies, income that belongs to one person is deemed for tax purposes to belong to another person stipulated by

---

[15] See Interpretation Bulletins IT-510, "Transfers and loans to related minors" (1987); IT-511R, "Interspousal transfers and loans" (1994); Young, "The Attribution Rules" (1987) 35 *Can. Tax J.* 275.

the Act. The income is said to be "attributed" to the person stipulated by the Act. The three most important attribution rules are:

1. Subsection 74.1(1), which provides that, where a person has transferred (or loaned) property to or for the benefit of his or her spouse, the transferee's income from the property is attributed to the transferor;

2. Subsection 74.1(2), which provides that, where a person has transferred (or loaned) property to or for the benefit of a related minor, the transferee's income from the property is attributed to the transferor; and

3. Section 74.2, which provides that, where a person has transferred (or loaned) property to or for the benefit of his or her spouse, any capital gain from the disposition of the property by the transferee is attributed to the transferor.

The purpose of these rules is to prevent a high-income taxpayer from diverting taxable income to a low-income taxpayer. If it were not for the attribution rules, a transfer of income-yielding property from a high-income taxpayer to a low-income taxpayer would have the effect of reducing the tax payable on the income yielded by the transferred property. When the attribution rules apply, the income from the transferred property is deemed to continue to be the income of the transferor. For example, if high-income wife (W) has given to low-income husband (H) a $1,000 – 10% bond, upon which H earns $100 of interest, the $100 of interest income that has been derived by H is deemed to be the income of W (s. 74.1(1)).

The attribution rules, like the other provisions of the Income Tax Act, are addressed only to income tax consequences. For all other purposes, the transfer is perfectly valid and effective: the transferee will become the owner of the transferred property and of the income which it yields. If the transferor has a non-tax reason for making a gift to a family member, then the transferor may still decide to make the gift; indeed, the transferor may be happy to pay the tax on the transferee's income. However, the attribution rules must operate as a disincentive to substantial intrafamily gifts, because when the rules apply the donor has to be willing not only to give away property, but to continue to pay the tax on the income yielded by the property. Thus, the rules tend to reinforce existing accumulations of wealth by discouraging the sharing of property with spouses and children.

(b)   Spouses

Attribution of property income under s. 74.1(1) and of capital gains under s. 74.2(1) occurs if property is transferred (or loaned) to the transferor's "spouse". The term is defined in s. 252(4) of the Income Tax Act as including not only formal marital relationships, but common law relationships as well. Under s. 252(4), persons "of the opposite sex" who are cohabiting "in a conjugal relationship" are deemed to be "spouses" where (a) they have been cohabiting for the preceding 12 months, or (b) they are the natural or adoptive parents of the same child. (Note that same-sex couples are excluded; so are family units lacking a conjugal relationship, such as parent and adult child.) This definition of "spouse" applies not only to the attribution rules but for all income tax purposes.[16] Attribution under ss. 74.1(1) and 74.2(1) will continue for so long as the transferee remains the "spouse" of the transferor, and the transferor remains a resident of Canada. An end of the spousal relationship, or the death of either spouse, or the permanent departure from Canada of the transferor, will bring attribution to an end.

Where spouses remain married, but are separated pursuant to a court order or written separation agreement, s. 74.5(3) provides that attribution of income under s. 74.1 is suspended for as long as the separation continues; attribution of capital gains under s. 74.2 is not suspended automatically, but will be suspended if both spouses jointly elect to suspend attribution of capital gains. If the separation is ended by reconciliation, the attribution rules will return to force. If the marriage is ended by divorce, the attribution rules will cease to apply.

(c) Related minor

Attribution of property income under s. 74.1(2) occurs if property is transferred or loaned to or for the benefit of "a person who was under 18 years of age". Before 1985, there was no requirement that the minor transferee be related to the transferor, but now s. 74.1(2) stipulates that the minor transferee "(a) does not deal with the individual [transferor] at arm's length, or (b) is the niece or nephew of the individual [transferor]". The effect of paragraph (a) is to include a sibling or child (or other descendant) of the transferor (see the definitions of "arm's length" in s. 251(1)(a), of "related persons" in s. 251(2)(a), and of "blood relationship", "marriage" and "adoption" in s. 251(6)).[17] Paragraph 74.1(2)(b) adds a niece or nephew of the transferor (who would not be automatically included in the definition of arm's length). The practical effect of these limitations is that a transfer (or loan) to a minor attracts attribution only if the minor transferee is the child,[18] grandchild, brother, sister, niece or nephew of the transferor. For the rest of this chapter, the term "related minor" will be used as shorthand for these relatives.

---

[16] Prior to 1992, common law couples were excluded from those provisions of the Act which applied to "spouses". Under the current definition, couples fulfilling the requirements of s. 252(4) are not only subject to the attribution rules, but also have the burden or benefit of all of the other provisions of the Act recognizing spouses of taxpayers; these were listed earlier in the chapter in the text accompanying note 12, above.

[17] In addition, a person under 18 who, although not a sibling, child or other descendant of the transferor, was not in fact at arm's length to the transferor will be caught by s. 74.1(2). See generally Interpretation Bulletin IT-419R, "Meaning of arm's length" (1995).

[18] The term "child" is defined in s. 252(1) to include (among other persons) the spouse of a child.

Attribution under s. 74.1(2) will continue for so long as the transferor remains a resident of Canada, and the transferee remains under the age of 18. In the taxation year in which the transferee attains 18, attribution ceases. The death of either transferor or transferee will also bring the attribution to an end.

(d)   Transfer or loan

The attribution rules apply where a taxpayer has "transferred or loaned" property to a spouse or a related minor. The application of the rules to a gift, a sale, a loan, a trust for a spouse or related minor, and a corporation of which a spouse or related minor is the shareholder are considered in the following sections of this chapter.

(e)   Gift

A gift is obviously a transfer, and a gift is the transaction at which the attribution rules are primarily aimed. The gift divests the donor of the income produced by the transferred property, and, since the donor receives no consideration, the divested income is not replaced by income from assets received in return for the transferred property. If husband (H), paying tax at the top marginal rate, gives Blackacre to his wife (W), who has no taxable income, there would be a substantial loss of tax revenue if Blackacre's income were not attributed back to H. Subsection 74.1(1) accomplishes that result, and s. 74.1(2) would accomplish the same result if Blackacre had been given to a related minor.

(f)   Sale

A sale is also a transfer within the meaning of the attribution rules. But s. 74.5(1) exempts a sale for fair market value. The reason for the exemption is that, if fair market value has been paid by the transferee spouse or related minor, then the transferor has simply substituted another potentially income-producing asset for the one transferred; there is no income-splitting and the transaction is outside the mischief of the attribution rules. However, s. 74.5(1)(a) stipulates that the consideration must be equal in value to the property transferred, and s. 74.5(1)(b) stipulates that if the consideration includes indebtedness the purchaser must be obliged to pay a commercial rate of interest and must actually regularly pay the interest.[19] These stipulations ensure that artificial sales for inadequate consideration or for consideration in the form of an interest-free debt cannot be

---

[19] More precisely, s. 74.5(1)(b) stipulates that the interest rate must be no less than the lesser of (a) the "prescribed rate" that was in effect at the time that the indebtedness was incurred, and (b) the market rate at that time. The prescribed rate is set quarterly by Revenue Canada under reg. 4301: see note 27, below. The interest agreed upon must be paid not later than 30 days after the end of the year throughout the term of the indebtedness.

used as devices to divert property income from the "vendor" to a "purchaser" who is a spouse[20] or a related minor.

(g)   Loan

The attribution rules apply to a loan as well as a transfer. This is an important change in the rules dating from 1985. The pre-1985 rules applied only to a transfer, and it had been held by the courts that a loan was not a transfer.[21] Even an interest-free loan was held to be outside the attribution rules;[22] and the interest-free loan became a common method of avoiding the attribution rules. The lender would derive no income from the money lent, because no interest was payable. The borrowing spouse or minor would invest the borrowed money in income-producing investments, and the resulting income would not be attributed back to the lender. In this way, a diversion of income was achieved.

This gap in the attribution rules was finally plugged in 1985. A loan of cash (or other property) to a spouse or related minor now attracts the same attribution rules as a "transfer". Subsection 74.5(2) exempts a loan if the loan is made at a commercial rate of interest and if the borrower actually regularly pays the interest.[23] The reason for this exemption is that, if the debt bears interest, the lender has acquired an income-producing asset (the debt) for the money lent; there is no income-splitting and the transaction is outside the mischief of the attribution rules.[24]

(h)   Trust

The attribution rules apply to property settled on trust[25] for a spouse or related minor. This was decided by the courts in 1948,[26] and since then the position has been reinforced by express references to a trust in the rules. Where the person entitled to income from a trust is the settlor's spouse or a related minor, the income is attributed to the settlor. The attribution rules cannot be avoided by the interposition of a trust between the transferor and the transferee.

---

[20] In the case of a spouse, s. 74.5(1)(b) adds the further requirement that, on the sale, the transferor-spouse must have elected against the s. 73(1) rollover.

[21] *Dunkelman* v. *M.N.R.*, [1959] C.T.C. 375, 59 D.T.C. 1242 (Ex. Ct.).

[22] *Oelbaum* v. *M.N.R.*, [1968] C.T.C. 244, 68 D.T.C. 5176 (Ex. Ct.).

[23] The precise stipulations of s. 74.5(2) are the same as those of s. 74.5(1), described in note 19, above.

[24] If the borrowing spouse or minor can obtain a rate of return on the investments purchased with the borrowed money that is higher than the interest rate payable to the lender, then the net income is not attributed and an income-split is achieved.

[25] See ch. 21, Trusts, below.

[26] *Fasken Estate* v. *M.N.R.*, [1948] C.T.C. 265, 4 D.T.C. 491 (Ex. Ct.).

The pre-1985 rules were not sufficiently specific to provide clear answers to all the attribution issues raised by trusts for the benefit of spouses and minors. The basic attribution rules are now supplemented by s. 74.3, which spells out the attribution consequences whenever there has been a transfer or loan to a trust in which the settlor's spouse or a related minor is a beneficiary. Without going into detail, the results could be summarized as follows:

1. Where the trust's property income is paid or payable to a spouse or a related minor, there will be attribution under s. 74.1(1) or (2). Where the trust's capital gains are paid or payable to a spouse, there will be attribution under s. 74.2.

2. This is so, even if the payment is the exercise of a discretionary power by the trustee.

3. Where income is not paid or payable to a spouse or a related minor, there will be no attribution.

4. This is so, even if the income is being accumulated in the trust for the ultimate benefit of a spouse or a related minor.

Another section of the Act dealing specifically with trusts is s. 75(2), a provision that pre-dates the 1985 amendments and was not altered in 1985. Subsection 75(2) operates to attribute to the settlor income or taxable capital gains from property transferred to a trust in which a settlor has reserved to himself or herself a power to revoke the trust, or a power to change the beneficiaries, or a power to direct or veto dispositions of the trust property. Attribution occurs regardless of who are the beneficiaries of the trust: s. 75(2) is not confined to trusts for spouses and related minors. The idea is that a settlor should not be able to divert taxable income away to the beneficiaries of a trust while continuing to retain substantial control over the trust.

(i)   Corporation

Section 74.4 provides for attribution of income or capital gains from property transferred or loaned to a corporation of which the transferor's spouse or a related minor is the shareholder. Before 1985, there was a question whether attribution applied in this situation, because of course a corporation is an entity distinct from its shareholders, who have no proprietary interest in property that has been transferred or loaned to the corporation. Section 74.4 now makes clear that attribution applies, but only if "one of the main purposes of the transfer or loan [to the corporation] may reasonably be considered to be to reduce the income of the individual [transferor] and to benefit . . . [a spouse or a related minor of the transferor]". This "purpose test" involves an inquiry into the intention of the transferor at the time of making the transfer or loan to the corporation. This inquiry injects into s. 74.4 an element of uncertainty that is absent from the other attribution rules; the other rules simply rely on the objective legal effect of the transfer or loan.

Another unique feature of s. 74.4 is that it stipulates the amount to be attributed to the transferor, and that amount is derived by applying the Department's prescribed quarterly interest rate[27] to the value of the property transferred or loaned. This arbitrary figure is attributed regardless of whether or not a dividend is paid by the corporation to the spouse or minor.[28] Indeed, if a dividend is paid to the spouse or minor, there is no provision to exclude the dividend from the income of the spouse or minor, and the recipient will have to report the dividend for tax purposes. That amounts to double taxation, because the transferor also has to report the arbitrary attributed figure. Double taxation is scrupulously avoided in the other attribution rules, each of which stipulates that income attributed to the transferor is deemed not to be the income of the actual recipient (spouse or minor).[29]

Section 74.4 exempts a transfer or loan to a "small business corporation", which is defined in s. 248 as a Canadian-controlled private corporation (CCPC) with assets "all or substantially all" (generally considered to mean 90 per cent or more) of which were "used in an active business carried on primarily in Canada". This exemption reflects the policy of the attribution rules to apply to income from property, and not income from a business. (This policy is explained in a later section of this chapter.)[30] However, the narrowness of the definition of a small business corporation makes s. 74.4 somewhat underinclusive in its pursuit of this policy. A loan or transfer to a company that was not Canadian-controlled, or was not private, or was using more than 10 per cent of its assets to derive property income, could attract attribution, even though the company's income was wholly or mainly derived from carrying on a business.

(j)   Indirect transfer

The provisions just discussed that attribute income channelled to a spouse or a related minor through a trust or a corporation are designed to catch the more obvious varieties of indirect transfers or loans, and subject them to basically the same treatment as direct transfers or loans. The Act also specifically deals with "back-to-back transfers and loans", in which it is the intervention of a third party

---

[27] Regulation 4301 provides for a quarterly setting of the "prescribed rate of interest" based on the average yield of 90-day treasury bills in the first month of the previous quarter.

[28] The attributed figure is reduced by the amount of any dividends (grossed-up) or interest paid by the corporation to the transferor (but not to the spouse or minor for whose benefit the transfer or loan was made).

[29] But note s. 160 making the transferee liable as well as the transferor, and empowering the Minister to assess the transferee. Presumably, this power would be invoked only if the tax could not be collected from the transferor.

[30] The Act contains other preferences for the shareholders of "small business corporations", namely, the $500,000 lifetime capital gains exemption (ch. 15, Capital Gains, below), and the treatment of allowable capital losses as allowable business investment losses that are deductible from income other than taxable capital gains (ch. 18, Losses, below).

individual that masks the transfer of property to a spouse or a related minor. For example, Husband, instead of giving Blackacre to Wife, could give Blackacre to Third Party, who in turn gives Blackacre to Wife. Or, Husband could give Blackacre to Third Party, who in turn gives Greenacre to Wife. In both these examples, there is no direct transfer or loan from Husband to Wife, but Third Party is playing a purely intermediary role in what is in substance a gift from Husband to Wife. Both these cases are specifically provided for by s. 74.5(6), which treats the transactions as if the property had been given directly by Husband to Wife.

As well as the foregoing specific measures, each of the attribution rules applies where an individual has transferred or loaned property "either directly or indirectly" to a person to whom attribution would apply. The word "indirectly" would enable the court to penetrate to the reality of some hitherto unforeseen device for laundering a transaction the effect of which was to divert property income to a spouse or a related minor.[31]

(k) Property

The attribution rules apply only when there has been a transfer or loan of "property". If the transfer or loan was to a spouse or a related minor, ss. 74.1(1) and 74.1(2) attribute to the transferor any income (or loss) from the property. If the transfer or loan was to a spouse, s. 74.2(1) also attributes to the transferor any capital gain (or loss) from a later disposition of the property by the spouse.

The term "property" is defined in s. 248 in very broad terms. It means "property of any kind whatever whether real or personal or corporeal or incorporeal", and it includes "unless a contrary intention is evident, money". Of course, "money" by itself cannot yield income or capital gains, but as soon as the recipient of the money invests the money in income-yielding investments, the attribution rules will continue to apply to the investments that have been substituted for the money. This is because the rules apply not only to the property transferred or loaned, but also to "property substituted therefor". This phrase is considered in the next section of this chapter.

(l) Property substituted

As noted in the previous section, the attribution rules apply to "property substituted" for the property transferred or loaned. If the recipient of property to which the attribution rules apply sells the property and reinvests the proceeds of sale, the attribution rules continue to cling to the new investments. Income from the new investments or capital gains from their disposition will be attributed in

---

[31] E.g., *Naiberg* v. *M.N.R.*, [1969] C.T.C. 492, 69 D.T.C. 361 (T.A.B.), where attribution was applied to a complex scheme involving transfers of property among three married couples.

the same way as if the investments were the original subjects of the transfer or loan.

If the recipient of property to which the attribution rules apply invests the *income* yielded by the transferred property, the income yielded by the investments representing the income ("income on income" or "second generation income" is not attributed. Investments that represent income from the transferred property are neither property transferred nor property substituted therefor. For the same reason, interest on interest that is allowed to accumulate is also not attributed.[32]

(m)   Income from business

Subsections 74.1(1) and 74.1(2) do not attribute income from a business. This is because the provisions refer to income "from the property". Since the Act in its other provisions often distinguishes between income from "property" and income from a "business", it was perhaps inevitable that the attribution rules would be interpreted as not applying to income from a business.[33] Thus, if property is transferred to a spouse or a related minor, but the income derived from the assets (or substituted assets) is characterized for tax purposes as income from a business, rather than income from property, there will be no attribution. The transfer of an apartment building (yielding property income) will therefore attract attribution, while the transfer of an apartment hotel (yielding business income) will not.[34] This gap in the attribution rules may be explained on the basis that income from a business does not flow automatically from the ownership of property but requires activity on the part of the transferee (or his or her employees). In view of the difficulty of apportioning the transferee's income from the business between the assets transferred and the transferee's own efforts, the Act does not attribute any of the income from the business.

---

[32] This is recognized by the Department in Interpretation Bulletin IT-511R, "Interspousal transfers and loans" (1994), para. 6. The Department used to take the same view of income from investments that represented reinvested capital gains realized by the transferee, but the Department has now repented of this position. Now the Department takes the view that an investment representing the entire proceeds of disposition of property transferred or loaned, including any capital gain, is "property substituted" for the property transferred or loaned: IT-511R, para. 27. Therefore, there is no apportionment of the income of the new investment: all of the income, including the income from the reinvested capital gain, is attributed to the transferor.

[33] *Wertman* v. *M.N.R.*, [1964] C.T.C. 252, 64 D.T.C. 5158 (Ex. Ct.); *Robins* v. *M.N.R.*, [1963] C.T.C. 27, 63 D.T.C. 1012 (Ex. Ct.); Interpretation Bulletin IT-510, "Transfers and loans to related minors" (1987), para. 3; Interpretation Bulletin IT-511R, "Interspousal transfers and loans" (1994), para. 5.

[34] For the distinction between business and property income, see ch. 12, Income from Business or Property: Inclusions, under heading 12.1, "Business and property distinguished", below.

(n) Capital gains

As has already been noted, s. 74.2 attributes capital gains (or losses). Section 74.2 applies on a transfer or loan to the transferor's spouse. Subsection 74.1(1) has no application to capital gains, because it attributes only income or loss from property, and s. 9(3) provides that income or loss from property does not include a capital gain or loss from the disposition of property. Therefore, when property is transferred from one spouse to another, any income from the property will be attributed to the transferor-spouse by virtue of s. 74.1(1), and any capital gain arising from the later disposition of the property by the transferee-spouse will be attributed to the transferor-spouse by virtue of s. 74.2.

When property is transferred from a transferor to a related minor, and the transferee-minor later disposes of the property, any capital gain or loss on the disposition of the property by the transferee-minor is not attributed to the transferor. This is because s. 74.1(2), like 74.1(1), applies only to income or loss from property, and there is no equivalent of s. 74.2 applicable to transfers to minors. Section 75.1 does attribute capital gains and losses on the transfer of farming property from a taxpayer to his or her child; but this is a special case (explained in the next paragraph). In general there is no attribution of capital gains or losses on a transfer to a minor.

Why is there this difference in the attribution rules between transfers to spouses and transfers to minors? Part of the reason undoubtedly derives from the tax consequences of the initial transfer of the property to the spouse or the minor. On a transfer of property to a spouse, s. 73(1) provides a "rollover" for capital gains purposes.[35] This means that no capital gain or loss is recognized for tax purposes at that time, and the transferee-spouse is deemed to have acquired the property at its cost to the transferor-spouse, even if the fair market value of the property at the time of the transfer is substantially higher than its cost. On a subsequent disposition by the transferee-spouse, if the capital gain were not attributed, the transferor-spouse would have succeeded not merely in diverting future gains to the transferee-spouse but in actually diverting a gain which had already accrued in the transferor's hands at the time of the transfer. This would be a potentially serious tax avoidance procedure, and it would also violate the Act's general policy of freeing from tax consequences transactions between spouses. On a transfer of property from a taxpayer to a minor, by contrast, there is no rollover. Any accrued capital gain (or loss) at the time of the transfer has to be recognized by the transferor even if the transfer is by way of gift (s. 69).[36] Therefore, tax has to be paid on any gain accrued to that point, and the transferee is deemed to acquire the property at its fair market value at the time of the transfer. In the case of farming property, there is a rollover on

---

[35] See ch. 15, Capital Gains, under heading 15.15, "Rollovers", below.

[36] See ch. 15, Capital Gains, under heading 15.14, "Deemed dispositions", below.

a transfer from the taxpayer to his or her child (s. 73(3)), and that is the special case in which there is attribution of capital gains and losses (s. 75.1). The reasoning appears to be that, when a rollover is available on transfer, there should be attribution of capital gains and losses.

The rollover on the initial transfer of property to a spouse provided a powerful reason for attributing any capital gain realized by the transferee-spouse. There is no similarly powerful reason for attributing capital gains derived by a transferee-minor. Nonetheless, since income from property derived by the transferee-minor is attributed (s. 74.1(2)), one would expect capital gains to be attributed as well, unless there is a good reason not to do so. That good reason is to be found in the fact that, in the case of a related minor, attribution ceases in the year of the minor's eighteenth birthday. This temporal limitation on attribution means that a minor could avoid attribution of capital gains very easily, by not disposing of the transferred property until the year of the minor's eighteenth birthday. One way of precluding this result would be to provide for a "deemed disposition" of the transferred property at fair market value on the minor-transferee's eighteenth birthday. But the policy decision was evidently taken not to introduce that much complexity into the system. The result is that the Act makes no provision for attribution of capital gains derived by a transferee-minor.

(o)   Tax avoidance

Subsection 74.5(11) provides that the attribution rules do not apply to a transfer or loan of property "where it may reasonably be concluded that one of the main reasons for the transfer or loan" was to use the attribution rules to reduce the tax on the income or capital gain derived from the property. It is not easy to design transactions in which the attribution rules would accomplish a reduction in tax, but the Act has its anti-avoidance rule just in case.

(p)   Income diversion

The detailed attribution rules of ss. 74.1 through 74.5 are designed to stop income-splitting by the transfer of income-producing property from a high-income taxpayer to a low-income taxpayer. The rules are limited to transfers to spouses and related minors, because in other cases there is no reason why a genuine divestment of income-producing property should not be effective for tax purposes.

Where a taxpayer diverts income away from himself or herself without actually giving up the property or other source of the income, it seems obvious that the diversion should be ineffective for tax purposes regardless of the relationship between the taxpayer and the person to whom the income has been diverted. Otherwise, income-splitting would be an easy and (sometimes) costless exercise. For this reason, the attribution rules have to be supplemented by more general rules against diversions of income. Subsection 56(2) provides:

> 56(2) A payment or transfer of property made pursuant to the direction of, or with the concurrence of, a taxpayer to some other person for the benefit of the taxpayer or as a benefit that the taxpayer desired to have conferred on the other person . . . shall be included in computing the taxpayer's income to the extent that it would be if the payment or transfer had been made to the taxpayer.

What s. 56(2) does is to render ineffective diversions of income by a taxpayer to another person. For example, an employee might direct the employer to pay all or part of the employee's salary to a creditor of the employee. Or a creditor might direct the debtor to make payments of interest to the creditor's mother. Or a consultant might bill clients (for work done by the consultant) in the name of a company controlled by the consultant. All of these arrangements are perfectly legal and effective for other purposes, but s. 56(2) makes them ineffective for tax purposes.[37] They will not shift the tax liability away from the person who is entitled to the source of the income. In each case, the taxpayer would have to report the income, even though he or she did not actually receive it.

The application of s. 56(2) was considered by the Supreme Court of Canada in *McClurg* v. *Canada* (1990).[38] In that case, the taxpayer and an associate had incorporated a company to operate a truck dealership. The corporation had three classes of shares, two of which were held entirely by the taxpayer and his associate. The third class was held entirely by the taxpayer's wife and the wife of his associate. The articles of incorporation contained a discretionary dividend clause that entitled each class of shares to dividends only at the discretion of the directors. The taxpayer and his associate, who were the sole directors, exercised their power under this clause to declare a dividend of $10,000 only on the class of shares held by the wives. The corporation accordingly paid this dividend to the wives, and paid nothing to the taxpayer and his associate who held the other classes of shares. In assessing the taxpayer's income, the Minister applied s. 56(2) and attributed to him a portion of the dividend that had been paid to the taxpayer's wife. The Supreme Court of Canada, by a majority, held that the dividend payment in *McClurg* escaped attribution under s. 56(2). According to Dickson C.J. for the majority, the exercise by the directors of their power under the discretionary dividend clause in the company's articles of incorporation should not be regarded as a payment that was caught by s. 56(2). Had no dividend been declared, the income would have remained in the corporation; it would not have gone to the taxpayer. Subsection 56(2) was therefore blocked by the corporate veil, and the

---

[37] The taxpayer must have "desired" to confer a benefit on the recipient. Where there is no evidence of such a desire, as where a company transferred a property to Father at the direction of Son for a price that Son did not realize was less than fair market value, s. 56(2) does not apply: *Ascot Enterprises* v. *The Queen*, [1996] 1 C.T.C. 384, 96 D.T.C. 6015 (F.C.A.).

[38] [1990] 3 S.C.R. 1020, [1991] 1 C.T.C. 169, 91 D.T.C. 5001 (S.C.C.). For discussion, see Beam and Laiken, "Recent Developments on Subsection 56(2): Indirect Payments" (1995) 43 *Can. Tax J.* 447.

discretionary dividend clause was held to be successful in diverting income away from the higher-income taxpayer to his lower-income spouse.

In *McClurg*, Dickson C.J. made a puzzling reference to the fact that the taxpayer's wife had been active in the business, and he described the dividend payment to her as a "legitimate quid pro quo" for what she had contributed.[39] Since a dividend is income from property — the return on the capital invested in the company by the shareholder — it is odd to characterize it as a quid pro quo for services performed for the company. It also seems irrelevant to the Court's reasoning, which was that the taxpayer would not have received the income had no dividend been paid to his wife; this would be true regardless of the contribution made to the company by the wife. However, in *The Queen* v. *Neuman* (1996),[40] the Federal Court of Appeal relied on the dictum to apply s. 56(2) to attribute to a controlling shareholder a discretionary dividend that the company had paid on shares owned by his wife. In the *Neuman* case, unlike *McClurg*, the recipient wife had made no contribution to the company other than her subscription to the shares on which the dividend was paid. This was relevant, the Court said, because of the obiter dictum in *McClurg*, which they said was binding on them. With respect, the Court's reliance on the obiter dictum led to a result that was contrary to the ratio decidendi of the case (that the taxpayer would not be entitled to the dividend if it had not been paid to his wife). In our view, *Neuman* was wrongly decided. Leave to appeal to the Supreme Court of Canada has been granted, and we shall have to await the outcome of the appeal.[41]

A second general rule precluding the diversion of income from high-income earners to lower-income earners is s. 56(4). This section of the Act applies attribution to the assignment of rights to receive income by a taxpayer to a person with whom the taxpayer is not at arm's length. For example, an author might assign a right to royalties to his or her child (whether or not that child is a minor); the royalty income will be attributed back to the author by virtue of s. 56(4).

A third general rule precluding the diversion of income from high-income persons to low-income persons is s. 56(4.1). Subsection 56(4.1) applies to the case where a taxpayer makes a loan at little or no interest to a non-arm's-length individual, and that individual invests the loan in an income-producing property;

[39] *Id.*, 1054.

[40] [1996] 3 C.T.C. 270, 96 D.T.C. 6464 (F.C.A.).

[41] The facts of *Neuman* arose before 1985, when s. 74.4 was added to the Act. Section 74.4 would now lead to the attribution to the husband of an amount of income stipulated by the formula in that section: see heading 7.5(i), "Corporation", above. However, the decision remains important, because a transfer or loan to a "small business corporation" is exempt from s. 74.4; in that case, if *Neuman* is rightly decided, the express exemption from s. 74.4 would not avoid attribution under s. 56(2), which is an odd result.

in that case, attribution will apply, provided "it may reasonably be considered that one of the main reasons for making the loan . . . was to reduce or avoid tax". Subsection 56(4.1) differs from the three principal attribution rules of ss. 74.1(1), 74.1(2) and 74.2(1) in three important respects. First, s. 56(4.1) applies only where the lender of the money had a tax-avoidance reason for the loan; if the loan can be explained by a non-tax-avoidance reason, then s. 56(4.1) will not apply. (Of course, there will still be attribution if the loan was made to a spouse or related minor within the terms of s. 74.1(1), 74.1(2) or 74.2(1).) Secondly, s. 56(4.1), (like s. 56(4), discussed in the previous paragraph) applies to transactions that divert income to *any* non-arm's-length individual, and not just to spouses and related minors; for example, s. 56(4.1) will catch a loan to an adult child. Thirdly, s. 56(4.1) applies only to loans and not to outright gifts. As a result, a loan to an adult child of the taxpayer would be caught by s. 56(4.1), while an outright gift to an adult child is neither caught by that section nor by any other provision of the Act.[42] This has led one commentator to argue that s. 56(4.1) favours the wealthy, who can "afford parting irrevocably with their capital by making gifts rather than loans to their children".[43]

(q) Policy

The attribution rules have over the years become increasingly complicated, as loopholes have gradually been plugged. They now add considerable complexity to the Act. Ironically, as the rules have become more watertight, their importance has diminished. The rules are mainly directed to the family with two spouses only one of which possesses an income. It is the rapid decline in the number of two-spouse, one-income families that has reduced the usefulness of the rules. Where both spouses earn incomes, there is little scope for income-splitting between spouses (although the diversion of investments to children might still be attractive). Where both spouses earn incomes, and there is a considerable disparity between the two incomes, the attribution rules will continue to play a role in nullifying for tax purposes the transfer of income-yielding property from the high earner to the low earner. Some diversion of income can still be achieved without running afoul of the attribution rules. The couple can arrange their affairs so that consumption expenditures are made by the high earner and savings are made out of the lower income. In that way, future investment income will be derived by the lower-income spouse.

The attribution rules would not be needed at all in a flat-rate system, where all incomes, high or low, would bear tax at the same rate. The flattening of rates that occurred in 1988 has reduced the value of income-splitting, but the

---

[42] A sale in return for a non-interest-bearing promissory note probably also avoids the section, because a sale on deferred payment terms has not in the past been treated as a loan for tax purposes: Wolfe D. Goodman, Tax Column (1988) 9 *Estates and Trusts J.* 77, 79.

[43] *Ibid.*

availability of personal credits to each individual taxpayer, the three-bracket rate schedule and the various surtaxes have left the system sufficiently progressive that the savings from splitting continue to be substantial. This was demonstrated at the beginning of the chapter.

Should the attribution rules be repealed? Such a change would be regressive in that the income-splitting that it would allow would be available in practice only to the wealthier class of property owners. It is arguable, however, that the logic of accepting the individual as the tax unit should be carried forward to the elimination of the attribution rules. After all, the tax saving caused by income-splitting is purchased at the price of a legal divestment of the income-earning property in favour of another individual. It is true that the transferee is, we are assuming, a member of the transferor's family, but if the arguments in favour of the individual as the tax unit are valid, it is not silly to treat the transferor's loss of legal title to and control over income as having tax consequences. Moreover, the repeal of the attribution rules would provide an incentive to property-owners to share their property with spouses and children, which might contribute in some small way to a more equitable distribution of wealth, especially to women, who often lack the same opportunity to accumulate wealth as men.

8

Residence

8.1   Policy

(a)   The problem

A country cannot levy tax on everyone in the world. It must confine its taxes to people with some connection with the country. It would be impossible for Canada to enforce a tax against people lacking any connection with Canada; and even if it were possible, there is no moral justification for forcing such people to help finance Canada's government. Canada, like every other country, has to employ some factor or factors to identify the class of people liable to pay Canadian income tax. As we shall see, the dominant factor that is employed by Canada is residence — the topic of this chapter. But it is interesting to examine, albeit briefly, some of the other connecting factors which could be used as the basis for a nation's income tax.

(b)   Source

One possibility is to levy income tax on all income having its source in Canada. Such a tax would be relatively easy to assess and enforce. Moreover, if all countries taxed on the source principle (and adopted uniform rules to allocate income to source) double taxation would be eliminated. In fact, Canada and most other countries do use source as a connecting factor for some income taxation — in Canada's case for the taxation of non-residents.[1] But source alone would not be a satisfactory basis for an equitable income tax, because such a tax could not be assessed by reference to each taxpayer's total ability to pay. Wealthy taxpayers would be able to arrange to earn their income from several different countries and thereby obtain all the advantages of splitting income. The criterion of ability to pay[2] excludes source as the sole or primary basis of income tax liability, because ability to pay can only be fairly compared on the basis of each taxpayer's entire world income.[3]

(c)   Citizenship

Citizenship (or nationality) is used by the United States as the factor which identifies the people liable to pay income tax in the United States. The argument, no doubt, is that even the non-resident citizen is entitled to the protection of his or her person and property by the government of his or her citizenship. Moreover, citizenship enables the taxing country to tax those of its citizens who have moved to tax havens such as the Bahamas or Bermuda (although such people could change their citizenship, and even if they did not enforcement would be difficult).[4] But the disadvantage of citizenship is that it would sweep in many people whose links with the taxing country had become (for non-tax reasons) very tenuous, and it would exclude many people living permanently in the taxing country. The United States has had to modify the

---

[1] See sec. 8.3, "Taxation of non-residents", below.

[2] On ability to pay as the criterion of equity, see ch. 4, Objectives, under heading 4.3, "Equity", above.

[3] See Bale in Hansen, Krishna, Rendall (eds.), *Canadian Taxation* (1981), 23.

[4] *Id.*, 27.

principle of citizenship by also taxing resident aliens and by providing partial exemptions for the foreign income of non-resident citizens.[5]

(d)   Domicile

Domicile is another factor which could be used as the basis for income tax. The domicile of a deceased person has commonly been used in Canada as a primary basis for death taxation. (At this time, Canada has no death taxation, neither an estate tax nor succession duties.) But domicile is a concept that is encrusted with archaic and often artificial rules. A person's "domicile of origin" (which is determined at birth, usually by the father's domicile) and a person's "domicile of dependence" (under which a married woman assumes the domicile of her husband) may bear little relationship to a person's actual permanent home. Even a person's "domicile of choice", which involves residing in a country with the intention of remaining there permanently, is not an entirely satisfactory criterion for taxation: the element of intention raises difficult questions of proof and excludes people who may be longstanding residents of the taxing country although they lack the intention to stay permanently.[6]

(e)   Residence

Residence is the principal connecting factor which is used for Canadian income tax. The factor of residence, it would be argued, produces the largest class of taxpayers with strong social and economic ties with the country; they are all people with a moral obligation to finance the government; and they are all people against whom enforcement is practicable. It is probably the best of all the alternatives, although the taxation of a resident alien (who cannot vote) can be criticized as "taxation without representation", and the concept of residence (as we shall see) is far from precise.

8.2   Taxation of residents

Subsection 2(1) of the Income Tax Act provides:

> 2(1) An income tax shall be paid, as required by this Act, on the taxable income for each taxation year of every person resident in Canada at any time in the year.

Note the phrase "resident in Canada at any time in the year". The definition of "taxable income" in s. 2(2) points to the definition of "income" in s. 3. Section 3 makes clear that a person resident in Canada at any time in a taxation year ("taxation year" is defined in s. 249(1))[7] is liable to pay income tax on his or her *world* income (income "from a source inside or outside Canada") for that year. The harshness of imposing this regime on a person who was resident in

---

[5] *Id.*, 25-28.

[6] *Id.*, 28-30.

[7] See ch. 6, Taxation Year, above.

Canada "at any time in the year" is mitigated by s. 114, under which a part-time resident individual is not taxed as a resident for the part of the year when he or she was not resident.[8] The harshness of taxing income from non-Canadian sources, which may have already been taxed in the country of source, is mitigated by s. 126, which allows to Canadian residents a credit against Canadian tax for tax paid to another country (subject to certain limits). It should be noted here too that the problem of double taxation is addressed in treaties which Canada has entered into with many other countries.[9]

Effective for taxation years beginning in 1996, new rules are proposed which will require Canadian residents owning investments outside Canada with a total cost exceeding $100,000 to file an information return with Revenue Canada reporting those investments.[10] The purpose of these new foreign reporting rules is to ensure that Canadian residents are reporting their non-Canadian source income.

8.3   Taxation of non-residents

A person who is not resident in Canada is not liable to pay Canadian income tax, unless he or she received certain kinds of income from Canadian sources. Subsection 2(3) provides:

> 2(3) Where a person who is not taxable under subsection (1) for a taxation year
>
> (a)   was employed in Canada,
>
> (b)   carried on a business in Canada, or
>
> (c)   disposed of a taxable Canadian property,
>
> at any time in the year or a previous year, an income tax shall be paid, as required by this Act, on the person's taxable income earned in Canada for the year determined in accordance with Division D.

Subsection 2(3) applies only to a person who is not taxable under subsection (1), and that means a person who was not resident in Canada at any time in the taxation year. The non-resident becomes liable to Canadian tax if he or she was employed in Canada, carried on business in Canada or disposed of a taxable Canadian property. The reference to "a previous year" in s. 2(3) is to cover the case where a non-resident who, although no longer employed or carrying on business in Canada in the current year, receives some income from a previous year's employment or business activity.

---

[8]   Section 114 is discussed under sec. 8.4, "Taxation of part-time residents", below.

[9]   See sec. 8.10(c), "Tax treaties", below.

[10]   The information return is due on the filing-due date (which for most individuals is April 30 following the relevant taxation year), but the first reporting deadline has been delayed for one year, i.e., until 1998. Canadian residents must also file information returns in three other circumstances: (1) when they own an interest in a foreign affiliate; (2) when they transfer or loan property to a non-resident trust and (3) when they receive a distribution from a non-resident trust.

The non-resident, unlike the resident, is not liable to pay Canadian tax on his or her world income. Income earned by a non-resident from sources outside Canada is totally exempt from Canadian tax. Ordinary income tax (which is levied by Part I of the Act) is payable only on "taxable income earned in Canada". This phrase is defined in s. 115 of the Act. Essentially, it comprises employment income earned in Canada,[11] business income earned in Canada[12] and taxable capital gains (and allowable capital losses) from dispositions of "taxable Canadian property". "Taxable Canadian property" is defined in s. 115(1)(b). As Harris notes,[13] it consists of capital property "that has some reasonably permanent connection with Canada and where it is thought to be administratively feasible to collect the tax".[14] The most important inclusion is "real property situated in Canada"; it also includes (among other things) capital property used in carrying on business in Canada, shares in a private corporation resident in Canada and a capital interest in a trust resident in Canada. The most important exclusion from "taxable Canadian property" is stocks and bonds of public corporations, including public corporations resident in Canada.[15]

Taxable income earned in Canada by a non-resident is taxed under Part I of the Act, the same part that governs the liability of a resident. The non-resident individual's taxable income earned in Canada is therefore taxed under the same graduated rate schedule in s. 117 as is applicable to the taxable income of a resident. The difference is that, in the case of a resident, the rate schedule is applied to his or her entire income, whether earned or unearned, and whether it came from a Canadian source or a foreign source. In the case of a non-resident, the rate schedule is applied only to his or her taxable income earned in Canada as if that were the taxpayer's entire income for the year.

As Bale has pointed out,[16] it is rather peculiar to apply the graduated rate schedule to the non-resident's taxable income earned in Canada without regard for the amount of unearned or foreign income derived by the non-resident. The

---

[11] The residence of the employer is irrelevant in determining whether an individual earned employment income in Canada. The crucial question is where the individual carried out the duties of his or her employment.

[12] Section 253 sets out a list of activities in Canada that count as carrying on business in Canada.

[13] Harris, *Canadian Income Taxation* (4th ed., 1986), 89.

[14] Section 116 is an advance collection mechanism that applies whenever a non-resident disposes of a taxable Canadian property. By pre-paying the tax, or establishing the existence of a treaty exemption, the seller can obtain a s. 116 certificate, which will make it safe for the buyer to pay the seller the full purchase price. If a s. 116 certificate is not supplied on closing by the seller, the buyer is required to withhold and remit one-third of the purchase price. Without such a certificate, the buyer is required to withhold and remit one-third of the purchase price.

[15] There is an exception for the case where the non-resident owns or controls 25 per cent of the shares of the public corporation.

[16] Bale in Hansen, Krishna, Rendall (eds.) *Canadian Taxation*, (1981), 55.

justification for a graduated rate schedule is the attempt to relate tax to ability to pay,[17] and if no attempt is made to measure ability to pay, it is arguable that a flat rate of tax on the non-resident's Canadian-source income would be fairer. That is indeed how Canada taxes the non-resident's Canadian-source *property* income (see below), but the non-resident's Canadian-source employment and business income and capital gains are taxed under the graduated rate schedule.

The phrase "taxable income earned in Canada" not only excludes foreign-source income, it also excludes income from Canadian sources other than employment, business and dispositions of "taxable Canadian property". It thus excludes investment income (income from property), such as interest, dividends, rents, royalties and trust income. It also excludes certain other categories of income, such as maintenance, alimony, pensions and annuities. These classes of income are accordingly free of Part I tax when they are received by a non-resident. However, where these classes of income are paid to a non-resident by a resident, s. 212 in Part XIII of the Act imposes a special tax (Part XIII tax) on the income at the flat rate of 25 per cent.[18] The rate of 25 per cent (which is stipulated by s. 212) is reduced to 15 per cent (or occasionally 5 or 10 per cent) in nearly all the tax treaties that Canada has entered into;[19] each treaty is implemented by a statute which always provides that the treaty overrides the inconsistent provisions of the Act such as s. 212. The obligation to pay the Part XIII tax is imposed on the resident payor, who is required by s. 215(1) to deduct and withhold the tax from his or her payments to the non-resident payee,[20] and to remit the tax to the government.

The obligation to pay the Part XIII tax is also imposed (by s. 212) on the non-resident payee, but there is no requirement that the payee file a return or even notify the Department of an address. In other words, the collection of the Part XIII tax is in practice wholly dependent on the withholding of the tax by the resident payor. The reality is that it is usually impossible to enforce tax laws

---

[17] See ch. 5, Rates, under heading 5.2(e), "Justification for progressive rates", above.

[18] Section 216 allows a non-resident to elect to file a tax return reporting only his net rental income and to pay tax at the regular Part I personal rates. This will be advantageous if the tax at regular rates on the net rental income (after expenses) is less than the Part XIII tax, which is levied on the gross income. A similar election is allowed by s. 217, which applies to alimony, pension payments and certain other amounts subject to Part XIII tax. If the tax owing as a result of s. 216 and s. 217 elections is less than the tax withheld at source, the non-resident will get a refund. He or she may also apply to have the withholdings under Part XIII reduced in the future.

[19] See sec. 8.5(c), "Tax treaties", below.

[20] Paragraph 212(1)(b) exempts from non-resident withholding tax interest paid to foreign investors on various types of debt obligations, including bonds issued by a federal, provincial or municipal government. As a result of s. 212(1)(b), interest earned by foreign investors on such loans is effectively free of Canadian tax. These exemptions were originally designed as temporary measures to encourage foreign investment in Canada. However, the exemptions appear to have taken a permanent place in Canadian income tax law.

against persons who are no longer in the jurisdiction and who have left no assets in the jurisdiction. The general rule, applied by most countries including Canada itself,[21] is that the local courts will not entertain proceedings by foreign governments to enforce tax laws and will not even enforce foreign judgments which have been obtained by foreign governments for taxes.

8.4 Taxation of part-time residents

What is the tax liability of a person who is resident in Canada for only part of a taxation year? We have already noted that s. 2(1) applies to a person who is resident in Canada "at any time" in the taxation year. In the absence of any other provision, this would render a person who becomes resident in Canada during a year (or ceases to be resident in Canada during a year) liable to pay Canadian tax on his or her world income for the entire year. Subsection 2(1) uses the term "person", which is defined in s. 248(1) as including a corporation as well as an individual. For a corporation that is resident in Canada for only part of a taxation year, there is no relieving provision: s. 2(1) catches all of the corporation's world income for the entire year. For an individual, however, there is a relieving provision which applies in the year of immigration or emigration, namely, s. 114.[22]

Section 114 applies to an individual who was resident in Canada for part of the taxation year and was non-resident for the other part of the year. Section 114 deems the individual's income for the period of residence to be world income (as defined in s. 3) and the individual's income for the period of non-residence to be "taxable income earned in Canada" (as defined in s. 115). It is the treatment of the period of non-residence that is the relieving portion of s. 114. For that period, the part-time resident need only report "taxable income earned in Canada". As we noticed in the previous section of this chapter dealing with the taxation of non-residents, "taxable income earned in Canada" is limited to income from employment earned in Canada, income from business earned in Canada, and taxable capital gains (and allowable capital losses) from dispositions of taxable Canadian properties. The items most commonly recognized during a period of non-residence are deferred employment income, business income and taxable capital gains from dispositions of taxable Canadian properties.

By virtue of s. 114, during the period of non-residence, the part-time resident need not report or pay Part I income tax on income falling outside the definition of "taxable income earned in Canada". As we noted in the previous

---

[21] *United States* v. *Harden*, [1963] S.C.R. 366 (S.C.C.).

[22] Section 114 is only applicable in the year that an individual becomes resident in Canada or ceases to be resident in Canada. Aside from the year of immigration or emigration, an individual who spends part of the year in Canada and part of the year outside Canada would not be characterized as a part-time resident, but as either a resident or a non-resident for the full year: see discussion under sec. 8.5, "Residence of individuals", below.

section of this chapter, that phrase excludes employment and business income from non-Canadian sources, and it also excludes all investment income and other income not derived from employment or business. Income received from Canadian sources during the period of non-residence which is caught by Part XIII of the Act will be subject to the withholding tax of 25 per cent (reduced by treaty to 5, 10 or 15 per cent) imposed by s. 212. A tax of 5, 10 or 15 per cent will often be more favourable to the taxpayer than the tax that would be exigible if the income caught by Part XIII was instead part of the taxpayer's world income and was subject to the progressive rate schedule of s. 117.[23] That of course would be the result under s. 2(1) if s. 114 did not exist.

8.5 Residence of individuals

(a) Common law residence

There is no exhaustive definition in the Act of residence and there is a plethora of cases on the question. Two definitions that are often used are these:

Thomson v. *M.N.R.* (1946)[24] per Rand J.:

> For the purpose of income tax legislation, it must be assumed that every person has at all times a residence. It is not necessary to this that he should have a home or a particular place of abode or even a shelter. He may sleep in the open. It is important only to ascertain the spatial bounds within which he spends his life or to which his ordered or customary living is related.

Interpretation Bulletin IT-221R2, "Determination of an individual's residence status" (1983), para. 2:

> The Courts have held that an individual is resident in Canada for tax purposes if Canada is the place where he, in the settled routine of his life, normally or customarily lives. In making this determination, all of the relevant facts in each case must be considered.

Although Rand J. in the first definition points out that a taxpayer may not have a home, the homeless rarely raise issues of income tax. It is "the peripatetic lifestyle of the leisurely wealthy"[25] that raises residence questions. Such people usually have at least one home. The country in which the taxpayer makes his or her home will be "the place where he, in the settled routine of his life, regularly, normally or customarily lives". The availability of a place where the taxpayer has the right to stay is usually the critical element in determining the country of residence, although the courts will look at other factors as well, such as the frequency and duration of visits, and the presence of social and business connections. The object of the exercise, though, is to identify the country in

---

[23] Since Part XIII tax is imposed on gross income and Part I tax is based on net income (after expenses), the tax treatment which is the most favourable in the circumstances depends on the amount of expenses that can be deducted: see note 18, above, concerning the elections that non-residents can make to pay Part I tax on certain sources of income.

[24] [1946] S.C.R. 209, 224-225.

[25] *The Queen* v. *Reader*, [1975] C.T.C. 256, 260, 75 D.T.C. 5160, 5162 (F.C.T.D.).

which the taxpayer has his or her home. If more than one country is indicated, the courts will not hesitate to find a person to be resident in more than one country. Nor is there anything surprising in the proposition that a person may have a home in two countries — although it is rarely desirable from a tax standpoint.[26]

The leading Canadian case on residence is *Thomson v. M.N.R.* (1946),[27] in which the taxpayer, a wealthy Canadian citizen who had gone to a lot of trouble to give up Canadian residence, was held nonetheless to be a resident of Canada. In 1923, he sold his home in New Brunswick, announced that Bermuda was now his residence, and went to Bermuda. In the following years, he actually spent very little time in Bermuda, mainly living in the United States, where he built a house which was kept permanently ready for occupancy and where he spent most of his time. Starting in 1932, he began to regularly return to New Brunswick for four or five of the warmer months every year, and he eventually built a house there which was kept available all year long. Every year, however, he kept his stay in New Brunswick to less than 183 days (to avoid the sojourning rule).[28] The taxpayer's wife and child accompanied him in these regular migrations. The Supreme Court of Canada, by a majority, held that the taxpayer was resident in Canada. Rand J., who wrote the principal opinion, said that the taxpayer's time in Canada was not a temporary "stay" or "visit":[29]

> His living in Canada is substantially as deep rooted and settled as in the United States. In terms of time [the United States] may take precedence but at best it is a case of primus inter pares. He is [in Canada] as at his "home"; and the mere limitation of time does not qualify that fact. . . . That brings him within the most exacting of any reasonable interpretation of "resides" or "ordinarily resident".

Taschereau J., who dissented, held that the taxpayer was "a resident of the United States, making occasional visits to Canada".[30]

One point that emerges from the *Thomson* case is that the intention of the taxpayer, while obviously relevant in determining the "settled routine" of a taxpayer's life, is not determinative. In *Thomson* (as in many other cases), it was the external facts as to his customary mode of life which persuaded the Court that his home was in Canada, notwithstanding his intention not to be resident in Canada. Another point (which has already been mentioned) is that a person can

---

[26] For discussions of residence, see McGregor, "Deemed Residence" (1974) 22 *Can. Tax J.* 381; Hansen, "Individual Residence" [1977] *Can. Tax Found. Conf. Rep.* 682; Suarez, "Tax Planning for Departure from Canada" (1991) 39 *Can. Tax J.* 1; Bale in Hansen, Krishna, Rendall (eds.), *Canadian Taxation* (1981), ch. 2; Harris, *Canadian Income Taxation* (4th ed., 1986), 82-86; Krishna, *The Fundamentals of Canadian Income Tax* (4th ed., 1992), 81-93.

[27] [1946] S.C.R. 209, [1946] C.T.C. 51, 2 D.T.C. 812 (S.C.C.).

[28] See sec. 8.5(d), "Sojourning for 183 days", below.

[29] [1946] S.C.R. 209, 268.

[30] *Id.*, 220.

be resident in more than one country at the same time. In *Thomson*, it was clear that the Court thought that the taxpayer was resident in the United States as well as in Canada (and he was in fact being taxed in the United States as a resident).[31]

Thomson may be contrasted with *Beament* v. *M.N.R.* (1952),[32] another decision of the Supreme Court of Canada. In that case, the taxpayer was posted overseas with the Canadian army at the beginning of World War II in 1939, and, except for a visit of a few weeks in 1941, he did not return until May 1946. In the meantime, he had married in England, had children there, and established a matrimonial home there. The Court held that he was not resident in Canada until his actual return in 1946. The absence of any home in Canada "to which he could as of right return" negatived Canadian residence. This case, like *Thomson*, emphasizes that intention is not the crucial factor in determining residence. In *Beament*, the taxpayer always regarded his absence from Canada as temporary and intended to return. Nevertheless, he was held not to be a resident until his actual return.

Nor is physical presence, though obviously an important factor, necessary to residence. In *Russell* v. *M.N.R.* (1949),[33] a taxpayer who was absent from Canada for several years on war service, but who (unlike *Beament*) maintained a matrimonial home and family in Canada, was held to be resident in Canada.[34]

(b)   Ordinarily resident

Section 250(3) provides as follows:

> 250(3) In this Act, a reference to a person resident in Canada includes a person who was at the relevant time ordinarily resident in Canada.

This provision is often alluded to in the cases, but it is doubtful whether it adds anything to the common law. As Rand J. said in *Thomson*, if the common law concept of residence is given its full significance, "ordinarily resident" becomes "superfluous".[35] However, it certainly tends to reinforce the proposition that a temporary absence from Canada, even one lasting for the full taxation year in issue, does not necessarily involve a loss of Canadian residence; if a family household remains in Canada, or possibly even if close personal and business ties are maintained in Canada, then the taxpayer may be held to be "ordinarily resident" in Canada.

---

[31]   The tax treaty between Canada and the United States now has rules for allocating to one country or the other a taxpayer who is resident in both countries.

[32]   [1952] S.C.R. 486, [1952] C.T.C. 327, 52 D.T.C. 1183 (S.C.C.).

[33]   *Russell* v. *M.N.R.*, [1949] Ex. C.R. 91, [1949] C.T.C. 13, 4 D.T.C. 536 (Ex. Ct.).

[34]   Paragraph 250(1)(b) now deems a member of the Canadian Forces to be resident in Canada; this would confirm the result in *Russell* and change the result in *Beament*.

[35]   [1946] S.C.R. 209, 226.

(c) Giving up residence

Many people planning a temporary but lengthy period of absence from Canada, for example, on a transfer outside Canada, an exchange of jobs, a sabbatical leave or even an extended holiday, would like to establish non-resident status for Canadian tax purposes. The Department initially indicated a generous attitude, suggesting in an interpretation bulletin that the sale or extended lease of the taxpayer's home in Canada would usually suffice to establish non-residence. However, the Department has revised the interpretation bulletin, which now indicates that a Canadian resident who leaves the country for less than two years will be presumed to have continued as a Canadian resident throughout the time abroad unless the taxpayer "can clearly establish that he severed all residential ties on leaving Canada".[36] The Department's change of position was vindicated in a series of "sabbatical" cases decided by the Tax Review Board in 1980.[37] In each case, a university professor who had left Canada for up to one year on sabbatical leave was held to have retained his resident status. In each case, the professor had leased his home in Canada but had not severed all residential ties during his leave, and he had resumed teaching duties on returning to Canada.

For people leaving Canada permanently, there is usually little doubt that residence has been lost. A difficulty can arise, however, in determining the date at which Canadian residence ceased. The date will usually be important as marking the end of the period when Canada taxes world income.[38] It is also important as marking the time at which the "departure tax" becomes applicable.[39] In *Shujahn* v. *M.N.R.* (1962),[40] for example, the taxpayer was transferred by his employer to the United States on August 2, 1957. He departed Canada on that date and put his house up for sale. His wife and child remained in Canada in the house until it was sold, which was not until February 1958; then they joined the taxpayer in the United States. Was he a resident of Canada for the whole of 1957 or only until August 2? The Exchequer Court held that he had given up residence on August 2. The continued occupation of the Canadian house by his family would normally indicate continued residence, but in this case "was explained in a satisfactory manner" as being solely for the purpose of facilitating the sale.

---

[36] The "residential ties" are a dwelling place (or places), spouse and dependants, and personal property and social ties: Interpretation Bulletin IT-221R2, "Determination of an individual's residence status" (1983), paras. 4 and 6.

[37] *Saunders* v. *M.N.R.*, [1980] C.T.C. 2436, 80 D.T.C. 1392 (T.R.B.); *Mash* v. *M.N.R.*, [1980] C.T.C. 2443, 80 D.T.C. 1396 (T.R.B.); *Brinkerhoff* v. *M.N.R.*, [1980] C.T.C. 2441, 80 D.T.C. 1398 (T.R.B.); *Breskey* v. *M.N.R.*, [1980] C.T.C. 2445, 80 D.T.C. 1402 (T.R.B.); *Magee* v. *M.N.R.*, [1980] C.T.C. 2450, 80 D.T.C. 1403 (T.R.B.).

[38] See sec. 8.4, "Taxation of part-time residents", above.

[39] See sec. 8.9, "Departure tax", below.

[40] [1962] Ex. C.R. 328, [1962] C.T.C. 364, 62 D.T.C. 1225 (Ex. Ct.).

(d)   Sojourning for 183 days

Paragraph 250(1)(a) provides that a person shall "be deemed to have been resident in Canada throughout a taxation year" if the person:

> sojourned in Canada in the year for a period of, or periods the total of which is, 183 days or more.

Paragraphs 250(1)(b) through (f) also deem to have been resident in Canada members of the armed forces and federal and provincial civil servants who are stationed outside Canada. The most important and interesting provision is paragraph (a), quoted above, under which a person who "sojourned" in Canada for 183 days in a taxation year is deemed to have been resident for the entire year.[41]

The term "sojourn" means something less than residence. A sojourner is a person who is physically present in Canada, but on a more transient basis than a resident. A sojourner lacks the settled home in Canada which would make him or her a resident. A person who is a resident of another country and who comes to Canada on a vacation or business trip would be an example of a sojourner. In most cases, of course, a sojourner would stay in Canada for only a short period of time, but if the sojourner stays for a period of 183 days, or for several periods totalling 183 days, then the effect of s. 250(1)(a) is to tax the sojourner as if he or she were a resident for the whole year. The rationale is no doubt that a person spending so much time in Canada has a stake in the country which is not markedly different from that of a resident, and which entails a contribution to the financing of the government. There is also the administrative convenience that s. 250(1)(a) will eliminate some of the argumentation over whether a person is a resident or not.

In the *Thomson* case,[42] the taxpayer contended that he was a mere sojourner in Canada, and that since he had never remained in Canada for 183 days in any year, he could not be deemed a resident. But the Court held that his visits to Canada did not have the transient character of sojourning: they were not unusual, casual or intermittent. On the contrary, they were part of the permanent, settled routine of his life. The taxpayer was therefore held to be resident in Canada for the year, although he had spent less than 183 days in the country.[43] As we noticed earlier, the length of time spent physically present in Canada is not crucial in determining whether or not a person is a resident at common law. It is, however, crucial in applying the 183-day-sojourner rule, because physical presence is essential to sojourning and sojourning has no taxation relevance unless it continues for 183 days.

---

[41] For discussion, see McGregor, note 26, above.

[42] Note 27, above.

[43] Accord, *MacDonald* v. *M.N.R.*, [1968] Tax A.B.C. 502, 68 D.T.C. 433 (T.A.B.) (taxpayer held to be resident although he had spent only 166 days in Canada).

The sojourning rule of s. 250(1)(a) does not interact very happily with the part-time residence rule of s. 114. Take the case of *Shujahn*,[44] where the taxpayer was held to be a Canadian resident until August 2 of the year in question, and to be a non-resident thereafter. The taxpayer in *Shujahn* was entitled to the relief afforded by s. 114 and was taxed on his world income only until August 2. But if his presence in Canada until August 2 had not had the permanent or settled character of residence, so that he was a mere sojourner, then s. 250(1)(a) would have deemed him to have been resident in Canada "throughout" the taxation year. The word "throughout" makes s. 114 inapplicable, because s. 114 applies only where a person was a resident for "part" of a taxation year. Thus, if the taxpayer had been held to be a sojourner, and deemed resident under s. 250(1)(a), he would have had to pay tax as a resident for the entire year. This is anomalous: the more tenuous the connection with Canada the heavier the Canadian tax liability. At the very least, surely, the part-time 183-day-sojourner could be afforded relief similar to the part-time resident in respect of that part of the year when he or she was not present in Canada.[45]

8.6 Residence of corporations

(a) Common law residence

The primary taxing provisions of ss. 2 and 3 apply to "persons" and "taxpayers", and both these terms include corporations. It is therefore as necessary for a corporation as it is for an individual to determine the place of residence in order to decide whether the corporation is liable to Canadian tax on its world income. In the absence of any exhaustive definition of residence in the Act, the courts have had to develop a test of residence for corporations just as they have for individuals. The rule which developed in the United Kingdom and which has been adopted in Canada is that a corporation is resident in the country "where the central management and control actually abides".[46]

Corporate law confers on the board of directors of a corporation the legal power to manage the affairs of the corporation. In the ordinary case, therefore, the place where a corporation's board of directors meets will be the place where the central management and control actually abides. This was the result in *De Beers Consolidated Mines* v. *Howe* (1906),[47] in which the test was first enunciated. The corporation whose residence was in issue was incorporated in South Africa, had its head office in South Africa, and carried on its business of

---

[44] Note 40, above.

[45] McGregor, note 26, above, 390.

[46] *De Beers Consolidated Mines* v. *Howe*, [1906] A.C. 455, 458 (H.L.). For discussion, see Pyrcz, "The Basis of Canadian Corporate Taxation: Residence" (1973) 21 *Can. Tax J.* 374.

[47] Previous note.

mining in South Africa. But a majority of the board of directors lived in England; and the board always met in England and made all major policy decisions there. The House of Lords held that the corporation was resident in England.

Corporate law does not confer upon the shareholders of a corporation the power to manage its affairs. That is the task of the directors, who are not the servants or agents of the shareholders, and who are under no legal obligation to follow the wishes of the shareholders. Therefore, the residence of the shareholders is not normally relevant in determining the location of the central management and control of a corporation. However, the shareholders do own the corporation, and they do possess some important powers, in particular, the power to elect (or to remove) the directors. In a closely held corporation (or sometimes even in a widely held corporation), in which one shareholder or a group of shareholders wields effective voting power, the major shareholder will be able to influence the decisions of the directors, if he or she chooses to do so, and in some corporations the major shareholder will dictate the decisions of the directors.

In *Unit Construction Co.* v. *Bullock* (1960),[48] three corporations which were incorporated in Kenya, which carried on business in Kenya, and whose directors resided and met in Kenya, were held to be resident not in Kenya but in England. The three corporations were subsidiaries of an English corporation, and they were effectively controlled in fact from England by the directors of the parent corporation. The House of Lords held that the location of central management and control was a question of fact, and that in this case it actually abided in England.

It is usually difficult to determine whether the board of directors of a corporation is exercising an independent discretion, albeit influenced by a shareholder or other outsider, or whether the board has actually surrendered its discretion to the outsider. Even if the facts are known, the question is one of degree which is not easy to determine. In addition, however, there are often evidentiary problems in establishing that a board of directors actually acts under the dictation of an outsider. It is significant that in *Unit Construction Co.* v. *Bullock* it was to the advantage of the three Kenyan corporations and their parent for the corporations to be held resident in England, and the evidence of de facto control from England was therefore readily available.

There have been a number of Canadian cases in which the evidence appeared to establish de facto control by the major shareholder, and yet the courts refused to conclude that central management and control was exercised

---

[48] [1960] A.C. 351 (H.L.).

from outside the board of directors.[49] These cases have been criticized as reverting to a de jure control test, which was rejected by the House of Lords in *Unit Construction Co.* v. *Bullock*.[50] The results of these cases are admittedly hard to explain on any other basis. But the courts have continued to pay lip-service to the de facto control test, and there seems to be no reason to doubt that *Unit Construction* represents the law of Canada as well as the United Kingdom. Where it can be established that the board of directors of a corporation does not in fact exercise independent management and control, then the place of residence of the person who dictates the board's decisions is the place of residence of the corporation.

(b)   Incorporation in Canada

From a revenue point of view, the central management and control test suffers from the disadvantage that it is easy for a corporation to change the location of its central management and control and thereby change its residence. The Act therefore deems certain corporations with Canadian connections to be resident in Canada irrespective of the location of their central management and control. Paragraph 250(4)(a) deems all corporations which were incorporated in Canada after April 26, 1965 to be resident in Canada. Paragraph 250(4)(c) deals with corporations which were incorporated in Canada before April 27, 1965; they are deemed to be resident in Canada if at any time after April 26, 1965 they were resident in Canada or carried on business in Canada; even a short period of Canadian residence (central management and control in Canada) or carrying on business in Canada is sufficient to make the corporation a Canadian resident forever. These provisions mean that the only kind of corporation that can lose Canadian residence is the one that was not incorporated in Canada. Indeed, they come close to substituting a nationality test[51] as the basis for taxing corporations.

These deemed residence provisions mean that most corporations which were incorporated in Canada are deemed resident in Canada. The importance of the central management and control test is therefore much reduced for Canada. The deemed residence provisions also make it common for a corporation to have dual residence: the corporation that is deemed to be resident in Canada by virtue

---

[49] *Sifneos* v. *M.N.R.*, [1968] Tax A.B.C. 652, 68 D.T.C. 522 (T.A.B.); *Zehnder & Co.* v. *M.N.R.*, [1970] C.T.C. 85, 70 D.T.C. 6064 (Ex. Ct.); *Bedford Overseas Freighters* v. *M.N.R.*, [1970] C.T.C. 69, 70 D.T.C. 6072 (Ex. Ct.).

[50] Pyrcz, note 46, above, 380.

[51] Section 8.1(c), "Citizenship", above.

of Canadian incorporation after 1965, but which is controlled in the United States, would be an example.[52]

8.7　Residence of trusts

Subsection 104(2) provides that a trust shall be deemed to be "an individual". An individual is defined in s. 248(1) as "a person other than a corporation". It follows that a trust is a "person" and a "taxpayer" so that ss. 2 and 3 are applicable, and the question whether the trust is resident in Canada or not is as crucial as it is for genuine individuals and for corporations: if resident in Canada, the trust will be liable to Canadian tax on its world income; and if not resident in Canada, the trust will be liable to Canadian tax only on the Canadian-source income specified in Division D of Part I and Part XIII.

The Act does not supply any rules for determining the residence of a trust. It does not even include deemed residence rules comparable to those applicable to individuals and corporations. The Department has adopted the position that the residence of a trust is a question of fact depending on the circumstances of each particular case. The Department will generally consider a trust to reside where the managing or controlling trustee resides.[53] This position finds implicit support in s. 104(1) of the Act, which provides that a reference to a trust shall be read as a reference to "the trustee . . . having ownership or control of the trust property". If a trust has a single trustee, and the trustee is resident in Canada, then it is clear that the trust is resident in Canada. The case is more troublesome where the trustee is not a resident of Canada, but the bulk of the trust's business or property interests are in Canada. It seems wrong that such a trust should be able to claim non-resident status, but in the absence of any deeming provisions it is not easy to escape from that result.

The most difficult case is the trust with several trustees, each resident in a different country. If we go back to the language of s. 104(1), it is pertinent to ask: which trustee has the "ownership or control of the trust property"? The difficulty is that, under the general law of trusts, trustees own the trust property jointly, and, unless the trust instrument provides otherwise, trustees must act unanimously. As a matter of strict law, therefore, no single trustee, and not even a majority of trustees, has "ownership or control of the trust property". The factual situation may of course be quite different from what the law

---

[52] The common law test alone does occasionally yield dual residence if central management and control is found to be divided between two jurisdictions, as it was in *M.N.R.* v. *Crossley Carpets*, [1968] C.T.C. 570, 69 D.T.C. 5015 (Ex. Ct.), but this is unusual: one of the possible jurisdictions can usually be identified as the true seat of power. Note that under most tax treaties dual residence is not a problem, because corporate income is allocated among each of the countries where the corporation has a "permanent establishment".

[53] Interpretation Bulletin IT-447, "Residence of a trust or estate" (1980).

contemplates. One of several trustees may be the dominant figure in the administration of the trust with the others playing mainly a formal role. A possible approach, by analogy to the rule that has developed with respect to corporations, would be to fix the residence of the trust in the place where de facto management and control is exercised. This approach does not receive much encouragement from s. 104(2)'s stipulation that a trust is to be deemed an "individual", which of course does not include a corporation; but s. 104(2) is not specifically addressed to the issue of residence and should not be treated as precluding a sensible solution to a difficult problem.

There seems to be only one decided case on point, namely *Thibodeau Family Trust* v. *The Queen* (1978).[54] In that case, Gibson J. of the Trial Division of the Federal Court relied upon the cases dealing with the residence of corporations, and applied the central management and control test to determine the place of residence of a trust. There were three trustees, of whom two lived in Bermuda and a third lived in Canada. The Minister assessed the trust as a Canadian resident on the basis that the Canadian trustee was a member of the family for whom the trust had been established, was the chief executive officer of a corporation owned by the trust, and seems to have been active and influential in the investment programme of the trust. On the other hand, the trust instrument altered the general rule of unanimity by authorizing a majority of the trustees to make decisions binding on the trust. The day-to-day administration of the trust was in fact carried out in Bermuda by the Bermuda trustees, and there was evidence that they did not always follow the wishes of the Canadian trustee. Meetings of the trustees were held in Bermuda. In these circumstances, the Court held that the central management and control of the trust actually abided in Bermuda, and that the trust was not resident in Canada.

8.8 Provincial residence

The foregoing discussion has been addressed to the question whether a particular taxpayer is resident in Canada or not. However, for resident taxpayers, it is also necessary to determine in which province the taxpayer is resident. This determines liability for provincial income tax, and since rates of provincial income tax vary considerably,[55] it is a question of some importance.

For individuals, reg. 2601 of the Income Tax Regulations provides that the province in which the individual resided on the last day of the taxation year is entitled to tax the individual on his or her entire income for the year. It is immaterial that the individual may have resided in another province or provinces for most of the year, and (with one exception to be noted) it is immaterial that the individual's income may have been derived from sources outside the

---

[54] [1978] C.T.C. 539, 78 D.T.C. 6376 (F.C.T.D.).

[55] See ch. 5, Rates, above.

province.[56] Regulation 2601 makes an exception for an individual who has income from a business with a permanent establishment outside the province of last-day residence. In that case, the income attributable to the business is deemed to have been earned in the province or country where the permanent establishment is located.[57] Where an individual has permanent establishments in more than one province or country, reg. 2603 supplies rules for apportioning the income between the jurisdictions.

For corporations, reg. 402 allocates the income to the province in which the corporation had a permanent establishment in the taxation year. Where a corporation has permanent establishments in more than one province or country, rules similar to those for the business income of individuals enable the income to be apportioned between the jurisdictions.[58]

For trusts, the regulations are silent, but since a trust is deemed by s. 104(2) to be an individual, the rules for individuals would be applicable.

8.9   Departure tax

Section 128.1 has the effect of imposing a "departure tax" on persons giving up Canadian residence.[59] The policy is to prevent Canadian residents from leaving the country without paying tax on capital gains which had accrued (but not been realized) while they were residents of Canada. (As will be explained in chapter 15, Capital Gains, below, the general rule is that capital gains are taxed only when realized; that chapter also discusses in more detail the "deemed dispositions" of which the so-called departure tax is an example.) The technique employed by s. 128.1 is to provide that a taxpayer who has ceased to be a resident of Canada shall be deemed to have disposed of all of his or her property at fair market value immediately before ceasing to be a resident. This ensures that any accrued capital gains (or losses) are recognized for purposes of Canadian tax, and that they are recognized as falling into income during the period of Canadian residence.

---

[56] The constitutionality of a province taxing its residents in respect of income earned outside the province was upheld in *Kerr* v. *Supt. of Income Tax*, [1942] S.C.R. 435; *CPR* v. *Prov. Treas. Man.*, [1953] 4 D.L.R. 233 (Man. Q.B.).

[57] Income of an individual that escapes provincial tax (because it is income from a business with a permanent establishment outside Canada) is subject to a federal surtax of 52 per cent of the appropriate proportion of the federal tax payable by the individual. In other words, the federal government takes up the tax room left open by the absence of provincial tax.

[58] Various special kinds of corporations are subjected to special rules by regs. 403–413.

[59] Until 1994, these rules were contained in s. 48 of the Act, which was repealed and replaced by s. 128.1. For a discussion of s. 48, see Brown, "Can you take it with you?" (1972) 20 *Can. Tax J.* 470.

In October 1996, significant changes were proposed to make the departure-tax rules more onerous.[60] The proposals, which will apply to departures on or after October 1, 1996, came about because of an Auditor General Report concerning an income tax ruling that Revenue Canada had given to a trust which was emigrating to the United States.[61] This ruling (which had been given in 1991) confirmed that the deemed disposition on departure rules did not apply to shares owned by the trust (which were valued at $2 billion) because of the exception in the Act for "taxable Canadian property".[62] The tax policy reason for the "taxable Canadian property" exception (which the October 1996 proposals now amend to exclude shares) was that subsection 2(3) of the Act taxes capital gains realized by non-residents on the eventual disposition of taxable Canadian property.[63] As a practical matter, however, Canada's ability to tax capital gains on shares which are taxable Canadian property is restricted by a term in most of the tax treaties that Canada has negotiated with other countries which exempts capital gains from Canadian tax after the former Canadian resident has been a non-resident for 10 years.[64] Under the proposals, there is a deemed disposition of shares on departure so that the 10-year rule cannot be utilized to avoid the tax on any accrued gains. The taxpayer is allowed to postpone payment of the tax caused by the deemed disposition until the shares are actually sold (when cash will be available for the payment) if the taxpayer posts acceptable security with Revenue Canada to secure the ultimate payment of the postponed tax.[65] This rule mitigates the harshness of taxing unrealized gains.

---

[60] These changes are contained in the Notice of Ways and Means Motion tabled in the House of Commons on October 2, 1996. At the time of writing, the proposed changes have not been enacted.

[61] *Report of the Auditor General of Canada* (May, 1996), ch. 1, 1-12 to 1-23.

[62] Subparagraph 128.1(4)(b)(i). "Taxable Canadian property", as noticed earlier under sec. 8.3, "Taxation of non-residents", above, does not usually include stocks and bonds of public corporations. In this particular situation, however, the shares which were owned by the trust were public company shares which were deemed to be taxable Canadian property because they had been obtained in exchange for other shares which were taxable Canadian property (s. 85(1)(i)). The ruling was required on whether s. 85(1)(i) applied to residents of Canada (as well as non-residents) since it was not clear that property could be taxable Canadian property if a taxpayer was a resident of Canada. The October 2, 1996 Notice of Ways and Means Motion contains proposals to amend the Act to confirm that this is the case.

[63] A gain on the disposition of a taxable Canadian property is one of the three classes of income upon which Canada taxes non-residents (the others being Canadian employment income and Canadian business income: s. 2(3)).

[64] See, for example, the 10-year rule in Article V of the Canada-U.S. Tax Convention.

[65] The October 2, 1996 Notice of Ways and Means Motion also proposes to require individuals who emigrate from Canada after 1995, and who own property with a value of more than $25,000, to report their property holdings to Revenue Canada.

There are currently four major exceptions to the deemed disposition on departure from Canada. Assuming the October 1996 proposals are enacted, the first exception (which used to be for taxable Canadian property) is for two types of taxable Canadian property, namely, real property situated in Canada and capital property used in a business in Canada. Shares that are taxable Canadian property will not be included in this first exception to the deemed disposition. The Act, as it currently reads, permits an individual (other than a trust) to elect out of the first exception (which used to be for all taxable Canadian property) in order to have the property elected on deemed to be disposed of at fair market value (s. 128.1(4)(d)). At the time of writing, the Department of Finance has not decided whether this election will continue under the new rules to allow, for example, an accrued capital loss on Canadian real estate to be recognized in order to offset an accrued capital gain on shares which have suffered a deemed disposition. It would make sense from a tax policy perspective to continue to allow this election, providing that any property elected on remains a taxable Canadian property, as it currently does.[66]

The second exception to the deemed disposition on departure rules is for rights to receive payments from a registered retirement savings plan, a registered pension plan, the Canada Pension Plan and other pension plans (s. 128.1(4)(b)(iii)). The reason for this exception is that all these payments will be subject to Part XIII withholding tax when they are eventually made to a non-resident. This exception has not been changed.

The third exception to the deemed disposition on departure rules is any property in respect of which a taxpayer has filed an election to make s. 128.1 inapplicable (s. 128.1(4)(b)(iv)). This election, as it currently reads, enables a taxpayer to convert property that is not taxable Canadian property into taxable Canadian property if the taxpayer posts acceptable security with Revenue Canada to secure the ultimate payment of tax on the actual disposition (s. 128.1(4)(e)). The October 1996 proposals do not refer at all to this election, but, because the intent of the October proposals is to ensure that there is a deemed disposition of shares on departure, and because the tax owing on all deemed dispositions is proposed to be postponed until the asset is actually sold (providing acceptable security is posted), it seems unlikely that this election will continue to be available.

The fourth exception from the deemed disposition on departure rules applies to emigrants who, during the 10 years prior to the date of departure, were resident in Canada for a total of 60 months of less. Any property owned by such emigrants when they last became a resident of Canada and any property acquired by bequest or inheritance after that time will not be subject to the deemed

---

[66] Under the current rules, a taxpayer may not use an election under s. 128.1 to trigger allowable capital losses to apply against his taxable capital gains from *actual* dispositions during the year, just *deemed* dispositions (s. 128.1(4)(f)).

disposition on departure rules (s. 128.1(b)(v)). The intent of this rule is to accommodate the needs of Canadian business by exempting employees who are temporarily transferred to Canada.

Section 128.1 applies to arrivals as well as departures. When a taxpayer becomes a resident of Canada, he or she is deemed to have acquired all of his or her property (other than taxable Canadian property) at fair market value at the time of becoming a resident (s. 128.1(1)(c)). This does not trigger any liability to tax. What it does is to establish the cost base of the property at the fair market value on arrival. When the property is eventually disposed of, this is the figure from which any gain or loss will be computed. The effect is to exclude from Canadian tax recognition any gains or losses which had accrued before the taxpayer became resident in Canada.

The policy behind s. 128.1, including the recent changes proposed to it, is sound in principle. However, the working out of that policy does lead to a remarkably complex set of rules. Moreover, Canada is the only country to employ the technique of deemed acquisition on arrival and deemed disposition on departure. An emigrant from Canada may find therefore that when an asset is subsequently disposed of in the new country of residence, the new country will only recognize the actual historical cost of the asset for the purpose of computing the taxable capital gain. The increment in value already taxed by Canada in the year of departure would therefore be taxed a second time, with no credit available for the Canadian tax that was paid in the earlier year.

8.10 International aspects

(a) International anomalies

The fact that an individual or corporation may be resident in two countries at the same time, and the fact that most countries levy some taxes on non-residents (as Canada does for some types of Canadian-source income), guarantee that even very similar tax systems of various countries will overlap and some people will find that they are taxed by two different countries on the same items of income. Moreover, many countries use different criteria than Canada as to who should pay tax (for example, nationality rather than residence is the basis in some countries), and their rules differ in other crucial respects. Discrepant criteria of liability and differences in other basic rules may easily impose double taxation. Conversely, differing national systems may leave a gap in coverage which would permit avoidance or evasion. In particular, some jurisdictions (for example, the Bahamas)[67] are "tax havens" which impose little or no income tax. The most drastic (and most effective) avoidance measure is to actually move

---

[67] Other tax havens include Bermuda, British Virgin Islands, Cayman Islands, Channel Islands, Isle of Man, Liberia and Netherlands Antilles: see *Grundy's Tax Havens: A World Survey* (4th ed., 1983).

one's residence to a tax haven country. (It was not just the climate that led E.P. Taylor to establish his residence in the Bahamas.) But taxpayers who do not want to go that far, and especially those nasty multinational corporations, occasionally manage to divert some of their income into countries located in "the sunnier (both climatically and financially) parts of the world".[68]

(b)   Canadian solutions

Some of these problems can be and have to be solved by Canada unilaterally. With respect to double taxation, s. 126 of the Income Tax Act allows to a resident taxpayer a credit for taxes paid to foreign countries. With respect to avoidance, various provisions could be cited, but perhaps the two most important are the so-called departure tax of s. 128.1, which has already been discussed, and the foreign accrual property income (FAPI) rules of ss. 91-96.

The FAPI rules impose tax on investment income derived outside Canada ("foreign accrual property income") by a corporation controlled by a taxpayer resident in Canada ("controlled foreign affiliate"); they attribute to the Canadian taxpayer the investment income which he or she is allowing to accumulate in a corporation which he or she controls but which is resident offshore. Generally speaking, the FAPI rules do not attempt to tax active business income which is earned outside Canada by a non-resident corporation. In the past, this led Canadian corporations to establish offshore corporations in tax havens to purchase goods for, or provide services to, the Canadian corporation, and to avoid Canadian tax by setting the transfer price of the goods or services between the two corporations as high as possible. Since the offshore corporation's mark-up on the goods or services reduces the profit of the Canadian corporation, the offshore corporation's mark-up is thereby diverted away from Canada and into the offshore jurisdiction (where it may be free of tax). Starting in 1994, the definition of active business income was restricted to exclude income from businesses carried on by offshore purchasing companies such as those just described (s. 95(2)(a.1)).[69]

The Minister frequently attacks transfer-pricing schemes to divert income into low-tax jurisdictions, but if the FAPI rules do not catch the offshore income (because it is active business income), a variety of other anti-avoidance rules (none of which fits perfectly) have to be invoked. The results, in the past, have

---

[68] Brown, note 59, above, 632.

[69] Other types of income which were also excluded from the definition of active business income include income earned by offshore captive insurance companies (s. 95(2)(a.2)), income earned by offshore factoring, leasing and lending companies (s. 95(2)(a.3) and (a.4)), and income earned by offshore companies that trade in debt obligations (s. 95(2)(l)).

been mixed.[70] The recent growth in international trade has provided taxpayers around the world with increased opportunities to avoid paying tax in high-tax jurisdictions such as Canada by manipulating international transfer prices. The February 18, 1997 federal budget announced that the Canadian government intends to follow the U.S. government's lead by codifying a set of international transfer pricing rules and applying penalties if the rules are not complied with.[71] The extent of the problem is so great that, by 1999-2000, Revenue Canada expects that the number of auditors employed on international audits will be more than five times the number employed in 1992-93.[72]

(c) Tax treaties

The principal mechanism for harmonizing the tax systems of various countries so as to reduce double taxation and avoidance is the treaty. Canada has entered into tax treaties with over 50 countries, including the United States and the United Kingdom (but not including tax haven jurisdictions, needless to say). These treaties are not merely binding under international law; each one has been enacted into domestic Canadian law by a federal statute, and each implementing statute provides that the terms of the treaty are to take precedence over any inconsistent provisions of the Income Tax Act. In fact, each treaty does make significant changes in the Canadian law as it relates to tax questions which involve Canada and the country with which Canada has entered into the treaty.[73] The relevant treaty must always be consulted whenever the tax liability of a person with some connection with a treaty country is in issue.

For example, most of the treaties deal with cases of dual residence by establishing tie-breaker rules to identify only one country as being the one with the right to tax the person concerned. In the case of an individual, such factors as the place of permanent home, habitual abode and nationality are taken into account; where these factors do not supply an answer, the treaties allow "the competent authorities" of the two countries to determine the question "by mutual

---

[70] E.g., compare *Dominion Bridge Co.* v. *The Queen*, [1977] C.T.C. 554, 77 D.T.C. 5367 (F.C.A.) (Minister successful, but reasons unclear) with *The Queen* v. *Irving Oil*, [1991] 1 C.T.C. 350, 91 D.T.C. 5106 (F.C.A.) (Minister unsuccessful). These cases relate to taxation years before the introduction of the general anti-avoidance rule, discussed in ch. 22, under heading 22.4, "General anti-avoidance rule", below.

[71] The rules will be codified by amending the "reasonableness" requirement in s. 69 (discussed in ch. 13, under heading 13.13, "The 'reasonable' requirement", below) so that the principles and methods set out in the 1995 OECD international transfer pricing guidelines can be complied with. Rules will also be introduced to require contemporaneous documentation of transfer prices used in cross-border related-party transactions. See Department of Finance, "Tax Measures: Supplementary Information" in *February 18, 1997 Federal Budget*, 5-20 to 5-22.

[72] Revenue Canada, *Compliance: From Vision to Strategy*, (1997) 41.

[73] As well as the examples in the text that follows, note the 10-year rule discussed in the text accompanying note 64, above.

agreement". In the case of a corporation, a common provision is that "industrial and commercial profits" of an enterprise are to be allocated to the country where the corporation has its "permanent establishment", and these terms are defined in the treaty.

The treaties try to block evasion of tax by a mechanism for the exchange of information on the affairs of taxpayers. Major objects of scrutiny are the multinational corporations, which are constantly under suspicion of hiding income in tax havens and not paying their fair share of taxes in the countries in which they operate.

Another objective of the tax treaties is to promote increased investment between the two countries involved by allowing lower rates of withholding tax on the flow of income between residents of the two countries. That is why Canada's Part XIII tax on payments to non-residents is reduced from 25 per cent to 15 per cent (and occasionally 5 or 10 per cent) in nearly all of Canada's treaties.[74] This concession is normally reciprocated by the other country. In practice, many other countries would be amenable to a lower rate than 15 per cent, but Canada's concerns about its level of foreign investment and about the revenue loss which would be entailed have normally made Canada unwilling to grant a rate below 15 per cent.[75] Canada's policy means that other countries are not willing to grant a rate of less than 15 per cent to Canadian investors, even when those countries have granted lower rates (often as low as 5 per cent or 0 per cent) to investors from other countries. The same concerns about the level of foreign investment and about revenue loss have led Canada to refuse to extend the dividend tax credit[76] to non-residents, although other countries with similar gross-up-and-credit systems for the taxation of shareholders have made such credits available by treaty to non-residents.

---

[74] See heading 8.3, "Taxation of non-residents", above.

[75] The rate of 5% is very rare. Starting in 1997, the Canada-U.S. Tax Convention provides for a 5% rate in cases where a shareholder owns at least 10% of the voting stock of a company (Art. X(2)(a); for 1996, the rate was 6%, and from October 1984 to the end of 1995, the rate was 10%). In all other cases, the Canada-U.S. rate is 15% (Art. X(2)(b)).

[76] See ch. 19, Corporations and Shareholders, under heading 19.4, "Taxation of shareholders", below.

9

Tax Base

9.1   Definition of tax base

A "tax base" is the base upon which a tax is levied. "Income tax, if I may be pardoned for saying so, is a tax on income".[1] However, income is not a self-defining term, and the question of what items come into income for tax purposes and thereby form part of the tax base is one of the major problems of income tax policy. The term "tax base" properly includes all of the rules respecting the measurement of income, including exemptions and deductions, as well as inclusions.

---

[1] *London County Council* v. *A.G.*, [1901] A.C. 26, 35 per Lord Macnaghten.

9.2   Source theory

Ideally, an income tax Act would reflect a consistent theory as to the nature of income. Unfortunately, this cannot be said of the Canadian Act. However, there is a theory that has been influential in the drafting and interpreting of the Act. The theory is that income is a yield from a productive source. That "source" theory takes as its metaphor the fruit and the tree. The tree is "capital" while the fruit is "income". Increases in the value of the tree, even if realized by sale, are still capital (the source of income); only the fruit is income.

It has been suggested that the source theory of income arose in the United Kingdom at a time when the economy was primarily agricultural and it was natural to think of income in those terms.[2] Another factor was probably the distinction between capital and income that the courts had developed for the law of trusts, where it was necessary to distinguish between the rights of a life tenant (or income beneficiary) and those of a remainderman (or capital beneficiary).[3] The idea that income was the yield from a productive source, and that the source itself was capital, became part of the Anglo-Canadian way of thinking about income. Accordingly, the Income Tax Acts of the United Kingdom and Canada, while taxing income from employment, business or property, did not at first attempt to tax capital gains, gifts, inheritances or windfalls and many other miscellaneous receipts.

We shall see that the tax base in Canada has been broadened by the express inclusion of many items that would be excluded by the source theory. Capital gains, which became partially taxable in 1972, are the most important example. But the Income Tax Act still contains no comprehensive definition of income; and s. 3 of the Act, which is the closest thing to a comprehensive definition, refers to a taxpayer's income for the year "from a source inside or outside Canada". The reference to a source has encouraged the courts to exclude from income for tax purposes accretions to a taxpayer's wealth that lack the characteristics of periodic payments for services rendered to an employer (where the employment is the source) or for business activity (where the business is the source) or for the use of property (where the property is the source).

For example, the Act says nothing about the strike pay that a union pays its members while they are on strike. In *Canada* v. *Fries* (1990),[4] the Supreme Court of Canada decided that strike pay was not taxable. The Court said that it was not satisfied that strike pay was "income . . . from a source" within the

---

[2] *Report of the Royal Commission on Taxation* (Carter Report), vol. 3, 64-65.

[3] *Id.*, 65.

[4] [1990] 2 S.C.R. 1322, [1990] 2 C.T.C. 439, 90 D.T.C. 6662 (S.C.C.).

meaning of s. 3; and "the benefit of the doubt" should go to the taxpayers.[5] The Court's doubt arose from the source theory of income. Under a more comprehensive theory of income, the payments to striking workers in replacement of their employment income would obviously have to count as income for tax purposes.

In *Schwartz* v. *Canada* (1996),[6] the Supreme Court of Canada held that a payment of damages for breach of contract was not income from a source that was caught by the Income Tax Act. The contract was a contract of employment, which the prospective employer had rescinded before the prospective employee had actually started work. The prospective employer paid the prospective employee $360,000 as damages for the breach of contract. The Supreme Court of Canada held that this sum was not liable to tax, because it was not income. It was not income from employment, because it was not possible to determine what portion of the damages related to foregone income under the contract of employment and what portion related to other factors. Nor was the sum a taxable retiring allowance, because the Act's definition of a retiring allowance called for a "loss" of employment, and since the employment had never commenced it had not been lost. The Court refused to treat s. 3's reference to income from a source as a general provision that captured amounts that narrowly escaped the more specific provisions of the Act. Although the payment in *Schwartz* was held to be a non-taxable windfall, La Forest J. for the majority affirmed the conventional view that the sources specifically mentioned in s. 3, namely, "office, employment, business and property", were not the only sources of income. He also referred with approval to the proposition that all accretions to wealth "regardless of source" should be included in the tax base in order to measure a taxpayer's ability to pay.[7] However, Major J. in a separate concurring opinion pointed out that the Canadian Act had never endorsed the tax policy idea that all accretions to wealth should be taxed. He even doubted whether there were any sources of income other than those expressly recognized by the Act.[8] The latter view seems wrong as a matter of interpretation of s. 3, which clearly leaves open the possibility of non-specified sources of income. However, Major J. may be right as a matter of practical reality: the courts are very reluctant indeed to impose tax on receipts that are not specifically covered by the Act. The reluctance stems from the absence of a comprehensive theory of income.

---

[5] *Id.*, 1323.

[6] [1996] 1 S.C.R. 254, [1996] 1 C.T.C. 303, 96 D.T.C. 6103 (S.C.C.).

[7] *Id.*, paras. 48-49.

[8] *Id.*, paras. 67-76.

9.3   Haig-Simons theory

When economists put their minds to the definition of income for tax purposes, they found the source theory to be "narrow", "artificial", "eccentric" and "little less than absurd".[9] Why? Because the source theory of income was poorly adapted for tax purposes, where the object was to measure a taxpayer's ability to pay tax. Robert Murray Haig, an American economist writing in 1921, proposed a more comprehensive definition of income. Haig said that, for tax purposes, the definition of income should be "the money value of the net accretion to one's economic power between two points of time".[10] Under this definition, any accretion to economic power in the course of a taxation year, regardless of its source, would count as income for the year.

In 1938, Henry C. Simons, another American economist, proposed a more elaborate version of Haig's definition. Simons said: "Personal income may be defined as the algebraic sum of (1) the market value of rights exercised in consumption and (2) the change in the value of the store of property rights between the beginning and the end of the period in question".[11] This definition was fundamentally the same as Haig's, but Simons' definition explicitly took account of consumption, treating the value of the goods and services consumed by the taxpayer during the year as part of the taxpayer's accretion to wealth for that year.

The Carter Commission, which was much influenced by Haig and Simons, restated the Haig-Simons theory in these terms:[12]

> The comprehensive tax base has been defined as the sum of the market value of goods and services consumed or given away in the taxation year by the tax unit [the taxpayer], plus the annual change in the market value of the assets held by the unit.

According to Haig-Simons theory, income equals consumption plus gain in net worth over a taxation year. It does not matter whether the gain in net worth consists of periodic payments from a source (such as salary, wages, business income or property income) or profits from the sale of property (capital gains), or transfers from other people (such as gifts, inheritances or gambling winnings) or the direct products of one's own labour (such as home-grown fruit and vegetables or home renovation) or the direct benefits of one's own property (such as the right to occupy one's own home). Nor does it matter whether the gain in net worth is expected or unexpected, regular or irregular, deliberate or accidental, realized or accrued, in cash or in kind. All gains should be taken into account in measuring a taxpayer's income for tax purposes.

---

[9] Haig in Haig (ed.) *The Federal Income Tax* (Columbia University Press, 1921), 54.

[10] *Id.*, 59.

[11] Simons, *Personal Income Taxation* (University of Chicago Press, 1938), 50.

[12] Carter Report, vol. 3, 39.

9.4   Carter's comprehensive tax base

The Carter Commission, following the Haig-Simons theory, argued that the definition of income should be suited to the purpose for which the definition was to be used. If the definition was to be the basis of an equitable tax system, then it should be a reasonably comprehensive measure of the annual increase in a taxpayer's ability to pay tax. The traditional, source-based concept of income, however apt to other purposes (such as trust accounting), was not a satisfactory measure of the annual increase in a taxpayer's ability to pay tax, because it excluded from income so many accretions to wealth. In principle, income should include every accretion to wealth, regardless of its source, because every accretion to wealth increases the recipient's ability to pay tax. This theory, which became the Commission's guiding principle, was aptly characterized as "a buck is a buck is a buck".

The Carter Commission proposed that the traditional definition of income be replaced by a "comprehensive tax base", a concept that drew heavily on Haig-Simons theory. The "comprehensive tax base" that the Carter Commission recommended was not quite as comprehensive as the pure Haig-Simons definition. If income were defined as consumption plus gain in net worth, the measurement of a taxpayer's income for a year would involve placing a value on (1) all goods and services (whether purchased on the market or supplied by his or her own efforts) that had been consumed by a taxpayer in the year, and (2) all gains or losses (whether realized or not) which had accrued over the year in all the assets owned by the taxpayer. The Carter Commission recognized that many of the required valuations were impracticable, and the Commission modified the definition so that for the most part it was confined to items which could readily be measured in dollars. Even so, the Commission's recommendations would have resulted in a remarkably comprehensive definition of income, at least by comparison with any existing national income tax system.

There is a close relationship between the tax base and tax rates. In order to raise a given amount of revenue, a tax can be levied on a narrow base at high rates or on a wider base at lower rates. Most proposals to widen the tax base are revenue-neutral, that is, they are accompanied by proposals to reduce rates. The argument for the wider base is that it produces a fairer system of taxation, not that it produces a greater amount of revenue, which it will only do if rates remain the same as they were on the narrower base. When the tax base was widened in 1972 (after the Carter report), rates were lowered substantially, and the further widening of the tax base that occurred in the tax reform of 1988 was also accompanied by a lowering of rates.

9.5   Capital gains

The most important (and perhaps the least radical) new element of Carter's comprehensive tax base, which was excluded from income under the traditional definition, was capital gains. The argument for the inclusion of capital gains as income is, of course, that they increase the wealth of the recipient, and therefore the ability to pay taxes, just as surely as does income from employment, business or property.

Moreover, the exclusion of capital gains seriously undermined the progressivity of the system. In both the United States, where capital gains have been taxed for a long time, and Canada, where capital gains have been taxed since 1972, capital gains comprise a very small proportion of the income reported by low-income individuals, and a very large proportion of the income reported by high-income individuals. The Carter Report displayed figures which showed that in the United States in 1963, when the percentage of capital gains to all other income reported by all individuals was 4 per cent, for individuals earning between $100,000 and $200,000 the relevant percentage was 48 per cent, and for individuals earning in excess of $200,000 the relevant percentage was 128 per cent.[13] The Carter Commission concluded that in Canada taxes were "probably a decreasing proportion of comprehensive income for upper income individuals and families", despite the fact that marginal rates at the time rose to 80 per cent.[14] We have already seen that the Commission concluded that the adoption of the comprehensive tax base (which of course would include gifts, inheritances and windfalls as well as capital gains) would allow a lowering of tax rates at all levels and a drastic lowering of rates at the upper levels. The Commission would have lowered the top marginal rate from its level of 80 per cent all the way down to 50 per cent. After this drastic lowering of rates, the tax system would not only yield the same revenue as before, but would be *more* progressive than before.

The Carter Commission departed from the pure Haig-Simons theory in recommending against the inclusion of unrealized (or accrued) capital gains. The Commission recognized "that income arises where there is an increase in economic power, and that economic power increases when the market value of property increases".[15] The Commission also recognized that it was inequitable to tax gains only when realized "in that taxpayers who retain investments which have appreciated in value are, in effect, allowed a tax-free investment of the accumulated gains that are built up free of tax, while others, who turn over their investments, are denied this privilege".[16] Nevertheless, with some hesitation, the Commission concluded that the administrative problems involved in taxing accrued gains were too difficult, and accordingly recommended that capital gains be taxed only when realized by the disposition of the property. However, in order to limit the period for which recognition of gains could be postponed, the

---

[13] *Id.*, 332.

[14] *Id.*, vol. 2, 261.

[15] *Id.*, vol. 3, 378.

[16] *Id.*, 379.

Commission recommended that there should be a "deemed disposition" of capital property on death, on the making of a gift and on giving up Canadian residence, even though no gain would actually be realized on those occasions.

The government was initially receptive to the Carter proposal that realized capital gains be included in full in income. The government's white paper that followed the Carter Report mainly accepted the proposal.[17] But the government altered its position during the period of debate on its white paper. The final decision, embodied in the 1971 Income Tax Act, was to tax gains only on a realization basis (except for Carter's deemed dispositions, which were accepted), and to include only one-half of realized gains in income. Thus the Carter Report did succeed in adding capital gains to the tax base, albeit on a preferential basis. (The tax reform of 1988 moved the inclusion rate up from one-half to three-quarters.)[18]

9.6   Gifts and inheritances

The traditional concept of income did not include gifts and inheritances. If anyone had asked why they were not income, the answer probably would have been that they were transfers of "capital". In 1966, when the Carter Commission reported, gifts and inheritances were not free of tax. They were taxed by federal estate and gift taxes and, in Ontario, Quebec and British Columbia, by provincial succession duties and gift taxes. However, these taxes were entirely independent of the income tax, and the rates and exemptions did not take account of the recipient's income.

Carter's recommendation was to include gifts and inheritances in the comprehensive tax base. The argument was essentially the same as the argument for the inclusion of capital gains. Like capital gains, gifts and inheritances increase the economic power of those who receive them, and should therefore be included in a tax base that purports to measure ability to pay. Again like capital gains, gifts and inheritances are received disproportionately by high-income individuals, so that their inclusion would steepen the progressivity of the income tax system.

Carter naturally recommended the repeal of the other taxes on gifts and inheritances. However, the inclusion of gifts and inheritances in the income of the recipient, where they would be taxed at the graduated rates that applied to all of the recipient's ordinary income as well, would undoubtedly have increased the total burden of tax on gifts and inheritances. The severity of including a large gift or inheritance in the income of a single year (the problem is the same with capital gains and other non-recurring receipts) was mitigated by recommendations

---

[17] Benson, *Proposals for Tax Reform* (1969), 40. (An exception was to be made for publicly-traded Canadian corporate securities, the gains from which were to be only one-half included.)

[18] The taxation of capital gains is the subject of ch. 15, Capital Gains, below.

for generous provisions for "forward averaging", which would have enabled taxpayers to smooth out their income by spreading the recognition (and enjoyment) of unusual income receipts over a period of years.[19] The problem of keeping track of numerous small gifts was addressed by a recommendation for the exemption of gifts up to an annual limit, so that only large gifts would need to be recorded and reported.

The Carter proposal to tax gifts and inheritances as income was never accepted by the government and was not part of the 1971 Income Tax Act. However, as will be explained in a later section of this chapter,[20] the federal government repealed its estate and gift taxes in 1971, giving as its reason the introduction of capital gains taxation with deemed dispositions on death and on gifts. Over the next 14 years, all of the provinces withdrew from (or never entered) the field of death and gift taxation. Ironically, the indirect effect of the 1971 tax reform has been to substantially reduce the taxes exigible on gifts and inheritances. This is unfortunate because the taxation of wealth at the time of a gift or inheritance has a place in a mix of taxes which seeks to reflect ability to pay. This point is argued later in the chapter,[21] and need not be elaborated here.

9.7 Windfalls

Windfalls, such as a lottery prize or a valuable find, were not taxed when Carter reported. No doubt this reflected the "source" concept of income. However, since windfalls increase taxable capacity no differently than dollars received in other ways, the Carter Commission recommended their inclusion in income.[22] Gambling winnings would also be taxed under this recommendation,[23] although this raised the question whether gambling losses should be deductible, to which the Commission answered no (except against gambling winnings).[24] The government did not accept the Commission's recommendations with respect to windfalls, which accordingly remain untaxed.[25]

---

[19] Averaging is briefly discussed in ch. 6, Taxation Year, under heading 6.4, "Income fluctuation", above. Since 1988, the Income Tax Act has contained no averaging provisions.

[20] Section 9.10, "Wealth tax", below.

[21] *Ibid.*

[22] Carter Report, vol. 3, 70.

[23] *Id.*, 526-527.

[24] The growth of lottery and casino gambling in Canada has led to the revisiting of this issue: see Canada, House of Commons, *Confronting Canada's Deficit Crisis — Tenth Report of the Standing Committee on Finance* (1994), 32, recommending the taxation of lottery and casino winnings over $500, with losses deductible against winnings. Perhaps because of opposition by the provinces that operate lotteries and casinos, the recommendation has not been implemented.

[25] For more discussion of windfalls, see ch. 12, Income from Business or Property: Inclusions, under headings 12.2(c), "Organized activity", and (d), "Gambling winnings", below.

9.8   Government transfer payments

In 1966, when the Carter Commission reported, there was a wide variation in the tax treatment of government transfer payments, such as worker's compensation benefits, unemployment insurance benefits, pensions, scholarships and bursaries. Naturally, the Commission recommended that all of these receipts be included in income, because they added to the recipient's ability to pay tax.[26] The Commission recognized of course that those payments not then taxed would have to be increased in order to make up for the new tax liability. Most of the Commission's recommendations in this area were accepted by the government, so that in 1971 there was a substantial broadening of the tax base. Worker's compensation is an anomaly: it continues to be untaxed.[27] The exemption costs about $600 million in foregone tax revenue.[28]

9.9   Imputed income

(a)   Definition

The reader may have wondered why the Haig-Simons definition of income[29] would include the value of goods and services *consumed* in the year by the taxpayer as well as the annual change in the taxpayer's net worth. Why should the taxpayer's consumption be relevant? Surely, an income tax should look to what the taxpayer received in the year rather than what he or she consumed?

The relevance of consumption to the measurement of income is that not all things which are used or consumed are purchased in ordinary market transactions. To the extent that consumption is purchased in ordinary market transactions, it will be reflected in ordinary income receipts or (through borrowing or spending savings) in reductions of net worth. But when a person uses (or consumes) his or her own personal services or his or her own property there is no actual receipt in cash or kind. Nevertheless, the benefit increases economic power and the capacity of the user to pay taxes. It is clear, therefore, that a completely comprehensive definition of income must include the benefit of the personal services and personal property consumed by the taxpayer in the year. This benefit must be valued and "imputed" to the consumer as income. Imputed income was not taxed when the Carter Commission reported, and the

---

[26] Carter Report, vol. 3, ch. 18.

[27] Worker's compensation is included in "income" by s. 56(1)(v); however, s. 110(1)(f)(ii) allows the deduction of worker's compensation payments in arriving at "taxable income". As a result of this arrangement, worker's compensation is effectively untaxed, but is taken into account in determining whether a person is a dependant and in calculating the refundable tax credits.

[28] Department of Finance, *Government of Canada Tax Expenditures* (1995), 26 ($610 million in 1992, $610 million in 1993).

[29] Section 9.3, "Haig-Simons theory", above.

Carter Commission recommended that it continue to be exempt from tax. It is still untaxed.

(b)   From services

The consumption of personal services is one element of imputed income. Most people buy clothes out of after-tax earnings. A person who makes his or her own clothes receives the same benefit tax-free (apart from the cost of materials). Home repairs or improvements, home-grown food and automobile maintenance by the owner are similar. In a family where one spouse earns income and the other remains at home to care for children and keep house, the homemaker's duties are unpaid and consequently untaxed. Yet the unpaid household work confers a considerable benefit on the family, because the family is spared the cost of paying for child care and housework which the two-earner family would have to purchase. The failure to tax the value of unpaid household labour is a tax benefit to the one-earner family.[30]

The failure to tax imputed income is one factor tending to discourage women from seeking work outside the home. Since the value of work performed by women in the home is not taxed, and the value of work performed outside the home would be taxed, there is a tax disincentive to seeking work outside the home. The loss of the income-earning spouse's credit for a dependent spouse (s. 118(1)(a)) is another disincentive. Running in the other direction is the partial deductibility of child-care expenses (s. 63), which helps to reduce the barrier against work outside the home. Much more valuable, however, is the income-split which is achieved by the family with two earning spouses. Despite the economies of maintaining only one household, in Canada each spouse is taxed as a separate individual. The two incomes are not aggregated, as occurs in many jurisdictions. We have already noticed[31] the income-splitting advantage enjoyed by the two-earner family. The Carter Commission would have eliminated this advantage by taxing the family as one unit, although the family was to be taxed under a separate rate schedule which was lower than the rate schedule for individuals. However, the Carter Commission did not recommend bringing into the taxable income of a family the imputed income of a spouse who performed unpaid housework.[32]

---

[30] Although self-performed services are technically a form of tax avoidance, people do not resent this form of avoidance as it is achieved through personal initiative and effort rather than class privilege or expensive tax advice. Indeed, the largest amounts of imputed income from services would probably be concentrated in the lower-income groups, who cannot afford to pay for services such as house-cleaning, gardening or home repair.

[31] Chapter 7, Taxation Unit, under heading 7.1, "Individual as taxation unit", above.

[32] Carter Report, vol. 3, 118-119.

(c)   From property

The use of one's own property is another element of imputed income. The imputed rent of an owner-occupied home provides the clearest example. The tenant has to pay rent out of his or her after-tax earnings in order to obtain the benefit of accommodation. The homeowner receives no taxable income from his or her investment in a home, which therefore provides the homeowner with a tax-free benefit of accommodation. If you doubt the great advantage enjoyed by the homeowner, consider the following example.

> A homeowner (H) with a marginal tax rate of 50 per cent owns a house, free and clear, which could be rented for $500 per month. He lives in the house. He moves to another city, letting his house in the old city for $500 per month and renting an equivalent house in the new city for $500 per month. Work out why this move leaves him worse off to the tune of $250 per month.

Before H moved, he paid no rent and received no rental income. After he moved, he paid rent of $500 per month and received rental income of $500 per month. If we disregard tax liability, his rental payment and his rental income cancel each other out perfectly. But the $500 he pays is not deductible from taxable income, while the $500 he receives is subject to tax at 50 per cent. Therefore, he becomes liable to pay an extra $250 per month in tax. The net result is that he is worse off by $250 a month.

How would the position be changed if imputed rent were brought into income for tax purposes? Before H moved he would have had to include in his income a notional rent of $500 per month, and this would increase his tax by $250 per month. He would still pay no rent, and receive no rental income, but he would pay an additional amount of tax, namely $250 per month. After H moved, his tax liability would not increase and his new rental income and outgo would exactly cancel each other out.

If imputed rent were taxed, the homeowner would not receive a concession from the tax system. The investment of money to save a personal expense (rent) would not offer any tax advantage over the investment of money to earn income. Homeowners would pay more tax, although their mortgage interest would be deductible as an expense incurred to earn income. The advantage of the extra tax would be that the system would be more equitable as between homeowner and renter, and rates could be lowered somewhat for everybody.

The tax advantage which the homeowner enjoys over the renter by virtue of the failure of the tax system to bring imputed rent into income is exacerbated in the United States, where not only is the homeowner's imputed rent untaxed, but the homeowner is allowed to deduct from income the mortgage interest and property taxes on his or her home. The homeowner is allowed to deduct expenses incurred to generate a benefit (the imputed rent) which is untaxed.

The tax advantage which the homeowner enjoys by virtue of the failure of the tax system to bring imputed rent into income[33] could be corrected in one of two ways. The most obvious way is to bring imputed rent into income. However, as noted by the Carter Commission, this raises the administrative problems of assessing the rental value of all owner-occupied dwellings in Canada, and it raises the problem of policy whether it is fair to tax imputed rent without also taxing other forms of imputed income. A second way of roughly equalizing the positions of owners and renters would be to allow renters to deduct for tax purposes some portion of the rent on their homes. This second approach was suggested by the Carter Commission as an alternative to taxing imputed income.[34] It is obviously administratively feasible, but it was not implemented in the 1971 Income Tax Act.[35]

(d) Reasons for exclusion

Both equity and neutrality suggest that imputed income should be taxed. Its exclusion from the tax base violates the stipulation of equity that tax should be levied in accordance with ability to pay. It also violates neutrality by encouraging people to by-pass the market to supply themselves with the property and services needed for personal living and leisure instead of devoting their capital and time to other, more productive ends. But there are great administrative difficulties in including imputed income in the tax base. The essence of imputed income is that it is not received in cash or any other measurable unit of value, and that it arises outside the market place. In order to tax an item of imputed income it would be necessary to place a monetary value on the equivalent item in the market place. This task of valuation would be a massive administrative burden, because nearly every taxpayer would have some items of imputed income, and their valuation would nearly always be difficult and would often give rise to dispute. If the tax system lightened the burden by taxing only those items of imputed income which could be more easily valued (imputed rent, for example), or those items upon which a standard arbitrary figure could be placed (household labour, for example), then a serious question of equity would be raised by the resulting discrimination against only some kinds of imputed income.

---

[33] A complete analysis of the effect of the tax system on the relative costs of owning and renting a home would also have to take account of the exclusion from capital gains tax of the principal residence. This is another concession to the homeowner relative to the renter, because the renter must pay tax on any capital gains on all of his or her investments.

[34] Carter Report, vol. 3, 48.

[35] It is possible that the tax system provides an indirect subsidy to renters through the generous capital cost allowances for depreciation that are allowed to landlords by the Act. If the market for rental housing is competitive, or if rents are controlled by law, the landlord's tax savings will be shifted forward to the tenants in the form of lower rents: see Clayton, "Income Taxes and Subsidies to Homeowners and Renters" (1974) 22 *Can. Tax J.* 295.

For these reasons, while economists generally agree that all of a person's consumption plus saving over a period of time should be treated as income, every income tax system is much less ambitious and for the most part taxes only those receipts in cash or kind which arise in the market place.[36] Even the Carter Commission, whose commitment to equity and neutrality was not easily diverted, decided not to recommend the inclusion of imputed income in the Commission's comprehensive tax base, on the ground that "the valuation and administrative problems" were "insuperable".[37] Therefore, the 1971 Income Tax Act did not bring imputed income into the tax base.

9.10 Wealth tax

Income is not the only measure of a person's ability to pay taxes. The mere possession of wealth or property represents an addition to ability to pay. Compare the case of the beggar who has no property and no income with the miser who has a hoard of gold but no income. Neither person pays any income tax, but there can be no doubt that the miser has the ability to pay some tax. Similarly, a person who receives income from property is much better off than the person who receives the same amount of income by working. The property-owner's income is derived with little effort, and will continue perpetually. The person without property derives his or her income from personal effort and must provide for the accidental or eventual decline and loss of his or her earning power. In addition, the property-owner can borrow on the security of the property, or sell some of the property, and thereby increase his or her consumption above the level that could be financed by his or her income. Yet a tax system that is based solely on income and that does not discriminate between different sources of income, would exact the same amount of tax from persons receiving the same incomes.

It seems obvious, therefore, that, if taxes should be levied in accordance with ability to pay, an income tax should be supplemented by a wealth tax. The case for a wealth tax does not need to depend upon a desire to reduce large concentrations of wealth and to make the distribution of wealth in Canada more even, although those goals presumably also appeal to most people. The case for a wealth tax may be rested simply upon the proposition that taxes should be levied in accordance with ability to pay. In other words, in order to raise the government's revenue requirements as fairly as possible, there is a place for a wealth tax in the mix of taxes that should be levied.[38]

---

[36] For an account of the Canadian exceptions to this general rule, and a good discussion of imputed income in general, see A.F. Sheppard, "The Taxation of Imputed Income and the Rule in *Sharkey* v. *Wernher*" (1973) 51 *Can. Bar Rev.* 617.

[37] Carter Report, vol. 3, pp 41, 47-49, 118-119.

[38] See generally Smith, *Personal Wealth Taxation* (Can. Tax Foundation, 1993).

A wealth tax could take the form of a periodic levy based on the assessed value of all of each taxpayer's property; such a levy could be imposed annually, or every five years, or other recurring date. Some European countries impose a wealth tax of this kind. In Canada, the municipal taxes on real estate are a limited form of periodic wealth tax, as are the federal and provincial capital taxes on large corporations.[39] But Canada (like the other common law countries) has never attempted to levy a periodic wealth tax on all types of property. It has always been assumed that the task of valuing all of a person's wealth is too difficult and controversial to be undertaken with any frequency. Traditionally, therefore, wealth taxes in Canada (and elsewhere in the common law world) have taken the form of wealth transfer taxes that are levied only when wealth is transferred, either on the death of the owner or when the wealth is given away.

At death, the task of valuing the deceased's property is no easier than it would be while the owner lived, but death occurs only once for each taxpayer and some measure of accounting for assets is necessary at that time anyway for the purpose of administering and distributing the estate. Thus, a death tax is much easier to administer than an annual or quinquennial levy. Moreover, a death tax is not necessarily less productive of revenue, since a less frequent tax can be imposed at much higher rates than a more frequent one. Death and distribution to successors is a break in continuity which creates a convenient and (in view of the windfall element of an inheritance) fair opportunity to collect a substantial tax. (Special relief can be provided for inheritance by a spouse and for the preservation of family farms and businesses — the three most common possibilities of hardship.) Various forms of death taxation have been levied in Canada ever since 1892 when Ontario discovered and enacted a constitutional form of inheritance tax.[40]

The second type of wealth transfer tax is levied on gifts of property. A gift tax is usually regarded as a supplement to a death tax to prevent the erosion of the death tax base by inter vivos gifts. In Canada, the various forms of death tax have always been accompanied by a gift tax.

In 1966, when the Carter Commission reported, there was a federal estate tax and a federal gift tax (and the proceeds of both taxes were shared with the provinces). As well, there was a provincial succession duty and a provincial gift tax in Ontario, Quebec and British Columbia, but not in the other provinces. As

---

[39] Chapter 19, Corporations and Shareholders, under heading 19.5(b)(ii), "Large corporations tax", below.

[40] An estate tax is levied on the entire estate of the deceased person, and is paid by the personal representative (executor or administrator) of the deceased person. A succession duty (or inheritance tax) is levied on each beneficiary's inheritance, and is paid by the beneficiary. Because an estate tax is regarded as an indirect tax, it is competent only to the federal Parliament, but a succession duty is competent to either the federal Parliament or the provincial Legislatures.

explained earlier in this chapter,[41] Carter's proposal for a "comprehensive tax base" involved the inclusion of inheritances and gifts in the taxable income of the recipient. Carter accordingly recommended the abolition of separate death and gift taxes.

In the tax reform of 1971, the federal government, while rejecting the proposal to tax inheritances and gifts as income, unexpectedly repealed the federal estate and gift taxes. The reason given was that there was to be a deemed disposition on death or gift, under which any accrued capital gain on property at the time of death or gift was to be deemed to be realized at that time and taxed as income. The reason seems entirely inadequate. In the first place, the new capital gains tax did not touch wealth that had accumulated before 1972, because gains accrued before the start of the new system were exempt. Secondly, even assuming that it was appropriate to exempt from tax all wealth accumulated before 1972, the new capital gains tax is levied on a far narrower base than the old estate tax. Capital gains are only the increases in the value of capital property; if property has not increased in value there is no tax, and if property has declined in value there is a deduction for the loss. An estate tax, by contrast, is levied on all of a deceased person's property — not just any appreciation in value — and whether or not the property has gained or declined in value during the ownership by the deceased.

After the repeal in 1971 of the federal estate and gift taxes, there was an initial rush by the provinces to enter the field. Ontario, Quebec and British Columbia were already levying succession duties and gift taxes, and they were quickly joined by all the other provinces except Alberta. But the restoration of the taxes was short-lived. The attraction of becoming a tax haven like Alberta led all the Atlantic provinces to repeal their new taxes in 1973 and 1974. British Columbia, Manitoba and Saskatchewan repealed their taxes in 1977, Ontario did so in 1979, and Quebec followed in 1985. At the time of writing (1995), no jurisdiction in Canada levies a death tax or a gift tax.[42]

---

[41] Section 9.6, "Gifts and inheritances", above.

[42] Wealth taxes have been attracting interest as governments cast about for new sources of revenue to reduce their deficits: see, e.g., Crawford, "Provincial Wealth Taxes?" (1993) 41 *Can. Tax J.* 150; Ontario Fair Tax Commission, *Wealth Tax Working Group Report* (1993). Ontario has surreptitiously imposed the equivalent of an estate tax by a threefold increase in 1992 in the "fee" that the province charges for the issue of probate. This fee, which is based on the value of the estate, has been challenged as an indirect tax, but has been upheld as a fee: *Re Eurig Estate* (1997), 31 O.R. (3d) 777 (C.A.).

10

Income from Employment

10.1   Structure of the Act

Part I of the Income Tax Act contains the provisions that levy the ordinary income tax on individuals, corporations, trusts and partnerships. Parts I.1 to XIV levy a variety of special taxes which supplement or complement the ordinary income tax. Part XV provides for administration and enforcement; Part XVI deals with tax evasion; and Part XVII is an interpretation part, giving definitions of most of the terms used in the Act.

Part I of the Income Tax Act is divided into Divisions. Division A (headed "Liability for Tax") consists only of s. 2, a section which has already been examined in the chapter on Residence. It will be recalled that s. 2(1) provides:

> 2(1) An income tax shall be paid, as required by this Act, on the taxable income for each taxation year of every person resident in Canada at any time in the year.

We have already considered the meanings of the terms "taxation year"[1] and "resident in Canada".[2] The term "taxable income" is defined in s. 2(2) as follows:

> 2(2) The taxable income of a taxpayer for a taxation year is the taxpayer's income for the year minus the deductions permitted by Division C.

According to s. 2(2), "taxable income" is arrived at by subtracting "the deductions permitted by Division C" from "income". Before 1988, the deductions permitted by Division C used to include the personal, marital (or spousal) and dependant deductions (the personal exemptions), and additional deductions for age, pension, disability, tuition, education, Canada Pension Plan, Unemployment Insurance, medical expenses and charitable contributions; these deductions were all eliminated in the tax reform of 1988, and converted into credits against tax. These credits are found in ss. 118-118.9, which are in Division E (headed "Computation of Tax"). As the result of the 1988 reform, there are only a few Division C deductions remaining.[3] Most individuals have no Division C deductions, which means that their "income" is the same as their "taxable income".

Division B (headed "Computation of Income") prescribes the rules for the measurement of a taxpayer's "income", which is commonly described as net

---

[1] Chapter 6, Taxation Year, above.

[2] Chapter 8, Residence, above.

[3] The most common remaining Division C deductions are the employee stock option deduction (s. 110(1)(d), (d.1)) (exempting 25 per cent of employee stock option benefits); the social assistance deduction (s. 110(1)(f)) (exempting welfare, workers' compensation, guaranteed income supplement and other social assistance payments); the home relocation loan deduction (s. 110(1)(j)) (exempting some of the benefit of a home relocation loan); the charitable donation deduction for corporations (s. 110.1); the loss carryover deduction (s. 111) (allowing deduction of losses incurred in other years); the intercorporate dividend deduction (ss. 112, 113) (exempting dividends paid by a corporation to a corporation); and the part-time residence deduction (s. 114).

income, because it is net of deductions other than the Division C deductions. Division B starts with s. 3, which defines the income of a taxpayer for a taxation year as including, among other things, the taxpayer's "income for the year from each office, employment, business and property" (s. 3(a)). The Act then goes on to supply detailed rules for the computation of income from these sources. Subdivision a of Division B provides the rules for income from "an office or employment"; subdivision b provides the rules for income from "a business or property";[4] subdivision c provides the rules for capital gains;[5] and subdivisions d and e provide for a miscellaneous group of "other sources of income" and "other deductions".[6] There are more subdivisions, which will be examined in the appropriate places.

The following chart summarizes the computation of net income, taxable income and tax for individuals:

Exhibit 10-1

OVERVIEW OF COMPUTATION OF NET INCOME, TAXABLE INCOME AND TAX FOR INDIVIDUALS

Subdivision a: Income from an office or employment
Subdivision b: Income from a business or property
Subdivision c: Net taxable capital gains
Subdivision d: Other sources of income
Subdivision e: Other deductions
Division B Net Income
[Division C Deductions]
Taxable Income
× Tax Rates (3)
Tax
[Tax Credits]
Basic Federal Tax*
[Other federal tax credits]
Part I Federal Tax
Part I.1 Surtax*
Total Federal Income Tax
Provincial Income Tax*
Total Income Tax

*Federal Surtax and Provincial Tax are a percentage of Basic Federal Tax (or Alternative Minimum Tax, if it is greater).

---

[4] Discussed in chs. 11-14, below.

[5] Discussed in chs. 15-16, below.

[6] Discussed in ch. 17, below.

10.2 Office or employment

The subject of this chapter is income from an office or employment, which is provided for in subdivision a of Division B of Part I of the Act. The subdivision opens with s. 5(1), which provides:

> 5(1) Subject to this Part, a taxpayer's income for a taxation year from an office or employment is the salary, wages and other remuneration, including gratuities, received by the taxpayer in the year.

The various elements of s. 5(1) will be examined in succeeding parts of this chapter.

10.3 Timing of recognition of income

Subsection 5(1) stipulates that a taxpayer's income from an office or employment for a taxation year must be "received by the taxpayer in the year". It has been held that an item of income is "received" when it is received in cash or the equivalent of cash. In *Vegso* v. *M.N.R.* (1956),[7] for example, a father employed his daughter to work on the father's tobacco farm at an annual salary of $800. However, the daughter was entitled to be paid only $100 per year, the arrangement being that the father would pay the balance when she married. The daughter did eventually marry, at which time $8,283 of employment income, which had accumulated over a period of ten years, was paid to her. The Minister assessed the entire sum of $8,283 as income for the year of payment. This assessment was upheld by the Tax Appeal Board. The income, being income from employment, was taxable in the year of receipt, not the years in which it had been earned or become payable to the employee.

This result was rather harsh, because the salary of $800 per annum was too low to attract tax if reported on an annual basis. The result would have been different if the daughter (employee) had each year been entitled to demand payment of her full annual salary of $800, and had voluntarily agreed to leave it with her father (employer). In that case, she would have been deemed to have received the payments that it was within her power to demand. This happened in *Blenkarn* v. *M.N.R.* (1963),[8] where an employee was paid a portion of his 1960 wages in 1961. In that case, the money paid in 1961 had to be recognized in 1960, because the payment was available to him in 1960, and he had voluntarily chosen not to requisition the cheque to which he was entitled. The payment was "received" as soon as he had an unconditional right to be paid, which was in 1960.

The Act provides rules for when items that are mailed are deemed to have been received (s. 248(7)). The general rule, which would be applicable to payments of salary or wages, is that items that are mailed are deemed to have

---

[7] (1956), 14 Tax A.B.C. 451 (T.A.B.).

[8] (1963), 32 Tax A.B.C. 321 (T.A.B.).

been received on the day that they are mailed. Thus a paycheque mailed by the employer on December 31, 1997 and actually received by the employee in January 1998 would be deemed to have been received by the employee in 1997. The amount of the cheque would form part of the employee's income for 1997.

Whenever an employee is paid salary or wages in a different calendar year (the taxation year for individuals being the calendar year) than the year in which the pay was earned, the pay will be taxed in the year of receipt. This commonly occurs when an employee receives a late (retroactive) pay raise: the payment will be taxed in the year that the payment was received, not the year in which it was earned.[9] Where an employee is paid in advance — in December for January — the income will have to be recognized in the December year, not the January year.[10]

The effect of the word "received" in s. 5(1) is to require that employment income be reported for tax purposes on a "cash basis".[11] Business income is usually reported for tax purposes on an "accrual basis".[12] Because an employer will usually be reporting his or her (business) income on an accrual basis, the employer will usually deduct an item of employee's salary in the year in which it was earned, even if it was not paid until a later year. The employee on the other hand will report the salary on a cash basis and will therefore not recognize an item of salary for tax purposes until it is received. This difference in the timing of the recognition of the salary item has been accepted by the courts.[13] The early deduction of the salary expense and late inclusion of the salary income -for businesses results in a postponement of tax. If payment of the salary could be delayed for a long time, the postponement of tax would become exceedingly valuable. The Act has accordingly been amended to limit the availability of salary deferral.[14] Subsection 78(4) requires that any remuneration deducted by the employer that

---

[9] *Markman* v. *M.N.R.*, [1989] 1 C.T.C. 2381, 89 D.T.C. 253 (T.C.C.).

[10] *Randall* v. *M.N.R.*, [1987] 2 C.T.C. 2265, 87 D.T.C. 553 (T.C.C.). The cases distinguish between an advance on account of future earnings, which is taxable in the year of receipt, and a loan from the employer to the employee, which is not: *Park* v. *M.N.R.* (1950), 1 Tax A.B.C. 391 (advance against future employment income held to be income); *Ferszt* v. *M.N.R.*, [1978] C.T.C. 2860, 78 D.T.C. 1648 (T.R.B.) (advance against future commissions held to be income). The distinction is explained in Interpretation Bulletin IT-222R, "Advances to employees" (1976).

[11] The word "received" appears in other provisions as well, always calling for the "cash method" of accounting: see ch. 11, Income from Business or Property: Profit, under heading 11.6(b), "Cash method", below.

[12] Chapter 11, Income from Business or Property: Profit, under heading 11.6(c), "Accrual method", below.

[13] E.g., *M.N.R.* v. *Rousseau*, [1960] C.T.C. 336, 60 D.T.C. 1236 (Ex. Ct.); *The Queen* v. *V & R Enterprises*, [1979] C.T.C. 465, 79 D.T.C. 5399 (F.C.T.D.); *Earlescourt Sheet Metal* v. *M.N.R.*, [1988] 1 C.T.C. 2045, 88 D.T.C. 1029 (T.C.C.).

[14] As well as s. 78(4) (discussed next), the Act contains detailed provisions for the taxation of "salary deferral arrangements" (s. 6(11)).

remains unpaid 180 days after the year-end must be added back into the employer's income. As a result of this provision, the employer will usually pay any such item within 179 days of its year-end, which will force the employee to recognize the item as income when received.

10.4　Office and employment defined

(a)　Statutory definitions

Subsection 5(1) refers to a taxpayer's income "from an office or employment". The word "office" is defined in s. 248(1):

> "office" means the position of an individual entitling the individual to a fixed or ascertainable stipend or remuneration and includes a judicial office, the office of a minister of the Crown, the office of a member of the Senate or House of Commons of Canada, a member of a legislative assembly or a member of a legislative or executive council and any other office, the incumbent of which is elected by popular vote or is elected or appointed in a representative capacity and also includes the position of a corporation director; and "officer" means a person holding such an office.

The word "employment" is also defined in s. 248(1):

> "employment" means the position of an individual in the service of some other person (including Her Majesty or a foreign state or sovereign) and "servant" or "employee" means a person holding such a position.

Although s. 5(1) uses the word "taxpayer", which is defined in s. 248(1) in terms which include a corporation as well as an individual, the definitions of "office" and "employment" both use the word "individual", which is defined in s. 248(1) as not including a corporation. It follows that for tax purposes a corporation cannot receive income from an office or employment.

(b)　Distinction between office and employment

What is the difference between an "office" and "employment"? The definition of office says that an office entitles the holder to "a fixed or ascertainable stipend or remuneration", the contrast being with an entitlement to an uncertain figure such as the profit of an enterprise. But an employment nearly always has this characteristic as well, although it is not mentioned in the definition of employment.

The key to the difference is a phrase in the definition of employment which is missing from the definition of office, namely, "in the service of some other person". This requires a contract of service (or employment) between the taxpayer and an employer; where such a contract exists, the taxpayer is "employed" and his or her remuneration will be income from employment. Where however there is a fixed or ascertainable remuneration but no contract of service, the taxpayer will be an "officer" and his or her remuneration will be income from an office. The examples of offices which are given in the definition of office are judges, ministers of the Crown, members of legislative bodies and directors of corporations. These examples illustrate that an office, unlike employment, is not created by or dependent upon a contract of service between an employer and the particular holder. The position is created by statute or some other instrument, independently of the person who fills the position, and the position is filled in succession by successive holders.[15]

The distinction between an office, on the one hand, and employment, on the other, is not important for taxation purposes. Income from an office and income from employment are lumped together under subdivision a and are computed in accordance with the same set of rules. The importance of the definitions is to enable a distinction to be drawn between income from an office or employment, on the one hand, and income from a business, on the other. Income from a business is computed under subdivision b, which provides a different set of rules for the computation of income than the rules of subdivision a.

(c) Distinction between office and business

The difference between income from an office and income from a business depends upon the requirement for an office of "a fixed or ascertainable stipend or remuneration". A business, by contrast, yields a profit which is not fixed or ascertainable in advance. A partner in a law firm derives business income, because he or she is not employed by anyone and his or her remuneration is calculated by reference to the profit of the firm. If the lawyer is appointed a judge or ombudsman or to a statutory board or commission, he or she is still not employed by anyone, but the fixed remuneration will make the taxpayer an officer, deriving income from an office.

(d) Distinction between employment and business

The difference between income from employment and income from a business depends upon the requirement for employment that the employee be "in the service" of an employer. In most cases the distinction between the self-employed individual who receives income from a business and the employee who receives salary or wages is perfectly clear: the partner in the law firm and his or her secretary illustrate the two cases. The employee receives income under a contract of service. The self-employed person receives income under contracts for the supply of the goods or services which his or her business produces.

Where a taxpayer supplies services (as opposed to goods) to one person (or to very few people, as opposed to many people), it is not always easy to determine whether the taxpayer is "in the service of" that other person. The

---

[15] *MacKeen* v. *M.N.R.*, [1967] Tax A.B.C. 374 (T.A.B.).

answer depends upon the general law defining the employment relationship.[16] The general law of all the provinces, including Quebec, draws a distinction between a "contract of service", which creates an employment relationship between the employer and the employee (or the master and the servant), and a "contract for services", which creates an independent contract relationship between the employer and the "independent contractor". The distinction arose first (and is still important) in the context of the law of torts: an employer (master) is vicariously liable for torts committed in the course of employment by an employee (servant); but an employer is not vicariously liable for torts committed by an independent contractor. In the context of the Income Tax Act, we would say that a person receiving remuneration as an employee, that is to say, under a contract of service, is receiving income from "employment"; a person receiving remuneration as an independent contractor, that is to say, under a contract for services, is receiving income from "a business".

The courts use four tests to distinguish between a contract of service and a contract for services: (1) the "control" test; (2) the "integration" test; (3) the "economic reality" test; and (4) the "specified result" test.

Of the four tests, it is the control test that has the longest pedigree. The control test looks to the degree of control possessed by the employer over the work that is to be performed. In a contract of service, the employer has a good deal of control: the employer has the power to specify not only the result to be accomplished by the employee, but also the manner of doing the work. In a contract for services, the employer will specify the result to be accomplished by the independent contractor, but it will be left to the independent contractor to determine the manner of achieving the result. For example, in a contract of service, the employer will normally specify the times at which the employee must start and stop work, and the employer will normally specify and supply the place of work, any required equipment and any assisting employees; these are illustrations of an employer's control over an employee's manner of work.[17] In a contract for services, by contrast, the independent contractor is usually hired simply to achieve a particular result: an architect will be hired to design a building, a lawyer will be hired to incorporate a company, and a courier will be hired to deliver a parcel. The employer of an independent contractor will not tell

---

[16] This is one of many examples where the Income Tax Act, a federal statute, relies upon concepts created by provincial law — presumably, where there is variation, the law of the province in which the issue arises: *M.N.R.* v. *Smith*, [1960] S.C.R. 477, [1960] C.T.C. 97, 60 D.T.C. 1102 (S.C.C.) (liability to succession duty turns on effect of disclaimer under Quebec law); *Sura* v. *M.N.R.*, [1962] S.C.R. 65, [1962] C.T.C. 1, 62 D.T.C. 1005 (S.C.C.) (liability to income tax turns on effect of Quebec's community property law); Noel, "Contract for Services" [1977] *Can. Tax Foundation Conf. Rep.* 712, 716.

[17] Part-time university lecturers have been held to be employees, on the basis of the control and integration tests: *Rosen* v. *The Queen*, [1976] C.T.C. 462, 76 D.T.C. 6274 (F.C.T.D.); *Molot* v. *M.N.R.*, [1977] C.T.C. 2170, 77 D.T.C. 111 (T.R.B.).

the contractor what hours he or she should work or what equipment he or she should use or what assistance he or she should retain. Those are matters to be left to the discretion of the contractor: the contractor fulfills his or her contract simply by accomplishing the promised result.

The control test has been much criticized in recent years. It has been pointed out, for example, that an employer will in fact exercise very little control over an employee who holds a senior managerial position. It has also been pointed out that an employer cannot control the working practices of an employee with special skills, such as an airline pilot or an engineer. These criticisms depend upon an overly literal and unrealistic conception of control. Surely, if the employer has the *power* to stipulate the manner of work, it should not matter that the power is not exercised. And, surely, if the employer has the power to stipulate such matters as the time and place of work, it should not matter that the employer is not sufficiently skilled to direct every detail of the work.

While much of the criticism of the control test is misconceived, the critics have been right to emphasize that control is not the only feature which distinguishes a typical contract of service from a contract for services. Other distinguishing features exist, and have occasionally been used as alternatives to control in formulating a test to separate employees from independent contractors. The "integration" test asks whether the person whose status is in issue is an integral part of (economically dependent on) the employer's business, which would indicate that he or she is an employee. The "economic reality" test asks whether the person whose status is in issue has the chance of profit and the risk of loss, which would indicate that he or she is an independent contractor. The "specified result" test asks whether the person whose status is in issue has placed his or her services at the disposal of the employer for a period of time without reference to a specified result, which would indicate that he or she is an employee. The tendency of the cases is to look at all four tests in order to characterize "the total relationship" between the parties.[18]

(e)   Tax consequences of distinctions

We have already noticed that income from an office or employment is computed under subdivision a while income from a business is computed under subdivision b. The distinction has two important tax consequences, each of them favourable to income from a business. First, the payer of income from an office or employment is required to withhold from the employee the tax (and Canada Pension Plan contributions and Employment Insurance premiums) that is payable

---

[18] E.g., *Wiebe Door Services* v. *M.N.R.*, [1986] 2 C.T.C. 200, 87 D.T.C. 5025 (F.C.A.); *Moose Jaw Kinsmen Flying Fins* v. *M.N.R.*, [1988] 2 C.T.C. 2377, 88 D.T.C. 6099 (F.C.A.). See Magee, "Whose Business is it?: Employees versus Independent Contractors" (1997) 45 *Can. Tax J.* (forthcoming).

on the income; income from business is not subject to withholding at source.[19] Secondly, while the rates of tax are the same for both classes of income when received by individuals,[20] income from an office or employment is entitled to fewer deductions than income from business; the reason for this difference is explained next.[21]

Section 5 defines income from an office or employment as "salary, wages and other remuneration, including gratuities". This figure is the *gross* revenue of the taxpayer. Section 8 allows certain deductions from this figure, and the section (by subsection (2)) makes it explicit that no other deductions are allowed. There is no general allowance of expenses incurred to produce income from an office or employment. As a result, if a taxpayer's revenue is characterized as income from an office or employment, as opposed to income from a business, the taxpayer is confined to the limited deductions stipulated by s. 8. These do not include many of the expenses which some employed persons incur by virtue of their employment. For example, in most cases,[22] the cost of premises, equipment, a car and other travelling expenses, tools, uniforms, books, periodicals and entertainment are not deductible from employment income; if the employer does not supply or pay for these things, no deduction is available to the employee who has supplied them out of his or her own pocket.

The tax situation of a person who receives income from a business is much more favourable. Subdivision b opens with s. 9, which defines income from a business (or property) as the "profit" therefrom. The term profit does not

---

[19] The withholding obligation is explained later in this chapter, under heading 10.10, "Withholding of tax", below.

[20] A Canadian-controlled private corporation is eligible for the small business deduction (credit) of 16 per cent of active business income, which yields a low rate of tax on the first $200,000 of active business income: ch. 19, Corporations and Shareholders, under heading 19.5, "Taxation of corporations", below. In order to take advantage of the low rate, as well as the more generous deductions available to business income, an employee (with a cooperative employer) used to be able to incorporate a corporation and interpose the corporation between the employer and the employee. The corporation would agree with the employer to supply the personal services of the former employee to the employer. The corporation would be entitled to the low rate and the full range of deductions from business income. The Act has blocked this means of avoidance by creating the category of a "personal services business" (s. 125(7)), which is excluded from the definition of "active business" (s. 125(7)) and denied the benefit of the small business deduction (credit); the personal services business is also denied many of the deductions available to other businesses (s. 18(1)(p)).

[21] A third feature of business income is the ability of the individual recipient to report business income on the basis of a fiscal period other than the calendar year. Before 1995, the use of an off-calendar fiscal period caused a deferral of tax. This privilege was repealed in 1995. From 1995 on, while an off-calendar fiscal period can still be used, the income has to be adjusted to a calendar-year basis, so that there is no significant deferral of tax: see ch. 6, Taxation Year, above.

[22] In some cases, s. 8 specifically allows expenses of the kind listed. The rules are discussed later in this chapter, under heading 10.9, "Deductions from employment income", below.

mean gross revenue, but the net figure which is arrived at after deducting from gross revenue all expenses incurred to produce that revenue.[23] Subject to some limiting rules in the Act, the independent contractor therefore has the full range of deductions available for tax purposes which would be allowed by generally accepted accounting principles in ascertaining profit. Obviously, these will include many expenses which are not allowed to the employee. The examples given earlier — premises, equipment, a car and other travelling expenses, tools, special clothing, books, periodicals and entertainment — are expenses or capital outlays which are deductible either currently or over a period of time for accounting purposes, and therefore (subject to some statutory limitations) for tax purposes as well. This assumes, of course, that each outlay was incurred for the purpose of producing income: personal or living expenses are not deductible from business income for either accounting or tax purposes.

Why should a taxpayer who earns $50,000 a year under a contract *of service* be treated differently from a taxpayer who earns $50,000 a year under a contract *for services*? Distinctions based on the source of income violate equity by failing to tax equal incomes equally, and they violate neutrality by creating a tax incentive to earn income in the form of business income rather than employment income. It is not surprising therefore that the Carter Commission condemned the distinction which the tax system drew between employment and business income. The Commission recommended that "all expenditures reasonably related to the gaining or producing of income" should be deductible from income, regardless of the type of income involved.[24]

Carter's recommendation to allow the deduction from employment income of all employment-related expenses was not accepted by the government. In the 1969 white paper which was issued after the Carter Report,[25] the government criticized the recommendation on the grounds that employed taxpayers do not keep the kinds of detailed records that would be entailed, and that the administrative task of processing the claims would be too great. Instead, the government proposed a standard deduction for expenses incurred to earn employment income. The 1971 Act implemented this proposal, allowing all employees a deduction of 3 per cent of their income up to a ceiling of $150. (The deduction was later raised to 20 per cent with a ceiling of $500.) This deduction went some way towards alleviating the unfairness of the prohibition against the deduction of employment-related expenses, and for most employees the deduction was quite generous. However, in the tax reform of 1988, the employment expense deduction was eliminated. No reason was given, and no alternative provision was made for the deduction of employment-related

---

[23] See chs. 11-14, below.

[24] *Report of the Royal Commission on Taxation* (Carter Report), (1966), vol. 3, pp. 76-87, 289-290.

[25] Benson, *Proposals for Tax Reform* (1969), 10, 16.

expenses. The 1987 white paper simply made the point that the value of the basic personal tax credit, which was introduced at that time, would more than compensate for the elimination of both the employment expense deduction and the basic personal exemption (which was also eliminated).[26] The removal of the standard employment expense deduction returns the tax system to the pre-1972 state of the law, which the Carter Commission had justly criticized as flouting both equity and neutrality.

10.5 Salary and wages

Subsection 5(1) brings into income from an office or employment "the salary, wages and other remuneration, including gratuities, received by the taxpayer in the year". The terms "salary" and "wages" are not defined for the purpose of s. 5, although the phrase "salary or wages" is used elsewhere in the Act to mean income from an office or employment (s. 248(1): "salary or wages"). There is no distinction in principle, or in tax treatment, between "salary" and "wages". In common parlance, however, salary is usually computed by reference to a relatively long period, often a year, while wages are usually computed by reference to a relatively short period, often an hour or a week.

10.6 Benefits

(a)   Inclusion in income

Paragraph 6(1)(a) of the Income Tax Act includes in a taxpayer's income from an office or employment:

> 6(1)(a) the value of board, lodging and other benefits of any kind whatever received or enjoyed by the taxpayer in the year in respect of, in the course of, or by virtue of an office or employment. . . .

(The paragraph goes on to list a number of benefits that are exempted from the general rule of taxability.)

If the Act taxed only an employee's "salary, wages and other remuneration, including gratuities" — the obvious items of income from an office or employment specified in s. 5(1) — then employers and employees would become very fond of fringe benefits. Assuming that a fringe benefit is deductible by the employer as an expense of doing business, it is immaterial to the employer whether he or she pays an employee a full salary of $80,000 or a salary of $70,000 plus fringe benefits worth $10,000. But if the fringe benefits were not taxed as part of the employee's income, then (assuming that the employee's marginal rate is about 50 per cent) the fringe benefits would be worth nearly twice as much to the employee as they cost the employer, and the latter alternative would be equivalent to a fully-taxed salary of nearly $90,000. In effect, Revenue Canada would be making a contribution to the employee's

---

[26] Wilson, *Tax Reform 1987: Income Tax Reform* (1987), 88.

pay by foregoing tax on part of the pay. "A disparity in the tax treatment of an employee who receives all his compensation as salary and wages and one who receives the same amount of compensation but partly in the form of fringe benefits is not defensible."[27] Nor is the erosion of the tax base that would result from a failure to tax fringe benefits. The purpose of s. 6(1)(a) is to ensure that the more significant fringe benefits are brought into income.[28] ie. board, lodgings, etc.

Section 6 then continues on for some 12 pages, bringing into income other specific taxable benefits. For example, if an employer provides an employee with a company car, there is a formula in section 6 which is used to compute the employee's taxable benefit (ss. 6(1)(e), 6(2)). If the employer pays for an employee's car expenses, this would also give rise to a taxable benefit (ss. 6(1)(k), (l)).

If an employer provides an employee with an interest-free or low-interest loan, there is a formula in s. 80.4(1) that computes a taxable benefit based on the prescribed interest rate[29] and the amount of interest paid on the loan (s. 6(9)). This deemed "interest" benefit may have an offsetting deduction. For example, low-interest and interest-free loans are often provided to encourage employees to purchase shares of the employer corporation and to assist relocating employees in the purchase of a home. If the loan is used to purchase shares, the deemed "interest" benefit can be claimed as a deduction for tax purposes, just as regular interest expense can be deducted (ss. 80.5, 20(1)(c)).[30] If the loan qualifies as a home relocation loan,[31] there is an offsetting Division C deduction: the maximum deduction is the lesser of the employee's interest benefit or $25,000 multiplied by the prescribed interest rate (s. 110(1)(j)). The stated objectives of this deduction are to "facilitate mobility of employees and take account of the fact that housing loans are an effective way for an employer to compensate employees who must move to an area where living costs are higher".[32]

Following s. 6 is s. 7, which computes the taxable benefit in cases where shares of the employer company (or a related company) are issued to an employee (s. 7(5)). The taxable benefit is computed as the difference between the fair market value of the shares acquired by the employee and the amount that he

[27] *McNeill* v. *The Queen*, [1986] 2 C.T.C. 352, 363, 86 D.T.C. 6477, 6485 (F.C.T.D.).

[28] A summary of non-taxable benefits is provided in Exhibit 10-2 later in this chapter, under heading 10.6(f), "Untaxed benefits", below.

[29] The "prescribed rate of interest" is set each quarter by Revenue Canada based on the average yield of 90-day treasury bills in the first month of the previous quarter: reg. 4301.

[30] Chapter 13, Income from Business or Property: Deductions, under heading 13.8 "Interest expense", below.

[31] An employee must move 40 kilometres or closer to a new work location in order for a housing loan to qualify as a home relocation loan (s. 248(1)).

[32] Department of Finance, 1985 Budget Supplementary Information.

or she has paid for them (s. 7(1)(a)). For example, if an employee earning $100,000 receives his or her "pay" in shares (rather than cash), the taxable benefit would be $100,000 since the employee has not paid anything for the shares. Alternatively, if an employer provides an employee with an option to purchase shares worth $100,000 for a price of $20,000, then, if the option is exercised, the employee's taxable benefit will be the $80,000 difference between the $100,000 fair market value of the shares and the $20,000 paid.[33]

There is an important exception to this rule in the case of arm's length[34] employees of Canadian-controlled private corporations (CCPCs),[35] which, in many cases, are incorporated small businesses. For an employee of a CCPC who acquires shares in the CCPC, the time at which the taxable benefit must be recognized is changed from the year in which the shares are acquired by the employee (the general rule) to the year in which the shares are disposed of by the employee (s. 7(1.1)). This preferential tax treatment is designed to help employees of CCPCs (other than controlling shareholders or their family members) to purchase shares issued by the employer. This tax treatment is very beneficial since it is difficult for an employee to pay tax on a stock option benefit when the employee has not received any cash from the transaction. In fact, the employee may actually be short of cash because of the cost of exercising the option and purchasing the shares. Thus, for employees of CCPCs, the tax consequences are deferred until the shares are sold (and cash is received).

When a stock option benefit has to be included in income, a Division C deduction can generally be claimed equal to 25 per cent of the stock option benefit (ss. 110(1)(d), (d.1)).[36] The net inclusion in taxable income is thus comparable to a capital gain, which is only three-quarters taxable.[37] The s. 7 stock option benefit is added to the cost of the shares acquired in calculating the

---

[33] Note that there is no taxable benefit when the employee is given or "granted" an option to purchase shares. There is generally no taxable benefit until the stock option is actually "exercised" and the shares are acquired, unless the employee disposes of the option prior to exercise. Detailed rules in ss. 7(1)(b) to 7(1)(e) cover the tax consequences when options are disposed of prior to exercise.

[34] The concept of "arm's length" is defined in s. 251. In this context, it would exclude an employee who is a controlling shareholder of the CCPC and his or her family members.

[35] Chapter 19, Corporations and Shareholders, under heading 19.1(d), "Canadian-controlled private corporations", below.

[36] The 25 per cent deduction can only be claimed (1) if the stock option price is greater or equal to the fair market value of the shares on the date that the options are granted (s. 110(1)(d)); or (2) if the stock option benefit qualifies under s. 7(1.1) and if the shares are held for two years.

[37] Chapter 15, Capital gains, under heading 15.4(c), "Three-quarters taxable", below.

adjusted cost base of the shares (s. 53(1)(j)),[38] which is relevant in determining the capital gain on the eventual sale of the shares.[39]

(b) Convertible into money

In the United Kingdom, it has been held that an item is not taxable as a benefit of employment unless it is money or something capable of being converted into money. The leading case is *Tennant* v. *Smith* (1892),[40] in which it was held that a bank employee, who was required to live in part of the bank premises, did not have to report the value of the accommodation as a benefit of his employment. Since the employee could not assign or sublet his right to occupy the premises, he had received no benefit that could be converted into money. Lord Macnaghten conceded that the employee had received a benefit in the sense of having been relieved of the expense of providing his own accommodation, but he asserted that a person is chargeable for income tax "not on what saves his pocket, but on what goes into his pocket".[41]

The reasoning in *Tennant* v. *Smith* appears remarkably unsophisticated to those who have been exposed to the Haig-Simons theory of income[42] — or even to purposive statutory interpretation. The case was decided under a United Kingdom income tax statute which contained no equivalent of s. 6(1)(a). In *Waffle* v. *M.N.R.* (1968),[43] Cattanach J. included in income the value of a Caribbean cruise supplied by the Ford Motor Company to the taxpayer, who was the employee of a Ford dealer. The judge found as a fact that the taxpayer could not have assigned his right to go on the cruise or otherwise have converted it into cash; he either went on the cruise or he received nothing. To an argument founded on *Tennant* v. *Smith*, the judge replied that in his view the language of s. 6(1)(a) "overcomes the principle laid down in *Tennant* v. *Smith*". He pointed out that "board which has been consumed and lodging which has been engaged cannot be converted into money by the taxpayer either subsequently or prior thereto and, in my view, identical considerations apply to 'other benefits of any kind whatsoever'". With respect, this seems correct. Paragraph 6(1)(a)'s inclusion of "board, lodging and other benefits of any kind whatever" clearly contemplates the inclusion of benefits that are not convertible into money.

---

[38] *Id.*, under heading 15.11, "Adjusted cost base", below.

[39] The gain on the eventual sale of the shares will usually be a capital gain: see ch. 16, Investing and Trading, below.

[40] [1892] A.C. 150 (H.L.).

[41] *Id.*, 164.

[42] Chapter 9, Tax Base, under heading 9.3, "Haig-Simons theory", above.

[43] [1968] C.T.C. 572, 69 D.T.C. 5007 (Ex. Ct.).

(c)   Reimbursements distinguished

If an employee incurs an expense for his or her employer, the reimbursement of that expense is not a taxable benefit. For example, if an employee purchases supplies for office use at the local stationery store and is reimbursed by the employer, the employee has received no benefit. But a reimbursement which covers a personal or living expense is taxable as a benefit under s. 6(1)(a). For example, if an employee purchases a television for personal use and is reimbursed by the employer, the employee has received the benefit of the television, and the value of that benefit is taxable.

In *Huffman* v. *The Queen* (1989),[44] a plainclothes police officer was reimbursed by his employer for clothing expenses, despite the fact that the clothes he had to wear were regular suits and shirts. The Court accepted the taxpayer's evidence that he could not wear the clothes off duty because they were loose-fitting in order to accommodate the equipment carried by plainclothes officers and because of rapid wear and tear. Although clothes are generally a personal consumption expense, the Court was persuaded that this taxpayer had received no personal benefit from the clothes he had purchased for his employment. The reimbursement for his purchase of the clothes was therefore properly classified as the reimbursement of an employment-related outlay, and was accordingly not a taxable benefit.

The difficulty in drawing the line between benefits and reimbursements is illustrated by a series of cases concerning the payment by an employer of an employee's moving expenses. The first of these cases is *Ransom* v. *M.N.R.* (1967).[45] Ransom, who was an employee of Dupont of Canada, was transferred by Dupont from Sarnia to Montreal. The housing market in Sarnia was depressed at the time of the transfer with the result that Ransom incurred a loss on the sale of his house in Sarnia. The loss was reimbursed to him by Dupont. The Exchequer Court (as well as holding that the payment by Dupont of the amount of the loss was not an allowance)[46] held that the reimbursement was not taxable as a benefit because the loss had been incurred "by reason of" his employment. This part of the decision seems open to criticism. While it is true that the employer's decision to move Ransom to Montreal was the reason for the sale of the house, the loss on sale is probably best regarded as one of the costs of Ransom's accommodation in Sarnia. The location of one's employment is ordinarily an important factor in choosing a house or apartment, but the costs associated with the house or apartment are consumption expenses nonetheless.[47] It is arguable, therefore, that the payment to Ransom was a reimbursement of a

---

[44] [1989] 1 C.T.C. 32, 89 D.T.C. 5006 (F.C.T.D.).

[45] [1967] C.T.C. 346, 67 D.T.C. 5235 (Ex. Ct.).

[46] See sec. 10.7, "Allowances", below.

[47] Cf. commuting expenses, which are also held to be personal expenses: notes 92–93, below.

personal expense, not an employment expense, and as such it should have been treated as a taxable benefit. However, *Ransom* has been followed in later cases,[48] and is accepted by Revenue Canada,[49] which treats the reimbursement by an employer of an employee's reasonable moving expenses, including any loss on the sale of the employee's old house, as non-taxable.[50]

Where a taxpayer is relocated by his or her employer and does not incur a loss on the sale of the old home, but is required to pay more for a similar home in the new (more expensive) location, any payment made by the employer to offset the extra cost of the new home is a taxable benefit under s. 6(1)(a). This was decided by the Federal Court of Appeal in *The Queen* v. *Phillips* (1994).[51] In that case, the taxpayer had been employed by the Canadian National Railway in New Brunswick. When CN closed its New Brunswick facility, the taxpayer was transferred to CN's Winnipeg facility, and was provided with $10,000 as a relocation payment. The purpose of this payment was to offset the higher cost of housing in Winnipeg, as the taxpayer was required to sell his home in Moncton and purchase another house in the new location. The Court distinguished *Ransom* on the ground that the taxpayer in that case had been reimbursed for an actual loss on the sale of his home, while the taxpayer in *Phillips* had not. In *Phillips*, the taxpayer had been assisted by his employer in the purchase of a new and more valuable home: his net wealth had been increased by the employer's payment, which was therefore taxable under s. 6(1)(a).

In *Canada* v. *Hoefele* (1995),[52] Petro-Canada assisted employees who were relocated from Calgary to Toronto by paying them a mortgage-interest subsidy, based on a finding that housing in Toronto cost 55 per cent more than housing in Calgary. The employee who moved to Toronto was reimbursed for the additional interest on his or her mortgage caused by the larger principal sum that had to be borrowed in order to buy a home in Toronto; the subsidy was capped at the average price differential for a comparable home in Calgary and Toronto. The Federal Court of Appeal held, by a majority, that the subsidy was

---

[48] *The Queen* v. *Splane*, [1990] 2 C.T.C. 199, 90 D.T.C. 6442 (F.C.T.D.); affd. [1991] 2 C.T.C. 224, 92 D.T.C. 6021 (F.C.A.); *Canada* v. *Hoefele*, discussed at note 52, below; Arnold and Li, "The Appropriate Tax Treatment of the Reimbursement of Moving Expenses" (1996) 44 *Can. Tax J.* 1.

[49] Interpretation Bulletin IT-470R, "Employees' fringe benefits" (1988), para. 37.

[50] Section 62 permits the deduction from employment income (as well as business income) of moving expenses incurred on a change of work, provided that they have not been reimbursed by the employer.

[51] [1994] 1 C.T.C. 383, 94 D.T.C. 6177 (F.C.A.).

[52] Reported as *Krull* v. *Canada* as well as *Canada* v. *Hoefele*, [1996] 1 C.T.C. 131, 95 D.T.C. 5062 (F.C.A.). The majority opinion was written by Linden J.A., MacGuigan J. concurring; the dissenting opinion was written by Robertson J.A.

not a taxable benefit, because the net worth of the employees had not been increased by the subsidy: they had comparable homes and no additional equity in those homes. As the dissenting opinion of Robertson J.A. pointed out, the majority's reasoning ignores the fact that the mortgage-interest subsidy, like the lump-sum payment in *Phillips*, helps the employee to purchase a more valuable home.[53] It is true that the lump-sum payment in *Phillips* had the effect of immediately increasing the net worth of the employee, whereas the interest-subsidy in *Hoefele* had no immediate effect on the employee's net worth. But, in identifying an economic benefit, it is hard to see why the distinction between principal and interest should make any difference. The economic benefit to the employee of the interest subsidy does not disappear simply because the employer's payments are made over a period of time rather than once and for all. Indeed, a present value[54] can be placed on the future stream of payments by the employer — and that is the value of the benefit to the employee.

(d)   Relationship to employment

Once it has been determined that a benefit has been conferred upon the employee, s. 6(1)(a) stipulates that the benefit must have been received "in respect of, in the course of, or by virtue of an office or employment". It used to be widely accepted that this phrase implied that there must be a causal relationship between the services rendered by the employee and the conferral of a benefit, or, in other words, that the benefit must have the character of remuneration for services rendered. The Supreme Court of Canada has now decided that this is too narrow an interpretation of s. 6(1)(a)'s broad words of relationship.

In *The Queen* v. *Savage* (1983),[55] the taxpayer, who was employed by a life insurance company, had received a payment of $300 from her employer. The employer had offered its employees $100 per course as a "prize" for passing courses in life insurance, and the taxpayer had passed three courses. The employer did not require its employees to take the courses; they were taken voluntarily. Obviously, the $300 was a benefit, and the benefit had been provided by the taxpayer's employer; but was it received "in respect of, in the course of, or by virtue of" the taxpayer's employment? The Supreme Court of Canada answered yes. To be sure, the payment was not made for services rendered to the employer; it was made for passing courses. But s. 6(1)(a) did not require that a

---

[53] Compare *The Queen* v. *Splane*, note 48, above, where a mortgage-interest subsidy on relocation compensated only for a rise in interest rates, covering the difference in interest payments between the old and the new mortgage on the same principal amount. Held, no taxable benefit to the employee.

[54] The present value of a future payment is explained in ch. 6, Taxation Year, under heading 6.5 "Postponement of tax", above.

[55] [1983] C.T.C. 393, 83 D.T.C. 5409 (S.C.C.).

benefit represent a form of remuneration for services rendered; a looser connection to the employment was sufficient. In this case, the courses were taken by the taxpayer to improve her employment skills, not for any recreational motive; and this was enough to decide that the employer's payment to the taxpayer was "in respect of" her employment. The $300 was therefore held to be a taxable benefit under s. 6(1)(a).

In *The Queen* v. *Blanchard* (1995),[56] the taxpayer was employed by a mining company that required him to work in Fort McMurray, Alberta. In order to make the move to Fort McMurray more attractive, the employer had a housing policy under which the employer agreed to buy back the homes of employees if they were relocated or if they left the company. The employer later terminated this housing policy, and paid $7,240 to the taxpayer (and the other employees who had the same right) as compensation for the rescission of the buy-back right. Was this payment taxable as a benefit of employment? The taxpayer argued that the payment had nothing to do with his past or future services to the employer; the payment was to compensate him for relinquishing a contractual right. The Federal Court of Appeal held that the payment was a benefit of employment. The Court followed *Savage* to the conclusion that "the smallest connection to employment" was required to trigger s. 6(1)(a) of the Act. Since the taxpayer was eligible for the payment only by virtue of his employment, the payment should be treated as being "in respect of" the employment within the meaning of s. 6(1)(a).

When an employee receives a benefit from his or her employer, the decisions in *Savage* and *Blanchard* in effect establish a presumption that the benefit is received in respect of employment. In some cases, however, it will be possible to establish that the connection between the benefit and the employment is too tenuous for s. 6(1)(a). For example, a person might receive a wedding present or a birthday present from a friend who was also the donee's employer; the present would not be a benefit in respect of employment.[57] Revenue Canada has established a policy of not attempting to tax such a gift, provided that the value of the gift does not exceed $100, that only one gift is received by the employee in the course of the year (two in the year that the employee marries), and that the employer does not claim the gift as a business expense.[58]

When an employee receives a benefit from someone other than the employer, there is obviously no presumption that the benefit is received in respect of employment. However, there are cases in which third-party benefits

---

[56] [1995] 2 C.T.C. 262, 95 D.T.C. 5479 (F.C.A.).

[57] Cf. *Busby* v. *The Queen*, [1986] 1 C.T.C. 147, 86 D.T.C. 6018 (F.C.T.D.) (stock option plan received by reason of taxpayer's personal relationship with employer).

[58] Interpretation Bulletin IT-470R, note 49 above, para. 9.

have been held to be benefits in respect of employment. The *Waffle* case,[59] discussed earlier, is an example; in that case, the Ford Motor Company gave a Caribbean cruise to the employee of one of its dealers. There are other cases where a manufacturer or wholesaler has rewarded effort by the employee of a retailer; the result is that the employee must report a taxable benefit from employment.[60]

(e)   Valuation

Paragraph 6(1)(a) calls for the inclusion in employment income of the "value" of benefits. What is the correct basis of valuation?

In the United Kingdom, it has been held that the value of an employment benefit is its disposable value to the employee. The leading case is *Wilkins* v. *Rogerson* (1960),[61] in which an employer had given to an employee a new suit as a Christmas bonus. It was agreed that the cost of the suit to the employer had been £14.15, but that if the employee had immediately sold it as a second-hand suit he would only have realized £5. The court held that the value of the suit as a benefit of employment was the disposable value of £5.

The decision in *Wilkins* v. *Rogerson* is consistent with the English decision in *Tennant* v. *Smith* which decided that a benefit is only taxable if it is money or convertible into money.[62] Since the suit was a taxable benefit only because it was convertible into money, it was logical to value the suit at the price for which it could be converted into money. But this approach is not correct for Canada. We have already noticed[63] that *Tennant* v. *Smith* is not good law in Canada, because s. 6(1)(a) taxes "any" benefit, and not merely those which are convertible into money. The policy of s. 6(1)(a) would be stultified if benefits were to be valued at their disposable value, because it would mean that benefits which were not convertible into money would have to be valued at nil. If such benefits were to be valued at nil it would be futile to include them in the tax base. It seems clear, therefore, that s. 6(1)(a) implicitly calls for a different basis of valuation than that adopted in England.

Once disposable value to the employee has been rejected, the only plausible basis of valuation would seem to be fair market value. The "classic test" of fair market value is "the price that would be willingly paid by a buyer who does not have to buy to a seller who does not have to sell".[64] This test

[59] Note 43, above.

[60] *Philp* v. *Cairns*, [1970] C.T.C. 330, 70 D.T.C. 6237 (Ex. Ct.); *Ferguson* v. *M.N.R.*, [1972] C.T.C. 2105, 72 D.T.C. 1097 (T.R.B.).

[61] [1960] Ch. 437 (H.C.).

[62] Section 10.6(b), "Convertible into money" above.

[63] *Ibid.*

[64] *Steen* v. *Canada*, [1988] 1 C.T.C. 256, 257, 88 D.T.C. 6171, 6172 (F.C.A.).

does not require that there be an actual market for the benefit. The test is based on a hypothetical market, and it requires an estimate to be made of the price upon which a willing seller and a willing buyer would agree for a similar benefit. On this basis, the suit in *Wilkins* v. *Rogerson* would have to be valued at about £14.15. This may seem somewhat harsh in that benefits provided by an employer are rarely the free choice of the employee, and are undoubtedly less valuable to the employee than something which the employee freely purchased for himself. However, this consideration introduces a speculative and subjective element to the task of valuation which it is probably not feasible to take into account.

The cost of the benefit to the employer cannot, in principle, be the basis of valuation. To be sure, that measures the deduction which the employer may take in respect of the benefit, but it does not necessarily measure the value to the employee, and it is the employee's tax liability with which we are now concerned. However, the fact remains that in many situations the cost to the employer provides a figure which it is reasonable to accept as being also the fair market value to the employee. Small differences between cost and fair market value would sometimes result from the employer's entitlement to some form of volume discount which would not be available to an individual purchaser of a single suit or vacation or other benefit. But this order of discrepancy could perhaps be overlooked or tolerated as a minor if arbitrary recognition of the lesser value to the employee of something that was selected for him or her as opposed to something that he or she selected.

Sometimes a payment by an employer to or for the benefit of an employee has a dual character, that is, it covers expenses incurred partly for the employer and partly for the personal benefit of the employee. The common cause of difficulty is the cost of transportation and accommodation for purposes which are partly employment-related and partly vacation. If the employer pays the entire bill, then the cost has to be apportioned between business and vacation, and the vacation element assessed to the employee as a benefit. Thus, a trip to the Bahamas supplied by a wholesaler to the employees of I.G.A. supermarkets and their spouses, which involved a mixture of business and pleasure, was assessed as a taxable benefit to the extent of half of the cost.[65] A trip to Greece supplied by a wholesaler to the employee of a retailer to attend a business convention which left time for several pleasure tours in Athens was assessed as a taxable benefit only to the extent of one-tenth.[66] A conference held by an insurance company in Phoenix, which included a full schedule of business activity for the company's employees, but which employees' spouses also attended at the employer's expense, was held not to include any element of

---

[65] *Philp* v. *Cairns*, [1970] C.T.C. 330, 70 D.T.C. 6237 (Ex. Ct.).

[66] *Ferguson* v. *M.N.R.*, [1972] C.T.C. 2105, 72 D.T.C. 1097 (T.R.B.).

benefit to the employees.[67] In other cases, however, the cost of the spouse's trip has been assessed as a benefit to the employee.[68]

Apportionment is also an issue where the employer's payment to or for the employee is for business purposes, but involves the provision of facilities which are unreasonably luxurious (and therefore expensive). In that situation, it is arguable that part of the cost should be attributed to a luxury element which was unnecessary for the business purpose and should be assessed as a benefit to the taxpayer. This line of argument was successful in *Zakoor* v. *M.N.R.* (1964),[69] where the employer supplied its president with a Cadillac. Although the car was used for employment purposes most of the time, so that (it was agreed) the proportion of personal use was only one-fifth, it was held that the personal benefit from the provision of the car was enhanced by its luxurious character and should be assessed at one-third of the operating expenses. In a case of this kind, our present concern is whether the luxury element should be added to the income of the employee, but it is worth mentioning that a question may arise whether the luxury element should be stripped from the employer's deduction under s. 67, the section which disallows the deduction of any expense except to the extent that the expense was "reasonable in the circumstances".[70]

(f)　　Untaxed benefits

There are a number of employment benefits that are expressly excluded by s. 6 of the Act from the general rule of taxability. These include, for example, employer contributions to a registered pension plan, a group sickness or accident insurance plan, and a private health care services plan (such as a dental plan or a drug plan). These benefits are often valuable. Their exclusion from the tax base violates both equity and neutrality.

In addition to the employment benefits that are expressly excluded from income, there are many fringe benefits that escape taxation as a practical matter, because they are of a minor nature and not readily susceptible of calculation. Thus, free parking in the employer's parking lot, free use of the employer's

---

[67] *Hale* v. *M.N.R.*, [1968] C.T.C. 477, 68 D.T.C. 5326 (Ex. Ct.).

[68] *Shambrook* v. *M.N.R.*, (1965), 40 Tax A.B.C. 28 (T.A.B.); *Paton* v. *M.N.R.*, [1968] Tax A.B.C. 200 (T.A.B.).

[69] (1964), 35 Tax A.B.C. 338 (T.A.B.). Note that, since 1987, deductions for expensive cars have been restricted by statute. Deductions for capital cost allowance and lease costs are limited to amounts based on a car costing $24,000 (ss. 13(7)(g) and 67.3) and the deduction for interest on a car loan is limited to $10 per day (s. 67.2). These limits apply both to the deductions available for employers (in computing business income) and for employees owning their own cars (under s. 8); however, the benefit of an employer-provided car is still based on the full price of the car or car lease (s. 6(1)(e)).

[70] See ch. 13, Income from Business or Property: Deductions, under heading 13.13, "The reasonable requirement", below.

telephone for personal calls, free coffee, subsidized meals in the employer's restaurant, discounts on merchandise, and transportation to the job are among the benefits which appear to be caught by the language of s. 6(1)(a), but which the Department makes no attempt to assess.[71]

Exhibit 10-2 summarizes the major non-taxable employment benefits.

Exhibit 10-2

NON-TAXABLE BENEFITS

By Specific Statutory Provision:

Employer contributions to a registered pension plan, group sickness/accident insurance plan (e.g., a disability insurance plan), private health care services plan (e.g., a drug or dental plan), supplementary unemployment insurance plan, deferred profit sharing plan (s. 6(1)(a)(i))

Counselling services relating to mental health and re-employment or retirement (s. 6(1)(a)(iv))

Certain reasonable allowances (s. 6(1)(b))

Board and lodging at a special work site (s. 6(6))

Disability-related employment benefits (s. 6(16))

Case Law and Interpretation Bulletin IT-470R:

Uniforms

Employee discounts

Reimbursement of reasonable relocation expenses

Subsidized meals if at least the cost of the food and preparation is recovered

Gifts of $100 per year not deducted by employer ($200 in the year of marriage)

Memberships in social clubs principally for the employer's advantage rather than the employee's

Reasonable business trip expenses

Tuition paid for courses taken primarily for employer's benefit

---

[71] Interpretation Bulletin IT-470R, note 38, above, Part B.

10.7 Allowances

(a) Inclusion in income

Paragraph 6(1)(b) of the Income Tax Act includes in a taxpayer's income from an office or employment:

> all amounts received by the taxpayer in the year as an allowance for personal or living expenses or as an allowance for any other purpose. . . .

A number of allowances are exempted from the general rule of taxability by s. 6(1)(b) itself and by other provisions of the Act.[72]

(b) Definition

The term "allowance" is not defined in the Act. It has been defined by the Department in these terms:[73]

> In this bulletin, the word "allowance" means any periodic or other payment that an employee receives from an employer, in addition to salary or wages, without having to account for its use.

The purpose of an allowance is to compensate the employee for expenses that he or she is likely to incur in the course of employment. But the allowance is set at a figure which does not precisely match the expenses; it is available for the personal use of the employee; and it need not be accounted for.

In *Campbell* v. *M.N.R.* (1955),[74] the taxpayer was a hospital nurse who was paid (in addition to her salary) the sum of $50 per month by her employer, the hospital, to compensate for her using her own car at her own expense to transport patients between the hospital and other locations of treatment.[75] In *M.N.R.* v. *Bherer* (1967)[76] the taxpayer was an employee of the Catholic School Commission who was paid (in addition to his salary) the sum of $2,000 per annum as an allowance for entertainment and travelling. In each case, the sums paid were held to be taxable allowances. In each case, the sums paid were intended to compensate the employee for extra expenses incurred in the course of employment, and they may have been a reasonable estimate of those expenses, but the sums paid were fixed in advance, irrespective of the actual expenses incurred, and they did not have to be accounted for.

It has already been mentioned that only limited deductions are available from income from an office or employment. Since none of those deductions covered Campbell's situation, she could not offset the addition to her income of

---

[72] E.g., ss. 6(6), 81(2), 81(3), 81(3.1).

[73] Interpretation Bulletin IT-522, "Vehicle and other travelling expenses" (1989), para. 41.

[74] (1955), 13 Tax A.B.C. 273 (T.A.B.).

[75] Although it is now possible to create a tax-free allowance for the use of an employee's motor vehicle (s. 6(1)(b)(vii.1)), this was not possible at the time.

[76] [1967] C.T.C. 272, 67 D.T.C. 5186 (Ex. Ct.).

the allowance by deducting any of her expenses of running the car. Bherer was more fortunate, because s. 8(1)(h) does allow the deduction of travelling expenses, although not entertainment expenses. He was therefore able to partly offset the addition to his income of the allowance by deducting from his income his actual travelling expenses. The court in *Bherer* commented on the harshness of taxing expense allowances, and on the facts of *Campbell* and *Bherer* it did work harshly. However, if allowances were not taxed, remuneration would be disguised in the form of over-generous expense allowances. For precisely the same reasons that fringe benefits must be brought into income, so must allowances. The criticism would be better directed at the inadequacy of the deductions allowed from income from an office or employment.

(c)   Reimbursements distinguished

An "allowance" should be contrasted with a "reimbursement", which is a payment by an employer to an employee to repay actual expenses incurred by the employee in the course of employment. A reimbursement is not an allowance.[77] Nor is an "accountable advance" an allowance. An accountable advance is an amount given by an employer to an employee for expenses to be incurred by the employee on the employer's business, which advance is to be accounted for by the employee after expenses have been paid by the production of vouchers and the return of any amount not so spent.[78] Clearly, with competent tax advice, Campbell's and Bherer's expenses could have been paid tax-free.

10.8   Compensation for loss of employment

Upon termination of employment, the departing employee may receive from the employer a lump sum payment as compensation for the loss of employment.[79] The amount of the severance payment is normally calculated by reference to the salary the departing employee would have received during a legally-required period of notice. The period of notice may be stipulated by the contract of employment (or collective agreement) or by employment standards legislation or by a common law standard of reasonableness. Such payments are

---

[77] *Ransom* v. *M.N.R.*, [1967] C.T.C. 346, 67 D.T.C. 5235 (Ex. Ct.); *The Queen* v. *Huffman*, [1990] 2 C.T.C. 132, 90 D.T.C. 6405 (F.C.A.). Contrast *Can.* v. *MacDonald*, [1994] 2 C.T.C. 48, 94 D.T.C. 6262 (F.C.A.) (monthly housing subsidy paid by employer to compensate for higher cost of accommodation — a consumption expense — after transfer of employee to Toronto; held, taxable allowance).

[78] See Interpretation Bulletin IT-522R, "Vehicle and other travelling expenses"(1996), para. 50(b).

[79] Sometimes the payment takes the form of a continuation of salary payments for an agreed period of time after the termination of employment.

usually characterized as income from employment,[80] and are taxed accordingly.[81]

Before 1978, if the departing employee sued the employer for wrongful dismissal and recovered damages, then the damages would be received free of tax.[82] This was because an award of damages for breach of contract (or for a tort or other cause of action) is not income for tax purposes. This was so, even though the amount of a damages award for wrongful dismissal would be computed by reference to exactly the same considerations (that is, the amount of salary that would have been paid during a required period of notice) as would be applied to the computation of a consensual severance payment. Since court-awarded damages were free of tax, it was also held that an out-of-court settlement of a wrongful dismissal action also escaped tax.[83] This created an incentive for a dismissed employee to at least initiate proceedings for wrongful dismissal, so that any agreement with the employer on a severance package could be characterized as the settlement of litigation.

In 1978, the Act was amended to subject all types of severance payments to tax. This was initially done by the introduction of the concept of a "termination payment", which was partially taxed. The termination-payment provision was repealed only four years later in 1981 when the definition of a "retiring allowance" (s. 248) was amended to perform the same function. A retiring allowance was then and is now fully taxed (not as income from employment, but as other income under subdivision d by virtue of s. 56(1)(a)(ii)). The 1981 amendment added to the definition of a retiring allowance an amount received "in respect of a loss of an office or employment of a taxpayer, whether or not received as, on account or in lieu of payment of, damages or pursuant to an order or judgment of a competent tribunal" (s. 248). This definition catches the damages awards and out-of-court settlements that used to escape tax.[84]

---

[80] Interpretation Bulletin IT-365R2, "Damages, settlements and similar receipts" (1987), para. 15. Section 5 of the Act, which taxes "remuneration", is extended by s. 6(3) to include payments made under agreements entered into before or after the period of employment. A signing bonus, paid under an agreement made before employment starts, is caught, for example. A severance payment, even if made under an agreement entered into after employment ends, is also caught.

[81] In some cases, it will be arguable that the payment is a "retiring allowance", discussed in following text, as well as in ch. 17, Other Income and Deductions, under heading 17.7, "Retiring allowances", below.

[82] *The Queen* v. *Atkins*, [1976] C.T.C. 497, 76 D.T.C. 6258 (F.C.A.).

[83] *Brackstone* v. *Canada*, [1980] C.T.C. 89, 80 D.T.C. 6060 (F.C.T.D.).

[84] The retiring allowance provisions have introduced some awkward complexity into the tax treatment of severance payments. It is often unclear whether a payment should be taxed under ss. 5 and 6(3) as income from employment, or under s. 56(1)(a)(ii) as a retiring allowance, and, although both types of payments are fully taxed, not all of the tax consequences are the same. Income from employment is subject to the normal rules respecting withholding of tax, Canada Pension Plan contributions and Unemployment Insurance premiums. The withholding rules are

However, where a dismissed employee recovers damages for defamation[85] or for breach of a "pre-employment contract",[86] the damages will still escape tax provided that they can be characterized as being neither income from employment nor a retiring allowance. Damages for breach of a contract of employment before the employment has actually commenced will also escape tax.[87]

10.9 Deductions from employment income

(a) Deductions denied

The deductions that are allowed against employment income are confined to the specific expenses enumerated in s. 8 of the Act. This is explicit in subsection (2) of s. 8. There is no general allowance of all expenses laid out to earn employment income. It has already been pointed out that this is a violation of equity and neutrality, because the full range of expenses is deductible from business income.[88] Until 1988, the discrimination against employment income was mitigated by a standard employment expense deduction, which was available to all recipients of employment income, and which was intended to offset the absence of a general deduction of employment-related expenses. However, as has already been explained, the standard employment expense deduction was repealed in 1988.[89] No reason was given; the only possible one could be the deduction's high cost in foregone revenue.

(b) Deductions permitted

The deductions that are allowed by s. 8 include legal expenses incurred to collect salary or wages, union dues, professional membership dues and contributions to a registered pension plan.[90] Sales personnel who are remunerated by commission are entitled to extra deductions akin to those available against business income (s. 8(1)(f)).

---

different for a retiring allowance (reg. 103(4)), and (subject to limits) the retiring allowance (but not income from employment) can be rolled into the employee's registered retirement savings plan (s. 60(j.1)). See generally Interpretation Bulletin IT-337R2, "Retiring allowances" (1984); Collins, "The Terminated Employee" [1993] *Can. Tax Foundation Rep.* 31: 1-46. The topic is also discussed in ch. 17, Other Income and Deductions, under heading 17.7, "Retiring allowances", below.

[85] *Bedard* v. *M.N.R.*, [1991] C.T.C. 2323, 91 D.T.C. 573 (T.C.C.); see also Collins, previous note.

[86] *Richardson* v. *M.N.R.*, [1988] 1 C.T.C. 2219, 88 D.T.C. 1134 (T.C.C.); see also Collins, note 84, above.

[87] *Schwartz* v. *Canada* [1996]1 S.C.R. 254; [1996] 1 C.T.C. 303; 96 D.T.C. 6103 (S.C.C.).

[88] Section 10.4(e), "Tax consequences of distinctions", above.

[89] *Ibid.*

[90] See Interpretation Bulletin IT-352R2, "Employee's expenses, including work space in home expenses" (1994).

Travelling expenses (including car expenses)[91] are only allowed in closely defined circumstances. There is a provision allowing deduction of travelling expenses for an employee who "was ordinarily required to carry on the duties of the employment away from the employer's place of business or in different places" (s. 8(1)(h)). To fall within this provision, the employee must be required to travel, must be required to pay the travelling expenses incurred, and must not have received an allowance for travelling expenses that was exempted from taxation under s. 6(1)(b). Unless these conditions are met, the expenses are not deductible.

Travelling expenses incurred in the course of employment, whether deductible or not, must be distinguished from the expenses of travelling to or from the place of employment. Such commuting expenses are regarded as personal or living expenses. The journey from home to work is outside the scope of employment. It is true, of course, that the journey is made by reason of the employment, but it is not made in the course of the employment. This is well settled by authority,[92] and it also makes good sense as a matter of tax policy. A line has to be drawn somewhere, and arrival at the place of work is a better point than departure from home. The nature of the journey from home to work is after all dictated primarily by a consumption decision as to the location of the home. The classification of commuting expenses as personal expenses means, of course, that they are not only not deductible from employment income, they are not deductible from business income either.[93]

In those cases where an employee is required by the contract of employment to pay office rent, or to hire an assistant, or to purchase supplies, those expenses are deductible (s. 8(1)(i)).[94] The deduction for supplies is confined to consumable supplies such as stationery. It does not apply to items with longer lives such as books, tools, equipment, special clothing and uniforms.[95] These kinds of expenses are not deductible from employment income. Nor is there any provision for the deduction of entertainment expenses

---

[91] See Interpretation Bulletin IT-522R, note 78, above.

[92] *Ricketts* v. *Colquhoun*, [1926] A.C. 1; *The Queen* v. *Diemert*, [1976] C.T.C. 301, 76 D.T.C. 6187 (F.C.T.D.).

[93] Chapter 13, Income from Business or Property: Deductions, under heading 13.3, "Commuting expenses", below.

[94] The expense of a home office could be deductible under s. 8(1)(i) (as office rent and supplies), or under s. 8(1)(f) (for sales personnel remunerated by commission), or under s. 8(1)(q) (for artists' expenses not exceeding $1,000). The home-office deduction under s. 8(1)(i) and (f) is strictly regulated by s. 8(13), which imposes conditions virtually identical to those imposed by s. 18(12) on the home-office deduction from business income: see ch. 13, Income from Business or Property: Deductions, under heading 13.4, "Home-office expenses", below.

[95] *Komarniski* v. *M.N.R.*, [1980] C.T.C. 2170, 80 D.T.C. 1134 (T.R.B.).

from employment income (except, as noted above, for sales personnel remunerated by commission).

(c)   Reimbursement of expenses

Expenses incurred in the course of employment that would not be deductible may of course be reimbursed by the employer. If so, the reimbursement is not taxed as a benefit. Expenses that are really personal or living expenses are not deductible, of course, and, if they are reimbursed, the reimbursement constitutes a taxable benefit.[96]

10.10   Withholding of tax

(a)   Supplement to the self-assessment system

The income tax system relies on each taxpayer's assessment of his or her own income, deductions and credits for the year, and the remittance of the income tax due at the appropriate time. Not all individuals can always be relied upon to be unfailingly honest, to keep complete financial records, to meet filing and payment deadlines, and to be in possession of enough cash when payments are due. Accordingly, the self-assessment system is supplemented by the requirement that the payor of specified types of income, primarily salary and wages, withhold tax from payments of income and remit the withheld tax to Revenue Canada on account of the payee's tax for the year (s. 153(1)). It is actually somewhat misleading to speak of withholding as merely supplementary to the self-assessment system, as the great majority of Canadian taxpayers receive most of their income in the form of salary or wages, and therefore have most of their tax withheld at source.

The amount of tax withheld by an employer is calculated using a formula set out in Part I of the regulations. Essentially, the employer must estimate the tax that will be owed by the employee, taking into account the annual remuneration and some of the deductions and credits to which the employee will be entitled; then the employer must withhold from each pay cheque (or envelope) an amount equal to the tax owing divided by the number of pay periods in the year.

(b)   Refunds

If the amount of tax payable for the year is more than the tax withheld, the taxpayer must pay the remainder by the balance-due day, which is April 30 of the following year (s. 153(2)). If the tax payable for the year is less than the tax withheld, the taxpayer will receive a refund from Revenue Canada (s. 164(1)). The taxpayer will also receive interest at the (quarterly adjusted) rate prescribed by the regulations (reg. 4301). However, the Department only pays

---

[96] Section 10.6(c), "Reimbursements distinguished", above.

interest from June 14 following the end of the taxation year (which is 45 days after the balance-due day of April 30) or 45 days after the actual date of filing, whichever date is later (s. 164(3)). In effect, the government receives an interest-free loan from the taxpayer between the time the tax was remitted by the employer and at least June 14 of the next year — a period that could be as long as 17 months, and even longer for the taxpayer who is foolish enough to file late.

(c)   Failure to withhold or remit

Section 227 establishes penalties for failure by an employer to withhold tax at source, and for failure to remit to Revenue Canada any tax that was withheld; the delinquent employer is liable for the amount that should have been withheld or remitted, plus penalties, plus interest. Where it is a corporation that has failed to withhold or remit, s. 227.1 imposes personal liability on the directors of the corporation, subject to a defence of due diligence. The employee is also liable for tax that was never withheld, but the employee is not liable for tax that was withheld but was never remitted.[97]

---

[97] *Lalonde* v. *M.N.R.*, [1982] C.T.C. 2749, 82 D.T.C. 1772 (F.C.A.).

11

Income from Business or Property: Profit

11.1 Structure of the Act

It will be recalled that s. 3(a) of the Income Tax Act includes in a taxpayer's income for a taxation year "the taxpayer's income for the year from each office, employment, business and property". In the previous chapter, we examined income from an office or employment, which is computed in accordance with the rules in subdivision a of Division B of Part I of the Act. In this chapter, and in the next three chapters, we shall examine income from business or property, which is computed in accordance with the rules in subdivision b. This chapter will examine the concept of profit; chapter 12 will examine specific inclusions in business or property income; chapter 13 will examine specific deductions (not including deductions for capital expenditures) from business or property income; and chapter 14 will examine deductions for capital expenditures from business or property income.

Subdivision b opens with s. 9 of the Act, subsection (1) of which states:

> 9(1) Subject to this Part, a taxpayer's income for a taxation year from a business or property is the taxpayer's profit from that business or property for the year.

Section 9 is the starting point for the calculation of a taxpayer's income from a business or property. We shall see that the reference to "profit" in s. 9 draws in a set of implicit rules (mainly based on generally accepted accounting principles) with respect to the items of income and expense that must (or may) be included and deducted in the determination of profit. The other provisions of subdivision b (ss. 10 to 37) modify (or in some cases reinforce) the general rules for the calculation of profit by allowing, disallowing or otherwise regulating particular inclusions and deductions. The main provisions are ss. 12, 18 and 20: s. 12 is a list of revenue items that must be included in income;[1] s. 18 is a list of expenditure items that may not be deducted; and s. 20 is a list of expenditure items that may be deducted.[2]

11.2   Business and property

Subdivision b provides the rules for the computation of income "from a business or property". The terms "business" and "property" are both defined in s. 248(1) of the Act. Those definitions will be examined in chapter 12. Because subdivision b includes income from both "business" and "property", the rules for the computation of income are usually the same for both types of income, and it is not usually necessary to distinguish between them. Those distinctions that do exist are also listed in the next chapter.[3]

11.3   Generally accepted accounting principles

The preparation of financial statements involves many judgments as to the proper interpretation of transactions entered into by the person or enterprise which is the subject of the statements. Differing judgments as to the recognition of receipts and expenditures and other questions can produce very different pictures of the profits or losses and assets and liabilities of a business. In order to provide comparability between the financial statements of different enterprises, and between the financial statements of the same enterprise for different years, the accounting profession has developed "generally accepted accounting principles".

Generally accepted accounting principles (GAAP) may be defined as the rules which are used by accountants in the preparation of financial statements, and are accepted by the accounting profession as producing accurate information about the financial condition of the person or enterprise which is the subject of the statements. These "principles" become "generally accepted", not by legislation or other formal imprimatur, but simply by their acceptance and use

---

[1] See ch. 12, below.
[2] See chs. 13, 14, below.
[3] Chapter 12, under heading 12.1, "Business and property distinguished", below.

by competent accountants. In court, generally accepted accounting principles are established by the expert evidence of accountants.[4]

An accounting practice will be regarded as "generally accepted" if it meets "at least one and usually more" of the following conditions:[5]

— the practice is actually followed in a significant number of cases;

— the method has support in pronouncements of professional bodies;

— the method finds support in the writings of academics and others.

The latter two elements are of relatively recent origin. Before the crash of the New York stock market in 1929, the accounting profession had not established standard-setting bodies and there was little theoretical writing. After the crash, concerns about inadequate financial reporting, which received some of the blame for the market excesses that led to the crash, contributed to academic interest in accounting, and caused the accounting profession in the United States to establish standard-setting procedures.[6] In Canada, standard-setting did not occur until 1946, when the Canadian Institute of Chartered Accountants (CICA) formed a committee for that purpose. Now standards are set by the Accounting Standards Board of the CICA, and they are published as "recommendations" in the *CICA Handbook*.

When there is dispute about the existence or the terms or the applicability of a generally accepted accounting principle, the *CICA Handbook* will often be a useful source. The Handbook has not, however, obviated the need for expert evidence. This is because the Handbook is silent on many issues, including some general issues, such as the timing of the recognition of revenue, and many industry-specific accounting practices. Even when the Handbook does speak, it is not conclusive. The Handbook itself cautions that "no rule of general application can be phrased to suit all circumstances" and "nor is there any substitute for the exercise of professional judgment" as to the appropriate practice in a particular case.[7] That is why a court that has to resolve a dispute about GAAP will require the expert evidence of accountants as to the appropriate practice in that case.[8]

Generally accepted accounting principles often permit alternative treatments of similar situations. For example, we shall see that there are several generally accepted methods of determining inventory costs, despite the fact that the method selected may make a considerable difference to the amount of profit reported by a business. The same is true of accounting for depreciation, where

---

[4] In *Moore* v. *M.N.R.*, [1987] 1 C.T.C. 377, 87 D.T.C. 5215 (F.C.A.), the Court noted that judges must be informed of generally accepted accounting principles by expert evidence, rather than by reference to textbooks or other reference materials, unless the texts are properly introduced in evidence or consented to by the parties.

[5] Arnold, *Timing and Income Taxation* (Can. Tax Foundation, Toronto, 1983), 7.

[6] Skinner, *Accounting Standards in Evolution* (Holt, Rinehart and Winston, 1987), 513.

[7] *CICA Handbook* (looseleaf), vol. 1, 9.

[8] Note 4, above.

a variety of methods are accepted. Where there is more than one generally accepted treatment, comparability of a kind is achieved by disclosure in the financial statements of exactly what has been done, and by consistent use from year to year of the same procedure. It is the function of the auditor of a business to examine carefully the financial statements prepared by the business's accountants, including their accounting procedures and their records, and to provide his or her opinion as to whether the statements "present fairly" the financial position of the business "in accordance with generally accepted accounting principles".

11.4 Profit and accounting principles

According to s. 9, a taxpayer's income for a taxation year from business or property is his or her "profit" therefrom for the year. Profit is not defined in the Act and conformity with generally accepted accounting principles is not specifically required.[9] However, as a general rule, both Revenue Canada[10] and the courts[11] apply generally accepted accounting principles to the determination of profit, except where the Income Tax Act specifically requires a departure from those principles.

On most issues, there is conformity between the financial accounts of a business and its tax accounts. However, where more than one accounting method exists under generally accepted accounting principles, the courts have said that the accounting method to be used for tax purposes is the method that is most appropriate in the circumstances, that results in a "truer picture" of income and that better matches expenses with revenues.[12] In MacGuigan J.'s words:

> . . . it would be undesirable to establish an absolute requirement that there must always be conformity between financial statements and tax returns and I am satisfied that the cases do not do so. The approved principle is that whichever method presents the "truer picture" of a taxpayer's revenue, which more fairly and accurately portrays income, and which matches revenue and expenditure, if one method does, is the one that must be followed.[13]

---

[9] An explicit requirement to use generally accepted accounting principles to compute profit for income tax purposes was considered and rejected twice by the Canadian government: Magee, "The Profit GAAP", *CA Magazine*, April 1995, 32-35.

[10] See Reed, "The Dilemma of Conformity: Tax and Financial Reporting: A Perspective from Revenue Canada" [1981] *Corp. Management Tax Conf.* 20; Interpretation Bulletins IT-95R, "Foreign exchange gains and losses" (1980); IT-417R, "Prepaid expenses and deferred charges" (1982).

[11] *Dominion Taxicab Assn.* v. *M.N.R.*, [1954] C.T.C. 34, 54 D.T.C. 1020 (S.C.C.); *The Queen* v. *Metropolitan Properties Co.*, [1985] 1 C.T.C. 169, 85 D.T.C. 5128 (F.C.T.D.).

[12] *West Kootenay Power & Light Co.* v. *The Queen*, [1992] C.T.C. 15, 92 D.T.C. 6023 (F.C.A.); *Maritime Telegraph and Telephone* v. *The Queen*, [1992] 1 C.T.C. 264, 92 D.T.C. 6191 (F.C.A.); Meghji, "The role of GAAP in computing Taxable Profit" [1995] *Can. Tax Foundation Conf. Rep.* 33:1; Magee, note 9, above; Arnold, note 5, above, ch. 1; Strain, "Now You See It, Now You Don't: The Elusive Relevance of GAAP in Tax Accounting" [1985] *Can. Tax Foundation Conf. Rep.* 38:1; Philp, "Is it Time to Place More Reliance on GAAP?" [1991] *Can. Tax Foundation Conf. Rep.* 25:1.

[13] *West Kootenay Power & Light Co.* v. *The Queen*, previous note, 33 and 6028.

The Act contains a number of specific provisions that require a departure from generally accepted accounting principles. There are a number of reasons for these departures. One reason is that a policy of the Act is to maximize taxable income, and some accounting practices are deemed to be too conservative,[14] for example, the creation of reserves, contingent accounts or sinking funds to provide for future contingencies[15] and the valuation of long term investments of financial institutions at cost.[16] A second reason is that the Act's policies of equity and administrative convenience require the uniform treatment of taxpayers in matters which are allowed to vary under generally accepted accounting principles, for example, rates of depreciation of fixed assets and the treatment of goodwill.[17] A third reason is that the use of the Act to pursue non-tax policies leads to preferential treatment of some items of revenue or expense about which accountants would be neutral, for example, the fast write-off of research equipment, pollution abatement equipment, manufacturing and processing machinery and motion picture production costs. A fourth reason is that in order to pay tax, a taxpayer must have some cash to pay the tax. This liquidity concern is the reason why it has been suggested from time to time that unrealized gains and losses should not be recognized for tax purposes (an issue that is discussed below). The liquidity concern explains why reserves for certain long-term receivables exist under the Act.[18]

In addition to specific provisions of the Income Tax Act that require departure from generally accepted accounting principles, courts have occasionally refused to accept for tax purposes a generally accepted accounting principle, even

---

[14] In *Symes*, note 31, below, Iacobucci J. suggested (at the pages referred to in note 32) that generally accepted accounting principles presented too "conservative" (i.e., too low) a picture of profit. That may be true of some principles, but it is not true in general. For example, the Act's requirements for capital cost allowances and goodwill (note 17, below) often result in a business proprietor's income for tax purposes being *lower* than the proprietor's income for accounting purposes. In *Symes* itself, acceptance of the taxpayer's argument would have produced a lower figure for tax purposes than that yielded by generally accepted accounting principles.

[15] Paragraph 18(1)(e).

[16] Section 142.5 requires financial institutions to value temporary and long-term investments in securities on a mark-to-market basis and to recognize unrealized profits and losses. Under generally accepted accounting principles, financial institutions only use the mark-to-market method for temporary investments (it is one of three alternatives allowed by section 3010 of the *CICA Handbook*). Section 3050 of the *CICA Handbook* requires long-term investments to be accounted for at cost and to be written down to market value if there is a permanent decline in value. (The cost method is always used for financial accounting purposes unless an investor is able to "significantly influence" an investee: a 20% or more ownership interest is usually required for significant influence. If an investor is able to significantly influence an investee, the equity method, which requires that the investor's cost of the investment be increased (or decreased) by its share of the investee's profit (or loss) each year (with some adjustments). If the investee is controlled, combined financial accounting statements — called "consolidated" financial statements — are prepared using the principles of the equity method. The equity method and consolidated financial statements are not used for income tax purposes.)

[17] Both topics are discussed in ch. 14, below.

[18] Paragraph 20(1)(n) and subparagraph 40(1)(a)(iii), discussed in ch. 15, below, under heading 15.12(b), "Proceeds due in future".

though it has not been explicitly modified or prohibited by the Act.[19] The most dramatic Canadian example of this is the decision in *M.N.R.* v. *Anaconda American Brass* (1956),[20] in which the Privy Council, reversing both the Exchequer Court and the Supreme Court of Canada, held that the LIFO method of determining the cost of inventory, although acceptable under generally accepted accounting principles, was not acceptable for the determination of "profits" under Canada's Income War Tax Act. This case is discussed later in this chapter,[21] where it is criticized as wrongly decided.

The courts used to insist upon the actual receipt of cash for the recognition of income. However, the Act was amended to require that an amount be included in income when it becomes receivable in respect of the sale of most goods and services in the course of a business (s. 12(1)(b)) and the courts eventually recognized the gross distortions in the measurement of income that are produced by the cash method of accounting (which is discussed later in this chapter). The courts now follow generally accepted accounting principles by insisting that most businesses recognize profit when amounts are receivable.[22]

A surprising regression from generally accepted accounting principles occurred in *Friedberg* v. *Canada* (1993),[23] where the Supreme Court of Canada held that the mark-to-market accounting method (which recognizes unrealized gains and losses on futures contracts and other securities on an accrual basis) was not appropriate for income tax purposes, even though the evidence indicated that it was the preferred method for financial accounting purposes. Iacobucci, J. for a unanimous Court stated that:

> while the "marked to market" accounting method proposed by the [Minister] may better describe the taxpayer's income position for some purposes, we are not satisfied that it can describe income for income tax purposes, nor are we satisfied that a margin account balance is the appropriate measure of realized income for tax purposes.[24]

The reasoning in *Friedberg* is very brief (the judgment runs less than a page), but Iacobucci J. does use the phrase "realized income" in the quoted passage. This has led commentators to suggest that the case stands for the legal principle that any generally accepted accounting principle that recognizes unrealized profits is not appropriate for tax purposes.[25]

The rationale for a legal requirement of realization would be the concern that taxes should not be imposed until income is certain and there is a reliable

---

[19] See Arnold, note 5, above, 27-31.

[20] [1956] A.C. 85 (P.C.).

[21] Text accompanying note 62, below.

[22] *Ken Steeves Sales* v. *M.N.R.*, [1955] C.T.C. 47, 55 D.T.C. 1044 (Ex. Ct.); *West Kootenay and Light Co.* v. *The Queen*, note 12, above. See discussion in Arnold, note 5, above, 25, 44, 81.

[23] [1993] 4 S.C.R. 285, [1993] 2 C.T.C. 306, 93 D.T.C. 5507 (S.C.C.).

[24] *Ibid.*

[25] E.g., McDonnell, "More on GAAP and Profit" in "Current Cases", [1994] 42 *Can. Tax J.* 452; Sykora, "The Income Tax Web Surrounding Derivatives" [1995] *Can. Tax Foundation Conf. Rep.*, 30:1, at 30:15-18. The existence of a realization principle is also discussed in Arnold, note 5, above, ch. 4; Strain, note 12, above, 38:8.

prospect of cash to pay the tax. However, generally accepted accounting principles are also conservative about the recognition of paper gains or losses, and so there is not much room for divergence between legal and accounting rules. In the rare cases where generally accepted accounting principles do recognize unrealized profits, income tax law often accords the same recognition. For example, in *Canadian General Electric Co.* v. *M.N.R.* (1961),[26] the Supreme Court of Canada held that unrealized gains and losses on foreign currency transactions made on income account, which were recognized for financial accounting purposes, must also be recognized for tax purposes.[27] Further, financial institutions are now required to use the mark-to-market method for securities.[28] The true position seems to be that generally accepted accounting principles rarely recognize unrealized gains or losses, but, when they do, the recognition is usually acceptable for tax purposes.

Both financial accounting and tax accounting have evolved over the years from simplistic systems based on cash and the realization of profit to more complex systems that reflect the complexity of business transactions today. Although tax accounting has several objectives which financial accounting does not have (such as the collection of tax, equity among taxpayers and providing the proper environment for economic growth), the objective of a meaningful measure of annual income is an objective which is common to both systems.

It is true that generally accepted accounting principles have little relevance in determining whether an item should be included or excluded from the tax base in the first place (and the occasional departures by the courts from generally accepted accounting principles often deal with issues of this type).[29] But accounting principles have a great deal of relevance in determining the appropriate timing of the inclusion of a revenue item and the appropriate timing of the deduction of an expense item. The better view, it is therefore submitted, is that, where the Act does not specifically require a different method of accounting, generally accepted accounting principles should be applied by the courts to the determination of profit under s. 9 of the Act.

Unfortunately, the Supreme Court has gone out of its way to cast doubt on whether generally accepted accounting principles have any relevance at all to the determination of profit under s. 9. We have already noticed the decision in

---

[26] [1961] C.T.C. 512, 61 D.T.C. 1300 (S.C.C.).

[27] The decision has been described as a "somewhat confused judgment": Strain, note 12, above, 38:27. In Interpretation Bulletin IT-96R5, "Foreign exchange gains and losses" (1980), para. 7, Revenue Canada states that either the realized or accrual basis may be used but that "the method used should be the same for financial statement and income tax purposes". (Note that the cases now indicate that conformity is not required as long as the accounting method used for tax purposes satisfies the "truer picture" test: text accompanying note 12, above.)

[28] Section 142.5, discussed in note 58, below, which was announced in a federal budget less than a year after the decision in *Friedberg*. However, proprietors carrying on an adventure in the nature of trade, like Friedberg, are now required to use cost: proposed s. 10(1.01), discussed in note 58, below

[29] See Meghji, note 12, above, 33:14 to 17.

Friedberg,[30] where the Court rejected a generally accepted accounting practice without any real explanation. In *Symes* v. *Canada* (1993),[31] the question was whether child care expenses were deductible as a business expense. The Court concluded that they were not. Since they would also not have been deductible under generally accepted accounting principles, the case did not call for any ruling on the relevance of generally accepted accounting principles. Nonetheless, in a long discussion of the determination of "profit" for the purpose of s. 9, Iacobucci J. for the majority of the Court said that it was not "appropriate" to rely on generally accepted accounting principles; rather, reliance should be placed on "well accepted principles of business (or accounting) practice" or "well accepted principles of commercial trading".[32]

Iacobucci J.'s obiter dictum is, with respect, confusing. The confusion is caused by his failure to provide any definition of the "well accepted principles of business (or accounting) practice" or "well accepted principles of commercial trading". Obviously, they are not the same as generally accepted accounting principles; otherwise, there would be no point in insisting on the distinction. And yet, in the two phrases offered, what does "well accepted" mean if it does not mean generally accepted by accountants? Where are the alternative "principles" to be found if not in the practices of accountants? How are the principles to be proved in court if not by the expert evidence of accountants? Until answers are provided to these questions, it seems unwise to abandon generally accepted accounting principles as the primary measure of profit for income tax (as well as general accounting) purposes.[33]

Subsequent cases have cited *Symes* as standing for the principle that the calculation of profits under s. 9 is a question of law which is unaffected by generally accepted accounting principles[34] but no court has ever explained what the rules of "law" are that would replace generally accepted accounting principles. As one commentator put it, "The vast majority of case law simply mouths the mantra that profit is computed in accordance with ordinary commercial principles and that taxable profit is a question of law."[35]

---

[30] Note 23, above.

[31] [1993] 4 S.C.R. 695, [1994] 1 C.T.C. 40, 94 D.T.C. 6001 (S.C.C.).

[32] *Id.*, 723; 52; 6009. Compare this dictum to the holding of the English Court of Appeal in *Gallagher* v. *Jones*, [1993] Simon's Tax Cases 537, in which the Court held that generally accepted accounting principles must be used for the purpose of determining business profits for tax purposes. Sir Thomas Bingham M.R. said (at p. 555) that he could not "understand how any judge made rule could override the application of a generally accepted rule of commercial accountancy". In that case (decided under a U.K. taxing statute), the Court held that prepaid rents must be amortized over the initial term of the lease in accordance with generally accepted accounting principles, rather than deducted when incurred in accordance with some judicial decisions.

[33] Compare Arnold, note 5, above, 19: "there is no distinction in Canadian income tax between ordinary commercial principles and ordinary accounting principles".

[34] E.g., *The Queen* v. *Toronto College Park*, [1996] 3 C.T.C. 94, 96 D.T.C. 6407 (F.C.A.).

[35] Meghji, note 12, above, 33:10.

At present, business proprietors rely upon generally accepted accounting principles in preparing their financial statements. They then use the same statements for tax purposes, accompanied by a form making only those adjustments to the figures that are specifically required by the Income Tax Act. Revenue Canada accepts this practice. At least for the time being, the dictum in *Symes* should not be interpreted as prohibiting this convenient practice. Without more guidance as to the content of the accounting principles that should be applied for tax purposes, it would be difficult for business proprietors to move away from generally accepted accounting principles for the purpose of their income tax returns. We conclude that it is probably still a fair generalization that profit will be determined for tax purposes according to generally accepted accounting principles unless the Income Tax Act modifies or prohibits the application of those principles.

The purpose of the rest of this chapter is to convey some basic information about accounting terminology and procedures. This information is necessary in order to understand the taxation of business or property income.

11.5 Balance sheet

(a) Definition

The "balance sheet" of a business presents the position of the business at a particular point in time. The conventional mode of presentation in Canada is to show "assets" at the top of the page, followed by "liabilities" and "shareholders' equity" (or "owner's equity") at the bottom. An alternative presentation is to list assets on the left-hand side and liabilities and shareholders' equity on the right-hand side.

(b) Assets, liabilities and equity

The terms "assets", "liabilities" and "equity" have special meanings for accountants. Assets are defined in the *CICA Handbook* as "economic resources controlled by an entity as a result of past transactions or events and from which future economic benefits may be obtained".[36] These will, of course, include all things of value which are used in the business; but, for reasons which will become evident later, the accountant treats all expenditures that have a continuing value to the business as assets, even if they are not represented by things with a realizable value. Thus, assets will include not only cash, accounts receivable, inventory, land, plant, equipment, goodwill and other things which would generally be accepted by lay people as assets, but also such items as "prepaid taxes", or "unamortized expenses of bond issue", whose status as assets depends upon acceptance of the accounting procedure of "deferral" which is explained later.

Liabilities are defined in the *CICA Handbook* as "obligations of an entity arising from past transactions or events, the settlement of which may result in the

---

[36] *CICA Handbook*, section 1000.29.

transfer or use of assets, provision of services or other yielding of economic benefits in the future".[37] Liabilities will, of course, include all legally enforceable obligations, such as debts owing to creditors, but the accountant also recognizes obligations based on ethical or moral or practical considerations even if they are not grounded in a legally enforceable duty.[38]

Equity is defined in the *CICA Handbook* as "the ownership interest in the assets of a profit-oriented enterprise after deducting its liabilities".[39] This consists of the capital which has been contributed by the owner of the business (if it is a sole proprietorship) or the owners (if it is a partnership) or the shareholders (if it is a corporation), as well as the profits that have been retained in the business. The owners' contribution, share capital and retained earnings are akin to liabilities in that they are sums that the owners or shareholders hope to get back if the business is ever sold or wound-up. What the liabilities and the equity on the bottom (or right-hand side) of the balance sheet really show is the sources of the funds used to purchase the assets on the top (or left-hand) side. Since the purchase of every asset must have involved the expenditure of funds which came from some source, the sum of the assets must always equal the sum of the liabilities and the equity; in other words, the two parts of the balance sheet must always balance.

(c)   Current and capital assets

A balance sheet will often distinguish between "current assets" and "capital assets". Current assets are cash and other assets which in the normal course of operations are expected to be converted into cash or consumed within a year. Current assets include cash, short-term bank deposits, marketable securities (stocks, bonds and other securities held on a temporary basis), accounts receivable (sums owing by customers or clients) and inventory (goods intended for sale).

Capital assets (which used to be called "fixed assets") are assets that are held for use in the production or supply of goods or services on a continuing basis, and which are not intended to be sold.[40] Capital assets may be tangible or intangible. Tangible assets include land, buildings, vehicles, machinery, tools and office equipment. Intangible assets include patents, copyrights, trademarks, franchises and licences. Capital assets are listed in the balance sheet at their cost price less any "accumulated depreciation" (or "accumulated amortization"). The accumulated depreciation of each asset is the amount by which the cost of the asset has been written off (i.e., deducted as an expense) in the years since its purchase. The net figure of cost less depreciation is the "book value" of the asset. Note that the book value makes no claim to be the actual market value of the asset or the cost of replacing the asset. The book value is the historical cost

---

[37] *Id.*, section 1000.32.
[38] *Id.*, section 1000.34.
[39] *Id.*, section 1000.35.
[40] *Id.*, section 3060.04.

of the asset less the accumulated amortization which has been deducted from income as depreciation. Depreciation (or amortization) is deducted from income in recognition of the fact that capital assets other than land gradually wear out. Depreciation spreads the cost of the asset over the period of its estimated life or estimated useful life, depending on the circumstances.[41] The book value of the asset is the part of the cost of the asset which has not yet been "used up" and deducted from income.

Current and capital assets should be distinguished from "long term investments". An individual or corporation may hold assets which are neither used in a business nor are intended to be sold within a year, but are held simply to produce income or capital gains. Such assets are long term investments. The most common forms of long term investment are stocks and bonds which are not intended to be sold within a year, but land, mortgages, gold, or any other kind of asset which offers the prospect of income or capital appreciation or both may be a long term investment.

(d)   Current and long-term liabilities

A balance sheet will often distinguish between current and long-term liabilities. "Current liabilities" are liabilities which the business could be obliged to discharge within a year. They would include bank indebtedness on account of overdraft or short-term loans, accounts payable (sums owing to suppliers or employees), taxes payable on the income for the year ending on the balance sheet date, and the current portion of long-term debt (bonds, mortgages or other long-term obligations which are due for repayment within a year). Current liabilities would not include debt that is not due for repayment within a year. This would be listed separately in the liabilities section of the balance sheet as long-term debt.

(e)   Working capital

The "working capital" of a business consists of its current assets less its current liabilities. Sometimes the relationship between current assets and current liabilities is expressed as a ratio — the "current ratio" — which is obtained by dividing the current assets by the current liabilities. A business cannot use its capital assets to discharge current liabilities or to provide a return to the proprietor or shareholders. These obligations can be met only out of current assets (and future earnings) and that is why the relationship between current assets and current liabilities is an important index of the health of a business, at least for the short term.

---

[41] *Id.*, section 3060.31.

11.6 Income statement

(a) Definition

The income statement (or statement of profit and loss) of a business sets out the position of the business over a period of time, such as three months or six months or (usually) one year. The income statement will show the gross revenue from the business for the year (or other accounting period) and all the expenses incurred to produce that revenue. The "net income" or "profit" is the revenue after deduction of the expenses.

If the net income is paid out to the proprietor of the business or the shareholders (if the proprietor is a corporation), then it will disappear from the balance sheet. If it is not paid out, but is retained in the business, then it will be represented by assets such as cash on the top of the balance sheet and by equity (retained earnings) on the bottom of the balance sheet.

The income from a business can only be determined with complete accuracy over the whole life of the business. After a business has been wound up or sold, a statement could be prepared which would include all receipts and expenditures since the commencement of the business, and the net gain or loss to the proprietors could be ascertained. However, this fact is not particularly helpful to the proprietors or managers of a business, who require regular information about the profitability of the business in order to make the decisions necessary to operate the business. Creditors, suppliers and customers of the business may also need regular information in order to decide whether to allow or extend credit and whether to accept and rely upon commitments by the managers. That is why every business must prepare financial statements at regular intervals of time. The preparation of accurate balance sheets at regular intervals does not present as much difficulty as the preparation of income statements. For the income statement, the question is how to ensure that the statement presents an accurate picture of the income of the business for the year (or other accounting period) which it covers. In accounting terms, the issue is: which receipts and expenditures should be "recognized" (included in the income statement) for the year or other accounting period?

(b) Cash method

The "cash method" of accounting is one way of determining which items of income and expense should be "recognized" (included in the income statement) for a particular year. Under the cash method, all items of income actually received in the accounting period are recognized for that period, and all expenses actually paid in the accounting period are recognized for that period. The income statement does not take account of amounts receivable or amounts payable. (The balance sheet will include these items of course.)

The cash method of accounting has the advantage of simplicity, but has little else going for it. It will often fail to provide a realistic statement of the result of business operations for a particular period. For example, if revenue earned over two years was received in a lump sum in the second year, the cash method would make the first year (without the income) look unjustifiably bad, and the second year (with the income) look unjustifiably good. If a two-year supply of inventory was acquired in a single purchase, the cash method would make the first year (with its large inventory expense) look unjustifiably bad and the second year (with no inventory expense) look unjustifiably good. Under the cash method, even the cost of a capital asset, such as a building, machinery or vehicle, which would be useful to the business for many years, would be recognized as an expense in the year in which it was paid for. (It may be noted in parentheses that this method of accounting for capital assets has never been permitted for tax purposes, even for cash-method taxpayers, because of the Income Tax Act's prohibition on the deduction of "capital" outlays.)[42]

Section 28 of the Income Tax Act expressly permits income from a "farming or fishing business" to be computed by the cash method. This might be thought to carry the negative implication that other kinds of business may not use the cash method for tax purposes. But, where the Act is silent, other businesses may also use the cash method for tax purposes, provided that (1) the cash method would be appropriate to that business under generally accepted accounting principles, and (2) the cash method has been used consistently.[43] However, as noted earlier, the cash method is rarely appropriate under generally accepted accounting principles and the Act specifically requires amounts to be included in income when they become receivable in the case of the sale of goods and services which are sold in the course of a business other than farming or fishing (ss. 12(1)(b), s. 28).

Generally speaking, income from property (as opposed to a business) may be computed by either the cash method or the accrual method, provided that (1) either method would produce an appropriate statement of income, and (2) the method chosen is used consistently.[44] In the case of interest income, while the cash method is acceptable (s. 12(1)(c)), the Act contains special rules that preclude the use of the cash method to postpone recognition of the income (s. 12(3)(4)).[45] In the case of dividends from corporate shares, the Act requires the use of the cash method.[46] The Act contains no specific provisions for other kinds of property income, such as rents and royalties.

Income from an office or employment must be computed by the cash method.[47]

---

[42] Chapter 14, below.

[43] *Publishers Guild of Canada* v. *M.N.R.*, [1957] C.T.C. 1, 17, 57 D.T.C. 1017, 1026 (Ex. Ct.); *Boosey and Hawkes* v. *M.N.R.*, [1984] C.T.C. 2871, 84 D.T.C. 1728 (T.C.C.); Arnold, note 5, above, 81. This is not the position taken by Revenue Canada in Interpretation Bulletin IT-261R, "Prepayment of rents" (1980), para. 5 ("As a general rule taxpayers must use the accrual method of accounting to calculate income from a business or property, unless the Income Tax Act provides otherwise in respect of specific items of income or expense.").

[44] Arnold, note 5, above, 84. But compare IT-261R, previous note.

[45] See ch. 12, Income from Business or Property: Inclusions, under heading 12.3(e), "Interest", below.

[46] See ch. 19, Corporations and Shareholders, under heading 19.4, "Taxation of shareholders", below.

[47] See ch. 10, Income from Employment, under heading 10.3, "Timing of recognition of income", above.

Capital gains are taxed under a special code of rules in subdivision c.[48] It is not appropriate to describe those rules as either the cash method or the accrual method, but they are closer to the cash method, because they generally tax only realized gains.

The miscellaneous types of income which are taxed under subdivision d[49] include pensions, unemployment insurance, alimony, scholarships and bursaries, among other items, and most of the provisions refer to amounts "received", which would direct the use of the cash method.[50]

(c)   Accrual method

For most businesses, the "accrual method" of accounting is the only one which is acceptable under general accounting principles. Under the accrual method, all items of revenue are recognized as income at the time when they are earned (even if they have not been received), and all expenditures are recognized as charges against income at the time when they are incurred (even if they have not been paid).[51] The general idea is that revenues should be matched to the period they relate to and expenses should also be so matched. This is often described as the "matching" principle for financial accounting purposes.[52] Recognizing an item of revenue before it has been received or recognizing an expense before it has been paid, is known as making an "accrual", which leads to the description of the accrual method of accounting. The opposite process to accrual, namely, deferral, is, as we shall see, an equally important part of the so-called accrual method of accounting.

Revenue[53] is normally treated as "earned" for financial accounting purposes in the period in which the recipient substantially completes performance of everything he or she is required to do as long as the amount due is ascertainable and there is no uncertainty about collection. Thus a lawyer or other supplier of services will normally recognize a fee as revenue when he or she

---

[48] Chapter 15, Capital Gains, above.

[49] See ch. 17, Other Sources of Income and Deductions, below.

[50] Arnold, note 5, above, 80.

[51] The following more technical definition of accrual accounting was provided by the U.S. Financial Accounting Standards Board in *Objectives of Financial Reporting by Business Enterprises, Statement of Financial Accounting Concepts No. 1* (Stamford: FASB, 1978) para. 44: "Accrual accounting attempts to record the financial effects on an enterprise of transactions and other events and circumstances that have cash consequences for an enterprise in the periods in which those transactions, events, and circumstances occur rather than only in the periods in which cash is received or paid by the enterprise".

[52] The "matching principle" which is used for tax purposes is similar: an expense must be matched to a particular revenue stream if matching provides a truer picture of profit, unless the Act specifically provides otherwise or the expense is a "running expense". See *The Queen* v. *Canderal*, [1995] 2 C.T.C. 22, 95 D.T.C. 5101 (F.C.A); *The Queen* v. *Toronto College Park*, note 34, above, discussed in ch. 14, under heading 14.1(d) "Running expenses", below.

[53] According to section 1000.37 of the *CICA Handbook*, "Revenues are increases in economic resources, either by way of inflows or enhancements of assets or reductions of liabilities, resulting from the ordinary activities of an entity".

completes a client's work and is ready to render a bill. A seller of goods will normally recognize a sale as revenue when the goods are delivered. Of course, much of the lawyer's work may have been done in a year prior to the year of completion; and the seller of goods may have acquired and packaged the goods in a year prior to that of delivery. But revenue is not usually recognized prior to the point of completion, because until completion it is not clear how much (if any) revenue will be received.

An expense[54] is "incurred" when a cost is used up in the business to earn revenue. All of the costs which relate to the current period must be recognized in that period even if they have not yet been paid, and even if there is no immediate liability to pay them. For example, a telephone bill may not be received until several weeks after the calls have been made. Under the accrual system of accounting, the bill must be recognized as an expense of the period when the calls were made. This is also normally the case for tax purposes, unless the Act provides otherwise.[55]

Accrual is the process which occurs when no cash has moved, and yet an item of revenue or expense is recognized because it properly belongs in the current period. The reverse situation is when cash has moved but the amount received or paid is not recognized as revenue or expense of the current period. This is referred to as "deferral". Note that the term deferral in this context does not mean that receipt of the income or payment of the expense has been deferred or postponed. On the contrary, the income has been received or the expense has been paid, and it is only its recognition in the income statement of the business that has been deferred. If a business received a fee or price in the year before it had substantially completed performance of its side of the agreement, it would normally defer the item of income until it had substantially completed performance. The fee or price would increase the assets of the business by increasing cash. But it would not appear in the income statement for the year of receipt. Instead, it would be carried on the balance sheet as a liability. It is a liability in the loose accounting sense that if the recipient did not complete performance he or she would have to repay it. Then in the year of completion the receipt will be recognized as a revenue item in the income statement of that year, and the liability will disappear from the balance sheet. This is normally the case for tax purposes as well.[56]

---

[54] According to section 1000.38 of the *CICA Handbook*, "Expenses are decreases in economic resources, either by way of outflows or reductions of assets or incurrences of liabilities, resulting from an entity's ordinary revenue generating or service delivery activities".

[55] E.g., s. 20(1)(aa) allows a deduction for landscaping expenses only if they have been paid in the year.

[56] For tax purposes, the deferral of an income receipt is regulated by I.T.A., ss. 12(1)(a) and 20(1)(m).

(d)   Accounting for capital assets

We have already noticed that an expense is incurred when a cost is used up in the business to earn revenue. For example, the rent of the business premises and the salaries of employees may be regularly paid at the end of each month. These will be wholly recognized as expenses of the period to which they relate. They are costs which expire at the end of the period to which they relate. No question of deferral arises. But some costs have a continuing value to the business, meaning that they will benefit not only the current accounting period but future periods as well. For example, the purchase cost of buildings, machinery, vehicles and other things is not used up in the current accounting period, but will continue to benefit the business for as long as the things purchased continue to be useful. Such costs are not recognized as expenses of the current period. Instead of appearing in the income statement as expenses, they will appear in the balance sheet as assets. The process of holding back an expense from the current period, with the consequent creation of an asset, is another example of deferral; and an asset might equally be called a "deferred expense" or a "prepaid expense".

An asset other than land does not last forever, and the matching principle requires that the cost of the asset must be charged against income for the period in which the asset benefits the business. In each year one of the expenses is the wearing out of part of each of the capital assets other than land. Land is deemed to be a permanent asset which never wears out. The accrual method of accounting requires that part of the cost of each capital asset except land should be treated as used up in each accounting period for which it is useful. The part of the cost which is deemed to be used up in an accounting period is usually called "depreciation" (or "amortization") and it is treated as an expense which is incurred in the period. The rate of depreciation should be calculated so that at the end of the asset's useful life its cost has been wholly amortized by the depreciation charges in the income statements for the period. For accounting purposes it is accurate to regard assets as simply prepaid expenses which eventually will be used up and disappear.

Depreciation (or amortization) is, as we have seen, the systematic allocation of costs which benefit more than one accounting period. The depreciation charge which is debited as an expense to the profit and loss account each year is simply a book entry; it requires no outlay of cash.

The Income Tax Act calls depreciation charges "capital cost allowances" and calls capital assets "depreciable property". Capital cost allowances are deductible for tax purposes against income from business or property. The deduction is explained in chapter 14, below.

(e)   Accounting for inventory

In a merchandising or manufacturing business, there will be assets which have been purchased either for immediate resale or for resale after they have been assembled or used in the manufacture of some product. Such assets are called "inventory" or "stock-in-trade". What assets constitute inventory depends upon the nature of the business. Motor vehicles, which would be capital assets for most businesses, will be inventory for an automobile dealer. Stocks and bonds, which would normally be investments, will be inventory for a security dealer. Even a business which supplies services, such as a law firm, will have an inventory of work in progress, meaning those tasks upon which work has been done but which have not yet been completed and billed.[57]

The cash method of accounting cannot be used by a merchandising or manufacturing business with substantial inventories. Under the cash method, the cost of all inventory purchased in one year would have to be treated as an expense for that year even if only some of the inventory was sold in that year. This would probably result in poor profits or a loss for that year. Next year, when the rest of the inventory was sold, the cost of those goods sold would not be reflected as an expense and the year's profit would be high. This is a mismatching of revenue and expenses which does not fairly present the actual operation of the business.

The accrual method of accounting will recognize as an expense for an accounting period only the cost of those goods sold during the period, and will carry the goods still on hand at the end of the period as an asset on the balance sheet. Actually, the cost of inventory is treated in exactly the same way as other costs incurred by a business. To the extent that inventory has been sold (goods sold), its cost has been used up in the current period and is accordingly recognized as an expense. To the extent that inventory has not been sold (closing inventory), its cost has a continuing value to the business and is accordingly carried on the balance sheet as an asset of the business. The treatment of closing inventory is of course just another example of the deferral of an expense.

It is important to note that if the fair market value of a closing inventory item is lower than its cost, generally accepted accounting principles require the inventory item to be written down to its market value. This results in the fair market value of the item being reported on the balance sheet and the amount of the write-down being recognized as an expense of the period. The Act contains two alternatives for valuing closing inventory: the "lower of cost or fair market value" method (s. 10(1)) and the "fair market value" method (reg. 1801) but a change from one method to another other cannot be made without Revenue Canada's permission (s. 10(2.1)). The write-up (or write-down) required under the fair market value method is added or deducted in computing the profit for the period.[58]

---

[57] I.T.A., s. 34, provides an exception to full accrual accounting by permitting a taxpayer who is a professional ("accountant, dentist, lawyer, medical doctor, veterinarian or chiropractor") to determine income without taking into account the value of work in progress.

[58] There are two major exceptions to these rules. The first applies to financial institutions, which are required to value the securities they own at fair market value (s.142.5, effective for taxation years ending after October 31, 1994). The second exception is for inventories of a business that is an adventure in the nature of trade. (The definition of an adventure in the nature of trade is discussed in ch. 16, under heading 16.3, "Adventure in the nature of trade", below.) Under proposed s. 10(1.01), such inventories must be valued at cost, (although accounting rules would require the

Each year (or other accounting period), a business with an inventory has to allocate part of the accumulated inventory costs to the goods sold during the year (those costs will be charged as a current expense), and the balance to the goods still on hand at the end of the year (those costs — or the fair market value, if it is lower — will appear as an asset — closing inventory — on the balance sheet).[59]

The most obvious way of calculating the cost of goods sold is to keep a record of the actual cost of each item in stock, and to keep a record of the sale of each item sold. At the end of the year all of the costs of the items sold can be totalled and recognized as an expense (cost of goods sold), and all of the costs of the items unsold can be totalled and included as an asset in the balance sheet (closing inventory). This method of determining inventory cost is called "specific identification", and it is acceptable for accounting purposes. It is however normally used only by businesses with a relatively small volume of high-cost, heterogeneous inventory and a relatively low turnover, such as dealers in automobiles, antiques or pictures. For businesses which manufacture or sell a high volume of homogeneous goods, such as bread or shoes or nuts and bolts, it is not feasible to keep the kinds of records which would be entailed by the method of specific identification.

For most businesses, the best that can be done is to keep records of the cost of (a) inventory on hand at the beginning of the accounting year ("opening inventory"), (b) inventory purchased during the year ("purchases"), and (c) inventory on hand at the end of the year ("closing inventory" — generally ascertained by a physical count known as "taking inventory"). These three figures enable the business to calculate the cost of goods sold in that year. The formula is as follows: Cost of goods sold = opening inventory + purchases − closing inventory.

The calculation of the cost of goods sold presents difficulty when (as is usual) inventory has been purchased at different prices. Where this is the case, there are a number of methods of placing a value on the cost of goods sold. One is the "average cost" method, which assumes that the cost of each unit of closing inventory and of goods sold was the average of the cost of all units held at the beginning of the year (opening inventory) and purchased during the year

---

"lower of cost or fair market value" method to be used). Proposed s. 10(1.01) was a legislative response to reverse the decision in *Friesen* v. *Canada*, [1995] 2 C.T.C. 369, 95 D.T.C. 5551 (S.C.C.). In *Friesen*, the Supreme Court ruled that s. 10(1) (as it then read) could be used to claim a deduction for an inventory write-down even if the taxpayer owned only one asset in inventory (such as a single parcel of land inventory). This change is one of the few examples of tax legislation in Canada that was made retroactive to a time prior to the announcement of the change (see ch. 2, above, under heading 2.2(b), "Budget"). Taxpayers who had not filed notices of objection or tax returns based on the decision in *Friesen* by the date the new rules were announced by press release (December 20, 1995) were made subject to the new rule.

[59] To ensure that a business calculates its cost of goods sold properly, the Act also requires that the amount used for closing inventory in one year be used again in the next year for opening inventory (s. 10(2.1)).

(purchases). Another is the FIFO method (first in, first out), which assumes that the goods sold were the first goods purchased, and allocates the most recent costs to closing inventory and the oldest costs to the goods sold. The LIFO method (last in, first out) makes the opposite assumption, allocating the oldest costs to closing inventory and the most recent costs to the goods sold. Each of these methods is generally accepted for accounting purposes; each has its advantages and disadvantages from an accounting standpoint; the details are beyond the scope of this work.

The LIFO method is (as has just been explained) generally acceptable for accounting purposes, although in Canada it is not as widely used as FIFO. However, in *M.N.R.* v. *Anaconda American Brass* (1956),[60] the Privy Council held that the LIFO method was not acceptable for tax purposes. Since the Income Tax Act was then (and still is) entirely silent as to the mode of determining the cost of inventory, and since it was clear from the expert evidence of accountants that the LIFO method produced the fairest picture of Anaconda's operations, this was an unfortunate result. Their lordships could not accept that a proper matching of expenses against related revenue could involve disregard of the physical flow of goods. Of course, the FIFO method which Anaconda had to substitute for tax purposes is not necessarily consistent with the physical flow of goods where they are non-perishable as in Anaconda's case. But the fundamental objection to their lordships' reasoning is that the accrual basis of accounting often requires that items of revenue and expense be recognized in an accounting period in disregard of the actual movement of goods or cash. The only questions are whether the recognition involves a matching of related outgo and income, and whether it otherwise presents a fair picture of the year's operations. Once competent accountants have given affirmative responses to these questions, as they did in Anaconda's case, it is very difficult to see why their lordships should be worrying about whether the metals used by the brass mill were taken off the top or the bottom of the pile. In the Exchequer Court,[61] Thorson P. wrote a long judgment which clearly set out the rationale of the LIFO method of determining inventory cost, which showed why it was especially appropriate to Anaconda's operations, and which concluded that it should be accepted for tax purposes. After reading this judgment, which was affirmed by a majority of the Supreme Court of Canada,[62] it is difficult to take seriously the unsophisticated opinion of the Privy Council. However, the Privy Council's decision is the law, at least for the time being. The LIFO method is therefore unacceptable for tax purposes.

(f) Accounting for taxes

In an unincorporated business, it is not usual to account for income taxes in the financial statements of the business. This is because an unincorporated

---

[60] [1956] A.C. 85 (P.C.).
[61] [1952] Ex. C.R. 2970 (Ex. Ct.).
[62] [1954] S.C.R. 737 (S.C.C.).

business is not taxed as a separate entity. Any income or loss of the business will affect the tax liability of the owner (or owners), but his or her total tax liability will depend upon his or her income or losses from other sources, and the exemptions, deductions and credits which are available to the taxpayer. It would be entirely arbitrary, and therefore misleading, to treat part of the owner's income taxes as a cost of the business.

In an incorporated business, however, it is usual to account for income taxes in the financial statements which are drawn up for submission to the shareholders. The corporation is taxed as a separate entity, and accountants have always treated corporate income tax as one of the costs properly attributable to the corporation's operations. The matching principle of the accrual method requires, of course, that tax (like any other cost) be recognized as an expense of the period in which the related revenues are reflected in the accounts. Obviously, this means that the accounts for fiscal year 1997 (for example) must be charged with the tax for fiscal year 1997, even though some of the tax will not be paid until fiscal year 1998. If the precise total of 1997 tax is not known when the 1997 financial statements are prepared, then an estimate must be made and charged.[63]

11.7 Balance sheet and income statement compared

Historically, the balance sheet was the only financial statement. It was considered most important to know what were the assets and liabilities of a business, and of course the balance sheet was the place to look. If one wanted to know how much a business had earned over the years one simply examined the change in net assets in successive balance sheets. At the same time revenue and expenses were normally recognized on the cash basis, and with such an unrefined concept of income the income statement added little information. It is only in the twentieth century that the cash basis of accounting has given way to accrual accounting, which makes possible a more refined and meaningful picture of what has happened between successive balance sheet dates. As a corollary there has been a shift of emphasis from the balance sheet to the income statement as the significant measure of the progress of a business enterprise. The general thrust of modern accounting is to produce the most meaningful possible income statement, even if this results in a less meaningful balance sheet.

It is the shift in emphasis from the balance sheet to the income statement which has led accountants to treat all deferred expenses as assets. This practice

---

[63] The tax expense consists of a current and a deferred portion. The current portion is the actual (or estimated) liability for the year. The deferred portion represents the taxes that the corporation has deferred by claiming larger deductions for tax purposes than it claimed on its financial statements. A common cause of deferred income taxes is that the corporation's capital cost allowance claim for tax purposes is higher than the depreciation charged in its financial statements. The deferred portion of tax is carried on the balance sheet as a liability called "deferred income taxes". Such entries cause great excitement among politicians and journalists who do not understand the matching principle that drives accrual accounting, and who believe that the entries show that corporations are avoiding paying taxes.

means that some of the so-called assets have no realizable value, for example, an advertising expense paid in advance. It also means that all assets are listed at cost (less any accumulated depreciation), even though their realizable value may be more or less than their cost. Most assets on a balance sheet must simply be viewed as the unexpired balance of previously incurred costs. It is a grave error to treat balance sheet figures as indicating the "value" of the assets used in the business. Prospective creditors or investors must concentrate their attention on a firm's earning record, as disclosed in a series of income statements, in order to determine whether to extend credit or to invest. Of course, a creditor who seeks security will be interested in the assets listed in the balance sheet as well as the firm's profitability, but he or she will not obtain valuations of the assets from the balance sheet figures. One exception to this general proposition concerns current (or liquid) assets such as cash, accounts receivable and inventory. Short-term creditors will be more interested in the liquidity of the firm's assets than in its long-term prospects, and they may place some reliance on the balance sheet figures for current assets in extending credit. Accordingly, accountants accept that the balance sheet treatment of current assets should not depart too seriously from their realizable value. In the case of cash and accounts receivable, the balance sheet figures should constitute realizable value. In the case of inventory, however, there is a potential conflict between income statement and balance sheet objectives, and it is unwise to place any reliance on the balance sheet figure without obtaining information (which may appear in notes to the balance sheet) as to how it is calculated.

11.8 Sample financial statements

MASSIVE MERCHANDISING COMPANY LTD.

BALANCE SHEET (in thousands)
as at December 31, 1997

ASSETS

CURRENT ASSETS:

Cash		$ 570
Short-term deposits		10
Accounts receivable		103
Inventory (FIFO)		6,827
INVESTMENTS:		
Stocks and bonds (at cost)		20
Mortgages (at cost)		30
CAPITAL ASSETS:		
Land (at cost)		1,550
Building & equipment		
Cost	10,000	
Less accumulated depreciation	5,400	
		4,600
		$ 13,710

LIABILITIES and EQUITY

CURRENT LIABILITIES:
Bank indebtedness	$ 366
Accounts payable	2,973
Income taxes payable	950
Current portion of long-term debt	57

LONG-TERM DEBT	2,672
DEFERRED INCOME TAXES	740

SHAREHOLDERS' EQUITY:
Capital stock (50,000 common shares of $100 each)	5,000
Retained earnings	952
	$ 13,710

MASSIVE MERCHANDISING COMPANY LTD.
INCOME STATEMENT (in thousands)
year ended December 31, 1997

REVENUES:
Sales		$111,222

EXPENSES:
Cost of goods sold and expenses except those shown below	$ 93,645	
Salaries	13,637	
Depreciation	1,007	
Municipal taxes	777	
Interest on long-term debt	228	
Interest on short-term debt	24	
Loss on investment	4	109,322

INCOME BEFORE INCOME TAXES:	1,900
Income taxes	850
NET INCOME FOR YEAR	$ 1,050

RETAINED EARNINGS:
Retained earnings, beginning of year	$ 502
Net income for year	1,050
Dividends paid to shareholders	(500)
Retained earnings, end of year	$ 1,052

12

Income from Business or Property: Inclusions

12.1 Business and property distinguished

(a) Distinction

Income "from a business or property" is computed in accordance with the rules of subdivision b of Division B of Part I of the Income Tax Act. The distinction between the two types of income depends on whether the income is derived primarily from the ownership of property, in which case it is income from property, or whether the income is derived primarily from the activity of the owner or the owner's employees, in which case it is income from business. The question has chiefly arisen with reference to income from apartment buildings, office buildings and shopping centres. It is considered later in this chapter, under heading 12.3(d), "Rent", below.

(b) Tax consequences of distinction

Because income from a business and income from property are both computed in accordance with the rules in subdivision b, for most purposes there is no difference in the tax treatment of the two types of income, and it is not necessary to distinguish between them.

The Act does, however, draw some distinctions between business and property income in provisions that are scattered around the Act. The following is a partial list:

1.   The attribution rules of ss. 74.1 and 74.2 apply to income from "property", but not income from a business.[1]

2.   The non-resident "who carried on a business in Canada" (s. 2(3)) is liable to pay Part I tax on his or her business income, but not if he or she received income from property; if the non-resident taxpayer received any of various classes of income from property, including "interest" (s. 212(1)(b)) and "rent" (s. 212(1)(d)), the taxpayer is liable to pay Part XIII tax on the income from property.[2]

3.   The person who was resident in a particular province on the last day of the taxation year is deemed to have earned his or her income for the year in that province for the purpose of computing provincial income tax (reg. 2601), but there is an exception for income from a "business", which must be allocated to the province or provinces in which the business had a permanent establishment.[3]

---

[1] Chapter 7, Taxation Unit, under heading 7.5, "Attribution rules", above.

[2] Chapter 8, Residence, under heading 8.3, "Taxation of non-residents", above.

[3] *Id.*, under heading 8.8, "Provincial residence", above.

4.   The definition of "foreign accrual property income" (FAPI) for the purpose of the FAPI rules[4] excludes income from "active businesses" (s. 95(1)).

5.   The capital cost allowance rules preclude the use of capital cost allowance deductions to create losses on income from "rental property" (reg. 1100(11)),[5] but where the income is from a business the restrictions do not apply.

6.   The deductions from cumulative eligible capital (for the amortization of intangibles) are available "in respect of a business", but not property (s. 20(1)(b)).[6]

7.   The rules regarding the taxation of corporations distinguish between income from an "active business", in respect of which the "small business deduction" is available to Canadian-controlled private corporations (s. 125), and "Canadian investment income" and "foreign investment income" (both of which exclude income from an active business), in respect of which a partial refund of tax is available (s. 129).[7]

12.2   Income from business

(a)   Definition of business

The word "business" is defined in s. 248(1) as follows:

> "business" includes a profession, calling, trade, manufacture or undertaking of any kind whatever and . . . an adventure or concern in the nature of trade but does not include an office or employment;

In practice, this definition is not particularly useful. From the numerous cases one can derive the following definition: a business is an organized activity that is carried on with a reasonable expectation of profit. The next section of this chapter will examine the requirement of a reasonable expectation of profit; the following section will examine the requirement of an organized activity.

A point that is sometimes overlooked is that income from a business is reported by the owner of the business. The owner of the business may be an individual or a corporation. A business that is owned by a corporation may once have been owned by an individual, who "incorporated" the business. When an individual incorporates a business what really happens is that the individual incorporates a company and transfers all of the assets of the business to the company in return for shares in the company. After this has taken place, it is the

---

[4]   *Id.*, under heading 8.10, "International aspects", above.

[5]   Chapter 14, Income from Business or Property: Capital Expenditures, under heading 14.2(f), "Rental and leasing properties", below.

[6]   *Id.*, under heading 14.3, "Eligible capital expenditures", below.

[7]   Chapter 19, Corporations and Shareholders, under heading 19.5, "Taxation of corporations", below.

company that is the owner of the business, and therefore it is the company that will report the income from the business. The former owner will no longer have business income to report. The former owner will continue to benefit from the success of the business, but the benefit will not take the form of business income. If the company distributes its profits to the shareholder, it will do so by paying dividends on the shares; dividends are a species of income from property (the property being the shares). If the individual has lent money to the company, the company may pay interest on the loan; interest is a species of income from property (the property being the loan, which is a chose in action). If the individual is a director of the company, the company may pay a director's fee; a director's fee is income from an office. If the individual is an employee of the company, the company may pay a salary or a bonus; a salary or bonus is income from employment. If the individual decides to sell his or her shares in the company, and does so at a profit, the profit will be a capital gain.

(b)   Reasonable expectation of profit

A business activity involves a degree of financial risk. Indeed, the taxation of business income softens the financial risk by allowing the deduction of business losses (and carryovers to other years if necessary). If a taxpayer engages in a business-like activity that consistently incurs losses (farming is the most common one), can the losses be deducted by the taxpayer (who may have other income, perhaps professional income, which would be sheltered by the losses)? The courts have answered no to this question. For an activity to be a business, there must be a "reasonable expectation of profit". This means that losses can be deducted during a start-up period, and from time to time when a generally profitable enterprise falls on hard times, but losses cannot be deducted indefinitely. An activity that is conducted without a reasonable expectation of profit is not a business. It must be a hobby or a recreation. Losses from such an activity are personal consumption expenses, which are not deductible for tax purposes.

If a taxpayer is unable to establish a reasonable expectation of profit, then an organized, business-like activity that generates some revenue, but not enough to cover expenses, will not be a business. The "hobby farmer" (or Bay Street farmer) has given rise to most of the cases,[8] but losses have been disallowed in other kinds of cases where a taxpayer could not show a reasonable expectation of profit: an author who had published six books,[9] a professional racing car driver who occasionally won prize money,[10] a restaurateur whose restaurant

---

[8] The best discussion is in *Moldowan* v. *The Queen*, [1977] C.T.C. 310, 77 D.T.C. 5213 (S.C.C.).

[9] *Payette* v. *M.N.R.*, [1978] C.T.C. 2223, 78 D.T.C. 1811 (T.R.B.).

[10] *Cree* v. *M.N.R.*, [1978] C.T.C. 2472, 78 D.T.C. 1352 (T.R.B.).

regularly attracted customers,[11] a producer of machine tools intended for sale,[12] and a lawyer with only two clients.[13] Of course, in the rare case where a hobby does yield a gain, as where a taxpayer's race horse unexpectedly produces net winnings in a particular year,[14] the gain is not taxable; it is not income from a business; it is a windfall.[15]

The determination that a taxpayer has no reasonable expectation of profit does not depend upon the subjective view of the taxpayer, who is likely to be overly optimistic about the prospects of his or her money-losing venture. The expectation of profit must be reasonable, which is "an objective determination to be made from all of the facts".[16] The Supreme Court of Canada has suggested four relevant factors: the profit and loss experience in past years, the taxpayer's training, the taxpayer's intended course of action to convert present losses into future profits, and the capability of the venture, as capitalized, to show a profit after capital cost allowance.[17] The amount of time the taxpayer spends on the activity in question is also relevant.[18] A heavy commitment of time helps to support a reasonable expectation of profit; a part-time commitment, for example, weekends or evenings on top of a day job, points in the opposite direction.

In *Tonn* v. *The Queen* (1995),[19] the Minister had disallowed the first three years of losses of a business venture in which revenue had fallen way below the proprietors' expectations as a result of the recession of the early 1990s. The Federal Court of Appeal pointed out that the venture did not have any recreational, hobby or other consumption motive, and was not a tax-avoidance scheme, but was intended to be a purely business proposition, although it had not turned out successfully. The Court held that, in the absence of any non-business motive, "the [reasonable expectation of profit] test should be applied sparingly and with a latitude favouring the taxpayer, whose business judgment may have been less than competent." The Court allowed the deduction of the losses, commenting that the tax system should not "discourage, or

---

[11] *Sirois* v. *M.N.R.*, [1988] 1 C.T.C. 2147, 88 D.T.C. 1114 (T.C.C.).

[12] *Knight* v. *M.N.R.*, [1993] 2 C.T.C. 2976, 93 D.T.C. 1255 (T.C.C.).

[13] *Landry* v. *The Queen*, [1995] 2 C.T.C. 3, 94 D.T.C. 6624 (F.C.A.).

[14] *Hammond* v. *M.N.R.*, [1971] C.T.C. 663, 71 D.T.C. 5389 (F.C.T.D.).

[15] On the non-taxability of windfalls, see the next heading in this chapter, 12.2(c), "Organized activity", below.

[16] Note 8, above, 313; 5215.

[17] *Id.*, 314; 5215.

[18] *Sipley* v. *The Queen*, [1995] 2 C.T.C. 2073, 2075 (T.C.C.).

[19] [1996] 1 C.T.C. 205, 96 D.T.C. 6001 (F.C.A.).

penalize, honest but erroneous business decisions".[20] As a result, another relevant factor is whether the business operation is intended to be purely commercial or whether it has some personal or non-business motive.[21]

(c)   Organized activity

The second characteristic of a "business" for tax purposes (the first being a reasonable expectation of profit) is that it involves organized activity on the part of the taxpayer (or his or her employees). A gain acquired without systematic effort is not income from a business. It may be income from property, such as rent, interest or dividends. If the gain does not have a property source, it is a windfall. The classic example of a windfall is finding something of value. However, the product of *organized* finding will be income from a business. This was the result in *MacEachern* v. *M.N.R.* (1977),[22] where the systematic effort of three deep-sea divers, who recovered gold and silver coins from a sunken ship, was held to be a business.[23]

A prize in a lottery or contest or the winnings of a bet are not as unplanned or unexpected as a lucky find, but they are windfalls nonetheless. However, as the next section of this chapter explains, if gambling winnings are the product of an organized effort, accompanied by a reasonable expectation of profit, then the winnings will be income from a business.

A windfall is not liable to tax as income. It is not income from a business for the reasons that have just been given. It is not caught by any of the other specific provisions of the Act, and it is not caught by the general language of s. 3, because s. 3 requires income to be "from a source", which a windfall is not.[24]

(d)   Gambling winnings

Profits derived from bookmaking or operating a betting shop constitute income from a business because the two characteristics of a business, namely, an organized activity and a reasonable expectation of profit, are obviously present. (It makes no difference to the Income Tax Act if the business is illegal:

---

[20] See also Owen, "The Reasonable Expectation of Profit Test: Is There a Better Approach?" and Magee, "Real Estate Rental Losses and the Application of the Reasonable Expectation of Profit Test after the Tonn Decision" in [1996] 44 *Can. Tax J.* 979 and 1150.

[21] This factor was applied in *Walls* v. *The Queen*, [1996] 2 C.T.C. 14, 96 D.T.C. 6142 (F.C.T.D.) (losses from a mini-warehouse operated by limited partnership denied: the partnership was structured as a tax shelter); *Joseph* v. *The Queen*, [1996] 2 C.T.C. 2388 (T.C.C.) (losses from a rental operation with no personal element allowed).

[22] [1977] C.T.C. 2139, 77 D.T.C. 94 (T.R.B.).

[23] Accord, *Tobias* v. *The Queen*, [1978] C.T.C. 113, 78 D.T.C. 6028 (F.C.T.D.).

[24] See ch. 9, Tax Base, under heading 9.7, "Windfalls", above.

the profits from an illegal business are taxable on the same basis as those from a legal business.)[25] At the other end of the spectrum is the casual gambler whose activity is a hobby or recreation and whose winnings are therefore treated as windfalls (and whose losses are treated as consumption expenses).[26]

When an individual devotes a great deal of time and effort to gambling, it is often difficult to determine whether the activity falls into the hobby category or the business category. In *M.N.R.* v. *Morden* (1961),[27] the taxpayer, an hotel proprietor, was an "inveterate gambler", who "was prepared to place a bet on the outcome of baseball, hockey and football matches, and on card games, whether he was a player or merely placed side bets". Despite the evidence of extensive gambling, the Court held that the evidence did not establish that the taxpayer "in relation to his betting activities conducted an enterprise of a commercial character or had so organized these activities as to make them a business calling or vocation". On the other hand, in *Walker* v. *M.N.R.* (1951),[28] the taxpayer, a farmer, was held to be engaged in the business of gambling and to be taxable on his winnings. In this case, the taxpayer regularly attended horse races in four cities and bet substantially and successfully at them; he was a part-owner of several horses and moved in a racing milieu which gave him access to inside information. The Court held that the gambling activity was not a mere hobby, but was sufficiently extensive and systematic to constitute a business.

From the point of view of Revenue Canada, gambling winnings are an addition to the tax base which might prove to be of little or no value. The player who wins at the Saturday-night poker game is matched by a player who loses. The inclusion of winnings in income seems to require the deduction of losses. As Rendall comments, "given the likelihood that losers would have longer memories than winners, Revenue Canada could find itself in a net loss position with respect to gambling transactions".[29] The Carter Commission proposed a straightforward solution to this difficulty: the Commission would have made all gambling winnings taxable on the ground that they increased ability to pay, but would have disallowed the deduction of losses (except against winnings) on the ground that they were a consumption expense.[30] This proposal was not adopted. The result is that gambling winnings are taxable only when the gambling activity is a business, and gambling losses are fully deductible when the gambling activity is a business.

---

[25] Chapter 13, Income from Business or Property, Deductions, under heading 13.12, "Expenses of illegal business", below.

[26] Rendall in Hansen, Krishna, Rendall (eds.), *Canadian Taxation* (1981), 75.

[27] [1961] C.T.C. 484, 61 D.T.C. 1266 (Ex. Ct.).

[28] [1951] C.T.C. 334, 52 D.T.C. 1001 (Ex. Ct.).

[29] Rendall, note 26, above, 76.

[30] *Report of the Royal Commission on Taxation* (Carter Report) (1966), vol. 3, 526-527.

(e)   Employment income compared

Where a taxpayer provides services to a single person, or to a few people, it may be unclear whether the taxpayer's remuneration is income from a business or income from employment. (Although both types of income are taxed, income from a business is treated more favourably in several respects.) The answer turns on whether the taxpayer's services are supplied under a contract *for services*, in which case the taxpayer is an independent contractor and the remuneration is income from a business, or whether the taxpayer's services are supplied under a contract *of service*, in which case the taxpayer is an employee and the remuneration is income from employment. This distinction has been described in chapter 10, Income from Office or Employment, above.[31]

(f)   Capital gains compared

Where a taxpayer makes a profit from the sale of property, it may be unclear whether the profit is income from a business (in which case it will be fully taxed) or is a capital gain (in which case it will be three-quarters taxed). The answer usually turns on whether the property was purchased as an investment, in which case the profit will be a capital gain, or whether the property was purchased for resale, in which case the profit will be income from a business. This distinction (and other refinements) is described in chapter 16, Investing and Trading, below.

12.3   Income from property

(a)   Definition of property

The word "property" is defined in s. 248(1) as follows:

"property" means property of any kind whatever whether real or personal or corporeal or incorporeal and, without restricting the generality of the foregoing, includes
(a) a right of any kind whatever, a share or a chose in action,
(b) unless a contrary intention is evident, money. . . .

The breadth of this definition means that it is rare that any dispute arises as to whether or not something of value is property for tax purposes. It is normally clear that it is.

(b)   Reasonable expectation of profit

It is possible to incur a loss from property. In the typical case, the taxpayer has borrowed money for the purpose of acquiring the property and the interest on the borrowed money and other carrying costs exceed the income that is yielded by the property. In most such cases, the taxpayer will be entitled to report a loss from the property. However, the courts have insisted that the taxpayer have a reasonable expectation of profit from the property before a loss

---

[31] Under heading 10.4(d), "Distinction between employment and business", above.

is deductible. This is the same idea as is used to deny the deductibility of endless losses from a taxpayer's alleged "business", and the same rules apply.[32]

For example, in *Maloney* v. *M.N.R.* (1989),[33] a taxpayer who let a house property to his mother at a rent that was far below the mortgage interest, property taxes, and other maintenance expenses of the property was not allowed to deduct his annual losses. It was found that the taxpayer had no reasonable expectation of profit from the property. The annual losses were in the nature of gifts to his mother, and gifts are non-deductible consumption expenses. This element of personal benefit has been present in many of the cases in which rental losses have been denied for lack of a reasonable expectation of profit: for example, the property is rented to friends[34] or relatives,[35] the rental property is part of the taxpayer's principal residence[36], the rental property is in a resort area[37] or the property is intended to be a future retirement or vacation home.[38] In purely commercial situations, where there is no personal or tax avoidance motive, the requirement of a reasonable expectation of profit is not to be applied strictly.[39]

In *Ludmer* v. *M.N.R.* (1993),[40] taxpayers were denied the deduction of interest paid by them on funds borrowed to acquire the shares of two corporations. The taxpayers admitted that they had acquired the shares knowing that the dividends from the shares could not possibly cover the interest cost. However, the taxpayers claimed that they had acquired the shares for the purpose of capital gains, rather than dividend income. The Tax Court held that, in determining whether the taxpayers had a reasonable expectation of profit, only the dividend income should be taken into account. Capital gains were not income from property,[41] and the Act did not allow the deduction of interest in anticipation of future capital gains. Once the anticipated capital gains were excluded from the expected return on the shares, it was clear that the taxpayers

---

[32] Section 12.2(b), "Reasonable expectation of profit", above.

[33] [1989] 1 C.T.C. 2402, 89 D.T.C. 314 (T.C.C.).

[34] *Trojanowski* v. *M.N.R.*, [1984] C.T.C. 2841, 84 D.T.C. 1705 (T.C.C.).

[35] *Maloney*, note 33, above; *Huot* v. *M.N.R.*, [1990] 2 C.T.C. 2364, 90 D.T.C. 1818 (T.C.C.); *Carew* v. *The Queen*, [1994] 2 C.T.C. 2008, 94 D.T.C. 1415 (T.C.C.).

[36] *Saleem* v. *M.N.R.*, [1984] C.T.C. 2660, 84 D.T.C. 1579 (T.C.C.); *Cecato* v. *M.N.R.*, [1984] C.T.C. 2125, 84 D.T.C. 1110 (T.C.C.).

[37] *Perratt et al.* v. *M.N.R.*, [1985] 1 C.T.C. 2089, 85 D.T.C. 101 (T.C.C.); *Meech* v. *M.N.R.*, [1987] 1 C.T.C. 421, 87 D.T.C. 5251 (F.C.T.D.).

[38] *Mason* v. *M.N.R.*, [1984] C.T.C. 2003, 84 D.T.C. 1001 (T.R.B.); *Dallos* v. *M.N.R.*, [1985] 2 C.T.C. 2021, 85 D.T.C. 417 (T.C.C.).

[39] Note 19, above.

[40] [1993] 2 C.T.C. 2494, 93 D.T.C. 1351 (T.C.C.).

[41] The distinction is explained in the next section of this chapter.

had no reasonable expectation of profit. Their interest expense was therefore not deductible.

(c)   Capital gains compared

The Act distinguishes between income from property and capital gains. Subsection 9(3) expressly provides that income from a property does not include any capital gain from the disposition of that property. Income from a property is the return that is obtained simply by owning the property, for example, rent on real estate, interest on bonds or dividends on shares. A capital gain arises only on the disposition of property; it is the return that is obtained when a property is disposed of for more than it cost.

The Act's distinction between income from property and capital gains is required because income from property is computed under subdivision b while capital gains are computed under subdivision c. The main tax distinction between the two categories of income is that income from property is fully included in income, while capital gains are only three-quarters included in income. However, as the *Ludmer* case[42] illustrates, there are other tax differences with respect to the deductibility of expenses and other matters.

(d)   Rent

It is obvious that the letting of property yields to the owner income from property. However, it is also obvious that a business will usually have a number of "capital assets",[43] and yet the income yielded by those assets is simply part of the business income of the owner.

The distinction between income from property and income from a business, when it is relevant for tax purposes,[44] has proved most difficult to draw in respect of the rental of real estate. Prima facie, of course, the rents derived from letting an apartment building, office building or shopping centre, are income from property. The rents are paid for the use of the property, not for services provided by the landlord. The difficulty arises from the fact that a landlord will often supply to the tenants, in addition to the right to occupy the rented premises, services of various kinds. Where the services supplied consist of only those services which are of a kind customarily included with rented premises, for example, maintenance of building, heating, air conditioning, water, electricity, and parking, the rent is still regarded as income from property. But if the services supplied go beyond those which are customary for an office building or apartment building or shopping centre (or whatever the property is),

---

[42] Note 40, above.

[43] Chapter 11, Income from Business or Property: Profit, under heading 11.5(c), "Current and capital assets", above.

[44] See sec. 12.1, "Business and property distinguished", above.

it becomes more plausible to characterize the owner's operation as a business rather than the mere letting of property. Services indicative of a business classification would include a commissionaire or other protective service, a restaurant, mail service, maid service, linen and laundry service. The extreme case is, of course, a hotel, where the extent of the services supplied to guests makes it obvious that it is a business. Where the range of services supplied by the landlord falls below hotel level, it becomes a question of degree whether the nature and extent of the services makes it appropriate to characterize the income as earned from a business.[45]

Another situation in which the distinction between income from a business and income from property becomes unclear is where a landlord owns many apartment buildings (or other rental properties), and employs an extensive staff to manage them. In that case, the courts apply a level-of-activity test to determine whether the landlord is engaged in a business. This is consistent with the requirement, noted earlier in this chapter,[46] of an organized activity as a leading characteristic of a business. Where many people are occupied in the management of a landlord's properties, the level of organized activity will usually lead the courts to find that the landlord is engaged in a business, even if the level of activity involved in managing an individual property is low.[47]

The level-of-activity test applies to other kinds of property income as well. A bank, for example, earns its profits primarily from making loans to borrowers and charging them interest. Interest on a loan is normally income from property, as is explained in the next section of this chapter. But the level of organized activity that is involved in making many loans, with all the supervisory and ancillary services that are required, transforms income from property into income from a business. (In the banking example, it is also arguable that the provision of banking services, such as cash withdrawals, chequing facilities, safety deposit boxes, foreign exchange transactions and the like, would in any case distinguish the banker from the mere lender of money.)

---

[45] See generally Interpretation Bulletin IT-434R, "Rental of real property by individual" (1982); *Wertman* v. *M.N.R.*, [1964] C.T.C. 252, 64 D.T.C. 5158 (Ex. Ct.); *Walsh and Micay* v. *M.N.R.*, [1965] C.T.C. 478, 65 D.T.C. 5293 (Ex. Ct.).

[46] Section 12.2(c), "Organized activity", above.

[47] For examples, see *Malenfant* v. *M.N.R.*, [1992] 2 C.T.C. 2431, 92 D.T.C. 2081 (T.C.C.); *Etoile Immobiliere S.A.* v. *M.N.R.*, [1992] 2 C.T.C. 2367, 92 D.T.C. 1984 (T.C.C.); and *Burri* v. *The Queen*, [1985] 2 C.T.C. 42, 85 D.T.C. 5287 (F.C.T.D.). The latter two cases also demonstrate the rebuttable presumption that income earned by a corporation pursuing the objects of its incorporation is income from a business.

(e)   Interest

(i)   Definition

The Income Tax Act contains no definition of "interest". Interest is not a technical term, however, and may be broadly defined as the price of borrowed money. Interest is any sum that has to be paid by a borrower (debtor) to the lender (creditor) as the price for the loan.[48] Interest is usually expressed as a percentage per annum of the principal amount of the loan, although under the contract of loan the interest will usually be payable more frequently than annually, and will occasionally be paid less frequently than annually. The borrower's obligation to pay interest will cease when the loan is repaid (redeemed), which will normally occur at a time (the maturity date) stipulated in the contract of loan. Interest rates are fixed by market forces. Some factors that bear on the interest rate are particular to each loan, namely, the creditworthiness of the borrower, the value of any security provided by the borrower and the term of the loan. Other factors are of general application, and the most important one is the expected rate of inflation over the term of the loan.

Every lender of money will want to be compensated for the expected decline in the purchasing power of the principal sum. For example, if inflation is expected at the rate of 5 per cent per annum over the life of the loan, it will be impossible to borrow money at rates that do not provide a return of several percentage points over 5 per cent. To the extent that interest simply compensates for the decline in the purchasing power of the principal of the loan, it ought not to be taxed at all. Only the real rate of interest (the actual rate minus the rate of inflation in a particular year) should have to be reported by the lender. The Income Tax Act is remiss in not making any allowance for inflation in computing interest income. The full amount of the nominal interest, including the portion that merely compensates for inflation, must be included in the lender's income for tax purposes.

Interest is income from property.[49] The property is the borrower's obligation to repay the loan, the details of which are to be found in the contract of loan, which is commonly called a debt obligation. A debt obligation is a chose in action, because what the lender has is the right to enforce the obligation against the borrower by legal action. A debt obligation may be called a personal loan, a promissory note, a bank account, a term deposit, a guaranteed investment certificate, a mortgage, a treasury bill, a bond, a debenture or a note. The

---

[48] Some courts have called for narrower and more technical definitions of interest. See, for example, *A.G. Ont.* v. *Barfried Enterprises*, [1978] 1 S.C.R. 974, [1978] C.T.C. 169 (S.C.C.), which (in a non-tax context) required "daily accrual" for an amount to qualify as interest.

[49] Interest on money invested short-term for use in a business is income from the business: *The Queen* v. *Marsh & McLennan*, [1983] C.T.C. 231, 83 D.T.C. 5180 (F.C.A.); *The Queen* v. *Ensite*, [1983] C.T.C. 296, 83 D.T.C. 5315 (F.C.A.); affd. [1986] 2 C.T.C. 459, 86 D.T.C. 6521 (S.C.C.); *The Queen* v. *Brown Boveri Howden*, [1983] C.T.C. 301, 83 D.T.C. 5319 (F.C.A.).

nomenclature varies according to the personality of the borrower (issuer of security), the nature of the security, the term of the loan, and other characteristics of the obligation.

(ii) Timing of recognition

Interest is specifically provided for in s. 12(1)(c) of the Income Tax Act, which includes in income:

12(1)(c) any amount received or receivable by the taxpayer in the year (depending on the method regularly followed by the taxpayer in computing the taxpayer's profit) as, on account or in lieu of payment of, or in satisfaction of, interest to the extent that the interest was not included in computing the taxpayer's income for a preceding taxation year;

Paragraph 12(1)(c) gives to a taxpayer the choice of reporting interest income by the "cash" method or by the "receivable" method. Under the cash method, the income is recognized when it is "received" by the taxpayer. Under the receivable method, the income is recognized when it is "receivable", that is, when the taxpayer has a legal right to receive it, even if it has not actually been received. Under the "accrual" method, interest is recognized as accruing from day to day, regardless of when the interest is received or receivable. While s. 12(1)(c) does not expressly authorize the accrual method of reporting interest income, the Department permits the use of that method too.[50] As s. 12(1)(c) implies, a taxpayer must follow the same method of reporting interest from a particular source from year to year. However, the Department does not require that interest from various sources all be reported by the same method.[51] For example, a taxpayer might choose the receivable basis of reporting interest on fully secured debts, and the cash (received) basis for more speculative investments.

The choice of reporting method offered by s. 12(1)(c) is subject to the overriding provisions of ss. 12(3) and 12(4) of the Act. The purpose of these provisions, which were added to the Act in 1980 (in the case of s. 12(3)) and 1990 (in the case of s. 12(4)), is to preclude the postponement of income that would be possible under the cash method and the receivable method. For example, government and corporate bonds often have interest coupons attached which may be clipped and cashed as they fall due. Taxpayers reporting bond interest by the cash method used to be able to postpone recognition of the interest on a corporate bond by not cashing the coupons as they fell due. Of course, if the uncashed coupons earned no interest, there would be no advantage in this practice, but some bond issues have a compounding feature under which uncashed coupons do earn interest. As another example, Canada Savings Bonds are available on a compound basis, under which no interest is payable during the term of the bond, and on the maturity date all of the interest, compounded, is

---

[50] Interpretation Bulletin IT-396R, "Interest income" (1984), paras. 1, 5.

[51] Id., para. 6.

paid to the bondholder (along with the principal sum). Taxpayers reporting bond interest by either the cash or the receivable method used to be able to postpone recognition of the interest on a compound bond until the maturity of the bond.

Subsections 12(3) and 12(4) of the Act do not directly amend s. 12(1)(c), but for most debt obligations[52] the effect of ss. 12(3) and 12(4) is to make the choices offered by s. 12(1)(c) illusory. Subsection 12(3) applies to corporations and partnerships, and it requires that all interest "accrued . . . to the end of the year" be reported annually, whether the interest is received, receivable or merely accrued. For example, if a corporation with a December 31 year-end held a bond upon which interest was payable on October 31 of each year, the corporation would be obliged to report not only the interest received or receivable on October 31 (after subtracting the two-month portion that would have been recognized in the previous year), but also the interest accrued from November 1 to December 31. In effect, s. 12(3) requires corporations and partnerships to report interest income by the accrual method.

Subsection 12(4) applies to individuals, and it requires that all interest on an "investment contract", that has accrued to each "anniversary day of the contract", must be reported annually. An investment contract is broadly defined to cover the standard forms of debt obligation, although there are some exclusions (s. 12(11)). The anniversary day is the annual anniversary of "the day immediately preceding the date of issue of the contract" (s. 12(11)). For example, the holder of a Canada Savings Bond that was issued on November 1, 1996 would have to report in 1997 the 12 months' interest accrued to October 31, 1997, even if the bond was a compound one on which no interest was received or receivable in 1997. The same obligation to report the 12 months' interest accrued to October 31 would arise in 1998 and each succeeding year that the bond is retained. Subsection 12(4) does not completely eliminate the choice of reporting methods in s. 12(1)(c). The cash or receivable method could be used if they would unfailingly yield each year all of the interest accrued to the anniversary day of the investment contract. Subsection 12(4) allows this, because it requires the inclusion of interest accrued to the anniversary day only "to the extent that the interest was not otherwise included in computing the taxpayer's income for the taxation year or any preceding taxation year". However, s. 12(4) does not allow the cash or receivable methods to be used if their effect would be to postpone the recognition of interest income that had accrued to the anniversary day of the investment contract.

(iii)   Blended payments

Subsection 16(1) of the Income Tax Act deals with "blended payments", that is, payments that combine interest and capital. Many residential mortgages,

---

[52] Some debt obligations are exempted from ss. 12(3) and 12(4); for them, s. 12(1)(c) continues to govern.

for example, require the borrower to make regular payments that are partly interest and partly the repayment of the principal sum; the amount of the principal sum is steadily reduced over the life of the loan. Subsection 16(1) provides that, where an amount that is payable under a contract or other arrangement "can reasonably be regarded" as in part interest and in part capital, then the part that can reasonably be regarded as interest shall be "deemed to be interest". This requires the recipient of the blended payments (the mortgagee in the case of a mortgage) to unblend them for tax purposes so that the income component can be reported as income. (The repayment of the principal sum has no tax consequences.)

Subsection 16(1) will catch the case where there is a concealed income element in a loan-repayment or instalment-purchase arrangement. In *Groulx* v. *M.N.R.* (1967),[53] for example, the taxpayer sold a farm to a purchaser for $395,000, of which $85,000 was payable immediately and $310,000 was payable in instalments over a period of six years; no interest was payable by the purchaser on the outstanding balance of the purchase price. The Supreme Court of Canada held that the payments of $310,000 which were received in instalments by the vendor-taxpayer could reasonably be regarded as being in part a payment of interest by the purchaser. What the Court found in effect was that the purchaser had agreed to pay a price above the market value of the farm, in return for the vendor's agreement to forego interest on the unpaid balance of the purchase price. The Court therefore upheld the Minister's assessment under s. 16(1) and treated a portion of the instalments of purchase price as interest which was taxable to the taxpayer-vendor.[54]

Where property is sold for a price that is payable in instalments, as in *Groulx*, and the instalments are "genuinely" interest-free, the instalments have been held not to attract s. 16(1),[55] and this position is accepted by the Department.[56] This is understandable where the parties are not dealing at arm's length, for example, where a parent sells property to a child. However, it is difficult to see why s. 16(1) should not always be applicable where the parties are at arm's length; surely, the purchaser must in every case have paid more for the property than he or she would have had to pay with customary terms of financing.

In many cases, the borrower of money or the purchaser of property uses the money borrowed or property purchased to earn business or property income.

---

[53] [1967] C.T.C. 422, 67 D.T.C. 5284 (S.C.C.).

[54] See also *Club de Courses Saguenay* v. *M.N.R.*, [1979] C.T.C. 3022, 79 D.T.C. 579 (T.R.B.), where the purchase price exceeded fair market value by $100,000.

[55] *Carter* v. *M.N.R.* (1965), 37 Tax A.B.C. 174, [1980] C.T.C. 2050, 65 D.T.C. 31 (T.A.B.); *Martin* v. *M.N.R.*, [1980] C.T.C. 2043, 80 D.T.C. 1050 (T.R.B.).

[56] Interpretation Bulletin IT-265R3, "Payments of income and capital combined" (1991), para. 8.

If so, then any interest payable to the creditor (lender or vendor) will be deductible by the debtor (borrower or purchaser) as an expense of earning the business or property income (s. 20(1)(c)).[57] If the debt were interest-free, the debtor would lose the deduction. Therefore, the debtor has little incentive to agree to pay a higher capital sum in lieu of interest. (Although a higher price for property purchased could provide a stepped-up cost base for the purpose of computing subsequent capital gains or losses, this would not normally be as valuable as the interest deduction.) Where the debtor is in a much lower tax bracket than the creditor, or where the debtor is using the money or property for a personal use such as to buy a house or a car, so that interest would not be deductible, there may well be an incentive to create an interest-free debt. It is immaterial to the debtor whether he or she makes payments of principal and interest, or simply larger principal payments, and yet the latter alternative would save the creditor tax. Here the parties' interests are not adverse with respect to tax, and s. 16(1) is needed to protect the tax base.

Where s. 16(1) is applied to payments made by a debtor to a creditor the deemed interest element is added to the income of the creditor. Since s. 16(1) deems the interest portion of blended payments to be interest on a debt obligation, s. 20(1)(c) allows the debtor to deduct the deemed interest payments where the money borrowed or property purchased was used to earn income from a business or property. In that case, there may be no advantage to the revenue in the application of s. 16(1), because the increase in the income of the creditor will be matched by a reduction in the income of the debtor. Presumably, if the debtor is a purchaser of property, he or she is required to reduce the cost base of the property for capital gains purposes by the amount of the deemed interest.

(f)　　Discounts

(i)　　Definition

A bond or mortgage or other debt obligation may be issued at a discount, and may be traded at a discount. If a bond is issued by the borrower to the lender for a price (the loan) which is less than the face value or principal sum of the bond, then the bond is issued at a discount. For example, if a $1,000 bond were issued by the borrower (debtor, issuer) for $900 (which is all that the lender (creditor, bondholder) would have to lend), then the bond would have been issued at a discount of $100. If a bond is sold by its owner for a price which is less than its face value or principal sum, then the bond is traded at a discount. For example, if the holder of a $1,000 bond sold the bond for $700, then the bond would have been traded at a discount of $300. A bond or mortgage or other debt obligation may be issued at a premium, and may be traded at a premium. A bond is issued at a premium if the issue price (the loan) is more than the face

---

[57] See ch. 13, Income from Business or Property: Deductions, under heading 13.7, "Interest expense", below.

value or principal sum of the bond; and a bond is traded at a premium if it is sold by its owner for a price which is more than its face value or principal sum.

When a bond or mortgage or other debt obligation matures (reaches the due date for repayment), the debtor is obliged to pay the precise amount of the principal sum to the creditor (the holder of the obligation) regardless of the price for which the holder acquired the obligation. This means that, if the holder acquired the bond (either on issue or by purchase) at a discount, on maturity the holder will make a gain (the discount) over and above the (discounted) price that the holder paid to acquire the bond. If, on the other hand, the holder acquired the bond at a premium, then on the maturity of the bond the holder will receive less (by the amount of the premium) than the price that the holder paid for the bond.

Interest rates in the financial markets vary from time to time in response to the supply of and demand for money, which is affected by a wide variety of factors, including the anticipated rate of inflation and the general economic outlook. There is no single current interest rate at any one time for all classes of debt obligations, because bonds, mortgages and other obligations differ in their maturity dates, in the security that they provide, and in the creditworthiness of the issuer. A discount or premium is the adjustment of the market to an interest rate that differs from the rate that is current at the time when a debt obligation is issued or traded. If a mortgage or bond or other debt obligation carries a right to interest at a rate which is less than the rate currently available for that class of obligation, the market value of the obligation will be "discounted" to a figure below the face value of the obligation — a figure which will make the effective yield to the purchaser closer to the current interest rate. If a debt obligation carries a right to interest at a rate which is higher than the rate currently available for that class of obligation, the obligation will issue or trade at a premium — a figure higher than the face value which will make the effective yield to the purchaser closer to the current interest rate. (This is the reason for a phenomenon that some investors find puzzling: when interest rates rise, the bond market falls, and when interest rates fall, the bond market rises.)

(ii)   Position of creditor

When a person acquires a bond, mortgage or other obligation, whether on its original issue or by purchase from an existing holder, the yield from the investment must be measured not merely by the rate of interest stipulated to be paid on the principal sum (or face value), but also by taking into account any discount or premium at which the holder acquired the obligation. A discount increases the yield to the holder above the rate of interest stipulated on the obligation. A premium reduces the yield to the holder below the rate of interest stipulated on the obligation.

Suppose P purchases from B (the mortgagee) a mortgage for $10,000 at 5 per cent at a time when current mortgage rates are in excess of 10 per cent, and suppose P pays $6,000 for the mortgage. Until redemption, P (the new mortgagee) will receive from the mortgagor $500 per annum ($10,000 x 5 per cent) for an effective yield to P of 8.33 per cent (500/6000 x 100/1 = 8.33%). Years later, on redemption, the mortgagor (who originally borrowed $10,000 at 5 per cent from B) must repay the full $10,000, and will pay the full $10,000 to P. This represents a further gain to P of $4,000, because he only paid $6,000 for the mortgage. The prospect of this gain on redemption obviously influenced the market price of the mortgage. P has put up with a lower interest rate in the knowledge that he will receive the full face value of the mortgage on redemption — and that the market value of the mortgage will rise as the redemption date approaches.

In the example given, when P purchased a debt obligation at a discount and then held it to maturity, the situation seems to call for the application of s. 16(1).[58] Surely, a part of the redemption proceeds, namely, the discount, should "reasonably be regarded as being in part interest". If not, then P makes a substantial tax saving in comparison with his simply investing his $6,000 at the current interest rate. In fact, s. 16(1) has generally been confined by the courts and the Department to cases where an interest-free element in a transaction has been arranged by agreement between the parties. Accordingly, where an obligation is traded at a discount as the result of market forces outside the control of the parties, s. 16(1) will not apply to the discount. This was decided by the Supreme Court of Canada in *Wood* v. *M.N.R.* (1969),[59] where it was held that an investor who purchased a mortgage at a substantial discount, and then held the mortgage until maturity, did not have to report any part of the redemption proceeds as interest income.[60]

It is hard to support the result that a yield on debt which is taken in the form of a discount should be tax-free. Now that capital gains are taxed (they were not when *Wood* was decided), it is clear that the discount would be a capital gain, because s. 54(c) expressly includes the redemption of a debt obligation in its definition of a "disposition" of property (which gives rise to capital gains). However, this redresses the anomaly only partially, because one quarter of a capital gain is tax-free (s. 38). By the same token, if the purchaser of a debt obligation paid a premium on purchase, and then held the obligation to maturity, the loss on redemption (of the amount of the premium) would be a

---

[58] Section 12.3(e)(iii), "Blended payments", above.

[59] [1969] C.T.C. 57, 69 D.T.C. (S.C.C.).

[60] This decision is somewhat weakened by the fact that in the Supreme Court of Canada the Minister abandoned the argument (which had succeeded before the Tax Appeal Board) that the discount should be treated as interest. The argument in the Supreme Court of Canada was accordingly addressed to the issue whether the taxpayer was an investor or a trader. He was held to be an investor; and his gain on redemption was accordingly tax-free, because capital gains were not then (before 1972) taxable.

capital and not an income loss, and only three-quarters of the loss would be deductible for tax purposes (and then only from taxable capital gains).[61]

The decision in the *Wood* case, that the discount there was not caught by s. 16(1), is not necessarily a reliable guide to the tax treatment of a discount which arises on the original issue of a debt obligation (an "original-issue discount"). In *Wood*, the debt obligation had been purchased from an existing holder, and the discount had arisen because of a fall in the market value of the obligation. Where a discount arises on the original issue of the obligation, then it must have been deliberately created by the borrower-issuer, either of its own motion or at the insistence of the lender. In that situation, the case for applying s. 16(1) and treating the discount as interest income is strong. In *Satinder* v. *The Queen* (1995),[62] the Federal Court of Appeal held that an original-issue discount was indeed interest income.

The Act contains a specific provision to cover debt obligations that pay no interest at all. Non-interest-bearing bonds are sometimes issued by a borrowing company, in which case they are called "zero coupon bonds". Sometimes they are created by a stockbroker who will strip the interest coupons off a conventional bond, which is then described as a "stripped bond". The principal (residue) of the bond and the interest coupons are then sold separately as non-interest-bearing obligations. Zero coupon bonds and stripped bonds are issued or sold at a sufficient discount to make up for the lack of interest; the return to the bondholder consists solely of the discount at which the bond was purchased; nothing will be received until the maturity of the bond. When interest rates are high, zero coupon bonds and stripped bonds are attractive to investors who wish to lock-in a long-term rate of return, and who do not want to bother with reinvesting periodic income payments. If the Income Tax Act made no specific provision for interest-free obligations, then the discount would not be taxed under s. 16(1) until it was "paid or payable" on the maturity of the bond; in some cases, it would be arguable, following *Wood*, that the discount was only three-quarters taxable as a capital gain. The Act, by s. 12(9) and reg. 7000, deems the full amount of the discount on an interest-free debt obligation to accrue to the holder in annual instalments during the term of the bond; by virtue of ss. 12(3) and 12(4) the holder is required to report as interest income a

---

[61] If the holder of a debt obligation is engaged in the business of trading in debt obligations, then any realized discount would be taxable in full as income from a business, and any realized premium loss would be deductible in full: see ch. 16, Investing and Trading, below. This was the issue in the *Wood* case, previous note.

[62] 95 D.T.C. 5340 (F.C.A.).

prescribed amount of the discount in each taxation year that the obligation is held.[63]

(iii)   Position of debtor

Up to this point we have been considering the tax consequences to the holder (creditor) of a discounted debt obligation. Now let us consider the position of the issuer (debtor). Suppose a company wishes to borrow money through the issue of bonds (or other debt instruments). Even when tax considerations are neutral, a company may wish to issue its bonds at a discount, because "that is the easiest way of honing the effective interest rate".[64] In order to make its bonds saleable at the time of issue, the company has to fix an interest rate at which they will be attractive to investors, but of course the company does not want to pay any more than it has to. The precise adjustment between supply and demand might involve an interest rate going as far as four decimal places. In order to avoid this, the company will often fix the rate of interest on its bonds at an even figure which is slightly below what it judges the market will require, and it will achieve the final adjustment between supply and demand by varying the purchase price of the bonds, for example, by issuing $1,000 bonds at $995. The discount has the effect of increasing the yield to the investors who purchase the bonds. If the company's judgment as to the market proves wrong, or if the market later falls before the issue has been fully sold, then the discount can be increased.

There does not seem to be any good reason why a discount should not be fully deductible by the borrower, just as interest is fully deductible when the borrowed money is acquired for the purpose of earning income from a business or property. This is the treatment that the Act accords to a "shallow" discount,[65] which is a discount of less than 3 per cent of the principal amount of the bond;[66] such a discount is fully deductible (s. 20(1)(f)(i)). But a "deep"

---

[63] Subsection 12(9) applies to a "prescribed debt obligation", which is defined in reg. 7000(1) as including a debt obligation on which no interest is payable; some other obligations on which interest is payable, but the interest rate increases over the life of the obligation, are also included. Regulation 7000(2) stipulates the rules for computing the prescribed amount of the annual inclusion of accrued interest.

[64] Grover and Iacobucci, *Materials on Canadian Income Tax* (3rd. ed., 1976), 193. (The statement is not in the current edition of this casebook, now edited by Arnold, Edgar and Li.)

[65] Subparagraph 20(1)(f)(i) does not permit the deduction until the discount is "paid", that is, on the maturity of the bond. The correct accounting treatment would be to amortize the discount over the life of the loan. On the other hand, the holder of the bond does not have to report the discount as income under s. 16(1) until it is "paid or payable".

[66] Subparagraph 20(1)(f)(i) imposes a second condition as well, namely, that the actual yield on the sum paid for the bond must not exceed 4/3 of the interest payable on the face value of the bond. This condition will always be satisfied when the discount is 3 per cent or less, except in the case of short-term obligations (when the discount has a larger impact on the yield).

discount, that is, a discount of more than 3 per cent, is only three-quarters deductible (s. 20(1)(f)(ii)).[67] A deep discount is thus treated as comparable to a capital loss, which is also only three-quarters deductible. This would make sense if the discount were treated as a capital gain in the hands of the bondholder, but, as noted in the previous section of this chapter, an original issue discount is normally taxed in full as interest under s. 16(1) when it is paid to the bondholder on the maturity of the bond.[68]

(g)   Dividends

Dividends on the shares of a corporation are a form of income from property which must be reported on a cash basis under subdivision b (see ss. 12(1)(j), 12(1)(k)). However, there are a number of special rules regarding dividends, and so this topic is postponed to chapter 19, Corporations and Shareholders, below.

---

[67] In the case of a tax-exempt entity, such as a municipality, the restriction on the deductibility of deep discounts is of no significance. Subsection 16(3) discourages the issue of deep discount bonds (defined by reference to the 4/3rds rule, previous note) by requiring that deep discounts on bonds issued by tax-exempt entities must be included in the income of the lender for the year in which he or she acquired the bond. This is a harsh rule, because the discount will not be received until the maturity of the bond. Therefore, tax-exempt entities do not issue deep-discount bonds.

[68] Text accompanying note 62, above.

13

Income from Business
or Property: Deductions

13.1 Structure of the Act

We have already noticed that subdivision b of Division B of Part I of the Income Tax Act contains the rules for the computation of income from a business or property. Chapter 11 dealt with s. 9 of the Act and the concept of profit. Chapter 12 dealt with the principal *inclusions* in income from a business or property. This chapter deals with *deductions* from income from a business or property, other than the deductions for capital expenditures, which are covered in chapter 14.

Section 9 of the Act, which brings into income a taxpayer's "profit" from a business or property, is the starting point for the calculation of income from a business or property. As was explained in chapter 11,[1] the term "profit" in s. 9 is not defined in the Act, but comprises net income computed (for the most part) in accordance with generally accepted accounting principles. It is the reference to "profit" in s. 9(1) that provides the primary rule governing the deduction of expenses in the computation of income from business and property.[2] Generally speaking, if an expense is deductible for accounting purposes, then it will be deductible for tax purposes as well, unless it is disallowed by some provision of the Income Tax Act. Likewise, if an expense is not deductible for accounting purposes, then it will not be deductible for tax purposes either, unless it is permitted by some specific provision of the Act. It follows that in determining whether or not a particular expenditure or loss is deductible for tax purposes, the first enquiry must be whether the item would be deductible under generally accepted accounting principles. The answer to that enquiry will in most cases yield the final answer for tax purposes as well as for accounting purposes. But for tax purposes a second enquiry is also necessary, namely, whether the item is specifically allowed or disallowed by the Act.

There are numerous provisions of the Act which specifically disallow or allow various deductions from business or property income. Most (but by no means all) of these provisions are to be found in ss. 18 and 20 of the Act. Section 18 contains a list of deductions that are specifically disallowed, while s. 20 contains a list of deductions that are specifically allowed. Some of these provisions depart from generally accepted accounting principles.[3] Others are consistent with generally accepted accounting principles and are presumably in the Act out of an abundance of caution. In the latter category, in our view, are ss. 18(1)(a) and 18(1)(h), provisions which are frequently quoted in the cases. As mentioned, s. 18(1) disallows a number of deductions. Paragraph 18(1)(a) of the prohibited list is as follows:

> 18(1)(a) an outlay or expense except to the extent that it was made or incurred by the taxpayer for the purposes of gaining or producing income from the business or property;

Paragraph 18(1)(h) of the prohibited list is as follows:

> 18(1)(h) personal or living expenses of the taxpayer, other than travel expenses incurred by the taxpayer while away from home in the course of carrying on the taxpayer's business;

There has been some reliance on these provisions in the cases, and suggestions from time to time that they stipulate a different result than would be produced

---

[1] Under heading 11.4, "Profit and accounting principles", above.

[2] *Daley* v. *M.N.R.*, [1950] C.T.C. 251, 4 D.T.C. 877 (Ex. Ct.); *Royal Trust Co.* v. *M.N.R.*, [1957] C.T.C. 32, 57 D.T.C. 1055 (Ex. Ct.); *Symes* v. *Canada*, [1993] 4 S.C.R. 695, 722, [1994] 1 C.T.C. 40, 51, 94 D.T.C. 6001, 6009 (S.C.C.).

[3] E.g., s. 18(1)(l), disallowing certain club fees after their allowance in *Royal Trust* v. *M.N.R.*, note 4 below; s. 20(1)(cc), allowing certain lobbying expenses after their disallowance in *No. 237* v. *M.N.R.* (1955), 12 Tax A.B.C. 230 (T.A.B.).

by the application of generally accepted accounting principles. However, no example has ever been offered of an expense that would be allowed by generally accepted accounting principles but would be disallowed by s. 18(1)(a) or s. 18(1)(h). The better view is that generally accepted accounting principles call for precisely the same results as the two paragraphs, namely, the disallowance of expenditures which are not made "for the purpose of gaining or producing income" (s. 18(1)(a)) and "personal or living expenses" (s. 18(1)(h)). In this sense the two paragraphs are otiose, but they do codify and draw attention to two principles of great importance. →functionless - serving no practical purpose

Another provision that is frequently referred to in the cases is s. 18(1)(b), which prohibits the deduction of an expenditure "on account of capital". This provision, and ss. 13 and 14, which go on to permit and regulate the amortization over time of capital expenditures, are covered in the next chapter.

This chapter does not attempt to provide a comprehensive account of the various deductions from income from a business or property. The chapter explains the principles that underlie the specific rules, and deals with some of the more interesting deductions — those that raise issues of principle.

13.2 Entertainment expenses

The prohibition on the deduction of personal or living expenses, which is explicit in s. 18(1)(h) and implicit in s. 18(1)(a) and s. 9(1) (through its incorporation of generally accepted accounting principles), has the effect of disallowing deductions for consumption expenses, such as expenses for travel, meals, hotel lodging, entertainment and recreation. However, it is settled that where expenses of this kind are incurred for a business purpose they are not to be treated as consumption expenses and they are deductible.

In *Royal Trust Co.* v. *M.N.R.* (1957),[4] the Exchequer Court held that a trust company could deduct for tax purposes fees paid by the company that were incurred by various of its officers in belonging to social and recreational clubs. The Court found that such payments were a normal business practice of the trust companies which produced business contacts and opportunities for the companies. The Court held that the payments were made for the purpose of gaining or producing income from the business and were deductible. The actual result in *Royal Trust* was reversed by legislation. Paragraph 18(1)(l) now prohibits the deduction of membership fees in social and recreational clubs as well as the expenses of the use or maintenance of a yacht, a camp, a lodge or a golf course.[5] But outside these specific prohibitions the principle remains intact.

---

[4] [1957] C.T.C. 32, 57 D.T.C. 1055 (Ex. Ct.)

[5] Since the expenses were held to be sufficiently business-related, they were deductible by the trust company, and would not have to be reported as taxable benefits from employment by the employees who belonged to the clubs. If the expenses had been held to be insufficiently

Royal Trust establishes the principle that entertainment expenses that have a dominant business purpose are deductible by the proprietor of the business.[6] The qualifying business purposes are those of acquiring and keeping customers or clients and making business connections. Expenses that are incurred primarily for pleasure are consumption expenses, which come within the prohibition of personal or living expenses in s. 18(1)(h), and are therefore not deductible.[7]

If an expenditure is incurred for both business and pleasure, then generally accepted accounting principles and s. 18(1)(a) would both require an apportionment of the expenditure between business (the deductible portion) and pleasure (the non-deductible portion). A clear example is the trip to a business convention in a pleasant setting in which the businessperson stays on for a few extra days as a vacation; in this case, the cost of the trip has been incurred partly for business and partly for pleasure, and an apportionment is necessary and not particularly difficult, based on the number of days spent on each purpose.

Much less clear is the case of a meal or entertainment or other benefit which is provided by the taxpayer to business associates primarily for a business purpose, but which at the same time gives personal pleasure to the taxpayer. In many cases, and especially if the business companions are congenial, the meal or show (or whatever) will be enjoyed by the taxpayer for its own sake quite apart from its business purpose. It is obvious that the difficulty of isolating and valuing the element of personal enjoyment on a case-by-case basis is insurmountable. In order to overcome this problem, s. 67.1 was introduced into the Act in 1988. Section 67.1 limits the deductibility of expenses for "food or beverages or the enjoyment of entertainment" to 50 per cent of the amount actually paid, or 50 per cent of the "amount in respect thereof that would be reasonable in the circumstances".[8] This provision effectively deems 50 per cent

---

business-related, the company would still have been able to deduct them under its salary line as fringe benefits to senior employees, but in that case the employees would have to report them as taxable benefits from employment. It would seem, therefore, that the real point of the litigation was to save the employees from having to pay tax on the benefits that they received. Since the enactment of s. 18(1)(l), the prohibited expenses can neither be deducted as regular business expenses nor as a salary item: see Interpretation Bulletin IT-148R2, "Recreational properties and club dues" (1981), paras. 11, 12. Cf. *Sie-Mac Pipeline Contractors* v. *The Queen*, [1993] 1 C.T.C. 226, 93 D.T.C. 5158 (S.C.C.) (expense of renting recreational lodge for meeting not deductible by virtue of s. 18(1)(l); renting a hotel would have been deductible). Since *Sie-Mac Pipeline Contractors*, Revenue Canada has interpreted the prohibited expenses as including the cost of a meal at a golf course if the meal was linked to the recreational use of the club (e.g., a game of golf before or after the meal): see, e.g., "Revenue Canada Questions and Answers", *Toronto West Revenue Canada & Tax Practioners Breakfast Seminar* (February 14, 1997), 4 (Question #2).

[6] *Riedle Brewery* v. *M.N.R.*, [1939] S.C.R. 253, [1938-39] C.T.C. 312, 1 D.T.C. 499-29 (S.C.C.) (brewery could deduct cost of free beer to customers).

[7] *Roebuck* v. *M.N.R.* (1961), 26 Tax A.B.C. 11 (T.A.B.) (lawyer could not deduct cost of bath mitzvah, although many clients were invited).

[8] The allowable percentage was 80 per cent until it was reduced to 50 per cent in 1994.

of "reasonable" entertainment-style expenses to be personal expenditures, and allows the remainder to be deducted as business expenses. Where an expenditure for food or beverages or entertainment is unreasonable within the meaning of s. 67.1, the section allows a deduction of 50 per cent of a "reasonable" portion of the expense.[9]

The rule that limits deductibility of business expenses for food, beverages or entertainment to 50 per cent of the actual expense is arbitrary, but in many cases is probably a realistic apportionment. It is also desirable as a matter of tax policy. In the first place, the old rule of full deductibility was open to abuse by the incurring of excessively high or excessively frequent expenses which had only a tenuous relationship to business income but which the Department could not in practice effectively police. In the second place, full deductibility violated neutrality by artificially stimulating the consumption of entertainment-type goods and services and thereby diverting to that sector of the economy resources that would in the absence of taxes be deployed elsewhere. In the third place, full deductibility violated equity since the element of untaxed personal benefit accrued mainly to taxpayers in business on their own account or employed in managerial positions (the expense being paid and the deduction being taken by the employer) and was not available to the majority of taxpayers. The inequity was regressive (a breach of vertical as well as horizontal equity) since the advantage accrued disproportionately to high-income people.[10]

13.3 Commuting expenses

Commuting, like business-related entertainment, is a dual-purpose expense. On the one hand, it could be said that the journey to work is a precondition of earning income. On the other hand, the nature of the journey to work is dictated by the consumption decision as to where to locate one's home. The courts have consistently preferred the latter view, and have disallowed commuting expenses as deductions from business income. They are expenses that make a taxpayer available for work, but they are not incurred in the course of the business.

Once a taxpayer has travelled from home to office, any business-related travel from the office, other than the journey home, is incurred in the course of

---

[9] Subsection 67.1(2) creates a number of exceptions to the 50 per cent rule: (a) where the taxpayer is in the business of providing food, beverages or entertainment (e.g., a restaurant or hotel); (b) where the cost of a ticket to a charity function includes food, beverages or entertainment; (c) where the taxpayer has been compensated for food, beverages or entertainment (as where the expense is billed to a client); (d) where the food, beverages or entertainment are paid for by an employer and have to be reported by an employee as a taxable benefit; and (e) where food, beverages or entertainment are available to all persons employed at a particular place (e.g., free coffee or an office party).

[10] See Brooks in Hansen, Krishna, Rendall (eds.), *Canadian Taxation* (1981), 202-203.

the business and is a deductible business expense. Thus, the lawyer who travels from his or her office to the courthouse, and back again, does incur a deductible expense.

In *Cumming* v. *M.N.R.* (1967),[11] the taxpayer was a doctor, an anaesthetist, who rendered all his professional services at a hospital near his home. However, he had no office at the hospital in which he could do the bookkeeping and paperwork of the practice, or read medical journals. He established an office at his home that was used exclusively for those purposes. The Exchequer Court held that the home office was the base from which the practice was operated. Therefore, the journeys to and from the hospital were not commutes, but were journeys made in the course of the practice. The expense of these journeys was accordingly deductible.[12]

13.4 Home-office expenses

The home office is another dual-purpose expense. If a businessperson does some business-related work at home, then the expenses of maintaining the home have a dual character. However, the courts have been unwilling to permit any part of the home expenses to be deducted unless the businessperson maintained a separate room in the house as an office, and used the room exclusively for business purposes. In that case, the businessperson would be permitted to deduct a proportion of the home expenses based on the proportion of floor space that the office bore to the total floor space of the home. In *Logan* v. *M.N.R.* (1967),[13] for example, a doctor was permitted to deduct the portion of home-related expenses that were attributable to a room in his home that was used as an office. The taxpayer was able to establish that the office was used exclusively for work-related activities, such as medical writing, bookkeeping, and meeting with other doctors. In *Mallouh* v. *M.N.R.* (1985),[14] by contrast, a doctor was denied a deduction for costs related to a home office that occupied half of the basement in the doctor's home. In that case, the office was more of a general study or den in which business-related work was not the exclusive activity.

---

[11] [1967] C.T.C. 462, 67 D.T.C. 5312 (Ex. Ct.).

[12] Accord, *The Queen* v. *Cork*, [1990] 2 C.T.C. 116, 90 D.T.C. 6358 (F.C.A.), in which a mechanical draftsman's expenses of travelling from "home" to work were held deductible. As was the case in *Cumming*, the taxpayer in *Cork* used his home as the base of operations from which he carried on his business. The trips from his home-office to various job sites were therefore not commutes, but trips made in the course of doing business, and were accordingly deductible from income.

[13] [1967] Tax A.B.C. 276 (T.A.B.).

[14] [1985] 1 C.T.C. 2297, 85 D.T.C. 250 (T.C.C.).

In 1988, s. 18(12) was added to the Income Tax Act to establish more precise, and more restrictive, rules with respect to the deductibility of a home office.[15] Paragraph 18(12)(a) provides as follows:

> 18(12) Notwithstanding any other provision of this Act, in computing an individual's income from a business for a taxation year,
>
> (a)   no amount shall be deducted in respect of an otherwise deductible amount for any part (in this subsection referred to as the "work space") of a self-contained domestic establishment in which the individual resides, except to the extent that the work space is either
>
> > (i)   the individual's principal place of business, or
> >
> > (ii)   used exclusively for the purpose of earning income from business and used on a regular and continuous basis for meeting clients, customers or patients of the individual in respect of the business;

Paragraph 18(12)(a) does not render the prior case-law irrelevant, because the provision applies only to a home-office expense that is "otherwise deductible". When a home-office expense would satisfy the prior cases, so as to be otherwise deductible, it must also satisfy one of the two tests in paragraph (a): either the office must be the individual's "principal place of business" (subparagraph (i)),[16] or, if the office is not the principal place of business, it must be "used on a regular and continuous basis for meeting clients, customers or patients" (subparagraph (ii)).[17] Where a home office fails to satisfy one of these two tests, no deduction will be allowed.

Many people operate small businesses out of their homes, sometimes on top of regular employment. Such businesses are often not particularly profitable. If they incur losses, the losses are deductible against the taxpayer's other income.[18] Paragraph 18(12)(b) provides that the deduction for a home office that satisfies the requirements of paragraph (a) is allowed only to the extent that the taxpayer has positive income from the business. In other words, the home-office deduction cannot be used to create a loss or increase a loss. Paragraph (c) provides that expenses that are disallowed by paragraph (b) can be carried forward indefinitely so long as the home office continues to qualify for the deduction under paragraph (a). Therefore, the portion of the home-office expenses that cannot be deducted in a particular year will be deductible in a

---

[15] The rule permitting the deduction of home-office expenses by employees (s. 8(13)), which is discussed in ch. 10, under heading 10.9(b), "Deductions permitted", above, contains the same restrictive language.

[16] The word "principal" is not defined. It is considered by Revenue Canada to have a meaning similar to "chief" or "main": Interpretation Bulletin IT-514, "Work space in home expenses" (1989), para. 2.

[17] Subparagraph 18(12)(a)(ii) also repeats the requirement, already established in the cases, that the office be used exclusively for the purpose of earning business income.

[18] Chapter 18, Losses, under heading 18.1, "Income losses", below.

future year if the income from the business is sufficient in that year.[19] For example, suppose that in year 1 a taxpayer operating a home-based business has (in thousands) revenue of $10, home-office expenses of $3 and other expenses of $9; in year 1, only $1 is deductible for the home office. In year 2, if revenue has risen to $15 and expenses have remained the same, the full current home-office expenses of $3 will be deductible, as well as the $2 disallowed prior year's home-office expenses; this will leave a profit for tax purposes from the home-based business of $1.

13.5 Housekeeping expenses

The cost of housekeeping may play a role in the earning of business income, because it relieves the taxpayer of non-income-earning work and frees up time for income-earning purposes. It is however a personal or living expense which is non-deductible. Like commuting, housekeeping may make the taxpayer available for work, but it is not done in the course of the business or as part of the income-earning process. The concern here is that the tax base would be seriously eroded if all expenses that were preconditions to working were deductible. Food, clothing and housing, for example, are all necessary in order to maintain the ability to function at work.

Nevertheless, the disallowance of housekeeping expenses can lead to arbitrary results. In *Benton* v. *M.N.R.* (1952),[20] the Tax Appeal Board disallowed a farmer's cost of hiring a housekeeper. The farmer was in poor health and could not manage both the farm and housekeeping duties. Because housekeeping is a personal or living expense, the wages paid to the housekeeper were not deductible from the farmer's income. Had the farmer done the housework himself and hired a farm hand to work the farm, the farm hand's wages would have been deductible as an expense incurred to earn income from the farming business.[21]

13.6 Child care expenses

Section 63 of the Act confers partial deductibility on child care expenses. Section 63 is in subdivision e because it is not confined to business income. It is confined to "earned income", which is defined as including income from an office or employment as well as income from a business (s. 63(3)(b)). Section 63 is subject to three important limitations: (1) only the lower-income parent can claim the deduction, which therefore cannot be claimed at all if one parent has

---

[19] The carryforward rule of paragraph (c) is explained in IT-514, note 16, above, para. 5.

[20] [1952] 6 Tax A.B.C. 230 (T.A.B.).

[21] Indeed, a portion of the wages paid to the housekeeper were held to be deductible, reflecting time spent by the housekeeper doing farm work.

no income;[22] (2) the deduction cannot exceed two-thirds of the "earned income" of the lower income parent; and (3) the deduction cannot exceed $5,000 per child under the age of seven and $3,000 per child between the ages of seven and 16, inclusive.[23]

Beyond the general deduction offered by s. 63, can child care expenses be deducted as an expense of doing business? In *Symes* v. *Canada* (1993),[24] the Supreme Court of Canada answered no. The taxpayer in that case, a self-employed lawyer with two small children, paid a nanny to look after her children. The taxpayer testified that less expensive forms of child care were not satisfactory in light of the long and irregular hours of her litigation practice, and that she and her husband (who was employed) had made a "family decision" that she would pay for the nanny. In 1985, for example, she paid wages of $13,000 to the nanny, and claimed the full amount as a business expense. The Minister allowed a deduction of only $4,000, which was (in 1985) the maximum deduction allowed by s. 63 for a taxpayer with two children. (It has since been increased, as noted in the previous paragraph.)

The majority of the Supreme Court of Canada, in an opinion written by Iacobucci J., held that child care expenses would not be deductible as business expenses according to traditional tests of deductibility. Although the child care expenses had to be borne in order to allow the taxpayer to go to the office, they were not incurred in the income-earning process,[25] but merely to "make the taxpayer available to the business".[26] The deductibility of an expense was traditionally governed by the commercial needs of the business rather than by the personal circumstances of the proprietor.[27] Iacobucci J. acknowledged that this rule respecting deductibility had developed at a time when businesspersons were mostly males with home-based wives to look after their children. In this situation, child care was a private matter, quite separate from a taxpayer's business activity. Now that businesspeople include women as well as men, and the care of their children is an inescapable part of their business arrangements,

---

[22] There are some exceptions to this rule to meet the case where both incomes are equal (in which case a joint election determines eligibility) (s. 63(2.1)), and where the lower-income person is separated from the taxpayer, infirm, confined to a bed or wheelchair, in prison or in full-time attendance at a secondary school or a designated educational institution (in which cases, the higher-income parent may claim a deduction) (s. 63(2)).

[23] There is no deduction for the care of a child after the year of his or her 16th birthday, except in the case of a child with a mental or physical infirmity (s. 63(3) definition of "eligible child"). If a child is eligible for the disability credit (s. 118.3), the $5,000 limit, instead of shrinking to $3,000, continues to apply after the child turns seven (s. 63(1)(e)(ii)(A)(II)).

[24] [1993] 4 S.C.R. 695, [1994] 1 C.T.C. 40, 94 D.T.C. 6001 (S.C.C.).

[25] *Id.*, 730; 55; 6012.

[26] *Id.*, 739; 60; 6015.

[27] *Id.*, 743; 62; 6017.

it might be appropriate for the courts to "reconceptualize" the nature of a business expense, and in particular to re-examine the rule that disallows expenses that are incurred to make the taxpayer available to the business.[28] However, Iacobucci J. did not pursue this interesting suggestion, because he held that it was "unnecessary to determine whether reconceptualization is appropriate having regard to the presence of s. 63 in the Act".[29]

Section 63 of the Act, according to Iacobucci J., was an exhaustive provision for the deductibility of child care expenses, leaving no room for their deductibility as business expenses. Section 63 explicitly applied to child care services purchased "to enable the taxpayer . . . to carry on a business", and the cap on the deduction was defined by reference to the taxpayer's "earned income", which explicitly included income from business. The cap on the s. 63 deduction, as well as its limitation to the lower-earning parent,[30] would be undermined if child care expenses were fully deductible from business income by whichever parent had actually paid the expenses. In this case, for example, the "family decision" as to which parent should pay for child care placed the obligation on the wife, who earned business income, rather than the husband, who earned employment income. There was no suggestion that this decision had been driven by tax considerations, but the decision did make possible the argument that the expenses were business expenses. Iacobucci J. commented that "in many cases there would be more bookkeeping than reality about such a decision".[31] In the end, therefore, the majority of the Court[32] concluded that s. 63 made clear that child care expenses were not deductible as business expenses. The Minister's assessment, which confined the taxpayer to the s. 63 deduction, was accordingly upheld.

If the argument by the taxpayer in *Symes* had been successful, then self-employed persons, who earn income from a business, would be able to deduct child care expenses in full, while employed persons, who earn income from employment, would be subject to the restrictions of s. 63. This difference

---

[28] *Id.*, 743-744; 62; 6017.

[29] *Id.*, 744; 62; 6017; he added (at 750-751; 66; 6020): "It is not necessary for me to decide whether, in the absence of s. 63, ss. 9, 18(1)(a) and 18(1)(h) are capable of comprehending a business expense deduction for child care.".

[30] The majority of the Court also rejected an equality-based Charter challenge to s. 63's restrictions on the deductibility of child care expenses. The majority rejected the argument that the restrictions had a disproportionate impact on women: although women were more likely to bear the social costs of child care, there was no evidence that women were more likely to bear the financial costs of child care; and the restrictions affected only the financial costs of child care.

[31] [1993] 4 S.C.R. 695, 746, [1994] 1 C.T.C. 40, 63, 94 D.T.C. 6001, 6018.

[32] L'Heureux-Dubé and McLachlin JJ. dissented, holding that the child care expenses were fully deductible as business expenses; that s. 63 did not preclude their deduction as business expenses; and that, if s. 63 had precluded the deduction, it would have contravened the equality guarantee of the Charter of Rights.

in treatment would be bad tax policy, violating both neutrality and equity, because it confers an advantage on self-employed taxpayers (as do other provisions of the Act, to be sure) and, on average, self-employed taxpayers have higher incomes than employed taxpayers.

The deduction for child care expenses can be seen as a "tax expenditure",[33] designed for the purpose of assisting parents with the costs of child care and lowering a barrier to the entrance of women to the workplace. From this standpoint, even s. 63 is open to criticism. Although s. 63 treats employed and self-employed taxpayers equally, it possesses the fundamental disadvantage of all deductions: it delivers a larger benefit to the high-income earner than to the low-income earner, and no benefit at all to the person without taxable income. Other policy instruments, such as the direct provision of day care, or the direct subsidization of low-income parents, might be more effective uses for the amount of revenue foregone by s. 63. If the tax system is to be the vehicle of assistance, s. 63 would be better targeted as a credit, especially a credit that was refundable and income-tested (or vanishing).[34]

13.7   Interest expense

(a)   Paragraph 20(1)(c)

Interest on money borrowed by the taxpayer to earn income from a business or property is deductible from business or property income under s. 20(1)(c) of the Act. Paragraph 20(1)(c) provides for the deduction of:

> 20(1)(c) an amount paid in the year or payable in respect of the year (depending on the method regularly followed by the taxpayer in computing the taxpayer's income), pursuant to a legal obligation to pay interest on
>
> (i)   borrowed money used for the purpose of earning income from a business or property
>   . . .
>
> (ii) an amount payable for property acquired for the purpose of gaining or producing income from the property or for the purpose of gaining or producing income from a business. . . .

---

[33] Chapter 4, Objectives, under heading 4.6, "Tax expenditures", above.

[34] *Id.*, under heading 4.5, "Deductions and credits", above.

In order for interest "paid" or "payable"[35] to be deductible,[36] s. 20(1)(c) specifies that the "borrowed money"[37] (or the property purchased on credit) must be "used for the purpose of earning income from a business or property". This follows the principle that expenses must be related to a source of income. If money is borrowed to purchase a home, a cottage, a personal car or a vacation, the interest cost is not deductible, because these are consumption expenditures that yield no taxable income from a business or property.[38] Less obvious, perhaps, is that, where money is borrowed to purchase property in anticipation of capital gains, rather than income from a business or property, the interest cost is also not deductible.[39]

---

[35] Paragraph 20(1)(c) requires that the method of deducting interest depends on the method regularly followed by the taxpayer. In most cases, that will be the accrual method: for a discussion of the received (paid), receivable (payable) and accrual methods of accounting for interest income, see ch. 12, Income from Business or Property: Inclusions, under heading 12.3(e), "Interest", above. But deferred interest payments are not deductible under s. 20(1)(c) because no amount is paid or payable in the year and the amounts represent a contingent liability (s. 18(1)(e)): see *Barbican Properties* v. *The Queen* (1996), [1997] 1 C.T.C. 2383, 97 D.T.C. 5008 (F.C.A.). Paragraph 20(1)(d) provides that interest on interest (compound interest) must be deducted for tax purposes on a paid basis. There are some other specific provisions relating to interest that override the general rule of s. 20(1)(c), e.g., ss. 18(2), 18(3.1), 67.2.

[36] The Supreme Court of Canada seems to have committed itself to the proposition that, if there were no statutory allowance for the deduction of interest, an interest expense would not be deductible because it is an outlay "on account of capital", which is not deductible according to s. 18(1)(b): *Canada Safeway* v. *M.N.R.*, [1957] S.C.R. 717, 722-723, 727, [1957] C.T.C. 335, 340-341, 344, 57 D.T.C. 1239, 1241-1242, 1244 (S.C.C.); *Bronfman Trust* v. *The Queen*, [1987] 1 S.C.R. 32, 45, [1987] 1 C.T.C. 117, 124, 87 D.T.C. 5059, 5064 (S.C.C.). The proposition is clearly incorrect, being inconsistent with the accepted definition of "capital" expenditures (ch. 14, under heading 14.1, "Definition of capital expenditures", below), with the tax treatment of interest as income in the hands of the recipient, and with generally accepted accounting principles. However, unless and until the Supreme Court reverses itself on the point, it means that s. 20(1)(c) must be complied with in order for an interest expense to be deductible.

[37] For an example of interest on a legal obligation which is not "borrowed money", see *Parthenon Investments* v. *The Queen*, [1993] 2 C.T.C. 2872, 93 D.T.C. 1711 (T.C.C.), in which the Court found that interest paid on a note issued as payment of a dividend was not deductible since the note was not "borrowed money". This appears to be the correct result according to a strict reading of s. 20(1)(c) but it does not seem equitable since, if the dividend had been paid in cash and the cash had been loaned back to the company, the interest on the loan would then have been deductible (since the loan would constitute "borrowed money").

[38] If the tax system recognized the recurring benefits from taxpayer-owned property as imputed income, then of course interest expenses related to the purchase of a home, cottage or car would become deductible: see ch. 9, Tax Base, under heading 9.9, "Imputed income", above.

[39] *Ludmer* v. *M.N.R.*, [1993] 2 C.T.C. 2494, 93 D.T.C. 1351 (T.C.C.); and see ch. 12, Income from Business or Property: Inclusions, under heading 12.3(b), "Reasonable expectation of profit", above, which explains that a reasonable expectation of profit is a requirement for the deductibility of all expenses when property yields losses.

(b)   Current use of borrowed funds

The general rule is that it is "the current use rather than the original use of borrowed funds" that determines eligibility for a deduction.[40] If funds were originally borrowed for an ineligible use (to buy a cottage, for example), and the ineligible use was changed to an eligible use (by the sale of the cottage and the use of the proceeds to purchase income-earning investments, for example), then the interest expense on the loan, which had been non-deductible, would become deductible as from the commencement of the eligible use. Conversely, if funds were originally borrowed for an eligible use (to buy a rental property, for example), and the eligible use was changed to an ineligible one (by the taxpayer occupying the property as a personal residence, for example), then the interest expense on the loan, which had been deductible, would cease to be deductible as from the commencement of the ineligible use.

The current-use rule was applied relentlessly by the courts to deny the deductibility of the interest expense where the income source that funds were borrowed to acquire had disappeared. For example, a taxpayer who borrowed to purchase shares in a company that subsequently went bankrupt was denied a deduction for the continuing interest expense on the loan once the shares had ceased to be a source of income.[41] And a taxpayer who borrowed money to buy shares that he sold at a loss, leaving the loan outstanding, was denied a deduction for the continuing interest expense after the shares had been sold and had ceased to be a source of income.[42] In these cases, although the unfortunate taxpayer was under a continuing obligation to make interest payments to a creditor, the borrowed money no longer had an income-earning use to the taxpayer because the income source had disappeared. Therefore, the current-use rule required a denial of deductibility for the interest payments.

The denial of the deduction of a continuing interest expense after the loss of the source of income that was acquired with the borrowed money was a harsh rule. In 1994, the Act was amended to abrogate this rule. Section 20.1 creates an exception to the current-use rule by allowing the deduction of the continuing interest expense after the loss of the income source. When a property[43] purchased with borrowed money ceases to earn income (or a business purchased with borrowed money ceases to be carried on), and there is still a portion of the loan outstanding, s. 20.1 deems the unpaid balance of the loan to continue to be

---

[40] *Bronfman Trust* v. *The Queen*, [1987] 1 S.C.R. 32, 47, [1987] 1 C.T.C. 117, 129, 87 D.T.C. 5059, 5066 (S.C.C.).

[41] *Lyons* v. *M.N.R.*, [1984] C.T.C. 2090, 84 D.T.C. 1633 (T.C.C.).

[42] *Emerson* v. *The Queen*, [1986] 1 C.T.C. 422, 86 D.T.C. 6184 (F.C.A.).

[43] The section does not apply to real estate or depreciable property, which is used to provide rental or leasing income. The property most commonly covered by s. 20.1 will be stocks and bonds.

used for the purpose of earning income from a business or property.[44] Because of this deeming rule, the related interest expense continues to be deductible under s. 20(1)(c).

In *Tennant* v. *M.N.R* (1996),[45] the taxpayer borrowed $1 million to purchase 1 million common shares at $1 per share. The shares were an income-earning property, and so the interest on the loan was deductible under s. 20(1)(c). The taxpayer later used one of the Act's rollover provisions to exchange the shares for some other shares with a declared fair market value of $1,000.[46] The full amount of the loan remained outstanding and the question was whether the taxpayer could continue to deduct the interest on the entire principal sum of $1 million. The Minister took the position that only $1,000 of the loan could now be traced to an eligible use and the only interest that was deductible was interest on $1,000 of the principal sum. The Supreme Court of Canada held that the full amount of the interest continued to be deductible. When the taxpayer exchanged the original shares for the replacement shares, he was continuing to invest the entire proceeds of the loan in an eligible income-earning use. The ability to deduct the full amount of the interest depended on the use to which the proceeds of the loan, or any property substituted for the proceeds, was put. It did not matter whether the property had declined in value, just as it would not have mattered if the property had increased in value. The interest deduction was based on the amount of the loan, not on the value or cost of the replacement property.

(c)   Direct use of borrowed funds

In classifying the use to which borrowed funds have been put, it is the direct use that is determinative. For example, a taxpayer who borrows money for the purpose of purchasing a personal residence is denied a deduction for the interest payments on the loan even if the loan enabled the taxpayer to retain income-earning investments.[47] In that case, the ineligibility of the direct use of the borrowed funds (to purchase the home) disqualifies the interest payments from deductibility, despite the fact that the indirect use (to preserve investments) did yield income from property.

The direct-use rule was confirmed in *Bronfman Trust* v. *The Queen* (1987),[48] where a trust made a payment of capital to a beneficiary. Judging that the time was not right to sell any of the trust's investments, the trustees borrowed the money to make the capital payment. Three years later, the trustees

---

[44] In order to preclude abuse, s. 20.1 contains detailed rules to determine the portion of the borrowed money that is truly applicable to the lost source of income.

[45] [1996] 1 S.C.R. 305, [1996] 1 C.T.C. 290, 96 D.T.C. 6121 (S.C.C.).

[46] *Id.*, 308.

[47] *Toolsie* v. *The Queen*, [1986] 1 C.T.C. 216, 86 D.T.C. 6117 (F.C.T.D.).

[48] [1987] 1 S.C.R. 32, [1987] 1 C.T.C. 117, 87 D.T.C. 5059 (S.C.C.).

did sell off some of the trust's investments and repaid the loan. The trust (which is deemed to be an individual for tax purposes) sought to deduct the interest payments in each of the three years that the loan was outstanding. In this case, the direct use of the borrowed funds was ineligible for the deduction, because the payment to the beneficiary yielded no income from business or property. The trust argued, however, that the indirect use of the borrowed funds had yielded income from property, because the trust had retained investments that without the loan would have been sold, and those investments had produced income. The Supreme Court of Canada held that it was the direct use that was determinative, and denied the deduction. Dickson C.J., who wrote for the Court, pointed out that, if the preservation of income-producing assets counted as an eligible use, then any loan for any purpose (a vacation, for example) would give rise to deductible interest, provided the borrower owned income-producing assets. This would be unfair as between rich and poor (the rich would always qualify for the deduction), and "would make a mockery of the statutory requirement that, for interest payments to be deductible, borrowed money must be used for circumscribed income-earning purposes".[49]

It is not always easy to determine what is a direct use of borrowed money, and what is an indirect use. If a company borrows money in order to honour a guarantee that it gave to its parent company to enable the parent company to obtain a bank loan, is that a borrowing for the purpose of earning income from the business? The Federal Court of Appeal has suggested, in obiter, that the answer is no, even if the guarantor-company received consideration for the guarantee.[50] Superficially, it is easy to say that the direct use of the funds is to pay the parent company's debt, which is not an income-producing use. But, at least if consideration were given for the guarantee, the payment could as easily be analyzed as satisfying an obligation of the guarantor-company, which (assuming the obligation was incurred for business purposes) would seem to satisfy the direct-use rule.[51]

---

[49] *Id.*, 49; 126; 5065. After the *Bronfman* decision, Revenue Canada cancelled Interpretation Bulletin IT-80, "Interest on money borrowed to redeem shares, or to pay dividends" (1972), but announced that, despite its cancellation, IT-80 would continue to represent its administrative policy regarding interest deductibility. At about the same time, the Department of Finance released draft legislation dealing with the deductibility of the interest expense, not in the actual Bronfman situation of the distribution of capital by a trust, but in related situations where the income-earning use was only indirect: "Draft Legislation on Interest Deductibility", Department of Finance, December 20, 1991. This legislation, which would confirm Revenue Canada's pre-*Bronfman* assessing practices, has not yet (1997) been enacted and Revenue Canada continues to apply IT-80.

[50] *74712 Alberta v. The Queen*, [1997] 2 C.T.C. 30, 97 D.T.C. 5126 (F.C.A.)

[51] Interpretation Bulletin IT-445, "The deduction of interest on funds borrowed either to be loaned at less than a reasonable rate of interest or to honour a guarantee given for inadequate consideration in non-arm's length circumstances" (1981), para. 3, provides that interest on money borrowed to honour a guarantee is deductible providing adequate consideration was given for the guarantee.

13.8 Other costs of financing

As well as the interest expense on borrowed money, the raising of capital (whether by issuing shares or by borrowing) involves many other costs, for example, the fees that must be paid to lawyers, accountants, banks, underwriters and appraisers. Unlike interest, these costs do not recur: they are incurred once and for all, and they provide an enduring benefit to the business, because the business will make use of the capital for a long time. We shall see in the next chapter, which deals with capital expenditures, that expenditures to provide an enduring benefit to a business are classified as capital expenditures and (subject to important exceptions) their deductibility is denied by s. 18(1)(b).[52] In order to encourage new capital investment, before 1988 s. 20(1)(e) allowed a full deduction for financing expenses[53] in the year that they were incurred. In 1988, s. 20(1)(e) was amended to spread the deduction over a five-year period on a straight-line basis: one-fifth of the expenses is deductible in each year. The purpose of spreading the deduction was "to achieve a better matching of expenses and revenues".[54]

13.9 Damages and similar payments

In *Imperial Oil* v. *M.N.R.* (1947),[55] the issue was whether Imperial Oil (the taxpayer) could deduct for tax purposes a damages settlement of $526,995 which it was obliged to pay as the result of a collision between one of its ships and another ship. The Exchequer Court held that the item was deductible. It was argued for the Minister that the expenditure had been made not for "the purpose of gaining or producing income" (as stipulated by s. 18(1)(a)), but to discharge a legal liability. Thorson P. pointed out that that was true of every expense. The language of s. 18(1)(a) could not be taken literally, because an expense by itself could never directly accomplish the purpose of gaining or producing income. The issue, his lordship said, was whether the liability which made the expense necessary arose "as part of the operations, transactions or services by which the taxpayer earned the income". If so, then it was part of the income-earning

---

[52] Chapter 14, Income from Business or Property: Capital Expenditures, below.

[53] The eligible costs are defined in s. 20(1)(e), which requires that they be "not otherwise deductible". Costs which are otherwise deductible include annual financing fees on debt (s. 20(e.1)), premiums on life insurance required as collateral (s. 20(1)(e.2)), interest on debt (s. 20(1)(c)) and discounts on debt (s. 20(1)(f)). "Participating interest" paid on company bonds, which was computed as 15% of the company's operating surplus, was not interest deductible under s. 20(1)(c) but qualified for deduction under s. 20(1)(e)(ii): *Sherway Centre* v. *The Queen*, [1996] 3 C.T.C. 2687, 96 D.T.C. 1640 (T.C.C.).

[54] Department of Finance, *Technical Notes* (Carswell), s. 20(1)(e).

[55] [1947] C.T.C. 353, 3 D.T.C. 1090 (Ex. Ct.).

process, and it was deductible.[56] The Court reasoned that the transportation of petroleum products was one of Imperial Oil's business operations, and the risk of collision at sea (even when caused by the negligence of an employee) was a normal hazard of those operations. Therefore, any resulting liability for damages was one of the costs of Imperial Oil's operations and was therefore deductible.

Imperial Oil establishes the principle that s. 18(1)(a)'s requirement that an expense be "for the purpose of gaining or producing income" will not preclude the deduction of damages (and similar liabilities) where the damages flow from a normal risk of business operations. It is implicit in this reasoning that a payment to discharge a liability that did not flow from a normal risk of operations would not be deductible. However, if the payment were characterized as conferring an "enduring benefit" on the business, the payment would be "on account of capital", and, as is explained in the next chapter,[57] would qualify as an eligible capital expenditure which could be amortized over a period of years. If the payment satisfied neither the *Imperial Oil* test nor the enduring benefit test,[58] it would probably not be deductible at all.[59] Even if the payment satisfied the *Imperial Oil* test, the deduction would normally be disallowed if the liability were a fine or other sanction for illegal activity; that point is taken up later in the chapter.[60] And any deduction would be disallowed to the extent that it was not reasonable in the circumstances; that point is also taken up later in the chapter.[61]

A liability of any kind is deductible only if the liability has actually been paid or if the liability is a legal obligation at the end of the taxation year. The Income Tax Act generally prohibits the deduction of liabilities that are merely contingent, or of "reserves" to provide for expected future liabilities (s. 18(1)(e)). A number of reserves are, however, specifically authorized by the Act.[62]

---

[56] Accord, *Premium Iron Ores* v. *M.N.R.*, [1966] S.C.R. 685, [1966] C.T.C. 391, 66 D.T.C. 5280 (S.C.C.) (legal expenses incurred in contesting United States tax assessment deductible, although directed to saving money rather than making it).

[57] Chapter 14, Income from Business or Property: Capital Expenditures, below.

[58] The uninsured loss or destruction of a capital property would give rise to a capital loss, three-quarters of which would be allowable under subdivision c: ch. 15, Capital Gains, under heading 15.9, "Disposition", below.

[59] Interpretation Bulletin IT-467R, "Damages, settlements and similar payments" (1992); see also the next section of this chapter, under heading 13.10, "Theft", below. An extraordinary loss is the negative counterpart of a windfall, which need not be recognized as income.

[60] Section 13.11, "Fines", below.

[61] Section 13.13, "The 'reasonable' requirement", below.

[62] E.g., ss. 20(1)(l), 20(1)(m), 20(1)(m.1), 20(1)(n), 20(1)(o), 20(26), 40(1)(a)(iii), 61.2–61.4. Most reserves that are claimed as a tax deduction in one year are added back into income the following year under s. 12.

13.10 Theft

In *General Stampings of Canada* v. *M.N.R.* (1957),[63] the issue was whether a corporation could deduct for tax purposes a sum of $36,571.33 which had been embezzled by the corporation's general manager. The Tax Appeal Board disallowed the loss on the basis that the defalcation was a unique event, possible only for an official with extensive control over corporate funds, and having "nothing whatever to do with the conduct of the company's income-earning activities". The Board contrasted this loss, "so unusually experienced", with losses resulting from purloinings by more lowly employees which were normal hazards of a business and accordingly deductible.[64] Similarly, losses caused by outside criminals, such as burglars, have been held to be deductible.[65]

13.11 Fines

Is there any principle of public policy which would deny the deduction of expenses which would otherwise be deductible under the Income Tax Act? This question is commonly posed when a business proprietor attempts to deduct fines levied against him or her for illegal acts committed in the course of the business.[66] The same question is raised by attempts to deduct bribes and other illegal expenditures.[67] The Income Tax Act specifically deals with some kinds of payments. Interest and penalties under the Income Tax Act itself are not deductible (s. 18(1)(t)). Nor are certain expenditures that are prohibited by the Criminal Code (s. 67.5); these include bribes to judges, public officials and law enforcement officers, payments made for the purpose of influencing municipal

---

[63] (1957), 17 Tax A.B.C. 1 (T.A.B.).

[64] Subsequent cases have suggested that it is not so much the level of the thieving employee in the employment hierarchy that determines deductibility of embezzled funds or employee theft, as whether or not the money or property was taken in the course of business operations, and whether the risk of theft was inherent in those operations. See *Cassidy's* v. *M.N.R.*, [1990] 1 C.T.C. 2043, 89 D.T.C. 686 (T.C.C.); *Parkland Operations* v. *The Queen*, [1991] 1 C.T.C. 23, 90 D.T.C. 6676 (F.C.T.D.); Interpretation Bulletin IT-185R, "Losses from theft, defalcation or embezzlement" (1991).

[65] *Weidman Bros.* v. *M.N.R.* (1950), 2 Tax A.B.C. 223 (T.A.B.); *Thayer Lumber Co.* v. *M.N.R.* (1957), 18 Tax A.B.C. 284 (T.A.B.).

[66] See Krishna, "Public Policy Limitations on the Deductibility of Fines and Penalties" (1979) 16 *Osgoode Hall L.J.* 19; Brooks in Hansen, Krishna, Rendall (eds.), *Canadian Taxation* (1981), 242-246; Krasa, "The Deductibility of Fines, Penalties, Damages and Contract Termination Payments" (1990) 38 *Can. Tax J.* 1399.

[67] Political contributions are not deductible (s. 18(1)(n)), but they do give rise to a credit against tax (s. 127(3)); the credit is denied if the taxpayer acquired a financial benefit from the contribution (s. 127(4.1)(b)).

officers and payments made to buy an official appointment.[68] When a taxpayer incurs an expense for these purposes, the expense is non-deductible regardless of whether it resulted in the production of business or property income.

The Income Tax Act is silent on the question whether fines can be deducted from business income. There are cases which have denied the deduction of business-related fines on the basis that a fine is not an expense that is incurred for the purpose of earning income. The leading case is *I.R.C.* v. *Alexander Von Glehn* (1920),[69] where it was held that a fine for trading with the enemy was not deductible, because it was not really a "commercial loss". *E.H. Pooler* v. *M.N.R.* (1962)[70] decided that a fine of $2,000 levied by the Toronto Stock Exchange on a member was not deductible by the member, because the fine was not incurred "for the purpose of producing income". It is possible that these decisions proceeded from an inarticulate premise of public policy, but taking them at their face value they seem open to criticism. On the basis of the *Imperial Oil* case,[71] one must surely conclude that if the activity which gave rise to the fine was income-producing business activity, then the fine is properly regarded as one of the costs of earning the revenue.

Von Glehn and *Pooler* may be contrasted with *Day and Ross* v. *The Queen* (1976),[72] in which a trucking company was permitted to deduct a large number of fines, most of them for violations of provincial laws imposing weight restrictions on the loads of its trucks. The trucking company established that such fines were inevitable in the trucking business, and the Federal Court accepted that they were deductible expenses of the business.[73] An earlier, similar decision is *Rolland Paper Co.* v. *M.N.R.* (1960),[74] although no fine was in issue in that case. In that case, a paper company was permitted to deduct the legal expenses of defending an anti-trust prosecution. The company was convicted and fined, but apparently did not attempt to deduct the fine. The Exchequer Court held that the company's illegal trade practices were "followed for the purpose of earning

---

[68] Only bribes to Canadian officials are included in this list. Bribes to foreign officials are deductible, unless the courts develop a public-policy objection to deductibility: cf. the cases dealing with fines, discussed in following text.

[69] [1920] 2 K.B. 553 (C.A.).

[70] [1962] C.T.C. 527, 62 D.T.C. 1321 (Ex. Ct.).

[71] Note 55, above.

[72] [1976] C.T.C. 707, 76 D.T.C. 6433 (F.C.T.D.).

[73] In *Amway of Canada* v. *The Queen*, [1996] 2 C.T.C. 162, 96 D.T.C. 6135 (F.C.A.), it was held that if a penalty was "avoidable" it was not incurred for a business purpose and was not deductible. Avoidability is a much stricter test than *Imperial Oil*, note 55, above, stipulates for a business purpose.

[74] [1960] C.T.C. 158, 60 D.T.C. 1095 (Ex. Ct.).

income from the business", and the legal expenses of defending the practices from prosecution were deductible.[75]

Once it is established that a fine was paid for the purpose of producing income from a business, the question arises whether there is a principle of public policy which requires or justifies a denial of deductibility. The existence of such a principle was asserted in *Luscoe Products* v. *M.N.R.* (1956),[76] in which the Tax Appeal Board refused to allow a drug company to deduct a fine which had been imposed for manufacturing a cough remedy with too much alcohol in it. The Board said that it would be "preposterous" if the company were allowed to deduct the fine "and thus be enabled to share equally with the public revenue the loss to which it was condemned by reason of its own unlawful act". There are echoes of this kind of reasoning in *Day and Ross*, where the Court, while allowing the deduction of the fines, stressed that the taxpayer's unlawful acts (the violations of the weight restrictions) were not intentional, and were not "outrageous transgressions of public policy". Similarly, in *Rolland Paper*, the Court, in allowing the deduction of the legal expenses of defending the anti-trust prosecution, was careful to repeat a statement made by the sentencing court that the directors of the company had not been "guilty of moral turpitude or wicked intention". The implication of these dicta is, of course, that deliberate or outrageous or morally culpable illegality would require a tax court to deny the deductibility of a fine or associated legal expenses. That is the position that is asserted by Revenue Canada.[77]

It is undeniable that if a taxpayer can deduct a fine from income, then (depending upon the taxpayer's marginal rate) the sting of the fine is much reduced. However, this is not a very strong reason for disallowing the deduction of the fines, because, if it were clearly settled that business-related fines were deductible, then sentencing courts would presumably impose heavier fines on illegal business activity to offset the advantage of deductibility. Nor is it "irrational" for the impact of a fine to "depend upon the marginal bracket of the taxpayer".[78] The real impact of a fine always depends upon the wealth of the defendant, and where the sentencing court has a discretion it always has to make a judgment about the defendant's capacity to pay in fixing an appropriate fine.

---

[75] See also *TNT Canada* v. *The Queen*, [1988] 2 C.T.C. 91, 88 D.T.C. 6334 (F.C.T.D.) (fines deductible); *United Color and Chemicals* v. *M.N.R.*, [1992] 1 C.T.C. 2321, 92 D.T.C. 1259 (T.C.C.) (kickbacks deductible).

[76] (1956), 16 Tax A.B.C. 239 (T.A.B.).

[77] Interpretation Bulletin IT-104R2, "Deductibility of fines or penalties" (1993) para. 2, asserts a general rule of non-deductibility; para. 3 allows deductibility in certain cases not involving "deliberate disobedience of the law". Accord, *Amway of Canada*, note 73, above, where the Federal Court of Appeal expressly rejected the arguments advanced in this book against such a rule of public policy.

[78] Brooks, note 66, above, 243.

It is surely an exaggeration to say that allowing the deduction of fines would "frustrate" the objectives of the statute under which the fine is imposed.[79]

The overriding principle of tax policy is that tax should be levied in accordance with ability to pay; this entails the consequence that only net income should be subject to tax; and this leads to the conclusion that business-related fines should be deductible. To be sure, the ability-to-pay principle is occasionally departed from, but it should only be departed from in pursuit of a very strong competing policy. The question is whether the policy of giving full effect to the statutes under which the fines are imposed is sufficiently strong to outweigh the ability-to-pay principle.

The difficulty in giving effect to vague notions of public policy is well illustrated by the kinds of distinctions contemplated by the dicta in *Day and Ross* and *Rolland Paper*, which require the tax court to inquire into the moral turpitude of the taxpayer in order to decide whether or not the fine is deductible. Such an inquiry is surely inappropriate to a tax court, especially when blameworthiness has already been determined by the sentencing criminal court in fixing the fine. Professor Brooks, who argues that fines should generally be non-deductible, would make an exception for the "compensatory" portion of a fine, and he suggests that the tax court inquire into the purpose of a fine for which deduction is claimed, apportion it between the compensatory element (if any) and the deterrent element, and allow a deduction for the former but not the latter.[80] But this inquiry would be even more difficult than that into moral turpitude. Certainly, neither determination could be made with any confidence by a taxpayer preparing his or her income tax return, or by Revenue Canada in assessing it. The important objectives of self-assessment and ease of administration would be far better served by a blanket prohibition on the deduction of fines than by these compromises. While the issue is difficult, perhaps the best solution is to allow fines to be deductible if they were incurred in the course of business operations. — Hogg argument (administrative simplicity argument)

13.12 Expenses of illegal business

There is no doubt that the income from an illegal business, such as bootlegging, bookmaking or prostitution, is subject to tax.[81] This is an easier question than the deductibility of fines, because in taxing illegal income the tax policy of taxing increases in ability to pay and the public policy of discouraging illegal activity work in harmony. The only possible objection to taxing illegal

---

[79] *Ibid.*

[80] Brooks, Case Comment (1977) 25 *Can. Tax J.* 16.

[81] *Minister of Finance* v. *Smith*, [1927] A.C. 193, [1917-27] C.T.C. 251, 1 D.T.C. 92 (P.C.) (bootlegging); cf. *The Queen* v. *Poynton*, [1972] C.T.C. 411, 72 D.T.C. 6329 (Ont. C.A.) (proceeds of embezzlement taxable income, although not business income).

income would be a feeling that the state should not live off the avails of prostitution or accept money which is otherwise tainted with illegality. But the Canadian tax system (in common with those of other countries) has not been troubled by such a scrupulous morality and has been happy to accept whatever money it can lay its hands on.[82]

Once it is accepted that the revenue of an illegal business is subject to tax, there is no plausible argument for disallowing the expenses of an illegal business. To disallow expenses would be to tax a gross income figure that is more than the "profit" from the business, and s. 9 only purports to tax the "profit" — the revenue net of expenses. The courts surely have no mandate to use the tax system as a vehicle to impose extra penalties on illegal activity which is already penalized by other statutes. Most of the expenses of an illegal business will in any case be perfectly legitimate in themselves, for example, rent, utilities, supplies and equipment; those expenses that are illegitimate, for example, fines or protection payments or bribes, surely do not raise any different issue than attempts by a legal business to deduct such expenses (which was the topic of the previous section of this chapter).

In *M.N.R.* v. *Eldridge* (1964),[83] the Exchequer Court had to decide whether the Minister had properly assessed the tax of the proprietor of a call girl business. It was common ground that the business was illegal; and it was common ground that the income was liable to tax. The dispute centred on the deductibility of expenses, but here the difficulties were caused by the poor recordkeeping (apparently common in this line of business) and hence inadequate proof of expenses rather than any issue of principle. Those expenses which could be proved were allowed. The legal costs of defending one of the call girls who had been charged under the Criminal Code were allowed as an expense laid out for the purpose of gaining income, because her acquittal enabled her to return to income-earning activity, which would have been precluded by a sentence of imprisonment. No fines were in issue in this case, apparently because most charges had been laid after the business had been brought to an end by the police.

13.13 The "reasonable" requirement

Section 67 of the Act provides as follows:

> 67. In computing income, no deduction shall be made in respect of an outlay or expense in respect of which any amount is otherwise deductible under this Act, except to the extent that the outlay or expense was reasonable in the circumstances.

---

[82] In the debate about the deductibility of fines (under the previous heading, 13.11, "Fines", above), it has never been doubted that, when a legitimate business commits illegal acts that enhance its revenue (adding alcohol to a cough syrup, disregarding weight restrictions on truck loads, or price fixing, for example), the additional revenue is taxable.

[83] [1964] C.T.C. 545, 64 D.T.C. 5338 (Ex. Ct.).

Section 67 prohibits the deduction of an expense except to the extent that the expense was "reasonable in the circumstances". Section 67 is in subdivision f of Division B of Part I (which is a miscellaneous collection of rules relating to the computation of income), rather than subdivision b, because s. 67 is applicable to deductions from income from every source, not just business and property income. However, its main application is to deductions from business and property income, because the deductions from other kinds of income are more closely regulated and less susceptible of abuse.

The section is framed in terms of an objective standard of reasonableness. It does not give to the Minister a discretion to disallow expenses which in his or her opinion are unreasonable. In practice, however, departmental policy in identifying and initially disallowing certain classes of expenditure is the key to the actual operation of the section. To judge by the numerous decided cases, the section is principally employed in two situations: (1) where a particular expense is excessive in relation to the purpose for which it was incurred; and (2) where non-arm's-length management fees or rents or salaries are paid to artificially reduce the income of the payor or achieve some other tax-avoidance purpose.

In the first category are a number of cases in which expenses have been wholly or partially disallowed on the ground that they purchased excessively luxurious facilities for the purpose sought to be achieved. The purchase of a Cadillac or Rolls Royce automobile has attracted successful challenge on this ground,[84] as have extravagant entertainment expenses[85] and travelling expenses.[86]

An unusual case is *No. 511* v. *M.N.R.* (1958),[87] in which the taxpayer, a lumber company, sought to deduct the cost of sponsoring a baseball team. The Tax Appeal Board accepted that this was a legitimate and deductible form of advertising, but held that the actual expense of $22,500 was too high because it was more than half of the company's profits. The Board held that $5,000 would be the cost of a reasonable advertising campaign using newspaper and radio advertisements and the Board allowed a deduction of $5,000. Underlying this decision is probably an unexpressed factual judgment that the sponsorship of the baseball team was essentially a hobby for the principal shareholder of the taxpayer-corporation, so that the expense was only partially laid out for a business purpose. In this case, and in the luxury cases, s. 67 is the vehicle by which an element of personal consumption is disallowed or stripped from an otherwise legitimate business expense. This could be done without recourse to

[84] E.g., *Kent and Co.* v. *M.N.R.*, [1971] Tax A.B.C. 1158 (T.A.B.).

[85] E.g., *Chabot* v. *M.N.R.* (1961), 26 Tax A.B.C. 204 (T.A.B.).

[86] E.g., *No. 589* v. *M.N.R.* (1959), 21 Tax A.B.C. 153 (T.A.B.).

[87] (1958), 19 Tax A.B.C. 248 (T.A.B.).

s. 67, since ss. 9, 18(1)(a) and 18(1)(h) all prohibit the deduction of non-business expenditures,[88] but s. 67 is a convenient tool for the purpose.

There have been two cases where the total of a taxpayer's business expenditures has been reduced, not on the ground that any particular expenditure was unreasonable, but on the ground that the total of all expenditures was excessive in relation to the revenue of the business.[89] These cases are more difficult to understand, and a dictum in one of the cases that expenses should not ordinarily exceed one-third of revenue will astonish most business proprietors. If the Tax Appeal Board in each of these cases was covertly suggesting that particular expenditures must have been extravagant or unnecessary, then s. 67 does seem properly applicable. But a theory that all businesses must be profitable, or a theory that tax tribunals can assess the efficiency of a business operation, seem unsafe bases from which to apply s. 67.

The second category of case to which s. 67 has been applied is the payment of non-arm's-length management fees, rents or salaries. A good example is *Mulder Bros.* v. *M.N.R.* (1967).[90] In that case, a corporation controlled by two brothers, A and B, paid salaries as follows:

Brother A	$20,000
Brother B	$13,000
Brother B's wife	$13,000

All three persons genuinely worked as employees of the corporation, but the Minister took the view that the wife's services were only worth $6,000. In his opinion, the total salary of $26,000 paid to the B family had been divided between B and B's wife to produce the most favourable income-split rather than to reward their actual contributions of work. The Minister therefore used s. 67 to reduce the company's tax deduction for the wife's salary to $6,000. The Tax Appeal Board raised the reasonable figure to $8,500, still disallowing the balance.

While corporate salaries have attracted the most frequent applications of s. 67, other non-arm's-length payments are also vulnerable. For example, a dentist who sought to deduct $12,000 as rent for premises owned by his wife was limited to $5,000,[91] although a lawyer who sought to deduct $1,000 per month as a management fee to a corporation owned by himself and his wife successfully resisted an attack based on s. 67.[92]

---

[88] See sec. 13.2, "Entertainment expenses", above.

[89] *Ramsay* v. *M.N.R.* (1954), 10 Tax A.B.C. 386 (T.A.B.); *Elliot* v. *M.N.R.*, [1971] Tax A.B.C. 175 (T.A.B.).

[90] [1967] Tax A.B.C. 761 (T.A.B.).

[91] *Cohen* v. *M.N.R.* (1963), 31 Tax A.B.C. 216 (T.A.B.).

[92] *Shulman* v. *M.N.R.*, [1961] C.T.C. 385, 61 D.T.C. 1213 (Ex. Ct.); affd. by S.C.C. without reasons.

The only effect of s. 67 is to disallow the deduction of an unreasonable expense to the extent that it is unreasonable. This has the effect of increasing the income of the payor. Section 67 says nothing however about the tax liability of the payee (recipient). The payee must recognize for tax purposes the full amount of the payment received. In the *Mulder* case, the wife would have to report as income her full $13,000 salary, even though $4,500 of it had been denied to the employer as a deduction. The unreasonable portion of the salary would therefore be taxed twice. On the other hand, B would only have to report his salary of $13,000, even though it had in effect been found to be artificially low.

capital expenditure: an outlay of funds for the acquisition or improvement of a fixed asset which extends the life or increases the productivity of the asset. The expenditure for the acquisition of an asset should be capitalized and depreciated over the estimated useful life of the asset

14

Income from Business or Property: Capital Expenditures

14.1 Definition of capital expenditures

(a)　Significance of "capital" classification

Paragraph 18(1)(b) prohibits the deduction from income of:

> an outlay, loss or replacement of capital, a payment on account of capital or an allowance in respect of depreciation, obsolescence or depletion except as expressly permitted by this Part;

The expenditures which are referred to in s. 18(1)(b) are expenditures which are made for a business purpose, but which are "capital" in nature. The classification of an expenditure as on account of capital means that it is not deductible in full in the year in which it was made. But it does not mean that the expenditure is not deductible at all. Paragraph 18(1)(b) prohibits the deduction of a capital expenditure "except as expressly permitted by this Part". And the Act does expressly permit the amortization over a period of years of most capital expenditures. As this chapter goes on to explain, the Act allows the deduction of "capital cost allowance" in recognition of the depreciation of most tangible property,[1] and the deduction of 7 per cent of three-quarters of "eligible capital expenditures" in recognition of the depreciation of most intangible property.[2] Only if a capital expenditure is not made to acquire depreciable property, and is not an eligible capital expenditure, is the deduction absolutely prohibited by s. 18(1)(b). There are only a few such expenditures; they are tax "nothings".[3] Of course, it is usually more favourable to the taxpayer for an expenditure to be classified as a current expense, for it can then be deducted immediately (or over a short period of years),[4] whereas a capital expenditure may only be deducted over a period of years in strict compliance with the rules governing depreciable property and eligible capital expenditures.

(b)　Enduring benefit test

There are many cases in which the courts have had to determine whether or not a particular expenditure is on account of capital. While a variety of definitions of "capital" have been offered,[5] most of the cases have used the

---

[1] Section 14.2, "Depreciable property", below.

[2] Section 14.3, "Eligible capital expenditures", below.

[3] Section 14.4(f), "Nothings", below.

[4] Section 14.1(c), "Prepaid expenses", below.

[5] See Brooks in Hansen, Krishna, Rendall (eds.), *Canadian Taxation* (1981), 206-223.

"enduring benefit" test. The test was formulated by Viscount Cave L.C. in *British Insulated and Helsby Cables* v. *Atherton* (1926)[6]:

> But, when an expenditure is made, not only once and for all, but with a view to bringing into existence an asset or an advantage for the enduring benefit of a trade, I think there is very good reason (in the absence of special circumstances leading to an opposite conclusion) for treating such an expenditure as properly attributable not to revenue but to capital.

The expenditure in issue in *British Insulated* was a large lump sum paid by a company to provide the initial funding to establish a new pension scheme for its employees. The House of Lords held that this payment could not be deducted in full from current revenue as the company claimed. The benefit of the payment would last for many years beyond the current year, because it would "obtain for the company the substantial and lasting advantage of being in a position throughout its business life to secure and retain the services of a contented and efficient staff". It followed that the expenditure had brought into existence "an asset or an advantage for the enduring benefit of a trade". The expenditure was therefore a capital one.

The "enduring benefit" test asks the right question. If an expenditure is made to produce a benefit to the business that will last beyond the current taxation year, then it should not be deducted in full in the current year. That would understate the income for the current year. The accounting theory which requires that expenditures be matched against the revenues which they help to produce is designed to yield accurate annual statements of net income. The tax system should pursue exactly the same objective. An accurate determination of net income is the best measure of ability to pay.

Both accounting and tax policy would agree that expenditures that produce an enduring benefit to the business should not be immediately deductible in full. The corollary of this proposition is that such expenditures should be amortized over the period for which they do confer a benefit on the business. The accountant accomplishes this by deducting from each year's income the portion of the expense which was used up in that year, and deferring the unused portion of the expenditure by carrying it on the balance sheet as an asset to be written off in future years.[7] The tax system should permit exactly the same procedure to be used for tax purposes. For the most part, as we shall see in the discussion of capital cost allowance, it does so, although it closely regulates the maximum annual write-off. But we shall also see that some capital expenditures, those which are outside the capital cost allowance provisions, were not deductible at all before 1972 (even if an accountant would have amortized them over a period of years); they were tax "nothings". The 1971 Act introduced the concept of eligible capital expenditures, which includes most of the former "nothings", and

[6] [1926] A.C. 205, 213 (H.L.).

[7] Chapter 11, Income from Business or Property: Profit, under heading 11.6(d), "Accounting for capital assets", above.

the Act makes provision for their amortization. But only three-quarters of the eligible capital expenditures may be amortized, and then over a long period of time — 7 per cent by the declining-balance method, which is approximately a 30-year amortization.

(c)   Prepaid expenses

It is not helpful to think of a capital expenditure as the acquisition of an asset. This is true, but it is not helpful because any prepaid expense creates an asset, although the asset may be short-lived. If a tenant (who is a business proprietor) pays one month's rent in advance for business premises, the tenant acquires an asset, namely, the right to occupy the rented premises for one month. Yet the rent is obviously an expense that is fully deductible from income under the accrual method of accounting and for tax purposes under s. 9. If the tenant pays two years' rent in advance, then the tenant acquires a similar asset, namely, the right to occupy the rented premises for two years. However, as we have seen, under the accrual method of accounting,[8] the full two years' rent would not be deductible from income in the year of payment. The portion of the rent which applies to the current accounting year would be recognized as an expense of that year. The unused balance of the expenditure would be recognized as an expense of the following year. This is accomplished by the accounting procedure of deferral. At the end of the first year, the unused part of the prepaid rent will be deferred (held back) and will appear on the tenant's balance sheet as an asset. The difference in accounting treatment between the prepayment of one month's rent and the prepayment of two years' rent is that the benefit of the one month's rent will be wholly used up in the current accounting period, while the benefit of the two years' rent will extend beyond the current accounting period.

The "enduring benefit" test identifies capital expenditures as those which confer an enduring benefit on the business. But how long is enduring? An extreme position would be that any expenditure which confers a benefit lasting (however briefly) beyond the current taxation year is a "capital" expenditure. But the consequence of this definition would be that s. 18(1)(b) would prohibit the deduction of every prepaid expense, except in accordance with the rules governing depreciable property and eligible capital expenditures. The courts have not accepted this position. On the contrary, what the courts have decided is that some prepaid expenses may be amortized over the period to which they relate in accordance with the generally accepted accounting procedure of deferral.

In *M.N.R.* v. *Tower Investment* (1972),[9] the taxpayer sought to defer and deduct over a three-year period the cost of an advertising campaign. The purpose of the advertising campaign was to find tenants for 24 apartment buildings built

---

[8] *Id.*, under heading 11.6(c), "Accrual method", above.

[9] [1972] C.T.C. 182, 72 D.T.C. 6161 (F.C.T.D.).

by the taxpayer. The taxpayer in its own accounts only deducted a small portion of the advertising expenditure in year 1 when rental income was low and wrote off the rest of the expenditure in years 2 and 3 when the apartments were fully rented. The taxpayer sought to treat the expenditure in the same way for tax purposes. The Minister took the position that the process of deferral was not authorized by s. 18(1)(a), and that the entire expenditure had to be deducted from income for tax purposes in year 1 — the year in which it was actually incurred. The Federal Court agreed with the taxpayer that the advertising expenditures were "not current expenditures in the normal sense" because they had been "laid out to bring in income not only for the year they were made but for future years". The Court held that since the deductions had been made in accordance with generally accepted accounting principles they were allowed under what is now s. 18(1)(a).

In *Tower*, the Minister argued that the advertising expenditures had to be deducted in the year in which they were made, and the taxpayer argued that they should be spread over several years. In most cases, of course, the taxpayer will prefer an immediate deduction for tax purposes of costs which have been deferred for accounting purposes. One would expect Revenue Canada to turn the loss in *Tower* to its own advantage and require taxpayers to defer prepaid expenses, at least where that is in accordance with their accounting treatment. The Department did do this in *Neonex International* v. *The Queen* (1978),[10] where the taxpayer had claimed for tax purposes the immediate deduction of expenditures incurred in the manufacture of signs which were sold in a future accounting period. The taxpayer had deferred the expenditures for accounting purposes. The disallowance of the deduction was upheld by the Federal Court of Appeal, Urie J. commenting that the taxpayer's profit "would not be portrayed fairly or accurately if it were permitted to adopt this method [immediate deduction] for tax purposes".

Neither in *Tower* nor in *Neonex* did the Minister argue that the prepaid expenses were on account of capital and therefore prohibited from deduction under s. 18(1)(b). The two courts therefore did not address that issue. Yet the decisions effectively establish a middle ground between expenses which are currently deductible, on the one hand, and capital expenditures, on the other hand. The expenditures in *Tower* and *Neonex* conferred benefits which lasted beyond the current accounting period; yet the benefit did not last for so long a time as to constitute an "enduring benefit". Other examples would be rent or municipal taxes paid in advance of the period to which they relate, insurance premiums on multi-year policies, and expenditures on promotional material (catalogues, brochures, etc.) to be used in a future year. Deferral is the only way in which these expenditures can be matched with the revenue to which they

---

[10] [1978] C.T.C. 485, 78 D.T.C. 6339 (F.C.A.).

relate, and it should obviously be used for tax purposes as well as for accounting purposes.

In 1981, the Income Tax Act was amended by the enactment of s. 18(9), which expressly stipulates that certain categories of prepaid expenses must not be deducted in full in the year of payment, and must be deducted in the years to which they relate. The stipulated categories of prepaid expenses are payments for future services, interest, taxes, rent, royalties and insurance. It is not clear why s. 18(9) is limited to those categories of prepayments. The Department takes the view that s. 18(9) was "enacted for greater certainty", and, although it does not cover all categories of prepaid expenses, there is a general requirement that "all costs that could clearly be related to future periods be expensed in those periods, if they are material and if failure to defer the expense would distort the net profit not only of the year during which the expense was incurred but also of the subsequent year or years to which the benefit relates".[11] In other words, the Department now assesses on the basis that there is a general rule requiring that all prepaid expenses (whether or not covered by s. 18(9)) be deferred and deducted "in accordance with the matching principle as required in generally accepted accounting principles".[12]

The position now seems to be well established that where an expenditure provides a benefit extending beyond the current accounting period, but not for a very long period, the timing of its recognition is governed by generally accepted accounting principles without running into the prohibition of s. 18(1)(b). Where the benefit would extend for a long period, it is an "enduring" benefit, which makes the expenditure on account of "capital". In that case, s. 18(1)(b) will apply, and the expenditure will be deductible only in accordance with the rules respecting depreciable property or eligible capital expenditures, and only if those rules are applicable. (The rules are discussed later in this chapter.) The distinction between capital and other expenditures is, as the Carter Commission commented,[13] "one of timing and not of any inherent quality". The Carter Commission would have dropped the use of the term capital altogether, but it is unfortunately still with us.

(d)   Running expenses

An expenditure that confers a benefit on a business that will last beyond the current accounting period has sometimes been allowed as a full deduction in the year of the expenditure on the basis that it is a "running expense". The courts have said that the matching principle does not apply to the "running expense of the business as a whole even though the deduction of a particularly heavy item

---

[11] Interpretation Bulletin IT-417R, "Prepaid expenses and deferred charges" (1982), para. 3.

[12] *Id.*, para. 2.

[13] *Report of the Royal Commission on Taxation* (Carter Report) (1966), vol. 4, 249.

of running expense in the year in which it is paid will distort the income for that particular year".[14] Stated simply, the "running expenses" of a business are deductible in the year they are incurred.

The term "running expense" is not an accounting term: it is an invention of Anglo-Canadian income tax law. In *Vallambrosa Rubber Co.* v. *Farmer* (1910),[15] the court used a milk and cow analogy to describe "running expenses" and to explain why they should be fully deductible: "Supposing a man conducted a milk business, it really comes to the limits of absurdity to suppose that he would not be allowed to charge for the keep of one of his cows because at a particular time of the year, towards the end of the year of assessment, that cow was not in milk, and therefore the profit which he was going to get from the cow would be outside the year of assessment . . .".[16] In *Naval Colliery Co.* v. *Commissioners of Inland Revenue* (1928),[17] Rowlatt J. defined a "running expense" as an "expenditure incurred on the running of the business as a whole in each year".[18] In *Oxford Shopping Centres* v. *The Queen* (1979),[19] Thurlow A.C.J. referred to a running expense as an "expense that is not referable or related to any particular item of revenue".[20] On the basis of these cases, "running expenses" can be defined as expenses which are not "related to any particular item of revenue" but relate to "the running of the business as a whole".

In *Oxford Shopping Centres*, the taxpayer-developer paid a municipality $490,050 for improvements to roadways near one of the taxpayer's shopping centres. The taxpayer deducted that amount in full in computing its income for tax purposes for 1973, but deferred the amount and amortized it over 15 years for accounting purposes. The first line of argument of the Minister was that the expenditure was on account of capital. The second line of argument was that the expenditure, if current, had to be deferred and amortized. In deciding in favour of the taxpayer, the Federal Court of Appeal held that the expenditure was not on account of capital and that, because the amount was a running expense that "is not referable or related to any particular item of revenue",[21] it could be deducted in full in 1973.

---

[14] *Oxford Shopping Centres* v. *The Queen*, [1981] C.T.C. 128, 81 D.T.C. 5065 (F.C.A.); affd without written reasons [1980] C.T.C. 7, 18, 79 D.T.C. 5458, 5466 (F.C.T.D.).

[15] (1910), 5 T.C. 529 (Sess. Ct.).

[16] *Id.*, 535.

[17] (1928), 12 T.C. 1017 (HL).

[18] *Id.*, 1027.

[19] Note 14, above.

[20] *Id.*, 18; 5466-5467.

[21] *Ibid.*

In *Canderel* v. *M.N.R.* (1995),[22] a tenant inducement payment was held not to be a "running expense". The taxpayer was in the business of managing and developing commercial real estate properties and, in 1986, had paid a tenant the amount of $1,208,369 as an inducement to enter into a lease. The taxpayer deducted the full amount of this payment in computing its income for tax purposes for 1986. The Minister disallowed the amount and recomputed the deduction as $69,274 by amortizing the payment over the initial term of the related lease. In deciding in favour of the Minister, the Federal Court of Appeal held that the tenant inducement payment was not a "running expense" of the taxpayer's business because of the direct contractual relationship between the payment and a specific stream of rental income to be earned over a future period. The correct treatment for tax purposes (as well as accounting purposes) was to amortize the payment over the term of the lease that would yield the stream of related income.

The decision in *Canderel* reaffirms the legal principle that the "running expenses" of a business are fully deductible, but it illustrates how difficult it is to determine whether or not an expenditure is a "running expense". The question is whether the expenditure relates to the taxpayer's business as a whole or to a particular revenue stream. If it can be matched with a specific source of revenue, then it must be amortized over the period during which the revenue is received.[23] The case of tenant inducement payments seems clear-cut, because each payment relates to a specific lease and can therefore be matched with a particular revenue stream. However, some payments may have wider implications than simply inducing the signing of a particular lease. They may be used as a form of advertising to attract other tenants to the landlord's properties, in which case it would be arguable that they were running expenses.[24]

(e)   Recurring expenditures

It has been suggested, although not as a conclusive test, that a "capital expenditure is a thing that is going to be spent once and for all, and an income expenditure is a thing that is going to recur every year".[25] This theory that a capital expenditure is made "once and for all" is perhaps true for some small businesses, but a large business will purchase new capital assets every year. The

---

[22] [1995] 2 C.T.C. 22, 95 D.T.C. 7, 5101 (F.C.A.).

[23] See also *The Queen* v. *Toronto College Park*, [1996] 3 C.T.C. 94, 96 D.T.C. 6407 (F.C.A.), in which *Canderal* was followed; Robertson J. said (at 101, 6411) that generally accepted accounting principles were not relevant to the decision. See also text accompanying note 34 in ch. 11, Income from Business or Property: Profit under heading 11.4 "Profit and Accounting Principles", above.

[24] See Carr, "Lease Inducement Payments" [1993] *Can. Tax Foundation Conf. Rep.* 32:26-35; Thomas, "The Matching Principle: Legal Principle or a Concept?", (1996) 44 *Can. Tax J.* 1693, 1698 (where the decisions in *Toronto College Park* and *Canderel* are discussed).

[25] *Ounsworth* v. *Vickers*, [1915] 3 K.B. 267, 273.

expenditures laid out to purchase new machines, trucks, etc., are recurring, but they are capital expenditures because each provides an enduring benefit to the business. On the other side of the coin, a current expenditure, which provides a benefit to the business which is exhausted in the current year, could be of an unusual or non-recurring kind, for example, a severance payment on the dismissal of a senior employee.

Nevertheless, in businesses where a particular kind of expenditure regularly recurs, and there is no risk of serious income distortion, the regular recurrence will usually justify treating the expenditures as current. Many businesses treat the purchase of books or tools as current expenses, even though the books or tools provide a value to the business which lasts for several years. For accounting purposes this is justified, since the recurring expenditures are not large in relation to the size of the business, are similar each year, and are not markedly different from the depreciation charges which would be available if the books and tools were treated as capital assets and depreciated. Of course, the latter treatment would also be acceptable for accounting purposes, although it involves a lot more work.

[handwritten margin note: ie fully deductible in year expense incurred]

There is no reason why relatively small recurring expenditures which are currently deductible for accounting purposes should not also be currently deductible for tax purposes. This has been accepted by the Privy Council in a tax appeal from Australia;[26] and it appears to be accepted in Canada by Revenue Canada.[27]

(f)   Repair of tangible assets

The relative size and recurrent character of an expenditure is also helpful in answering the question whether an expenditure on a capital (fixed) asset is properly regarded as the maintenance or repair of the existing asset, in which case it is currently deductible, or whether it is an improvement or addition to the asset, in which case it is a capital expenditure. Every business has to expend money regularly to repair or maintain damaged or worn equipment. Often the repair or maintenance will involve the purchase and installation of new parts, for example, a new window for a building or a new muffler for an automobile, and those parts have a life that is expected to last long beyond the current accounting period. Yet no one would doubt that the cost of the window or the muffler should be treated as a currently deductible expense. The cost is small in relation to the asset being repaired, the cost is of a kind that will regularly recur, and its purpose is simply to restore the original asset to its normal operating capacity. However, where the cost is large in relation to the asset being repaired (or

---

[26] *B.P. Australia* v. *Commr. of Taxation*, [1966] A.C. 224 (P.C.); but see the criticism by Brooks, note 5, above, 211.

[27] Brooks, note 5, above, 209.

improved), where it is not of a kind that will regularly recur, and where the purpose is to improve the quality of the asset substantially beyond its original condition, then the cost will be treated as a capital expenditure.[28]

In *Earl* v. *M.N.R.* (1993),[29] the taxpayer had spent $33,039 on the purchase of a new roof for a commercial rental property. In reporting her income for tax purposes for the year, the taxpayer claimed the entire amount as an expense of the year in which it was incurred. The Minister disagreed, arguing that the amount was a capital expenditure. The Tax Court of Canada agreed with the Minister's assessment, and found that "the new pitched roof created an improvement to the building of an enduring nature and was different in kind from the old flat roof".[30] The Court concluded that the expense was a capital expenditure rather than a current expense.

The difficulty in drawing the line when the various considerations do not all point in the same direction is illustrated by a comparison between *Canada Steamship Lines* v. *M.N.R.* (1966)[31] and *Shabro Investments* v. *The Queen* (1979).[32] In the *Canada Steamship* case, the taxpayer had replaced the floors and walls of the cargo-carrying holds in its ships. The expenditures involved were substantial in relation to the value of the ships and in relation to the repair-experience of previous years. On the other hand, the work was necessitated by normal wear and tear (so that it was recurrent in one sense), and the new floors and walls did no more than restore the holds of the ships to full operating capacity (so that there was no substantial improvement or addition to the ships). The Exchequer Court held that the expenditures were current expenses.[33]

In the *Shabro Investments* case, the issue concerned the replacement of a concrete floor in a commercial building. The original floor had consisted of concrete slabs reinforced by wire mesh laid directly on land fill; the floor broke when the underlying ground subsided. The taxpayer spent $95,000 in 1973 in removing the broken floor, in driving new piles to properly support the new floor, and in pouring a new reinforced concrete floor supported by the new piles. The result of all this effort was simply to provide a ground floor that was suitable for its intended use, and to restore the building to normal operating condition. On the other hand, the expense was substantial and unlikely to recur,

---

[28] See generally IT-128R, "Capital cost allowance — depreciable property" (1985), para. 4; Brooks, note 5, above, 216-220.

[29] [1993] 1 C.T.C. 2081, 93 D.T.C. 65 (T.C.C.).

[30] *Id.*, 2087; 68.

[31] [1966] C.T.C. 255, 66 D.T.C. 5205 (Ex. Ct.).

[32] [1979] C.T.C. 125, 79 D.T.C. 5104 (F.C.A.).

[33] However, on another issue, the cost of replacing boilers on one of the steamships, the Court treated the expenditure as capital: the new boilers were of a different and superior kind than those they were purchased to replace.

and the new floor was an improvement in quality over its inadequate predecessor. The Federal Court of Appeal held that the expenditure was capital.

(g)   Protection of intangible assets

In the leading case of *Canada Starch Co.* v. *M.N.R.* (1968),[34] the Court said that an expenditure on account of capital contributes to the "business entity, structure, or organization", whereas an expenditure on account of revenue contributes to the "process" of earning income. The case involved a payment made by Canada Starch to a competitor to settle a dispute about Canada Starch's right to use a particular trade mark. As a result of the settlement the competitor withdrew its opposition to the use of the trade mark. The Court held that the settlement payment by Canada Starch was a current expenditure because it related to "process" rather than the "business entity, structure, or organization". This distinction has been applied in other cases as well,[35] but it is very difficult to understand. Perhaps it is an obscure way of saying that capital expenditures have a longer period of usefulness to the business than current expenditures. In *Canada Starch*, the Court went on to apply the "enduring benefit" test as well to reinforce its conclusion. If the two tests are the same, then the enduring benefit test surely employs the clearer and more appropriate language.

The decision in *Canada Starch* was that the cost of settling the trade mark dispute was not a capital expenditure. A similar decision was reached in *Kellogg Co. of Canada* v. *M.N.R.* (1943),[36] where the cost of litigating a dispute about Kellogg's right to use the name "Shredded Wheat" was held not to be a capital expenditure. These cases have been defended on the basis that "expenses made to preserve capital assets should be deductible as current expenses".[37] There is an implicit analogy to the repair of a tangible asset.[38] But, while the litigation in *Canada Starch* and *Kellogg* did have the effect of protecting an asset (an intangible asset), it did not simply restore the situation as it existed before the litigation. The effect of the litigation was to remove a cloud on the taxpayer's title to use a particular business mark or name. The removal of that cloud improved the quality of the taxpayer's title. The removal of that cloud conferred a benefit on the business which would last long after the end of the current accounting period. In addition, and again unlike the repair of tangible assets, the expenditures in *Canada Starch* and *Kellogg* were made "once and for all" and were unlikely to recur.

---

[34] [1968] C.T.C. 466, 69 D.T.C. 5320 (Ex. Ct.).

[35] Brooks, note 5, above, 215-216.

[36] [1943] C.T.C. 1, 2 D.T.C. 601 (S.C.C.).

[37] Brooks, note 5, above, 221.

[38] Section 14.1(f), "Repair of tangible assets", above.

Canada Starch and *Kellogg* are also hard to reconcile with *M.N.R.* v. *Dominion Natural Gas Co.* (1940),[39] where the legal costs of defending a challenge to Dominion Natural Gas's licence to supply gas to a particular locality were held to confer an enduring benefit and therefore to be capital expenditures. In our opinion, the case was rightly decided.[40] After the litigation, the taxpayer had a less vulnerable, more valuable licence than it had ever had before. That is an enduring benefit. *if lost case, then no enduring benefit on a legal expenses treated as current*

The effect of the decisions in *Canada Starch* and *Kellogg* was to permit the expenditures in question to be wholly deducted in the year in which they were incurred. It is possible that the Courts' reluctance to hold that the expenditures were capital in nature was related to the fact that if the expenditures were capital they could not be deducted at all. This was the position before 1972, because at that time most capital expenditures for intangibles were "nothings". The harshness of this result may well have influenced courts to lean in favour of treating expenditures for intangibles as current expenses.[41] The 1971 Act eliminated most of the former nothings by treating most capital expenditures for intangibles as "eligible capital expenditures", three-quarters of which are "eligible capital property" which may be amortized under rules similar to the capital cost allowance rules.[42] The expenditures in *Canada Starch* and *Kellogg*, if classified as capital expenditures, would now be deductible as eligible capital expenditures. Admittedly, eligible capital expenditures are only three-quarters deductible, and then only at the rate of 7 per cent (of the declining balance), but it is submitted that the present Act's explicit recognition of capital expenditures for intangibles makes any pre-1972 judicial propensity in favour of classifying intangibles as current expenses no longer appropriate.

(h)　Business purpose

The question of whether an expenditure is capital or not must not be confused with the question of whether an expenditure has been made for the purpose of earning income from a business or property. The latter question is logically prior to the former. An expenditure which lacks an income-producing purpose (such as a personal consumption expenditure) is not deductible for that reason, and it is never necessary to decide whether it is capital or current. A capital expenditure in the present context is invariably an expenditure which is made for an income-producing purpose. It differs from a current expense only in respect of the timing of the benefit: the benefit of the capital expenditure will

---

[39] [1940-41] C.T.C. 155, 1 D.T.C. 499-133 (S.C.C.).

[40] Contra, Brooks, note 5, above, 221.

[41] See also *Algoma Central Ry.* v. *M.N.R.*, [1968] C.T.C. 161, 68 D.T.C. 5096 (S.C.C.), where the cost of a survey designed to encourage the future development of the area served by the Algoma Central Railway was held to be currently deductible.

[42] Section 14.3, "Eligible capital expenditures", below.

continue for a substantial period of time, whereas the benefit of the current expense will not last beyond the current accounting period.[43]

14.2 Depreciable property

(a)   Definition of depreciable property

It will be recalled that s. 18(1)(b) prohibits the deduction from business or property income of "capital" expenditures "except as expressly permitted by this Part". Paragraph 20(1)(a) goes on to expressly permit the deduction from business or property income of:

> such part of the capital cost to the taxpayer of property, or such amount in respect of the capital cost to the taxpayer of property, if any, as is allowed by regulation;

Paragraph 20(1)(a) authorizes regulations permitting the deduction from income of "capital cost allowance", which is the Income Tax Act's term for depreciation. The property in respect of which capital cost allowance may be claimed is called "depreciable property".

"Depreciable property" is defined in s. 13(21) of the Act. Subsection 13(21) provides that "depreciable property" means any property of the taxpayer in respect of which a deduction under s. 20(1)(a) is allowed. The deduction under s. 20(1)(a) is provided for by Part XI of the Income Tax Regulations, which describes the deduction as a "capital cost allowance". Regulation 1100(1) permits a taxpayer to deduct a capital cost allowance in respect of property comprised in any of 46 prescribed classes,[44] each of which is allocated a particular rate of capital cost allowance. Property that was not acquired for the purpose of gaining or producing income is excluded from the prescribed classes (reg. 1102(1)(c)).[45]

---

[43] As to expenditures which will benefit short periods beyond the accounting period, see sec. 14.1(c), "Prepaid expenses", above.

[44] That is, Class 1 to Class 44, including Class 10.1 and proposed Class 43.1.

[45] In advance income tax rulings, Revenue Canada has considered property to be depreciable property in situations where it held for the purpose of gaining or producing income for periods as short as two months. See Sinclair, "Intra-Group Loss Utilization" in "Current Tax Issues" [1996] *Can. Tax. Conf. Rep.*1 (forthcoming). *Hickman Motors* v. *The Queen*, [1995] 2 C.T.C. 320, 95 D.T.C. 5575 (F.C.A.) is an interesting recent case which deals with the interaction of reg. 1102(1)(c) and the rules which apply on the winding-up of a subsidiary into a parent (under s. 88(1)). The case concerns a 1984 capital cost allowance claim on property acquired on a winding-up on December 28, 1984, held at the parent company's year end of December 31, 1984 and disposed of on January 2, 1985. The Federal Court of Appeal, relying on its decision in *Mara Properties Ltd.* v. *Canada* (which has since been reversed by the Supreme Court) found that the property was not depreciable property (because of reg. 1102(1)(c)) and concluded that s. 88(1) did not result in depreciable property of a subsidiary becoming depreciable property of a parent (thus creating an independent right to capital cost allowance). Application for leave to appeal to the Supreme Court has been granted and it is not at all clear what the result will be when the case is heard by the Supreme Court since, in its decision *R.* v. *Mara Properties Ltd.*, [1996] 2 S.C.R. 161, [1996] 2 C.T.C. 54, 96 D.T.C. 6309 (S.C.C.), the Supreme Court found that s. 88(1) resulted in inventory of a subsidiary retaining its character as inventory in the hands of the parent (which allowed the parent company a full loss on land sold shortly after it was acquired).

Schedule II of the Regulations lists the contents of each class. It is the property listed in all the classes of Schedule II which comprises "depreciable property". The classes for some of the more common types of depreciable property are as follows:

Class 1:   buildings, including component parts, such as air-conditioning
(4%)   equipment, heating equipment and elevators;

Class 8:   tangible capital property that is not included in another class
(20%)   (e.g., furniture);

Class 10:   computer hardware, automotive equipment (including
(30%)   automobiles costing $25,000 or less) and films;

Class 10.1:   automobiles costing more than $25,000;
(30%)

Class 12:   computer software, videos, and tools costing less than $200;
(100%)   and

Class 43:   manufacturing and processing equipment.
(30%)

Class 8 (20 per cent) is a catch-all that includes "a tangible capital property that is not included in another class". The classes of Schedule II therefore include the costs of nearly all tangible property which was acquired "for the purpose of gaining or producing income" (reg. 1102(1)(c)), but was not deductible in the year it was paid because it was a "capital" expenditure (reg. 1102(1)(a)).

Inventory is excluded (reg. 1102(1)(b)), since the cost of inventory is not a capital expenditure and is accounted for by the normal accounting device of deferral.[46]

Land is also excluded (reg. 1102(2)), because, although the cost of land acquired for the purpose of gaining or producing income is a capital expenditure, land does not wear out and it is not appropriate to make any deduction for its depreciation. Since buildings are included, the capital cost allowance system requires the cost of developed land to be apportioned between land and building, with only the building portion eligible for capital cost allowance.

Section 68 requires a single purchase price to be allocated between different categories of property where that is relevant for tax purposes. The most

---

[46] Chapter 11, Income from Business or Property: Profit, under heading 11.6(e), "Accounting for inventory", above.

common case is land and building, since these are normally sold together.[47] Section 68 imposes a test of reasonableness on the allocation of values. The parties to a sale and purchase normally have adverse interests with respect to the allocation. The vendor would prefer a higher allocation to the land since any gain on the land is only three-quarters taxed as a capital gain, and a lower allocation to the building to minimize recapture of capital cost allowance. The purchaser would prefer a higher allocation to the building so as to maximize future capital cost allowance, and a lower allocation to the land so that future appreciation will be taxed as a capital gain. When the parties' interests are adverse, if they reach an agreement on the allocation of value, the agreement will usually be respected by Revenue Canada as a reasonable allocation in compliance with s. 68.[48] If Revenue Canada regards the agreement as unreasonable, or if there is no agreement, then Revenue Canada will make an allocation and assess accordingly. Either party can then use the process of objection and appeal to challenge the assessment and secure a court ruling as to the reasonable allocation.

Most intangible property is excluded from Schedule II of the Regulations and is therefore not eligible for the capital cost allowance deduction.[49] Expenditures for intangible property qualify instead as "eligible capital expenditures", three-quarters of which may be amortized under a system similar to the capital cost allowance system, which is described later.[50]

(b) Depreciation and capital cost allowance

"Capital cost allowance" is the Income Tax Act's term for depreciation. Since the proprietor of a business or property may well want to amortize his or her capital assets at a different rate or by a different method for accounting purposes than that permitted for tax purposes, it is convenient to use the term

---

[47] Another common case is the allocation of the purchase price of a business among the various categories of tangible property that are eligible for different rates of capital cost allowance and goodwill, which is an eligible capital expenditure (discussed under sec. 14.3, "Eligible capital expenditures", below).

[48] Paragraph 13(21.1)(a) will adjust this allocation if the proceeds of disposition allocated to the building is less than the undepreciated capital cost of the building, where, at the same time, the vendor is claiming a capital gain on the subjacent land. The purpose of this rule is to prevent the vendor from having a terminal loss on the building (which is deductible) while at the same time having a capital gain on the land (which is three-quarters taxable). Accordingly, the purchaser of the property is not affected.

[49] Intangible properties which do qualify as depreciable properties are listed in Class 14 ("patent, franchise, concession or licence for a limited period in respect of property") and Class 44 ("a patent, or a right to use patented information for a limited or unlimited period"). A Class 44 asset can be treated as a Class 14 asset (if it has a limited life) or as an eligible capital expenditure (if it has an unlimited life), if the taxpayer so elects. Since the Class 44 capital cost allowance rate is 25 per cent (declining-balance), which allows for a relatively fast write-off, it is usually advantageous to treat the asset as a Class 44 asset.

[50] Section 14.3, "Eligible capital expenditures", below.

capital cost allowance for the tax write-off, and depreciation for the accounting write-off.

Depreciation is the accounting device by which the costs of long-term assets are spread over several years. If one considers the example of a business firm paying ten years' rent in advance in one lump sum, it is obvious that only one-tenth of that sum should be recognized as having been used up each year, and that the unused balance should be regarded as an asset. More commonly, of course, a long-lived asset is acquired by purchase than by prepayment of rent, but the same basic analysis holds. The cost of buying a building with a life of ten years is like paying ten years' rent in advance. The total cost must be amortized over the period of the life of the building. The idea is to match the cost of the asset against the revenues which it helps to produce. The primary purpose of depreciation is to provide an accurate statement of profit or loss for each year's operations. The actual value of the asset may or may not diminish by the amount of depreciation charged to income each year.

(c) Straight-line depreciation

The simplest method of depreciation is the "straight-line" method, under which the cost of the asset is allocated evenly over the useful life of the asset. Thus, if a machine with a useful life of five years is acquired for $1,000, the business will deduct a depreciation expense of $200 each year for five years. The income statement will show a depreciation expense of $200. The balance sheet will show as the "net book value" of the machine the unused balance of the cost of the machine (waiting for use in future years).

Year	Unrecovered Cost (net book value)	Rate (% of cost)	Depreciation Expense
1	$ 1,000	20%	$ 200
2	$ 800	20%	$ 200
3	$ 600	20%	$ 200
4	$ 400	20%	$ 200
5	$ 200	20%	$ 200

At the end of year 5, the asset has been completely written off ($200 - $200 = $0), and it will disappear from the balance sheet. No further depreciation expense will be available in respect of that asset.

The straight-line method is the one which is most commonly used by public companies in Canada to calculate depreciation for accounting purposes.[51] However, the straight-line method is not permitted for the calculation of capital

---

[51] Private companies often use the capital cost allowance rates, which follow a declining-balance method (discussed in following text).

cost allowance under the Income Tax Act, except for specified classes of depreciable property[52] as well as depreciable property owned by fishermen and farmers.[53]

(d) Declining-balance depreciation

Another method of depreciation is the "declining-balance" method. The declining-balance method involves applying a uniform rate of depreciation to the unrecovered cost of the asset. Calculation of the appropriate rate is more difficult than with the straight-line method: normally about twice the straight-line rate would be used. Under the declining-balance method, the book value of an asset never reaches zero, reflecting perhaps the reality that there is usually some salvage value at the end of the asset's useful life. Assume again that in year one a business acquires a machine with a useful life of five years for a cost of $1,000, and now assume that the declining-balance method at a rate of 40 per cent is employed.

Year	Unrecovered Cost (net book value)	Rate (% of cost)	Depreciation Expense
1	$ 1,000	40%	$ 400
2	$ 600	40%	$ 240
3	$ 360	40%	$ 144
4	$ 216	40%	$ 86.40
5	$ 129.60	40%	$ 51.84

At the end of year 5, the asset has been written down to $77.76 ($129.60 − $51.84 = $77.76). The figure of $77.76 is the net book value which will appear in the balance sheet.

Under the declining-balance method, depreciation charges are heavier in the earlier years of an asset's life and decline progressively each year. A number of reasons can be advanced for this method. First, it recognizes the fact that assets are normally acquired in expectation of fairly early advantage, and it therefore seems prudent to write off their cost more rapidly in the early years when the anticipated economic benefits are more certain. Secondly, it recognizes the fact that maintenance charges for the asset are likely to increase as the asset gets older, and therefore depreciation charges should decline in order to even out the total annual expenses attributable to that asset. Thirdly, it recognizes the fact that a fall in value is likely to be greater in the early rather than the later years, and therefore more of the capital cost should be charged as an expense in the early years. This point also makes the book value of the asset in the balance

---

[52] Regs. 1100(1)(b), (c), (p), (q), (t), (v).
[53] Regs. 1700-1704.

sheet (cost less depreciation) more accurate, but this is not as important a factor as reflecting true expenses in the income statement. Despite these apparent advantages, the declining-balance method is less widely used for accounting purposes in Canada than the straight-line method. For tax purposes, however, it is the declining-balance method which the Income Tax Regulations insist upon for calculation of capital cost allowance in all except the exceptional cases mentioned earlier.

(e)   Discrepancy between capital cost allowance and depreciation

On the whole, the rates of capital cost allowance allowed by reg. 1100 are fairly generous, so that a taxpayer rarely has to write off an asset more slowly for tax purposes than for accounting purposes. Moreover, the declining-balance method produces high capital cost allowance deductions in the early years of an asset's life and thereby reduces tax in those years. No tax is actually avoided, because the high deductions of the early years will be offset by lower deductions in the later years. But some tax is postponed until the later years, and we have already noted that the postponement of tax is advantageous, leaving money which would otherwise have been paid in taxes available for use in the business. Another advantage of the Act's capital cost allowance system is that capital cost allowance need not be claimed in full, or at all, in a particular year, if it is advantageous to a taxpayer because of poor profits to defer until later years all or part of the deduction.

The liberality of the capital cost allowance system is no doubt designed to make a set of uniform and necessarily arbitrary rules as acceptable as possible. Without uniform rules for all taxpayers, the system would be difficult to administer, and it would give rise to the possibility of taxpayers in similar situations paying different amounts of tax. This was the situation before 1948, when the Act gave the Minister a discretion as to whether to allow a taxpayer's depreciation charges, and the Minister normally accepted the taxpayer's book depreciation. Since various different methods and rates were acceptable under generally accepted accounting principles, the same variety was accepted by the tax system. Uniform rules for income tax purposes were introduced into the Act in 1948, but with the restriction that taxpayers could not claim a capital cost allowance deduction for tax purposes that was greater than their book depreciation. In 1954, the restriction was lifted, so that the tax rules operated independently of a taxpayer's accounting practices.

Because of the liberality of the present system, it happens quite often that the capital cost allowance which is permitted by the Income Tax Regulations is more favourable to the taxpayer than the depreciation expense which the taxpayer deducts for accounting purposes. This will often be the case where the taxpayer uses the straight-line method of depreciation for accounting purposes. When the regulations' rate of capital cost allowance is about right for the asset in question, the initial capital cost allowance deducted on a declining-balance basis will be substantially greater than the depreciation charged on a straight-line basis for accounting purposes. In addition, the Act (or regulations) permits especially fast write-offs of some assets, where it is the policy of the government to provide taxation incentives to encourage certain kinds of investment or activity, for example, pollution abatement equipment and equipment used in scientific research and development in Canada.[54] A firm which is able to employ a fast write-off for tax purposes would of course normally do so as a means of postponing tax, but would employ a lower write-off for accounting purposes for the current year. As explained above, before 1954, corporate taxpayers could not claim capital cost allowances greater than the depreciation charges in their accounts, but this limitation was removed in 1954, inaugurating the current dual system.

(f)   Rental and leasing properties

The capital cost allowance permitted by the Act and regulations may give rise to a loss for tax purposes, although no loss has really been suffered. The capital cost allowance on an apartment building or office building, in particular, will provide substantial annual deductions to the owner, especially in the early years of the building's life, although the building may not be declining in value at all. If the capital cost allowance exceeded the net rental income from the property (before capital cost allowance), then a loss would be generated for tax purposes. Not only would the owner report no income from that property, the loss would be available to offset some of the owner's income from other sources as well.[55]

Regulation 1100(11) was adopted in 1972 to restrict the capital cost allowance that may be claimed on a "rental property".[56] A rental property is defined in reg. 1100(14) as a building used "principally for the purpose of gaining or producing gross revenue that is rent".[57] The effect of reg. 1100(11) is to limit the capital cost allowance which may be claimed on a rental property to a maximum of the rental income less all deductions other than capital cost allowance. This provision means that capital cost allowance on a rental property

---

[54] Equipment used for scientific research and development in Canada is not only fully deductible (s. 37(1)), it is eligible for an investment tax credit (s. 127(5)). Related expenses (e.g., salaries) receive the same treatment.

[55] Chapter 18, Losses, under heading 18.1, "Income losses", below.

[56] There is also a requirement that each rental property acquired for more than $50,000 be placed in a separate class (reg. 1101(1ac)). This prevents the sheltering of recapture of capital cost allowance on the disposition of the property: see sec. 14.2(m), "Recapture", below.

[57] The word "principally" is considered to mean more than 50 per cent, generally based on floor space: *Mother's Pizza Parlour* v. *The Queen*, [1988] 2 C.T.C. 197, 88 D.T.C. 6397 (F.C.A.). If the "principally" test is met, the entire building is classified as a rental property: *Canada Trust Co.* v. *M.N.R.*, [1985] 1 C.T.C. 2367, 85 D.T.C. 322 (T.C.C.).

can be deducted only to the point where the income from the property for tax purposes is reduced to zero; the capital cost allowance may not be used to create or increase losses which would shelter the owner's income from other sources.[58]

Similar restrictions apply to "leasing property" (reg. 1100(15)), which is moveable depreciable property used "principally for the purpose of gaining or producing gross revenue that is rent, royalty or leasing revenue" (reg. 1100(17)).[59] Examples would be construction equipment, boats or aircraft, which are rented out to users.

A subset of leasing property is "specified leasing property", which is leasing property worth more than $25,000, which is subject to additional restrictions (regs. 1100(1.1) to (1.3)). These restrictions were introduced in 1989 in response to a proliferation of sale-leaseback transactions by non-taxable entities, such as government agencies, municipal bodies, charities and corporations with large losses or loss carryforwards. A transit authority (for example) might own a fleet of buses upon which it would not be able to claim capital cost allowance, because the authority was tax-exempt. The transit authority would sell the buses to a taxable entity (the lessor), which could claim capital cost allowance on the buses, and which would lease the buses back to the transit authority. The authority would receive not only the purchase price of the buses, but also favourable rental rates as the lessor would pass on part of the tax savings generated by the lessor's capital cost allowance deduction on the buses. Both the lessor and the lessee (the transit authority) would be better off — at the expense of the Canadian taxpayer. This practice has now been blocked by deeming the sale-leaseback of "specified leasing property" to be a loan of the purchase price by the lessor to the lessee at Revenue Canada's prescribed interest rate (adjusted quarterly under reg. 4302), so that the rent received by the lessor is deemed to be a blended payment of interest and principal on the loan. The

---

[58] If the taxpayer owns more than one rental property, capital cost allowance on one rental property can be used to offset rental income on another rental property. This is because the income and losses for all rental properties (after deducting expenses but before claiming capital cost allowance) are added together in order to determine the limit for the overall capital cost allowance claim. For example, consider a taxpayer with two Class 1 buildings with an undepreciated capital cost of $40,000 each, the first with a rental profit of $1,000 before capital cost allowance and the second with a rental profit of $5,000 before capital cost allowance. The total capital cost allowance claim on the buildings is $3,200 — the lesser of $3,200 (4% capital cost allowance rate × 2 assets at $40,000 each) and $6,000. The capital cost allowance on the first building is not restricted to $1,000 because the taxpayer's overall rental profit is $6,000. However, if there were a rental loss of $5,000 on the second building (rather than a $5,000 profit), no capital cost allowance could be claimed on either building because there is a net rental loss of $4,000 on the two buildings.

[59] Corporations are exempt from the rental and leasing property restrictions if their "principal business" (accounting for 90 per cent of gross revenues) is the leasing, rental, development or sale of real property (reg. 1100(12), in the case of the rental property restriction) or the renting or leasing of leasing property (reg. 1100(16), in the case of the leasing property restriction).

lessor's capital cost allowance claim[60] is restricted to the amount of principal notionally repaid on the loan each year.[61]

Quite apart from the "specified leasing property" rules, a "lease" of property can sometimes be characterized as a sale of the property from the lessor to the lessee for debt consideration. Accountants call such a lease a "capital lease", and there are generally accepted accounting principles to identify a capital lease.[62] For tax purposes, the characteristic of a capital lease is that "the object of the transaction at its inception is to transfer the ownership in property from a lessor to a lessee".[63] This will be the case if the lessee will acquire title to the leased property at the term of the lease, or if there is a "bargain purchase option" allowing the lessee to acquire title at the term of the lease at a price below the expected fair market value of the property. A capital lease is characterized as a sale for tax purposes, which means that the lessee (purchaser) will deduct capital cost allowance (and deemed interest) rather than rent.

(g)   Retirement of depreciable property

What is the tax treatment of the retirement of a depreciable property? Consider the case of a business proprietor with one depreciable property. The asset may be sold before the end of its useful life, or it may have a salvage value at the end of its useful life. Either way, the owner receives some value for the asset, which the Act, in s. 13(21), describes as "proceeds of disposition".

If the proceeds of disposition exceed the undepreciated capital cost (book value for tax purposes) of the asset, then it is evident that too much capital cost allowance has been claimed in prior years. In order to correct the understatement of taxable income in prior years, the proceeds of disposition in excess of the asset's undepreciated capital cost should be added to income for the year in which the proceeds were received. The Act, by s. 13(1), accordingly requires that the amount of the excess must be added to income. This is known as the "recapture" of capital cost allowance.

If the proceeds of disposition of depreciable property exceed the original capital cost of the property (as opposed to the undepreciated capital cost) then obviously the full amount of capital cost allowance claimed over the prior years will be recaptured, but what about the amount by which the proceeds exceeds the

---

[60] There is also a requirement that each specified leasing property be placed in a separate class (reg. 1100(1.1)), as is the requirement for rental properties acquired for more than $50,000 (note 56, above).

[61] See, generally, Athanassakos and Klatt, "Lease or Buy? How Recent Tax Changes have affected the Decision" (1993) 41 *Can. Tax J.* 444.

[62] *CICA Handbook*, section 3065.

[63] Interpretation Bulletin IT-233R, "Lease-option agreements; Sale-leaseback agreements" (1983), para. 3.

original cost? There is no justification for including this latter figure in income from a business or property, because it has never provided a deduction from prior years' income. It is a capital gain. It is taxed, as we shall see, but on the more favourable basis accorded capital gains.[64] It is not recaptured under s. 13. Section 13 makes clear that the maximum sum that can be recaptured is the amount of the capital cost allowances that have been claimed in prior years. It accomplishes this result by providing that the amount of the recapture is calculated by subtracting from the undepreciated capital cost the lesser of the proceeds of disposition and the original capital cost (s. 13(21), definition of "undepreciated capital cost").

If the proceeds of disposition of a depreciable asset are less than the undepreciated capital cost of the asset, then it is evident that too little capital cost allowance has been claimed in prior years. Subsection 20(16) accordingly provides that where the proceeds of sale of depreciable property are less than the undepreciated capital cost of the property, the amount of the shortfall may be deducted from income. This is known as the deduction of a "terminal loss".

Consider the example of four depreciable properties, each acquired in 1992 for $100, each depreciated at different rates for tax purposes (because each was in a different class with no other assets in the class), and each disposed of in 1997 for various proceeds of disposition.

		Asset 1	Asset 2	Asset 3	Asset 4
1.	Cost in 1992	100	100	100	100
2.	Undepreciated capital cost before sale in 1997	40	50	60	70
3.	Proceeds of disposition	40	70	110	30
4.	Recapture of capital cost allowance	Nil	20	40	Nil
5.	Capital gain	Nil	Nil	10	Nil
6.	Terminal loss	Nil	Nil	Nil	40

Asset 1 yielded proceeds of disposition equal to its undepreciated capital cost, which showed that capital cost allowances had exactly matched the actual decline in value and that no recapture or terminal loss was required. Asset 2 yielded proceeds of disposition which exceeded its undepreciated capital cost by $20, requiring recognition of a recapture of that amount in income for 1997. Asset 3 yielded proceeds of disposition which exceeded the original capital cost of the asset by $10, requiring recognition of a capital gain of that amount (three-quarters taxable) and a recapture of $40 (all the capital cost allowance claimed) in income for 1997. Asset 4 yielded proceeds of disposition which were

[64] Only three-quarters of a capital gain must be reported as income: ch. 15, Capital Gains, below.

$40 less than undepreciated capital cost, showing that actual depreciation had exceeded the capital cost allowance claimed and requiring recognition of a terminal loss of $40.

(h) Class method of depreciation

So far we have considered the case of a business proprietor with one depreciable property. If he or she has a number of similar depreciable properties, then for accounting purposes he or she could either depreciate each property individually or depreciate all the properties as a single class (or pool or group). The Income Tax Act and regulations require that the "class method" of depreciation accounting be used for tax purposes.

The advantage of the class method for accounting purposes is that some assets may last longer than their estimated life while others may have to be retired prematurely. In a group of related assets, any under-depreciation on some assets will probably be balanced by over-depreciation on others. It is not even necessary that all assets in the class have the same estimated useful life, so long as a single rate can be established for the whole class which is about the average of the various estimated useful lives. (For tax purposes, of course, the rates are fixed by regulation.) Nor is it necessary that the assets in the class be purchased at the same time or for the same price. On the purchase of a new asset, its cost is added to the undepreciated capital cost of the class.

On the sale or retirement of an existing asset, the proceeds of its disposition (or its original capital cost, if that is less than the proceeds of disposition) are subtracted from the undepreciated capital cost (UCC) of the group. It is obvious that, when an asset is retired which is worth something, a subtraction has to be made from the group's UCC. The proprietor cannot continue to depreciate an asset that he or she no longer owns and uses. What is not so obvious is why it is the actual proceeds of disposition (up to the asset's original capital cost) that should be deducted from the group's UCC. Suppose an asset in the group is disposed of for precisely its individual UCC. Here the amount realized on disposition shows that the capital cost allowances claimed in prior years have been precisely right in respect of that particular asset. No adjustment is needed to make up for over- or under-depreciation. The proper subtraction is the proceeds of sale. If an asset is disposed of for more than its individual UCC, then its actual proceeds of disposition are subtracted from the group UCC, because that asset was over-depreciated and the over-depreciation can now be indirectly and gradually corrected by subtracting from the group's UCC not only the UCC of the individual asset retired but also the excess over UCC for which it was sold — but only up to original cost. The deduction from the group's UCC of the actual proceeds (up to original cost) will reduce the group's UCC by more than the UCC of the particular asset retired, and thereby diminish future capital cost allowance on the remaining assets in the group. If a depreciable asset is disposed of for less than its individual UCC, then that means that the asset was under-depreciated in prior years. The under-depreciation can now be indirectly and gradually corrected by subtracting from the group's UCC, not the full UCC of the asset, but only the actual proceeds of sale. In this way future capital cost allowances will be diminished by less than they would be if the full UCC of the asset retired were deducted from the group.

At any given time, the group's UCC will not necessarily be the sum of the UCCs of all the assets in the group, because the group's UCC will also reflect any gains and losses on the disposition of former assets of the group. This discrepancy between the group's UCC and the sum of the individual assets' UCCs is not a real concern, because the whole theory of the class method of depreciation is that gains and losses will roughly cancel each other out in the long run.

The interesting point to notice about the class method is that the gain or loss on the retirement of a particular asset is reflected in the group's UCC, but is not directly reflected in taxable income. If the disposition of a depreciable asset yields a gain over UCC, and if there are other assets of the same class with a combined (group) UCC sufficient to cover the gain, there is no recapture. There is, of course, an effect on future income in that future capital cost allowance will be reduced by the fact that the group's UCC has been reduced by more than the UCC of the asset retired, which in effect reduces the UCC of the remaining assets. These assets will now support capital cost allowance deductions in future years which are lower than the total of their individual UCCs would have permitted. But this is less severe for the taxpayer than would be the immediate recapture of the entire gain. Only when the group balance is completely wiped out by the subtraction of the proceeds of a disposition, and the balance becomes a negative figure, is there a recapture. So long as this does not occur, the tax liability on a gain is "sheltered" by the other assets in the group. This is an example of the deferral of an item of taxable income — and it is favourable to the taxpayer.[65]

By the same token, when an asset is sold for less than its undepreciated capital cost, then, so long as there is at least one asset remaining in the group, the taxpayer cannot claim a terminal loss against income. The subtraction of the proceeds of sale will simply have the effect of diminishing the group balance by less than the UCC of the asset retired, which in effect adds to the UCC of the remaining assets. These assets will now support higher capital cost allowances in future years than the total of their individual UCCs would have permitted, but this is not as favourable to the taxpayer as would be the immediate deduction of a terminal loss. This is an example of the deferral of a tax deduction — and it

---

[65] This deferral advantage, and the introduction in 1972 of the separate-class rule for rental properties costing $50,000 or more, is discussed under heading 14.2(m), "Recapture", below. There is also a separate class rule for Class 10.1 (automobiles costing more than $25,000): reg. 1101(1af).

is unfavourable to the taxpayer.[66] Only if all the assets of a particular class are disposed of, leaving a positive balance in the empty group's UCC, may a terminal loss be claimed.

(i) Capital cost allowance

It is now time to look at the mechanisms by which the Act and regulations accomplish the results which have so far been explained in very general terms.

Regulation 1100(1) stipulates the rate of capital cost allowance which may be deducted in respect of each class of depreciable property. The rate is applied to the "undepreciated capital cost" to the taxpayer "as of the end of the taxation year (before making any deduction under this subsection for the taxation year) of property of the class". This makes it clear that the declining-balance method must be employed ("undepreciated capital cost"); that the class method must be employed ("property of the class"); and that it is the undepreciated capital cost of the class at "the end of the taxation year" which provides the base from which the deduction is calculated (subject to the half-year rule, explained below).[67] Thus the general rule is that if the class has no undepreciated capital cost at the end of the year, then no capital cost allowance can be claimed for the class.[68]

(j) Undepreciated capital cost

"Undepreciated capital cost" is defined by s. 13(21), which provides (in part) as follows:

> "undepreciated capital cost" to a taxpayer of depreciable property of a prescribed class as of any time means the amount determined by the formula
>
> $(A + B + C + D) - (E + E.1 + F + G + H + I + J)$

---

[66] In response to this problem there is a separate-class rule for certain assets commonly purchased by business proprietors which often decline in value rapidly after a few years because of technological obsolescence (as well as wear and tear). This separate class rule allows taxpayers the choice of putting any photocopier (Class 8), facsimile (fax) machine (Class 8) or computer and systems software (Class 10) costing $1,000 or more into a separate class for capital cost allowance purposes (reg. 1101(5p)) rather than pooling it with other Class 8 or 10 assets. If a taxpayer chooses to use the separate-class rule, a full terminal loss can be deducted in the year of sale if the asset is sold for an amount which is less than its UCC within four years. If, after the fourth taxation year in which the asset is owned, it has not been sold, the asset is transferred back to the regular Class 8 or 10 at the beginning of year five (reg. 1103(2g)).

[67] Section 14.2(k), "Half-year rule", below.

[68] There is one exception to this general rule: Class 10.1, which is the class for automobiles costing more than $25,000 having a separate-class rule. In the case of Class 10.1, one-half of the capital cost allowance that would have been allowed in respect of the automobile, had it not been disposed of, may be claimed if the automobile was owned by the taxpayer and included in Class 10.1 at the end of the preceding year (reg. 1100(2.5)). Class 10.1 automobiles are also exempt from the recapture (s. 13(2)) and terminal loss (s. 20(16)) rules.

where

A   is the total of all amounts each of which is the capital cost to the taxpayer of a depreciable property of the class acquired before that time,

B   is the total of all amounts included in the taxpayer's income under this section for a taxation year ending before that time, to the extent that those amounts relate to depreciable property of the class . . .

[C and D are special cases.]

E   is the total depreciation allowed to the taxpayer for property of the class before that time,

[E.1 is a special case.]

F   is the total of all amounts each of which is an amount in respect of a disposition before that time of property . . . of the taxpayer of the class, and is the lesser of

    (a)   the proceeds of disposition of the property minus any outlays and expenses to the extent that they were made or incurred by the taxpayer for the purpose of making the disposition, and

    (b)   the capital cost to the taxpayer of the property,

[G, H, I and J are special cases.]

The definition of undepreciated capital cost (UCC) includes positive elements, namely, items A, B, C and D, which are those things to be added to the UCC of depreciable property of a prescribed class, and negative elements, namely, items E, E.1, F, G, H, I and J, which are those things to be subtracted from the UCC of the class.

The first positive element of UCC is item A, which requires that when depreciable property of a prescribed class is acquired the capital cost[69] of the property must be added to the UCC of the class.

The second positive element of UCC is item B. The function of item B is to bring the UCC back to zero after there has been a recapture. Suppose that at the end of year 1 there was a recapture, but there were still some assets remaining in the class. If in year 2 more depreciable property of that class were acquired, item B would wipe out the former negative balance of the UCC account so that the full capital cost of property acquired in year 2 is available for capital cost allowance at the end of year 2. (This will be clearer after the recapture rule, explained below,[70] has been understood.) (Items C and D are also positive elements added into UCC, but they deal with special cases outside the scope of this book.)

---

[69] The term capital cost generally means the "full cost to the taxpayer of acquiring the property", which will include not only the purchase price, but also legal, accounting, engineering and other fees incurred on the acquisition: Interpretation Bulletin IT-285R2, "Capital cost allowance — general comments" (1994), para. 8.

[70] Section 14.2(m), "Recapture", below.

The first negative element of UCC is item E. It makes the requirement — essential for a system which amortizes on the basis of declining-balance — that when capital cost allowances are deducted from income under s. 20(1)(a) they must also be subtracted from the UCC of the class.

The second negative element of UCC is item F. It requires that, when depreciable property of a prescribed class is disposed of, the proceeds of disposition up to a maximum of the capital cost of the property must be subtracted from the UCC of the class. If the property is disposed of for more than its capital cost, only the capital cost is subtracted from the class. As explained earlier, the gain over capital cost is left out of account in this subdivision of the Income Tax Act (subdivision b) because it is a capital gain, three-quarters taxable under the next subdivision (subdivision c). (The definition of undepreciated capital cost also includes four more negative elements, items G through J, which deal with special cases outside the scope of this book.)

(k) Half-year rule

We noticed earlier in this chapter that the capital cost allowance for each year is calculated as a percentage of the undepreciated capital cost "as of the end of the taxation year". Before 1981, when a depreciable property was acquired during the year — even close to the end of the year — the taxpayer was able to deduct the full amount of capital cost allowance in respect of the property, even though it had not been owned for the full year. In that case, of course, the taxpayer had not in fact suffered a full year of depreciation. In 1981, reg. 1100(2) introduced the "half-year rule", the effect of which is to deny to the taxpayer 50 per cent of the capital cost allowance that would otherwise be available in respect of a depreciable property acquired during the taxation year.[71]

The half-year rule still provides some tax advantage for the taxpayer who acquires a depreciable property after the half-way point of the year. The more accurate method would be to prorate the capital cost allowance according to the number of days in the year that the property was owned (and available for use).[72] This would present no special difficulty if each depreciable property were depreciated individually. As we have noticed, however, the Act and regulations require that capital cost allowance be calculated by the class method,

---

[71] Certain classes of depreciable property are exempted from the application of the half-year rule, either because they have their own version of the half-year rule, namely, Classes 13, 24, 27, 29 and 34, or because they have other special features, namely, Classes 12, 14, 15.

[72] This is what the regulations require when a taxpayer has a short taxation year (less than 365 days) (reg. 1100(3)). A short taxation year will occur in a variety of situations, for example, if a business is started or ended during a taxation year, or if an individual carrying on business dies, or if a corporation carrying on business is wound up, undergoes a change of control, or amalgamates with another company, or if a change of fiscal period is approved by the Minister.

and it would be quite complicated to arrange a system of prorating for the portion of the capital cost allowance attributable to those assets in the class that were acquired during the last taxation year. The half-year rule is easier to apply than a more refined rule would be. *– given class method of calculating the CCA*

Regulation 1100(2) applies only when a taxpayer acquired a depreciable property in the taxation year. In that case, the capital cost allowance for the year of acquisition is calculated on the basis of a notional UCC defined by reg. 1100(2), rather than the actual UCC. The notional UCC is derived by first calculating the actual UCC as of the end of the year (including the full capital cost of acquisitions), and then subtracting 50 per cent of the capital cost of acquisitions during the year. If depreciable property of the same class was disposed of in the year, then 50 per cent of the net figure (cost of acquisitions minus proceeds of dispositions up to capital cost) is subtracted from the UCC. (If the proceeds of dispositions exceeded the cost of acquisitions, then reg. 1100(2) does not apply; there must be a net increase in the UCC account for reg. 1100(2) to apply.) The notional UCC is used only to calculate capital cost allowance for the year of acquisition. The opening balance of the UCC for the next year is the actual UCC, that is, the UCC calculated with the total cost of acquisitions and proceeds of dispositions taken into account. Of course, the opening balance will be higher than it would have been if reg. 1100(2) did not exist, because the capital cost allowance for the previous year (which will have been subtracted from the UCC) was artificially reduced by the operation of reg. 1100(2).

notional UCC

Suppose at the beginning of 1997 T has a UCC account of $300 for T's class 8 assets. During 1997, T acquires another class 8 asset for $100. The UCC at the end of 1997 (before deducting capital cost allowance) is $400 ($300 + $100). Because of the acquisition in 1997, reg. 1100(2) applies, requiring the calculation of a notional UCC, which is $350 ($400 − 50% of $100). Capital cost allowance for 1997 is calculated on the basis of the notional figure of $350, yielding a capital cost allowance deduction (at the rate of 20 per cent for class 8) of $70 (20 per cent of $350). The calculation of the capital cost allowance for 1997 exhausts the usefulness of the notional UCC. The opening balance of the UCC account for the next year, 1998, will be the actual UCC, namely, $330 ($400 − $70).

example

(l)   Available for use

Another restriction against claiming capital cost allowance for recently acquired property is the "available for use" rule of s. 13(26). Subsection 13(26) provides that the cost of property purchased by a taxpayer may not be added to the UCC of a class until the property purchased becomes "available for use". Subsection 13(27) provides that property becomes available for use when "the property is first used by the taxpayer for the purpose of earning income".[73] The purpose of this rule is to prevent a taxpayer from claiming capital cost allowance on depreciable property that is not being used in the business, for example, machinery that had been bought but was still sitting in its packing case at the end of the taxation year.

(m) Recapture

Subsection 13(1) provides as follows:

> 13(1) Where, at the end of a taxation year, the total of the amounts determined for E to J in the definition "undepreciated capital cost" in subsection (21) in respect of a taxpayer's depreciable property of a particular prescribed class exceeds the total of the amounts determined for A to D in that definition in respect thereof, the excess shall be included in computing the taxpayer's income for the year.

When the negative elements of the definition of undepreciated capital cost in s. 13(21) exceed the positive elements, so that for a prescribed class of depreciable property there is a negative balance in the UCC account at the end of the taxation year, that negative balance must be included in income. A negative balance could only arise by dispositions of property in the class for proceeds which exceed the positive balance of the UCC of the class immediately before the dispositions.[74] As we noted earlier, when this occurs it means that the capital cost allowance that has been deducted in previous years has been greater than the actual decline in value of the property in the class. The recapture puts back into income the difference between the capital cost allowance that was previously claimed and the actual decline in the value of the property.

Subsection 13(1) only effects a recapture if the UCC account has a negative balance "at the end of a taxation year". This means that when a depreciable property is sold for more than the UCC of its class, the recapture will be avoided if another depreciable property of the same class costing more than the amount of recapture is acquired before the end of the taxation year. The new property will shelter the tax liability arising on the disposition of the old property, because, at the end of the taxation year, the UCC will show a positive balance and s. 13(1) will be inapplicable. In the case of "rental property" (buildings used to earn rental income),[75] the deferral of tax by this means has been deemed sufficiently important to warrant an exception to the normal class basis of capital cost allowances. Reg. 1101(1ac) provides that each rental

---

[73] This is the straightforward case. The definition of "available for use" in ss. 13(27), 13(28) and 13(29) is long and complicated and includes special rules for special kinds of property.

[74] Note that the amount deducted from the UCC of the class is the lesser of the proceeds of disposition and the capital cost of the property disposed: s. 13(21)F. Where the proceeds of disposition of a depreciable property exceed the capital cost of the property, the excess must be recognized as a capital gain (three-quarters taxable): see sec. 14.2(g), "Retirement of depreciable property", above.

[75] Section 14.2(f), "Rental and leasing properties", above.

property acquired after 1971 for more than $50,000 must be placed in a separate capital cost allowance class. This means that on the disposal of a rental property any recapture (or terminal loss) will have to be immediately recognized even if another rental property is owned or is acquired in the same year.

After a recapture has been recognized under s. 13(1), the negative balance in the UCC account rises to nil for the following year. This occurs because the second positive element of the UCC definition (item B of s. 13(21)) adds the amount of the recapture to the UCC.[76]

(n)   Terminal loss

Subsection 20(16) provides as follows:

> 20(16) Notwithstanding paragraphs 18(1)(a), (b) and (h), where at the end of a taxation year,
>
> (a)   the total of all amounts used to determine A to D in the definition "undepreciated capital cost" in subsection 13(21) in respect of a taxpayer's depreciable property of a particular class exceeds the total of all amounts used to determine E to J in that definition in respect of that property, and
>
> (b)   the taxpayer no longer owns any property of that class,
>
> in computing the taxpayer's income for the year
>
> (c)   there shall be deducted the amount of the excess determined under paragraph (a), and
>
> (d)   no amount shall be deducted for the year under paragraph (1)(a) in respect of property of that class
>
> and the amount of the excess determined under paragraph (a) shall be deemed to have been deducted under paragraph (1)(a) in computing the taxpayer's income for the year from a business or property.

When there is a positive balance in the undepreciated capital cost account of a class of depreciable property at the end of a taxation year, but no longer any property remaining in the class, then the entire positive balance in the class "shall be deducted" from income as a terminal loss. (The taxpayer must take the deduction; there is no discretion in the matter.) A terminal loss only arises if the taxpayer no longer owns any property of the class. If there were still some property in the class, then as long as the UCC is positive the taxpayer would take the regular capital cost allowance deductions allowed by s. 20(1)(a) and reg. 1100. It is only if all the property in the class has been disposed of, and there is still a positive balance remaining in the UCC of the class, that a terminal loss must be recognized. It is then evident that a loss has been incurred, because the proceeds of disposition of all the property in the class has failed to yield the full amount of the undepreciated capital cost of the property sold. As we noted earlier, when this occurs it means that the capital cost allowance taken in previous years has been less than the actual decline in the value of the property

---

[76] Section 14.2(j), "Undepreciated capital cost", above.

of the class. The terminal loss deduction takes out of income the difference between the capital cost allowance that was previously claimed and the actual decline in value of the property.

Subsection 20(16) (like s. 13(1)) is addressed to the situation "at the end of a taxation year". This means that if the conditions of s. 20(16) are satisfied at some time in a taxation year, but another depreciable property of the same class is acquired before the end of the year, then no terminal loss can be claimed. The ordinary capital cost allowance, consisting of the appropriate percentage of the balance in the UCC account, is all that can be deducted.

After a terminal loss has been deducted under s. 20(16), the balance in the UCC account falls to nil for the following year. This occurs because s. 20(16) deems the terminal loss to have been deducted under s. 20(1)(a), and this would cause it to be subtracted from the UCC by virtue of the first negative element of the UCC definition (item A of s. 13(21)).

Example

	UCC class 16 (40%)
Year 1	
T purchases two aircraft (his only class 16 assets) for use in his airline business at a cost of $100,000 each (s. 13(21)A).	$ 200,000
UCC at end of year 1	200,000
Capital cost allowance for year 1 (reg. 1100(1), Schedule II, class 16, 40%) based on notional UCC of $100,000 ($200,000 – 50% of $200,000): reg. 1100(2) (the half year rule).	(40,000)
Note that T may claim less than full capital cost allowance if he chooses (reg. 1100(1) "not exceeding"), and this choice might be made to minimize current losses or to utilize loss carryovers from earlier years.	
Year 2	
T purchases aircraft #3 for $20,000 (s. 13(21)A).	20,000
T sells aircraft #1 for $90,000 (s. 13(21)F(b)).	(90,000)
T sells aircraft #2 for $130,000 (i.e., $30,000 more than capital cost) (s. 13(21)F(a)).	(100,000)
Note that capital gain of $30,000 will have to be recognized on the sale of aircraft #2.	
UCC at end of year 2 (negative balance)	(10,000)
Recapture for year 2 (s. 13(1), s. 13(21)B)	10,000

Note that no capital cost allowance can be claimed for year 2.

Note that the half-year rule (reg. 1100(2)) has no application if no capital cost allowance can be claimed. Even if there were a positive balance in the UCC account for year 2, so that capital cost allowance could have been claimed, the half-year rule would still not apply because in year 2 the proceeds of dispositions exceeded the cost of acquisitions.

Year 3

T purchases aircraft #4 for $60,000 (s. 13(21)A).	60,000
Note that if this aircraft had been purchased in the previous year, it would have avoided the recapture in year 2.	
UCC at end of year 3	60,000
Capital cost allowance for year 3 (reg. 1100(1), Schedule II, class 16, 40%) based on notional UCC of $30,000 ($60,000 – 50% of $60,000): reg. 1100(2) (the half-year rule).	(12,000)

Year 4

T sells aircraft #3 and #4 for a total of $30,000 (s. 13(21)F(a)).	(30,000)
Note that T no longer owns any class 16 assets.	
UCC at end of year 4 (positive balance)	18,000
Terminal loss for year 4 (s. 20(16), s. 13(21)E)	(18,000)
	NIL

14.3 Eligible capital expenditures

It will be recalled that current expenses incurred for the purpose of gaining income from a business or property are deductible in computing "profit" for tax purposes, but "capital" expenditures incurred for the purpose of gaining income from a business or property are by s. 18(1)(b) not deductible, except as expressly permitted by the Act. Paragraph 20(1)(a) authorizes regulations permitting the deduction from income of capital cost allowance with respect to "depreciable property", but depreciable property, as listed in Schedule II of the Income Tax Regulations, consists primarily of tangible property such as buildings, machinery, and equipment. Land is not listed in Schedule II and is specifically excluded by reg. 1102(2). Some intangible property is listed in

Schedule II,[77] but most intangible property, and notably goodwill, is not listed in Schedule II and is therefore not "depreciable property".

Before 1972, capital expenditures which were not laid out to purchase depreciable property were not deductible at all. Expenditures of this kind, of which the most important was the cost of goodwill, came to be called "nothings". The Carter Commission proposed that the cost of purchased goodwill (and other intangible assets of more or less permanent life) should continue to be non-deductible for tax purposes, on the basis that goodwill, like land, generally does not depreciate.[78] Other classes of expenditures for intangibles which have a long-run but not permanent value to the business were to be listed and pooled in a new capital cost allowance class with a rate of 20 per cent. Any other costs of intangibles were to be deductible in full when incurred.

The government did not accept Carter's recommendations in detail, but it did ameliorate the treatment of "nothings". The 1971 Act provided for the amortization of most of the former nothings (including purchased goodwill) by the creation of a category of capital expenditures called "eligible capital expenditures". One-half of eligible capital expenditures were to be placed in a pool called "cumulative eligible capital" and amortized at a maximum rate of 10 per cent per annum by the declining-balance method.

As part of the tax reform of 1988, the Act was amended to increase the portion of an eligible capital expenditure that is added to the pool of cumulative eligible capital from one-half to three-quarters. At the same time, the rate at which the cumulative eligible capital could be written off each year was reduced from 10 per cent to 7 per cent, still on a declining-balance basis. The rate reduction nearly offsets the effect of the increase in the size of the pool, so that since 1988 annual deductions from cumulative eligible capital have become only slightly higher than they were before 1988 (e.g., for an eligible capital expenditure of $200, 10 per cent of $100 = $10; 7% of $150 = $10.50). The reason for the 1988 amendment was to mirror the increase in the inclusion rate of capital gains from one-half to three-quarters, which was also part of the tax reform of 1988. The idea was that any "recapture" of cumulative eligible capital should continue to be taxed on roughly the same preferential basis as capital gains.

The 1988 regime is the one that is now in place. "Eligible capital expenditure" is defined in s. 14(5) of the Act as "an expenditure on account of capital for the purpose of gaining or producing income from the business", subject to a number of exclusions. The definition excludes capital expenditures for tangible property (whether land or depreciable property) and for those types of intangible property that are depreciable property. This leaves within the

---

[77] Note 49, above.

[78] Carter Report, vol. 4, 245.

definition a residuary class of capital expenditures that includes most capital expenditures for intangibles, for example, purchased goodwill, trade marks, quotas, franchises and licences for an unlimited period,[79] customer lists, "know-how", stock exchange seats and organization costs.[80]

The most important of these expenditures is the cost of goodwill, and a brief explanation of what goodwill is may be desirable. When a person buys a business, he or she is concerned primarily with the earning capacity of the business as a going concern. The value of particular tangible capital assets in the business such as land, buildings, machinery, and so on, is not particularly significant since the purchaser does not plan to sell the assets but to use them in the business. (They may be of considerable significance to the purchaser's bank or other lender of money who desires security.) But the price of the business will normally exceed the value of all the tangible assets; otherwise the vendor would "break up" the business and sell each individual asset rather than selling the business as a going concern. A common method of valuing a business is to multiply the last year's earnings (or the average earnings of several prior years) by a figure called an "earnings multiple" (or "price earnings ratio"). The appropriate multiple would be obtained by negotiation between vendor and purchaser, but would depend primarily on the price at which similar businesses are being traded. Thus, if a business earns $40,000 after tax, and its earnings multiple is 10, the value of the business will be $400,000.

Suppose that a purchaser acquires a business for $400,000, and the tangible assets acquired are worth a total of $150,000. What did the purchaser acquire for the remaining $250,000? The answer is goodwill: the difference between the value of a business as a going concern and the value of its tangible assets is goodwill.[81] Goodwill is "the capitalized value of the earning power of a going-concern business over and above a reasonable return on the value of its other assets".[82] Goodwill consists of all the intangible advantages possessed by an established business: its name and reputation, its location, the nature of its competition, its connections with suppliers, the expertise of its employees, the loyalty of its customers, and other hard-to-define characteristics which spell the difference between business success and business failure. The accounting treatment of purchased goodwill is to show the asset on the balance sheet at cost,

---

[79] Note 49, above.

[80] For example, legal fees for incorporation of a company. Costs of financing are not eligible capital expenditures, because they are specifically deductible under s. 20(1)(e) over a five-year period: ch. 13, under heading 13.8, "Other costs of financing", above.

[81] Carter Report, vol. 4, 244.

[82] Harris, *Canadian Income Taxation* (4th ed., 1986), 171. See, generally, Durnford, "Goodwill in the Law of Income Tax" (1981) 29 *Can. Tax J.* 759.

and to amortize it on a straight-line basis over the estimated life of the goodwill. The period selected for amortization is inevitably arbitrary.[83]

The intangible property that is purchased with an eligible capital expenditure is described in the Act as "eligible capital property" (defined in s. 54).

Three-quarters of each eligible capital expenditure is added to the "cumulative eligible capital" account of the business. Paragraph 20(1)(b) allows a deduction not exceeding 7 per cent of the cumulative eligible capital at the end of each year.[84] The deduction is taken on a declining-balance basis, and the cumulative eligible capital account, which is defined in s. 14(5), is operated in much the same way as the undepreciated capital cost account of a class of depreciable property. The cumulative eligible capital account is increased by three-quarters of each eligible capital expenditure (purchase of eligible capital property), and it is diminished by three-quarters of the proceeds of disposition of eligible capital property. A recapture and a terminal allowance (terminal loss) each causes the account to be reset to zero. A recapture (income inclusion) under s. 14(1) occurs if the account falls to a negative figure as the result of a disposition of eligible capital property.[85] A terminal allowance (deduction) under s. 24(1) occurs if the account has a positive balance when the taxpayer ceases to carry on the business.

---

[83] The period of amortization cannot exceed 40 years, according to the *CICA Handbook*, para. 1580.58.

[84] There is no half-year rule to reduce the deduction that can be taken in the year that an eligible capital expenditure is made. The half-year rule of reg. 1100(2) with respect to depreciable property is described under heading 14.2(k), "Half-year rule", above.

[85] The full amount of the proceeds of disposition is deducted from the cumulative eligible capital account, even if part of the proceeds represents a gain over the original cost. There is no need to give the capital gain portion preferential treatment, because any amounts that go into income are calculated with reference to only three-quarters of the proceeds of disposition, and are therefore taxed on a preferential basis analogous to that applied to capital gains (which are only three-quarters taxable). The gain over original cost is only relevant for a private corporation, because one-quarter of this gain (i.e., the non-taxable portion) is added to the corporation's capital dividend account (see paragraph (c) of the definition of capital dividend account in s. 89(1)). As discussed in ch. 19, Corporations and Shareholders, under heading 19.5(c)(v), "Capital gains", below, a private corporation can elect to pay tax-free dividends to its shareholders out of its capital dividend account.

Example

	Cumulative eligible capital
<u>Year 1</u>	
T purchases goodwill for $100,000 (s. 14(5)).	$ 75,000
Cumulative eligible capital (CEC) at end of year 1	75,000
Deduction for year 1 under s. 20(1)(b) (7%)	(5,250)

Note that T may claim less than the full deduction if he chooses (s. 20(1)(b) "not exceeding 7%"), and this choice may be sensible in a situation of current losses or available loss carryovers.

<u>Year 2</u>

T sells goodwill for $140,000 (s. 14(5)).   (105,000)
Note that the full three-quarters of proceeds is subtracted from CEC despite the fact that part of the proceeds represents a gain over original cost of $100,000.

T purchases new "customer lists" in the same business for $80,000 (s. 14(5)(a)(i)).   <u>60,000</u>

Note that this purchase restores the CEC account to a positive balance and shelters the inclusion in income under s. 14(1) of $35,250 which would otherwise have been caused by the sale of goodwill.

Cumulative eligible capital (CEC) at end of year 2	24,750
Deduction for year 2 under s. 20(1)(b) (7%)	(1,733)

<u>Year 3</u>

T ceases to carry on business.

Cumulative eligible capital (CEC) at end of year 3	23,017
Terminal allowance (s. 24(1))	(23,017)

Note that no deduction can be taken under s. 20(1)(b) for year 3 (s. 24(1)(b)), and the CEC is reduced to nil by s. 24(1)(c).   NIL

14.4 Classification of business or property expenditures

(a) Current expenses

Current expenses, for example, salary, wages, rent, utilities, supplies, etc., are deductible in the year incurred under s. 9.[86]

(b) Prepaid expenses

Expenditures that provide a benefit to the business for a period which lasts beyond the current year but is not long enough to be "enduring" are not capital expenditures within the prohibition of s. 18(1)(b). They may be deferred and amortized over the period of their usefulness, either in accordance with s. 18(9) (if the expense is one of those listed in that section) or in accordance with generally accepted accounting principles (for prepaid expenses not listed in s. 18(9)).[87]

(c) Cost of depreciable property

The cost of purchasing depreciable property is not deductible in the year incurred because of s. 18(1)(b)'s prohibition of the deduction of capital expenditures. However, capital cost allowance may be claimed on the "undepreciated capital cost" (defined in s. 13(21)) of each class of depreciable property under s. 20(1)(a) and Part XI of the regulations.[88]

(d) Eligible capital expenditures

Eligible capital expenditures (defined in s. 14(5)) are not deductible in the year incurred because of s. 18(1)(b)'s prohibition of the deduction of capital expenditures. However, three-quarters of eligible capital expenditures are accumulated in the cumulative eligible capital account (defined in s. 14(5)), and annual deductions may be taken from the account under s. 20(1)(b).[89]

(e) Cost of land

The cost of land is a capital expenditure (except for a business which trades in land, in which case the land would be inventory). Its deduction is therefore prohibited by s. 18(1)(b). Land is not depreciable property (reg. 1102(2)), nor an eligible capital expenditure (s. 14(5)). The cost of land is therefore not deductible at all in computing income from a business or property. It is probably best not to describe it as a tax "nothing", however, because the cost of land is deductible under subdivision c in computing any capital gain or

---

[86] Chapter 13, Income from Business or Property: Deductions, above.

[87] Section 14.1(c), "Prepaid expenses", above.

[88] Section 14.2, "Depreciable property", above

[89] Section 14.3, "Eligible capital expenditures", above.

loss on the ultimate disposition of the land.[90] In effect, land, even if it is used in a business, is treated as if it were an investment (like stocks and bonds).

(f)   Nothings

"Nothings" are expenditures that are not deductible at all. The following are the main classes of nothings: (1) the cost of intangible property acquired to earn income from property (as opposed to income from business), which is not an eligible capital expenditure;[91] (2) expenditures disallowed by specific provisions of the Act, for example, expenses of recreational facilities or clubs (s. 18(1)(l)), expenses of advertising in foreign periodicals (s. 19) or foreign radio and television stations (s. 19.1), and the non-deductible portion of meals and entertainment (s. 67.1);[92] and (3) perhaps some kinds of fines.[93] In addition, of course, personal and living expenses are not deductible (s. 18(1)(h)), but unlike the three listed classes of nothings these are not expenses incurred to earn business or property income.

---

[90] Chapter 15, Capital Gains, below.

[91] Section 14.3, "Eligible capital expenditures", above.

[92] Chapter 13, Income from Business or Property: Deductions, under heading 13.2 "Entertainment expenses", above.

[93] *Id.*, under heading 13.11, "Fines", above.

15

Capital Gains

15.1 History

The history of the tax treatment of capital gains has already been related. Capital gains were initially excluded from the tax base by virtue of the "source theory" which dominated the Anglo-Canadian conception of income.[1] Under the Haig-Simons conception of income,[2] capital gains (along with all other accretions to net worth) had to be taxed. The "comprehensive tax base" urged by the Carter Commission also included capital gains, although the Commission conceded that it was impracticable to assess capital gains which had accrued but had not been realized, and so the Commission recommended that (with some

---

[1] Chapter 9, Tax Base, under heading 9.2, "Source theory", above.

[2] *Id.*, under heading 9.3, "Haig-Simons theory", above.

exceptions) only realized gains should be included.[3] The ultimate compromise, which was enacted in the 1971 Income Tax Act, was to include only one-half of realized capital gains in income, and to allow the deduction of one-half of capital losses against those gains. In this way, capital gains became taxable for the first time in 1972,[4] but on a basis more favourable than other classes of income. The tax reform of 1988 increased the inclusion rate from one-half to three-quarters, thereby reducing but not eliminating the tax preference for capital gains.

While it is common to refer to the "capital gains tax", the description is not really accurate. There is no separate tax on capital gains. Capital gains are simply another source of income, three-quarters of which are included in a taxpayer's income, along with the taxpayer's income from other sources, such as employment, business or property.

15.2 Policy issues

The issues of policy to be addressed in this chapter are: (1) Should capital gains be taxed at all? (2) If so, should they be taxed on a preferential basis? (3) Should the system be adjusted for inflation?

15.3 Inclusion in the tax base

(a) Equity

The first issue, whether capital gains should be taxed at all, raises for reconsideration the arguments in favour of a reasonably comprehensive tax base. If tax is to be levied in accordance with ability to pay, then every increase in a taxpayer's ability to pay should be included in income, subject only to considerations of administrative feasibility. Since a capital gain represents an increase in the taxpayer's ability to pay tax, the capital gain should be included in income (and a capital loss should be deducted from income). This argument is of course grounded in the idea of tax equity: in comparing the taxable capacity of different taxpayers, "a buck is a buck is a buck". The taxpayer who makes a dollar in the form of a capital gain should be treated no differently than the taxpayer who makes a dollar in the form of income from employment or business or property.

The equity argument is reinforced in the case of capital gains by the fact that capital gains are derived disproportionately by high-income individuals. The

---

[3] *Id.*, under heading 9.5, "Capital gains", above.

[4] This raised the transitional problem of how to exempt from tax those capital gains accrued on property owned on January 1, 1972, the date of commencement of the new system. The solution turned out to be quite complicated: Income Tax Application Rules, s. 26(3) (tax-free zone rule), s. 26(7) (election of valuation day value). The significance of these provisions has not yet disappeared, because some taxpayers continue to own capital properties that they owned on January 1, 1972. However, the transitional provisions are outside the scope of this book.

Carter Commission used statistics from the United States, where capital gains had been taxed for a long time, to show that capital gains tend to form a small proportion of the income reported by low-income individuals, and a large proportion of the income reported by high-income individuals. Indeed, the Commission concluded that the inclusion of capital gains in income would permit a drastic lowering of tax rates at the upper levels of income while actually improving the true progressivity of the system.[5] In fact, as Carter predicted, the capital gains reported in Canada since tax reform in 1971 have been disproportionately concentrated in the upper-income classes. The inclusion of capital gains, even on a preferential basis, has therefore contributed to the progressivity (vertical equity) of the system.[6]   *: capital gains claimed by high-income individuals.*

(b)   Neutrality

The case for full taxation of capital gains may also be placed on the ground of neutrality. When capital gains are untaxed, taxpayers will go to great lengths to arrange their affairs so that profit is obtained in the untaxed form of a capital gain instead of ordinary income. The most important example of this technique in Canada was the use of corporations to accumulate (or "store") income, so that the gain to the shareholder was reflected in the enhanced value of the corporation's shares, which could be realized (by the sale of the shares) as a tax-free capital gain. "Surplus stripping" (or dividend stripping) in this way was countered by complex provisions in the Act which were hard to administer and never completely effective. If a tax system were neutral in its treatment of capital gains and other forms of income, there would be no tax incentive to take profits in the form of capital gains, and no need for complicated anti-avoidance measures.[7] Since the present Act gives preferential treatment to capital gains, the incentive to take profits in the form of capital gains still exists, although the particular problem of surplus-stripping has been much reduced by also according preferential treatment to corporate dividends, and many of the anti-avoidance measures have been repealed.

(c)   Certainty

Finally, the full taxation of capital gains would increase the certainty of the law by eliminating the difficult task of distinguishing between capital gains and ordinary income. No issue has generated more litigation than the question whether a profit realized on the sale of property is business income or a capital gain. If the sale of the property is held to be a trade or an "adventure or concern in the nature of trade", then the profit is business income. If, on the other hand,

---

[5] Chapter 9, Tax Base, under heading 9.5, "Capital gains", above.

[6] For details, see Allan, Poddar, LePan, "The Effects of Tax Reform" (1978) 26 *Can. Tax J.* 1; Revenue Canada, *Taxation Statistics* (1996), Table 9, 120.

[7] *Report of the Royal Commission on Taxation* (Carter Report) (1966), vol. 3, 334-335.

the sale is held to be the realization of an investment, then the profit is a capital gain. The difficulty in formulating satisfactory legal tests to distinguish between these kinds of transactions, and the evidentiary problems involved, could all be forgotten if the system taxed capital gains and business income in the same way.[8] Since the present Act gives preferential treatment to capital gains, the problem of distinguishing between capital and income transactions is still with us, as a glance at every volume of reported tax cases will demonstrate.[9]

15.4 Preferential treatment

(a) Preferences

Under the present system, capital gains are given preferential treatment in three respects: (1) capital gains are brought into income only when realized so that the payment of tax is postponed until realization occurs; (2) only three-quarters of capital gains are included in income; and (3) there is a lifetime exemption from tax for $500,000 of capital gains on the disposition of farm property and shares in a small business corporation.[10] The next three sections of this chapter discuss each of these preferences.

(b) Realization basis

The general rule is that a capital gain (or capital loss) on a property is not recognized for tax purposes until it has been realized by the sale (or other disposition) of the property. A gain that has accrued through the appreciation in value of a property, but has not been realized, is not recognized for tax purposes. There are two reasons why capital gains are not taxed until they have been realized: (1) the administrative problem for government in annually evaluating all capital property so as to assess accrued capital gains; and (2) the liquidity problem for taxpayers in finding the cash to pay tax on gains that have not yielded any cash.

Since the realization basis permits tax to be postponed while the gain accrues, it is a tax preference. The economic advantage of postponement of tax was described earlier.[11]

A disadvantage for the taxpayer of the realization basis is that there is a "bunching" of several years' gains into one taxation year, the year of realization. This may cause the gains to be taxed at a higher rate than if they had been recognized annually over the period of accrual. However, even if bunching

---

[8] Carter Report, vol. 3, 335-336.

[9] Chapter 16, Investing and Trading, below, is devoted to this issue.

[10] The exemption for the gain on the disposition of a principal residence (sec. 15.17, "Principal residence", below) could also be added to the list.

[11] Chapter 6, Taxation Year, under heading 6.5, "Postponement of tax", above.

pushes the taxpayer into a higher tax bracket, that disadvantage would normally be more than offset by the advantage of having postponed payment of tax for the period of accrual. In addition, the Income Tax Act used to offer relief from "bunching" by allowing persons with "lumpy incomes" to take advantage of averaging provisions. These averaging provisions have now been repealed, however, which removes the statutory relief against the bunching of several years' income into a single taxation year. Of course, a large proportion of capital gains are derived by taxpayers in the top rate bracket, who cannot be pushed into a higher bracket by gains realized in a particular year.

The realization basis gives to the taxpayer control over the timing of the recognition of capital gains. This is itself an important tax preference. To be sure, sometimes circumstances outside the taxpayer's control will require a sale of capital property at a time which is inopportune for tax purposes. For the most part, however, the sale of property is a voluntary act, and the taxpayer will not do it without regard for tax considerations. An example of an opportune time to sell an asset that is sheltering a capital gain would be when a loss has accrued on another asset. On selling both assets, the gain on one would be absorbed by the loss on the other. For example, in 1974, there was a drop in the stock market and taxpayers reported more losses than gains on corporate shares. In the same year, taxpayers reported gains on real estate which totalled 300 per cent above the gains reported the previous year. It may be surmised that there was a connection between the two figures: what probably happened was that many taxpayers took advantage of their stock exchange losses to realize gains on real estate.[12]

One effect of the realization basis of capital gains taxation is to discourage an owner from selling an asset that has appreciated substantially in value. As long as the asset is retained, no tax has to be paid; as soon as the asset is sold, tax has to be paid on the capital gain that has been realized. The owner feels "locked in" by the potential tax liability. Of course, an owner will still sell if he or she needs the money or if the asset is expected to fall in value. But the owner will be reluctant to sell to put the money to another use, because there would be less money available for the other use. This lock-in effect is a disincentive for the owner to put his or her property to its most profitable (efficient) use. While economists are not agreed on the seriousness of this problem, it seems intuitively obvious that it must have an adverse effect on the nation's productivity. The present system places limits on the lock-in effect by providing that on the death of a taxpayer there is a "deemed disposition" of all of the deceased's capital property at fair market value (s. 70(5)). On death, therefore, all accrued capital gains have to be recognized. Nor can property be passed from generation to generation by inter vivos gift without recognizing accrued capital gains, because on a gift of capital property there is also a deemed

---

[12] Perry, "The Yield of the Capital Gains Tax" (1976) 24 *Can. Tax J.* 395.

disposition at fair market value (s. 69(1)). The new owner by inheritance or by gift takes the property fully tax-paid, and is not locked-in until new gains have accrued.[13]

(c)   Three-quarters taxable

The second (and more obvious) element of the preferential treatment of capital gains is that only three-quarters of a capital gain is included in income. The Carter Commission recommended that capital gains should be fully taxable. The Income Tax Act of 1971 included in income only one-half of capital gains. The tax reform of 1988 raised the inclusion rate from one-half to three-quarters.

In a world without inflation, the arguments for full taxation of capital gains which were canvassed earlier[14] are overwhelming. But, as long as many capital gains are caused mainly by inflation, it would be inequitable to move to full taxation of capital gains without at the same time adjusting the system for inflation. The three-quarters inclusion of capital gains could conceivably be defended as a crude adjustment for inflation. The defence would be difficult, however, because the adjustment is so arbitrary. Compare the following three cases:

Case A:

A in a taxation year earns $20 of income from employment. *fully taxed*

Case B:

B in a taxation year sells an asset for $40 which he had bought for $20 just a few weeks earlier. *- 3/4 taxed - should be fully taxed*

Case C:

C in a taxation year sells an asset for $40 which she had bought for $20 ten years earlier. In that ten years the consumer price index has advanced by 100 per cent, or in other words the dollar has depreciated by 50 per cent. *3/4 taxed - shouldn't be taxed @ all*

A's capacity to pay tax has increased by $20 and he should be taxed on that figure. B's capacity to pay has also increased by $20 and he should be taxed on that figure. C's capacity to pay has increased not one iota, because the increase in the nominal dollar value of her property simply reflects the decline in the value of the dollar; C's gain should not be taxed at all.[15] The present system will impose full taxation on A's gain, as it should; but only three-quarters taxation on B's gain, which should be fully taxed; and three-quarter's taxation

---

[13] The deemed dispositions are discussed later in this chapter: sec. 15.14, "Deemed dispositions", below.

[14] Section 15.3, "Inclusion in the tax base", above.

[15] In *MacDonald* v. *M.N.R.*, [1984] C.T.C. 2624, 84 D.T.C. 1602 (T.C.C.), a taxpayer argued that his inflation-induced capital gains on real property should not be subject to tax. The Tax Court of Canada held that in the absence of statutory provisions exempting inflationary gains from taxation, the inflation-induced component of capital gains cannot be deducted in computing the amount of a taxable capital gain.

on C's gain, which should not be taxed at all. Only case A is appropriately taxed. The results of cases B and C do not reflect the taxpayers' increases in their ability to pay, and are therefore inequitable.

As long as capital gains are only three-quarters taxed, the system is inequitable (and not neutral) as between the taxpayer who makes ordinary income (A, above) and the taxpayer who makes a real (not inflation-caused) capital gain (B, above). But, as long as the system is not adjusted for inflation, even three-quarters taxation is too severe for the taxpayer whose gain has simply matched the rate of inflation (C, above). The required reforms are twofold: (1) capital gains should be fully taxed, but (2) the system should be adjusted to cancel out the effect of inflation. If the system were changed in these two ways, A and B would be taxed equally, reflecting their equal increases in ability to pay; and C would not be taxed at all, reflecting the illusory character of her gain. There is no technical difficulty in implementing the first change to full taxation of capital gains. Indeed, it would greatly simplify the tax system, as Carter pointed out.[16] Nor is it technically difficult to adjust capital gains for inflation, although any adjustment will increase the complexity of the tax system. The topic of adjusting capital gains for inflation is discussed in greater detail under heading 15.5, "Adjustment for inflation", below.

(d)   Lifetime exemption

In 1985, the Income Tax Act was amended to introduce a lifetime exemption for $500,000 of capital gains (s. 110.6). All capital gains derived by an individual (corporations were not eligible) were exempt from tax up to a lifetime limit of $500,000. This exemption formed a third tax preference for capital gains compared with other forms of income. As such, it violated equity and neutrality, and its implementation was exceedingly complex, requiring numerous amendments to the Act. The exemption was to be phased in over a period of six years. In 1987, the phase-in process had brought the exemption up to a limit of $100,000, which was due to rise by a further $100,000 each year until it reached $500,000 in 1990. The tax reform of 1988 capped the exemption at its 1987 level of $100,000. The resulting $100,000 lifetime exemption remained in the Act until 1994, when it was repealed.

Unfortunately, the repeal of the lifetime exemption in 1994 was not complete. When the exemption was capped at $100,000 in 1988, two classes of property were exempt from the cap: "qualified farm property" (real property used in the business of farming)[17] and "qualified small business corporation shares" (shares in a Canadian-controlled private corporation engaged in active business

---

[16] Notes 7 and 8, above.

[17] As well as real property, an interest in a family farm partnership and shares in a family farm corporation are eligible for the exemption.

in Canada). For these two categories of capital property, the original lifetime exemption of $500,000 was unchanged. When the exemption was repealed in 1994, the repeal did not touch these two privileged categories. The lifetime exemption of $500,000 therefore continues to apply to qualified farm property and qualified small business corporation shares. When these properties are disposed of by a taxpayer, the capital gain is exempt from tax until the taxpayer's lifetime limit of $500,000 has been reached. The figure of $500,000 represents the full amount of capital gains; the Act uses the figure of $375,000, which is three-quarters of $500,000, and which constitutes the limit in terms of taxable capital gains.

The repeal of the lifetime exemption in 1994 for all capital property other than qualified farm property and qualified small business corporation shares was accompanied by an ingenious and generous transitional provision. For persons owning capital property on February 22, 1994 (the date of the budget announcing the repeal of the exemption), a special election was available, which enabled the taxpayer to report all or part of any accrued (but unrealized) capital gains on the property up to that date. Any gain recognized by the election that was eligible for the $100,000 capital gains exemption would be untaxed. The election worked by treating taxpayers as having sold their capital property on February 22, 1994, and as having immediately purchased the property back at its fair market value or at an elected lower figure. This allowed taxpayers to take advantage of the capital gains exemption before it disappeared. The election also created a new cost base for the property in respect of which the election was made. Following the election, the cost base of the property is its fair market value on February 22, 1994, or other elected figure, rather than its actual cost on the date it was acquired. The new cost base of capital property in respect of which the election was made is the only continuing consequence of the general lifetime exemption, and it will remain significant for quite some time.

15.5 Adjustment for inflation

It is important to recognize at the outset that the indexing of the personal income tax which is accomplished by s. 117.1 of the Act, and which has earlier been described,[18] does not address the problem of inflation-induced capital gains. The purpose of the indexing formula of s. 117.1 is to ensure that increases in income which simply reflect the rate of inflation (minus 3 per cent) do not increase the rate of tax payable by the taxpayer. To this end, the tax brackets and most of the fixed-dollar deductions and credits are annually expanded by that year's rate of inflation (minus 3 per cent). The taxpayer's increase in income is subject to tax; all that is necessary to cancel out the effect of inflation, and all that indexing does, is to reduce the average rate of tax. However, this is not a solution to the problem of inflation-induced capital gains. For example, it will

---

[18] Chapter 5, Rates, under heading 5.3, "Indexing for inflation", above.

be recalled that in case C above,[19] C had purchased a property for $20, held it for a period of years while the consumer price index advanced by 100 per cent, and then sold the property for $40. C's nominal gain has been wholly created by inflation. The effect of inflation on the gain cannot be cancelled out by adjusting the *rate* of tax payable by the taxpayer on the gain. The only way in which the effect of inflation can be cancelled out is by eliminating the *gain itself*. The gain is totally illusory and should not be taxed at all.

One way in which capital gains could be adjusted for inflation is by indexing the cost base of capital property.[20] In the example given, the taxpayer's actual cost was $20, but over a period of 100 per cent inflation the cost should be notionally increased by 100 per cent (the rate of inflation) to $40. A disposition for $40 would not then involve the recognition of any gain, because the proceeds of disposition would not exceed the indexed cost base. A disposition for $45 would involve the recognition of a gain of $5 because that would be a real gain in purchasing power — a gain over and above the rate of inflation. A disposition for $35 would involve the recognition of a loss of $5 since the nominal gain of $15 would represent a loss in real purchasing power of $5.

Another way in which capital gains could be adjusted for inflation is by "tapering". This consists of including in income a smaller portion of a capital gain the longer a capital property is held. For example, a gain realized during the first year of ownership might be fully taxable, with the inclusion rate declining by (say) 10 percentage points for each year of ownership. A gain realized during the third year of ownership would be 70 per cent taxable. After a period of ownership of ten years, the gain would be exempt.

15.6 Taxable capital gains

The Income Tax Act, by s. 3(b), includes in income "taxable capital gains" less "allowable capital losses". Subdivision c of Division B of Part I of the Act, which is entitled "Taxable Capital Gains and Allowable Capital Losses", and which comprises ss. 38-55, then supplies the rules for the computation of taxable capital gains and allowable capital losses.

A "taxable capital gain" is defined in s. 38(a) as three-quarters of a "capital gain"; and an "allowable capital loss" is defined in s. 38(b) as three-quarters of a "capital loss". Since it is "taxable capital gains" rather than

---

[19] Text accompanying note 15, above.

[20] Indexing the cost base would apply even where capital property has been acquired with borrowed money. Although borrowed money provides the leverage to increase the owner's equity by far more than the rate of inflation, the interest payable to the lender will reflect the anticipated rate of inflation at the time of the loan, so that much of the owner's apparent gain has been paid to the lender in the form of higher interest rates.

"capital gains" which are brought into income, and "allowable capital losses" rather than "capital losses" which are deductible, it is the definitions of taxable capital gains and allowable capital losses which implement the policy of including only three-quarters of capital gains in income.

15.7 Capital gains

The essence of a capital gain or capital loss may be drawn from s. 40 of the Act, a provision that will later be considered in more detail. It is a gain or loss which is derived from a "disposition" of "property". It is measured by taking the difference between the "proceeds of disposition" of the property and the "adjusted cost base" of the property. If the proceeds of disposition are more than the adjusted cost base of the property, the excess is a capital gain. If the proceeds of disposition are less than the adjusted cost base of the property, the deficiency is a capital loss.

The next four sections of this chapter will examine what kinds of "property" give rise to capital gains and losses, what kinds of transactions are "dispositions", and the meanings of "proceeds of disposition" and "adjusted cost base".

15.8 Capital property

(a)   Definition

A capital gain or loss is a gain or loss from a disposition of "property". If there is no disposition of property, there is no capital gain or loss. However, there are some exceptional classes of property the disposition of which does not give rise to a capital gain or loss. "capital property" is a convenient term to describe property the disposition of which will give rise to capital gains or losses.[21]

Capital property is defined in s. 54 as follows:

"capital property" of a taxpayer means

(a) any depreciable property of the taxpayer, and

(b) any property (other than depreciable property), any gain or loss from the disposition of which would, if the property were disposed of, be a capital gain or a capital loss, as the case may be, of the taxpayer;

In order to determine what property is capital property it is necessary to turn to s. 39 of the Act, which specifies which kinds of property do not give rise to capital gains or losses. The excluded property is not capital property. All property not excluded is capital property.

---

[21] The special case of depreciable property, giving rise to capital gains but not capital losses, is considered under heading 15.8(c), "Depreciable property", below.

(b)   Exclusions

The major exclusion from capital gains treatment (and hence from the definition of capital property) is derived from the words in brackets in ss. 39(1)(a) and (b). These words have the effect of excluding from capital gains treatment any property the disposition of which gives rise to ordinary income — ordinary income being income from employment, business, property or any other source except taxable capital gains.

The most important example of property excluded by the bracketed words of ss. 39(1)(a) and (b) is the inventory of a business. For example, if an automobile dealer sells a car at a profit, he or she has made a gain from the disposition of property; but the gain is not a capital gain, because the profit of a trader on the sale of his or her inventory is ordinary income — income from a business. Another example is property bought on speculation as an "adventure or concern in the nature of trade". For example, if a person sells a parcel of real estate which he or she acquired with the intention of making a profit by early resale, this person too has made a gain from the disposition of property; but again it is not a capital gain because the profit of an adventure or concern in the nature of trade is ordinary income — income from a business. It is often difficult to determine whether a taxpayer who has profited (or lost) from transactions in property is (1) a trader, in which case the property is inventory and the profit is business income, or (2) a speculator, in which case the property is speculative property and the profit is also business income, or (3) simply an investor who has realized an investment, in which case the profit is a capital gain. These distinctions have produced more case-law than any other issue under the Income Tax Act, and are discussed in chapter 16, "Investing and Trading", below.

The important point for present purposes is that the capital gains category is a residuary category, including only those gains from the disposition of property which would not otherwise be taxed. Not only does this exclude profits from trading or from an adventure in the nature of trade, it also excludes any other gain which is taxed elsewhere in the Act. For example, gains on stock options granted to employees are included in employment income by s. 7, and property appropriated to a shareholder by a corporation is included in income from property by s. 15. Any gain caught by s. 7 or 15 (or any other provision of the Act outside subdivision c) is automatically excluded from the capital gains provisions.[22]

---

[22] Paragraph 39(1)(a) reinforces the general exclusion of gains taxed elsewhere with a number of specific exemptions of property that receives distinctive tax treatment elsewhere: eligible capital property, cultural property, Canadian resource property, foreign resource property, timber resource property and insurance policies. Paragraph 39(1)(b), dealing with capital losses, contains the same set of exclusions, but with the important addition of depreciable property. The special case of depreciable property, giving rise to capital gains but not capital losses, is considered in the next section.

(c)   Depreciable property

Depreciable property is anomalous in that its disposition may give rise to capital gains, but not to capital losses. Nevertheless, s. 54 includes depreciable property in the definition of capital property.

Depreciable property is defined by s. 13(21) as property in respect of which capital cost allowance ("deductions under paragraph 20(1)(a)") may be claimed; that means, of course, property which has been acquired "for the purpose of gaining or producing income" (reg. 1102(1)(c)) and which is included in Schedule II of the Income Tax Regulations.[23] The reason why depreciable property is excluded from *capital loss* treatment is that losses on depreciable property are fully deductible from business or property income under subdivision b through the regular deduction of capital cost allowances under s. 20(1)(a) as adjusted by the provisions for recapture (s. 13(1)) and terminal loss (s. 20(16)).[24] The reason why depreciable property is not excluded from *capital gains* treatment is because any gain over capital cost on the disposition of depreciable property is not taxed under subdivision b and must therefore be included in the capital gains category. Of course, any recapture of capital cost allowance on the disposition of depreciable property is taxed under subdivision b as business income or property income (depending upon whether the depreciable property had been used to earn business income or property income). But, if the proceeds of disposition of depreciable property exceed the capital cost of the property (as opposed to the undepreciated capital cost of the property), the portion of the proceeds which exceeds capital cost is a capital gain.[25]

15.9 Disposition

(a)   Significance

The policy of taxing realized, rather than accrued, gains[26] is implemented in the Act by the rule that a capital gain arises only on a "disposition" of property.[27] This rule is complemented by s. 9(3), which provides that income (or loss) from a property, which is computed under subdivision b, does not include any capital gain (or loss) from the disposition of that property. It is the disposition which distinguishes capital gains from property income, such as rent, interest or dividends, to which the property-owner is entitled by virtue of merely holding the property.

---

[23] Chapter 14, Income from Business or Property: Capital Expenditures, under heading 14.2, "Depreciable property", above.

[24] *Ibid.*

[25] *Id.*, under heading 14.2(g), "Retirement of depreciable property", above.

[26] Section 15.4(b), "Realization basis", above.

[27] See especially ss. 38–40.

(b)   Definition see s. 54

"Disposition" is defined in s. 54 as including "any transaction or event entitling a taxpayer to proceeds of disposition of property".[28] This definition points to the definition of "proceeds of disposition", also in s. 54, which includes "the sale price of property that has been sold"; "compensation for property taken under statutory authority"; the insurance proceeds on loss or injury to property; and a number of other kinds of compensation. When the two definitions are read together, it is clear that a disposition includes a sale of property, an expropriation of property for compensation, an insured loss or injury to property, and the redemption or cancellation of a loan.[29] By far the most common form of disposition would be a sale of property. But a disposition need not be a voluntary act by the owner of property: expropriation, loss and redemption would normally be involuntary.[30] A disposition need not involve the continued existence of the property or the acquisition of the property by someone else: destruction of property by fire or the redemption of a debt would lead to the disappearance of the property; yet those events are dispositions.

(c)   Gratuitous transactions

Can there be a "disposition" without "proceeds of disposition"? The definition of a disposition as "any transaction or event entitling a taxpayer to proceeds of disposition" would suggest that the existence of proceeds of disposition is essential. But the definition of disposition is not exhaustive: it uses the word "includes" rather than the word "means"; and there is no policy reason why a total loss, such as an uninsured casualty loss, should be excluded when a partial loss, such as an underinsured casualty loss, is included. The Department takes the view that a disposition occurs "where possession, control and all other aspects of property ownership are relinquished", even if "there is no consideration flowing to the person disposing of the property".[31] On this view, which seems sound, there would be a disposition if a capital property were stolen, destroyed, lost, abandoned or confiscated without any right to compensation or insurance. In such a case, the proceeds of disposition would be zero for the purpose of computing the capital loss from the disposition.

An inter vivos gift would also be a disposition under the Department's definition. This conclusion is reinforced by the terms of s. 69(1)(b), which provides that, where a taxpayer has "disposed of" anything "by way of gift", he

---

[28] The definition goes on to list a number of specific transactions that are included or excluded.

[29] The redemption or cancellation of a loan is expressly mentioned in the definition of disposition.

[30] In the case of involuntary dispositions, where the taxpayer uses the proceeds of disposition to purchase a replacement property, s. 44(1) enables the taxpayer to elect to defer recognition of any capital gain until the replacement property is disposed of.

[31] Interpretation Bulletin IT-460, "Dispositions — absence of consideration" (1980), para. 1.

or she shall be deemed to have received proceeds of disposition therefor equal to its fair market value. This paragraph provides that the proceeds of disposition are deemed to be the fair market value of the gift rather than the actual proceeds of zero. Similarly, the effect of the passing of property on death is not left to the operation of the general capital gains provisions. Subsection 70(5) provides that, where a taxpayer has died, the taxpayer shall be deemed to have disposed, immediately before his or her death, of all of his or her capital property and to have received proceeds of disposition equal to the property's fair market value. These deemed dispositions on a gift and on death, as well as the Act's other deemed dispositions, are discussed later in this chapter.[32]

(d)   Timing

It is sometimes necessary to determine the time at which a disposition has occurred. A typical situation would be where a contract of sale is entered into in one taxation year, and the closing date (when, normally, legal title and possession is given and the bulk of the consideration is received) occurs in the next taxation year. In which year must any gain or loss on the sale be recognized? This depends upon whether the disposition takes place for tax purposes on the contract date or on the closing date.

It will be recalled that the definition of a disposition is "a transaction or event entitling the taxpayer to proceeds of disposition of property". The time of a disposition therefore depends upon the question when the taxpayer becomes "entitled" to the proceeds of disposition. Is that the contract date or the closing date? In support of the contract date, it could be said that on the making of a contract of sale the vendor becomes entitled to the proceeds of disposition in the sense that the vendor has legally enforceable rights against the purchaser. As well, at that point the price is fixed so that any future change in the value of the property will affect the tax position of the purchaser and not the vendor. On the other hand, in support of the closing date, it could be said that the vendor's right to be paid is normally subject to the fulfilment of conditions by the vendor, and in particular the delivery of clear title and vacant possession on the closing date. If the definition of disposition were read as calling for an unconditional entitlement to proceeds of disposition, the closing date would normally be indicated. As well, it could be added that the owner should not become liable to pay tax until he or she has actually received or obtained the indefeasible right to receive the gain upon which he or she is taxed.

The timing of a disposition is also relevant to the right of the vendor or purchaser to claim capital cost allowances on depreciable property. Where a sale of depreciable property straddles the end of the taxation year, the question will arise whether it is the vendor or purchaser who can claim capital cost allowance

---

[32] Section 15.14, "Deemed dispositions", below.

on the property for that year. The definition of "disposition" for capital cost allowance purposes (s. 13(21)) is essentially the same as that for capital gains purposes (s. 54). For capital cost allowance purposes, the closing date would seem more appropriate than the contract date, because the vendor normally has the continued use of the property until the closing date, and the purchaser has not normally obtained the use of the property until then.[33]

The better view is that the date of disposition for capital gains purposes and the dates of disposition and acquisition for capital cost allowance purposes should be the same, and that the relevant date should be the closing date.[34]

15.10   Proceeds of disposition

On a disposition of capital property, any capital gain or loss is measured by the difference between the "proceeds of disposition" of the property and the "adjusted cost base" of the property (s. 40). The definition of proceeds of disposition is contained in s. 54, and is explained in the earlier section of this chapter on the definition of disposition.[35] Essentially, it consists of the gross proceeds realized by the disposition: the price received on sale, the compensation received on expropriation, the insurance proceeds received on loss, and so on. In certain situations, such as succession on death or inter vivos gift, the Act stipulates "deemed" proceeds of disposition; these situations are discussed later under deemed dispositions.[36]

15.11   Adjusted cost base

The final element to be brought into account in computing a capital gain is the "adjusted cost base" of the property (s. 40). This term is defined in s. 54, which reads (in part) as follows:

> "adjusted cost base" to a taxpayer of any property at any time means, except as otherwise provided,
>
> (a) where the property is depreciable property of the taxpayer, the capital cost to the taxpayer of the property as of that time, and
>
> (b) in any other case, the cost to the taxpayer of the property adjusted, as of that time, in accordance with section 53. . . .

---

[33] In the case of the purchaser, the "put in use" rule would normally postpone any right to claim capital cost allowance until after the closing date: ch. 14, Income from Business or Property: Capital Expenditures, under heading 14.2(l), "Available for use", above.

[34] Accord, Interpretation Bulletin IT-133, "Stock exchange transactions — date of disposition of shares" (1973), para. 3. For a discussion of the acquisition date for capital cost allowance purposes, see Interpretation Bulletin IT-285R2, "Capital cost allowance — General Comments" (1994), paras. 16-19.

[35] Section 15.9(b), "Definition", above.

[36] Section 15.14, "Deemed dispositions", below.

With respect to depreciable property, the "adjusted cost base" is the "capital cost" of the property, which is the figure upon which capital cost allowances under s. 20(1)(a) are computed. It is essential that those two figures be the same so that the capital gain provisions work in harmony with the capital cost allowance provisions. "capital cost" is not defined in the Act; it is simply the actual cost of the property, including along with the purchase price any expenses or fees required to complete the acquisition.[37]

With respect to non-depreciable capital property, the adjusted cost base is the "cost" of the property, "adjusted" in accordance with s. 53. "Cost" is not defined in the Act, and it simply means the actual cost of the property, including expenses of acquisition.[38] Thus the "cost" of non-depreciable property is no different from the "capital cost" of depreciable property. Non-depreciable property differs from depreciable property in that the cost of non-depreciable property is subject to adjustment under s. 53, whereas the capital cost of depreciable property is not subject to adjustment. It is the possibility of actual cost being adjusted under s. 53 which, although only applicable to non-depreciable property, gives rise to the term *adjusted* cost base. Section 53 provides for either upward (s. 53(1)) or downward (s. 53(2)) adjustments to actual cost which are basically designed to make the taxation of capital gains compatible with the other parts of the Act. For example, property taxes and interest charges on non-income-producing land are not deductible by the owner (s. 18(2)), but they can be added to the adjusted cost base of the land under s. 53(1)(h) (an upward adjustment). Many of the s. 53 adjustments are technical in nature and have no application to the majority of capital transactions.

Property owned in 1972, when the taxation of capital gains was introduced, is subject to special deemed cost provisions which are designed to ensure that gains accrued prior to 1972 are not subject to tax.[39] Property owned in 1994, when the lifetime capital gains exemption was abolished, may also have an artificial cost base, namely, its elected value on February 22, 1994; the election that produces that result was explained earlier in this chapter.[40] In addition, the various "deemed dispositions" give rise to deemed cost as well as deemed proceeds of disposition; the deemed dispositions are discussed later in this chapter.[41] Finally, the "rollovers" give rise to deemed cost as well as

---

[37] Interpretation Bulletin IT-285R2, note 34, above, paras. 8-9.

[38] In *The Queen* v. *Sterling*, [1985] 1 C.T.C. 275, 85 D.T.C. 5199 (F.C.A.), it was held that interest on money borrowed to purchase gold (which was not tax deductible) was not part of the gold's adjusted cost base. The interest payments related to the source of the funds used to make the purchase, and not directly to the cost of acquiring the property purchased.

[39] Note 4, above.

[40] Section 15.4(d), "Lifetime exemption", above.

[41] Section 15.14, "Deemed dispositions", below.

deemed proceeds of disposition; the rollovers are discussed later in this chapter.[42]

15.12   Computation of gain

(a)   Proceeds due immediately

The computation of a capital gain or capital loss is governed by s. 40(1) of the Act. The straightforward case is where the taxpayer who has disposed of capital property is entitled to be paid in full in the year of the disposition. In that case, if the proceeds of disposition exceed the adjusted cost base of the property plus the expenses of the disposition, the excess is the amount of the capital gain. If the adjusted cost base plus the expenses of the disposition exceed the proceeds of disposition, the excess is the amount of the capital loss. For example, if T sells a capital property with an adjusted cost base of $80 for proceeds of disposition of $100, incurring selling expenses of $5, T has to recognize a capital gain of $15 ($100 − ($80 + $5) = $15). If the proceeds of disposition were $60, he or she would have to recognize a capital loss of $25 ($80 + $5 − $60 = $25). Of course, only three-quarters of these figures would constitute the "taxable capital gain" and the "allowable capital loss".

Subsection 40(1) refers specifically to the expenses of the dispositions ("any outlays and expenses to the extent that they were made or incurred by the taxpayer for the purpose of making the disposition"), but makes no reference to the expenses incurred on the acquisition of the property. As noted earlier, however, the Department accepts that the expenses of acquisition may be treated as part of the cost of capital property,[43] so that the expenses of acquisition also reduce the capital gain or increase the capital loss.

(b)   Proceeds due in future

Subsection 40(1) permits the establishment of a "reserve for future proceeds" where the taxpayer who has disposed of capital property is not entitled to full payment of the proceeds of disposition in the year of disposition. The common case is a sale where part of the price is payable at the time of the disposition and the balance is payable by instalments over a period of years.[44] The general idea, consistent with the realization-basis of the system, is that as long as the taxpayer has not become entitled to receive the full proceeds of disposition the taxpayer should not have to recognize the full gain for tax purposes. This idea is implemented by permitting the taxpayer to deduct from his or her capital gain in the year of disposition a "reasonable" reserve to reflect the

---

[42] Section 15.15, "Rollovers", below.

[43] Notes 37-38 and accompanying text, above.

[44] A sale and mortgage back attracts the same treatment: Interpretation Bulletin IT-152R3, "Special reserves — Sale of land" (1985), paras. 10-13.

fact that a portion of the proceeds of disposition are not due in the year of disposition. A reasonable reserve would consist of the proportion of the capital gain that equals the proportion of the proceeds of disposition that are "not due to the taxpayer until after the end of the year". For example, if Vendor sold a capital property to Purchaser on terms that only one-third of the purchase price was payable in the year of disposition, this would leave two-thirds of the purchase price due after the end of the year of disposition, which would enable Vendor to claim a reserve of two-thirds of the gain. In later years, as instalments of the price are paid, portions of the reserve are recognized until in the year of the last payment the reserve is eliminated. In this way, recognition of the capital gain is spread over the years in which the proceeds of disposition are payable.

Before 1981, the reserve for future proceeds could be used to achieve lengthy postponements of tax. For example, Mother could sell a capital property to Child for its fair market value in the form of a non-interest-bearing promissory note payable by Child on demand. So long as Mother made no demand for payment, 100 per cent of the proceeds of disposition remained "not due to the taxpayer [Mother] until after the end of the year", and a reserve of 100 per cent of the capital gain could be claimed by Mother. This would allow the full amount of the capital gain to be sheltered from tax. The reserve could be claimed every year until the death of Mother, when the reserve would have to be brought into Mother's income for the terminal taxation year. In 1981, the reserve provisions of s. 40(1) were amended to limit the period for which a reserve could be claimed to five years, and to require that at least 1/5 of the gain be recognized in each of the five years.[45] The way in which this works is explained below.

The reserve established by s. 40(1)(a)(iii) must not exceed the lesser of (1) the proportion of the gain which equals the proportion of the proceeds of disposition that are not payable until after the end of the taxation year (s. 40(1)(a)(iii)(C)), and (2) 1/5 of the gain multiplied by an amount equal to 4 minus "the number of preceding taxation years of the taxpayer ending after the disposition of the property" (s. 40(1)(a)(iii)(D)). It is the second limitation, established by s. 40(1)(a)(iii)(D), that limits the life of the reserve to five years, and requires the taxpayer to recognize at least 1/5 of the capital gain over each year in which the reserve is claimed.

In the year of disposition of a capital property for future proceeds, s. 40(1)(a)(i) requires the full capital gain to be reported, but s. 40(1)(a)(iii) then permits the taxpayer to reduce the gain by the amount of a reasonable reserve, up to a maximum of 4/5 of the gain (s. 40(1)(a)(iii)(D)). In the second year, s. 40(1)(a)(ii) becomes applicable, requiring the previous year's reserve to be reported, but, if some portion of the proceeds are still not due until after the end of the second year, s. 40(1)(a)(iii) will again permit the taxpayer to claim a

---

[45] The life of the reserve is extended to ten years in respect of dispositions of farming property to a child: s. 40(1.1).

reasonable reserve, up to a maximum of 3/5 of the gain (s. 40(1)(a)(iii)(D)). In the third year, the second year's reserve will have to be reported, but, if some portion of the proceeds are still not due until after the third year, s. 40(1)(iii) will again permit the taxpayer to claim a reasonable reserve, this time up to a maximum of 2/5 of the gain (s. 40(1)(a)(iii)(D)). This process will continue until the earliest of (1) the year in which the taxpayer has received the entire proceeds of disposition, and (2) the fifth taxation year after the disposition of the property, at which point s. 40(1)(a)(iii)(D) establishes a maximum reserve of 0/5 of the proceeds of disposition, which of course equals $0, requiring the taxpayer to recognize the remainder of the gain, whether or not any proceeds of disposition remain outstanding. There are two further limitations on the life of the reserve: a reserve cannot be claimed by a person who becomes non-resident (s. 40(2)(a)(i)) or in the year of death (s. 72(1)(c), but there is an exception for a spouse or spouse trust: s. 72(2)(b)).

The operation of s. 40(1)(a) may be illustrated by an example:

Example

T in year 1 disposes of a capital property with an adjusted cost base of $100 for proceeds of disposition of $300, payable as to $75 in year 1, a further $75 in year 2, and as to the remaining $150 in year 10 (with interest).

In this example, T has made a capital gain of $200 ($300 − $100 = $200) in year 1, the year of disposition. However, since the proceeds of disposition are payable over ten years, T may claim a reserve under s. 40(1), thereby spreading the gain over five years (the maximum life of the reserve under s. 40(1)(a)(iii)(D), even though the last of the proceeds will not become payable for ten years). T's gain for the five taxation years ending after the disposition would be as follows:

Year 1 (year of disposition)

Gain otherwise determined (s. 40(1)(a)(i)):

P.O.D. *proceeds on disposition*	$ 300	
A.C.B. *adjusted cost base*	100	
	$ 200	$ 200

Less: reserve for future proceeds
    Lesser of:

s. 40(1)(a)(iii)(C)
(proportion of gain which equals the
proportion of the proceeds of
disposition that are not payable
until after the end of the taxation year)
200 × 75% = $150

s. 40(1)(a)(iii)(D)
(1/5 of the gain multiplied by an
amount equal to 4 minus the number
of taxation years ending after the disposition)
200/5 × (4 − 0) =   160   (150)

Gain for year 1: $ 50

Year 2

Reserve claimed in preceding year
(s. 40(1)(a)(ii)) $ 150

Less: reserve for future proceeds
    Lesser of:

s. 40(1)(a)(iii)(C)
200 × 50% = $ 100

s. 40(1)(a)(iii)(D)
200/5 × (4 − 1) =   120   (100)

Gain for year 2: $ 50

Year 3

Reserve claimed in preceding year $ 100

Less: reserve for future proceeds
    Lesser of:

s. 40(1)(a)(iii)(C)
200 × 50% = $ 100

s. 40(1)(a)(iii)(D)
200/5 × (4 − 2) =   80   (80)

Gain for year 3 $ 20

Year 4

Reserve claimed in preceding year		$ 80
Less: reserve for future proceeds		
Lesser of		
s. 40(1)(a)(iii)(C)		
200 × 50% =	$ 100	
s. 40(1)(a)(iii)(D)		
200/5 × (4 − 3)	(40)	(40)
Gain for year 4		$ 40

Year 5

Reserve claimed in preceding year		$ 40
Less: reserve for future proceeds		
Lesser of		
s. 40(1)(a)(iii)(C)		
200 × 50% =	$ 100	
s. 40(1)(a)(iii)(D)		
200/5 × (4 − 4)	0	0
Gain for year 5		$ 40

In year 6 nothing will be reported — no reserve was claimed in the preceding year. The capital gain of $200 has now been fully recognized.

The reserve for future proceeds is expressed in s. 40(1)(a)(iii) as "such amount as the taxpayer may claim . . .". These words make the reserve optional. The taxpayer is not required to claim the reserve, nor, if the taxpayer does claim the reserve, to claim the full "reasonable amount". Ordinarily, of course, the taxpayer will want to claim the maximum reserve possible, since the claim enables the taxpayer to postpone payment of some tax. But special circumstances could make it desirable not to claim the reserve, for example, a year of exceptionally low income, or the availability of capital losses to offset the gain.

The computation of capital losses is provided for in s. 40(1)(b), which makes no provision for a reserve for future proceeds. Thus if a capital loss is suffered on a disposition for future proceeds the full loss must be recognized in the year of disposition. The taxpayer will be happy to recognize the full loss as soon as possible. If the loss cannot be fully deducted in the year of disposition (allowable capital losses can only be deducted against taxable capital gains), the loss carryover rules would be applicable, permitting (at the discretion of the taxpayer) a carryback for three years and an indefinite carryforward.[46]

---

[46] Chapter 18, Losses, under heading 18.2(b), "Net capital losses", below.

15.13   Capital losses

We have already noted that a capital loss is calculated in the same way as a capital gain, that is to say, it is the difference between the adjusted cost base of the property disposed of and its proceeds of disposition. And, just as the system recognizes only three-quarters of a capital gain, calling the taxable portion a "taxable capital gain", so the system recognizes only three-quarters of a capital loss, calling it an "allowable capital loss" (s. 38(b)). Allowable capital losses are deductible only against taxable capital gains. This restriction on deductibility and other aspects of the treatment of capital losses are best understood in the context of the tax treatment of other losses. More detailed consideration of the current deductibility of allowable capital losses, and of the carryover to other years of unused capital losses, including the concept of an "allowable business investment loss", is therefore postponed until chapter 18, Losses, below.

15.14   Deemed dispositions

(a)   Description

The Income Tax Act provides for a number of "deemed dispositions", under which a taxpayer is deemed to have received proceeds of disposition equal to the fair market value of a capital property, although that capital property has not in fact been converted into cash or otherwise realized. On the death of a taxpayer, for example, all of his or her capital property is deemed to have been disposed of at its fair market value, thereby forcing recognition of any accrued gains or losses. On a gift of capital property, the donor is deemed to have disposed of the property at its fair market value, and must therefore recognize any accrued gain or loss on the property. In the case of death or gift, there is in fact a disposition since property passes from the taxpayer to a successor or donee, but there are no proceeds of disposition. The provisions for the so-called deemed dispositions on death or gift really supply only deemed proceeds of disposition. However, there are also deemed dispositions on the 21st anniversary of a trust, on the change of use of capital property, and on becoming non-resident. In these cases, the taxpayer continues to own the property; there has been no relinquishment of ownership and therefore no actual disposition; the deemed disposition provisions supply both a deemed disposition and deemed proceeds of disposition.

(b)   Purpose

The realization basis of capital gains taxation, if adhered to without exceptions, would enable the owners of capital property to postpone paying tax on accrued gains for as long as the gains were not realized. This would not be tolerable as a matter of tax policy, because of the loss of revenue to the government, the inequity of according such a valuable preference to owners of capital property, and the lock-in effect of unrealized capital gains. Each of the deemed dispositions, by forcing recognition of a gain (or loss) which has not been realized, constitutes an exception to the realization basis of capital gains taxation. The purpose of the deemed dispositions is to place limits on the period for which capital gains taxation can be postponed.

The deemed dispositions raise the twin problems associated with accrual-basis capital gains taxation. First, there is the administrative problem for the government of using valuations for the calculation of tax on a gain that has not been realized. Secondly, there is the liquidity problem for the taxpayer of finding cash to pay tax on a gain that has not been realized. However, most jurisdictions seize upon death or a gift as an occasion for the payment of a tax of some kind. It is certainly administratively feasible, and it is probably not normally especially harsh to taxpayers, considering that a major liquidity problem can be foreseen and provided for, for example, by life insurance.

(c)   Death

The most important of the deemed dispositions occurs on the death of an owner of capital property. There is of course an actual disposition on death in the sense that the deceased's property passes immediately by operation of law to the personal representative (called the "legal representative" in the Income Tax Act), and ultimately to the deceased's successors designated by will or (if there is no will) the provincial intestacy law. However, neither the legal representative nor the successors provide any proceeds of disposition and so the tax consequences of death have to be treated specifically by the Income Tax Act. The policy of the Act is to require the capital gains accrued during the deceased's lifetime to be recognized for tax purposes in the deceased's last taxation year (the terminal year). This is accomplished by s. 70(5), which provides that, on the death of a taxpayer, the deceased taxpayer is deemed to have disposed of all of his or her capital property for proceeds of disposition equal to the fair market value of the property.

The deemed disposition of a deceased taxpayer's capital property is deemed to have occurred "immediately before the taxpayer's death". This brings any taxable capital gains (or recapture of capital cost allowances) into the income of the deceased's terminal year, rather than into the income of the deceased's estate (which becomes a new taxpayer). Thus, recognition of capital gains cannot be postponed beyond the lifetime of the owner of the appreciated property. The lock-in effect caused by unrealized capital gains is therefore also limited to the lifetime of the owner. The successor to the capital property (the person inheriting the property) is deemed to acquire the property at its fair market value (s. 70(5)(b)). The successor is not locked-in, because the inherited property is no longer sheltering any untaxed capital gains, and until fresh gains have accrued the successor has no tax incentive not to sell the property.

The deemed disposition of capital property on death can be avoided by the owner giving the property away before death. But there is also a deemed disposition at fair market value on the making of an inter vivos gift of capital property (s. 69(1)(b)); so that an inter vivos gift has the same effect as death in forcing the recognition of accrued capital gains or losses. Where a deceased taxpayer's property is inherited by a spouse or spouse trust, or (in the case of farming property) a child of the taxpayer, recognition of accrued gains can be postponed through rollover provisions which are applicable to those dispositions, as well as to inter vivos gifts to a spouse or spouse trust or (in the case of farming property) a child.[47]

(d) Gift

As noted in the previous paragraph, a deemed disposition on a gift of capital property is necessary to complement the deemed disposition on death. The deemed disposition on death can be avoided by an inter vivos gift to the next generation, but the Income Tax Act exacts the price of immediate recognition by the donor of any unrealized gains accrued up to the time of gift. Under s. 69(1)(b), where a person has made an inter vivos gift of property (or has made a non-arm's-length sale for inadequate consideration), the donor is deemed to have received proceeds of disposition equal to the fair market value of the property. Thus any accrued gains (or losses) must be recognized by the donor at the time of the gift. Under s. 69(1)(c), the donee of the gift is deemed to acquire the property at its fair market value, the intent being to step up the donee's cost base so that the donee never has to pay tax on the gain that was taxed at the time of the gift.[48]

When a donor makes a gift of property to a registered charity, the donor can claim a tax credit or deduction for the fair market value of the donation,[49] but, because of the deemed disposition, the donor must generally report a taxable capital gain equal to 75 per cent of the accrued capital gain on the donated property.[50] However, for gifts of publicly-traded securities made to a registered charity after February 18, 1997 and before 2001, only 37.5 per cent of the accrued capital gain is included in income.[51] The stated purpose of this rule, *exception*

---

[47] See sec. 15.15, "Rollovers", below.

[48] The language of s. 69(1)(c) does not precisely match that of s. 69(1)(b) in that s. 69(1)(c) makes no reference to a non-arms-length sale for inadequate consideration. Accordingly, it seems that s. 69(1)(c) would not step up the cost base in that situation, leading to double taxation of the deemed gain.

[49] Individuals may claim a tax credit under s. 118.1(3) for the fair market value of the gift (s. 118.1(1)). Corporations may claim a deduction under s. 110.1(1).

[50] An exception exists when property meeting criteria set out in the Cultural Property Export and Import Act is given to an authority or institution designated under that Act. There is deemed to be no capital gain on such gifts (s. 39(1)(a)(i.1)).

[51] In order to qualify for the 37.5% inclusion rate, the securities must be listed on a prescribed stock exchange in Canada and must be given to a charity other than a private foundation.

except for

which violates the Canadian income tax system's fundamental principles of equity and neutrality, is to provide a level of tax assistance for donations of "eligible appreciated capital property which is comparable to that in the U.S.".[52] The rule is to be terminated after 2001 if it has not been effective in both increasing donations and distributing them fairly among charities.[53]

(e)　　Trust

A gift of property to a trust, whether on death or inter vivos, gives rise to a deemed disposition under s. 70(5) or s. 69(1)(b), just like a gift to an individual. A sale of property to a trust gives rise to the normal rules requiring recognition of any realized gain or loss, again just like a sale to an individual. Indeed, a trust is deemed to be an individual by s. 104(2). However, once capital property has been acquired by a trust, it is sheltered for a long time from the deemed disposition on death. A trust never dies, and it can be made to last as long as a hundred years despite the rule against perpetuities (which requires that all interests be vested within a life in being and 21 years). Even on the termination of a trust, the distribution of capital property to the capital beneficiaries does not involve recognition of accrued capital gains (s. 107(2)). The Income Tax Act therefore had to make special provision to preclude the use of a trust to postpone for excessive periods of time the recognition of capital gains. To this end, s. 104(4) imposes, at 21-year intervals, a deemed disposition at fair market value on all capital property held by a trust. This deemed disposition occurs on the 21st anniversary of the creation of the trust, and again on the 42nd anniversary, and again on the 63rd anniversary, and so on every 21 years until the trust is terminated.[54]

The 21-year deemed disposition of capital property in a trust differs from the deemed dispositions on death or gift in that the 21-year deemed disposition is not triggered by any event akin to a disposition, but simply by a passage of 21 years. Its purposes are the same as those of the deemed disposition on death, that is to say, to limit the period for which tax on accrued capital gains can be postponed, and to reduce the lock-in effect of a realization-based capital gains tax.

---

[52] Department of Finance, *1997 Budget*, "Supplementary Information", 5-17. The United States tax rules are far more generous: all donations of appreciated capital property are exempt from capital gains tax.

[53] Department of Finance, *1997 Budget*, "Building the Future", 7-11.

[54] This is the general rule to which there are a variety of exceptions and qualifications. The taxation of trusts is the topic of ch. 21, below; and the 21-year deemed disposition is more fully discussed under heading 21.3(b), "Capital Gains", below.

(f) Change of use

Subsection 45(1) provides for a deemed disposition at fair market value where property which was acquired for a non-income-producing use is converted to an income-producing use (s. 45(1)(a)(i)), and vice versa (s. 45(1)(a)(ii)). For example, if an automobile acquired for the personal use of the owner was later used for business purposes, on the change of use there would be a deemed disposition. If a cottage acquired to earn rental income was later used for recreational purposes by the owner, on the change of use there would be a deemed disposition. Where a property is used for both non-income-producing and income-producing purposes a change in the proportion of use for each purpose gives rise to a partial deemed disposition (s. 45(1)(c)).

One reason for the deemed disposition on the change of use of property is the distinctive capital gains treatment of "personal-use property": while gains on personal-use property are taxable, losses are not allowable. The reason for this treatment is discussed later in this chapter.[55] One consequence of the distinctive treatment of personal-use property is that on a change of use of a capital property it is necessary to segregate a period of personal use (non-income-producing), when losses are not allowable, from a period of income-producing use, when losses are allowable. Another reason for segregating a period of non-income-producing use from a period of income-producing use is that capital cost allowances may not be claimed against non-income-producing property, but may be claimed against some kinds of income-producing property (those that qualify as depreciable property).[56] The deemed disposition on the change of use thus draws a line which marks the end or the beginning of the allowability of capital losses and the deductibility of capital cost allowances.

It is the distinction between non-income-producing and income-producing uses which is critical for the recognition of both capital losses and capital cost allowances. Other changes of use will usually make no difference. That is why there is no deemed disposition under s. 45(1) if a change of use of capital property does not move that property from the income-producing category to the non-income-producing category, or vice versa. For example, there would be no deemed disposition under s. 45(1) if a building acquired to earn rental income were converted into an office for the owner's business; there would have been a change of use from an investment to a capital asset in a business, but since both uses are income-producing s. 45(1) would not apply.

Subsections 45(2) and (3) offer an election to the taxpayer to postpone the deemed disposition on a change of use from non-income-producing to income-producing, and (in the case of a principal residence only) vice versa. The

---

[55] Section 15.16, "Personal-use property", below.

[56] Chapter 14, Income from Business or Property: Capital Expenditures, under heading 14.2, "Depreciable property", above.

elections are discussed in the later section of this chapter on principal residence.[57]

(g)   Departure from Canada

Subsection 128.1(4) of the Act provides that when a taxpayer ceases to be a resident of Canada there is a deemed disposition at fair market value of all of the departing taxpayer's property, with certain exceptions. The purpose is to tax the gains that accrued while the taxpayer was resident in Canada; otherwise the gains would escape Canadian tax altogether. This deemed disposition is often called a "departure tax", and is discussed under that heading in chapter 8, Residence.[58]

15.15   Rollovers

(a)   Definition

A "rollover" occurs when a capital property passes from one person to another in a transaction that is a "disposition" (or a deemed disposition), in circumstances where the Income Tax Act exempts the transaction from the general requirement that any capital gain or loss be recognized. This favourable treatment is accorded to certain dispositions of property within a family, namely, dispositions of capital property from one spouse to another and dispositions of farm property from a parent to a child. These intrafamily rollovers are designed to eliminate tax consequences from at least some transactions within a family, and they constitute a rudimentary recognition of the family as a single taxation unit.[59] Rollover treatment is also accorded to transfers of property to a corporation in return for shares of the corporation and certain transfers of property between related corporations. These corporate rollovers are designed to remove tax obstacles to the formation of corporations and the reorganization or amalgamation of corporations. There are comparable rollovers for partnerships.[60] There is also a rollover on the distribution of property to the capital beneficiaries of a trust.[61]

The way in which the rollovers work is best explained by looking at a specific example, namely, the interspousal rollover which is examined in the next section of this chapter.

---

[57] Section 15.17(g), "Change of use", below.

[58] Chapter 8, Residence, under heading 8.9, "Departure tax", above.

[59] Chapter 7, Taxation Unit, under heading 7.3, "Present recognition of family", above.

[60] Chapter 20, Partnerships, under heading 20.4, "Partnership property", below.

[61] Chapter 21, Trusts, under heading 21.6, "Termination of trust", below.

(b) Transfer to spouse

(i) Inter vivos

Subsection 73(1) of the Act provides for a rollover when capital property is transferred inter vivos by a taxpayer to the taxpayer's spouse. Consider the following example. → ∴ no tax consequences from such a transfer

Example

H transfers to W, his wife, as a gift, a capital property with an adjusted cost base of $20 and a fair market value of $30.

If this transaction were not between spouses, so that s. 73(1) did not apply, the gift of capital property would be deemed by s. 69(1)(b)[62] to be a disposition for proceeds equal to the fair market value of the property; this would require the donor (H) to recognize the accrued capital gain ($10). But, in this example, s. 73(1) applies, because there is a transfer of capital property from "a taxpayer" (H) to "the taxpayer's spouse" (W). Subsection 73(1) provides for a rollover of the property from H to W; the property is said to roll over to W, meaning that it passes to W without any tax consequences.

The rollover of s. 73(1), like the others in the Act, is not accomplished by denying that there has been a disposition from H to W. On the contrary, the property is "deemed to have been disposed of . . . by the taxpayer". The rollover is accomplished by deeming the proceeds of disposition to be the adjusted cost base of the property (in the case of depreciable property, the undepreciated capital cost). This means that the gain or loss to the transferor will always be nil. In our example, H's deemed proceeds of disposition are $20, and the adjusted cost base of the property is $20; when the latter is subtracted from the former the remainder is nil. H need not recognize the accrued gain of $10.

The transferee (recipient) of the property is deemed to have acquired the property for an amount equal to the deemed proceeds, that is, the adjusted cost base of the property (undepreciated capital cost in the case of depreciable property). In this way, the transferee steps into the shoes of the transferor, taking over the property at its adjusted cost base to the transferor. Any accrued gain waits in the property until the property is disposed of. The rollover does not eliminate the liability to pay tax on the accrued capital gain; it simply postpones the liability until the transferee-spouse disposes of the property (or is deemed to dispose of it). In our example, where W acquired property with an adjusted cost base of $20 and a fair market value of $30, if W subsequently sold the property for $35 she would have to recognize a capital gain of $15 ($35 − $20 = $15). This capital gain would consist of the $10 gain which had accrued while H owned the property and the $5 gain which had accrued after W acquired the

---

[62] Section 15.14(d), "Gift", above.

property. (The entire taxable capital gain (3/4 of $15) will be attributed to H by virtue of the attribution rule of s. 74.2.)[63]

The rollover provided by s. 73(1) is not confined to gifts. The section speaks of property "transferred". A sale for fair market value from one spouse to another is covered by the section. Thus, in our example, even if W paid H the fair market value of $30, so that H actually realized the gain of $10, H need not recognize the gain for tax purposes.

The term "spouse" is defined in s. 252(4) as including a person of the opposite sex cohabiting with the taxpayer "in a conjugal relationship", who has either cohabited with the taxpayer for the preceding 12 months or is a parent of a child of the taxpayer. The definition employs the term "includes" rather than "means", meaning that the definition is not exhaustive. Clearly, parties to a legally valid marriage are also "spouses" for the purposes of the Act, even though they are not part of the definition in s. 252(4). Under s. 252(3), the term "spouse" in s. 73(1) is defined as also including a party to a void or voidable marriage. Subsection 73(1) includes "a former spouse of the taxpayer", but allows for a rollover in that case only where capital property is transferred to the former spouse "in settlement of rights arising out of their marriage" (s. 73(1)(b)).

The rollover also applies on a transfer of property to a "spouse trust", which is a trust created by the taxpayer under which the spouse is the income beneficiary, and no person except the spouse is able to obtain either income or capital during the lifetime of the spouse (s. 73(1)(c)). The definition of a spouse trust and the rollover to a spouse trust are discussed in chapter 21, Trusts, below.[64]

Subsection 73(1) permits the transferor-spouse to elect "not to have the provisions of this subsection apply". This provision allows the transferor-spouse to elect against rollover treatment. If the election is made, the ordinary capital gains rules will apply, which means in the case of a gift that s. 69(1)(b) will deem the disposition to have taken place at fair market value. If no election is made, the rollover occurs automatically. In most cases, the transferor-spouse will prefer rollover treatment because it permits the postponement of tax on accrued capital gains. In some cases, however, it will be advantageous to exercise the right of election, for example, where the transferor-spouse has incurred capital losses which could be used to offset any gain on the property transferred.[65]

---

[63] Chapter 7, Taxation Unit: under heading 7.5, "Attribution rules", above.

[64] Chapter 21, Trusts, under heading 21.2(c), "Spouse trust", below.

[65] No capital loss can be created on a transfer to a spouse of property that has declined in value; such a loss is a "superficial loss" (s. 54) and is deemed to be nil by s. 40(2)(g)(i).

(ii)   On death

Subsection 73(1) applies only to inter vivos transfers between spouses. However, s. 70(6) provides a similar rollover on the death of a taxpayer for capital property inherited by the spouse of the deceased taxpayer.

The general rule for capital property is, as we have noticed,[66] that on the death of the owner there is a deemed disposition at fair market value. This is imposed by s. 70(5). Subsection 70(6) constitutes an exception to s. 70(5). Where on the death of a taxpayer a capital property is inherited by the taxpayer's spouse (s. 70(6)(a)) or spouse trust (s. 70(6)(b)), then the deemed disposition of s. 70(5) does not apply. Instead, s. 70(6) deems the property to have been disposed of by the deceased for proceeds of disposition equal to the adjusted cost base of the property, and to have been acquired by the spouse or spouse trust for the same figure. This creates a rollover on death similar in design to that created for inter vivos dispositions by s. 73(1).

The rollover under s. 70(6), like its inter vivos counterpart under s. 73(1), can also be avoided by an election. Subsection 70(6.2) enables the legal representative of the deceased taxpayer to elect against the rollover. If this election is made, s. 70(5) will apply to the property passing to the spouse or spouse trust so that there will be a deemed disposition at fair market value. If no election is made, the rollover occurs automatically. The election would be especially advantageous if the property passing to the spouse had accrued gains, and the deceased was otherwise in a loss position in the terminal year; in that case, the losses could be used to eliminate the gains on the spousal property. (Since losses cannot be carried forward beyond the terminal year, unused losses would be wasted.) Even if the deceased had income in the terminal year, if the income was particularly low an election might be worthwhile to take advantage of the low rate of tax. If the spousal property had accrued losses, but the deceased did have income in the terminal year, an election would enable the losses to be used to reduce income in the terminal year.[67] (In the terminal year, allowable capital losses and net capital losses are deductible against income from all sources, not just taxable capital gains: s. 111(2)).[68]

(c)   Transfer to child

On a transfer of capital property by a parent to a child, there is no general rollover provision equivalent to those applicable to transfers between spouses. The idea of the family as the taxation unit has not progressed that far yet. However, on a transfer from a parent to a child, there is a rollover provision for

---

[66] Section 15.14(c), "Death", above.

[67] A deemed disposition under s. 70 is exempted from the definition of a "superficial loss": note 60, above.

[68] Chapter 18, Losses, under heading 18.2, "Capital losses", below.

one class of capital property, namely, farming property (ss.70(9) to (11), 73(3) to (4)). The purpose of this rollover is to facilitate the retention within a family of a farm. If tax were payable on the accrued gain in a farm when the property passed from parent to child, the resulting requirement of cash might force the sale of the farm. The solution is the rollover, allowing farming property to pass (either inter vivos or on death) from parent to child without the need to recognize any accrued capital gains. This rollover is not essentially different from the spousal rollover, although it includes a more complicated elective provision. The rollover on the disposition of farming property to a child of the taxpayer will not be discussed in detail in this book.

(d)   Transfer to corporation

On a transfer of property to a corporation in return for shares of the corporation, s. 85 makes a rollover available. The idea is to eliminate any tax cost from the incorporation of a business, which obviously involves the transfer of business assets to the new corporation in return for shares of the corporation. The rollover is also available where property is transferred to an established corporation in return for shares of the corporation. To the extent that the transferor receives from the corporation non-share consideration such as cash or a debt (non-share consideration is often called "boot"), there is a genuine realization of the property transferred which should attract normal capital gains treatment. Section 85 accordingly regulates how much non-share consideration can be received without losing (or partially losing) the rollover. The section is hedged with other restrictions as well, and is elective. The resulting law is quite complex, and will not be discussed in this book.

There are other corporate rollovers in addition to the s. 85 rollover: on a share-for-share exchange (where one corporation takes over the shares of another in return for treasury shares of the acquiring corporation: s. 85.1), on certain corporate reorganizations and amalgamations (ss. 86, 87) and on the winding-up of a corporation's wholly owned subsidiary (s. 88(1)). These rollovers are all automatic and are provided to remove tax impediments to changes in corporate structure that do not involve a genuine realization of capital assets. These rollovers are outside the scope of this book.

15.16   Personal-use property

(a)   Definition

Personal-use property is defined in s. 54 as property owned by a taxpayer "that is used primarily for the personal use or enjoyment of the taxpayer" or of "a person related to the taxpayer". It thus includes such things as cottages, cars, bicycles, boats, sporting or recreational equipment, household appliances, furniture and clothing. It also includes principal residences, but the unique tax treatment of the principal residence is explained separately later in this chapter.[69]

(b)   No-loss rule

Subparagraph 40(2)(g)(iii) provides that a loss from the disposition of personal-use property (other than "listed personal property", discussed below) is deemed to be nil. The reason for the no-loss rule is that the depreciation of personal-use property is normally the result of its having been used for the personal enjoyment of the taxpayer. The decline in value is therefore treated as an expense of consumption which, like other expenses of consumption, should not be recognized for tax purposes. The same argument does not apply to *gains* on personal-use property: they are real additions to the owner's wealth and are accordingly taxed as capital gains (subject to the $1,000 rule, discussed below).

Example (A)

Taxpayer A purchases a car for his personal use for $7,000, and sells it three years later for $4,000. Subparagraph 40(2)(g)(iii) deems the loss to be nil. The actual loss of $3,000 is treated as the cost of using a car for personal use.

Example (B)

Taxpayer B purchases a cottage for her personal use for $80,000, and sells it four years later for $90,000. The gain of $10,000 must be recognized as a capital gain, three-quarters taxable.

(c)   Listed personal property

There is an exception to the rule that there can be no capital losses on personal-use property, and that relates to "listed personal property". Listed personal property is defined in s. 54 as follows:

> "listed personal property" of a taxpayer means the taxpayer's personal-use property that is all or any portion of, or any interest in or right to, any
>
> (a)   print, etching, drawing, painting, sculpture, or other similar work of art,
>
> (b)   jewellery,
>
> (c)   rare folio, rare manuscript, or rare book,
>
> (d)   stamp, or
>
> (e)   coin;

LPP

Although listed personal property is personal-use property (as the definition states), capital losses on listed personal property are deductible, but only against capital gains from listed personal property. The reason for this special treatment is that art, jewellery, rare books, stamps and coins, while they are used for the personal use or enjoyment of the owner, also have the characteristics of

---

[69]   Section 15.17, "Principal residence", below.

investments. Declines in their value would not normally be attributable to use, but to changing market conditions similar to those which affect other forms of investment. Since a decline in the value of listed personal property is not likely to be a consumption expense, there is no reason to treat it any differently than the decline in the value of capital property generally. However, the Act strikes a compromise between treating it as personal-use property, in which case losses would be disallowed, and treating it as non-personal-use property, in which case losses would be allowed in accordance with the general capital loss rules. The compromise is to permit losses on listed personal property to be deducted, but only against gains on listed personal property.

The compromise tax treatment of losses on dispositions of listed personal property may be seen by examining s. 3(b), the provision which brings taxable capital gains and allowable capital losses into the computation of income. Clause 3(b)(i)(B) brings into income a taxpayer's "taxable net gain for the year from dispositions of listed personal property"; the "net gain" is a figure which is derived by deducting losses from gains on personal-use property in accordance with the rules established by s. 41(2); and the "taxable net gain" is three-quarters of the net gain (s. 41(1)). If losses on dispositions of listed personal property exceed gains in a taxation year, the net loss is not deductible under s. 3(b)(ii) or s. 3(e). The net loss is called the taxpayer's "listed-personal-property loss" for the year (s. 41(3)), and it may be carried back three years and forward seven years and deducted against gains on listed personal property in those years in accordance with the rules in s. 41(2).[70]

(d) $1,000 rule

Another peculiarity of the tax treatment of personal-use property is the $1,000 rule, which is contained in s. 46(1):

> 46(1) Where a taxpayer has disposed of any personal-use property of the taxpayer, for the purposes of this subdivision
>
> (a)   the adjusted cost base to the taxpayer of the property immediately before the disposition shall be deemed to be the greater of $1,000 and the amount otherwise determined to be its adjusted cost base to the taxpayer at that time; and
>
> (b)   the taxpayer's proceeds of disposition of the property shall be deemed to be the greater of $1,000 and the taxpayer's proceeds of disposition of the property otherwise determined.

The effect of s. 46(1) is to exempt small transactions with personal-use property from capital gains. By deeming the adjusted cost base and the proceeds of disposition of personal-use property to be the higher of the actual figures or $1,000, s. 46(1) ensures that, where personal-use property with an adjusted cost base of less than $1,000 is sold for proceeds of disposition of less than $1,000,

---

[70] Chapter 18, Losses, under heading 18.3(b), "Listed-personal-property losses", below.

no capital gain is recognized. This is because both the adjusted cost base and the proceeds of disposition are deemed to be the same figure, namely, $1,000.

Example (C)

Taxpayer C disposes of a sailboat with an adjusted cost base of $700 for proceeds of disposition of $900. By s. 46(1), the adjusted cost base is deemed to be $1,000 and the proceeds of disposition are deemed to be $1,000, yielding a capital gain of zero.

Where the adjusted cost base is less than $1,000, but the proceeds of disposition exceed $1,000, a capital gain will have to be recognized, but s. 46(1) will still bump the adjusted cost base up to $1,000, reducing the capital gain. In the previous example, if C's proceeds of disposition of the sailboat were $1,200, her actual gain would be $500 ($1,200 – $700 = $500), but her deemed gain would be only $200 ($1,200 – $1,000 = $200). Where the adjusted cost base and the proceeds of disposition are each more than $1,000, s. 46(1) will have no application, and any capital gain will be computed on the basis of the actual figures. (In order to preclude abuse of the $1,000 rule, there are special rules for the disposition of part of a personal-use property or part of a set of personal-use properties: ss. 46(2), (3).)

Subsection 46(1) can have the effect of eliminating capital losses as well as capital gains:

Example (D)

Taxpayer D disposes of a painting with an adjusted cost base of $2,500 for proceeds of disposition of $400. Since a painting is listed personal property (s. 54), s. 40(2)(g)(iii) does not deem the loss to be nil. However, s. 46(1) deems the proceeds of disposition to be $1,000, thereby reducing the capital loss from its actual figure of $2,100 ($2,500 – $400 = $2,100) to a deemed figure of $1,500 ($2,500 – $1,000 = $1,500).

The elimination or reduction of losses on the disposition of personal-use property is relevant only for listed personal property, since by virtue of s. 40(2)(g)(iii) losses on the disposition of other kinds of personal-use property are not recognized anyway.[71]

15.17 Principal residence

(a) Rationale of exemption

A taxpayer's home is, of course, "personal-use property". Normally, gains on the disposition of personal-use property have to be recognized for tax purposes, although losses are not allowable.[72] However, it is widely accepted

---

[71] Section 15.16(b), "No-loss rule", above.
[72] *Ibid.*

that a capital gain on the sale of a home should not attract tax. Where a home is sold, and a new home is to be purchased, any capital gain on the disposition of the old home is an illusory gain in the sense that the new home will have to be purchased in the same inflated market as the old home was sold. On the other hand, a similar comment could be made about many other capital gains, especially where they are solely the result of inflation. Certainly, the gain on a home would not seem to warrant special treatment in cases where the taxpayer buys the new home in a town where prices are lower (or buys a cheaper home), or if the taxpayer moves into rented accommodation, or if the taxpayer died and the family assets are being realized. In these cases, however, there still seems to be an emotional objection to levying tax on any gain on the home.

Even the Carter Commission was willing to allow an exemption for at least part of the capital gain on a taxpayer's home. The Commission recommended that there be an exemption of $1,000 gain per year, plus the value of improvements. The government's white paper accepted the Carter recommendations, but the final governmental decision was to exempt altogether (in most situations) any gain on the disposition of a taxpayer's "principal residence".

(b)   Definition of principal residence

"Principal residence" is defined in s. 54 of the Act. For a property to qualify as a principal residence in a particular taxation year it must satisfy three basic requirements: (1) the property must be "owned, whether jointly with another person or otherwise . . . by the taxpayer" (opening words of the definition); (2) the property must be "ordinarily inhabited" in the year by the taxpayer or the taxpayer's spouse (or former spouse) or child (paragraph (a) of the definition); and (3) the property must be "designated" by the taxpayer to be his or her principal residence for the year (paragraph (c) of the definition).[73] Some other elements of the definition, which are contained in paragraphs (b) and (d), are concerned with changes in the use of the property, and are considered later.[74]

Each of the three basic elements of the definition will now be considered.

(c)   Ownership

Ownership is an obvious element of the definition of principal residence, because only the owner would be entitled to receive, and be liable to pay tax on, any capital gain on the disposition of a property.

---

[73] A principal residence may also be owned by a trust, provided similar requirements are satisfied: references to "personal trust" in s. 54 definition of "principal residence".

[74] Section 15.17(g), "Change of use", below.

It will be noted that s. 54 does not require that the taxpayer be the sole owner of a principal residence. However, in cases of co-ownership, the question whether the entire gain on a principal residence is exempt will depend upon whether or not all of the co-owners are entitled to claim the exemption. When a property owned by more than one person is sold, the co-owners will be entitled to share the proceeds of disposition; any gain on the sale will thus be shared. Whether each co-owner has to recognize his or her share of the gain for tax purposes will depend upon whether each co-owner is entitled to designate his or her interest in the property sold as a principal residence for the period of ownership.

Example

A and B jointly own a house (a capital property). A and B are not (and have never been) married to each other (within the meaning of the Act).[75] A but not B has "ordinarily inhabited" the house for the period of their joint ownership. A and B sell the property for a capital gain otherwise determined of $20,000, of which they are each entitled to one-half.

In this example, A, who has ordinarily inhabited the property, will be able to designate the property as his principal residence for the period of ownership, which will eliminate any capital gain for him. But B, who has not ordinarily inhabited the property, will be unable to designate the property as her principal residence and will therefore have to recognize for tax purposes her share of the gain on sale. If B had ordinarily inhabited the property, then B as well as A would be able to designate the house as her principal residence and she too would obtain exemption for her share of the gain.

If A and B were married (within the meaning of the Act), or formerly married but separated, then, even if only A ordinarily inhabited the house, B (as well as A) would be entitled to designate the house as her principal residence for the period of ownership (s. 54 permits occupation by the taxpayer's "spouse or former spouse"), which would eliminate any capital gain to B (as well as A). This shows that two spouses who are co-owners of the same property can both designate that property as a principal residence. (We shall see that two spouses cannot designate *different* properties as their principal residences at the same time.)[76]

(d)   Ordinarily inhabited

Paragraph (a) of the definition of "principal residence" stipulates that, in order to qualify as a principal residence for a particular year, the property must

---

[75] Note that s. 252(4) includes common-law relationships.

[76] Section 15.17(e), "Designation", below.

have been "ordinarily inhabited" in the year by the taxpayer, the taxpayer's spouse or former spouse or the taxpayer's child.

The term "ordinarily inhabited" is not defined in the Act, but the Department has issued an interpretation bulletin[77] which gives its interpretation of the term, as follows:

> The question of whether a housing unit is "ordinarily inhabited" in a taxation year by a taxpayer or by the spouse, former spouse or a child of the taxpayer must be resolved on the basis of the facts in each particular case. Where a housing unit is occupied by such a person for only a short period of time in the year (e.g., a seasonal residence occupied during a taxpayer's vacation or a house sold early or bought late in the year), it is the Department's view that the person ordinarily inhabits the housing unit in the year, provided that the principal reason for owning the property is not for the purpose of gaining or producing income.

This interpretation, which will grant principal residence status to a cottage or other seasonal residence which is only occupied for a short time in the year,[78] is a liberal one. The interpretation obtains some support by analogy from the cases interpreting the phrase "ordinarily resident", which have not insisted that a person spend most of his or her time in the particular country as long as time is spent there as part of the person's usual way of life, and which have decided that a person may be resident in several countries at the same time.[79]

The Department's liberal interpretation of "ordinarily inhabited" is carried forward to the conclusion that a taxpayer, who must be a Canadian resident to take advantage of the principal residence exemption (s. 40(2)(b)(i)), can have a principal residence outside Canada, such as a condominium in Florida, a ski lodge in Austria or a villa in the south of France.[80] While this appears implausible, the Act does not stipulate that the principal residence be in Canada, and since a person can be resident in more than one country at a time, it can hardly be doubted that a person could be resident in Canada and still "ordinarily inhabit" a property outside Canada.[81] Under the Department's interpretation of ordinarily inhabited, a taxpayer may own more than one property that is "ordinarily inhabited" by the taxpayer in a taxation year. The word "principal" in "principal residence" is not regarded as excluding a cottage in the country (for example) even if the taxpayer also owns a house in the city. However, a taxpayer is precluded from having more than one principal residence in any given year by

---

[77] Interpretation Bulletin IT-120R4, "Principal residence" (1993), para. 12.

[78] Cf. *Ennist* v. *M.N.R.*, [1985] 2 C.T.C. 2398, 85 D.T.C. 669 (T.C.C.) (taxpayer occupied newly-purchased condominium for only 24 hours, because of transfer to another city; held, condominium not ordinarily inhabited; principal residence designation denied).

[79] See ch. 8, Residence, under heading 8.5(a), "Ordinarily resident", above; McGregor, "Principal Residence" (1973) 22 *Can. Tax J.* 116, 120.

[80] IT-120R4, note 77, above, para. 41.

[81] McGregor, note 79, above, 121.

the restrictions on designation, which are explained in the next section of this chapter. The taxpayer is permitted to designate either the city house or the country cottage (in our example), but he or she cannot designate both.

Sometimes a taxpayer will use a house property partly to earn business or property income. For example, a homeowner may use one room as a home office; or the homeowner may operate a day care business in the home; or the homeowner may rent a room to a lodger; or the owner of a cottage (or other seasonal residence) may rent it for part of the year. The Department takes the position[82] that the whole of the property still qualifies as ordinarily inhabited by the owner so long as (a) the income-producing use "is ancillary to the main use of the property as a residence";[83] (b) the taxpayer did not make structural changes to the property to accommodate the income-producing use; and (c) the taxpayer does not claim capital cost allowance on the property. If these conditions are not satisfied, then the portion of the house used for the income-producing purpose would be ineligible for principal residence status. The rest of the property, which is used as a residence, would be ordinarily inhabited by the owner and therefore eligible for principal residence status.

(e) Designation

Paragraph (c) of the definition of "principal residence" in s. 54 stipulates that in order to qualify as a principal residence for a particular year the property must be "designated" by the taxpayer to be his or her principal residence for that year. The designation does not need to be made each year. It is made in the income tax return for the year in which the property is disposed of; at that time, the taxpayer designates the property as his or her principal residence for all the years for which he or she claims the property as a principal residence.[84]

In each year, a taxpayer may designate only one property as a principal residence, even if the taxpayer owned and ordinarily inhabited more than one property. Before 1982, it was possible for two spouses to each designate a property as his or her principal residence. The pre-1982 designation rule limited the designation to one principal residence per person, not per family unit, so that, if the city house were owned solely by one spouse and the country house were owned solely by the other spouse, the capital gains on both properties could be

---

[82] IT-120R4, note 77, above, para. 38.

[83] In *Saccamono* v. *M.N.R.*, [1986] 2 C.T.C. 2269, 86 D.T.C. 1699 (T.C.C.), it was held that the taxpayer ordinarily inhabited the whole of a property that was 70 per cent rented to existing tenants when the taxpayer acquired it; the taxpayer, although occupying only 30 per cent of the property, intended to occupy the entire property.

[84] Income Tax Regulations 2301. Revenue Canada's administrative position is more lenient. Form T2091, upon which the designation is made, need not be filed unless there is some remaining taxable capital gain on the residence after making the designation: IT-120R4, note 77, above, para. 13.

eliminated under the principal residence exemption. In 1982, the definition of principal residence was amended to limit the designation to one property per family unit. Now a taxpayer may designate a property to be his or her principal residence for a particular year only if no other property has been designated for that year by the taxpayer *or by the taxpayer's spouse* (or by the taxpayer's unmarried children under 18). The reference to the spouse (and child) restricts the designation to one principal residence per family.[85]

(f)   Surrounding land

Paragraph (e) of the definition of principal residence in s. 54 provides that the principal residence shall be deemed to include "the land subjacent to the housing unit and such portion of any immediately contiguous land as can reasonably be regarded as contributing to the use and enjoyment of the housing unit as a residence". If the total area of land under and around the principal residence exceeds half a hectare (which is approximately one acre), then the definition stipulates that "the excess shall be deemed not to have contributed to the use and enjoyment of the housing unit as a residence unless the taxpayer establishes that it was necessary to such use and enjoyment". In rural municipalities, there are often zoning restrictions that impose on residential land minimum lot sizes in excess of half a hectare. Where such a restriction is in force at the time that a residential property was purchased,[86] and where none of the property is used for an income-producing purpose,[87] the Department accepts that the full amount of the minimum lot is necessary to the use and enjoyment of the residence.[88] If the restriction is later relaxed "by circumstances or events beyond the taxpayer's control", and the owner subdivides and sells off some of the land, the portion sold will be eligible for principal residence designation.

---

[85] Subsection 40(6) is a transitional rule that grandparents a property that could have been designated before 1982. Under s. 40(6), the gain is split into two parts: the gain accrued to December 31, 1981 (when two spouses could each designate a different principal residence in the same year), and the gain accrued after December 31, 1981 (when two spouses could designate only one principal residence in the same year). If this s. 40(6) formula yields a higher exemption than the s. 40(2)(b) formula, then the s. 40(6) formula is applied. If not, then the s. 40(2)(b) formula is applied. The principal residence form T2091 sets out all the required calculations.

[86] Query correctness of *The Queen* v. *Yates*, [1986] 2 C.T.C. 48, 86 D.T.C. 6296 (F.C.A.); affg. [1983] C.T.C. 105, 106, 83 D.T.C. 5158, 5159 (F.C.T.D.), asserting, obiter, that it is the restrictions in place at the time of disposition that are critical.

[87] Query correctness of *The Queen* v. *Yates*, previous note, allowing principal residence status to portion of residential lot that was sold separately from the house, and that had always been rented to a farmer who grew crops on it.

[88] IT-120R4, note 77, above, paras. 21-23. The Department's positions seem to be more consonant with sound policy than those of the leading case, notes 86, 87, above.

(g) Mechanism of exemption

The exemption of the gain on the disposition of a principal residence is contained in s. 40(2)(b), which provides as follows:

> 40(2)(b) where the taxpayer is an individual, the taxpayer's gain for a taxation year from the disposition of a property that was the taxpayer's principal residence at any time after the date, (in this section referred to as the "acquisition date") that is the later of December 31, 1971 and the day on which the taxpayer last acquired or reacquired it, as the case may be, is the taxpayer's gain therefrom for the year otherwise determined minus that proportion thereof that
>
> > (i) one plus the number of taxation years ending after the acquisition date for which the property was the taxpayer's principal residence and during which the taxpayer was resident in Canada,
>
> is of
>
> > (ii) the number of taxation years ending after the acquisition date during which the taxpayer owned the property whether jointly with another person or otherwise;

Paragraph 40(2)(b) does not simply exempt from tax the capital gain on the disposition of a principal residence. Instead, it provides a formula for the calculation of the gain which is designed to yield a zero gain for a property which has been the taxpayer's principal residence for the entire period of the taxpayer's ownership, and to yield a proportionately reduced gain for a property which was the taxpayer's principal residence for only part of the period of his or her ownership. The formula may be stated as follows (G.O.D. meaning "gain otherwise determined"):

$$\text{Gain} = \text{G.O.D.} - \left(\text{G.O.D.} \times \frac{1 + \text{no. of years principal residence}}{\text{no. of years owned}} \right)$$

Under the s. 40(2)(b) formula, one first calculates the capital gain on the disposition of the principal residence in the usual way, namely, by subtracting the adjusted cost base from the proceeds of disposition. That is the gain "otherwise determined". The gain otherwise determined is then reduced by subtracting from it an amount calculated by multiplying the gain otherwise determined by a fraction of which the numerator (the top of the fraction) is one plus the number of taxation years ending after 1971 for which the property was the taxpayer's principal residence and the taxpayer was resident in Canada, and the denominator (the bottom of the fraction) is the number of taxation years ending after 1971 during which the taxpayer owned the property. The term "taxation year" includes the whole or any part of a taxation year.

Where the numerator and denominator of the fraction are equal, then the amount to be deducted from the gain otherwise determined will be equal to the gain otherwise determined. In the result, therefore, the capital gain on the property will be zero. Because this formula includes "one plus" in the numerator, it will sometimes yield a numerator which is one more than the denominator. This produces the clumsy result that the amount to be deducted from the gain will be larger than the gain. This will give a negative figure. The Act provides by s. 257 that the negative figure is to be treated as nil.

The reason for including "one plus" in the formula for the numerator is to allow for the situation where the taxpayer is unable to designate the property as a principal residence for one of the years in which he or she owned it. This will arise where the property was purchased in the same year that a previous principal residence was sold. Only one property can be designated as a principal residence in any one taxation year (paragraph (c) of the definition of "principal residence" in s. 54), and in the year of sale and purchase the taxpayer probably will have designated the property sold as his or her principal residence. On the sale of the second residence, the taxpayer is only able to designate it as his or her principal residence for one less than the actual number of years that he or she owned it. The addition of one year to the numerator corrects this problem by bringing the fraction up to one, thereby cancelling out all of the capital gain.

Example

A house was purchased by T in 1995 for $200,000, was ordinarily inhabited by T, and was sold by T in 1997 for $230,000.

The sale of the house in 1997 has yielded a gain of $30,000. If T, in her taxation return for 1997 (reg. 2301), were to designate the house as her principal residence for 1996 and 1997, a total of two years, her gain under s. 40(2)(b) would be zero, calculated as follows:

Gain Otherwise Determined (G.O.D.) (1):	$30,000
Less Exemption (2): $30,000 \times \dfrac{1+2}{3}$:	30,000
Gain [(1) − (2)]	0

In this example, T did not designate the house as her principal residence for 1995. The designation would not have been available for 1995 if it had been used to exempt the gain on a previous residence disposed of in 1995. However, the "one plus" rule of s. 40(2)(b) makes up for the missing year and enables the gain to be reduced to zero. If T had been able to designate the house as her principal residence for 1995, then she would only need to use 1995 and 1996 to reduce her gain to zero. She could then save 1997 for her next principal residence.

If a taxpayer owns more than one property that she ordinarily inhabits (within the meaning of the principal residence definition in s. 54), things become more complicated. Now she must calculate the gain per year on each property, and factor in the "one plus" rule, to determine how best to allocate each year of principal residence designation.

Example

A house was purchased by T in 1993 for $100,000, was ordinarily inhabited by T, and was sold in 1997 for $150,000.

A cottage was purchased by T in 1994 for $80,000, was ordinarily inhabited by T, and was sold in 1997 for $140,000.

A ski chalet was purchased by T in 1995 for $120,000, was ordinarily inhabited by T, and was sold in 1997 for $140,000.

In this example, T has sold three properties in 1997, and each of them is eligible for the principal residence designation. Only one can be designated each year. Which should be selected? The first step is to calculate the gain per year on each property:

— the house has a $10,000 gain per year ($50,000/five years);

— the cottage has a $15,000 gain per year ($60,000/four years); and

— the ski chalet has a $6,667 gain per year ($20,000/three years).

Since the cottage has the highest gain per year ($15,000), it should be designated for three of the four years of its ownership, using the "one plus" rule to cover off the fourth year. Since the house has the second highest gain per year ($10,000), it should be designated next. A designation of four of the five years of ownership would completely exempt the gain, but three of those years have been used up for the cottage. Two years are available for the designation of the house, but two is not the best answer, because if one year were allocated to the ski chalet the one plus rule would make that designation more valuable than allocating a second year to the house.

There is room for some variation in the actual calendar years designated for each property (although the property must be owned in the year of designation). One possible allocation would look like this:

	House	**Cottage**	**Ski chalet**
G.O.D. (1)	$50,000	$60,000	$20,000
# of years owned	5 (1993-97)	4 (1994-97)	3 (1995-97)
gain per year	$10,000	$15,000	$ 6,667
years designated	1 (1993)	3 (1994-96)	1 (1997)
Exemption (2)	$50,000 × $\frac{1+1}{5}$	$60,000 × $\frac{3+1}{4}$	$20,000 × $\frac{1+1}{3}$
	= $20,000	= $60,000	= $13,334
Gain [(1)−(2)]	$30,000	0	$6,666

In this example, we assumed that the three principal residences were sold in the same year, which would not often happen in practice. If, for example, the ski chalet was not sold in 1997, and T had no intention of selling it in the near future, then the eventual gain on the property would be uncertain (it might even fall in value). Even if the property were likely to increase in value, the time value of money[89] would diminish the value of any tax savings to be derived many years hence from the designation of the ski chalet. On these facts, it might be better not to save a year of designation for the ski chalet, and to obtain the immediate tax saving that would be derived by designating the house for a second year.

Paragraph 40(2)(b) will result in an apportionment of the gain in some situations where the property disposed of was used as a principal residence for some of the period of the taxpayer's ownership, and as an income-producing property for the rest of the taxpayer's ownership. However, in order to identify the situations where this occurs, we must first consider the provisions of the Act that deal with a change of use of capital property.

(h)   Change of use

(i)   Deemed disposition

Paragraph 45(1)(a) provides for a deemed disposition at fair market value when property is converted from a non-income-producing use to an income-producing use, and vice versa. This deemed disposition has already been briefly discussed.[90] It is of general application within subdivision c of the Act, but our present concern is with its application to a house acquired as a principal residence and subsequently used to earn rent. In that case, the conversion to rental use would result in a deemed disposition at fair market value. There would be no taxable capital gain, even if the property had increased in value, because the property had been used exclusively as the taxpayer's principal residence. Nor would there be an allowable capital loss, even if the property had declined in value, because the property would be personal-use property in respect of which capital losses are not allowable. However, there would be three indirect tax consequences: (1) the property could no longer be designated as a principal residence; (2) the fair market value of the building (exclusive of the land) at the time of the change of use would become the capital cost of the property from which capital cost allowances could be claimed (s. 13(7)(b)); and (3) the fair market value of the property (land and building) at the time of the change of use would become the adjusted cost base of the property for capital gains purposes (s. 45(1)(a)(iv)).

If the former principal residence, now used to earn rent, were sold, then any gain (or loss) over fair market value at the time of the change of use would have to be recognized for tax purposes. There would be no apportionment of the gain under s. 40(2)(b), because the tax-free status of the principal residence was

---

[89] See ch. 6, Taxation Year, under heading 6.5, "Postponement of tax", above.

[90] Section 15.14(f), "Change of use", above.

recognized at the time of the change of use; the deemed disposition at that time marked a fresh break with a new cost base.

(ii)   Election against deemed disposition

The deemed disposition on a change from a non-income-producing use to an income-producing use can be avoided by making an election under s. 45(2).[91] Subsection 45(2) permits a taxpayer who has changed property from a non-income-producing use to an income-producing use to elect to "be deemed not to have begun to use the property for the purpose of gaining or producing income"; in that case, no deemed disposition occurs until "the taxpayer rescinds the election". An election under s. 45(2), by avoiding the deemed disposition, will postpone the recognition of any accrued capital gain or loss: the property will retain its existing adjusted cost base. The election will also prevent the taxpayer from claiming capital cost allowance in respect of the property, because reg. 1102(1)(c) excludes from the classes of depreciable property any property "that was not acquired by the taxpayer for the purpose of gaining or producing income". Needless to say, the income yielded by the property will be subject to tax as business or property income under subdivision b, and all applicable expenses except capital cost allowances will be deductible.

When a principal residence is converted to an income-producing use, paragraph (b) of the definition of "principal residence" in s. 54 makes clear that a s. 45(2) election will enable the property to continue to be designated as a principal residence, notwithstanding the fact that the property is no longer "ordinarily inhabited by the taxpayer". However, paragraph (d) of the definition provides that the designation as a principal residence can continue for only four years; at the end of four years, the designation is no longer available.[92] Paragraph (d) is designed to meet the case of the taxpayer who moves out of his or her principal residence with the intention of returning to it within four years. A disposition of a principal residence which has been rented for four years or less, and in respect of which a s. 45(2) election has been made, will accordingly attract no taxable capital gain.

The four-year period, in which a principal residence designation continues to be available in respect of income-producing property, is indefinitely extended by s. 54.1. Section 54.1 applies where a taxpayer has moved out of his or her home as the result of the relocation of the taxpayer's place of employment by his or her employer, and where the taxpayer subsequently moves back into the house

---

[91] The s. 45(2) election should be filed with the tax return for the year in which the change of use occurs, although Revenue Canada's administrative practice is to accept late-filed elections as long as no capital cost allowance has been claimed: IT-120R4, note 77, above, para. 31.

[92] The expiry of the four-year designation window does not cause a deemed disposition of the property. That will not occur until the s. 45(2) election is actually rescinded.

while still employed by the same employer or immediately following the termination of his or her employment by that employer.

Example

> T, who occupies a principal residence in Toronto, is employed in Toronto by Imperial Oil. Imperial Oil moves T to Calgary, where she remains for ten years. On the move to Calgary she rents her Toronto home, making an election under s. 45(2). At the end of ten years, while still employed by Imperial Oil, T moves back to Toronto and resumes occupation of her house.

When T eventually sells her house, s. 54.1 will apply and the designation as a principal residence will be available for the entire ten-year period when the taxpayer was located in Calgary. If the taxpayer had moved to Calgary to a job with a new employer, then s. 54.1 would not apply. Nor would s. 54.1 apply if, after having been moved to Calgary by Imperial Oil, T had changed jobs in Calgary and had not resumed occupation of her Toronto home before the end of the following taxation year.

The election under s. 45(2) to avoid the deemed disposition is available only where property is converted from a non-income-producing use to an income-producing use. It does not apply to the opposite case, where property is converted from an income-producing use to a non-income-producing use, despite the fact that this change of use also causes a deemed disposition under s. 45(1)(a). However, s. 45(3) provides an election in this case, so long as the property "becomes the principal residence of the taxpayer". This covers the case where a taxpayer acquires a house for the purpose of earning income, rents it to a tenant, and later on, after the tenant leaves, the taxpayer moves into the house himself and occupies it as a personal residence. Subsection 45(3) allows the taxpayer to elect against the deemed disposition that would otherwise be caused by the change of use that occurred when he began to occupy the property. This election enables the taxpayer to postpone the recognition of any capital gain on the property that had accrued up to the time of the change of use.[93] When the property is eventually disposed of, the principal residence designation will be available for four of the years that the house was rented[94] as well as the later years when the house was actually occupied by the taxpayer.

---

[93] Subsection 45(4) provides that the s. 45(3) election is not available if the taxpayer has been deducting capital cost allowance in respect of the property. The restriction means that s. 45(3) cannot be used to postpone the recapture of capital cost allowance.

[94] Paragraphs (b) and (d) of the definition of principal residence (s. 54) allow the four-year window to a property that is subject to a s. 45(3) election as well as a s. 45(2) election. In addition, the "one plus" formula in s. 40(2)(b)(i) and the rule that part of a year equals a taxation year may have the effect of subtracting one or two years from the income-producing period and adding them to the principal residence period.

(iii) Partial change of use

Where a property, including a principal residence, has a partial change of use, s. 45(1)(c) provides for a partial deemed disposition. There is no provision in the Act allowing this deemed disposition to be avoided by election.

With respect to a principal residence, a common situation is where the owner, who used to use the property exclusively as a residence, takes in a boarder or uses one room as an office. In this kind of case, where the business or rental use of the property is ancillary to the main use of the residence, the Department takes the position that a change of use is not deemed to have occurred and that the entire property continues to qualify as a principal residence.[95] Moreover, provided that the taxpayer has set aside and used a certain area of the residence solely for the purpose of producing income, the taxpayer "may claim the expenses (other than capital cost allowance) pertaining to the portion of the property used for income-producing purposes". However, the taxpayer may not claim capital cost allowance on any portion of the residence; if the taxpayer does so, the Department's position is that a change of use has occurred.[96]

If a partial change of use in a principal residence is deemed to have occurred, whether because the new income-producing use is more than merely ancillary to the residential use, or because the owner wishes to claim capital cost allowance on the portion of the building used for the income-producing purpose, then a deemed disposition under s. 45(1)(c) occurs. Under s. 45(1)(c), the taxpayer is deemed to have disposed of the income-producing portion of the property for proceeds equal to the proportion of the fair market value of the property which the new income-producing use of the property bears to the total use of the property. Any gain will of course be tax-free because of the principal residence exemption of s. 40(2)(b), but on a subsequent disposition of the property any gain which is attributable to the income-producing portion of the property will be subject to tax as a capital gain. Any recaptured capital cost allowance will also come back into income.

The apportionment between residential and income-producing uses is made on the basis of the number of square feet or the number of rooms used for each purpose.[97] This apportionment has to be made even where the income-producing use is ancillary, and there has been no deemed disposition under s. 45(1)(c), if the taxpayer wishes to deduct "a reasonable portion of expenditures for maintenance of the residence".

---

[95] IT-120R4, note 77, above, para. 38. See also text accompanying note 82, above.

[96] *Ibid.*

[97] *Id.*, para. 29.

(i)   Residence requirement

In order to become entitled to the principal residence exemption for a particular year, s. 40(2)(b)(i) stipulates not only that the property sold must be designated as the taxpayer's principal residence for that year, but also that the taxpayer must be resident in Canada during that year. A taxpayer who leaves his or her principal residence in Canada, rents it (making an election under s. 45(2)), and who becomes non-resident for a period, cannot count the period of non-residence in reduction of the gain on a subsequent disposition of the house. Of course, the "one plus" formula in s. 40(2)(b)(i), and the rule that part of a year equals a taxation year, may suffice to overcome one or two years of non-residence, but more than that will result in a portion of the gain being recognized for tax purposes.

(j)   Business or property income

The tax-exempt status of the principal residence is of course referable only to capital gains. We have already noted that, if the principal residence is used to earn rent, or for business purposes, then the income must be reported and tax paid in the usual way. A less obvious point, perhaps, is that the acquisition and disposition of a principal residence, or more likely a series of principal residences, could be held to be trading in the properties, which is the carrying on of a business.[98] Any gain on trading activity would of course have to be recognized in full as business income,[99] and no principal residence exemption would be applicable.

---

[98] E.g., *May* v. *M.N.R.*, [1980] C.T.C. 2457, 80 D.T.C. 1413 (T.R.B.).

[99] Chapter 16, Investing and Trading, below.

16

Investing and Trading

16.1 Capital or income

When a profit is made on the sale of property the profit may be either a capital gain or income from a business. It cannot be income from property.[1]

---

[1] Chapter 12, Income from Business or Property: Inclusions, under heading 12.3(c), "Capital gains compared", above.

We have already noticed the exclusion of capital gains from the traditional Anglo-Canadian concept of income,[2] the Carter Commission's recommendation that they be fully taxed, and the eventual compromise embodied in the 1971 tax reform, which was that only one-half of capital gains were to be included in income. The preferential treatment of capital gains continues, although the 1988 tax reform increased the taxable portion of capital gains from one-half to three-quarters. A consequence of this preferential treatment is that the distinction between a capital gain and income from a business, which is of course fully taxed, continues to be important under the Act.

It is not difficult to describe the usual cases:

1. Investment
    T, a dentist, sells her Bell Canada stock, which she acquired as an income-producing investment. Any profit is a capital gain.

2. Personal-use property
    T, a bank employee, sells his cottage, which he acquired for recreation. Any profit is a capital gain.

3. Capital asset
    T, a shoe manufacturer, intending to move the location of her business, sells the factory for more than she paid for it. The profit (excess over capital cost) is a capital gain. (There may also be included in income a recapture of capital cost allowance.)

4. Inventory
    T, an automobile dealer, sells a car in the course of his business. Any profit is income from a business.

5. Speculation
    T, a lawyer, sells gold, which she acquired with a view to resale at a profit. Any profit is income from a business.

The Income Tax Act is not particularly helpful in distinguishing between even these usual cases. The definition of a "capital gain" in s. 39(1)(a) says in effect that a capital gain is a gain from the disposition of property which would not be taxed as ordinary income. The definition of a "capital loss" in s. 39(1)(b) is similar. This sends us to the definitions of various kinds of ordinary income, and specifically for present purposes to the definition of income from a business. "Business" is defined in s. 248(1) as follows:

> "business" includes a profession, calling, trade, manufacture or undertaking of any kind whatever and . . . an adventure or concern in the nature of trade but does not include an office or employment;

This is also not very helpful, although the reference to a "trade" includes the automobile dealer (case 4, above), and the reference to "an adventure or concern

---

[2] Chapter 9, Tax Base, under heading 9.5, "Capital gains", above.

in the nature of trade" includes the speculator (case 5, above). The exclusion from ordinary income of the profit on the sale of an investment (case 1, above), or of a property used for personal use (case 2, above) or of an income-producing business asset (capital asset or fixed asset) (case 3, above) depends on the traditional Anglo-Canadian assumption that income must be a yield from a productive source,[3] rather than on anything specific in the Income Tax Act. Yet those results are well settled: where property is purchased for some purpose other than resale, any gain realized when the property is eventually sold is not ordinary income. Before 1972, any such gain was entirely free of tax. Under the present Act, any such gain is a capital gain, three-quarters of which is taxed.[4]

16.2 Trade

(a)   Systematic buying and selling

As the case of the automobile dealer (case 4, above) shows, the profit from trading in property is income from a business. Anyone who buys and sells property in an organized way, with a reasonable expectation of profit, is a trader.[5] This is so even if trading in property is not the person's main line of business. In *Scott* v. *M.N.R.* (1963),[6] for example, the Supreme Court of Canada held that a lawyer who over a period of eight years had purchased 149 agreements and mortgages at a discount, using both his own and borrowed money, and who had then realized a profit by holding the obligations to maturity, was a trader whose gains were income from a business. By contrast, in *Wood* v. *M.N.R.* (1969),[7] the Supreme Court of Canada held that a lawyer who over a period of seven years purchased 13 mortgages at a discount, using only his own money, and then realized a profit by holding the mortgages to maturity, was an investor whose gains were capital gains (which were then untaxed). The Court in *Wood* emphasized that small factual differences could change the result in these cases, and held that the smaller volume of transactions and the exclusive use of savings (as opposed to borrowings) "was consistent with the making of personal investments out of his savings and not with the carrying on of a business".[8]

---

[3] *Id.*, under heading 9.2, "Source theory", above.

[4] The sale of "depreciable property" (upon which capital cost allowance may be claimed) may yield income in the form of recapture of capital cost allowance (ch. 14, under heading 14.2(m), "Recapture", above), but profit in excess of capital cost is a capital gain. The sale of "eligible capital property" by an individual, but not by a corporation, may also yield a capital gain: ch. 14, under heading 14.3, "Eligible capital expenditures", note 53, above.

[5] A business is an organized activity that is carried on with a reasonable expectation of profit: ch. 12, under heading 12.2(a), "Definition of business", above.

[6] [1963] S.C.R. 223, [1963] C.T.C. 176, 63 D.T.C. 1121 (S.C.C.).

[7] [1969] S.C.R. 330, [1969] C.T.C. 57, 69 D.T.C. 5073 (S.C.C.).

[8] *Id.*, 334; 60; 5075.

(b)   Relationship to taxpayer's other work

Where a series of transactions are related to the taxpayer's ordinary work, that will strengthen the inference that he or she is engaged in trading rather than personal investment. In *Cooper* v. *Stubbs* (1925),[9] for example, a member of a firm of cotton brokers, who also purchased and sold cotton futures on his own account, carrying out about 50 transactions per year, was held to be in the business of trading in cotton futures. Similarly, in *Morrison* v. *M.N.R.* (1928),[10] a member of a firm of grain commission merchants, who also bought and sold grain on his own account, carrying out 260 transactions in the taxation year in issue, was held to be a trader. In *Whittall* v. *M.N.R.* (1967),[11] a member of a firm of stockbrokers who bought and sold corporate shares and oil and gas rights on his own account was held to be a trader. In all these cases, the skill and experience of the taxpayer, coupled with the frequency of the transactions, led the courts to conclude that the profits were the product of organized business activity, namely, trading.

(c)   Inventory

Property that has been purchased for resale as part of a business is of course inventory or stock-in-trade,[12] whereas property that is used in a business to produce income over a period of time (plant, machinery, vehicles, etc.) is a capital asset (or fixed asset) (called "depreciable property" in the Income Tax Act).[13] A profit on the sale of inventory is income from a business, but a profit on the sale of a capital (fixed) asset is a capital gain.[14]

(d)   Change of use

Within a business, the classification of a particular asset will depend not only upon the purpose for which it was acquired, but upon the purpose for which it is used. In *Canadian Kodak Sales* v. *M.N.R.* (1954),[15] machines known as "recordaks" were rented by Kodak to customers; the recordaks were treated in

---

[9]   [1925] 2 K.B. 753 (C.A.).

[10] [1928] Ex. C.R. 75 (Ex. Ct.).

[11] [1967] C.T.C. 377, 67 D.T.C. 5264 (S.C.C.).

[12] Chapter 11, Income from Business or Property: Profit, under heading 11.6(e), "Accounting for inventory", above.

[13] Chapter 14, Income from Business or Property: Capital Expenditures, under heading 14.2(a), "Definition of depreciable property", above.

[14] The portion of the proceeds of disposition in excess of capital cost is a capital gain. If the proceeds are less than the capital cost, there is no capital loss; the tax consequences are governed by the rules respecting capital cost allowance, recapture and terminal loss: ch. 14, under heading 14.2, "Depreciable property", above.

[15] [1954] C.T.C. 375, 54 D.T.C. 1194 (Ex. Ct.).

Kodak's financial accounts as capital (fixed) assets and capital cost allowance was claimed for tax purposes. However, in 1951 there was a change of marketing policy and in that year and the following year half of all the leased recordaks were sold to the customers who had been renting them. Were the profits on these sales on account of capital or income? The Exchequer Court held that the profits were income. In effect, the Court decided that the change in corporate policy in 1951 and 1952, which had made the recordaks available for sale, had converted those recordaks that were sold from capital assets (the sale of which would have been on account of capital) to inventory (the sale of which gave rise to business income).

In *Edmund Peachey* v. *The Queen* (1979),[16] land which had been acquired for subdivision and sale was rezoned so that this plan became impossible. When the land eventually was sold, the corporate taxpayer argued that it had been converted from inventory to a capital asset so that the profit on sale was a capital gain. The Federal Court of Appeal rejected this argument on the facts, but the Court accepted that land (or other property) acquired as inventory could be converted to another purpose. What was required, however, and was lacking in this case, was an "unequivocal positive act implementing a change of intention". Presumably, constructing on the land a building for use by the taxpayer would have been an example of such an act.

16.3   Adventure in the nature of trade

(a)   Isolated transaction

When a taxpayer enters into an isolated transaction (or only a few transactions), he or she is not a trader; but if the transaction was a speculative one, intended to yield a profit, the profit will still be income from a business rather than a capital gain. This result flows from the inclusion of the phrase "adventure or concern in the nature of trade" in the Act's definition of "business".[17] It is well settled that a single transaction may be an adventure or concern in the nature of trade.[18]

---

[16] [1979] C.T.C. 51, 79 D.T.C. 5064 (F.C.A.).

[17] The definition is in s. 248(1); it is quoted under sec. 16.1, "Capital or income", above.

[18] *M.N.R.* v. *Taylor*, [1956] C.T.C. 189, 56 D.T.C. 1125 (Ex. Ct.); *Regal Heights* v. *M.N.R.*, [1960] C.T.C. 384, 60 D.T.C. 1270 (S.C.C.). Property that is the subject of an adventure in the nature of trade is inventory: *Friesen* v. *Canada*, [1995] 3 S.C.R. 103, [1995] 2 C.T.C. 369, 95 D.T.C. 5551 (S.C.C.). The inventory of an adventure in the nature of trade must be valued at cost (proposed s. 10(1.01)) rather than at the lower of cost or fair market value. See ch. 11, Income from Business or Property: Profit, under heading 11.6(e), "Accounting for Inventory", above.

(b)　Intention on acquisition

In distinguishing between an adventure in the nature of trade and an investment, the critical factor is the intention of the taxpayer at the time of the acquisition of the property. If the taxpayer's intention was to resell the property at a profit, then the transaction is an adventure in the nature of trade and any profit will be taxed as business income. If, on the other hand, the taxpayer's intention was to hold the property as a source of regular income (or any purpose other than resale), then the transaction is an investment and any profit will be taxed as a capital gain.[19]

It is often denied that there is any single test which will resolve the question whether a transaction is an adventure in the nature of trade. It is said that in addition to intention, many other factors must be considered: whether the property was acquired with borrowed funds; the period of ownership of the property; efforts made to attract purchasers or to make the property more marketable; the skill and experience of the taxpayer; the relationship of the transaction to the taxpayer's ordinary business; the nature of the property, especially whether it yields regular income; and the circumstances of the eventual sale, especially whether it arose from something unanticipated at the time of purchase.[20] It is true that the courts do consider a range of factors in determining whether or not a transaction is an adventure in the nature of trade, but it is submitted that these factors are no more than objective indicators of a speculative intention. In the nature of things, the taxpayer's oral evidence of his or her intention is self-serving and is bound to be suspect, and so the courts have tended to rely primarily on the objective facts surrounding the purchase of the property, the subsequent course of dealing and the circumstances of the sale in order to determine whether the taxpayer acquired the property as an investment or as a speculation. But the assertion that "every case depends upon its own facts", or that "no single test is determinative", is simply not satisfactory, because it seems to leave the issue to the unfettered discretion of the tribunal or court which is seized of it.

The issue cannot be discretionary because it requires the application of a legal concept — "adventure or concern in the nature of trade" — to a factual situation. The essence of "trade" is systematic buying and selling with a view to profit. An adventure or concern *in the nature of* trade is an isolated transaction (which lacks the frequency or system of a trade) in which the taxpayer buys property with the intention of selling it at a profit, and then sells it (normally at a profit, but sometimes at a loss). It is submitted that the only issue that is consistent with this analysis, and with the results of nearly all of the decided

---

[19] Beam and Laiken "Adventure or Concern in the Nature of Trade: Badges of Trade as the Key to Taxpayer Intention", (1996) 44 *Can.Tax. J.*, 888.

[20] See, e.g., Interpretation Bulletin IT-459, "Adventure or concern in the nature of trade" (1980).

cases,[21] turns on the intention of the taxpayer at the time when he or she acquired the property. If that intention was to realize a profit by resale, then the subsequent sale is the culmination of an adventure in the nature of trade and any profit (or loss) will be taxed as income (or loss) from a business. If that intention was something else, for example, to hold the property as an income-earning investment, or to use the property as a capital (fixed) asset in a business, or to use the property for personal purposes, then the subsequent sale of the property will be treated as a capital transaction. As the *Stikeman Tax Service*[22] pithily comments: "One of the first rules relating to true capital gains is that if one is to be had it should not be deliberately sought"!

(c)   Differing intentions

Since the intention of the taxpayer is the key, it follows that two parties to the same transaction may receive different tax treatment. When a farmer sells the farm to a developer, the farmer's gain is capital, because the property was acquired as a farm. But when the developer subdivides the property and sells off the lots, the developer's gain is income from a business, because the property was acquired for resale.

(d)   Change of intention

What is the legal position when a taxpayer's intention changes between the time of acquisition of the property and the time of sale? We have already noticed that assets in a business may be converted from inventory to fixed assets or vice versa.[23] Can a change of intention have a similar effect on an isolated transaction?

It is necessary to draw a distinction between property acquired as an investment (or for some other purpose not including resale) and property acquired for resale. In the former case (the investment), it is difficult to contend that a change of intention could convert the transaction into an adventure in the nature of trade. After all, the sale of an investment is inevitably preceded by a decision to sell the asset, and is often preceded by efforts to sell the asset. If this change in the intention of the taxpayer converted the transaction into an adventure in the nature of trade, then a capital gain could never be generated by a voluntary disposition, but only by an involuntary disposition such as an expropriation. That is of course ridiculous in light of the numerous cases which have held that the sale of an asset which was acquired to hold as an investment was on capital account. However, there are very few cases in which a court has

---

[21] *Irrigation Industries* v. *M.N.R.*, note 40 below, being an exception.

[22] Stikeman, *Canada Tax Service* (Carswell, looseleaf), vol. 2, commentary to s. 9.

[23] Section 16.2(d), "Change of use", above.

explicitly considered the effect of a taxpayer's decision to stop holding property as a source of income (or other purpose) and to turn it to account by sale.

One case in which the taxpayer's change of intention was considered is *McGuire* v. *M.N.R.* (1956).[24] In that case, the taxpayer had bought a small farm with the intention of living on it and working it as a farm, which is what he did for nine years. Then he subdivided the property into 52 lots, and sold the lots. This activity was relied upon by the Minister as showing that the taxpayer had embarked on a speculative venture. The Exchequer Court rejected the Minister's argument, holding that, since the property was not purchased for resale, the subsequent efforts to sell the property did not turn it into a speculative venture. The taxpayer's profit was held to be a capital gain. The English Court of Appeal reached the same result on similar facts in *Taylor* v. *Good* (1974).[25] These cases reflect the common-sense proposition that the decision to sell a property that was acquired for some purpose other than resale, and efforts to make the sale as advantageous as possible, do not convert the transaction into an adventure in the nature of trade.[26]

With respect to property acquired for resale, a change of intention evidenced by objective facts might well convert a speculative purchase into a capital transaction. If, for example, we reversed the chronology of *McGuire* and supposed that land purchased for subdivision and sale was converted by the owner into a farm upon which he lived and worked for a substantial period of time. When the property was eventually sold it would be arguable, on the analogy of the change of use of business assets,[27] that the property had lost its speculative character and the sale was on capital account. Less clear, perhaps, is the case where property purchased for resale is simply held for a very long time before resale. Here it would be arguable that some time in the long period of ownership the property must have ceased to be an object of trade and became an investment.[28]

---

[24] [1956] C.T.C. 98, 56 D.T.C. 1042 (Ex. Ct.).

[25] (1974), 49 T.C. 277 (C.A.).

[26] Contra, *Dawd* v. *M.N.R.*, [1981] C.T.C. 2999, 81 D.T.C. 887 (T.R.B.); *Turnbull* v. *M.N.R.*, [1984] C.T.C. 2800, 84 D.T.C. 1720 (T.C.C.). In both cases, the courts held that land originally purchased for reasons other than resale was converted to inventory by the owners' efforts to sell the land. The courts took the view that the amount of preparation for sale was more consistent with a business venture than with the steps an ordinary owner would take in preparing to sell a capital asset. As a result, the courts held that the properties were "converted" from capital assets to inventory when the owners committed themselves to subdividing and selling the properties. This required the courts to determine the dates at which the properties were converted to inventory: any gain in the value of the properties before the "conversion dates" would be on account of capital, while gains after the commitment to subdivide and sell would be on account of income.

[27] Section 16.2(d), "Change of use", above.

[28] Cf. *M.N.R.* v. *Thibeault*, [1964] C.T.C. 232, 64 D.T.C. 5151 (Ex. Ct.).

(e) Commodities

When a taxpayer buys and sells property which is not for personal use and which will not yield income there is a presumption that the taxpayer purchased the property with the intention of reselling it at a profit. The leading Canadian case is *M.N.R.* v. *Taylor* (1956),[29] in which the taxpayer purchased 1,500 tons of lead occupying 22 railway cars which he sold at a profit. This was an isolated transaction: the taxpayer had never made a similar purchase before. The Court held that the transaction was an adventure in the nature of trade, pointing out that the taxpayer could do nothing with such an asset except sell it; he could not have acquired it for any other purpose. The same conclusion has been reached with respect to the purchase and sale of commercial quantities of toilet paper,[30] whisky,[31] sugar,[32] and sulphuric acid.[33] These assets could be turned to account only by resale. They could not by their very nature be regarded as investments.

The presumption that a commodities transaction is an adventure in the nature of trade will be rebutted where the facts clearly point to an intention to invest. A commodity such as gold may be purchased without any intention of early resale. Being non-income-producing, gold can only be turned to account by resale, but there is a class of gold purchasers who do in fact have no intention of resale in the foreseeable future. They see gold as a "store of value", providing security against inflation, or against the volatility of paper currencies, or against the instability of governments; and notwithstanding the absence of regular income they buy gold with the intention of holding it for as long as possible. While there are no reported cases in which gold has been held to be an investment, there are cases in which undeveloped land has been held to be an investment on the ground that it was purchased as a long-term store of value.[34] These cases would apply to gold (or silver or other commodities) acquired for the same reason.[35]

Revenue Canada has issued an interpretation bulletin stating that "as a general rule" it is "acceptable" for "speculators" to report all their gains (or losses) from transactions in commodity futures or in commodities either as capital gains (or losses) or as business income (or loss), provided the same

---

[29] [1956] C.T.C. 189, 56 D.T.C. 1125 (Ex. Ct.).

[30] *Rutledge* v. *C.I.R.* (1929), 14 T.C. 490 (Ct. of Sess.).

[31] *C.I.R.* v. *Fraser* (1942), 24 T.C. 498 (Ct. of Sess.).

[32] *Atlantic Sugar Refineries* v. *M.N.R.*, [1948] C.T.C. 326, 4 D.T.C. 507 (Ex. Ct.).

[33] *Honeyman* v. *M.N.R.*, [1955] C.T.C. 151, 55 D.T.C. 1094 (Ex. Ct.).

[34] Section 16.3(i), "Real estate", below.

[35] See Eddy and Kerr, "Taxation and Commercial Law Aspects of Gold Transactions in Canada" (1980) 28 *Can. Tax J.* 401.

reporting is followed consistently from year to year.[36] This position allows a "speculator" to make a one-time-only election of the tax treatment he or she prefers. Since this election is not expressly authorized by the Act (unlike, for example, the election with respect to Canadian securities),[37] it is probably not technically binding on either the taxpayer or the Minister.

(f)   Foreign exchange

Gains or losses on foreign exchange are often incidental to other transactions. Property or services may be bought or sold by a Canadian resident in terms of a foreign currency, and the foreign exchange rate may change between the time when the obligation to pay is created and the time when payment is made. In this situation, the primary transaction is the sale or purchase of the property or services. If that transaction is on income account, for example, a purchase of inventory or a sale of professional services, then the foreign exchange gain or loss will also be on account of income. If the primary transaction is on capital account, for example, the purchase or sale of an investment, then any foreign exchange or loss will also be on capital account. Gains or losses experienced through buying and selling foreign currency are subject to the same tax treatment as commodities,[38] including the administratively-established election that has been described.[39]

(g)   Income-producing property

When a taxpayer buys and sells property that is a traditional kind of investment, in the absence of a pattern of trading, the normal inference would be that the transaction was an investment and that any profit was a capital gain. In *Irrigation Industries* v. *M.N.R.* (1962),[40] the Supreme Court of Canada held that the purchase of shares in a company, made with borrowed money, and followed by sale only a month later (when the loan was called), was not an adventure in the nature of trade, but merely an investment. It seemed clear on the facts, and did not seem to be denied by the Court, that the taxpayer's purchase of the

[36] Interpretation Bulletin IT-346R, "Commodity futures and certain commodities" (1978), paras. 7, 8. The term "speculator" is defined in para. 6 as a person who does not come within the following three categories: (1) a person whose transactions are part of business operations that use commodities (e.g., a distillery); (2) a person whose transactions are based on special insider information; and (3) a corporation whose prime or only activity is trading in commodities. Revenue Canada insists on income treatment for persons in the three categories.

[37] Section 16.3(h), "Canadian securities", below.

[38] Section 16.3(e), "Commodities", above.

[39] See generally Interpretation Bulletin IT-95R, "Foreign exchange gains and losses" (1980), para. 6. A difference is created by s. 39(2), which provides that only an amount in excess of $200 of an individual's gain or loss on the disposition of foreign currency is taxable or allowable as a capital gain or loss.

[40] [1962] C.T.C. 215, 62 D.T.C. 1131 (S.C.C.).

shares was speculative, not designed to yield income in the form of dividends, but rather to yield a quick profit on resale. If this is so, then the decision is wrong. Martland J. for the Court said that corporate shares were intrinsically an investment in contrast to articles of commerce; and it did not matter that the shares were purchased "with the intention of disposing of the shares at a profit as soon as reasonably possible". But, with respect, the nature of the property is relevant only as casting light on the intention of the taxpayer. Once it is established that the taxpayer's intention was to speculate, the Court should have held that the transaction was an adventure in the nature of trade.

The general thrust of Martland J.'s opinion in *Irrigation Industries* was to deny that an isolated transaction in corporate shares could ever be treated as an adventure in the nature of trade. Later decisions of the Supreme Court of Canada, however, have made clear that this implausible proposition is not good law. In *M.N.R.* v. *Foreign Power Securities Corp.* (1967),[41] for example, the taxpayer (an investment company) sold at a profit a number of shares from its portfolio. The Supreme Court of Canada held that the profit was a capital gain and not income. This decision was based not on any inherent quality of corporate shares, but on the intention of the taxpayer. The Court held that the taxpayer had acquired the shares "as investments to be held as a source of income". The taxpayer had not acquired the shares for the purpose of resale, and had sold them only because its officers had concluded that "the shares had reached a price that was unreasonably high". In *M.N.R.* v. *Sissons* (1969),[42] the Supreme Court of Canada held that a purchase of corporate debentures at a discount was an adventure in the nature of trade, so that the profit obtained on maturity was income from a business. This was an isolated transaction by an individual who was a dealer in postage stamps. Yet Pigeon J. said that it was an adventure in the nature of trade, because "the purpose of the operation was not to earn income from the securities but to make a profit on prompt realization".

Foreign Power and *Sissons* confirm that the classification of transactions in corporate securities (whether shares or debt) does not depend upon any inherent characteristics of such securities, but on the intention with which they are acquired. If that intention is to hold the securities as a source of income (as in *Foreign Power*), then any profit on sale will be capital; if that intention is to make a profit by prompt realization (as in *Sissons*), then any profit on sale will be income. In other words, the intention test has survived the dicta of *Irrigation Industries*.[43]

---

[41] [1967] S.C.R. 295, [1967] C.T.C. 116, 67 D.T.C. 5084 (S.C.C.).

[42] [1969] S.C.R. 507, [1969] C.T.C. 184, 69 D.T.C. 5152 (S.C.C.).

[43] Accord, *Bossin* v. *The Queen*, [1976] C.T.C. 358, 76 D.T.C. 6196 (F.C.T.D.); *Tamas* v. *The Queen*, [1981] C.T.C. 220, 81 D.T.C. 5150 (F.C.T.D.); *Becker* v. *M.N.R.*, [1983] C.T.C. 11, 83 D.T.C. 5032 (F.C.A.); *Placements Bourget* v. *M.N.R.*, [1988] 2 C.T.C. 8, 88 D.T.C. 6274 (F.C.T.D.); *Karben Holden* v. *M.N.R.*, [1989] 2 C.T.C. 145, 89 D.T.C. 5413 (T.C.C.); *McGroarty*

While the foregoing cases all concerned corporate securities, the same principles would apply to other income-producing assets, such as mortgages and other debt obligations and developed real estate. The income-producing character of the property (in contrast to commodities) will give rise to a presumption that the property is held as an investment, but that presumption will be rebutted if the facts clearly indicate that the property was acquired not to yield income but to yield a profit on early sale.

(h)   Canadian securities

The question whether transactions in corporate securities are on account of capital or income is now affected by subsections (4), (5) and (6) of s. 39, which were added to the Income Tax Act in 1977. Subsection 39(4) permits a taxpayer to elect capital treatment for all dispositions of "Canadian securities" made by the taxpayer in the year of election and in any future year. "Canadian security" is defined in s. 39(6) as meaning shares or debt of a corporation resident in Canada.[44] The s. 39(4) election is permanent: the taxpayer is bound to accept capital treatment of dispositions of Canadian securities in future years. Capital treatment is of course the most favourable treatment of gains, but it may be unwelcome if losses are incurred in future years.[45]

The election is available to both individuals and corporations, provided that they are Canadian residents. By s. 39(5), various classes of persons are excluded from the right to elect. Paragraph (a) excludes "a trader or dealer in securities". The terms "trader" and "dealer" are not defined in the Act. In the context of s. 39(5), the terms should be limited to persons who hold themselves out to the public as dealers in shares, bonds or other securities. Under general tax law, as we have noticed, any person who buys and sells a high volume of securities on his or her own account with a view to profit from their short-term resale is a trader. According to the Federal Court of Appeal in *The Queen* v. *Vancouver Art Metal Works* (1993),[46] the private trader is excluded from election by virtue of paragraph (a) of s. 39(5). This means that a purported election under s. 39(4) does not preclude litigation on the vexed question of whether a person is or is not a trader. The decision greatly reduces the usefulness of the s. 39(4) election. As we have seen, a person held not to be a trader would be entitled to capital gains treatment anyway, except in respect of a particular transaction held to be an adventure in the nature of trade. By virtue of the decision in *Vancouver Art Metal Works*, the only purpose served by a s. 39(4)

---

v. *M.N.R.*, [1989] 1 C.T.C. 2280, 89 D.T.C. 185 (T.C.C.); *Pollock* v. *M.N.R.*, [1994] 1 C.T.C. 3, 93 D.T.C. 6050 (F.C.A.). See generally Durnford, "Profits on the Sale of Shares" (1987) 35 *Can. Tax J.* 837.

[44] There is an exception for "prescribed" securities, which are defined in reg. 6200.

[45] Section 16.4, "Losses", below.

[46] [1993] 1 C.T.C. 346, 93 D.T.C. 5116 (F.C.A.).

election is to preclude the question whether a particular transaction by a non-trader is an adventure in the nature of trade.

(i)   Real estate

Developed land that produces income representing a reasonable rate of return on its capital cost may obviously be either an investment or a speculation, depending upon the intention with which it was acquired. If the intention was to hold the land as a source of income, then it is an investment and any profit (or loss) on sale will receive capital treatment. If the intention was to take a profit by reselling the land, then any profit (or loss) on sale will receive income treatment.

In *H. Fine and Sons* v. *M.N.R.* (1984),[47] for example, the taxpayer corporation purchased land and erected a warehouse on the site. The taxpayer began carrying on business at the site, but experienced financial difficulties several years later, forcing it to sell off some of the land. In reporting its income for the taxation year in question, the taxpayer reported the gain from the sale of the land as a capital gain. The Federal Court-Trial Division agreed with the taxpayer. The taxpayer had purchased the land not for a speculative purpose but with the intention of using it as a capital (fixed) asset of the business. Therefore, the transaction was not an adventure in the nature of trade, and the gain was on account of capital. In *Paquet* v. *M.N.R.* (1982),[48] the taxpayer had purchased a farm with the intention of working the land, and had only sold for a profit after receiving unsolicited offers from family and friends. As was the case in *H. Fine and Sons*, the taxpayer in *Paquet* was found not to have purchased the property with a speculative intention, and the profit from the sale was accordingly held to be a capital gain.

In many cases, of course, the acquisition of land will be motivated by both the intention to hold it as an investment as well as the intention of selling the property at a profit. An attempt is made to analyze that situation under heading 16.3(g), "Secondary intention", below.

What about undeveloped land which yields little or no income and which has not been purchased for recreation or development? On the one hand, undeveloped land is like a commodity (such as lead) in that it can produce a return to the owner only by being sold. On the other hand, undeveloped land is unlike most commodities in that it is sometimes purchased and held for a long time as a store of value.[49] In two cases, taxpayers have been able to establish that non-income-producing land was held as an investment. In both *M.N.R.* v.

---

[47] [1984] C.T.C. 500, 84 D.T.C. 6520 (F.C.T.D.).

[48] [1982] C.T.C. 2144, 82 D.T.C. 1148 (T.R.B.).

[49] Gold or silver are sometimes purchased for this reason too: sec. 16.3(e), "Commodities", above.

Lawee (1972)[50] and *Montfort Lakes Estates* v. *The Queen* (1980),[51] the Federal Court-Trial Division found that the land had been acquired to provide security against inflation over a long term without any intention of sale at an early opportunity. When resale did occur (after nine years in *Lawee* and 18 years in *Montfort*), the profit was held to be a capital gain.

The Department has issued an interpretation bulletin dealing with the sale of real estate,[52] but it simply purports to describe the general law, not offering any election comparable to that available for commodities[53] or Canadian securities.[54] The classification of transactions in real estate therefore continues to be a major field of battle in the courts.

(j)   Secondary intention

One of the difficulties of intention as the key to the classification of transactions is that a taxpayer may have more than one intention at the time when he or she purchases property. This fact has given rise to the "secondary intention" doctrine. If property is purchased with the primary intention of using it in some non-speculative way, but with a secondary (alternative) intention of selling it at a profit if the primary purpose proves impracticable, then if the secondary intention is carried out the transaction will be held to be on account of income rather than capital. For example, in the leading case of *Regal Heights* v. *M.N.R.* (1960),[55] the taxpayer acquired undeveloped land with the primary intention of building a shopping centre on the site. After some development work had been done, the plan was abandoned when it was discovered that another shopping centre was to be built only two miles from the taxpayer's property. The taxpayer then sold the land at a profit. In the Supreme Court of Canada, it was held that the profit was income from a business. The trial judge had found that the corporate taxpayer's primary intention was to develop the land into a shopping centre, but the judge had also found that there was a good chance that the shopping centre plan might not come off and that the taxpayer was aware of this and had a secondary intention to sell the land at a profit if the primary intention became impracticable. The Supreme Court of Canada accepted these findings and held that the existence of the secondary intention made the enterprise an adventure in the nature of trade.

---

[50] [1972] C.T.C. 359, 72 D.T.C. 6342 (F.C.T.D.).

[51] [1980] C.T.C. 27, 79 D.T.C. 5467 (F.C.T.D.).

[52] Interpretation Bulletin IT-218R, "Profit, capital gains and losses from the sale of real estate" (1986).

[53] Section 16.3(e), "Commodities", above.

[54] Section 16.3(h), "Canadian securities", above.

[55] [1960] C.T.C. 384, 60 D.T.C. 1270 (S.C.C.).

Since *Regal Heights* was decided, there has been a flood of cases on the secondary intention doctrine. While the cases have not been entirely consistent, two decisions of the Federal Court of Appeal (none of the cases have gone to the Supreme Court of Canada) have helped to define the state of mind that will qualify as a secondary intention. In *Reicher* v. *The Queen* (1975),[56] the taxpayer, who was a professional engineer, acquired land to construct an office building. The building was constructed, the taxpayer moved his offices into it, and excess space was rented to third parties. However, about a year later, the taxpayer sold the property at a profit, taking back a lease from the purchaser. The taxpayer testified that the sale-and-lease-back had been caused by financial difficulties which had arisen unexpectedly after the project was well under way. The Federal Court of Appeal accepted this explanation for the early sale and held that resale was not a motivating reason for the acquisition of the property; the transaction was therefore not an adventure in the nature of trade. A similar decision was reached in *Hiwako Investments* v. *The Queen* (1978),[57] where the taxpayer purchased a group of apartment buildings, and then sold them at a profit less than a year later. The sale had been made after it was discovered that the buildings were less profitable than anticipated, and in response to an unsolicited offer. The Federal Court of Appeal recognized that the taxpayer had purchased the property for capital appreciation as well as the rental income. But this alone did not amount to a secondary intention to sell. The Court held that resale was not a motivating reason for the purchase. Therefore, the secondary intention doctrine did not apply, and the transaction was not an adventure in the nature of trade.

What *Reicher* and *Hiwako* establish is that the secondary intention to sell must have existed at the time when the property was acquired, and that it must have been "an operating motivation" or a "motivating reason" for the acquisition of the property. This language is intended to emphasize that a secondary intention does not exist merely because the taxpayer contemplates the *possibility* of resale of the property. That would be too strict a test, because any prudent investor would have that possibility in mind when purchasing an investment. In other words, it is not necessary for the taxpayer who claims to be an investor to show that his or her *exclusive* purpose was to acquire an investment. McDonnell, in one of a series of excellent case comments on this question in the *Canadian Tax Journal*, goes so far as to suggest that the prospect of resale at a profit is a motivating reason only if the taxpayer would still have acquired the property as a speculation in the absence of the primary intention to build a shopping centre (or whatever).[58] This may pitch the test too high, but certainly the secondary

---

[56] [1975] C.T.C. 659, 76 D.T.C. 6001 (F.C.A.).

[57] [1978] C.T.C. 378, 78 D.T.C. 6281 (F.C.A.).

[58] McDonnell, case comment (1977) 25 *Can. Tax J.* 618, 620; see also case comments (1976) 24 *Can. Tax J.* 120; (1978) 26 *Can. Tax J.* 412.

intention doctrine will not be satisfied unless the prospect of resale at a profit was an important factor in the decision to acquire the property.

(k)   Corporate intention

In many of the foregoing cases, the taxpayer was a corporation. In determining the intention of the corporation, the courts have invariably lifted the corporate veil and attributed to the corporation the intention of those individuals who control the corporation. In particular, it is clear that statements of purpose in the corporation's memorandum of association or other constituting instrument are of little relevance to the present enquiry, which turns on actual and not fictional intention.[59] The rule which is applied in these tax cases seems to be no different from the "directing mind" principle, which is used to determine corporate intention in other branches of the law, such as tort[60] or crime.[61]

16.4 Losses

Most of the vast quantity of litigation concerning the proper classification of transactions with property is generated by the dissimilar treatment accorded by the Income Tax Act to capital gains, which are only three-quarters taxable, and income from a business, which is fully taxable. (The stakes were higher before 1988, when capital gains were only half taxable, and higher still before 1972, when capital gains were not taxed at all.) Where a transaction with property yields a profit, it is the taxpayer who argues that the transaction was an investment to be taxed on capital account, and it is the Minister who argues that the transaction was a trade or speculation to be taxed on income account. But a transaction with property does not always yield a profit. When it yields a loss, the same problem of classification arises, because the Income Tax Act accords dissimilar treatment to capital losses and business (or other income) losses.

Capital losses are only three-quarters deductible, and are only deductible against taxable capital gains (three-quarters capital gains). Business losses are deductible in full, and are deductible against income from all sources. Full detail of the tax treatment of losses, including the special case of "allowable business investment losses", and the loss-carryover rules, is provided in chapter 18, Losses, below. For the present purpose, it is sufficient to notice that a loss on a capital transaction is generally accorded worse tax treatment than a loss on an income transaction. Accordingly, when a loss is in issue we find the normal roles of taxpayer and Minister reversed. Now it is the taxpayer who argues that he or

---

[59] *Sutton Lumber and Trading Co.* v. *M.N.R.*, [1953] C.T.C. 237, 53 D.T.C. 1158 (S.C.C.); *C.W. Logging Co.* v. *M.N.R.*, [1956] C.T.C. 15, 56 D.T.C. 1007 (Ex. Ct.); *Regal Heights* v. *M.N.R.*, [1960] C.T.C. 384, 60 D.T.C. 1270 (S.C.C.).

[60] *Lennard's Carrying Co.* v. *Asiatic Petroleum*, [1915] A.C. 705 (H.L.).

[61] *Tesco Supermarkets* v. *Nattrass*, [1972] A.C. 153 (H.L.).

she was a trader or speculator, and it is the Minister who argues that the taxpayer was an investor. One example (of many) is *Bossin* v. *The Queen* (1976),[62] in which the taxpayer had lost money on the stock market, and in which Collier J. could not resist commenting that, if the taxpayer had made a profit, "the Minister would then, I suspect, have been making diametrically opposite arguments in this Court"![63]

---

[62] [1976] C.T.C. 358, 76 D.T.C. 6196 (F.C.T.D.).

[63] *Id.*, 371, 6205.

17

Other Income and Deductions

17.1 Structure of the Act

Subdivision d of Division B of Part I of the Income Tax Act includes in income certain amounts which are not income from an office or employment (subdivision a), nor income from a business or property (subdivision b) nor net taxable capital gains (subdivision c). These amounts, which are set out in sections 56 to 59.1 of the Act, are called "other income". Amounts which are not included in income in any of subdivisions a, b, c or d are not necessarily free of tax. An amount could still be characterized as income "from a source" within the meaning of s. 3, in which case it would be taxable. However, the courts have shown no disposition to add new sources of income to those covered by subdivisions a, b, c and d.[1] For practical purposes, if an amount is not caught by subdivisions a, b, c or d, it is very likely that it is not taxable. (For greater certainty, s. 81 contains a list of items that are definitely not taxable.)

Subdivision d brings into income several types of "other income". The most common ones are pension income,[2] income from registered retirement savings plans (RRSPs),[3] income from other deferred income plans,[4] retiring allowances,[5] spousal and child support,[6] workers' compensation and social assistance payments,[7] scholarship income in excess of $500,[8] research grants (net of expenses),[9] death benefits (in excess of $10,000),[10] unemployment

---

[1] *Canada v. Fries*, [1990] 2 S.C.R. 1322, [1990] 2 C.T.C. 439, 90 D.T.C. 6662 (S.C.C.); *Schwartz v. Canada*, [1996] 1 S.C.R. 254, [1996] 1 C.T.C. 303, 96 D.T.C. 6103 (S.C.C.); see also ch. 9, Tax Base, under heading 9.2, "Source theory", above.

[2] Section 17.2, "Pension income", below.

[3] Section 17.5, "Registered retirement savings plans (RRSPs)", below.

[4] Sections 17.3, "Registered pension plans (RPPs)", 17.4, "Deferred profit sharing plans (DPSPs)", 17.6, "Registered education savings plans (RESPs)", below.

[5] Section 17.7, "Retiring allowances", below

[6] Section 17.9, "Spousal and child support", below.

[7] Section 17.10, "Workers' compensation and social assistance", below.

[8] The first $500 of scholarship income is excluded from tax (s. 56(1)(n)).

[9] Paragraph 56(1)(o).

[10] Death benefits, which are included in income under s. 56(1)(a)(iii), are defined in s. 248(1) as amounts received "on or after the death of an employee in recognition of the employee's service in an office or employment. . .". The definition goes on to exclude the first $10,000 received and to allocate the $10,000 tax-free limit first to the employee's spouse. If any of the $10,000 limit remains, and payments are received by other taxpayers (e.g., the employee's children), the limit is allocated to others in proportion to the payments received by them. (The first $10,000 tax-free amount is technically not a death benefit.)

insurance benefits,[11] and the income portion of an annuity payment.[12] The first six items are discussed in greater detail later in this chapter.

Subdivision e allows a taxpayer to deduct a list of "other deductions" set out in ss. 60 to 66.8 of the Act. The only common characteristic of the subdivision e deductions is that they are not confined to income from an office or employment or to income from a business or property or to net taxable capital gains; deductions confined to those sources are allowed by subdivisions a, b and c. Some of the subdivision e deductions are related in some fashion to inclusions in subdivision d, for example, deductions for the capital element of annuity payments (s. 60(a)) and for spousal and child support (s. 60(b)), but others are not related to the subdivision d inclusions. Some of the subdivision e deductions can be claimed against any type of income, for example, the deductions for spousal and child support (s. 60(b))[13] and the deduction for the expenses of an objection or appeal under the Income Tax Act (s. 60(o)(i)).[14] However, the deductions for moving expenses (s. 62), child care expenses (s. 63), attendant care expenses (s. 64),[15] and RRSP contributions (ss. 60(i), (j.1) and (l)), all

---

[11] Subparagraph 56(1)(a)(iv).

[12] An annuity is a contract to receive a periodic payment and is usually purchased from a life insurance company. (The owner of the annuity contract is called the "annuitant".) There are two basic types of annuities: "life annuities" and "term annuities". A "life annuity" is an annuity that is paid for the remainder of the annuitant's life or his spouse's life. A "term annuity", on the other hand, has a fixed term, that is, the annuity will be paid for a fixed number of years only. A life annuity can also have a "guaranteed term", that is, payments will be guaranteed for a fixed number of years even if the annuitant dies before the end of that period. A life annuity can also have "joint and last survivor benefits", in which case the amount will be paid until the later of the dates of death of the annuitant or his spouse (i.e., the "last survivor's" date of death). The amount of the annuity that can be purchased for a certain dollar amount (e.g., $100,000) varies, depending upon interest rates and, if it is a life annuity, the age of the taxpayer (and his spouse, if the annuity has joint and last survivor benefits). The income portion of an annuity payment is included in income in the following manner: first, the entire amount of the annuity payment is included in income (s. 56(1)(d)) and then the capital element of the annuity payment is deducted (s. 60(a)) since the capital element is a return of the annuitant's invested after-tax capital. These rules apply only to annuities purchased with after-tax funds. Pension annuities and RRSP annuities, on the other hand, are fully taxed: there is no capital amount to deduct because they are purchased with tax-sheltered retirement savings: see secs. 17.2, "Pension income", 17.5(f), "RRSP annuities", and 17.5(g), "Registered retirement income funds", below.

[13] Section 17.9, "Spousal and child support", below.

[14] The deduction of expenses in connection with an objection or appeal (such as legal or accounting fees) is allowed even if the objection or appeal is not successful. If all or part of the expenses are reimbursed, there is an income inclusion for this amount (s. 56(1)(l)) which will offset all or part of the amount deducted in the year or a previous year.

[15] Section 64 was enacted so that a taxpayer eligible for the disability credit (s. 118.3) could claim a limited deduction for the cost of an attendant who enables the taxpayer to work. The deduction can only be claimed by the person eligible for the disability credit and cannot exceed two-thirds of his or her "earned income" (as defined). Before 1997, the maximum s. 64 deduction was $5,000; this limit has now been removed.

have restrictions requiring the taxpayer to have certain types of income in order to claim the deduction.

The deduction for child care expenses was discussed earlier in chapter 13.[16] The deductions for moving expenses,[17] alimony and maintenance payments,[18] and RRSP contributions[19] are discussed later in this chapter.

17.2 Pension income

Subdivision d opens with s. 56, which brings a variety of miscellaneous receipts into income. The several forms of pension income are caught, namely, pensions (and other benefits) from the following sources:

- the federal Old Age Security Act and similar provincial laws (s. 56(1)(a));
- the Canada Pension Plan and provincial pension plans (s. 56(1)(a));
- registered pension plans (RPPs) (s. 56(1)(a));
- deferred profit sharing plans (DPSPs) (s. 56(1)(i));
- registered retirement savings plans (RRSPs) (s. 56(1)(h)); and
- registered retirement income funds (RRIFs) (s. 56(1)(t)).

The first two items are the two sources of public pensions. The Old Age Security programme pays pensions, supplements and spouse's allowances to persons who have reached the age of 65.[20] The basic pension is paid to all longstanding Canadian residents, but since 1989 it has been "clawed back" through the income tax system, so that pensioners with incomes in excess of $53,215 (in 1997) have to repay, in accordance with a statutory formula, all or part of the payments that they receive.[21]

The Canada Pension Plan (CPP) (and its only provincial equivalent, the Quebec Pension Plan) also pays benefits to persons who have reached the age

---

[16] Chapter 13, Income from Business or Property: Deductions, under heading 13.6, "Child care expenses", above.

[17] Section 17.11, "Moving expenses", below.

[18] Section 17.9, "Spousal and child support", below.

[19] Section 17.5, "Registered retirement savings plans (RRSPs)", below.

[20] Effective January 1, 2001, a tax-free Senior's Benefit is to replace benefits which are currently available to seniors through the Old Age Security programme, the age credit (s. 118(2)) and the pension credit (s. 118(3)). The Senior's Benefit, which was proposed in the 1996 budget, is to be income-tested based on a couple's net income. Taxpayers who are 60 years of age or older on December 31, 1995 will have the choice of receiving benefits under the Old Age Security programme or the Senior's Benefit. The proposed Senior's Benefit is still under study and no legislation has been introduced to implement it.

[21] The amount that must be repaid (or "clawed back") is the lesser of the Old Age Security payments received and 30 per cent of the taxpayer's Division B income in excess of $53,215 (s. 180.2). The amount of Old Age Security so repaid is deductible in computing the taxpayer's income (s. 60(w)).

of 65. The Canada Pension Plan differs from the Old Age Security programme in two important respects. First, the CPP is contributory,[22] and benefits are paid only to those persons who have contributed to the Plan during their working years in Canada. Secondly, the CPP is not income-tested, and benefits are paid (and not clawed back) in accordance with the entitlement built up through contributions, regardless of the amount of other income received by the pensioner.

The other sources of pensions that are captured by s. 56 and listed above are registered pension plans, deferred profit sharing plans, registered retirement savings plans and registered retirement income funds. These are all privately funded and privately organized plans, but they receive tax assistance. That assistance takes the form of an exemption from tax for contributions to the plans and for income earned by the investments in the plans. Only when the pensions (or other benefits) are eventually paid are they taxable under s. 56(1). Because recognition of the income for tax purposes is deferred until the benefits are withdrawn from the plans (normally at retirement), the plans are often called "deferred income plans".[23] Each deferred income plan is discussed in more detail in the following sections of this chapter.

17.3 Registered pension plans (RPPs)

Registered pension plans (RPPs) are private employer-sponsored retirement savings plans which are regulated by Revenue Canada and by provincial pension benefit legislation and were first introduced into the income tax legislation in 1919. Normally, both the employer and the employee contributes to an RPP, although "non-contributory" plans (to which only the employer contributes) also exist. An RPP enjoys special status under the Income Tax Act: contributions to an RPP by employers and employees are tax deductible,[24] contributions by employers are not taxed to the employees as benefits from employment (s. 6(1)(a)(i)), and the investment income earned by the plan is not subject to tax (s. 149(1)(o)). The funds accumulated and invested in an RPP on a tax-free basis only begin to be taxed when a taxpayer withdraws amounts from the plan (s. 56(1)(a)(i)). In most cases, this occurs on retirement, when the taxpayer receives his or her pension income in the form of a monthly

---

[22] A taxpayer's CPP contributions are eligible for a 17 per cent tax credit (s. 118.7).

[23] A further, much less significant, tax advantage of the deferred income plans is the pension credit of 17 per cent of the first $1,000 of "pension income" (for persons aged 65 or over) or "qualified pension income" (for persons under 65) (ss. 118(3) and (7)).The maximum allowable federal credit is $170 ($1,000 × 17%).

[24] Paragraph 8(1)(m) allows an employee a deduction for his contribution (within limits) and paragraph 20(1)(q) allows an employer a deduction for his contribution in respect of an employee.

life annuity.[25] The first $1,000 of pension annuity income received from an RPP is eligible for the 17 per cent pension income credit (s. 118(3)).[26]

There are two types of RPPs: "defined benefit" plans and "defined contribution" plans (sometimes called "money purchase" plans).[27] In a defined benefit plan, the employer agrees to provide a "defined benefit" at retirement; the defined benefit is usually expressed as a percentage of the employee's earnings for each year of service. The earnings figure used is usually an average of earnings in the last years of service, such as the average earnings in the last three years of service. For example, if the employer agreed to provide a defined benefit of 2 per cent of earnings per year of service, and an employee had average earnings of $50,000 and 20 years of service, the employee's pension benefit would be $20,000. The amount required to be contributed to the plan to fund this defined benefit would be determined by an actuary, who would take into consideration such factors as the income expected to be earned on plan investments as well as employee turnover and mortality rates. The plan document would specify how the amount required to fund the defined benefit would be split between the employer and the employee. The maximum defined benefit that may be accumulated each year is $1,722.22.[28] A defined benefit plan which provides this maximum annual benefit would provide a maximum pension of $60,278 at age 65 after 35 years of service: 35 × $1,722.22.

In a defined contribution (or money purchase) plan, the employer agrees to make "defined contributions" to the plan on behalf of each employee. For example, the employer might agree to contribute a certain percentage of an employee's wages or a fixed dollar amount (the employee would usually also contribute a defined amount). In a defined contribution plan, there is no agreement or guarantee as to the amount of pension benefit that the employee will eventually receive (as is the case in a defined benefit plan). Instead, the pension benefit will be whatever is the amount of the pension annuity that can be purchased with the employee's share of the fund that has accumulated by the time of the employee's retirement. This will depend on the level of employer and employee contributions, the investment income earned on those contributions

---

[25] Under most provincial pension benefit legislation, an RPP becomes vested after two years of service. Once an RPP is vested, benefits cannot be received except in the form of a life annuity on retirement. See note 12, above, for the various types of annuities.

[26] Note 23 above.

[27] Some plans are a combination of the two types.

[28] Regulation 8500. $1,722.22 is one-ninth of $15,500, which is to be the RRSP money limit in 2004 (the current money limit is $13,500). In 2005, the annual defined benefit is to be indexed along with the RRSP money limit. As discussed in note 43, below, these increases have been postponed several times. The derivation of the amount of the RRSP money limit is discussed in the text accompanying note 43.

over the years to retirement and the interest rates at the time of purchase of the pension annuity.

If an employee changes jobs, the funds to which the employee is entitled in the former employer's pension plan can be transferred directly to the new employer's pension plan (or a registered retirement savings plan (RRSP)) on a tax-free basis. These and other direct transfers of tax-assisted retirement savings are discussed later in this chapter.[29]

17.4   Deferred profit sharing plans (DPSPs)

Deferred profit sharing plans (DPSPs) are private employer-sponsored profit-sharing plans. They were first introduced into the Income Tax Act in 1961. The Act sets maximum limits on contributions by an employer and does not allow an employee to contribute. The contributions by an employer to a DPSP are not fixed like contributions to a defined contribution RPP, but fluctuate according to the employer's profitability. However, a DPSP is similar to a defined contribution (or money purchase) RPP in that the pension benefit consists simply of what can be purchased with the accumulated fund at the time of retirement or withdrawal of benefits.

Contributions by an employer to a DPSP within the limits of the Income Tax Act are tax deductible (s. 147(8)), the contributions are not included in the employee's income as a benefit from employment (s. 6(1)(a)(i)), and the investment income earned by the plan is not subject to tax (s. 147(7)). Withdrawals from a DPSP may be made at any time (subject to any restrictions set out in the plan agreement), and, when they are made, they are taxed (s. 56(1)(i)).

17.5   Registered retirement savings plans (RRSPs)

(a)   Definition of RRSP

Registered retirement savings plans (RRSPs) are private retirement savings plans that can be established by individuals for their own retirement. They were first introduced into the Income Tax Act in 1957 to help those individuals who were not members of company pension plans. As will be explained in more detail, the Act sets limits on contributions, and allows a deduction for contributions. The investment income earned by the plan is not subject to tax. An RRSP is like a defined contribution (money purchase) RPP in that the amount of the pension annuity is not defined, but depends upon what can be purchased

---

[29]   Section 17.8, "Summary of transfers to RPPs, RRSPs, and DPSPs", below.

at the time of retirement.[30] Unlike a defined contribution RPP, however, no minimum annual contributions need be made to an RRSP. Withdrawals from an RRSP may be made at any time, and, when they are made, they are taxed (s. 56(1)(h)).

The RRSP differs from the RPP and the DPSP in that only the RRSP can be established by an individual, and only that individual (or his or her spouse) can make contributions to the RRSP. RPPs and DPSPs, on the other hand, must be sponsored by an employer, and the employer must make contributions for the employees who are members of the plan.

(b)   Postponement of tax

Despite the differences, the RRSP shares with the RPP and the DPSP the two characteristics that earn the description of deferred income plans. The first is the tax deductibility of contributions.[31] The second is the exemption from tax of plan income. The funds in the plans, both contributions and accumulated income, are not subject to tax until they are withdrawn. The tax deductibility of contributions and the tax-free status of plan earnings means that before-tax dollars can be invested and before-tax investment income can be reinvested. As a result, the amount of income that can be accumulated under such plans is far greater than could be earned by investing after-tax dollars in an investment vehicle that was not sheltered from tax.

For example, consider a taxpayer who is subject to tax at a combined federal-provincial rate of 40 per cent and who saves $10,000 of pre-tax income each year to provide for her retirement. If she could invest the $10,000 of pre-tax income each year in an RRSP or RPP and earn a pre-tax return of 10 per cent on her investment, at the end of ten years she would accumulate $159,370 before taxes ($10,000 × a present value factor of 15.937). A second taxpayer investing outside an RRSP or RPP could save and invest only the after-tax amount of $6,000 ($10,000 × (1 − 40%)) and, because the earnings each year would be

---

[30] RRSPs are purchased from banks and other financial institutions. The investment can take the form of a special savings account, a term deposit or a mutual fund, or the RRSP can be self-administered, in which case it can invest in a variety of items. Investments in an RRSP are subject to restrictions: there are restrictions on the amount of foreign investments and on investments in real estate and shares of private corporations. Financial institutions offering self-administered RRSPs often impose annual service charges which are not tax deductible (s. 18(1)(u)).

[31] Subsection 146(5) allows an individual a deduction for contributions to an RRSP (within limits). Paragraphs 20(1)(q) and 20(1)(y), respectively, allow an employer a deduction for contributions to an RPP and DPSP (within limits). Paragraph 8(1)(m) allows an employee a deduction for his contribution to an RPP (within limits). Contributions in excess of these limits may deregister the plan (which will cause the funds accumulated in the plan to be immediately taxable). Subparagraph 6(1)(a)(i) states that an employer's contribution to an RPP or DPSP is not a taxable benefit.

taxed at the rate of 40 per cent, the annual income earned on the investment would be only 6 per cent (10% × (1 − 40%)). At the end of ten years, the second taxpayer would have accumulated only $75,468 ($6,000 × 12.578), which is much less than the $159,370 in the RRSP or RPP of the first taxpayer. Even if the first taxpayer is still subject to tax at 40 per cent when she withdraws the funds from her RRSP or RPP at the end of the tenth year, she will have $95,622 ($159,370 × 60%) rather than $75,468, an increase of over $20,000 in ten years.[32]

To summarize then, tax-assisted retirement savings plans allow taxpayers to invest before-tax dollars and reinvest a before-tax return, which enables them to accumulate more retirement savings than under regular methods. This is the major advantage of tax-assisted retirement savings plans. Additional taxes can be saved if the taxpayer is at a lower marginal rate when funds are withdrawn from the plan, as is often the case after retirement. (Amounts can also be transferred between tax-assisted retirement savings plans on a tax-free basis.)[33] Also, the first $1,000 of pension income is effectively tax-free because of the $1,000 pension credit.[34] In the case of the RRSP (but not the RPP or the DPSP), there is a further advantage in that a taxpayer can contribute to the RRSP of his or her spouse (including a common-law spouse: s. 251(4)). If the spouse is in a lower tax bracket than the contributor when withdrawals are made and taxed in the spouse's hands, the tax payable will be lower than if the contributor had had to report the income.[35]

(c)   Policy objectives

The tax reform of 1988, which made a number of fundamental changes to the tax system, also included proposals for reform of the tax-assisted pension regime.[36] The pension reform proposals were not enacted until 1991. The reform of 1991 was designed with two objectives in mind. The first objective was to permit individuals to have an equal amount of tax assistance irrespective of the form of retirement plan utilized. The second objective was to provide

---

[32] The tax deferral advantage is not so great with respect to income that receives preferential treatment under the Act. For example, dividends from taxable Canadian corporations earned inside an RRSP do not receive the normal gross-up and tax credit treatment. Similarly, capital gains earned inside an RRSP are not taxed at the three-quarters rate. All income earned inside an RRSP is fully taxed when it is eventually withdrawn from the plan.

[33] Section 17.8, "Summary of transfers to RPPs, RRSPs and DPSPs", below.

[34] Note 23, above.

[35] Section 17.3(e), "Withdrawals", below.

[36] Department of Finance, *Improved Pensions for Canadians* (1985). The pension reform proposals were originally to be enacted in 1986 at the same time as the rest of the measures of the Tax Reform of 1986 (which were actually enacted in 1988). However, because of various implementation issues, the pension reform proposals did not become law until January 1, 1991.

taxpayers with flexibility as to the timing of contributions to retirement plans. This second objective was met by allowing taxpayers to carryforward their unused RRSP contribution limits for seven years starting in 1991.

The first objective was met by integrating the contribution limits for the various types of tax-assisted retirement savings plans in Canada. Prior to 1991, taxpayers who were members of the most generous defined benefit RPPs had a considerable advantage over other taxpayers. Pension reform attempted to put all types of tax-assisted retirement savings plans on an equal footing. Contribution limits were adjusted so that the amounts that members of defined benefit RPPs could save on a tax-assisted basis was no more than a taxpayer could save using a combination of a defined contribution RPP, DPSP and/or RRSP. All these measures resulted in increases in the tax-deductible contribution limits for defined contribution RPPs, RRSPs, and DPSPs.

The increases in the limits for tax-deductible contributions to RPPs, RRSPs and DPSPs reflect a decision by government to continue to use the tax system to encourage private saving for retirement. Regarded as tax expenditures,[37] one might well question the distributional effects of the measures, which, like all deductions, deliver a larger benefit to those with high incomes than to those with low incomes. Indeed, private saving for retirement is simply beyond the capacity of those whose incomes barely provide the necessities of life. A case can be made for the proposition that tax assistance for private saving should be reduced or eliminated, and the revenue saved should be directed to the enrichment of the public pensions provided by the (underfunded) Canada Pension Plan[38] and the (unfunded) Old Age Security programme.[39]

---

[37] Ontario Fair Tax Commission, *Fair Taxation in a Changing World* (U. Toronto Press, Toronto, 1993), 327, described tax assistance for private retirement savings as "the biggest tax expenditure in the personal income tax system and, arguably, the most important social program delivered through the tax system". The Government of Canada treats the tax assistance provided to RPPs, RRSPs and DPSPs as tax expenditures and valued them at $15.770 billion for 1993 and $13.720 billion for 1992: Government of Canada, *Tax Expenditures 1995*, (1996), 26. (These figures represent the net amount of six separate figures reported for the tax expenditures associated with RRSP and RPP contributions and withdrawals and the non-taxation of investment income earned in those plans. Data for DPSPs is not available.) The concept of tax expenditures is explained in ch. 4, Objectives, under heading 4.6, "Tax expenditures", above.

[38] Legislation to reform the Canada Pension Plan was introduced in 1997. Among the changes are increases in annual premiums over the period 1997 to 2003. Without these changes, actuaries estimate the Canada Pension Plan would have been exhausted by 2015: Godfrey, *Your Voice in Ottawa*, May 1997, 2 (mimeo).

[39] As discussed in note 20, above, effective January 1, 2001, the Old Age Programme and the age and pension credits are to be replaced by an income-tested Senior's Benefit. The Ontario Fair Tax Commission, note 37, above, 327–333, recommended that the upper limits for the deductions for contributions to RPPs and RRSPs be reduced, and that the deductions be converted to credits. Similar recommendations are made by Austin, "Policies, Preferences and Perversions in the Tax-assisted Retirement Savings System" (1996) 41 *McGill L. J.* 571.

However, in view of the current desire for tax cuts (rather than increases), the deeply indebted state of Canadian government finances and the steadily aging population of Canada, it is obvious that private saving will continue to be the major source of retirement income for most people. Measures to encourage taxpayers and their employers to make private provision for retirement during their working years, and thereby relieve the public purse from full responsibility, are easy to justify on these pragmatic grounds.

It is also possible to contest the view that tax assistance for private saving for retirement is a tax expenditure, that is, a "social programme delivered through the tax system".[40] It could be argued that, in calculating the amount of income earned each year by an individual for tax purposes, it is appropriate to set aside a portion of the income to provide for the individual's retirement. The analogy is that of the business proprietor, who sets aside a portion of the business income (depreciation charges or capital cost allowances) to allow for the wearing out of the capital assets employed in the business. It is arguable that an individual whose income is derived from his or her own effort should be permitted to make provision for the wearing out of his or her human capital — the decline in ability and energy that will inevitably come with old age. On this basis, the provisions in the Income Tax Act for retirement saving are not so much a social programme as tax measures to spread individual earned income over a longer period and thereby better measure income for tax purposes on an annual basis.[41]

The current system is based on the premise that the maximum tax-assisted pension benefit should be 2 per cent per year of the average of a person's best three years of earnings multiplied by his or her number of years of service (to a maximum of 35 years) and that the maximum benefit after 35 years should be restricted to $60,278.[42] To fund this $60,278 maximum pension benefit, the maximum benefit to be accrued each year is therefore $1,722.22 ($60,278/35 maximum years of service). The system also assumes that it takes $9 today to buy a $1 pension benefit per year starting at age 65. Since a pension of 2 per cent of earnings is the maximum pension to accrue annually, it follows that (1) a contribution of 18 per cent (9 × 2%) is required to fund this annual pension benefit, but that (2) the maximum contribution in any year should be limited to nine times the maximum benefit to be accrued, which is $15,500 ($1,722.22 × 9

---

[40] Note 37, above.

[41] Another tax-related way to characterize the retirement savings provisions is that, by exempting savings and taxing withdrawals, the retirement savings provisions convert the income tax system into "a modified form of expenditure tax". This was the view of the Carter Commission: *Report of the Royal Commission on Taxation* (Carter Report) (1966), vol. 3, 411–412.

[42] $60,278 was 2 1/2 times the average industrial wage in the year that these amounts were determined.

= $15,500). The $15,500 dollar limit is subject to a phase-in rule: the 1997 RRSP limit is $13,500.[43]

The above discussion tells us where the numbers that the system uses come from. Here is how the system works for 1997. (1) Employers report a taxpayer's "pension adjustment" (defined below) for the 1996 year (the previous year) in respect of RPP and DPSP plans on the taxpayer's 1996 T4 slip in February 1997. (2) The 1996 pension adjustment is reported (but not included in income) on the taxpayer's 1996 tax return which is generally due on or before April 30, 1997. (3) Revenue Canada uses the 1996 "pension adjustment" and other information reported in the taxpayer's returns for the years 1991 to 1996 to calculate the taxpayer's maximum deductible RRSP contribution for 1997 (s. 60(i)) and reports the amount to the taxpayer on a 1996 notice of assessment (which would normally be received within a few weeks or months of filing the 1996 return).[44]

The terms "earned income" and "pension adjustment" (PA) are defined in the following section of this chapter, but it is important, at this point, to note that the purpose of the PA is to integrate tax-assisted retirement savings through the various plans. The contribution limits for RPPs, DPSPs and RRSPs are set (based on the numbers above) so that the amount that an individual who is a member of a RPP and/or DPSP can save on a tax-assisted basis is (theoretically) no greater or less than if he or she was not a member of a DPSP or RPP and could only save using an RRSP. It is the PA that ties these three systems together: the PA reflects an estimate of a taxpayer's tax-assisted retirement savings for the year using an RPP or DPSP and is deducted from the taxpayer's RRSP contribution limit for the following year. For example, if a taxpayer's 1997 RRSP contribution limit before PA was $13,500 and her 1996 PA (in respect of contributions to an RPP and a DPSP in that year) was $9,000, she could only contribute $4,500 to an RRSP in 1997. The reason for the one-year lag is to allow the employer time to report the information to Revenue Canada and the taxpayer.

(d)   Contributions

If a taxpayer is not a member of an RPP or DPSP and has always contributed the maximum tax-deductible RRSP contributions in previous years,

---

[43] The phasing-in has been delayed three times since the rules were introduced in 1991. The 1996 budget froze the RRSP money limit at $13,500 until 2003. The money limit will be $14,500 in 2004 and $15,500 in 2005 and indexed based on increases in the average industrial wage after that. (RPP and DPSP limits are phasing-in in a similar, although not identical, manner.)

[44] Revenue Canada also has an Automated Tax Information Phone Service (called "TIPS") that a taxpayer can phone to find out his or her RRSP contribution limit. The taxpayer's social insurance number, birthday, and the total income reported on line 150 of the prior year's return must be entered to obtain this information.

his or her RRSP contribution limit for 1997 is the lesser of 18 per cent of the previous year's earned income and the $13,500 dollar limit for the year (s. 60(i)). In order to claim a deduction for 1997, this amount must be contributed in the year or within 60 days of the year (i.e., by March 1, 1998)[45] to either the taxpayer's RRSP or the taxpayer's spouse's RRSP (or a combination of the two) (ss. 146(5) and (5.1)). However, there is no doubling up.

Earned income is defined in s. 146(1).[46] Its principal components are employment income, business income and spousal and child support payments included in income under s. 56(1)(b). Property income is not included, except for real estate rental income and certain royalty income. Losses from employment or business, and spousal and child support payments which are deductible under s. 60(b), are deducted in arriving at the net figure of earned income.[47]

These rules are best illustrated by example. Assume that a taxpayer who is not a member of a RPP or DPSP earned a $50,000 salary in 1996 and paid $20,000 of alimony or maintenance to a former spouse in that year. His 1997 RRSP contribution limit would be $5,400, which is the lesser of 18 per cent of his $30,000 of earned income ($50,000 − $20,000) and $13,500. If he only contributed $4,000 to his RRSP (or his spouse's RRSP) by the February 29, 1998 deadline, he would be able to carryforward his undeducted RRSP contribution room of $1,400. If, in this example, the taxpayer had not made his maximum tax deductible RRSP contributions in a previous year, the amount of his maximum deductible 1997 RRSP contribution would be increased by the amount of the deficiency. Using the above example, but assuming that the taxpayer had undeducted RRSP contribution room from 1995 of $2,000, results in a maximum tax-deductible 1997 RRSP contribution limit of $7,400 ($5,400 from above plus $2,000). If the taxpayer still only contributes $4,000 to his RRSP for 1997, he will have a $3,400 undeducted contribution room to carry forward to future years.[48]

If a taxpayer is a member of an RPP or DPSP, the formula becomes more complicated. In that case, the concept of the "pension adjustment" (PA) is used to reduce the taxpayer's RRSP contribution limits for a particular year. Omitting

---

[45] In the case of a year which is a leap year, 60 days after the end of the year would be February 29. If any deadline occurs on a weekend, the deadline is extended to the next business day: Interpretation Act, R.S.C. 1985, c. I-21, s. 26.

[46] The definition of "earned income" in s. 146(1) is different from the definition of "earned income" for child care expenses purposes (s. 63(3)).

[47] The tax treatment of spousal and child support payments is discussed under heading 17.9, "Spousal and child support", below.

[48] See definition of unused contribution room in s. 146(1). Individuals who terminate employment after 1996 will also have added to their unused contribution room a Pension Adjustment Reversal (PAR), equal to the excess of the PAs reported over the years (from their former employer's RPP or DPSP) over the termination benefit actually received.

complications, a taxpayer's PA consists of (1) the amount of the contributions (by the employer as well as the employee) to a defined contribution RPP, plus (2) a figure derived from the benefit accrued under a defined benefit RPP,[49] plus (3) the amount of the contributions (by the employer) to a DPSP. As explained earlier, the PA will prevent a taxpayer from achieving extra tax assistance through membership of an RPP or DPSP as well as an RRSP.

RRSP contributions are commonly made in cash but can be made using investments if a taxpayer has a self-administered RRSP.[50] If an investment is transferred to an RRSP, the amount of the contribution is the fair market value of the investment and there is a deemed disposition at the fair market value of the investment (s. 69). Accordingly, if the investment is a Canada Savings Bond or other interest-bearing security, accrued interest to the date of transfer (which has not been previously included in the taxpayer's income) must be recognized in the year of the transfer. If the investment consists of stocks or bonds that have appreciated in value, a capital gain will have to be recognized on the transfer. If the investment has gone down in value, however, the capital loss is denied under s. 40(2)(g)(iv).[51]

What we have just discussed is the deduction for the regular "earned income" RRSP contribution that many Canadians make each year (s. 60(i)). There are two other RRSP deductions which are in addition to this regular RRSP contribution deduction. The first is a deduction for an RRSP contribution in respect of income from a retiring allowance (s. 60(j.1)); this deduction is discussed under heading 17.7, "Retiring allowances", below. The second is a deduction for an RRSP contribution in respect of a "refund of premiums" (s. 60(l)); this deduction is discussed under heading 17.5(h), "Tax consequences on death", below.

In summary then, it is possible for a taxpayer to make three different types of deductible RRSP contributions: the regular "earned income" contribution (s. 60(i)); the contribution of part of a retiring allowance (s. 60(j.1)); and the contribution of a "refund of premiums" (s. 60(l)). Only the regular "earned income" contribution can be made to either the taxpayer's RRSP or the taxpayer's spouse's RRSP. Contributions in respect of retiring allowances and "refunds of premiums" must be made to the taxpayer's own plan. All of these contributions must be made in the year that the deduction is claimed or within 60 days of the end of that year.

---

[49] The difference between defined contribution RPPs and defined benefit RPPs is discussed under sec. 17.3, "Registered pension plans (RPPs)", above.

[50] See note 30, above, for a discussion of the various types of RRSPs.

[51] See ch. 18, Losses, under heading 18.2(c), "Superficial losses", below.

(e)   Withdrawals

Withdrawals from an RRSP are generally taxable and tax is withheld on the withdrawal (reg. 103).[52] Any balance of tax owing is paid when the taxpayer files a tax return. (There is one exception to the general rule that withdrawals are taxable, namely, the RRSP Home Buyer's Plan, discussed below.)

If a taxpayer makes a withdrawal from his or her RRSP (or receives RRSP annuity payments), and his or her spouse has made a contribution to the RRSP in the year of the withdrawal or the previous two years, the withdrawal will be taxed in the spouse's hands to the extent of those contributions. The amount which is taxed in the spouse's hands (s. 146(8.3)) and not the taxpayer's hands (s. 146(8.6)) is the lesser of the RRSP withdrawal (or annuity payment) and the contributions made by the spouse in the year or the previous two years. For example, if the husband made a $5,000 withdrawal from his RRSP in 1997 and the wife had made contributions of $1,000 to the husband's RRSP in each of the years 1995, 1996 and 1997, $3,000 of the withdrawal would be taxed in the wife's hands and $2,000 would be taxed in the husband's hands. This "attribution" rule limits the amount of income splitting that can be done with spousal RRSPs.[53] In order to avoid this attribution rule, the contributing spouse must stop contributing to the RRSP for three years before any withdrawal is made.

The RRSP Home Buyer's Plan assists a taxpayer to buy a first home by allowing the taxpayer to withdraw up to $20,000 from his or her RRSP for this purpose without any tax (s. 146.01). Any money so withdrawn must be repaid to the RRSP in stipulated annual instalments over 15 years. In order to be considered a first-time home buyer, neither the taxpayer nor the taxpayer's spouse (while married to the taxpayer)[54] must have owned a home in any of the five years before the year of withdrawal. Contributions to an RRSP that are withdrawn under the RRSP Home Buyer's Plan within 90 days are not deductible.

(f)   RRSP annuities

If a taxpayer owns an RRSP at the end of the year in which he or she turns 69, then the total value of the RRSP is included in his or her income for

---

[52] The withholding tax is lowest (10 per cent) if amounts of $5,000 or less are withdrawn at a time (reg. 103).

[53] If an RRSP to which a spouse has contributed is converted to a registered retirement income fund (RRIF) (discussed in the next section of this chapter), any RRIF payment in excess of the minimum payment amount will be included in the spouse's income to the extent of spousal contributions made in the year of payment or the previous two years (s. 146.3(5.1)).

[54] For this purpose, spouse includes a common-law spouse (s. 252(4)(a)) and marriage includes a conjugal relationship with a common-law spouse (s. 252(4)(b)).

the year. In order to prevent this, a taxpayer must purchase either an RRSP annuity or a registered retirement income fund (RRIF) (or a combination of the two) with the funds in the RRSP before the end of the year in which the taxpayer turns 69. The funds in the RRSP are transferred directly to the RRSP annuity or RRIF on a tax-free basis[55] (s. 147(16)).

RRSP annuities can be life annuities or term annuities. Life annuities may have a guaranteed term and may have joint and last survivor benefits.[56] Term annuities must provide benefits up to age 90. If the taxpayer's spouse is younger than the taxpayer, the taxpayer may elect to have the term annuity pay benefits until the spouse reaches age 90.

(g)   Registered retirement income funds (RRIFs)

A registered retirement income fund (RRIF) is, as has just been explained, an alternative to the RRSP annuity as the vehicle by which the RRSP pension is delivered. A RRIF is basically an extension of an RRSP and can be self-administered.[57] RRIFs pay out a minimum amount which increases each year based on a formula, but the taxpayer may withdraw any amount in excess of this minimum amount. The major differences between an RRSP annuity and RRIF are as follows: (1) the RRIF provides greater tax deferral because (under the statutory formula) the RRIF payments increase over time; (2) the RRIF provides more flexibility as to investments and may be self-administered; (3) the payout under a RRIF does not depend on interest rates at the time of purchase; (4) the payout under a RRIF is more flexible since any amount in excess of the minimum amount can be withdrawn; and (5) the payout under an RRSP annuity is guaranteed whereas the payout under a RRIF is not.

(h)   Tax consequences on death

The general rule is that the value of a taxpayer's RRSP, RRSP annuity or RRIF is included in the taxpayer's income in the year of death unless the beneficiary of the plan is the deceased taxpayer's spouse (s. 146(8.8)). If the beneficiary of the plan is the deceased taxpayer's spouse, it is the spouse who will pay tax on the payments received rather than the deceased.[58] Any lump

---

[55] Before the 1996 budget, the age limit for these rules was 71. Taxpayers who turned 70 or 71 in 1997 have until the end of 1997 to purchase an RRSP annuity or RRIF and transfer the funds in their RRSP on a tax-free basis.

[56] See note 12, above, for an explanation of these terms.

[57] Financial institutions offering self-administered RRIFs often charge annual administration fees which are not tax deductible (s. 18(1)(u)).

[58] If the spouse is not named as the beneficiary under the RRSP or RRSP annuity document, the legal representative of the deceased and the spouse can jointly elect to treat the amount as a "refund of premiums" and have the amounts taxed in the spouse's hands, so long as the spouse is entitled to at least that amount under the will (s. 146(8.1)). (It is, however, preferable to name

sum payment received by a spouse out of a deceased taxpayer's RRSP is called a "refund of premiums" and the spouse can claim an offsetting s. 60(l) deduction if the amount of the refund of premiums is contributed by the spouse to an RRSP or is used by the spouse to purchase a RRSP annuity or RRIF annuity within the year of death or within 60 days of that year. Often, because of the amount of tax that would have to be withheld on the payment of the refund of premiums to the spouse, these contributions are made by arranging for the trustee of the deceased's plan to make the transfer directly to the spouse's plan.

An amount will also qualify as a refund of premiums if the deceased has no spouse at the date of death and the beneficiary of the deceased's RRSP is a child or grandchild who is "financially dependent".[59] As in the case of a refund of premiums received by a spouse, the amount included in the financially dependent child or grandchild's hands as a refund of premiums can be offset with a s. 60(l) deduction. In the case of financially dependent child or grandchild who is mentally or physically infirm, the s. 60(l) deduction may be used for a contribution to an RRSP for the child;[60] in the case of a financially dependent child or grandchild who is not mentally or physically infirm, the s. 60(l) deduction is available only for the cost of the purchase of a term annuity to age 18. If a child or grandchild is 18 years of age or older and not infirm, there is no s. 60(l) deduction and no deferral of tax.

Because a deceased's RRSP can yield a significant amount, the rules respecting a refund of premiums on death are important in estate planning. Consideration should always be given to leaving an RRSP by will to a spouse or qualifying child or grandchild so as to take advantage of the tax-free rollover.

17.6 Registered education savings plans (RESPs)

Previous sections of this chapter have discussed several deferred income plans, namely, registered pension plans (RPPs), deferred profit sharing plans (DPSPs) and registered retirement income funds (RRIFs). The policy rationale for all of these plans is to provide tax assistance for private saving for retirement. The Income Tax Act recognizes one other deferred income plan, namely, the registered education savings plan (RESP), the purpose of which is to enable a taxpayer (the "subscriber") to save for the post-secondary education of a "beneficiary", who is normally, but not necessarily, the child or grandchild of the subscriber. The RESP differs from the various retirement funds in that contributions to an RESP are not tax deductible. However, the RESP does offer

---

the spouse as beneficiary under the plan in order to avoid probate fees.) In the case of a RRIF, there is no such election.

[59] According to the definition of refund of premiums in s. 146(1), "financially dependent" means that the child earns less than the basic personal credit amount under s. 118(1)(a) ($6,456 in 1997).

[60] It can also be used for the purchase of a term annuity to age 18 or an RRSP annuity or an RRIF.

two tax advantages: (1) the income of investments in the plan is not taxed; and (2) when the income is withdrawn and distributed to the beneficiary (who must by then be a student in a post-secondary institution) the income is taxed as income of the beneficiary, not the subscriber. The rules for RESPs are contained in s. 146.1. A brief discussion follows.

Annual contributions to an RESP are limited to $4,000 per beneficiary. Contributions can be made for a period of 21 years but maximum contributions per beneficiary are limited to $42,000.[61] Excess contributions are subject to a penalty tax of 1 per cent per month (12 per cent per year).[62] Income earned from investments in an RESP can accumulate on a tax-free basis for up to 25 years but, after that time, the plan is deregistered.

Before 1997, the major disadvantage of an RESP was that the income earned inside the plan was forfeited if a beneficiary did not attend a post-secondary institution.[63] For many parents, the risk that their children would not attend a post-secondary institution was sufficiently serious to forego the potential tax deferral and income splitting advantages of an RESP, even though the RESP could name a substitute beneficiary in the event that the primary beneficiary did not go on to get a post-secondary education. The rules have therefore been changed, starting in 1997, in order to make RESPs more attractive. If the beneficiary of an RESP does not go on to a post-secondary education and the RESP has been running for 10 years, the contributor can withdraw the income accumulated in the RESP (up to a maximum of $40,000) and transfer it to his (or his spouse's) RRSP if he has unused RRSP contribution room. If the accumulated RESP income cannot be fully offset by RRSP contribution room, a special tax of 20% (as well as regular income tax) will apply to the excess amount withdrawn. RESPs have not been popular in the past and, while this change should make them more attractive, it is not clear whether

---

[61] The $42,000 (21 years × $2,000 per year) maximum limit is derived from the $2,000 annual contribution limit that was in place for 1996. The limit was increased to $4,000 for 1997 in light of increases in tuition fees and to help parents who had not made maximum use of RESPs make up for missed contributions. See Canada, *The Federal Budget*, February 18, 1997.

[62] Starting in 1997, if an individual under 21 years of age replaces a sibling as a beneficiary under an RESP (because the sibling is not going on to get a post-secondary school education), none of the contributions which have been made to RESPs in respect of the sibling are to be taken into account in determining whether excess contributions have been made in respect of the RESP of the individual.

[63] Starting in 1997, distance education courses, such as correspondence courses, also qualify.

they will become more popular in the future, since the effective tax rate on amounts withdrawn in excess of the amount that can be transferred to an RRSP is very high.[64]

17.7   Retiring allowances

(a)   Meaning of retiring allowance

A "retiring allowance" is included in income in the year of receipt (s. 56(1)(a)(ii)). However, it enjoys this tax advantage over other income, including income from employment: the "qualifying" portion of the retiring allowance may be contributed to a registered retirement savings plan (RRSP) or registered pension plan (RPP) and the contribution is deductible (s. 60(j.1)).[65] This deduction is discussed in more detail later in this section of the chapter. Because early retirement programs have become a popular way for public and private sector employers to "downsize" and reduce their employee costs, this tax deduction has become increasingly well-used and increasingly important.

A retiring allowance is defined in s. 248(1) as:

an amount . . . received

(a)   on or after retirement of a taxpayer from an office or employment in recognition of the taxpayer's long service, or

(b)   in respect of a loss of an office or employment of a taxpayer, whether or not received as, on account or in lieu of payment of, damages or pursuant to an order or judgment of a competent tribunal,

by the taxpayer or, after the taxpayer's death, by a dependant or a relation of the taxpayer or by the legal representative of the taxpayer.

In order to receive a retiring allowance, there must be a "retirement" from employment or a "loss" of employment, both of which involve a termination of employment. In *Schwartz* v. *Canada* (1996),[66] the taxpayer entered into a contract of employment with a prospective employer, but the employer rescinded the contract before the taxpayer had actually started to work for the employer. Following negotiations, the prospective employer paid the taxpayer $360,000 as

---

[64]   Before 1985, it was common for a father or mother (or a grandparent) to establish an inter vivos trust for a minor child (or grandchild) in order to save for the child's education. The income accumulating in the trust could be taxed in the hands of the beneficiary through the use of a preferred beneficiary election, and the income would not be attributed to the settlor if the funding of the trust had been made by loan (as opposed to gift). In 1985, the attribution rules were extended to loans as well as gifts, and trusts for minor children ceased to be a means of income-splitting for most taxpayers. In addition, starting in 1996, the preferred beneficiary election was no longer available in most cases. See generally ch. 21, Trusts, below.

[65]   The rules respecting withholding of tax, Canada Pension Plan contributions and Unemployment Insurance premiums are also different for a retiring allowance than for income from employment: reg. 103(4).

[66]   Note 1, above.

damages for breach of the contract. The Supreme Court of Canada held that the amount paid to the taxpayer was not a retiring allowance. The Court reasoned that, since the taxpayer was not in fact employed by the prospective employer at the time when the contract was rescinded, there had been no loss of employment. For the same reason (presumably), the Crown did not argue that the payment was income from employment. Therefore, the payment escaped tax altogether.

In *Schwartz*, there was no loss of employment because employment had not started. The more common source of doubt concerns the employee who is undoubtedly employed before the date of the "retirement" and continues to maintain a relationship with the employer after that time. In *Serafini* v. *M.N.R.* (1989),[67] it was held that an employee participating in an early retirement programme, who continued to receive full salary and benefits (and to accrue pension benefits) for 12 months after his so-called "retirement", was still employed, even though he did not perform any duties of employment. (After the 12-month period, the employee began to receive his pension.) The Tax Court of Canada decided that the payments during the 12-month period constituted regular employment income, stating that the taxpayer's situation was similar to "to a pre-retirement leave with full pay and benefits".[68] This case illustrates the risk that payments received under an early retirement programme will be taxed as employment income, in which case they will lose the benefit of the tax-free rollover for contributions to an RRSP or RPP. Care must be taken in the design of an early retirement programme to ensure that a former employee does not continue to receive full employee benefits, and in particular, to accrue pension benefits after "retirement". Because it is common practice for larger employers to provide medical and dental benefits to retired employees, it is unlikely that the provision of such limited "post-retirement benefits" would cause a problem. However, if the employee continues to be a member of a company pension plan, it is likely that the employment will not have been terminated for tax purposes and that any payment received (the quantum of which will often be based on his or her former salary) will be taxed as employment income rather than as a retiring allowance.[69]

In Revenue Canada's view, the termination of employment for any reason (other than death)[70] generally constitutes a retirement or loss of employment for the purpose of the definition of retiring allowance in s. 248(1). There are, however, some exceptions. Revenue Canada does not consider the employment

---

[67] [1989] 2 C.T.C. 2437, 89 D.T.C. 653 (T.C.C.).

[68] *Id.*, 2442; 657.

[69] See ch. 10, Income from Employment, under heading 10.8, "Compensation for loss of employment", above.

[70] If an employee dies prior to retirement, payments made by his employer are considered to be death benefits: note 10, above.

to have terminated if the employee continues to be employed in a different position by the same employer or by an affiliated company shortly afterwards. (Continuing as a director for nominal compensation is permissible.)[71] Where an employee is hired as a consultant to perform services for the former employer shortly after his or her "retirement", it is also possible (depending upon the facts of the situation) that there was, in fact, no loss of employment for tax purposes.[72] Similarly, where an employee of a law firm (or other partnership) is promoted to partner in that firm, it is not clear that he or she is eligible to receive a retiring allowance.[73]

Retiring allowances will often be a useful way of compensating the senior managers of a business when the business is sold. In *Henderson* v. *M.N.R.* (1991),[74] the taxpayer was the controlling shareholder and manager of a corporation that sold its drugstore business to Shopper's Drug Mart. The taxpayer continued to work on a part-time basis as a pharmacist for Shopper's Drug Mart, in the same location that his corporation had previously operated in as well as another location. Notwithstanding his employment by the new owner of the business, the Tax Court of Canada held that amounts paid to him by his corporation in the year of sale and the following year qualified as retiring allowances, since the payments were in recognition of long service and he had in fact retired from his employment with his corporation.

Paragraph (a) of the definition of retiring allowance in s. 248 (quoted above) captures a payment made "on or after retirement" in recognition of "long service".[75] For this type of retiring allowance, the amount must be related to long service, which Revenue Canada understands "to have reference to the total number of years in an employee's career with a particular employer or affiliated employers".[76] Revenue Canada takes the view that the payment of "accumulated sick leave credits" qualifies as a retiring allowance, but the payment of "accumulated vacation leave" does not. A payment of accumulated vacation leave is therefore taxed as ordinary income from employment (ss. 5, 6(3)).[77] It is difficult to justify such a distinction, and it would surely be better to accept that payment of accumulated vacation leave, as well as payments of accumulated sick

---

[71] Interpretation Bulletin IT-337R2, "Retiring allowances" (1984), paras. 3 and 4. See also Collins, "The Terminated Employee" [1994] *Can. Tax Foundation Rep.* 31:1, 31:6-31:13, for a discussion of Revenue Canada's position.

[72] See Collins, note 71, above, 31:13-31:14.

[73] *Window on Canadian Tax*, CCH Canadian, para. 1844 discussing a technical interpretation dated April 8, 1992. See also Collins, note 71, above, 31:14.

[74] [1991] 2 C.T.C. 2048, 91 D.T.C. 1116 (T.C.C.).

[75] E.g., *Adler* v. *M.N.R.*, [1995] 1 C.T.C. 181, 94 D.T.C. 6605 (F.C.A.).

[76] IT-337R2, note 71, above, para. 5.

[77] *Ibid.*

leave, are in recognition of long service, so that if they are paid on or after retirement they would qualify as a retiring allowance.

Paragraph (b) of the definition of retiring allowance in s. 248 (quoted above) captures a payment made "in respect of a loss of an office or employment of a taxpayer" whether or not it is "received as, on account or in lieu of payment of, damages or pursuant to an order or judgment of a competent tribunal". As was explained in chapter 10, Income from Employment, this means that most damages awards and out-of-court settlements in respect of a loss of office or employment are taxed as retiring allowances rather than being treated as tax-free payments of capital.[78] According to Revenue Canada, payments in respect of a loss of office or employment also include payments under voluntary early retirement programmes which "are essentially designed to eliminate a number of office or employment positions (albeit on an elective basis)".[79]

(b)   Deduction for contribution to RRSP

The "qualifying" portion of a retiring allowance which is eligible for contribution to an RRSP or RPP, giving rise to a deduction under s. 60(j.1), is $2,000 per year of service before 1996 (including part years) plus an additional $1,500 for each year (or part year) before 1989 for which no RPP or DPSP benefits were earned. Thus, a taxpayer who was not a member of an RPP or DPSP would be entitled to the additional $1,500 (for a total of $3,500) per year of service for each year (or part year) of employment before 1989. Similarly, a taxpayer who was a member of an RPP or DPSP but whose benefits had not vested[80] by the time he ceased to be an employee would be entitled to the additional $1,500 per year of service for each year (or part year) of employment before 1989.

Consider the following example. An employee ceases employment on October 1, 1997 after working for the same employer since March 1, 1985. The employee receives a retiring allowance of $50,000. All his pension benefits have vested. However, because of a one-year waiting period before he could join the company pension plan, he earned no pension benefits for 1985. In this example, the taxpayer would have to report the $50,000 retiring allowance as income under s. 56(1)(a)(iv), but he could make an RRSP or RPP contribution of $23,500 ($2,000 × 11 years before 1996 plus $1,500 × 1 non-vested year before 1989) and claim a deduction for the contribution under s. 60(j.1).

---

[78] Chapter 10, Income from Employment, under heading 10.8, "Compensation for loss of employment", above.

[79] IT-337R2, note 71, above, para. 6 (as amended by correction sheet no. 21, July 18, 1986).

[80] Vesting refers to the time that an employee becomes indefeasibly entitled to the employer's contributions. Most provincial pension benefit laws require vesting to take place after two years of employment.

Before 1982, there was no limit on the amount of the retiring allowance that could be rolled tax-free into an RRSP or RPP. According to the Minister of Finance in his budget speech in 1981 (when s. 60(j.1) was introduced), "senior executives . . . typically arrange to receive a large lump-sum payment upon retirement which they may then contribute tax-free to their RRSP. . . . The amount of these retiring allowances has increased dramatically in recent years and in some instances amounts to several hundreds of thousands of dollars".[81] In 1982, s. 60(j.1) was enacted to restrict the tax-free rollover of retiring allowances. The amount of RRSP and RPP contribution that was deductible under s. 60(j.1) was initially limited to $3,500 per year of service, which was the limit for employer contributions to RPPs at the time. In 1989, the limit was reduced to $2,000 per year of service, with the $3,500 limit still applying for pre-1989 years where RPP or DPSP pension benefits had not been earned. Because of the measures implemented with pension reform in 1991, increasing RRSP limits and enabling taxpayers to carryforward their unused contribution limits, the s. 60(j.1) deduction was eliminated for years of service after 1995. Persons retiring after 1995 are still be able to use the deduction, but only for years of service before 1996.

17.8 Summary of transfers to RPPs, RRSPs and DPSPs

Previous sections of this chapter have discussed the deduction for contributions to a registered pension plan (RPP) (s. 8(1)(m)),[82] as well as the three different deductions for RRSP contributions that are available to taxpayers.[83] The first RRSP deduction is the regular "earned income" deduction (s. 60(i)). The second RRSP deduction is the deduction for the qualifying portion of a retiring allowance (s. 60(j.1)). The third RRSP deduction is for the contribution of a "refund of premiums" received on another taxpayer's death (s. 60(l)). Only the regular "earned income" RRSP contribution can be made to either the taxpayer's or the taxpayer's spouse's plan. The effect of these deductions is to allow certain amounts of income received by a taxpayer to be contributed to an RPP or RRSP on a tax-free basis.[84]

While an individual normally contributes to an RPP through payroll deductions, RRSP contributions are usually made directly by the contributor. There are, however, employee "group RRSP" plans, which are funded by monthly payroll deductions of an amount determined by the employee and

---

[81] Federal budget of November 12, 1981 (MacEachen).

[82] Section 17.3, "Registered pension plans" (RPPs)", above.

[83] Section 17.5, "Registered retirement savings plans (RRSPs)", above.

[84] For the purpose of the alternative minimum tax (ch. 5, Rates, under heading 5.4, "The alternative minimum tax", above), however, all RPP and RRSP contributions, except for the "refund of premiums" contribution, must be added back into income (s. 127.52(1)(a)).

deducted as a regular "earned income" deduction under s. 60(i). As well, in many cases, contributions of the qualifying portion of a retiring allowance (s. 60(j.1)) and the refund of premiums (s. 60(l)) are made directly to the taxpayer's RRSP by the payer of the amount, in order to avoid the tax that would have to be withheld if the amounts were first paid to the taxpayer and then contributed by the taxpayer to his or her RRSP. In all these cases, the s. 60 deduction is available to the taxpayer, regardless of whether the contribution is made by the taxpayer or directly by someone else.

There are other so-called "direct transfers" to RRSPs, RPPs and DPSPs, which must be made directly by the plan trustee in order to be done on a tax-free basis. These "direct transfers" include:

- transfers from an RPP to an RPP or RRSP (s. 147.3);
- transfers from a DPSP to an RPP, RRSP or DPSP (s. 147(19)); and
- transfers from an RRSP to an RPP, RRSP or RRIF (s. 147(16)).

The first two transfers, under ss. 147.3 and 147(19), allow a taxpayer leaving his or her employment, who is entitled to funds or benefits under the employer's RPP or DPSP, to have the funds transferred on a tax-free basis directly by the trustee of the RPP or DPSP to a new employer's plan or an RRSP.[85] The third transfer, under s. 147(16), allows taxpayers with RRSPs to move their RRSPs to different financial institutions and to purchase RRSP annuities and RRIFs, all on a tax-free basis.

17.9   Spousal and child support

(a)   Deduction-inclusion system

Payments for the support of a spouse or former spouse or child are deductible by the payer under s. 60(b) of the Act, and must be included in the income of the recipient under s. 56(1)(b).[86] These rules do not apply to child support payments required to be made under agreements or orders made or varied after April 30, 1997 (or orders in place before May 1, 1997 if the payer and the recipient so elect). Payments made pursuant to such orders will not be

---

[85] Provincial pension benefit legislation generally restricts the transfer of RPP benefits to "locked-in" RRSPs and life income funds (LIFs, which are essentially "locked-in" RRIFs). Unlike normal RRSPs, no withdrawals can be made from a "locked-in" RRSP and accumulated funds in a "locked in" RRSP can only be used to purchase a life annuity (not a term annuity or RRIF). Unlike normal RRIFs, which continue to pay out benefits after age 80 (according to a formula), the funds remaining in a LIF at age 80 must be used to purchase a life annuity. For a further discussion of RRSP annuities and RRIFs, see headings 17.5(f), "RRSP annuities", 17.5(g), "Registered retirement income funds (RRIFs)", above.

[86] For a detailed discussion of all these provisions see Durnford and Toope, "Spousal Support in Family Law and Alimony in the Law of Taxation" (1994) 42 *Can. Tax J.* 1.

taxable in the hands of the recipient and will not be deductible in the hands of the payer.[87]

Paragraphs 60(b) (deduction) and 56(1)(b) (inclusion) contain the formula "A – (B + C)" to describe the payments that they cover. Amount "A" in the formula is the total of "support amounts" (i.e., spousal and child support payments) paid and received during the year when the payer and recipient were living separate and apart. Amount "B" in the formula is the total of "child support amounts" that became receivable during the year under an agreement or order made or varied after April 30, 1997 (or orders in place before May 1, 1997 if the payer and the recipient so elect). Amount "C" in the formula is the total of all "support amounts" included or deducted in a previous year. The net result of the formula is that all support amounts are deductible by the payer and included in the income of the recipient, except for tax-free child support payments (described in B) and support amounts received in the year but included in income in a prior year.

Subsection 56.1(4) contains the following definitions of support amount and child support amount:

> "support amount" means an amount payable or receivable as an allowance on a periodic basis for the maintenance of the recipient, children of the recipient or both the recipient and children of the recipient, if the recipient has discretion as to the use of the amount, and
>
>> (a) the recipient is the spouse or former spouse of the payer, the recipient and payer are living separate and apart because of the breakdown of their marriage and the amount is receivable under an order of a competent tribunal or under a written agreement or
>>
>> (b) the payer is a natural parent of a child of the recipient and the amount is receivable under an order made by a competent tribunal in accordance with the laws of a province.
>
> "child support amount" means any support amount that is not identified in the agreement or order under which it is receivable as being solely for the support of a recipient who is a spouse or former spouse of the payer or who is a parent of a child of whom the payer is a natural parent.

Part (a) of the definition of a support amount includes payments to a "spouse or former spouse" as the result of the "breakdown of the taxpayer's marriage" (remember that the definition of "spouse" and "marriage" in s. 252(4) includes common-law relationships).[88] In order for payments to a "spouse or former spouse" to qualify for the deduction-inclusion provisions of ss. 60(b) and 56(1)(b), the payments must satisfy the following requirements: (1) the payments must be an "allowance" (discussed below); (2) the payments must be made "on

---

[87] Amount B in the formula contained in ss. 60(b) and 56(1)(b) provides a deduction for amounts which are receivable under a child support agreement or order on or after its "commencement day." The circumstances provided in the text are set out in the definition of "commencement day" in s. 56.1(4).

[88] Chapter 7, Taxation Unit, under heading 7.5(b), "Spouses", above.

a periodic basis" (a lump sum payment is not deductible);[89] (3) the payer and recipient must be "living separate and apart" from each other; and (4) the payment must be made under the terms of either a court order or a "written agreement".

Part (b) of the definition of support amounts includes support payments where there has been no marriage (not even a common-law relationship) between the payer and the recipient, but the payer is the "natural parent" of a child of the recipient.[90] These payments must also be an "allowance", they must be made "on a periodic basis" and the payer must have been living "separate and apart" from the recipient. But part (b) of the definition is more restrictive than part (a) in that the payment must have been made under a court order; a written agreement will not suffice for such payments, let alone anything less formal.

In order for an allowance to qualify as a support amount, the recipient must have "discretion as to the use of the amount". As a result, payments made directly to third parties for the benefit of the spouse (or former spouse) or children are excluded from the definition of support amount, because in that case the recipient would have no "discretion as to the use of the amount". Common examples of third party payments include payment of rent, mortgage payments,[91] tuition fees, dental expenses and counselling. Subsections 56.1(2) and 60.1(2) create an exception to the general rule by deeming a third party payment to be an "allowance payable on a periodic basis" and deeming the recipient to "have discretion as to the use of that amount" if the order or written agreement provides that these subsections "shall apply". These provisions allow third party payments to be treated as "support amounts" if the payer and the recipient so agree and the payments are paid pursuant to a court order or written agreement (if applicable) which refers to ss. 56.1(2) and 60.1(2).

---

[89] See *McKimmon* v. *The Queen*, [1990] 1 C.T.C. 109, 89 D.T.C. 6088 (F.C.A.) in which the court distinguished between a periodic payment which is an allowance and a payment made as an instalment of a capital amount. Some of the criteria listed by the court in *McKimmon* are summarized in Interpretation Bulletin IT-118R3, "Alimony and maintenance" (1990), para. 12. According to paragraph 13 of this Interpretation Bulletin, a lump sum payment covering periodic payments which are in arrears will be considered to be a periodic payment; it will therefore be deductible to the payer and taxable to the recipient in the year of payment.

[90] Before 1997, former ss. 60(c) and 56(1)(c) covered the payments just described; former ss. 60(b) and 56(1)(b) applied only to payments made to a spouse or former spouse; and former s. 56(12) defined the term "allowance". The definition of "support amount" in 56.1(4) and new ss. 60(b) and 56(1)(b) incorporate the rules contained in all these provisions after 1996.

[91] *Gagnon* v. *The Queen*, [1986] 1 S.C.R. 264, [1986] 1 C.T.C. 410, 86 D.T.C. 6179 (S.C.C.) allowed such an amount to be deducted as an allowance; the result was reversed by the enactment of former s. 56(12), which required that the recipient have "discretion as to the use of the amount" in order for the amount to be a deductible. This requirement is now contained in the definition of support amount in s. 56.1(4).

Subsections 56.1(3) and 60.1(3) cover payments made before a written agreement or court order has come into existence; such payments are deemed to have "been paid and received thereunder" if the agreement or order so provides and the payments are made in the year that the agreement or order is made or in the previous year. This allows taxpayers to make payments which are deductible to the payer and taxable to the recipient under ss. 56(1)(b) and 60(b) and still have some time to negotiate a written agreement or obtain a court order.

Legal expenses paid to establish the right to support are treated as payments on account of capital and are therefore not deductible; however, legal fees paid to enforce the payments after the right has been established are deductible.[92]

Earned income for RRSP purposes is reduced by support amounts paid and deducted from income under s. 60(b) and increased by support amounts received and included in income under s. 56(1)(b).[93]

(b)   Policy objectives

The deductibility of payments for spousal and child support is an anomaly, because the payments have no connection to the earning of income. In an intact family, they are consumption expenses that are not deductible against any source of income. It is therefore odd that the payments should be deductible when a family has broken up. Once deductibility is allowed, however, it is sound tax policy to require the recipient to report the payments and pay income tax on them. Otherwise, the income represented by the payments would escape tax altogether.

The deduction-inclusion system was introduced into the Act in 1942 with the avowed purpose of providing a subsidy to split families to assist with the additional expenses of maintaining two households.[94] The system was based on the premise that the payer is usually in a higher tax bracket than the recipient; when that is the case, the diversion of some income from the payer to the recipient creates an income-split which reduces the total amount of tax that is payable.[95] The subsidy provided by the deduction-inclusion system is the difference between the cost in foregone revenue caused by the payer's deduction and the amount of revenue raised by the recipient's inclusion. The Government

---

[92] *Sembinelli* v. *M.N.R.*, [1994] 2 C.T.C. 378, 94 D.T.C. 6636 (F.C.A.). See also ch. 14, Income from Business or Property: Capital Expenditures, under heading 14.1(a), "Significance of capital classification", above, for a general discussion of the non-deductibility of certain capital expenditures.

[93] See paragraphs (b) and (f) of the definition of earned income in s. 146(1).

[94] The legislative history is related in *Thibaudeau* v. *Canada*, [1995] 1 C.T.C. 382, 390, 95 D.T.C. 5273, 5281 (S.C.C.).

[95] See ch. 7, Taxation Unit, under heading 7.4, "Income splitting", above.

of Canada treats the subsidy as a tax expenditure and valued it at $220 million for 1993 and $200 in 1992.[96] Since this figure excludes provincial taxes, which in the aggregate amount to more than 50 per cent of federal tax, the combined federal-provincial tax expenditure was in excess of $330 million in 1993 ($200 million × 1.5) and $300 million in 1992.

If the universe unfolded as it should, this subsidy would be reflected in a higher level of support payments: the deductibility of the payments for the higher-income payer should enable the lower-income payee to negotiate, or obtain in court, a higher level of support than could be provided if the payments were not deductible, and that higher level of support should more than offset the tax that the recipient would become liable to pay. The tax benefit will not, however, be shifted forward to the recipient if the amount of support is fixed without regard for the tax consequences to payer and recipient. And, in those cases where the recipient is in the same (or a higher) tax bracket as the payer, the deduction-inclusion system produces no tax benefit.[97]

In *Thibaudeau* v. *Canada* (1995),[98] a recipient of child-support payments challenged the validity of former s. 56(1)(b), the provision that required her to include the payments in her income. She argued that s. 56(1)(b) was a violation of the equality guarantee in s. 15 of the Charter, because s. 56(1)(b) discriminated against separated custodial parents by forcing them to pay the tax on support payments. The Supreme Court of Canada, by a majority, rejected the argument and upheld s. 56(1)(b). The Court held that the provision should not be assessed in isolation from s. 60(b) (which, it will be recalled, is the matching deduction for the payer spouse) and the family law system, under which support orders and agreements are made. The deduction-inclusion system resulted in a reduction of tax for the majority of separated couples. While it was the payer who received the benefit of the deduction, the deduction increased the payer's ability to pay support. While it was the recipient who suffered the tax burden, the family law system required that the tax burden be taken into account in fixing the amount of support, so that the amount should be grossed-up to fully compensate the recipient for the additional tax liability. In Thibaudeau's case, the family court had taken her additional tax liability into account, but it appeared that the liability had been under-estimated and that the gross-up for tax was,

---

[96] Government of Canada, *Tax Expenditures 1995* (1996), 26.

[97] If the recipient's child tax benefit and GST credit are being reduced by the inclusion, the recipient's marginal tax rate would include the rates at which these payments are phased out. The child tax benefit (s. 122.6) and GST credit (s. 122.5) are discussed in ch. 4, under heading 4.5(b), "Refundable and income-tested credits", above.

[98] [1995] 1 C.T.C. 382, 95 D.T.C. 5273 (S.C.C.). The principal majority opinion was written by Gonthier J. Short concurring opinions were written by Sopinka J., with whom La Forest J. agreed, and by Cory and Iacobucci JJ. Dissenting opinions were written by McLachlin J. and L'Heureux-Dubé J.

therefore, insufficient.[99] The Supreme Court of Canada, in deciding against Thibaudeau, held that this deficiency should be remedied by a review of the support order by the family court. Although some separated custodial parents did not benefit from the deduction-inclusion system, as a group custodial parents did benefit.[100] Therefore the Income Tax Act did not discriminate against them, and there was no breach of s. 15 of the Charter of Rights.

Although Thibaudeau lost the court battle, she won the war against the deduction-inclusion system for child support. The Government of Canada, in consultation with the provinces, announced its intention to reform the child support system within months of the decision of *Thibaudeau*. These reforms are now law: they include the introduction of a no deduction/no inclusion system for child support agreements or orders made or varied after April 30, 1997 (discussed above), guidelines for calculating the child support to be paid (to reduce legal costs and improve the fairness and consistency of amounts awarded), and improvements in the enforcement of court-ordered child support.[101]

17.10   Workers' compensation and social assistance

Workers' compensation and social assistance[102] payments are included in net income (ss. 56(1)(v) and (u)), but are deducted in computing taxable income (s. 110(1)(f)). This tax treatment results in these payments being included in income for the purpose of determining a taxpayer's eligibility for various income-tested tax credits (which are based on a taxpayer's net income rather than a taxpayer's taxable income). Such income-tested tax credits include the

---

[99]   The Court did not consider the question, upon which no evidence seemed to have been led, as to how much lower the support order would have been if the deduction in s. 60(b) did not exist. Without some estimate of this, it is not apparent, merely from the inadequacy of the tax gross-up, that Thibaudeau was worse off than she would have been in a world without the deduction-inclusion system.

[100]   McLachlin and L'Heureux-Dubé JJ. dissented primarily on the grounds that the family law system could not be relied upon to shift the tax benefit forward to the custodial spouse. By conferring the benefit of the deduction on the non-custodial spouse and imposing the burden of the tax on the custodial spouse, the Act was discriminatory.

[101]   A study of 708 cases of court-ordered child support contained in a Department of Justice data base, found that 77 per cent of the recipients would be better off under the new child support family law and tax rules (and 23 per cent of the payers would be worse off): Feltham and MacNaughton, "The New Child Support Rules and Existing Awards: Choosing the Best Tax and Family Law Regime", (1996) *Can. Tax J. 44*, 1265, 1285.

[102]   Social assistance payments are payments made by the federal, provincial and municipal governments to assist low-income taxpayers. The federal "guaranteed income supplement" and "spouse's allowance" benefits that low-income seniors receive are examples. Welfare payments are another example. The only social assistance payments that are specifically excluded from income are payments for foster care (s. 81(1)(h)).

refundable GST credit (s. 122.5),[103] the child tax benefit (s. 122.6),[104] claims for dependants by others (ss. 118(1)(a), (b) and (d))[105] and the age credit reduction (s. 118(2)).[106] However, because workers' compensation and social assistance payments are deducted in computing taxable income, these payments are not subject to tax.

It will be recalled that the Carter Commission recommended that workers' compensation and social assistance payments be subject to tax but that this recommendation was not implemented in the tax reform of 1972.[107] The debate on whether such payments should be taxed continues today. The Government of Canada treats the non-taxation of social assistance and workers' compensation as a tax expenditure, which the Government valued at $1.54 billion for 1993.[108] Including provincial taxes, which in the aggregate amount to more than 50 per cent of federal tax, the combined federal-provincial tax expenditure is in excess of $2.31 billion ($1.54 billion × 1.5). The main argument for taxing these government transfer payments to individuals is that the payments increase the recipient's ability to pay tax. In the case of workers' compensation payments, there is the additional argument that the premiums that employers pay are tax deductible.

17.11 Moving expenses

Section 62 allows a deduction for "moving expenses". The definition of moving expenses includes travel costs, transportation and storage of household effects, temporary lodging and meals, the costs of selling an old residence and the legal expenses of buying a new residence. The deduction is only available if the move was 40 kilometres or more and was caused by a change in the location of the taxpayer's work (or, in the case of a student, a change of university). The deduction can be taken from income from employment at the new location or income from business at the new location or scholarships or research grants at

---

[103] Chapter 4, Objectives, under heading, 4.4(d), "Refundable and income-tested credits", above.

[104] *Ibid.*

[105] Chapter 4, Objectives, under heading 4.4(c), "Conversion of deductions to credits", above.

[106] The Old Age Security clawback (note 21, above) is also based on the net income of an individual and the Senior's Benefit, which is to replace the Old Age Security programme in 2001, will be based on a couple's net income: see note 20, above.

[107] Chapter 9, Tax Base, under heading 9.8, "Government transfer payments", above. Workers' compensation payments were initially excluded from income (see s. 81(1)(h), as it read before 1982) until 1982, when the current inclusion-deduction system for these payments became effective (s. 56(1)(v)).

[108] Note 96, above. The $1.54 billion figure quoted is the sum of the figures reported for the guaranteed income supplement and spouse's allowance benefits ($225 million), social assistance benefits ($705 million), and workers' compensation benefits ($610 million).

the new location (s. 62(1)(f)). Any excess of deductible expenses over qualifying income can be carried forward for one year (s. 62(1)(d)).

The deduction for moving expenses is available only for expenses that were not reimbursed by the taxpayer's employer. In chapter 10, Income from Employment, above, the point was made that the rules allowing an employer to reimburse an employee for moving expenses on a tax-free basis are far more generous than the rules in s. 62, which allow an employee to deduct only those expenses listed in s. 62(3).[109] As a result, it is better for an employer to reimburse a taxpayer for non-deductible moving expenses (such as a $50,000 loss on the sale of a house) than to pay him or her an allowance for the same amount. For example, if an employee is reimbursed for a $50,000 loss on the sale of a house, the reimbursement need not be reported because it not considered to be a taxable benefit of employment.[110] However, if the taxpayer's employer pays him or her a $50,000 allowance in respect of this loss, the allowance would have to be reported as employment income (s. 6(1)(b)), but no amount would be deductible as a moving expense because a loss on the sale of a house is not one of the deductible moving expenses listed in s. 62(3). In the second case, the taxpayer would report $50,000 of income for tax purposes whereas, in the first case, the taxpayer would have nothing to report. This is an anomalous result.

---

[109] Chapter 10, Income from Employment, under heading 10.6(c), "Reimbursements distinguished", above. The restricted list of moving expenses is set out in s. 62(3). The rules state that a taxpayer deducting moving expenses must include any reimbursement or allowance received in respect of those expenses in his income in order to deduct the expenses (s. 62(1)(g)). Typically, however, any employer-reimbursed expenses would simply be left off the list of moving expenses to be deducted in the employee's tax return whereas any allowances would automatically be included in his income under s. 6(1)(b). Paragraph 62(1)(g) ensures that employer-reimbursed expenses are not deducted.

[110] *Ibid.*

18

Losses

18.1 Income losses

(a) Current losses

Subdivision a of Division B of Part I of the Income Tax Act provides the rules for the computation of "income *or loss* from an office or employment". Subdivision b provides the rules for the computation of "income *or loss* from a business or property". Both of those subdivisions provide for deductions as well as inclusions, so that the computation can yield a negative figure, namely, a loss. In the case of an office or employment, a loss would be very unusual, because the few available deductions would rarely exceed the income. In the case of a business or property, however, a loss is a common occurrence. This is especially the case with a business, where expenses may exceed expectations or revenue may fall below expectations or both. Even a successful business may incur losses in the early (start-up) years or for temporary periods; and of course many businesses are unsuccessful, consistently incurring losses until they are wound up. Income from property is obviously far less risky than income from business, but property can yield losses, especially where the property has been acquired with borrowed money, in which case the interest expense, when added to other carrying costs, may exceed (for example) the rent from the real estate or the dividends from the shares.

We have already noted the rule that losses that are incurred from business or property in circumstances where the taxpayer has no reasonable expectation of profit are not deductible at all.[1] Such losses are regarded as non-deductible consumption expenses. They are discussed later in this chapter.[2] What this section of the chapter is concerned with is losses that are incurred from a business or property in circumstances where there is a reasonable expectation of profit.

A loss from an income source, such as business or property, is deductible against income from all other sources, including taxable capital gains, derived in the same taxation year. This result is stipulated by s. 3(d) of the Act. For example, assume taxpayer A has income from employment of $60,000 (includible under s. 3(a)) and a taxable capital gain of $10,000 (includible under s. 3(b)). If in the same year A has incurred a business loss of $30,000, A may deduct (under s. 3(d)) the amount of the loss from the combined income from both other sources, giving A a total income for tax purposes of $40,000 ($60,000 + $10,000 − $30,000 = $40,000) (s. 3(e)).

Losses cannot be transferred from one taxpayer to another. If the taxpayer in our example had incorporated the business, so that the loss of $30,000 had been suffered by the corporation, then the individual taxpayer could not deduct the business loss. If the corporation had no positive income to offset the loss, then the loss would not be deductible by the corporation. The loss could be carried over to other years by the corporation, in accordance with the loss carryover rules that are described next. But, if the corporation never became successful, the loss carryover would not be able to be used. The deductibility of losses must be taken into account in determining whether or not to incorporate a business, especially if start-up losses are anticipated. It may be prudent to delay incorporation until it is clear that the business is successful. For the same reason,

---

[1] Chapter 12, Income from Business or Property: Inclusions, under headings 12.2(b), 12.3(b), both entitled "Reasonable expectation of profit", above.

[2] Section 18.6, "Hobby losses", below.

it is often imprudent for a corporation with more than one business to organize the different businesses as separate (subsidiary) corporations. If the separate businesses are operated within a single corporation, then, if losses are incurred by one of the businesses, the losses can be deducted from the profits from a profitable business. If the unprofitable business were operated by a separate corporation, the losses may be wasted for tax purposes.[3]

(b)   Non-capital losses

The point has been made that, when a taxpayer incurs an income-source loss in a taxation year, the loss must be deducted against any income derived by the taxpayer from other sources in the loss year. If the positive income for the loss year is not sufficient to offset the loss, the taxpayer will have no income for the year (s. 3(f)). The taxpayer's deficit for the year (excess of current loss over current income) is described by the Act as the taxpayer's "non-capital loss" for the year (s. 111(8)). For example, a taxpayer who in a taxation year had employment income of $50,000, a taxable capital gain of $9,000 and a business loss of $80,000, would have a non-capital loss for that year of $21,000 ($50,000 + $9,000 − $80,000 = −$21,000).

A non-capital loss is not deductible in the year that it was incurred, because the taxpayer has no more income in that year against which the loss could be applied. However, a non-capital loss for a particular taxation year may be carried over to other taxation years and deducted in those years. Paragraph 111(1)(a) provides as follows:

> 111(1) For the purpose of computing the taxable income of a taxpayer for a taxation year, there may be deducted such portion as the taxpayer may claim of the taxpayer's
>
> (a)   non-capital losses for the 7 taxation years immediately preceding and the 3 taxation years immediately following the year;

This provision allows the non-capital loss to be carried back three years and forward seven years from the year in which the loss was incurred.[4]

Paragraph 111(1)(a) is confusing at first until one realizes that it is drafted from the standpoint of the year in which the non-capital loss may be deducted, not the year in which the non-capital loss was incurred (the loss year). From the standpoint of the loss year, the loss may be carried back three years and forward seven years. From the standpoint of any other year, a non-capital loss is available as a deduction if it were incurred in the three years immediately following (from

---

[3] The Act does not permit the consolidation of the income and losses of related corporations; each corporation is taxed separately. The artificial arrangement in *Stubart Investments* v. *The Queen* (1984), ch. 22, note 8, below, was designed to get around this rule.

[4] Section 111 is located within Division C of Part I of the Act. This means that the deduction of carried-over losses is part of the computation of "taxable income", rather than "income" (s. 2(2)). The deduction of current losses is part of the computation of "income", because the deduction of current losses is allowed by s. 3, which is in Division B of Part I of the Act.

which it would have been carried back) or in the seven years immediately preceding (from which it would have been carried forward).

The loss carryover rules are restricted for a corporation that has undergone a change of control.[5] In that case, s. 111(5) provides that non-capital losses[6] arising before the change of control cannot be deducted after the change of control, unless they are business losses, and the business in which the losses were sustained is continued with a reasonable expectation of profit after the change of control. If those conditions are met, the losses can be deducted after the change of control, but only to the extent of income from the business in which the losses were sustained or from another similar business.[7] The purpose of s. 111(5) is to stop a market for loss companies, under which unprofitable corporations are taken over solely for the tax value of their unused losses, which could be used to shelter income from the business of the corporation that has taken over the unprofitable business. Where a corporation with unused losses is taken over, and the new managers make the acquired corporation's business profitable, then the acquired corporation's unused losses can be applied against the profits from the formerly unprofitable business, even though the profits were earned after the change of control. In that situation, the takeover has accomplished the sound commercial objective of making an unprofitable business profitable, and there is no reason why the unused pre-takeover losses should not continue to be available.[8]

Paragraph 111(1)(a) allows the deduction of "such portion as the taxpayer may claim" of the non-capital loss for a year. This language gives the taxpayer a discretion as to whether or not to deduct an available non-capital loss in a particular year, and a discretion to deduct only a portion of the loss in a particular year.[9] This makes it possible for the taxpayer to "spread" the loss as

---

[5] Technically speaking, these restrictions apply only when control of a corporation is "acquired", which will not necessarily occur on a "change of control". See Dean, "The January 15, 1987 Draft Amendments Relating to the Acquisition of Gains and Losses" [1987] *Corp. Man. Tax Conf.* 2:4 for a discussion of this distinction. Since the terms are synonymous in many cases, however, the use of the more common term "change of control" is sufficient for our purposes.

[6] The deductibility by a corporation of net capital losses (and non-capital losses arising from losses from property and allowable business investment losses) is also restricted after a change of control: note 15, below.

[7] See Interpretation Bulletin IT-302R3, "Losses of a corporation — The effect on their deductibility of changes in control, amalgamation and winding up" (1993), paras. 14, 15.

[8] There are other rules that deem a company to have a year-end on a change of control (s. 249(4)), and require that a variety of assets be written down to their fair market values, thus subjecting any resulting losses to the loss carryover restrictions: s. 111(4)(c) and (d) (non-depreciable capital property); s. 111(5.1) (depreciable property); s. 111(5.2) (eligible capital property); s. 111(5.3) (accounts receivable).

[9] Subsection 111(3) provides that the amount of a loss that may be deducted in a particular year is reduced by amounts that have been deducted in previous years.

advantageously as possible over the years of highest income. Of course, holding on to a non-capital loss in anticipation of future high earnings involves the risk that the earnings will not materialize before the expiry of the seven-year carryforward period, in which case the loss could be wasted.

When a taxpayer decides to carry a non-capital loss back to a previous taxation year, this involves re-opening the taxpayer's tax liability for the previous year. In the usual case, the taxpayer will have filed a return for that year; the Minister will have issued an assessment; and the taxpayer will have paid the tax due for the year. In order to deduct a loss carryback in a previous year, the taxpayer files with Revenue Canada a form entitled "Request for Loss Carryback", claiming the deduction. If the request is in order, the Minister reassesses the taxpayer for the previous year (employing that year's rules), and then sends the taxpayer a refund of the tax which, as the result of the new deduction, will be shown to have been overpaid. (Interest on the refund is payable only from the time that the loss is claimed: s. 164(5)(d).)

18.2 Capital losses

(a) Current losses

A loss from the disposition of capital property (other than depreciable property)[10] is a "capital loss" (s. 39(1)(b)).[11] Three-quarters of a capital loss is an "allowable capital loss" (s. 38(b)). An allowable capital loss is deductible only from taxable capital gains derived in the same taxation year. The deduction is allowed by s. 3(b) of the Act. For example, a taxpayer who in a taxation year has income from a business of $50,000 (includible under (s. 3(a)), a taxable capital gain of $9,000 (includible under s. 3(b)) and an allowable capital loss of $30,000, is only able to deduct (under s. 3(b)) $9,000 of the allowable capital loss, because that is the extent of the taxpayer's taxable capital gains for the year. The taxpayer must report income for tax purposes of $50,000.

The restriction on the deductibility of allowable capital losses stands in contrast to the treatment of losses from other sources, such as office, employment, business or property. These losses, as noted above,[12] are deductible from income from all other sources, including taxable capital gains. This result is accomplished by s. 3(d), but s. 3(d) does not apply to allowable capital losses; this means that allowable capital losses are deductible only under s. 3(b), which restricts the deductibility of allowable capital losses to taxable

---

[10] Losses from the disposition of depreciable property are recognized through the system of capital cost allowances, adjusted by the provisions for recapture and terminal loss; any ultimate loss is a loss from a business or property: ch. 14, Income from Business or Property: Capital Expenditures, under heading 14.2 "Depreciable property", above.

[11] Chapter 15, Capital Gains, under heading 15.13, "Capital losses", above.

[12] Section 18.1(a), "Current losses", above.

capital gains. The Act used to permit an individual (but not a corporation) to deduct allowable capital losses from income other than taxable capital gains, but only up to a limit of $2,000. In 1985, this deduction was repealed, leaving the current deductibility of allowable capital losses entirely dependent on the existence of taxable capital gains in the same taxation year.

The restriction on the deductibility of allowable capital losses also stands in contrast to the treatment of taxable capital gains. A taxable capital gain must be recognized in the year that it is derived, whereas an allowable capital loss is not necessarily deductible in the year that it is incurred. The asymmetrical treatment of gains and losses has been described as creating "a bias against risk-taking".[13] What is the reason for it? The answer is that it is an attempt to reduce the advantage of the realization basis of capital gains taxation. Capital gains that have accrued on a capital property do not have to be recognized for tax purposes until they are realized by the sale or other disposition of the property. This enables tax on capital gains to be postponed until a time of the taxpayer's choosing (a disposition usually being a voluntary act). If there was no restriction on the deductibility of capital losses, a taxpayer could dispose of a property with accrued losses and obtain an immediate deduction despite the fact that the taxpayer was continuing to hold other properties upon which gains had accrued but had not been realized. By restricting the deductibility of capital losses, the Act reduces the incentive to postpone the realization of capital gains and diminishes the ability of taxpayers to manipulate their capital-gains income.

The restriction on the deductibility of allowable capital losses is removed for the taxation year in which a taxpayer dies (the terminal year) and the immediately preceding year. In those two years, allowable capital losses are deductible from income from all sources, not just taxable capital gains. This is provided by s. 111(2), which also extends the same privilege to allowable capital losses carried over from other years ("net capital losses", discussed in the next section of the chapter). The terminal year, it will be recalled, is the year in which the deemed disposition on death takes place (s. 70(5)).[14] That deemed disposition, which applies to all of the deceased taxpayer's capital property, could give rise to more capital losses than capital gains. It would be unfair to maintain the normal restriction on deductibility for the losses of the terminal year when the carryforward of unused losses (discussed in the next section of this chapter) that is available to a living taxpayer is not available to the deceased taxpayer. The preceding year is included with the terminal year, because a taxpayer might die early in a taxation year when insufficient income had been earned to cover the allowable capital losses generated by the deemed disposition; in that case, it would be important to be able to carry the losses back and apply them against income from all sources in the previous year.

---

[13] Bossons, "Implementing Capital Gains Reforms" (1979) 27 *Can. Tax J.* 145, 152.

[14] Chapter 15, Capital Gains, under heading 15.14, "Deemed dispositions", above.

(b) Net capital losses

If in a taxation year a taxpayer incurs allowable capital losses that exceed the taxpayer's taxable capital gains in that year, the non-deductible excess of the allowable capital losses is described by the Act as the taxpayer's "net capital loss" for the year (s. 111(8)). Our previous example was a taxpayer who in a taxation year has $50,000 of business income, a taxable capital gain of $9,000 and an allowable capital loss of $30,000. That taxpayer has a net capital loss for the year of $21,000.

A net capital loss is not deductible in the year that it is incurred, because the taxpayer has no more taxable capital gains against which the loss could be applied. This is so even if, as in our example, the taxpayer does have positive income other than taxable capital gains in the same year. However, s. 111(1)(b) provides that a net capital loss for a particular year may be carried back three years and carried forward indefinitely (for the lifetime of the taxpayer).[15] Any such carried-over net capital loss is still subject to the same restrictions on deductibility: it is deductible only against taxable capital gains of the year into which the net capital loss has been carried. It is the existence of this restriction that explains why the carryforward period is not restricted to seven years, as it is for a non-capital loss. In the year of death and the immediately preceding year, s. 111(2) removes the restriction on deductibility. In those two years, net capital losses (as well as allowable capital losses incurred in the year of death) are deductible against income from all sources. The reason for the more generous treatment of the last two years is that the year of death is the end of the carryforward period, and any losses not deducted by then would be wasted.

In other respects, the rules for the carryover of a net capital loss are similar to the rules for a non-capital loss. In particular, the taxpayer has a discretion as to the year or years to which the loss is carried, and a discretion to deduct only a portion of the loss in a particular year.

---

[15] When a corporation undergoes a change of control, s. 111(4) stops the carryover of net capital losses (and non-capital losses arising from losses from property and allowable business investment losses). Net capital losses incurred before the change of control cannot be carried forward to the years after the change of control, and net capital losses incurred after the change of control cannot be carried back to the years before the change of control. However, s. 111(4)(e) permits the corporation to treat some or all of its capital properties as having been disposed of immediately before the end of the taxation year preceding the change of control. The corporation has an election, under which it is allowed to stipulate the amount of the deemed proceeds of disposition of each capital property, provided the elected amount is more than the adjusted cost base and not more than the fair market value of the property. This provision enables the corporation with unused net capital losses (and property losses and allowable business investment losses) to use up the losses against gains accrued before the change of control.

(c)   Superficial losses

The Act contains several "stop-loss" rules that deny a deduction for a capital loss in circumstances where, on policy grounds, no deduction should be permitted. One such rule, explained in chapter 15, Capital Gains,[16] is the rule that any loss on the disposition of personal-use property is deemed to be nil; the reason for that rule is that losses on personal-use property are really consumption expenses. Other stop-loss rules depend on the policy premise that no loss should be allowed where a disposition results in little or no change in the beneficial ownership of the property disposed of.[17] In this category is the superficial loss rule.

Subparagraph 40(2)(g)(i) deems a "superficial loss" to be nil. A superficial loss is defined in s. 54 as a taxpayer's loss from the disposition of a property in any case where:

(a)   during the period that begins 30 days before and ends 30 days after the disposition, the taxpayer or a person affiliated with the taxpayer acquires a property (in this definition referred to as the "substituted property") that is, or is identical to, the particular property, and

(b)   at the end of that period, the taxpayer or a person affiliated with the taxpayer owns or had a right to acquire the substituted property . . .[18]

An affiliated person includes a taxpayer, his or her spouse, a corporation controlled by the taxpayer or his or her spouse (and many others).[19]

Consider the example of T, who in 1995 holds 100 shares in XYZ Ltd. The shares have declined in value by $600, but T does not want to get rid of them because she believes that the value of the shares will eventually rise again. However, she would like to claim an allowable capital loss of $450 (three-quarters of $600), because she has a taxable capital gain of about that amount which could be sheltered by the allowable capital loss. If it were not for the superficial loss rule, T could sell the shares for their current price, which would result in a $600 loss, and immediately buy another 100 XYZ shares for the same price. That way, she would still have the same investment,[20] but she would have crystallized the accrued loss on the shares. The effect of the

---

[16] Chapter 15, Capital Gains, under heading 15.16, "Personal-use property", above.

[17] For example, losses are denied on a disposition of property to a registered retirement savings plan trust (s. 40(2)(g)(iv)(B)) and to a controlled corporation (s. 40(2)(g)(i) and proposed ss. 13(21.2), 40(3.3), as set out in Bill C-69, which has not been passed at the time of writing).

[18] As proposed in Bill C-69, which has not been passed at the time of writing.

[19] The full definition of affiliated person is quite extensive and is set out in proposed s. 251.1 contained in Bill C-69.

[20] The sale and purchase of the shares would normally involve transaction costs in the form of brokerage fees. These costs have been ignored in the example in the text, but T would obviously be attracted to the sale and purchase only if the tax benefit of the loss (if it were allowed) was worth more than the transaction costs.

superficial loss rule of s. 40(2)(g)(i) is to block this practice by deeming T's loss to be nil if she purchased the replacement shares[21] within 30 days of (before or after) selling the original shares.[22] If T waited more than 30 days to purchase the replacement shares (or if she bought them more than 30 days before selling the original shares), then the superficial loss rule would not apply and the loss would be allowable.

The definition of superficial loss (quoted above) includes the case where the taxpayer's property has been acquired (within the 30-day period) by the taxpayer's spouse.[23] This element of the definition precludes T from crystallizing the loss by giving her shares to her husband and electing against the s. 73 rollover. The gift coupled with the election causes a deemed disposition at fair market value (s. 69(1)(b)),[24] but the superficial loss rule deems the resulting loss to be nil. However, the superficial loss rule does not apply to a testamentary gift (a gift by will) from one spouse to another;[25] since a will is operative only on the death of the testator, a testamentary gift is unlikely to be motivated by tax avoidance, and there is no reason to disallow the loss.

18.3 Losses from listed personal property

(a) Current losses

A loss from the disposition of "listed personal property" is a kind of capital loss, but one to which even more restrictions on deductibility have been attached. Listed personal property has already been discussed in chapter 15, Capital Gains.[26] It will be recalled that listed personal property is defined in s. 54 as "personal-use property" (also defined in s. 54) that consists of works of art, jewellery, rare books and stamp and coin collections. Unlike other kinds of "personal-use property", the losses on which are not deductible at all, losses on dispositions of listed personal property may be deducted against gains on listed personal property, but not from other kinds of capital gains or other kinds of income.

---

[21] If T had purchased only 50 shares, instead of the full 100, then only half the loss would be a superficial loss.

[22] The lower adjusted cost base of the substituted property is adjusted upward by the amount of the superficial loss: s. 53(1)(f).

[23] The list of affiliated persons in s. 251.1 does not include a spouse trust.

[24] See ch. 15, Capital Gains, under heading 15.14, "Deemed dispositions", and 15.15, "Rollovers", above.

[25] The definition of superficial loss in s. 54 excludes a deemed disposition under s. 70. Therefore, if property is left by will to a spouse, and the legal representative elects against the s. 70(6) rollover, there is a deemed disposition at fair market value (s. 70(5)), and any resulting capital loss is allowable to the deceased.

[26] Chapter 15, Capital Gains, under heading 15.16(c), "Listed personal property", above.

The technique by which this result is achieved is seen from ss. 3(b) and 41 of the Act. Paragraph 3(b) includes in a taxpayer's income for a year "the taxpayer's taxable net gain for the year from dispositions of listed personal property". Subsection 41(1) defines the taxpayer's taxable net gain for the year from dispositions of listed personal property as three-quarters of "the taxpayer's net gain for the year from dispositions of such property". Subsection 41(2) then supplies the rules by which a taxpayer's net gain for a taxation year from dispositions of listed personal property is determined. If in a taxation year a taxpayer has an excess of gains over losses from dispositions of listed personal property, and there are no losses from other years entitled to be carried over into the year, the excess is the taxpayer's net gain for the year from dispositions of listed personal property. Three-quarters of that figure then becomes the taxpayer's taxable net gain for the year from dispositions of listed personal property (s. 41(1)); and that taxable net gain is the amount which the taxpayer must include in income for the year (s. 3(b)).

(b)   **Listed-personal-property losses**

If in a taxation year a taxpayer has an excess of losses over gains from dispositions of listed personal property, the excess is called the "listed-personal-property loss" of the taxpayer for the year (s. 41(3)). That listed-personal-property loss is not deductible in the current year, of course, but it may be carried back three years and carried forward seven years; the carried-over loss is still only deductible against any excess of gains over losses from dispositions of listed personal property (s. 41(2)).[27]

18.4   Business investment losses

(a)   **Current losses**

A capital loss from the disposition of shares or debt of a "small business corporation" is a special category of loss that receives more generous treatment than other kinds of capital losses. A small business corporation is defined in s. 248 as a "Canadian-controlled private corporation" (defined in s. 125(7))[28] that uses "all or substantially all" (90 per cent is the accepted standard) of its assets in "an active business carried on primarily in Canada".

A capital loss on the disposition of shares or debt of a small business corporation is described by s. 39(1)(c) as a "business investment loss". It is still only three-quarters deductible, the deductible portion being called an "allowable business investment loss" by s. 38(c). But an allowable business investment loss

---

[27] This is the only loss carryover in Division B of Part I of the Act. As explained in note 4, above, the other loss carryovers are in Division C.

[28] Chapter 19, Corporations and Shareholders, under heading 19.1(d), "Canadian-controlled private corporations", below.

then differs from other kinds of capital losses in that an allowable business investment loss is fully deductible against all other income of the taxpayer. This result is accomplished by s. 3(d), which places an allowable business investment loss on the same footing as a loss from income sources ("an office, employment, business or property"). By contrast, of course, other allowable capital losses are deductible only against taxable capital gains (s. 3(b)).

The definition of a business investment loss in s. 39(1)(c) describes the loss as a "capital loss", thereby excluding an income loss from trading or speculating in the shares or debt of a small business corporation.[29] An income loss is excluded because it is in any case entitled to more generous treatment than a business investment loss. Not only is an income loss deductible from all other kinds of income (a position now enjoyed by the allowable business investment loss), an income loss is deductible in full whereas only three-quarters of a business investment loss (described as an allowable business investment loss) is deductible (s. 38(1)(c)).

The reason for the full deductibility from current income of allowable business investment losses is to encourage investment in Canadian-controlled private corporations carrying on business in Canada. The theory is that, by making losses deductible on the same basis that gains are includible, the bias against risk-taking which is inherent in the asymmetrical treatment of capital gains and capital losses[30] will be eliminated for investments in Canadian-controlled private corporations that carry on business in Canada. This treatment of losses then complements the other tax advantages which are accorded to the business income of Canadian-controlled private corporations.[31] The policy is to encourage the growth of small Canadian-owned businesses.

(b) Non-capital losses

An allowable business investment loss is initially subject to the loss carryover rules of losses from income sources. The definition of a "non-capital loss" in s. 111(8) includes a taxpayer's allowable business investment loss for the year along with losses from income sources. A taxpayer's non-capital loss for the year is of course the excess of losses over income which is not deductible in the current year but is available for carryover to other years.[32] The definition of a "net capital loss" in s. 111(8) includes a matching exclusion of allowable business investment losses (subject to the seven-year rule described later). The

---

[29] Chapter 16, Investing and Trading, above.

[30] Note 13, above.

[31] The most important of these is the small business deduction of s. 125: ch. 19, Corporations and Shareholders, under heading 19.5(d), "Active business income of Canadian-controlled private corporations", above.

[32] Section 18.1(b), "Non-capital losses", above.

loss carryover rules for a non-capital loss, instead of those for a net capital loss, are thus made available to an unused allowable business investment loss. This means that the loss may be applied to income from all sources in the years to which the loss is carried.

The inclusion of unused allowable business investment losses in the definition of non-capital loss also means that the carryover period for a non-capital loss, namely, three years back and seven years forward, applies to the loss. This is a disadvantage, because the carryforward period for a net capital loss is not restricted to seven years. The Act employs an ingenious technique to remove this disadvantage from allowable business investment losses. The definition of "net capital loss" in s. 111(8) provides that a seven-year-old unused allowable business investment loss is to be included in the taxpayer's net capital loss for the seventh year — the year in which the loss would otherwise have expired. In that way, an allowable business investment loss that cannot be deducted in the carryforward period for non-capital losses can be carried forward indefinitely as a net capital loss. Of course, after the seventh-year transformation, the loss can only be applied against taxable capital gains.

18.5 Farming losses

(a)   Categories of farmer

The deductibility of losses from farming differs according to whether the taxpayer is (1) a full-time farmer for whom farming is the chief source of income; (2) a part-time farmer for whom farming, although engaged in with a reasonable expectation of profit, is not the chief source of income; or (3) a hobby farmer for whom farming provides no reasonable expectation of profit.[33]

(b)   Full-time farmer

A full-time farmer is a person who devotes the major part of his or her time and effort to farming.[34] For the full-time farmer, a loss from farming is a loss from a business, and the current loss is treated for tax purposes in the same way as any other loss from a business (or other income source). The loss may be deducted against income from all other sources, including taxable capital gains (s. 3(d)).[35]

With respect to loss carryovers, s. 111(1)(d) permits "farm losses" to be carried back three years and forward ten years. This is more generous than the general rule of s. 111(1)(a) which restricts the carryforward of non-capital losses

---

[33] See *Moldowan* v. *The Queen*, [1977] C.T.C. 310, 77 D.T.C. 5213 (S.C.C.); Interpretation Bulletin IT-322R, "Farm losses" (1978).

[34] This is the person referred to in s. 31 as having his or her "chief source of income" from farming: sec. 18.5(c), "Part-time farmer", below.

[35] Section 18.1(a), "Current losses", above.

to seven years. A "farm loss" is defined in s. 111(8) as the non-deductible portion of the taxpayer's loss for the year "from a farming or fishing business".[36] The definition of non-capital loss in s. 111(8) then excludes farm losses, thereby making inapplicable the general loss carryover rule of s. 111(1)(a). Therefore, if a taxpayer's loss for the year from a farming or fishing business exceeds the taxpayer's income from all other sources, the excess is a "farm loss" which is entitled to the ten-year carryforward (and the three-year carryback) provided by s. 111(1)(d).

(c)   Part-time farmer

For the part-time farmer, the general rules regarding the deductibility of losses have been replaced by more restrictive rules. The principal restriction is contained in s. 31, which defines a part-time farmer in these terms:

> Where a taxpayer's chief source of income for a taxation year is neither farming nor a combination of farming and some other source of income . . . .

The phrase "chief source of income" is not defined in the Act, and is rather obscure considering that the question of the recognition of farming losses arises only in the case of a taxpayer who has no income at all from farming, but has instead incurred a loss.

In *Moldowan* v. *The Queen* (1977),[37] the Supreme Court of Canada held that a taxpayer's "chief source of income" was not to be determined solely by comparing the amount of income earned from farming with the amount earned from other sources. It depended as well on the taxpayer's lifestyle. Thus, a taxpayer for whom farming was the main occupation in terms of time and effort would be held to have farming as his or her "chief source of income", even if other sources of income tended to be more profitable. Such a taxpayer would be free of the restrictions of s. 31.

Section 31's obscure reference to a taxpayer whose chief source of income is not "a combination of farming and some other source of income" contemplates only the case of the taxpayer whose main occupation is farming but who also has some ancillary sources of income. This was also decided in *Moldowan*. It renders the combination phrase redundant, since such a taxpayer's chief source of income would be farming anyway.

In the result, s. 31 applies to the taxpayer who operates a farm as a sideline business. The typical case is that of the taxpayer (often in a high tax bracket) whose chief source of income has nothing to do with farming (for example, a city lawyer) but who also owns a farm. If that person could deduct all farming losses, the deduction would enable him or her to shelter from tax some high-rate professional income. Of course, even if the losses only cost the

---

[36] "Farming" and "fishing" are defined in s. 248.

[37] [1977] C.T.C. 310, 77 D.T.C. 5213 (S.C.C.).

taxpayer 47 cents in the dollar, that is still a cost. However, the farm may also be a source of recreation for the taxpayer and may be appreciating in value (an appreciation which will eventually be taxed only as a capital gain). Section 31 accordingly restricts the deductibility of a part-time farmer's farming losses.

When s. 31 applies, it permits the recognition of the first $2,500 of losses from farming, and one-half of the next $12,500 of losses from farming. The result is that the part-time farmer cannot deduct more than $8,750 of farming losses from his or her non-farming income in any taxation year, and can deduct that much only if the farm suffered a loss of $15,000 or more. For example, a taxpayer who incurs a loss from farming of $5,500 would be entitled to recognize a loss for the current year of $2,500 plus one-half of $3,000 ($5,500 − $2,500 = $3,000), that is, a total of $4,000. The balance of the loss, namely, $1,500, would be disallowed by s. 31.

The portion of the loss from farming that is disallowed by s. 31 (in our example, $1,500) is described by s. 31 as the taxpayer's "restricted farm loss" for the year. Under s. 111(1)(c), a restricted farm loss may be carried back three years and forward ten years, which is the same period as is allowed for farm losses suffered by a full-time farmer. However, the carryover of restricted farm losses is specially restricted by s. 111(1)(c) in that the carried-over loss may be applied only against income from farming. Thus, the part-time farmer will be unable to use his or her restricted farm losses to shelter off-farm income; the restricted farm losses can be used only if and when the farm becomes profitable.

A part-time farmer with unused restricted farm losses receives a measure of tax relief when he or she sells the farm land. In that case, s. 53(1)(i) adjusts the cost base of the land by adding to it any unused restricted farm losses from prior years (and any disallowed farm loss from the year of disposition), but only up to the total of property taxes and interest charges paid on the land in each year. In this way, the portion of the unused losses which is attributable to property taxes and interest charges receives indirect tax recognition by bumping up the adjusted cost base of the land and thereby reducing any capital gain on the disposition of the land. The adjustment under s. 53(1)(i) could have the effect of eliminating any capital gain on the land, but it cannot have the effect of creating a capital loss; the latter result is expressly precluded by s. 53(1)(i)(iv).[38]

It can be argued that s. 31 is not really necessary, and that it contributes needless complexity to the Act. Section 31 applies only where the part-time farming operation is conducted with a reasonable expectation of profit. If there is no reasonable expectation of profit, the losses are completely disallowed as "hobby" losses. (This is the topic of the next two sections of the chapter.) It is certainly arguable that, where a farm is operated with a reasonable expectation

---

[38] See Interpretation Bulletin IT-232R2, "Non-capital losses, net capital losses, restricted farm losses, farm losses and limited partnership losses" (1987).

of profit, any losses should be fully recognized. However, in the case of the part-time farmer, the farm, although operated with a reasonable expectation of profit, often serves as a place of recreation as well. If the farm incurs a loss, it is often realistic to attribute part of the loss to the recreational benefit: to that extent the loss is a consumption expense (personal or living expense) which should not be deductible. Yet it is very difficult to determine on a case-by-case basis what portion of a farming loss is to be treated as a deductible business expense and what portion is to be treated as a non-deductible consumption expense. It is this difficulty which has led Parliament to create an arbitrary half-way house between the full-time farmer whose losses are recognized in full and the hobby farmer whose losses are not recognized at all. Section 31, by restricting the recognition of the losses of the part-time farmer, attempts to prevent the use of the tax system to finance what may be partly a hobby.

(d) Hobby farmer

The third category of farmer is the person who operates a farm with no reasonable expectation of profit. The best indication of the absence of any reasonable expectation of profit would be that the taxpayer had reported no, or very little, profit from the farm for a period of years.[39] For the person who operates a farm with no reasonable expectation of profit, farming is only a hobby or recreation. The farm is not a business, and the inevitable annual losses are not losses from a business. The losses are personal or living expenses which are disallowed by s. 18(1)(h). This point is elaborated in the next section of this chapter.

18.6 Hobby losses

The hobby farmer, who is the topic of the previous section of this chapter, is the commonest case of a person who carries on a business-like activity with no reasonable expectation of profit. But any activity, however business-like, that is carried on without a reasonable expectation of profit is a hobby. This was explained in chapter 12, in which the requirement of a reasonable expectation of profit was stipulated as an essential ingredient of a business for tax purposes.[40] In that chapter, cases were cited in which losses were disallowed from the rental of real estate, the writing of books, the racing of cars, the operation of a restaurant, the producing of machine tools and the practice of law. In each case, the absence of a reasonable expectation of profit denied to the activity the status of a commercial activity, and made the persistent rental or business losses non-deductible. In each case, the activity was a hobby and the losses were the costs of the hobby, which like other recreational costs are non-deductible consumption expenses.

---

[39] Interpretation Bulletin IT-322R, "Farm losses" (1978), para. 5.

[40] Chapter 12, Income from Business or Property: Inclusions, under headings 12.2(b) and 12.3(b), "Reasonable expectation of profit", above.

19

Corporations and Shareholders

19.1   Introduction

(a)   Scope of chapter

This chapter is about the taxation of corporations and shareholders. It will examine the policies and rules which are relevant to the taxation of income earned by corporations and income distributed by corporations to their shareholders. It will cover the most common kinds of Canadian corporations and the most common kinds of distributions. It will not deal with the numerous kinds of corporations that attract special tax treatment, such as non-resident corporations, non-resident-owned investment corporations, investment corporations, mortgage investment corporations, mutual fund corporations, cooperative corporations and insurance corporations. Nor will the chapter deal with the rollovers and other tax rules regarding the transfer of assets to corporations,[1] reorganizations, amalgamations, reductions of capital and the winding up of corporations.

(b)   Incorporation

A corporation or company (for present purposes these terms are synonymous) may be incorporated under either federal or provincial law. Once incorporated, the company is a legal person which is separate from its shareholders. The shareholders have no proprietary interest in the company's underlying assets, that is, the things that the company has acquired with the funds raised by issuing shares (or borrowing money or retaining earnings). What the shareholders own is shares in the company — a quite different kind of asset. Similarly, the liabilities of the company are its alone and they must be satisfied out of the assets of the company. In a sole proprietorship or partnership business, the proprietor or partners are personally liable to satisfy the liabilities incurred

---

[1] For a very brief treatment, see ch. 15, Capital Gains, under heading 15.15(d), "Transfer to corporation", above.

by the business, and in the event of business failure they may lose their own personal assets and become bankrupt. A prime reason for the incorporation of a company is that the shareholder's risk is limited to the sum paid for, or agreed to be paid for, his or her shares. The personal assets of the shareholder are not at risk. This is known as "limited liability".

(c)   Public and private corporations

Anglo-Canadian corporate law has traditionally distinguished between "public" and "private" companies. The private company was one with less than 50 shareholders, with restrictions on the sale of shares contained in the company's constitution, and which was prohibited from offering its shares to the public. This classification of companies was employed in order to exempt the private company from some of the reporting and regulatory requirements which had to be satisfied by a more widely-held company. The public-private dichotomy is still employed by the corporate law of several provinces, but the tendency of recent statutory amendments has been to substitute other nomenclature and qualifications, still with the general purpose of exempting the closely-held corporation (or "close corporation" as the Americans call it) from some of the regulations of the governing corporate statute.

The Income Tax Act draws important distinctions between public and private corporations, with private corporations being eligible for a number of tax advantages which are denied to public corporations. However, the terms "public corporation" and "private corporation" are specifically defined by the Act for its purposes. A "public corporation" is defined by s. 89(1) as a corporation resident in Canada whose shares are "listed on a prescribed stock exchange in Canada". The Income Tax Regulations, by reg. 3200, prescribe the stock exchanges of Toronto, Montreal, Vancouver, Alberta and Winnipeg for the purpose of this definition.[2] A "private corporation" is defined by s. 89(1) as a corporation resident in Canada which is "not a public corporation", and is not "controlled" by "one or more public corporations".[3]

---

[2] In addition, a corporation whose shares are not listed on a prescribed stock exchange may become a public corporation by (1) election, or (2) designation. As to election, s. 89(1)(g) allows a corporation to elect to become a public corporation if it complies "with prescribed conditions relating to the number of its shareholders, dispersal of ownership of its shares, public trading of its shares and size of the corporation". Those conditions are prescribed by the regulations, regs. 4801–4802. As to designation, s. 89(1)(g) gives to the Minister the power to designate a corporation as a public corporation where it complies with the same conditions as are stipulated for election as a public corporation.

[3] The meaning of "controlled" is discussed in the next section of the chapter.

(d)   Canadian-controlled private corporations

The Act, as well as distinguishing for various purposes between public corporations and private corporations, has a number of important provisions that are applicable to Canadian-controlled private corporations (CCPCs). The term "Canadian-controlled private corporation" is defined in s. 125(7) as follows:

> "Canadian-controlled private corporation" means a private corporation that is a Canadian corporation other than a corporation controlled, directly or indirectly in any manner whatever, by one or more non-resident persons, by one or more public corporations . . . or by any combination thereof. . . .;

As the name implies, a CCPC is a kind of private corporation. It must also be a "Canadian corporation", which is defined in s. 89(1) as a corporation that is resident in Canada and was incorporated in Canada. Finally, it must not be "controlled, directly or indirectly in any manner whatever" by non-residents of Canada or by public corporations.

The word "controlled" is used elsewhere in the Act as well, but there is no generally applicable definition of "control" or "controlled". The courts have held that the word "controlled", appearing elsewhere in the Act without the accompanying phrase "directly or indirectly in any manner whatever", means de jure control and not de facto control.[4] De jure control requires ownership of a majority of the voting shares in the corporation enabling election of a majority of the members of the board of directors. Therefore, if a majority of the voting shares of a private corporation are owned by non-residents (or public corporations), the corporation cannot be a CCPC. However, the definition does not require that the corporation be controlled by residents, so long as it is not controlled by non-residents. Therefore, if exactly 50 per cent of the shares are owned by non-residents, the corporation could be a CCPC.

Where non-residents (or public corporations) do not have de jure control of a private corporation, but do have de facto control, the de facto control will suffice to deny the corporation the status of a CCPC. Subsection 256(5.1) provides that the phrase "controlled, directly or indirectly in any manner whatever" (which, it will be recalled, is in the definition of a CCPC) includes the case where "the controller has any direct or indirect influence that, if exercised, would result in control in fact of the corporation". This expands the concept of control in s. 125(7) to include de facto control. An example of de facto control would be where a non-resident person owned only 49 per cent of the voting shares of a corporation, but the remaining shares were "widely dispersed among many employees of the corporation or held by persons who could reasonably be considered to act in respect of the corporation in accordance with his wishes".[5]

---

[4] *Buckerfields* v. *M.N.R,* [1964] C.T.C. 504, 64 D.T.C. 5301 (Ex. Ct.); *M.N.R.* v. *Dworkin Furs,* [1967] C.T.C. 50, 67 D.T.C. 5035 (S.C.C.).

[5] This example was given in the technical notes to s. 256(5.1) when it was introduced in Bill C-139 on June 30, 1988.

In that case, the non-resident owner of the 49 per cent block would be in actual (de facto) control of the corporation, even though the owner did not have the de jure control that would flow from ownership of a majority of the voting shares. De facto control can also arise in non-share ownership situations, such as where a non-arm's length person is a major creditor, customer or supplier. Any time non-residents (or public corporations) have de facto control, the corporation would not be a CCPC.

(e) Corporate distributions

While a company is a going concern, it will make various kinds of payments to persons associated with it. The company will pay "dividends" to its shareholders; dividends are declared at the discretion of the directors of the company. Dividends may only be paid out of profits, either current earnings or retained earnings from prior years. The company will pay "interest" to its debtholders. The company will be obliged by its contracts with the debtholders to pay them interest at agreed-upon rates, whether or not the company is earning sufficient money to afford it. Similarly, the company will be obliged by its employment contracts to pay salaries or wages to the company's employees, whether or not the company is earning sufficient money to afford them.

In computing the company's profit (or loss) for a year, interest and salaries or wages will be two of the expenses which are deducted from gross revenue. Any resulting profit is then available for payment to shareholders: it may be paid to the shareholders in whole or in part by declaration of a dividend, and any amount not so paid will be retained in the company as "retained earnings" (or "earned surplus"). Any sum retained by the company will be available for use in the company's business or for investment by the company. As such it will increase the value of the common shares, but it will not provide any direct benefit to any of the individuals associated with the company.

Payments received by an individual from a company are of course taxable in the hands of that individual if they constitute income within the meaning of the Income Tax Act. In the case of interest, salary and wages, there is no question of double taxation. These are costs which are incurred for the purpose of gaining or producing income, and therefore the company is permitted to deduct these payments from its taxable income, so that they are taxed only in the hands of the debtholder, employee or other recipient.[6] However, the company is not permitted to deduct dividends paid to shareholders from its taxable income. Dividends are not costs of earning revenue; they are distributions of profits.

---

[6] Paragraph 18(1)(a). In addition, most employee benefits must be included in the income of an employee (s. 6, discussed in ch. 10, under headings 10.6, "Benefits", and 10.7, "Allowances", above) and, with the exception of club dues (s. 18(1)(l)) and entertainment expenses (s. 67.1), discussed in ch. 13, under heading 13.2, "Entertainment expenses", above, most are fully deductible to the company.

Profits that are paid out to shareholders as dividends are therefore taxed twice: first at the corporate level as income of the company, and, secondly, at the shareholder level as income of the individual shareholders. We shall see in the next section of this chapter that it is possible to give shareholders credit against their tax liabilities for tax paid by the corporation, so that the total tax liability at both the corporate and shareholder level is no greater than if the income actually earned by the company had been earned directly by the individual shareholders. This "integration" of the corporate and personal income tax was recommended by the Carter Commission, but only partially adopted by the Income Tax Act of 1971.

Where integration (or other tax relief) is not provided for, corporate-source income is subjected to an element of "double taxation".[7] It is, of course, literally taxed twice, once at the corporate level and again at the shareholder level; but if the shareholder does not receive full credit for the tax paid at the corporate level, then the cumulative burden of the two taxes is heavier than the burden of tax which would be borne by the shareholder if he or she had earned the income directly. What is the actual incidence of this extra taxation? Who ends up paying it? It is possible that some or all of the "extra" tax is "shifted" to the consumer in the form of higher prices for the corporation's goods and services; to the corporation's employees in the form of lower wages; or to capital generally, by way of lower investment in the corporation and greater investment in other assets, which reduces the economic return of those assets. The extent to which this shifting occurs will depend upon the nature of the corporation's market, how competitive it is and from whom the competition comes. As we have already noticed, tax incidence studies have suggested that the corporate income tax is slightly progressive.[8]

---

[7] The cost of a benefit provided to a shareholder in her capacity as a shareholder (i.e., *qua* shareholder) is subject to "double taxation": such benefits are not deductible at the corporate level (s. 18(1)(a)) and, since they are not dividends, there is no dividend tax credit to reduce the tax at the shareholder level. A shareholder receives a benefit *qua* shareholder (as opposed to *qua* employee) in cases where she is not an employee (or is provided with a benefit that other employees do not have). Such benefits are included in a shareholder's income under s. 15(1) (rather than under s. 6, referred to in note 6, above). A shareholder who is an individual must also include the amount of any loan or indebtedness provided by the company in income (s. 15(2)), but certain exceptions are provided in cases where the shareholder is also an employee: see proposed ss. 15(2.2) to 15(2.6). If all or part of a shareholder's loan that has been included in income under s. 15(2) is subsequently repaid, the amount repaid can be deducted by the shareholder in the year of repayment: s. 20(1)(j). The objective of ss. 15(1) and 15(2) is to prevent shareholders from extracting cash from their companies without paying tax on the amount.

[8] Chapter 5, Rates, under heading 5.2(d), "Progressive rates", above.

19.2 Integration of corporation and shareholder taxes

(a) Double taxation of corporate income

In an ideal tax system, income passing through an intermediary such as a corporation (or a trust) should not attract any additional (or any less) taxation than income received by an individual directly. In other words, the corporate income tax should be eliminated. However, this is easier said than done.

One way of eliminating the double taxation of corporate-source income would be to levy no taxes on corporate income at all, and to levy taxes on individual shareholders on the basis of the dividends received by them. The trouble with this simple solution is that, if there were no tax on corporate income, individuals who could arrange to earn income through a corporation would be able to retain their savings untaxed in the corporation. In order to block this mode of tax avoidance without levying a tax on corporate income, it would be necessary to levy taxes on the individual shareholders on the basis not only of dividends received, but of the change in value of their shares during the year, that is, accrued gains or losses. The difficulty with this approach is the practical difficulty of valuing and taxing accrued capital gains, which, it will be recalled, had led the Carter Commission to recommend that in general capital gains should be taxed only when they were realized. The removal of taxes from corporate income would also mean a loss of revenue to Canada from the substantial proportion of corporate income which is attributable to those shares in Canadian corporations that are owned by non-residents of Canada.[9]

A second way of eliminating the double taxation of corporate-source income would be to levy a tax on corporate income at approximately the top individual rate, but to allow the corporation a deduction for dividends paid to shareholders. This would mean that the corporate income tax would apply only to retained earnings. Distributed earnings would bear no corporate income tax; they would be taxed only in the hands of individual shareholders. As we shall see, this is essentially the scheme of taxation of trusts.[10] The trust receives a deduction for income distributed to the beneficiaries; the trust itself pays tax only on income retained in the trust. The disadvantage of treating corporations in the same way as trusts is the large proportion of shares of Canadian corporations that are held by non-residents of Canada. If corporations were able to deduct dividends paid to shareholders, the dividends paid to non-residents of Canada would escape ordinary Canadian income tax at the shareholder level (because the shareholder would be non-resident) as well as at the corporate level (because the corporation would deduct the dividends). The dividends would attract the Part XIII withholding tax on payments to non-residents, but under the Act the Part XIII tax is only 25 per cent, and under Canada's tax treaties the rate is

---

[9] *Report of the Royal Commission on Taxation* (Carter Report) (1966), vol. 4, 4-5.

[10] Chapter 21, Trusts, below.

normally reduced to 15 per cent and occasionally to a lower rate.[11] Therefore, unless Canada raised the rate of its Part XIII tax, and renegotiated all of its tax treaties, the allowance to corporations of a deduction for dividends paid to shareholders would result in a loss of revenue.

A third way of eliminating the double taxation of corporate-source income would be to levy a tax on the corporation, but not on the shareholder: dividends would be received by individual shareholders free of tax. The difficulty with this idea is that it makes no adjustment for the differing ability of individual shareholders to pay tax. In effect, each shareholder of a corporation would bear a tax at the rate paid by the corporation. If the rate was low, this would be inappropriate for a high-income shareholder. If the rate was high, this would be inappropriate for a low-income shareholder.

A fourth way of eliminating the double taxation of corporate income is to levy taxes at both the corporate level and the shareholder level, but to "integrate" the two taxes so that the total of the two taxes is no greater than the single tax that would be paid by an individual receiving income directly (not through a corporation). Under a system of full integration, a corporation would pay tax on its income, but when the income was distributed to the shareholders they would report as their personal income not only the amount of corporate income received by them as a dividend, but also the amount of corporate income which had been paid by the corporation as tax. Then the shareholders would receive credit against their personal income tax liability for the full amount of tax paid by the corporation in respect of the distributed income. In order to remove any tax advantage from the retention of corporate earnings, the corporate income should be taxed at the same rate as the top rate of personal income tax.[12] An integration system was recommended by the Carter Commission; it is explained in the next section of the chapter.

(b)   Carter Commission's proposals

The Carter Commission concluded that the only practical way to eliminate the double taxation of corporate-source income was to integrate the corporate and personal income taxes. To this end, the Commission proposed an imputation (or gross-up and credit) system along the lines described in the previous paragraph.

The Carter proposal may be illustrated by the following example. Suppose that a shareholder receives a dividend of $50. This actually represents $100 of income received by the corporation, because (under the Carter proposals) the corporation would have paid tax at the rate of 50 per cent before it paid the dividend. For tax purposes, the additional corporate income is "imputed" to the shareholder. The shareholder in reporting his or her income for tax purposes

---

[11] Chapter 8, Residence, under heading 8.3, "Taxation of non-residents", above.

[12] Carter Report, vol. 4, 7.

"grosses up" the dividend by 100 per cent (the amount of tax paid by the corporation) in order to include the full amount of corporate income in his or her personal income. The shareholder then becomes liable to pay tax on the full $100 at whatever rate of tax his or her personal income attracts. From the resulting tax liability the shareholder receives credit for $50, the amount of the tax paid by the corporation (and also the amount by which the dividend was grossed-up for inclusion in the personal tax return). The result for taxpayers in various brackets is illustrated in the following table:[13]

Table 1			
	Tax bracket of shareholder		
	15%	35%	50%
1. Dividend received	50.00	50.00	50.00
2. Plus: Gross-up of 100%	50.00	50.00	50.00
3. Taxable income	100.00	100.00	100.00
4. Personal tax	15.00	35.00	50.00
5. Minus: tax already paid by corporation	(50.00)	(50.00)	(50.00)
6. Tax (refund)	(35.00)	(15.00)	—
7. Plus: cash dividend	50.00	50.00	50.00
8. Total cash received by shareholder	85.00	65.00	50.00

If you compare the last figure of each column (total cash received by shareholder) with the shareholder's tax bracket for that year, you will notice that the total cash received by the shareholder is exactly the sum that he or she would have received had the corporate income of $100 been received by him or her directly. Thus the taxpayer with a marginal rate of 15 per cent receives $85 ($100 less 15%), the taxpayer at 35 per cent receives $65 ($100 less 35%), and the taxpayer at 50 per cent receives $50 (100 less 50%). The gross-up and credit procedure thus eliminates the ultimate impact of corporate income tax by integrating it with the personal income tax.

The integration of corporate and personal income taxes would satisfy the basic demands of equity and neutrality by ensuring that the ultimate tax on income received through a corporation was the same as if the income had been received directly by individuals. An individual who could arrange to receive his or her income through a corporation would pay tax at the same rate as the taxpayer who received the same amount of income directly. Nor could the

---

[13] The table is a modification of Table 19-1 in the Carter Report, vol. 4, p. 8.

shareholder-taxpayer gain any advantage by causing the corporation to retain its earnings, because all corporate earnings were to be taxed at 50 per cent, which under the Commission's recommendations was also to be the top rate of personal income tax.

There were some other side effects of the Carter proposal. The gross-up and credit procedure would be available only in respect of dividends received by Canadian residents. This would improve the after-tax rate of return on shares in Canadian corporations for most Canadian residents, but not for non-residents. This would in turn lead to a rise in the price of Canadian shares, which would encourage non-residents (whose after-tax yield would not justify the higher price) to sell their shares to Canadians. The increase in price of Canadian shares would lower the cost of raising share capital in Canada which should increase the total amount of share capital raised in Canada, and encourage Canadian corporations owned by non-residents to raise new capital by issuing shares in Canada.[14] These side effects appear to conflict with Carter's goal of neutrality, but they were simply the inevitable consequences of applying the system of integration to the tax system of Canada but not the United States. In any event, the tendencies of the new system were all in the direction of increased Canadian ownership of Canadian corporations, a result of which most Canadians would presumably approve.[15]

(c)   Tax reform of 1971

The Income Tax Act that was enacted in 1971 did not fully accept any of the Carter Commission's proposals. First, the integration of all corporate and personal income taxes was not implemented, although it was implemented with respect to two classes of corporate income, namely, the Canadian investment income of private corporations and (within limits) the active business income of Canadian-controlled private corporations. Secondly, the taxation of all corporate income at the flat rate of 50 per cent was not implemented, although corporate income other than the Canadian investment income of private corporations and the active business income of Canadian-controlled private corporations was taxed at a "standard" flat rate of 50 per cent; the two exceptional categories of corporate income were taxed at a "low" rate of 25 per cent. Thirdly, the top rate of personal income tax (which was 80 per cent in 1971) was not brought down to 50 per cent — the same as the standard corporate rate — although it was reduced to a combined federal-provincial rate of approximately 61 per cent.

---

[14] Carter Report, vol. 4, 9.

[15] It would be possible by treaty to extend the benefits of an imputation (gross-up and credit) system of taxing dividends to Canadian-corporation shareholders who are resident in the United States or other countries. However, the rules would involve a complex relationship between the two national tax systems and would presumably have a large cost in lost revenue to Canada.

While the 1971 Act did not adopt full integration of corporate and personal income taxes, it did adopt an imputation system of taxing dividends. The Act required that the tax on dividends in the hands of individual shareholders be calculated by the gross-up and credit procedure recommended by Carter. However, the gross-up was not Carter's 100 per cent but 33 1/3 per cent, and the credit was not Carter's 100 per cent but 33 1/3 per cent. The 33 1/3 per cent gross-up and credit "imputed" to the shareholder (i.e., added to the shareholder's income, and credited against the shareholder's tax) corporate income tax at the rate of 25 per cent. The corporate rate of 25 per cent was the "low rate" of tax which the 1971 Act imposed on the Canadian investment income of private corporations and (within limits) the Canadian active business income of Canadian-controlled private corporations. In respect of this income, therefore, corporate and personal income taxes were integrated.

(d)   Tax reform of 1988

After 1971, the Act was frequently amended to alter the corporate tax system. The amount of the dividend gross-up and credit was changed in 1977 from 33 1/3 per cent to 50 per cent, and in 1987 was changed back to 33 1/3 per cent. In 1982, the low rate of tax on Canadian investment income of private corporations was extended to foreign (as well as Canadian) investment income, but the rate could be claimed only by Canadian-controlled private corporations (CCPCs) (instead of all private corporations). Various other changes were made and unmade in the period up to 1988. It was the tax reform of 1988 that put in place the rules that are in effect at the time of writing (1997).

These rules are as follows (ignoring surtax, and in a province that levies its corporate tax at a rate of 10 per cent). The standard rate of corporate income tax is 38 per cent. The low rate of corporate income tax on the investment income of CCPCs is 18 per cent, and on the Canadian active business income of CCPCs is 22 per cent. A manufacturing and processing credit of 7 per cent is available to corporations engaged in manufacturing and processing. The dividend gross-up and credit is 25 per cent, which compensates the shareholder for corporate tax at the rate of 20 per cent, which is close to the low rate of corporate income tax on the investment income and active business income of CCPCs. For those two categories of income, integration is approximately achieved. More detail on the present system is provided later in the chapter.

For the moment, it is sufficient to notice how the system is supposed to provide integration of the low-rate corporate income tax with the personal income tax. Assume that a corporation earns income of $100, which is taxed at the low combined rate of 20 per cent (as would be the case for a CCPC earning investment income subject to provincial tax of 12 per cent or a CCPC earning Canadian active business income subject to provincial tax of 8 per cent). Assume that the after-tax portion of the corporation's income, namely, $80, is paid to a shareholder, who resides in a province where the provincial personal income tax rate is 50 per cent, and whose total income places him or her in the top federal personal tax bracket of 29 per cent, which yields a combined rate (ignoring surtaxes) of 43.5 per cent (29% × 150% = 43.5%). That case is reflected in the first column of Table 2, below. The second column assumes that the shareholder is in the second federal personal tax bracket of 26 per cent, which yields a combined rate of 39 per cent (26% × 150% = 39%). The third column assumes that the shareholder is in the first federal personal tax bracket of 17 per cent, which yields a combined rate of 25.5 per cent (17% × 150% = 25.5%).[16]

Table 2

		Combined federal-provincial tax bracket of shareholder		
		43.5%	39%	25.5%
1.	Corporate income before tax	100.00	100.00	100.00
2.	Corporate income tax at (combined) rate of 20%	(20.00)	(20.00)	(20.00)
3.	Corporate income after tax	80.00	80.00	80.00
4.	Dividend paid to shareholder	80.00	80.00	80.00
5.	Gross-up of one-quarter	20.00	20.00	20.00
6.	Taxable amount	100.00	100.00	100.00
7.	Personal income tax at (combined) rate of 43.5% (col. 1) or 39% (col. 2) or 25.5% (col. 3)	43.50	39.00	25.50
8.	Dividend tax credit (combined) of one-quarter of dividend	(20.00)	(20.00)	(20.00)
9.	Net personal income tax	23.50	19.00	5.50
10.	Tax paid by corporation	(20.00)	(20.00)	(20.00)
11.	Total tax paid by corporation and shareholder	43.50	39.00	25.50
12.	Tax if shareholder had earned $100 directly	43.50	39.00	25.50

In Table 2, the shareholder is required to report as income $20 more than he or she actually received (the gross-up), and receives a tax credit of the same amount (the dividend tax credit). In this way, the tax paid by the corporation is imputed to the shareholder. In column 1, the result for the shareholder in the

---

[16] On the rates of personal income tax, see ch. 5, Rates, above.

43.5 per cent bracket is that he or she pays $23.50 of personal tax on the dividend; this figure, when combined with the $20 paid by the corporation, yields a total tax burden of $43.50 (line 11). That is precisely the amount of tax that the individual would have paid had he or she earned the $100 directly rather than through a corporation (line 12). In columns 2 and 3 of Table 2, which cover shareholders in the 39 per cent and 25.5 per cent brackets, lines 11 and 12 are again identical. This means that, regardless of the personal tax bracket of the individual shareholder, the corporate and personal income taxes are perfectly integrated. There is no difference in the tax treatment of a person who earns income through a corporation and a person who earns the same amount of income directly. The intervention of the intermediary (the corporation) in the flow of income does not increase (or reduce) the total burden of tax imposed on the income.

Corporate income that does not qualify for the low rate of 20 per cent is taxed at the standard rate of approximately 38 per cent assuming provincial tax of 10 per cent.[17] This includes all of the income of public corporations, all of the income of private corporations that are not CCPCs, and the income of CCPCs that does not qualify for the small business deduction (chiefly, Canadian active business income in excess of $200,000 and foreign business income). In respect of the corporate income taxed at 38 per cent, there is incomplete integration since the gross-up and credit imputes to the shareholder only corporate income tax at the rate of 20 per cent. In respect of corporate-source income which does not qualify for the low rate, there is an element of "double taxation": the same dollars of income are taxed twice, once at the corporate level and once at the shareholder level, and without giving to the shareholder full credit for the tax paid at the corporate level. This income is therefore ultimately taxed at higher effective rates than income received directly by individuals. As such the tax is no doubt usually passed on to the consumer in the form of higher prices for the goods and services produced by the corporation, or, to the extent that competition holds down the price of the product, the tax may lower the after-tax return on the corporation's shares and depress their value.

The next table shows the effect of the gross-up and credit rules on corporate-source income that is ineligible for the low rate of 20 per cent and is taxed at 38 per cent (28 per cent federal and 10 per cent provincial).

---

[17] An exception to this is the manufacturing and processing credit: sec. 19.5(e), "Manufacturing and processing credit", below.

Table 3

		Combined federal-provincial tax bracket of shareholder		
		43.5%	39%	25.5%
1.	Corporate income before tax	100.00	100.00	100.00
2.	Corporate income tax at (combined) rate of 38%	(38.00)	(38.00)	(38.00)
3.	Corporate income after tax	62.00	62.00	62.00
4.	Dividend paid to shareholder	62.00	62.00	62.00
5.	Gross-up of one-quarter	15.50	15.50	15.50
6.	Taxable amount	77.50	77.50	77.50
7.	Personal income tax at (combined) rate of 43.5% (col. 1) or 39% (col. 2) or 25.5% (col. 3)	33.71	30.23	19.76
8.	Dividend tax credit (combined) of one-quarter of dividend	(15.50)	(15.50)	(15.50)
9.	Net personal income tax	18.21	14.73	4.26
10.	Tax paid by corporation	38.00	38.00	38.00
11.	Total tax paid by corporation and shareholder	56.21	52.73	42.26
12.	Tax if shareholder had earned $100 directly	43.50	39.00	25.50

Table 3 illustrates that the gross-up and credit of one-quarter of the dividend produces a serious under-integration for corporate-source income that has borne tax at the standard rate of 38 per cent. An individual taxpayer in the 43.5 per cent tax bracket would receive an after-tax return of $43.79 ($100.00 – $56.21) on $100 of corporate-source income, compared with an after-tax return of $56.50 ($100.00 – $43.50) on $100 of income received directly. Similar disparities exist for the individual taxpayers in the 39 per cent and 25.5 per cent tax brackets. Because the gross-up and credit of 25 per cent of the dividend provides compensation to the shareholder for corporate tax of only 20 per cent of the corporate income, when the corporate tax is more than 20 per cent, the compensation is insufficient. The result is that income flowing through a corporation is more heavily taxed than income received by an individual directly.

19.3 Sheltering income in a corporation

(a) Carter Commission's proposals

The integration of corporate and personal income taxes would be perfectly achieved if corporate income was free of tax; the only tax would be levied at the individual shareholder level. But this regime would give rise to other problems. One is that corporate income attributable to shares owned by non-residents of Canada would escape Canadian tax, except for the withholding tax on payments to non-residents. Another is that corporations would be encouraged to retain their earnings rather than distribute them to the shareholders (where they would be taxed). Individuals with income in excess of their personal needs would make sure that their investments and their businesses were held by corporations; excess income would be retained in the corporations where it would be sheltered from tax. The only way to overcome this form of avoidance would be to tax the annual accrued gain on the shares held by the individual shareholders, which would present major administrative difficulties. These are the reasons that led the Carter Commission to recommend that taxes be levied at the corporate as well as the shareholder level, and that integration be achieved by the imputation method of taxing dividends.

The problems that would arise from a failure to tax corporate income at all also arise, albeit in less severe form, when corporate income is taxed at a lower rate than the top rate applicable to personal income. High-income individuals then have an incentive to store excess income in corporations where it will be at least partly sheltered from tax. In the absence of remedial provisions, a high-income investor would use an investment holding company to hold his or her investments, leaving the income in the corporation for reinvestment, so that the extra bite of personal income tax that would be triggered by the payment of a dividend is put off (or "deferred") for as long as possible. Even a corporation with a genuine business purpose would be powerfully influenced to retain profits in excess of the personal needs of a controlling shareholder so as to avoid that second bite of tax. As corporations became swollen with retained earnings, shareholders would search for ways of removing the earnings otherwise than through dividends which would attract tax. This would lead to complex "dividend stripping" or "surplus stripping" schemes, which, if they were successful, would have to be countered by amendments to the Act.

All of these problems existed in Canada when the Carter Commission reported in 1966. At that time, there was a "low rate" of tax on corporate income up to $35,000 of only 21 per cent; above that level, the "standard rate" was 50 per cent. Rates of personal income tax, by contrast, rose to 80 per cent. The Carter Commission recommended that there should be no "low rate" of corporate income tax. All corporate income should be taxed at the same rate of 50 per cent, and that rate of 50 per cent should also be the top rate of personal income tax. This would have eliminated any tax incentive for an individual to earn income through a corporation instead of directly, and (when combined with the

Commission's scheme of integration) would have eliminated any tax incentive for a corporation to retain its earnings rather than distributing them to its shareholders.

(b)   Tax reform of 1971

The government did not accept Carter's recommendations. The Income Tax Act of 1971 did reduce the top rates of personal income tax so that (when combined with the various provincial rates) the top rate fell from its 1971 level of 80 per cent to 61 per cent for residents of Ontario (and somewhat higher for residents of most other provinces). This was a step in Carter's direction, but it left the top personal income tax rate well above the rate of 50 per cent which was established as the standard rate for the income of corporations (s. 123). The standard corporate rate was set to decline by one percentage point per year down to 46 per cent in 1976, and that decline increased the discrepancy between the top personal rate and the standard corporate rate. In addition, the 1971 Act introduced the "small business deduction" which had the effect of reducing the standard rate of federal tax all the way down to 25 per cent for Canadian active business income of Canadian-controlled private corporations. This was the old "low rate" of tax in a new guise. The discrepancy between a top personal tax rate of over 60 per cent and a low corporate rate of 25 per cent created the same powerful incentive to retain earnings in a corporation, and thereby defer the payment of personal taxes by the shareholders.[18] That low rate persists to this day. It is now (in 1997) 20 per cent (if provincial tax is 8 per cent).

(c)   Tax reform of 1988

The tax reform of 1988 narrowed the discrepancy between the top personal rate and the standard corporate rate of income tax. The top personal rate was reduced to 29 per cent federal, which, in a province that levied provincial tax at 50 per cent, rose to a combined level of 43.5 per cent ($29\% \times 150\% = 43.5\%$). The standard corporate rate was reduced to 38 per cent, with a 10 per cent abatement to allow the provinces room to levy their own corporate income taxes. This yielded a rate of 38 per cent in a province that levied its tax at 10 per cent (the same level as the abatement).

The tax reform of 1988 did not get rid of the low rate of tax produced by the small business deduction (s. 125(1)), which continued as a tax credit for Canadian-controlled private corporations (CCPCs), reducing their federal tax rate by 16 per cent to 22 per cent (before abatement) ($38\% - 16\% = 22\%$). The 10 per cent abatement for income earned in a province also remained, so that, in a province that levied tax on income eligible for the small business deduction at

---

[18] It also led to much litigation of the question of what qualified as active business income. The term is now defined in s. 125(7), although the definition does not solve all problems: see sec. 19.5(d)(ii), "Active business income", below.

the rate of 8 per cent (which in 1997 is in fact about the average provincial rate for this type of income), the low rate fell to 20 per cent (22% − 10% + 8% = 20%). We have already noted that the tax reform of 1988 set the rate of gross-up and credit at 25 per cent of dividends. That is the level at which integration of personal and corporate income taxes is achieved for corporate-source income, when the tax at the corporate level is 20 per cent. Even with integration, the payment of a dividend out of this low-rate corporate income will generate a considerable personal tax liability for a high-income shareholder. Obviously, in order to defer that personal tax liability, the incentive to retain low-rate income in a CCPC remains.

(d) Budgets of 1994 and 1995

After the tax reform of 1988, steep increases in provincial personal income tax rates, as well as federal and provincial surtaxes, brought the top combined federal-provincial personal income tax rates up to above 50 per cent in all provinces except Alberta. At the same time, there were lesser increases in provincial corporate tax rates and federal and provincial corporate surtaxes, so that in most provinces the federal standard rate of 38 per cent rose to a combined federal-provincial corporate tax rate of about 45 per cent. A gap of seven or eight percentage points between the top personal rate and the standard corporate rate created an incentive for wealthy Canadians to incorporate investment holding companies to earn their investment income and shelter it from some personal tax.

The federal budgets of 1994 and 1995 increased the tax that a CCPC must pay on investment income not distributed to shareholders. The purpose was to reduce the gap between the corporate tax rate and the top personal tax rate and thus remove the opportunity to defer personal tax by retaining investment income in a corporation. The two budgets did not make any fundamental change in the taxation of the Canadian active business income of CCPCs. With respect to that income, the low rate caused by the small business deduction on the first $200,000 of income remains, although the budget of 1994 took the deduction away from very large CCPCs. The small business deduction is explained later in this chapter.[19]

With respect to the investment income of CCPCs, the budgets of 1994 and 1995 made two changes. The first was to increase the refundable Part IV tax that private corporations pay on dividends received from other taxable Canadian corporations from the 25 per cent rate that was imposed by the tax reform of 1988 to 33 1/3 per cent. The rate of 33 1/3 per cent is much closer to the top rate that individuals pay on dividends after gross-up and credit. The Part IV tax is explained later in this chapter.[20] The second change was to increase the tax

---

[19] Section 19.5(d)(i), "Small business deduction", below.

[20] Section 19.5(c)(iv), "Dividends", below.

on investment income other than dividends of CCPCs by a special 6 2/3 per cent additional refundable tax. When this is added to the average combined federal-provincial corporate rate, which is about 45 per cent in 1997 (with provincial taxes and surtaxes), it brings the rate of tax on the investment income of CCPCs up to a level that is close to the top personal tax rate. Both of these tax increases are refundable: they increase the taxes paid initially by an investment holding corporation, but they are refunded when investment income is distributed to individual shareholders. The mechanics of the system of refundable taxes on investment income is discussed later in this chapter.[21]

19.4 Taxation of shareholders

(a)   Integration and imputation

In an earlier section of this chapter it was explained that the corporate-level tax and the shareholder-level tax on corporate-source income could be integrated by notionally imputing to the shareholder the corporate-level tax already paid by the corporation.[22] The Carter Commission popularized the term "integration" in Canada to describe the gross-up and credit system which the Commission advocated. Similar systems have been enacted in Europe (though not in the United States), where they are described as "imputation" systems. The term "imputation" is probably the more useful one to describe a system which gives too little (or too much) credit to shareholders for the tax paid by the corporation and which accordingly leaves some part of the two taxes "dis-integrated".[23] The earlier section of this chapter showed how Canada's imputation system works in principle, but the earlier account omitted many complications. This section of the chapter will examine in more detail how shareholders are taxed, and the next section will examine how corporations are taxed.[24]

(b)   Gross-up and credit procedure

When a shareholder receives a dividend on his or her shares the dividend is income from property. Paragraph 12(1)(j) of the Act (in subdivision b) requires the inclusion in a taxpayer's income of:

> any amount required by subdivision h to be included in computing the taxpayer's income for the year in respect of a dividend paid by a corporation resident in Canada on a share of its capital stock;

---

[21] Section 19.5(c), "Investment income of Canadian-controlled private corporations", below.

[22] Section 19.2, "Integration of corporation and shareholder taxes", above.

[23] Gibson, "Imputation Tax Systems" (1979) 27 *Can. Tax J.* 347, 348.

[24] See Kellough and McQuillan, *Taxation of Private Corporations and their Shareholders* (Can. Tax Foundation, 2nd ed., 1992).

Subdivision h, which is headed "Corporations Resident in Canada and their Shareholders", opens with s. 82(1), which provides:

In computing the income of a taxpayer for a taxation year, there shall be included

(a) . . .

    (ii)(A) . . . all amounts received by the taxpayer in the year from corporations resident in Canada as, on account or in lieu of payment of, or in satisfaction of, taxable dividends. . . .

plus

(b) where the taxpayer is an individual, other than a trust that is a registered charity, 1/4 of the amount determined under subparagraph (a)(ii) in respect of the taxpayer for the year.

Paragraph 82(1)(a) refers to "corporations resident in Canada", which recalls the concept of residence, discussed earlier,[25] and to "taxable dividends", which are defined as meaning all dividends except for dividends which are exempt from tax (s. 89(1)). For practical purposes, taxable dividends are all dividends except those paid out of the capital dividend account of a private corporation. This chapter will be confined to the tax situation of taxable Canadian corporations and their shareholders.[26]

Paragraph 82(1)(a) requires the inclusion in the shareholder's income of a dividend "received" by him or her. (It will be recalled that the word "received" calls for the cash method of reporting income.)[27] Paragraph 82(1)(b) then requires the shareholder to include an additional amount equal to 1/4 of the dividend. The shareholder is thus required to "gross-up" the dividend actually received by a factor of 1/4, and to include the grossed-up figure (5/4 of the dividend) in his or her income. The shareholder therefore pays tax not only on the dividend that he or she received, but also on a quarter-dividend that he or she did not receive. However, against his or her total personal tax liability the shareholder is allowed a dividend tax credit which should, in principle, be equal to the gross-up. The simple method of computing the tax liability of a shareholder who receives a dividend of $100 in a province that levies personal income tax at the rate of 50 per cent is displayed in the following Table 4.

---

[25] Chapter 8, Residence, under heading 8.6, "Residence of corporations", above.

[26] Dividends from other corporations are included in income from property, but there is no gross-up and credit: ss. 12(1)(j), 12(1)(k), 82(1)(a), 90.

[27] Chapter 11, Income from Business or Property: Profit, under heading 11.6(b), "Cash method", above.

Table 4

		Combined federal-provincial tax bracket of shareholder		
		43.5%	39%	25.5%
1.	Dividend received (s. 82(1)(a))	100.00	100.00	100.00
2.	Gross-up (s. 82(1)(b))	25.00	25.00	25.00
3.	Taxable income	125.00	125.00	125.00
4.	Personal income tax at (combined) rate of 43.5%, 39%, 25.5%	54.38	48.75	31.88
5.	Dividend tax credit (combined)	25.00	25.00	25.00
6.	Net personal income tax	29.38	23.75	6.88

In principle, in an imputation system, the credit should equal the gross-up. Table 4 assumes that the tax credit is equal to the gross-up (one quarter of the dividend). However, this assumption is correct only in a province that levies personal income tax at the rate of 50 per cent. The actual tax credit is provided by s. 121 of the Act, which provides as follows:

> 121. There may be deducted from the tax otherwise payable under this Part by an individual for a taxation year 2/3 of any amount that is required by paragraph 82(1)(b) to be included in computing the individual's income for the year.

It will be seen that s. 121 allows to the shareholder a credit (a deduction from tax) of 2/3 of the gross-up (which is the amount required to be included under s. 82(1)(b)). In order to understand why s. 121 allows a credit of only 2/3 of the gross-up rather than the full amount of the gross-up, it is necessary to recall that the Income Tax Act imposes only federal income tax. A credit provided against federal personal income tax will also cause a reduction in provincial personal income tax because provincial personal income tax (except in Quebec) is levied as a percentage, not of income, but of federal personal income tax.[28] The idea is that by giving a credit from federal personal income tax of 2/3 of the gross-up, this will automatically result in a reduction of provincial personal income tax of about 1/3 of the gross-up. The full effect of the credit would be a reduction in tax about equal to the gross-up. This would work out perfectly in a province which levied its personal income tax at the rate of 50 per cent, because 50 per cent of 2/3 is 1/3: a federal credit of 2/3 gross-up would also reduce provincial tax by exactly 1/3 gross-up, making the total effect of the credit exactly equal to the gross-up.

---

[28] Chapter 5, Rates, above.

In fact the provinces levy personal income taxes at a variety of rates, ranging (in 1997) from 45.5 per cent (Alberta) to 69 per cent (Newfoundland). No province levies its tax at exactly 50 per cent, and only Alberta and Ontario levy tax at less than 50 per cent. All the other provinces impose rates above 50 per cent. In those provinces, the s. 121 credit of 2/3 gross-up causes a reduction in provincial personal income tax of more than 1/3 gross-up. In Ontario, which in 1997 levies personal income tax at the rate of 48 per cent of federal tax (ignoring two surtaxes), the reduction of provincial tax is 32 per cent (2/3 × 48% = 32%) of the gross-up, instead of being 33 1/3 per cent of the gross-up. The total effective dividend tax credit is 99 per cent (67% + 32% = 99%) of the gross-up, or 24.75 per cent of the dividend, instead of being equal to the gross-up, namely, 25 per cent of the dividend. The credit will vary from province to province, depending upon the provincial rate of personal income tax.[29]

The following Table 5 uses the long method to compute the tax on a $100 dividend received by a shareholder in Ontario in the federal tax bracket of (1) 29 per cent (29% × 148% = 42.92% combined federal-Ontario rate), (2) 26 per cent (26% × 148% = 38.48% combined) and (3) 17 per cent (17% × 148% = 25.16% combined). (Again, surtaxes have been ignored to avoid complication.)

	Table 5			
		Federal tax bracket of shareholder		
		29%	26%	17%
1.	Dividend received (s. 82(1)(a))	100.00	100.00	100.00
2.	Gross-up (s. 82(1)(b))	25.00	25.00	25.00
3.	Taxable income	125.00	125.00	125.00
4.	Federal personal income tax at 29%, 26%, 17%	36.25	32.50	21.25
5.	Federal dividend tax credit (25 × 2/3) (s. 121)	(16.67)	(16.67)	(16.67)
6.	Net federal personal income tax	19.58	15.83	4.58
7.	Provincial personal income tax at 48% of federal tax	9.40	7.60	2.10
8.	Combined personal income tax	28.98	23.43	6.68

[29] The perfect system would adjust the percentage of the gross-up to the actual rate of personal income tax in each province, so that the combined credit equalled the gross-up. Presumably, this was regarded as too complicated.

If the last figure in each column of Table 5 is compared with the same figure in Table 4, above, it can be seen that the total tax liability of the three shareholders in Table 5 is slightly lower than in Table 4. This is because the combined rates in Table 5 are lower than in Table 4: 42.82 per cent versus 43.50 per cent, 38.48 per cent versus 39 per cent, and 25.16 per cent versus 25.50 per cent. This illustrates that s. 121, when combined with Ontario's income tax, effectively provides a credit somewhat less than the amount of the gross-up figure.

(c)　　Effect of gross-up and credit

The gross-up and credit reduces the effective rate of tax on dividends from taxable Canadian corporations. The credit, when combined with the gross-up, is the same as additional taxable income. The effect of the 25 per cent gross-up and credit is to increase the after-tax yield on dividend income so that it is equivalent to the after-tax yield on other income which is 25 per cent higher. Thus, a dividend of $100 yields the same after-tax return as interest income of $125. The gross-up and credit therefore provides an incentive for Canadian residents (who alone are entitled to the gross-up and credit) to invest in the shares of Canadian corporations instead of those of foreign corporations.

The encouragement to invest in the shares of Canadian corporations is not, of course, the primary purpose of the gross-up and credit. The primary purpose is to impute to the shareholder all or part of the tax paid by the corporation on the gross income which is represented by the dividend. A tax of 20 per cent paid by the corporation will be wholly imputed by the 25 per cent gross-up and credit. On income which is taxed to the corporation at the rate of 20 per cent, the corporate-level tax (at 20 per cent) and the shareholder-level personal income tax (at every rate) are integrated. This was illustrated by Table 2 under heading 19.2(d) of this chapter. Table 2 shows income of $100 earned by a corporation, taxed in the corporation at the rate of 20 per cent, and then paid out in full (after tax) to three shareholders at marginal rates of combined federal and provincial personal income tax of 43.5 per cent, 39 per cent and 25.5 per cent. The table shows that, for each of the three shareholders, the total tax paid by both the corporation and the individual shareholder on the income that has passed through the corporation is the same as the tax that would have been paid by the individual if the $100 before-tax income had been received by the taxpayer directly. Thus, the taxpayer in the 43.5 per cent bracket ends up with $56.50 of after-tax dividend income, which is $100 minus 43.5 per cent; the taxpayer in the 39 per cent bracket ends up with $61.00, which is $100 minus 39 per cent; and the taxpayer in the 25.5 per cent bracket ends up with $74.50, which is $100 minus 25.5 per cent. This is integration.

The reason why integration is achieved is that when the corporate tax rate is 20 per cent, the gross-up of one quarter is equal to the corporate tax. The gross-up therefore restores the amount of the dividend to the figure received by the corporation before corporate tax: $80 (dividend) + $20 (gross-up) = $100 (corporate income before tax). The total grossed-up dividend is then included in the shareholder's income and taxed at his or her marginal rate, exacting the same tax as if the individual had received the full amount of the income directly. The tax credit of 25 per cent of the dividend is equal to the tax of 20 per cent of the full income which has already been paid by the corporation. The result is, therefore, that the individual has paid the same tax as if he or she had received the corporate income directly, minus the tax paid by the corporation.

The gross-up and credit procedure may be explained in another way. The individual shareholder reports as income not only the dividend actually received but his or her share of the company's pre-corporate-tax distributed profits; he or she then receives a credit for the tax paid by the corporation. The corporate tax is a kind of withholding tax. The net effect is to eliminate "double taxation" of corporate profits.

The gross-up and credit only achieves integration of corporate and personal income taxes in respect of income which is taxed at a combined rate of 20 per cent at the corporate level. As we shall see, the only income of which this is approximately true is the investment income and (within limits) the active business income of Canadian-controlled private corporations. Most corporate income is taxed at a combined rate which is approximately 38 per cent. For that income, integration is incomplete, and after distribution to shareholders the total burden of the two taxes is heavier than if the income had been received directly by the individual shareholder. However, the gross-up and credit does provide some relief against this "double taxation". Tables 2 and 3 under heading 19.2(d) of this chapter, above, show the effect of the gross-up and credit system on corporate-source income that has been taxed in the corporation at 20 per cent (Table 2) and 38 per cent (Table 3).

19.5 Taxation of corporations

(a) Tax base

(i) *General rule*

Generally speaking, the rules for computing "income" are the same for corporations as they are for individuals. This follows from the fact that a corporation is a "person" (s. 248(1)) and may be a "taxpayer" (s. 248(1)). Division A of Part I of the Act applies to a "person", and most of the provisions of Division B which define the tax base apply to a "taxpayer". There are a considerable number of exceptions to the general rule, that is to say, provisions which are applicable only to an "individual" or only to a "corporation". Subject to numerous but minor exceptions, the general rule is that the tax base is the same for corporations as it is for individuals. The important exception for intercorporate dividends is discussed next.

(ii)   Intercorporate dividends

We have already considered the problem of double taxation which arises because corporate-source income is subject to (1) the corporate income tax that is applicable when the income is earned by the corporation, and (2) the personal income tax that is applicable when the corporation's after-tax income is distributed to the shareholders by the payment of dividends. We have also considered the imputation method (gross-up and credit) of taxing dividend income, which provides a partial remedy to the problem. Up to now, however, our assumption has always been that the shareholders of the corporation would be individuals. Needless to say, this is not always true: the shareholders of a corporation may include other corporations. If a dividend received by a corporation-shareholder were taxable to the recipient corporation, a third layer of tax would be imposed, because the income which the dividend represents has already been taxed in the hands of the payor corporation (which earned the income), and will be taxed again in the hands of the shareholders of the payee corporation when the payee corporation pays it out as a dividend to its own shareholders. Indeed, if the payee corporation itself has some corporate shareholders, then a fourth layer of tax would be imposed and a fifth or sixth layer would be possible. To tax corporate-source income twice is bad enough; to tax it more than twice is ridiculous.

The solution of the Income Tax Act to the problem of multiple taxation is to effectively exempt from Part I tax (ordinary income tax) dividends received by a corporation (intercorporate dividends). The dividends have to be included in the "income" of the recipient corporation by virtue of s. 82(1)(a), although they are not grossed-up (s. 82(1)(b) applies only "where the taxpayer is an individual"). However, s. 112(1), which is in Division C of Part I, allows the amount of the dividends to be deducted from the income of the recipient corporation in computing its "taxable income". The net result is that intercorporate dividends are washed out of the taxable income of the recipient corporation.

The effective exemption from Part I tax (ordinary income tax) of intercorporate dividends applies whether the recipient is a "public corporation" or a "private corporation" (the definitions were discussed earlier in this chapter).[30] But dividends received by a private corporation are subject to a Part IV tax of 33 1/3 per cent, which is refundable when the dividend is passed on to the private corporation's shareholders. The purpose of this tax, which is discussed later[31] is to discourage a private corporation from sheltering dividend income by not paying it out to the corporation's shareholders. The refund is

---

[30] Section 19.1(c), "Public and private corporations", above.

[31] Section 19.5(c), "Investment income of Canadian-controlled private corporations", below.

made regardless of whether the private corporation's shareholder is an individual or another corporation.

(b)   Tax rates

(i)   Federal tax

The rules for the computation of tax (unlike those for the computation of income) are quite different for corporations than they are for individuals. Division E of Part I of the Act supplies the rules for the computation of tax. Subdivision a of Division E prescribes the rules applicable to individuals. It will be recalled that the leading features of subdivision a are the graduated rate schedule of s. 117 and the indexing provision of s. 117.1 which were examined in chapter 5, Rates, above. Subdivision b of Division E then prescribes the rules applicable to corporations. They are our present concern.

Corporate income is not taxed at graduated rates. In place of the graduated rate schedule for individuals (s. 117), the general rule for corporations is supplied by s. 123, which imposes a single rate of 38 per cent. This is the "standard" federal rate, and it is a flat rate which applies regardless of how much taxable income a particular corporation derives. Because a corporation is simply an intermediary, there is no attempt to make the tax on corporate income "progressive".

(ii)   Corporate surtax

Section 123.2 imposes a surtax of 4 per cent of corporate income tax. This raises the standard federal rate (after the provincial abatement of 10 per cent, which is discussed later) to 29.12 per cent ((38% − 10%) + (28 × 4%) = 29.12%).

(iii)   Large corporations tax

Another tax that is imposed on corporations is the "large corporations tax", which is levied by Part I.3 of the Income Tax Act at the rate of 0.225 per cent of the corporation's taxable capital employed in Canada in excess of $10 million.[32] This is a capital tax, not an income tax, but the corporation surtax may be used to offset the large corporations tax. A corporation is permitted to credit against its large corporations tax liability for a particular year its surtax liability for the year. If the surtax liability is not wholly absorbed in a particular year, the surtax can be carried over to other years (back three and forward seven)

---

[32] The $10 million limit for large corporations tax must be shared by a group of "related" corporations (s. 181.5), except in the case of Canadian-controlled private corporations, where the $10 million limit must be shared by "associated" corporations (s. 181.5(7)). Most of the detailed rules for determining if corporations are "related" (s. 251) or "associated" (s. 256) look at who controls the company. Associated Canadian-controlled private corporations also share the $200,000 annual limit for the small business deduction: see text accompanying note 51, below.

and credited against the large corporations tax in those other years. Only a corporation that is not liable to pay the corporation surtax must pay the full amount of the large corporations tax.

The provinces also levy capital taxes on large corporations' taxable capital. The definitions of the corporations that are subject to the tax, the formula for calculating the taxable capital and the rates all vary from province to province.

In the text that follows, for the sake of simplicity, the corporation surtax, the large corporations tax and the provincial capital taxes will all be ignored.

(iv)   Provincial abatement

The rate of tax stipulated by s. 123, like the graduated rates of s. 117, is of course the rate of federal income tax. We have already noticed how the provincial income taxes correlate with the federal income tax for individuals.[33] The way in which the two levels of government share the field of corporate income tax is different — and simpler. The federal rate of tax, namely, s. 123's 38 per cent, is subject to an abatement of 10 per cent, which is intended to allow the provinces "room" to levy their corporate income taxes. The abatement is provided by s. 124(1), which provides:

> 124(1). There may be deducted from the tax otherwise payable by a corporation under this Part for a taxation year an amount equal to 10% of the corporation's taxable income earned in the year in a province.

Subsection 124(1) allows a deduction from tax, not income, so that it is preferable to describe it as a credit. The amount of the credit is however expressed as a percentage of income, not tax. It is "10% of the corporation's taxable income earned in the year in a province". (The federal Interpretation Act defines a province as including a territory.) The rules for allocating income to a particular province are set out in the Income Tax Regulations, Part IV, which were briefly described in chapter 8, Residence.[34]

(v)   Provincial taxes

Seven of the provinces (and the two territories) levy corporate income taxes which are expressed as a percentage of the corporation's (federally-defined) taxable income earned in the province, and which is collected by Revenue Canada. That is because these provinces have entered into tax collection agreements[35] with the federal government, under which the federal government collects each agreeing province's corporate income tax free of charge on

---

[33]   Chapter 5, Rates, above.

[34]   Chapter 8, Residence, under heading 8.8, "Provincial residence", above.

[35]   The federal-provincial tax collection agreements are discussed in ch. 5, Rates, under heading 5.1, "Federal sharing of tax room", above.

condition that the provincial tax is levied on the same income base as the federal corporate income tax. Ontario, Quebec and Alberta have not entered into tax collection agreements with the federal government regarding corporations. They do levy corporate income taxes, of course, and the abatement is available in respect of corporate income earned in those provinces. However, the three provinces outside the collection agreements collect their own corporate income taxes and require separate provincial returns to be filed with each provincial government. Although Ontario, Quebec and Alberta are free to define the base of corporate income tax as they choose, for the most part taxable income in those provinces is defined by the same rules for provincial tax purposes as for federal tax purposes. For ease of exposition in the rest of this chapter no distinctions will be drawn between Ontario, Quebec and Alberta, on the one hand, and the remaining seven provinces, on the other.

The rates of tax levied by the provinces on corporate income in 1997 generally range between 14 and 17 per cent. Ontario's rate is 15.5 per cent. Each province has a lower rate, usually around 8 per cent, for income that is eligible for the federal small business deduction, discussed below.[36]

The rates of provincial tax have no relevance to corporate income earned outside Canada, for no provincial tax is levied on such income, and the abatement does not apply to such income. The rate of tax on such income is therefore the 38 per cent stipulated by s. 123. But, for corporate income earned anywhere in Canada, the effective rate of tax is 38 per cent minus the 10 per cent abatement of s. 124 plus the rate of provincial tax. In a province that levied tax on corporate income at the rate of 14 per cent, the combined rate of tax would be 42 per cent (38% − 10% + 14% = 42%).

(vi)   Standard corporate rate

The "standard" rate of corporate income tax, namely, 38 per cent minus the abatement plus the provincial rate, is the rate of tax which is applicable to corporate income whenever the Act has no provision to the contrary. But there are a lot of provisions to the contrary. The three most important ones are: (1) the refundable tax on the investment income of Canadian-controlled private corporations, which reduces the tax on that class of income after distribution to shareholders by 26 2/3 percentage points; (2) the small business deduction in respect of qualifying active business income of Canadian-controlled private corporations, which reduces the tax on that class of income by 16 percentage points; and (3) the manufacturing and processing credit in respect of "Canadian manufacturing and processing profits", which reduces the tax on that class of

---

[36] Section 19.5(d)(i), "Small business deduction", below. Many provinces also have lower rates for income that is eligible for the manufacturing and processing credit: see sec. 19.5(e), "Manufacturing and processing credit", below.

income by 7 percentage points. These three exceptions to the general rule are our next three topics.

(c)   Investment income of Canadian-controlled private corporations

(i)   Canadian-controlled private corporations

The statutory definition of a Canadian-controlled private corporation (CCPC) was examined earlier in this chapter.[37] A CCPC will often be closely held; in fact, the most common case is where the shares are all held by members of one family. Very often, the corporation is controlled by one person, who is the major shareholder and the principal manager of the corporation's investments and business.

(ii)   Policy

The rules concerning the investment income of CCPCs attempt to make the corporation an investment vehicle of little tax significance. This involves, in the first place, taxing the corporation and its shareholders so that the shareholders obtain the same after-tax return on the investments held by the corporation as they would have obtained if they had received the income from the investments directly. This "integration" of personal and corporate income tax is achieved, as we have seen, when the corporate tax rate is 20 per cent. Thus, the idea is to impose corporate income tax of approximately 20 per cent on the investment income of a CCPC that is distributed to the shareholders by the payment of dividends.

Secondly, however, the rules concerning taxation of the investment income of CCPCs try to discourage the retention of income in the corporation, which would of course postpone the tax payable at the individual shareholder level. This second objective is pursued by initially taxing the investment income of a CCPC at the standard corporate rate plus 6 2/3 percentage points, which gives a rate close to the top personal rate. Tax equivalent to 26 2/3 per cent of the investment income of the corporation is refunded to it when dividends are paid out to the corporation's shareholders. In general, the refund is designed to reduce the effective rate of corporation income tax to the theoretical rate of 20 per cent that achieves integration. The high initial rate of corporate income tax (before refund) will be an incentive to pay dividends to shareholders whose marginal rate is less than the standard corporate rate plus 6 2/3 per cent.

The mechanism of the refund is the refundable dividend tax on hand account which is briefly described next.

---

[37] Section 19.1(d), "Canadian-controlled private corporations", above.

(iii)   Refundable dividend tax on hand account

The way in which the refund provisions work is complicated and the details are outside the scope of this book. Briefly, a CCPC will establish a "refundable dividend tax on hand" (RDTOH) account, and will credit the account with 26 2/3 per cent of its "Canadian investment income" and "foreign investment income". Those terms comprise, essentially, income from property (except for dividends from taxable Canadian corporations: see next section) and taxable capital gains[38] (s. 129(4)). The investment income may be Canadian or foreign. This RDTOH account represents money that has been paid to the Revenue Canada, but which will be refunded if and when the corporation pays dividends, in accordance with a formula established by the Act. The effect of the formula is that every $3 of dividend will generate a $1 refund from the RDTOH account.

For example, take the case of a CCPC that in a taxation year has investment income of $100. The corporation will pay combined federal-provincial corporate income tax at the rate of 46 2/3 per cent in a province that levies provincial corporate income tax of 12 per cent (38% + 6 2/3% − 10% + 12% = 46 2/3%). The corporation will pay $46.67 of combined income tax, and will credit $26.67 (26.67% of $100) to its RDTOH account. After tax, the corporation has only $53.33 left out of the $100 income, but it can also regard the $26.67 in the RDTOH account as available for payment of dividends, because that sum is refundable to the corporation by Revenue Canada. The corporation can, therefore, pay a dividend of $80 to its shareholders. A dividend of $80 will entitle the corporation to a refund from the RDTOH account of $26.67 (i.e., $1 for each $3 of dividend paid). That refund, paid by Revenue Canada, lowers the tax on the corporation's investment income from 46 2/3 per cent to 20 per cent. Note that the full refund would only be made if the corporation paid a dividend of three times the amount in the RDTOH account, which in this example requires a dividend of $80 ($26.67 × 3 = $80). This ensures that the low rate of tax is applicable only to income that has been fully distributed by the corporation.

In the example given, after receiving the refund from the RDTOH account, the corporation pays a net tax of 20 per cent (46 2/3% − 26 2/3% = 20%). The rate of 20 per cent is, of course, the rate at which perfect integration is achieved by the gross-up and credit rules for the taxation of dividends received by individual shareholders. Unfortunately, the rate of 20 per cent is more theoretical than real, because most provinces levy corporate income tax at rates of 15 to 17 per cent, instead of the 12 per cent that was assumed in the example. In addition, there is a federal corporate surtax of 4 per cent and there are provincial surtaxes which further increase the standard rate of corporate tax. When the standard combined federal-provincial rate of corporate tax (including

---

[38]   The treatment of capital gains is explained under sec. 19.5(c)(v), "Capital gains", below.

surtaxes) plus 6 2/3 per cent is more than 46 2/3 per cent, then the refund from the RDTOH account will leave the net amount of corporate tax somewhat higher than the magic figure of 20 per cent, and integration will not be fully achieved.[39]

(iv)   Dividends

Dividends paid by taxable Canadian corporations are excluded from the definitions of Canadian investment income and foreign investment income. It will be recalled that dividends paid by taxable Canadian corporations to shareholders that are corporations must be reported by the corporation-shareholder as income from property, but are deductible under s. 112(1). The s. 112(1) deduction means that intercorporate dividends paid by taxable Canadian corporations are effectively exempt from Part I tax.[40] But in order to discourage the use of a private corporation to "store" tax-exempt dividend income, s. 186 of the Act (which is in Part IV of the Act) imposes a special tax (Part IV tax) on private corporations of 33 1/3 per cent of the dividends received by the private corporation that were deductible under s. 112(1). When a dividend is received by a private corporation and the Part IV tax is paid, the full amount of the Part IV tax goes into the "refundable dividend tax on hand" (RDTOH) account. It is therefore potentially refundable in full.[41]

The sole purpose of the Part IV tax is to encourage a private corporation to pass the dividends received by it along to the shareholders, in whose hands of course they will be taxable. In principle, in order to accomplish its purpose, the Part IV tax should be equal to the rate of personal income tax that would be payable on a dividend by an individual shareholder in the top tax bracket. After taking into account the reduction of tax on dividend income caused by the gross-up and credit procedure, the rate of 33 1/3 per cent is about right for this purpose. Therefore, a high-income individual cannot defer any tax by holding

---

[39] The federal budget of February 27, 1995, in Table 6.3 (Budget Plan, 158), assumed the federal surtax of 4 per cent and a provincial corporate tax rate of 15.50 per cent, yielding a combined federal provincial corporate rate of 51.29 per cent ((38 − 10) × 1.04 + 15.5 = 51.29). Assuming that the corporation, with $100 of before-tax investment income, could find some additional cash to pay an $80 dividend, which would be necessary to generate a full refund of $26.67 from the RDTOH account, (based on the ratio of $1 refund for $3 dividend), the refund of $26.67 would bring the net tax on $100 of corporate investment income down to $24.62 ($51.29 − $26.67 = $24.62), or 24.62 per cent. This rate is too high to achieve perfect integration with the taxes at the shareholder level. However, the initial rate of 51.29 per cent is likely to be an effective deterrent to retaining investment income in a private corporation.

[40] Section 19.5(a)(ii), "Intercorporate dividends", above.

[41] If the corporation pays a dividend equal to the entire dividend received, this will produce a full refund from the refundable dividend tax on hand account, which pays a refund of $1 for every $3 of dividend.

portfolio investments in a private corporation and retaining the investment income in the corporation.

The refundable Part IV tax is payable by all private corporations, not just CCPCs. This means that a private corporation that is not a CCPC will also have an RDTOH account. However, that account will include only the Part IV tax on intercorporate dividends. The tax on other kinds of investment income — income from property (other than dividends) and taxable capital gains — is not partially refundable for a private corporation that is not a CCPC.[42]

(v)   Capital gains

Taxable capital gains come within the definitions of Canadian investment income and foreign investment income. When received by a CCPC, they are treated in the same way as income from property (other than dividends), that is, they are initially taxed at the standard corporate rate plus 6 2/3 per cent, but, through the mechanism of the refundable dividend tax on hand account, a portion of the tax equivalent to 26 2/3 per cent of the taxable capital gains is refundable. When the taxable capital gains are distributed to the shareholders as dividends, the refund is obtained, reducing the rate of tax (in a province that levies corporate tax at the rate of 12 per cent) to 20 per cent, the rate that achieves integration.[43]

Taxable capital gains are three-quarters of capital gains. The non-taxable quarter of the capital gain, which has been received free of tax by the corporation, should not be taxable when it is distributed to the shareholders as a dividend. This would be a violation of integration, for the non-taxable quarter of a capital gain would be free of tax if received by an individual directly. The Income Tax Act, by s. 83(2), accordingly allows a private corporation, but not a public corporation, to set up a "capital dividend account" into which the non-taxable quarter of capital gains are placed. Out of that account, the corporation can "elect" (by filing special forms) to pay "capital dividends" to the shareholders. Capital dividends are tax-free in the hands of the shareholders. A capital dividend is the only remaining important example of a dividend that is not a taxable dividend.

---

[42] Before 1982, the partial refund of corporate tax on investment income other than dividends was available to all private corporations. Since 1982, it has been restricted to CCPCs. However, the Part IV tax on dividends is still payable by private corporations that are not CCPCs, and the tax is still refundable to private corporations that are not CCPCs.

[43] The mechanics of the refundable dividend tax on hand account for investment income are explained under sec. 19.5(c)(iii), "Refundable dividend tax on hand account", above. As is acknowledged, most provinces levy corporate tax at rates in excess of 12 per cent, and those higher rates, plus federal and provincial surtaxes, make the net corporate tax (after refund) closer to 25 per cent in most provinces.

(d)   Active business income of Canadian-controlled private corporations

(i)   Small business deduction

A Canadian-controlled private corporation (CCPC) receives the "low rate" of corporate income tax in respect of the first $200,000 of its Canadian active business income. Section 125 provides a "small business deduction" of 16 per cent of "the income of the corporation from an active business carried on in Canada" up to a "business limit" of $200,000. The deduction is from tax, not income, so that it is really a credit. The credit reduces the federal rate of tax on the qualifying active business income of a CCPC to 12 per cent (38% − 10% − 16% = 12%). This rate, when combined with provincial tax rates, which are also lower for this class of income (around 8 per cent), brings the combined rate to approximately 20 per cent. The rate of 20 per cent is, of course, the rate at which integration of the corporation's tax and the shareholder's personal tax is achieved.

The small business deduction is available only to a "Canadian-controlled private corporation". The definition of a CCPC was explained earlier in the chapter.[44] It excludes foreign-controlled private corporations, and public corporations, as well as individuals operating unincorporated businesses as sole proprietorships or partnerships. This obviously violates the stipulation of equity that equal incomes should be treated equally. As will be explained, the CCPCs that benefit from the low rate of tax include many large, established, flourishing businesses, which on the face of it do not seem to need the help. The new struggling business, which earns no income after paying salaries, or incurs losses, is not helped at all.

(ii)   Active business income

Only income "from an active business" qualifies for the small business deduction. The term "active business" is defined by s. 125(7) as follows:

> "active business carried on by a corporation" means any business carried on by the corporation other than a specified investment business or a personal services business and includes an adventure or concern in the nature of trade.

The reference to "any business" makes clear that there is no real force to the word "active" in the phrase "active business". If the CCPC's income is business income,[45] then it qualifies for the low rate, provided it does not come within one of the two exceptions. The first exception is a "specified investment business" (defined in s. 125(7)), which is a business the principal purpose of

---

[44] Section 19.1(d), "Canadian-controlled private corporations", above.

[45] See ch. 12, Income from Business or Property: Inclusions, under heading 12.2, "Income from business", above.

which is to derive income from property.[46] The second exception is a "personal services business" (defined in s. 125(7)), which covers "incorporated employees";[47] this exception is designed to prevent an employee from converting income from employment into low-rate active business income by interposing a corporation between the employer and the employee, the function of the corporation being to supply to the employer the personal services of the former employee.[48]

(iii) Investment income compared

It will be recalled that the investment income of a CCPC is also taxed at a low rate of approximately 20 per cent, so as to come close to achieving integration of the corporate tax on that income with the shareholder's personal tax. There are two important differences, however, between the tax treatment of investment income and that of active business income. First, there is no limit on the amount of investment income that can benefit from the low rate, whereas there is the "business limit" of $200,000 on qualifying active business income. Secondly, the low rate on investment income is implemented by the device of a refundable portion of the tax, which is initially levied at the standard corporate rate plus 6 2/3 per cent. The refundable tax is intended to discourage CCPCs from retaining tax-sheltered investment income in the corporation; only after distribution of the income and receipt of the refund does the tax fall to the low rate. The qualifying active business income of a CCPC, by contrast, never bears the full standard rate of corporate tax, let alone the addition of 6 2/3 per cent; it is entitled to the small business deduction whether or not the income is distributed to the shareholders. The small business deduction provides an

---

[46] There are two cases when income earned by a such a business will be considered to be active. First, if the business employs more than five full-time employees throughout the year, it will be an active business (s. 125(7)); this rule recognizes that, once a company earning property income has a certain level of activity, it should be regarded as active. Second, if the business earns income (e.g., rent, interest) from an associated company and the associated company deducts the amounts in computing its income from an active business, these income items will be considered income from an active business (s. 129(6)); this rule prevents an associated group of companies from reducing its overall active business income by using such intercompany transactions.

[47] There are two cases when income earned by a such a business will be considered to be active. First, if the business employs more than five full-time employees throughout the year, it will be an active business (s. 125(7)); this rule recognizes that, once a business has a certain level of activity, it should be regarded as active. Second, if the business earns income from services (e.g., consulting services) provided to an associated company, it will be an active business (s. 125(7)); this rule recognizes that no tax advantage is being gained in such situations since an associated group of companies must share the $200,000 annual limit for the small business deduction in any case.

[48] As well as the low rate of tax created by the small business deduction, the conversion of income from employment into income from business makes available additional deductions for business expenses. These additional deductions have also been denied to a "personal services business": s. 18(1)(p).

incentive for a CCPC to retain its active business income and thereby avoid the payment of tax in excess of the low rate of 20 per cent. This is a deliberate policy of the Act: by enabling CCPCs to accumulate partially tax-sheltered dollars, it is hoped to encourage the expansion of Canadian businesses.

(iv)   Excessive active business income

The "small" business deduction is available to large as well as small CCPCs. However, since 1994, there has been a limit on the size of CCPCs that can claim the deduction. Subsection 125(5.1) reduces the $200,000 business limit for CCPCs with "taxable capital employed in Canada" in excess of $10 million (the same threshold as that used for the large corporations tax)[49] according to a sliding scale which reaches nil for a CCPC with taxable capital of $15 million. Therefore, no small business deduction is available to a CCPC with taxable capital of $15 million, and less than the full deduction is available to CCPCs with capital of less than $15 million but more than $10 million. Even with these limits, the small business deduction continues to be available to relatively large corporations. A corporation with taxable capital of less than $10 million that earns before-tax profits of $200,000 after paying all expenses, including salaries to its managers, is not all that small.

Where a CCPC has active business income in excess of the $200,000 business limit, the excess will be taxed at the standard corporate rate of 38 per cent (or more in most provinces). When that high-rate income is distributed to the shareholders, there is a substantial additional burden of tax compared with the tax that would be payable if the shareholder had earned the active business income directly. This is illustrated by Table 3 under heading 19.2(c), above. This tax penalty creates an incentive for a CCPC to keep its active business income within the annual limit of $200,000. The Act accordingly strikes at certain devices which might be used to artificially reduce corporate income. One device is to take profits out of the corporation in the form of salaries (which are deductible, of course) rather than dividends. It is in fact common for prosperous CCPCs to pay substantial salaries (or bonuses) to senior employees (who are usually also shareholders) so as to get the income of the corporation down to $200,000. However, it is clearly established that s. 67 (the reasonableness requirement) applies to make such salaries deductible from corporate income only to the extent that they are "reasonable in the circumstances".[50] Another device is to create several small CCPCs instead of one large one, or to split a large CCPC into two or more smaller CCPCs. This is met by rules concerning "associated" corporations, which provide that when several CCPCs are "associated" with each other they must share a single limit of $200,000; if the

---

[49] Section 19.5(b)(iii), "Large corporations tax", above.

[50] See ch. 13, Income from Business or Property: Deductions, under heading 13.13, "The reasonable requirement", above.

corporations cannot agree on the allocations, the Minister has the power to divide up the limit among the associated corporations (s. 125(3)).[51]

(e)   Manufacturing and processing credit

Section 125.1 of the Act, which was introduced in 1973, allows a tax credit to reduce corporate income tax on "Canadian manufacturing and processing profits". The credit is not available to unincorporated businesses engaged in manufacturing and processing. It is however available to any corporation, public as well as private, and foreign-controlled as well as Canadian-controlled. The Act (s. 125.1(1)) and regulations (Part 52) provide rules for computing a corporation's "Canadian manufacturing and processing profits". The credit is equal to 7 per cent of Canadian manufacturing and processing profits that are not eligible for the small business deduction. Income eligible for the small business deduction does not receive the additional relief of the manufacturing and processing credit. The effect of the credit, therefore, is to reduce the standard rate of corporate tax by 7 per cent of qualifying income. The policy is to provide encouragement to manufacturing and processing industries, on the theory (which would no doubt puzzle economists) that those industries are more valuable than service industries.

(f)   Conclusion

It is a depressing exercise to review the foregoing chapter and to note that there are four different rates of corporate taxation for ordinary business corporations in Canada today. Ignoring surtaxes, the four rates (assuming, for simplicity, provincial tax at 10%)[52] are as follows:

1.   Corporate tax at 38 per cent (38% − 10% + 10%):
      Investment income of public corporations.

> Investment income of private corporations that are not Canadian-controlled private corporations.

> Business income of public corporations that is not eligible for the manufacturing and processing credit.

> Business income of private corporations that is not eligible for the small business deduction or the manufacturing and processing credit.

---

[51] The rules for determining whether corporations are "associated" are set out in s. 256. Many of these rules look at who controls a corporation using the de facto concept of control, i.e., "controlled directly, indirectly in any manner whatever". The same phrase is used in the definition of Canadian-controlled private corporation. In the latter context, the concept of control is briefly discussed earlier in this chapter: text accompanying note 4, above.

[52] As explained earlier in the text, provincial rates are in fact much higher, around 15 to 17 per cent, except for income eligible for the small business deduction, upon which most provinces have a low rate, around 8 per cent.

2.   Corporate tax at 31 per cent (38% − 10% + 10% − 7%):

Business income of public corporations that is eligible for the manufacturing and processing credit.

Business income of private corporations that is eligible for the manufacturing and processing credit but not the small business deduction.

3.   Corporate tax at 22 per cent (38% − 10% + 10% − 16%):

Business income of Canadian-controlled private corporations that is eligible for the small business deduction.

4.   Corporate tax at 18 per cent (38% − 10% + 10% + 6 2/3% − 26 2/3%):

Investment income of Canadian-controlled private corporations that is distributed to shareholders.

Of the four rates, only two (classes 3 and 4) are close to the 20 per cent figure which is imputed to the shareholder by the gross-up and credit rules, and which would yield integration. Income in classes 1 and 2, by the time it is received by a shareholder in the form of dividends, has been taxed more heavily than income earned directly by an individual. This complex situation is neither equitable nor neutral. Indeed, it departs so far from those ideals that it is hard to believe that it could possibly be the product of a process of tax reform which started with the Carter Commission's Report in 1966.

20

Partnerships

20.1 Introduction

This chapter provides a very brief account of the tax treatment of partnerships.[1] First, the chapter describes the general nature of partnerships, the calculation of partnership income for tax purposes, and the way in which the Act levies tax on that income. The chapter then goes on to deal with the nature and tax treatment of each partner's interest in the firm. Finally, the chapter considers the tax treatment of acquisitions and distributions of "partnership property".

20.2 Definition of partnership

The Act contains no definition of "partnership" for income tax purposes.[2] This means that a particular business relationship will be considered a partnership

---

[1] For more detailed accounts of the law, see Arnold and McNair, *Income Taxation of Partnerships and their Partners* (1981); Carson, Steiss, Tikku, *Taxation of Partnerships in Canada* (1983); McQuillan and Thomas, *Understanding the Taxation of Partnerships* (3rd ed., 1991).

[2] Section 102 does define "Canadian partnership" for the purpose of the rollover provisions, but that definition presupposes that there is a partnership, and there is no definition anywhere else in the Act. Interpretation Bulletin IT-90, "What is a partnership?" (1973) sets out Revenue Canada's views on the issue.

for tax purposes where it would be considered a partnership[3] under the applicable provincial laws. For present purposes,[4] it is a sufficient definition of a partnership (or firm)[5] to describe it as two or more persons "carrying on business in common with a view to profit",[6] and sharing the profits.[7] Corporations can enter into partnership, but usually the members of a partnership are individuals, and this chapter will be limited to partnerships of individuals.

Unlike a corporation, a partnership is not a legal person that is separate from its members (partners). Property used by a partnership is owned in law by the individual partners. Liabilities incurred by a partnership are owed in law by the individual partners and may have to be satisfied out of the personal assets of the partners. It is the lack of separate legal personality, and the consequent lack of limited liability,[8] that distinguishes the partnership from the corporation. For these reasons, the corporation will usually be the preferred form of business organization. However, professionals, such as accountants, lawyers and doctors, have traditionally practised in partnership, and in many jurisdictions are prohibited by law from incorporating their practices.

---

[3] A "joint venture" is very similar to a partnership, but it does not entail a continuing relationship between the co-venturers, who join together to carry out a specific project. Because a joint venture is not a partnership, it does not have the same tax characteristics as a partnership.

[4] The definition of a partnership at common law is not entirely clear, and the Partnership Acts that have been enacted in each common law jurisdiction (following the model of the English Act) supply only a very vague definition and associated rules, e.g., Partnership Act, R.S.O. 1990, c. P.5, ss. 2-3. The civil law position is similar to the common law, although the Civil Code does accord more legal personality to a partnership than does the common law: Brierley and Macdonald (eds.), Quebec Civil Law (1993), 667.

[5] The word "firm" is often used as a synonym for partnership, but the word firm is wider, often including sole proprietorships and corporations. The Income Tax Act consistently uses the word partnership.

[6] This phrase comes from the statutes, e.g., Partnership Act, R.S.O. 1990, c. P.5, s. 2.

[7] The sharing of profits is neither a necessary nor a sufficient characteristic of a partnership: *Cox and Wheatcroft* v. *Hickman* (1860), 8 H.L. Cas. 268, 11 E.R. 431 (H.L.); Partnership Act, R.S.O. 1990, c. P.5, s. 3. However, the sharing of profits is the arrangement that normally characterizes a partnership.

[8] It is possible (both under the common law and the civil law) to create a "limited partnership", in which a "limited partner" (or partners) has limited liability like that of a shareholder in a corporation, and a "general partner" (or partners) has unlimited liability. However, the limited partner must be an entirely passive investor: participation in the management of the business exposes the limited partner to the same liability as a general partner. Incorporation is normally the best way to achieve limited liability. Limited partnerships are sometimes used as tax shelters, because they can be used to "flow-through" deductions and losses to passive investors. This use of limited partnerships has resulted in restrictions on the deduction of limited partnership losses (e.g., s. 111(1)(e)).

20.3 Taxation of partnership

The Income Tax Act recognizes the lack of legal personality of a partnership, and does not treat the partnership as a taxpayer. Although it is the individual partners who are liable to pay tax on the partnership's income, the Act does require the income of the partnership to be calculated at the partnership level before the income is apportioned among the partners. The partnership does not file a tax return, but it does have to file an annual "information return" setting out the income of the partnership and details of the partners who are entitled to shares of the income (reg. 229).

Partnership income is calculated for tax purposes in a two-step process. The first step is to calculate the income of the partnership "as if the partnership were a separate person resident in Canada" (s. 96(1)(a)).[9] For this step, the partnership is required to recognize all income and take all deductions that would be applicable to a separate person resident in Canada. The second step is to apportion the partnership's income among the individual partners in accordance with their shares in the firm (s. 96(1)(f)). Each individual partner is then obliged to report his or her share of the partnership income[10] as part of his or her income for the year.

The income of each individual partner retains the source-characterization that it had when it was derived by the partnership. Accordingly, the appropriate share of income that was business income in the partnership is treated as business income in the hands of the partner; property income remains property income; and taxable capital gains remain taxable capital gains. This means that the individual partner is subject to the rules applicable to each source of income. For example, a partner's share of partnership dividends from taxable Canadian corporations is grossed up and eligible for the dividend tax credit in the partner's hands. As another example, although the partnership's business income will be a net figure from which all deductions that were applicable at the partnership level have been taken, the individual partner may have further deductions if he or she incurred expenses personally to earn the partnership income (for example, by using a personal automobile in the business or by attending a business

---

[9] Before 1995, a partnership, like a corporation, could select its own fiscal period. The partnership income was then recognized by each individual partner in the calendar year in which the fiscal period ended. For a partnership with an early year-end (e.g., January 31), this resulted in a regular postponement of tax on the partnership income. However, since 1995, any partnership of which a member is an individual (or a professional corporation or another partnership which has such members) has been required to use the calendar year as its fiscal period.

[10] The shares of the partnership income will be defined in the partnership agreement. However, s. 103 of the Act provides for the case where shares have been agreed to for the purpose of reducing tax; in that case, the shares are deemed to be those that are "reasonable" in the circumstances. For example, members of a family in partnership might agree to share profits so as to achieve the most favourable income split, rather than in accordance with the partners' contributions of property and work; s. 103 would apply in such a case.

conference). As another example, if an individual partner incurred an allowable capital loss in his or her private investments, the loss will be deductible against his or her share of any taxable capital gains derived by the partnership.

20.4 Partnership interest

Each partner in a partnership is said to have an "interest" in the partnership. It is the extent of each partner's interest in the partnership that determines his or her entitlement to share in the profits of the business and the extent to which he or she may participate in the distribution of partnership property when the partnership is dissolved. For income tax purposes, each partner's interest in the partnership is treated as a capital property, separate from the assets held by the firm.

Because a partnership interest is capital property, the disposition of the interest gives rise to a capital gain or loss. When a partner disposes of his or her interest for proceeds of disposition that exceed the adjusted cost base of the interest, the partner will have to recognize a capital gain, three-quarters of which will be taxed. If the proceeds of disposition are less than the adjusted cost base, then the partner will have to recognize a capital loss.

The adjusted cost base of a partnership interest is determined by reference to a set of rules laid out in s. 53 of the Income Tax Act. Obviously, the cost of the interest to the partner is the primary figure from which the adjusted cost base of the partnership interest is derived. Once this starting figure is ascertained, s. 53(1)(e) provides for various additions to be made, and s. 53(2)(c) provides for deductions from the cost figure. Under s. 53(1)(e), the main figures to be added to the cost base of the interest include the value of any property contributed to the firm by the partner and any amount of partnership income from a prior year to which the partner is entitled.[11] The reason that the amount of income from a prior year to which the partner is entitled must be added to the adjusted cost base of the interest is to ensure that the partner's share of partnership income, which has already been reported by the partner under s. 96, is not subject to double taxation by increasing the value of the partner's interest in the firm.[12] Similarly, the partner's share of any losses generated by the partnership in a prior year must be deducted from the partner's adjusted cost base, as these amounts will also have been reported under s. 96.[13] The other major deduction from the

---

[11] The income of the current year is not included: see the wording in the preamble of s. 53(1)(i) and Revenue Canada's comments in Income Tax Technical News No. 5 (1995).

[12] In order to avoid double taxation, the partner adds to the adjusted cost base the partner's share of the partnership's full capital gain (not just the three-quarter's portion that is a taxable capital gain): s. 53(1)(i)(A).

[13] The treatment of capital losses is similar to capital gains: see previous note. A partner must deduct from the adjusted cost base the partner's share of the partnership's full capital loss, not just the three-quarter's portion that is an allowable capital loss (s. 53(1)(i)(A)).

adjusted cost base of the partnership interest, provided for by s. 53(2)(c) of the Act, is the value of any distribution of capital or income which the partner has received from the partnership.[14]

If s. 53(2) deductions exceed (on a cumulative basis) the original cost of the interest and all s. 53(1) additions, the adjusted cost base of the partnership interest will be a negative amount. A partner with a partnership interest having a negative adjusted cost base will have to recognize a capital gain equal to this amount (s. 40(3)) and the adjusted cost base of the partnership interest will be adjusted to zero (s. 53(1)(a)). Owning a partnership interest with a negative adjusted cost base will not result in an *immediate* capital gain for partners who are active in their partnerships, as is generally the case when accountants, lawyers or doctors practise in partnerships. Instead, the amount will be added to the partner's capital gain arising in the year that the interest is disposed of (s. 98(1)(c)). But owning a partnership interest with a negative adjusted cost base will result in an immediate capital gain when a partner is a limited or passive partner (ss. 40(3.1) to (3.2)) or when the interest is a "residual interest" in a partnership.[15]

20.5 Partnership property

A partnership usually requires capital in order to operate its business. This will be supplied by the partners, each of whom will usually contribute property to the partnership in exchange for a partnership interest (discussed in the previous section of this chapter). When a partner (or potential partner) transfers property to the partnership, there is an elective rollover under s. 97(2) similar to the s. 85 rollover that is available on the transfer of property to a corporation in return for shares in the corporation.[16]

When a partnership disposes of capital property, the partnership will first recognize a taxable capital gain or allowable capital loss under the same rules as

---

[14] Similarly, the partner's share of charitable donations and political contributions which have been made by the partnership must be deducted from the adjusted cost base (s. 53(2)(c)(iii)). Since these amounts are eligible for a tax credit or deduction in the partner's income tax return (ss. 110.1, 118.1, 127(4.2)), there is no double taxation.

[15] Subsection 98.1(1). A person who has ceased to be a partner, but has a right to receive property from the partnership in respect of a partnership interest, owns a "residual interest" in the partnership (s. 98.1(1)(a)) and is not considered to have disposed of a partnership interest (s. 98.1(1)(b)). An example of a person with a "residual interest" in a partnership is a retired partner of a law firm who receives distributions of partnership capital after retirement. The retired partner may also receive an annual distribution of income during retirement. Providing the income amounts are received from a Canadian partnership, they are deemed to be income from a partnership because the former partner is deemed to be a member of the partnership for this purpose (s. 96(1.1)).

[16] The details of the s. 85 rollover are outside the scope of this book. For a brief explanation, see ch. 15, Capital Gains, under heading 15.15(d), "Transfer to corporation", above.

apply to a corporation or an individual. Any resulting gain or loss is then apportioned among the partners in accordance with their shares, and is reported by the partners as part of their personal income. This is the two-step process of calculating each partner's income that was described earlier in the chapter.

On the dissolution of a partnership, the Act provides for rollovers of capital property where the business is continued by a former partner as a sole proprietorship (s. 98(5)), or by some of the former partners in a new partnership (s. 98(6)), or by a corporation in circumstances where the s. 85 rollover is available (s. 85(2)). The policy of the Act in all these cases is to remove tax impediments to what are really changes in the organization of a business. Where a partnership is dissolved and the property of the partnership is distributed to the partners, there is another rollover (s. 98(3)),[17] recognizing that the distribution is a return of each partner's share in what is really the partners' own property.

---

[17] Under s. 98(3), each partner must take an undivided share in each property equal to his or her share of the partnership.

21

Trusts

21.1 Definition of trust

A trust[1] exists when the management and control of property is vested in one person (or persons), the "trustee", while enjoyment of the property is vested in another person (or persons), the "beneficiary" (or cestui que trust). Normally, the legal forms by which this division between management and enjoyment is accomplished are that legal title to the trust property is in the trustee, while equitable (or beneficial) title to the trust property is in the beneficiary. Normally, so long as there is a separation of the legal and equitable title to property, there is a trust.[2] Nothing more is required.

A trust may be created by a living person, called the settlor, in which case the trust is called an inter vivos (or living) trust. A trust may be created by will, which of course becomes operative only on the death of the testator, in which case the trust is called a testamentary trust.[3]

21.2 Creation of trust

(a) Inter vivos trust

A trust may be created inter vivos in two ways, namely, by transfer or by declaration. A trust by transfer is created when a property-owner, the "settlor", transfers property to a trustee (or trustees) to hold upon trust for certain beneficiaries. A trust by declaration is created when a settlor declares himself or

---

[1] For more detailed accounts of the taxation of trusts, see Waters, *Law of Trusts in Canada* (Carswell, 2nd ed., 1984), ch. 13; Cullity and Brown, *Taxation and Estate Planning* (Carswell, 3rd ed., 1992), chs. 3, 6; Raphael, *Canadian Income Taxation of Trusts* (CCH, 3rd ed., 1993); Christopoulos and Kolinsky, *Taxation of Trusts and Beneficiaries* (Carswell, loose-leaf service); Saunders, "Inter Vivos Discretionary Family Trusts: A Potpourri of Issues and Traps," [1993] *Can. Tax Found. Conf. Rep.*, 37:1-58; Krishna, "Trusts and the Preservation of Wealth", Mathew, "The Use of Trusts for Income Splitting", and Ouellette, "Use of Trusts in Succession Planning" in [1996] *Ont. Conf. Rep., Can. Tax. Foundation*, Tabs 10, 11 and 12; and Saunders, "Personal Trusts and the Amendments Arising out of the 1995 Federal Budget: Impact and Planning", [1996] *Can. Tax J.* 188.

[2] The general law of trusts denies some of the incidents of a trust to a "bare trust", where the trustee, although holding legal title to the trust property, has no independent discretion and acts solely under the direction of the beneficiary: see, e.g., *Trident Holdings* v. *Danand Investments* (1988), 64 O.R. (2d) 65 (C.A.) (trustee treated as agent of beneficiaries). Revenue Canada ignores a bare trust (where the trustee "has no independent power, discretion or responsibility pertaining to the trust property"), treating any income (or loss) of the bare trust as being the income of the beneficiary: Revenue Canada Bulletin B-068, "Bare Trusts" (1993). In effect, the trustee of a bare trust is treated as receiving income as the agent of the beneficiary. This seems to be the correct treatment.

[3] Unless otherwise stated, the rules which are discussed in this chapter apply to personal trusts which are resident in Canada and their Canadian resident beneficiaries. A personal trust is defined in s. 248(1) as (a) a testamentary trust or (b) an inter vivos trust in which the beneficiaries did not purchase their interests from the trust or from anyone who had made a contribution to the trust.

herself to be a trustee of property for certain beneficiaries. The mode of transfer is more common than the mode of declaration.

A transfer of property by a settlor to a trust (i.e., to the trustee) may be a gift or a sale, depending upon whether the trust gives consideration; and it may constitute a new trust or add to the assets of an existing trust, depending upon whether the trustee was already holding property on the terms stipulated by the settlor. In all of these situations, the transfer is a "disposition" for tax purposes, because the definition of "disposition" in s. 54 includes "any transfer of property to a trust". If the property transferred to the trust is capital property[4] to the settlor, then, to the extent that the "proceeds of disposition" of the property exceeds the "adjusted cost base" of the property, the settlor will have to recognize a capital gain on the disposition, three-quarters of which is taxable as income (ss. 38(a), 39(1)(a), 40(1)(a)).[5]

Where the transfer of property by the settlor to the trust is a sale at arm's length, then the proceeds of disposition is defined to be the "sale price" of the property (s. 54). Where the transfer of property by the settlor to the trust is not a sale at arm's length, but was a gift or a sale for inadequate consideration, then the proceeds of disposition is deemed to be the "fair market value" of the property (s. 69(1)(b)).

The effect of the extended definitions of disposition and of proceeds of disposition is to create a deemed realization of property transferred to a trust, even if no consideration was actually paid. The "spouse trust" is an exception to these rules. We shall see later that there is a tax-free rollover of assets into a spouse trust. Except in the case of a spouse trust, it follows that the creation of a trust by transfer, and any subsequent transfer of property to the trust, may give rise to a taxable capital gain (or loss) in the hands of the settlor.

Where a trust is created by the settlor declaring herself to be a trustee it is obvious that the tax consequences should be the same as where a trust is created by transfer. However, the definition of disposition in s. 54 as a "transfer" of property to a trust is not particularly apt to catch a declaration of trust. Nevertheless, it is likely that the courts would give a sufficiently broad reading to the word "transfer" to enable both modes of creating an inter vivos trust to attract the same tax consequences.

---

[4] Capital property is defined in s. 54: see ch. 15, Capital Gains, under heading 15.8, "Capital property", above.

[5] See generally ch. 15, Capital Gains, above. In the case of depreciable property, the disposition may also cause a recapture of capital cost allowance, which is taxable as income (s. 13(1)). See generally ch. 14, Income from Business or Property: Capital Expenditures, above.

(b)   Testamentary trust

(i)   Definition

A testamentary trust is one created by will, under which the testator gives property on his or her death to a person (the trustee) to hold upon trust for someone else (the beneficiary). A will is not effective until the death of the testator, so that a testamentary trust is created only when the testator dies.

(ii)   Distinction between trust and estate

When a person dies, his or her assets and liabilities are known as the deceased's "estate". The deceased's estate passes to the "personal representative" (or "legal representative", which is the phrase used by the Income Tax Act). A personal representative is known as an "executor" if he or she is appointed by the will of the deceased, and as an "administrator" if he or she is appointed by the court, which occurs if the deceased left no will (died "intestate") or if the deceased left a will which failed to appoint an executor. The duty of the personal representative is to "administer" the deceased person's estate. This involves ascertaining and getting in all the assets, paying the debts, filing tax returns and paying taxes, paying funeral expenses and the expenses of administration, and generally getting the estate into a form in which it can be distributed to the persons who are entitled to inherit it under the terms of the will (if there is one) or provincial intestacy law (if there is no will). Obviously, the relationship between the personal representative and the deceased's successors is very similar to the relationship between a trustee and beneficiaries, but there is authority for the proposition that a personal representative is not a trustee of the property in an unadministered estate.[6]

If the deceased died intestate, or if the will directs the immediate distribution of the deceased's property, the personal representative's final act will be to distribute the property to the deceased's successors. But if the will establishes a trust (in which case it is called a "trust will"), the personal representative's final act will be to transfer the assets given on trust to the person appointed trustee by the will. Thenceforth the trustee will hold the assets on trust for the beneficiaries designated in the will. In practice, a trust will often appoint the same person (or persons) to be both executor and trustee. At the time when that person has completed the administration of the estate, he or she ceases to be an executor administering an estate and becomes a trustee. It is often difficult to ascertain when that mysterious transformation occurs, but it is rarely necessary to do so because there are so few differences between a personal representative and a trustee that nothing usually turns on the question whether the person was acting in the capacity of a personal representative or in the capacity of a trustee. For tax purposes, the definition of a trust includes an estate (s. 104(1)), so that

---

[6] *Commr. of Stamp Duties (Queensland)* v. *Livingston*, [1965] A.C. 694 (P.C. Aust.).

tax consequences rarely flow from the shadowy distinction between an estate and a trust.[7]

(iii)   Taxation of capital property on death

On death, there is a deemed disposition of all of a deceased person's capital property. Capital property is deemed to have been disposed of, immediately before death, for proceeds of disposition equal to the fair market value of the property (s. 70(5)(a)). Any resulting taxable capital gains (or allowable capital losses) have to be recognized as income (or loss) of the deceased for the taxation period ending at his or her death (the deceased's terminal year).[8] These rules apply to all of a deceased person's capital property, not just property left on trust. However, as with the inter vivos trust, there is an exception for the "spouse trust".

(c)   Spouse trust

The "spouse trust" is an exception to the general rules that are designed to recognize for tax purposes capital gains (or losses) on inter vivos sales or gifts and on testamentary gifts. Capital property which is transferred to a spouse trust, either inter vivos or on death, is deemed to have been disposed of for proceeds of disposition equal to the adjusted cost base of the property (ss. 70(6), 73(1)).[9] This creates a "rollover", because it means that no capital gain or loss is caused by the transfer of property to the spouse trust.[10] However, the spouse trust is deemed to acquire the property at its adjusted cost base (tax cost to the settlor), not at its fair market value, so that any liability to tax waits in the trust until the property is actually disposed of by the trustee or until the spouse dies (when there is a deemed disposition). The same rollover occurs where property is given directly to a spouse, either inter vivos or on death. The general idea is to eliminate income tax consequences from transactions between spouses.

The spousal rollover can be elected against by the settlor in the case of an inter vivos trust (s. 73(1)) and by the legal representative in the case of a testamentary trust (s. 70(6.2)). The election makes the normal rules applicable, which will cause a deemed disposition at fair market value on the transfer of the property to the spouse trust (if inter vivos, under s. 69(1)(b); if testamentary, under s. 70(5)). The election would be advantageous if the settlor or the deceased

---

[7] For those tax consequences that do flow from the distinction, see Brown, "The Transfer of Property on Death" (1994) 42 Can. Tax J. 1449.

[8] In the case of depreciable property, the deemed disposition may also cause a recapture of capital cost allowance.

[9] In the case of depreciable property, the deemed proceeds of disposition is normally the undepreciated capital cost of the property (ss. 70(6), 73(1)).

[10] See ch. 15, Capital Gains, under heading 15.15, "Rollovers", above.

had capital losses or other deductions available to offset any capital gain caused by the deemed disposition, or if the property consisted of shares of a small business corporation or farming property qualifying for the lifetime $500,000 capital gains exemption.[11] The election would also be advantageous if the transferred property had declined in value and the settlor or the deceased could make use of a capital loss.[12]

The spouse trust enjoys another privilege with respect to capital gains. During the lifetime of the spouse, the spouse trust is exempt from the rules, discussed later,[13] which impose upon trusts generally a deemed disposition of all capital property every 21 years. In the case of a spouse trust, there is a deemed disposition on the death of the spouse, whether that occurs more or less than 21 years after the creation of the trust (ss. 104(4) and (5)). After the death of the spouse, if the trust continues (that is, if the property is not distributed to the capital beneficiaries), there will be a deemed disposition of all capital property every 21 years.

A spouse trust may be created either inter vivos or by will. It is defined in ss. 70(6)(b) and 73(1)(c) as a trust created by a taxpayer under which:

(i)   the taxpayer's spouse is entitled to receive all of the income of the trust that arises before the spouse's death, and

(ii)   no person except the spouse may, before the spouse's death, receive or otherwise obtain the use of any of the income or capital of the trust.

The simplest example of a spouse trust would arise if a settlor or testator transferred or bequeathed property to a trustee to hold upon trust for his wife for life, with remainder to his children. In this trust, only the wife is entitled to the income[14] from the property arising in her lifetime, and the children are not entitled to "the use of" the capital until the wife's death. If the trustee also had power to encroach on capital for the benefit of the wife, the trust would still qualify as a spouse trust. But if the trustee had power to allocate income or capital to anyone other than the spouse during the lifetime of the spouse, the existence of that power would "taint" the trust. A tainted trust is of course perfectly valid: it simply loses the benefit of the spouse trust's tax privileges.[15]

---

[11] *Id.*, under heading 15.4(d), "Lifetime exemption", above.

[12] In the case of transfers to a spouse (as opposed to a spouse trust), any capital loss would be deemed a "superficial loss" and would be disallowed (s. 40(2)(g)(i); "superficial loss" in s. 54): see ch. 18, Losses, under heading 18.2(c), "Superficial losses", above.

[13] Section 21.3(b), "Capital gains", below.

[14] The word "income" in the definition of a spouse trust in ss. 70(6) and 73(1) means income in the trust accounting sense, not the tax sense (s. 108(3)). It is not necessary, therefore, for the spouse to be entitled to capital gains: see also sec. 21.4(b), "Capital gains", below.

[15] On spouse trusts, see Cullity and Brown, note 1, above, 117-203, 401-405.

21.3 Income taxed to the trust

(a) Accumulating income

The rules governing the taxation of the income of trusts and their beneficiaries are to be found in subdivision k of Division B of Part I of the Income Tax Act (ss. 104-108). As noted earlier, the Act draws no distinction between a "trust" and an "estate": the term "trust" refers to both (s. 104(1)). For the purpose of subdivision k, it is immaterial whether a person who is administering property for others is doing so as a personal representative (executor or administrator) or as a trustee.

A trust is deemed to be an "individual" for income tax purposes (s. 104(2)); an individual is defined as a person other than a corporation (s. 248(1)). This means that a trust is taxed under the same rules as an individual taxpayer. However, a trust is an intermediary like a corporation, and it presents opportunities for tax avoidance. These facts have led to some changes in the general rules concerning the computation of income and the rates of tax.

The major change in the general rules, which will be explained more fully later, is that the trust is taxed only on income accumulating in the hands of the trustee. Income paid or payable to a beneficiary is generally taxed as income of the beneficiary, not the trust.[16] The same treatment is accorded to income which is subject to a preferred beneficiary election.[17]

(b) Capital gains

Capital gains earned by a trust are generally taxed to the trust in the same way as they are taxed to an individual, that is to say, dispositions of capital property by the trustee will produce capital gains (or losses) three-quarters of which are taxable (or allowable). However, in addition, s. 104(4) provides for a periodic deemed disposition at fair market value of all capital property held by a trust. For trusts other than spouse trusts, the deemed disposition occurs every 21 years. The 21-year periods are measured from the creation of the trust, or, in the case of trusts in existence at the beginning of 1972, from January 1, 1972 (ss. 104(4)(b) and (c)).[18] It is immaterial whether a particular capital property has

---

[16] The tax position of the beneficiary is discussed under sec. 21.4(a), "Income taxed to the beneficiary", below. The Act also contains an anomalous provision that enables income that is paid or payable to a beneficiary to be split between the trust and beneficiary: note 25, below.

[17] This election is discussed in detail under sec. 21.4(c), "Preferred beneficiary election", below.

[18] In 1991, subsections (5.3)–(5.7) were added to s. 104, which enabled a trust with at least one "exempt beneficiary" (a family member only one generation removed from the settlor, e.g., a child of the settlor) to elect to postpone the deemed disposition until the death of the exempt beneficiary. This election is not available after 1998 (s. 104(5.3)). Trusts which have made the election will have a deemed disposition on January 1, 1999 of any property they own on that date (s. 104(5.3)(a)(i)). It may be advantageous to distribute assets to beneficiaries on a tax-free basis in satisfaction of their capital interests before January 1, 1999 in order to defer the recognition of

been held for 21 years; the 21-year periods relate to the duration of the trust. Spouse trusts are not subject to these deemed dispositions during the lifetime of the spouse,[19] but there is a deemed disposition on the death of the spouse (s. 104(4)(a)) and (if the trust continues) every 21 years thereafter (ss. 104(4)(b) and (c)).

On the date of a particular trust's deemed disposition, all capital property held by the trust has to be given a "fair market value". The property is then deemed to have been disposed of and reacquired at fair market value (s. 104(4)), thereby forcing the trust to recognize for tax purposes all accrued capital gains and losses.[20]

The reason for the 21-year deemed realization is to preclude the indefinite deferral of capital gains (and recaptures) through the use of a long-term trust. An individual taxpayer can only defer capital gains for the period of his or her lifetime, because there is a deemed disposition of all capital property on death. A settlor who transfers capital property to a trust avoids that deemed disposition, but the trust will be subject to the 21-year deemed dispositions.

If a trust consists of portfolio investments which are being frequently changed, the 21-year deemed disposition will not have particularly serious tax consequences: the turnover of investments will result in the regular recognition of any capital gains and will keep the adjusted cost base of the trust property relatively up to date. But the 21-year deemed disposition would be very serious for a trust which held longstanding assets with substantial accrued gains. Where it is possible for a trust to last for longer than 21 years, it is often good practice to confer upon the trustees the power to distribute all or some of the assets at any time. This enables the trustees to avoid the 21-year deemed disposition by distributing appreciated capital property to the beneficiaries before the expiry of the 21-year period. As will be explained later,[21] a distribution of property to capital beneficiaries is a tax-free transaction.

---

accrued capital gains (s. 107(2), discussed under sec. 21.6, "Termination of trust", below).

[19] A trust created before 1972 cannot be a spouse trust (s. 104(4)(a)). Like other pre-1972 trusts, the pre-1972 spousal trust would therefore suffer a deemed disposition on January 1, 1993, regardless of when the spouse died. Because of this, in 1991, paragraph (a.1) was added to s. 104(4) to create a category of "pre-1972 spousal trusts". In the case of pre-1972 spousal trusts, if the spouse was still alive on January 1, 1993, then the 21-year deemed disposition is postponed until the death of the spouse. However, since a pre-1972 spousal trust is still not a spouse trust, it did not suffer a deemed disposition on the death of the spouse if the death occurred before January 1, 1993.

[20] In the case of depreciable property, the deemed disposition is required by s. 104(5), and of course it may also cause a recapture of capital cost allowances.

[21] Section 21.6, "Termination of trust", below.

(c)   Multiple trusts

Since a trust is taxed as an individual, an obvious measure of tax avoidance would be the creation of multiple trusts, each of which would be taxed at a low rate. However, the Act strikes at this form of income-splitting with a number of provisions which, cumulatively, are very effective.

First, s. 104(2) provides that, where there is a number of trusts in which:

(a)   substantially all the property of the various trusts has been received from one person, and

(b)   the various trusts are conditioned so that the income thereof accrues or will ultimately accrue to the same beneficiary, or group or class of beneficiaries,

the Minister has the power to lump all the trusts together and tax all of the income as the income of a single trust. In *Mitchell* v. *M.N.R.* (1956),[22] a way was found around this provision. The settlor in *Mitchell* had four children, and he created a separate trust for each of them. It was held that, because the beneficiary of each trust was different, s. 104(2) was inapplicable. After this decision, until the enactment in 1971 of the high, flat rate of tax on inter vivos trusts (described below), the use of separate trusts for children became a popular means of income-splitting.

A second measure against income-splitting is s. 122(1.1), which denies to a trust the personal credits allowed to individuals by s. 118 of the Act. The denial of these credits stops taxpayers from creating trusts in order to obtain the advantage of multiple personal credits.

A third measure against income-splitting is the attribution rules, which are discussed later in this chapter.[23]

The fourth, and most drastic, measure against income-splitting is s. 122, which imposes a high, flat rate of tax on post-1971 inter vivos trusts. It is discussed in the next section of this chapter. This provision, which was introduced in 1971 with effect from the budget date of June 18, 1971, has largely eliminated the income tax advantages of creating the separate trusts for children which had become popular after the *Mitchell* decision (described above).

(d)   Rates of tax

With respect to rates of tax, the general rule is derived from the premise that a trust is deemed to be an individual for tax purposes (s. 104(2)). This means that the trust will be taxed in accordance with the individual rate schedule of s. 117(2). Federal and provincial surtaxes will also apply.[24]

---

[22] (1956), 16 Tax A.B.C. 99, 56 D.T.C. 521 (T.A.B.). (Subsection 104(2) was s. 63(2) in the Act at that time.)

[23] Section 21.5, "Income taxed to the settlor", below.

[24] Chapter 5, Rates, above.

Section 122 creates an exception for inter vivos trusts created after June 18, 1971 (the budget date when the terms of the 1971 Act were officially announced). Section 122 imposes on these post-1971 inter vivos trusts a flat rate of federal tax of 29 per cent, which is the top rate in the individual rate schedule of s. 117(2). That rate has to be grossed-up by the applicable provincial rate in order to ascertain the combined federal-provincial rate, and the rate will be further increased by applicable federal and provincial surtaxes. In most provinces, the federal rate of 29 per cent grows to a combined rate of about 50 per cent. The purpose of the high rate, as previously noted, is to discourage income-splitting. The creation of an inter vivos trust to divert income away from the settlor cannot be advantageous with respect to income taxed to the trust, because the trust will be taxed at the same rate as that applicable to the top personal tax bracket.

Section 122 does not apply to testamentary trusts, presumably because these are operative only on the death of the settlor and are not effective vehicles for a living person to divert income to a lower-tax-paying entity. Of course, it would be possible for a living person to contribute property to a pre-existing testamentary trust. But the Act's definitions of "testamentary trust" and "inter vivos trust" (both definitions are in s. 108(1)) make clear that any inter vivos contribution of property to a testamentary trust (however small) will convert the trust into a deemed inter vivos trust for tax purposes. As an inter vivos trust, all of its income would become subject to the high, flat rate imposed by s. 122.

Section 122 does not have retrospective effect: it does not apply to inter vivos trusts created before June 18, 1971. However, these pre-1972 inter vivos trusts avoid the minimum rate only so long as they continue to satisfy a set of stipulations in s. 122(2), of which the most important is that the trust "has not received any property by way of gift since June 18, 1971". Any gift to a pre-1972 inter vivos trust will therefore "contaminate" it. This result cannot be avoided by the time-honoured device of a sale in return for a promissory note, because another of the criteria of s. 122(2) is that the trust has not since June 18, 1971 incurred a debt to a non-arm's length person. Even a gift by will after June 18, 1971 will contaminate a pre-1972 inter vivos trust. Thus, a "pour-over" provision in a will (which gives property to a pre-existing inter vivos trust) is treated entirely differently from a trust created by will: a pour-over trust is subject to s. 122's flat rate, whereas a testamentary trust is not.

21.4　Income taxed to the beneficiary

(a)　Income paid or payable in the year

Paragraph 104(6)(b) provides that income which is "payable" to a beneficiary in a taxation year may be deducted from the income of the trust for tax purposes.[25] Subsection 104(13) provides that the income must be included in the income of the beneficiary to whom it was payable. According to s. 104(24), income is "payable in a taxation year" to a beneficiary if it was "paid in the year" to the beneficiary, or, if, although it was not actually paid, the beneficiary "was entitled in that year to enforce payment thereof". According to s. 104(18), if a beneficiary is an infant or minor (who cannot under the general law give a trustee a valid receipt), and cannot enforce payment solely for that reason, the income is still deemed to be "payable" to the beneficiary.

Where the trustee has no discretion as to the payment of income, that income will automatically be "payable" to the income beneficiary as soon as it is earned by the trust. Where the trustee has a discretion as to whether or not to pay income to a particular beneficiary, the best way to make sure that the income is payable to the beneficiary is for the trustee to exercise the discretion and pay the income to the beneficiary before the end of the year. If the actual payment cannot be made before the end of the year, the next best thing is for the trustee to make sure that the beneficiary has become entitled to enforce the payment. This could be done by signing a written resolution before the end of the year, resolving to pay the desired amount, and issuing a demand promissory note to the beneficiary (or, preferably, paying the amount), as soon as it can be quantified.

When income is payable to a beneficiary, the deduction under s. 104(6)(b) and the inclusion under s. 106(13) will divert the income from the trust to the beneficiary for tax purposes. The only income that is taxed to the trust, as opposed to the beneficiary, is income that is earned by the trust in a taxation year and is not paid or payable in the year to a beneficiary.[26]

(b) Capital gains

The tax treatment of capital gains will often reflect a difference between the concept of income for tax purposes and the concept of income for trust accounting purposes. Taxable capital gains are of course income for tax purposes, but they are capital for trust accounting purposes (unless the trust instrument

---

[25] Paragraph 104(6)(b) was amended in 1988 to give to a trust the discretion to deduct less than the full amount that was paid or payable to a beneficiary ("such amount as the trust claims"), and there is a mechanism for excluding the undeducted amount from the beneficiary's income (ss. 104(13.1) and (13.2)). The purpose of the amendment seems to have been to allow a trust to take advantage of losses, but the discretion is entirely unlimited. It does provide an opportunity to split income between the trust and the beneficiary, which could be advantageous in the case of a testamentary trust or pre-1972 inter vivos trust that is in a lower tax bracket than that of the beneficiary. For discussion, see Goodman, "Some Trust Law Problems resulting from the 1988 Amendments to the Income Tax Act" (1989) 37 *Can. Tax J.* 660, 663-671.

[26] Income that is subject to a preferred beneficiary election is also not taxed to the trust. This election, which is available in limited circumstances, is discussed under sec. 21.4(c), "Preferred beneficiary election", below.

provides otherwise). Accordingly, capital gains which are earned by a trust will not normally be payable to the income beneficiary of the trust, but will be added to the capital of the trust. Even if all of a trust's income (for trust accounting purposes) is payable each year to an income beneficiary, capital gains will not be payable to the income beneficiary. Capital gains will ultimately be payable to the capital beneficiary, but not until the time comes to distribute the capital of the trust. It follows that capital gains earned by a trust in a taxation year will often not be payable to a beneficiary in the year and will therefore be treated for tax purposes as accumulating income of the trust. If so, the trust will be obliged to report the capital gains as its income.

(c)   Preferred beneficiary election

The only trust income which is actually taxed as the income of the trust (as opposed to a beneficiary) is income which is not paid or payable in the taxation year to a beneficiary. Until 1996, even with respect to this income however, a "preferred beneficiary election" used to be available which if exercised would allocate the accumulating income to the beneficiary for tax purposes, even though the beneficiary was not entitled to receive the income until the period of accumulation had ended (ss. 104(12), (14)). This election was available to trusts with "preferred beneficiaries", who were defined as the settlor of the trust, the spouse of the settlor, and the child, grandchild or great grandchild of the settlor or the spouse of any such person (s. 108). The election allowed trust income which had not in fact been distributed to be split among family members (including minors) for income tax purposes.

In 1996, the preferred beneficiary election was severely restricted. For trust taxation years commencing in 1996, the preferred beneficiary election could only be made for a beneficiary who met the eligibility criteria for the credit for mental or physical impairment provided in ss. 118.3(1)(a) and (b). For taxation years commencing after 1996, the February 18, 1997 budget proposes also to allow a preferred beneficiary election to be made in respect of a beneficiary who is a person who is 18 years of age or older and is dependent on another individual because of a mental or physical infirmity (and is therefore eligible to be claimed as a dependant under s. 118(1)(d)). The criteria that an individual must meet to be eligible under s. 118(1)(d) are far less onerous than those outlined in s. 118.3.[27] Apart from these two exceptions, the effect of the change is that accumulating trust income can no longer be diverted to beneficiaries for

---

[27] Compare Revenue Canada's position regarding s. 118(1)(d), as outlined in Interpretation Bulletin IT-513, "Personal Tax Credits" (1989), para. 33, to the criteria set out in s. 118.3(1)(a) and (b).

tax purposes.[28] Only if the income is paid or payable to the beneficiaries will it be taxed to the beneficiaries.

(d) Ancillary conduit provisions

The Income Tax Act gives different tax treatment to income from different sources. When a beneficiary reports income from a trust, because it was paid or payable to the beneficiary, the general rule is that the income must be reported as income from property under subdivision b of Division B of Part I of the Act (s. 12(1)(m)). This is the general rule, laid down by s. 108(5)(a), and it means that income derived by a trust from a variety of sources loses its differentiated character when it flows through to the beneficiaries.

The general rule is subject to important exceptions, where the Act stipulates that income flowing through a trust retains its character in the hands of the beneficiary. The most important of these "ancillary conduit provisions" are as follows. Subsections 104(19) and (20) permit corporate dividends received by the trust to retain that character when reported by a beneficiary; this enables the beneficiary to take advantage of the Act's preferential treatment of dividend income. Subsections 104(21) and (21.2) permit capital gains received by the trust to retain that character when reported by a beneficiary; this enables the beneficiary to take advantage of the Act's preferential treatment of capital gains. Subsections 104(22) and (22.1) permit foreign-source income received by the trust to retain that character when reported by a beneficiary; this enables the beneficiary to claim the foreign tax credit.

(e) Tax-free payments to beneficiaries

A beneficiary may become liable to pay tax on income which has been retained in the trust and which he or she has not received for two reasons: (1) because it was "payable" to him or her in the year but was not actually paid (s. 104(6)); or (2) because, although it was not payable to him or her in the year, it was the subject of a preferred beneficiary election (s. 104(14)). In both cases, when the income is subsequently paid out, it is not taxable to the recipient in the year of payment, because tax on the income has already been paid (ss. 104(13), (14)). It should be noted that the ultimate recipient of the income will not necessarily be the beneficiary who paid the tax on the income when it was accumulating. That beneficiary may have died, or become disqualified for some other reason; but in these cases the subsequent distribution is still free of tax.

---

[28] The presence of the exception presumably means that all the complex law respecting preferred beneficiary elections will be preserved. The main complexities turn on the definition of a "preferred beneficiary" (s. 108), which depends upon a relationship with a "settlor" (s. 108), and the definition of the "share" of the accumulating income of each preferred beneficiary (s. 104(15)). For discussion, see Cullity and Brown, note 1, above, 347-354, 6-8.

Income which has been retained in the trust and which is neither payable in the year to a beneficiary nor the subject of a preferred beneficiary election will of course be taxed as income of the trust and not of any beneficiary. When this income is subsequently paid to a beneficiary, it too should not be taxable to the beneficiary because tax on the income has already been paid. Curiously, the Act does not expressly say this, but it is clear that the subsequent distribution to the beneficiary is free of tax.

21.5 Income taxed to the settlor

(a)   Trusts for spouses or related minors

Section 74.1 of the Income Tax Act provides that when property is transferred (or loaned) to a spouse of the transferor, or to a related minor (person under 18 who is related to the transferor as a child or other descendant, brother or sister, niece or nephew), the income from the property is deemed for tax purposes to be the income of the transferor and not the transferee. Section 74.2 provides that when property is transferred (or loaned) to a spouse of the transferor, any capital gain or loss on the disposition of the property by the transferee is deemed to be a capital gain or loss of the transferor and not of the transferee. These "attribution rules", as they are called, have already been examined in chapter 7, Taxation Unit, above.[29] The purpose of the rules is to preclude income-splitting among members of a family. The rules expressly apply to transfers (or loans) to a spouse or related minor "by means of a trust".[30]

Where a person transfers (or loans) property to a trust, and the income from the property is payable by the trust to the transferor's spouse, or to a related minor, then the income will be attributed to the transferor. This result is produced by s. 74.1(1) (in the case of the spouse) and s. 74.1(2) (in the case of the minor). If the transferred property is disposed of by the trust, and if any capital gain is payable to the transferor's spouse, then the capital gain will be attributed to the transferor. This result is produced by s. 74.2(1). Note that s. 74.2 applies only to spouses: there is no attribution of capital gains on a transfer to a related minor.

Where payments of income from transferred property, or capital gains from transferred property, are made to a spouse or related minor (in the case of income only), in the exercise of a discretion conferred upon the trustee by the trust instrument, attribution will still apply. Payments made pursuant to a

---

[29] Under heading 7.5, "Attribution rules", above.

[30] See also s. 74.5(9). Section 74.3, which was added in 1985, applies to transfers and loans to trusts, and provides a formula for calculating what amount of income is attributed to whom in the circumstance where a trust has received property from more than one individual or where a trust has distributed income to several beneficiaries not all of whom are a spouse or related minor to whom attribution would apply.

discretion attract the same attribution consequences as payments made pursuant to a duty.[31]

Income accumulating in a trust for the ultimate benefit of a spouse or related minor is not subject to attribution. This was decided in *Pichosky* v. *M.N.R.* (1964).[32] The reasoning of the case was that the rules only apply to income that would otherwise be taxable to a spouse or related minor. Since income accumulating in a trust is taxed to the trust, not to the beneficiaries, the attribution rules do not apply.[33] The fact that income accumulating in a trust is exempt from attribution will not produce any tax savings, at least if the trust was created or added to after June 18, 1971. It will be recalled that post-1971 inter vivos trusts are subject to a flat rate of tax equal to the top personal marginal rate (s. 122).[34] Testamentary trusts are not subject to the flat rate of tax, but there is no attribution of income of testamentary trusts in any event, because the transferor of the trust property is deceased, and attribution ceases with the death of the transferor.

Before 1985, a trust funded by a loan escaped the attribution rules. At that time, the attribution rules applied only to a "transfer" of property, and it was decided in *Dunkelman* v. *M.N.R.* (1959)[35] that a loan was not a transfer. The attribution rules were revised in 1985, and ss. 74.1 and 74.2 now expressly apply to a loan as well as a transfer. Subsection 74.5(2) exempts a loan at a commercial rate of interest upon which interest is in fact regularly paid.[36] Thus, the pre-1985 practice of settling a trust with a nominal amount (which was never invested to earn income) and providing the bulk of the funding in the form of an interest-free loan payable on demand will no longer avoid the attribution rules. Of course, there will sometimes be a non-tax reason for a settlor to fund a trust at least in part by a loan payable on demand. The loan gives to the settlor (in his

---

[31] So held in *Murphy* v. *M.N.R.*, [1980] C.T.C. 386, 80 D.T.C. 6314 (F.C.T.D.), a result that is confirmed by s. 74.3 (previous note), which yields an amount to be attributed in this situation.

[32] [1964] C.T.C. 177, 64 D.T.C. 5105 (Ex. Ct.).

[33] This reasoning is far from compelling, but the result is confirmed by s. 74.3 (note 30, above), which yields a nil figure for the amount to be attributed when income or capital gains from transferred property are being accumulated in the trust. However, accumulating income that is allocated to a spouse or related minor by a preferred beneficiary election is attributed: *Sachs* v. *The Queen*, [1980] C.T.C. 358, 80 D.T.C. 6291 (F.C.A.); this result is confirmed by s. 74.3, which yields an amount to be attributed in this situation.

[34] Section 21.3(d), "Rates of tax", above.

[35] [1959] C.T.C. 375, 59 D.T.C. 1242 (Ex. Ct.).

[36] Subsection 74.5(2) requires the interest rate to be no less than Revenue Canada's "prescribed rate" (which is set quarterly under reg. 4301, based on the average yield of 90-day treasury bonds during the first month of the previous quarter) or the market rate of interest (whichever was lower at the time the loan was made); and that the interest actually be paid by the borrower every year within 30 days of the end of the year.

or her capacity as creditor) the power to withdraw the funds if he or she should need them later in life.

(b)   Trusts with reserved power of revocation or control

Subsection 75(2) of the Income Tax Act provides as follows:

> 75(2) Where, by a trust created in any manner whatever since 1934, property is held on condition
>
> (a)   that it or property substituted therefor may
>
>   (i)   revert to the person from whom the property or property for which it was substituted was directly or indirectly received (in this subsection referred to as "the person"), or
>
>   (ii)   pass to persons to be determined by the person at a time subsequent to the creation of the trust, or
>
> (b)   that, during the lifetime of the person, the property shall not be disposed of except with the person's consent or in accordance with the person's direction,
>
> any income or loss from the property or from property substituted therefor, any taxable capital gain or allowable capital loss from the disposition of the property or of property substituted therefor, shall, during the lifetime of the person while the person is resident in Canada be deemed to be income or a loss, as the case may be, or a taxable capital gain or allowable capital loss, as the case may be, of such person.

Subsection 75(2) is, of course, another of the attribution provisions.[37] Its scope is quite unclear and it has rarely been litigated.[38]

A point which is perfectly clear is that s. 75(2) will operate to attribute income from a trust in which the settlor has reserved to himself or herself a power to revoke the trust, or a power to change the beneficiaries, or a power to direct or veto dispositions of the trust property, or a reversionary interest in the trust property. Thus, the section operates as a powerful disincentive to the creation of revocable trusts or trusts in which the settlor retains substantial control. What is not clear is whether the section will apply to the income of a trust of which the settlor is a trustee. In that situation, the settlor in his or her capacity as trustee would possess controls over the trust of the kind contemplated by the section. It is obviously prudent to avoid creating a trust in which the settlor is the sole trustee. Indeed, even if the settlor is just one of several trustees,

---

[37] It is also important to note that the general rule that property is transferred on a tax-free basis to a beneficiary in satisfaction of his or her capital interest in a trust (s. 107(2), discussed under sec. 21.6, below) will not apply if s. 75(2) was applicable at any time to any property of the trust (s. 107(4.1)(a)). Instead, the transfer will take place at the property's fair market value in cases where (1) the property is distributed to a beneficiary who is neither a contributor of the particular property to the trust or his or her spouse (s. 107(4.1)(b)) and (2) the contributor of the particular property is still alive (s. 107(4.1)(c)).

[38] For discussion, see Cullity and Brown, note 1, above, 664-668. In private technical interpretations, Revenue Canada has indicated that it interprets s. 75(2) very broadly: See Saunders, "Inter Vivos Discretionary Family Trusts: A Potpourri of Issues and Traps", note 1, above, at 37:6-14.

if the trustees' decisions must be unanimous, there is a risk that s. 75(2) would apply. In the common case where the settlor does want to be a trustee, it is good practice to have two additional persons as trustees and for the three trustees to be empowered to act by a majority.

Where a settlor has funded a trust, in whole or in part, by loan, and the loan is secured by a promissory note payable on demand, the settlor's ownership of the note gives him or her a power over the trust that is akin to a power of revocation. Since this power is derived from the settlor's position as creditor, rather than from the trust instrument, it is probable that s. 75(2) does not apply, although no case has considered the point.

21.6 Termination of trust

A trust is brought to an end by the distribution of its property to the beneficiaries. In many cases, in order to make an equitable distribution, it will be necessary to realize some or all of the trust property. Any such sales will of course be dispositions which may give rise to taxable capital gains or allowable capital losses. These gains or losses will be brought into the income of the trust, unless they are paid or payable to a beneficiary in the year, as they may well be, if the realization was for purposes of distribution. Where taxable capital gains (or losses), are paid or payable in the year to a beneficiary, then they are brought into the income of the beneficiary who is entitled to payment. It will be recalled that, while capital gains are income for tax purposes, they will normally be capital for trust accounting purposes, so that they will be brought into the income for tax purposes of the capital beneficiary of the trust, not the income beneficiary.

When property is transferred in specie out of a trust in satisfaction of an *income* interest, that is, to a beneficiary who is an income beneficiary for trust accounting purposes, s. 106(3) provides that the trust is deemed to have disposed of the property at its fair market value. A distribution of property in satisfaction of an income interest is not a common occurrence, but it may occur if a trust is brought to an end prematurely. It would occur, for example, if a trust were terminated during the life of the life tenant (income beneficiary), and the capital property of the trust were divided in specie between the life tenant and remainderman (capital beneficiary) in proportion to the values of their interests. The property which is distributed to the income beneficiary in satisfaction of his or her interest will be deemed to have been realized at fair market value, which will force recognition of any accrued capital gain (or loss).[39] Is the deemed

---

[39] On a sale by an income beneficiary of his or her income interest in the trust, s. 106(2)(a) requires the vendor to bring the entire proceeds of the disposition into income. But s. 106(3) is expressly exempted from the operation of s. 106(2)(a). Under s. 106(3), when the income beneficiary gives up his or her interest to the trust in return for trust property, the income beneficiary is not required to bring into income the value of the trust property received. The only tax consequence to the

income of s. 106(3) taxable to the trust or to the person to whom the property
has been distributed? The gain has, of course, been transferred in specie to the
beneficiary. Does that mean that it has been "paid" to the beneficiary (s.
104(24)), and is therefore deductible by the trust (s. 104(6)), and includible in
the beneficiary's income (s. 104(13))? Probably the answer to this question is
yes, although the position is not clear.[40]

When property is transferred in specie out of a trust[41] in satisfaction of
a *capital* interest, that is, to a beneficiary who is a capital beneficiary for trust
accounting purposes, s. 107(2)(a) provides that the trust shall be deemed to have
disposed of the property for proceeds equal to its "cost amount" to the trust. The
cost amount of properties of various kinds is defined in s. 248(1). In the case of
capital property other than depreciable property, the cost amount is the adjusted
cost base of the property. (In the case of depreciable property, the cost amount
is the undepreciated capital cost.) The effect of s. 107(2), therefore, is that the
property rolls out of the trust to the capital beneficiary. The trust recognizes no
capital gain or loss (and no recapture or terminal loss) on the distribution.

The beneficiary to whom the distribution is made is deemed by s.
107(2)(b) to acquire the property at its cost amount to the trust, plus an
additional amount defined by s. 107(2)(b). In the usual case where the
beneficiary acquired his or her interest in the trust for a cost of nil on the
original creation of the trust (see s. 107(1.1)), then the additional amount will be
inapplicable, and the beneficiary will acquire the property at its cost amount to
the trust. The additional amount stipulated by s. 107(2)(b) applies only in those
cases where the beneficiary purchased the interest from a former beneficiary or
inherited the interest on the death of a former beneficiary.[42] In those cases, the
beneficiary's interest in the trust will have an adjusted cost base, namely, the

---

income beneficiary may be the recognition of any capital gain (or loss) accrued on the trust
property received by him or her. This is discussed in the following text.

[40] The same question arises in respect of the deemed income created by s. 104(4)(a) (death of spouse
in spouse trust) and s. 107(4) (distribution of spouse trust property to someone other than spouse),
but in these two cases the flow-through to the beneficiary is specifically denied by s. 104(6)(b),
which however makes no reference to s. 106(3).

[41] Subsection 107(2) was amended in 1988 to apply only to a "personal trust" and a "prescribed
trust". A personal trust is defined in s. 248(1) as (a) a testamentary trust or (b) an inter vivos trust
in which the beneficiaries did not purchase their interests from the trust or from anyone who had
made a contribution to the trust. The definition will catch ordinary family trusts, and will exclude
many commercial trusts. A prescribed trust is defined in reg. 4800.1 as one that falls within three
categories: (1) a trust to hold employer shares; (2) a trust to secure debts; and (3) a voting trust.
A trust that is neither a personal trust nor a prescribed trust suffers a deemed disposition at fair
market value when property is distributed to a beneficiary in satisfaction of a capital interest (s.
107(2.1)).

[42] Neither of these circumstances would cause the trust to lose its character as a "personal trust"
(previous note), because the beneficiary would not have bought the beneficial interest from the
trust or from anyone who had made a contribution to the trust.

price for which it was purchased, or (under s. 70(5)) the fair market value at the time it was inherited; and that adjusted cost base could be higher than the cost amount to the trust. In that case, the net effect of s. 107(2)(b) is to step up the cost amount of the property distributed to the beneficiary to the price he or she paid for the purchased capital interest or was deemed to pay for the inherited capital interest. Without this step-up there would be an element of double taxation when the beneficiary later disposed of the property.

The roll-out which is available under s. 107(2) provides a powerful tax incentive for trustees to distribute capital property to the beneficiaries in specie. That way, recognition of accrued capital gains is deferred until the beneficiary disposes of the property. However, if the trust directs a distribution among several beneficiaries in equal (or otherwise defined) shares, it may not be possible to accomplish that result by a specie distribution. Even when assets can be distributed in specie in accordance with the trust instrument, there may be difficulties in equalizing the shares of the beneficiaries since the adjusted cost base of each asset will have to be considered as well as its fair market value.

Take the case of a trust which at the time for distribution has two capital beneficiaries, both equally entitled, and two properties, Blackacre and Whiteacre, both of equal value. This looks like an easy case for a specie distribution. But now suppose that Blackacre, with a fair market value of $100,000, has an adjusted cost base of $40,000, and Whiteacre, also with a fair market value of $100,000, has an adjusted cost base of $90,000. In that case, the recipient of Blackacre faces a much larger future capital gain than does the recipient of Whiteacre. Even if the trust also has some cash to make an equalizing payment to the recipient of Blackacre, it will not be obvious how much that payment should be, because it will not be obvious what is the present value of the future tax liabilities inherent in the two properties. Unless agreement can be reached with the two beneficiaries, and releases obtained from them, a specie distribution in this situation is unsafe from the point of view of the trustees, who could be liable for a failure in their duty to make an "equal" distribution. The trustees can avoid these headaches by selling the trust assets and making an equal distribution in cash. If they do that, however, the disposition of capital property by the trustees will require the immediate recognition of any accrued capital gains so that the tax postponement allowed by s. 107(2) will be lost.

The roll-out under s. 107(2) on the distribution in specie of trust assets applies to a spouse trust as well as to a non-spouse trust. (There is one exception to this proposition, discussed in the next paragraph.) However, it will be recalled that, in the case of a spouse trust, s. 104(4)(a) imposes a deemed disposition of all capital property on the death of the spouse. If the assets of the spouse trust are distributed soon after the death of the spouse (which would commonly occur), the spouse trust will not benefit from the s. 107(2) roll-out: its capital property will have so recently suffered the deemed disposition under s. 104(4)(a) on the death of the spouse that the property is unlikely to have any accrued capital gains. Of course, if there is a substantial lapse of time between the death of the spouse and the termination of the trust, then the trust's capital property might well have accrued gains, and the s. 107(2) roll-out would be a benefit, enabling the recognition of those gains to be deferred.

The roll-out on the distribution in specie of trust assets does not apply to a spouse trust in one exceptional situation. If a spouse trust is terminated prematurely in the spouse's lifetime, and if capital property is distributed to someone other than the spouse, then s. 107(4) provides that there is a deemed disposition of the capital property for proceeds equal to the fair market value of the property. This provision is necessary, because otherwise a spouse trust could be terminated prematurely in order to avoid the deemed disposition under s. 104(4)(a) on the death of the spouse. The deemed disposition under s. 107(4) on premature termination applies only to property distributed to beneficiaries other than the spouse, because any property distributed to the spouse will suffer a deemed disposition under s. 70(5) on his or her death. As well, any property distributed to the spouse in satisfaction of his or her income interest will suffer an immediate deemed disposition under s. 106(3).

21.7 Tax planning with trusts

(a) Reasons for creating trusts

The majority of family trusts, especially testamentary trusts, are created for reasons that have nothing to do with tax. Some of those reasons are:

- management is separated from enjoyment, which enables the settlor to appoint an experienced trustee to manage property for beneficiaries who may be too young or otherwise incapable of managing the trust property;

- control over the settlor's property can be projected over two or more generations by the creation of a life interest (or interests) followed by remainder interests;

- beneficial interests can be created for minors, or persons not yet born (such as future grandchildren), or persons not yet ascertained (such as future spouses of unmarried children or grandchildren);

- beneficial interests can be made subject to postponed vesting so that interests do not vest until the holder has reached a stipulated age; and

- the trustee can be given discretion with respect to distributions of income and capital so that the future circumstances of the beneficiaries can be taken into account.

Tax considerations are still important for trusts that are created for non-tax reasons, because the settlor or testator will want to steer clear of as many as possible of the tax disadvantages that the Income Tax Act now visits on trusts. Where there are tax advantages to be gained, the settlor or testator will want to consider them, and decide whether any tax-driven suggestions for the structure of the trust are compatible with the non-tax objectives. In some cases, a trust is created primarily for a tax reason, which is usually to accomplish the splitting of income among children or other relatives of the settlor. The rest of this chapter will try and draw together some of the previously described tax doctrine that is relevant to planning the creation of a trust.

(b) Planning a trust

An initial disadvantage of the trust is that there are no general rollover provisions to facilitate its creation. The formation of corporations and partnerships is addressed by provisions that enable capital property to be rolled into the new organization without tax cost. In the case of trusts, only the spouse trust has the benefit of a rollover on its creation. In many cases, a spouse trust will not fit the settlor's non-tax objectives. If it does fit, in order to take advantage of the spousal rollover, care must be taken not to taint the trust, for example, by creating a power of encroachment in favour of persons other than the spouse. The rollover is available to both an inter vivos and a testamentary spouse trust (ss. 70(6), 73(1)).

Another disadvantage of the trust, again in comparison with a corporation or partnership, is that the trust suffers a deemed disposition at fair market value of all of its capital property every 21 years (s. 104(4)). The only way to escape from the deemed disposition is to distribute the trust's property to the capital beneficiaries (taking advantage of the s. 107(2) rollover on distribution) before the 21-year period has expired. This cannot be done if the trust does not authorize such a distribution, and so consideration should be given to including in a trust that may last for 21 years a power in the trustees to terminate the trust within 21 years.

The spouse trust is exempt from the 21-year deemed disposition during the lifetime of the spouse, but the spouse trust suffers a deemed disposition on the death of the spouse, which may occur before the 21-year period has expired. Moreover, the deemed disposition on the death of the spouse cannot be avoided by an early termination of the trust, because a distribution to anyone other than the spouse during the lifetime of the spouse gives rise to a deemed disposition at fair market value (s. 107(4)).

In order to preclude the use of a trust to split income, a post-1971 inter vivos trust is taxed at the top individual rate regardless of the amount of its income (s. 122). However, income that is paid or payable to the beneficiaries is washed out of the trust and is taxed in the hands of the beneficiaries (ss. 104(6), (13)). This does offer some opportunities for income splitting if the income beneficiaries are adult children of the settlor or are unrelated to the settlor. Payments of income to a spouse (who must be the income beneficiary of a spouse trust) or a related minor trigger the attribution rules of s. 74.1 and result in the income being attributed back to the settlor. Payments of capital gains to a spouse (but not to a related minor) also attract attribution (s. 74.2). From a tax standpoint, it is desirable that income be payable to persons who will not attract the attribution rules (such as adult children); that there be a power to pay out capital gains (to persons other than the spouse) as well as ordinary income (so that capital gains are not taxed in the trust); and that the trustees have a discretion as to whom to pay income (so that tax considerations as well as non-tax considerations can be taken into account). However, these kinds of powers cannot be included in a spouse trust without tainting it, and they may be inconsistent with the settlor's non-tax objectives (which may include providing for a spouse or minor children).

A testamentary trust offers more potential for income splitting. The trust is taxed at the graduated rates that are applicable to individuals, so that capital gains or other income accumulating in the trust is not taxed at a high rate (unless there is a lot of accumulating income). If the testator wishes to postpone payments of income to children (for example), a separate trust could be set up for each child, and each trust would be taxed on its accumulating income as a separate individual.[43] Income that is paid or payable to beneficiaries is taxed in the hands of the beneficiaries.[44] Because the donor of the property is deceased, there is no attribution; therefore, payments to spouses and related minors are taxed in their hands.

(c) Role of trust in estate freeze

An inter vivos trust is usually one element of an "estate freeze", which is a tax-driven transaction designed to "freeze" accruing capital gains on "growth assets", and transfer the future growth of the assets to the next generation. The simplest case, which will be described in the text that follows, is that of the settlor who owns all of the common shares of a small business corporation (a Canadian-controlled private corporation, with all or substantially all of its assets employed in an active business: definition in s. 248). The settlor is concerned about the tax liability on the capital gains that have already accrued on his shares, and about the liability on the capital gains that (he hopes) will accrue in the future. An estate freeze may be attractive to him.

The freeze can be carried out in a variety of ways. The simplest type is accomplished by the settlor causing the corporation (which he controls) to undergo a reorganization under which the settlor's common shares would be exchanged for preference shares and new common shares would be issued to the settlor's children (and/or other relatives). The preference shares that would be issued to the settlor would possess the following characteristics:

---

[43] *Mitchell* v. *M.N.R.* (1956), note 22, above.

[44] Income that is paid or payable to beneficiaries can be split between the trust and the beneficiaries: note 25, above.

- the shares would be fixed at their face value; they would not be entitled to share in any surplus assets if the corporation were wound up;

- the shares would not be entitled to dividends in priority to the common shares; the directors would have the power to declare dividends on the common shares and not the preference shares;

- the shares would be retractable (redeemable at the option of the holder), so that they are worth their full face value even though they will not necessarily receive dividends; and

- the shares would carry voting rights so that the settlor retains legal control of the corporation (in addition to the de facto control conferred by the right to require redemption of the shares).

The corporation would issue new common shares, which would be entitled to any surplus assets on the winding up of the corporation. However, the new common shares would not carry voting rights. The new common shares could be issued to the settlor's children (and/or other relatives). Because the face value of the settlor's preference shares will represent the entire value of the corporation (the fair market value of the common shares for which the preference shares were exchanged), the common shares have no value at the time of the reorganization, and they can be issued for a nominal consideration. The subscribers for the common shares should themselves supply the consideration for their shares. The settlor must not supply the consideration for any shares purchased by a spouse or related minor, because this would cause the attribution rules to apply to future dividends and (in the case of a spouse only) future capital gains (ss. 74.1, 74.2).

This reorganization of the company is known as a freeze, because the settlor's interest in the company is frozen at its value at the date of the freeze. Because the settlor's preference shares are fixed in value, it is the common shares that will increase in value if the company's business increases in value. This means that the settlor knows that his capital gains are limited to the amount of his capital gains on the common shares that he exchanged for the preference shares. He need not recognize the gains at the time of the freeze, because a s. 86 rollover is available to shelter the share exchange. But, having frozen his capital gains, he is in a good position to plan for the tax liability that will need to be paid when his death will cause a deemed disposition at fair market value of the preference shares that (under s. 86) are sheltering the gains. For example, the settlor might purchase life insurance to fund the future tax liability.

The simplest form of estate freeze (as described above) need not make use of a trust. But, in many cases, the settlor will prefer the post-freeze common shares to be held by a trust for his children (and/or other relatives). If the settlor wishes to benefit minors, or persons not yet born (such as future grandchildren), or persons not yet ascertained (such as the spouses of children or grandchildren not yet married), or if the settlor wishes to create some discretion as to who receives income and how much, then a trust is required. In that case, it will be the trust that subscribes for the post-freeze common shares, borrowing the small sum ($10 or $50 would be usual) that would be required. If the trust borrows the money from the settlor, the loan must be made at a commercial rate of interest and the interest must in fact be regularly paid in accordance with the rules of s. 74.5(2) (so as to prevent the application of the attribution rules). The small loan would be repaid, with interest, as soon as the corporation pays a dividend on the common shares. Apart from the retirement of the loan, when the corporation pays dividends on the common shares held by the trust, the income is available for distribution to the beneficiaries. If the income is distributed, and if the beneficiaries have little or no other income, there will be substantial tax savings in comparison to the income all being received by the settlor.[45]

With respect to the future growth of the corporation, the effect of the freeze is to cause all future growth to be reflected in the value of the common shares that are held by the trust. If the trust were to suffer the 21-year deemed disposition after the shares had appreciated substantially in value, the taxable capital gains would be taxed at the top personal rate (because the trust is a post-1971 inter vivos trust) and the lifetime capital gains exemption of $500,000 for the shares of a small business corporation would be unavailable (because the exemption is not available to a trust). But to the extent that the common shares of the trust are distributed in specie to the beneficiaries before the 21st anniversary of the trust, the 21-year deemed disposition will be avoided. If the common shares have been distributed before the 21st anniversary of the trust, the taxable capital gains will not have to be recognized until the individual beneficiaries dispose of the shares. When the taxable capital gains do have to be recognized, it will be in the hands of the individual beneficiaries, each of whom is entitled to the $500,000 lifetime exemption. The settlor himself is also entitled to the $500,000 lifetime exemption, and he may decide to recognize the accrued capital gains at the time of the freeze if he has room in his lifetime exemption to shelter the gain.[46] The effect of the freeze is to multiply the lifetime exemptions that are available to shelter future capital gains.

---

[45] Because the income paid to the beneficiaries is dividend income, the beneficiaries will be entitled to the gross-up and credit by virtue of the ancillary conduit rule of s. 104(19). An individual with no other income can receive approximately $23,000 of dividend income before becoming liable to pay any tax. (There is an exemption of $40,000 for the alternative minimum tax.)

[46] To do this, the settlor and the corporation would jointly elect under s. 85(1) to transfer the settlor's common shares of the corporation to the corporation (in exchange for new preference shares of the corporation) at a price which is sufficient to trigger capital gains of $500,000 in the settlor's hands. If such an election is made, the automatic s. 86 rollover rules will not apply.

22

Avoidance

22.1 Tax evasion

Tax "avoidance" must be distinguished from tax "evasion". Evasion involves a deliberate breach of the Income Tax Act, for example, by failing to file a return, or by failing to report all taxable income, or by deducting non-existent expenses, or by concealing or falsifying other relevant information. Evasion is illegal, and is subject to both civil and criminal penalties under the

Act. The process of audit, investigation, search, seizure and prosecution have been described in an earlier chapter.[1]

22.2 Tax avoidance

Avoidance differs from evasion in that it is legal. It does not involve fraud, concealment or any other illegal measure. What it does involve is the ordering of one's affairs in such a way as to reduce the tax that would otherwise be payable. Avoidance presupposes that the taxpayer has a choice as to the ordering of his or her affairs, and the taxpayer chooses the course that would minimize tax liability. Where the course of tax-minimization is taken for predominantly personal or business reasons, with tax-saving only a subsidiary consideration, then the taxpayer's action can hardly be objected to; and, indeed, it may not be appropriate to describe it as "avoidance" at all. Thus, a taxpayer may accomplish both the deferral of some tax and the splitting of some income by transferring his or her business to a corporation in which he or she and members of his or her family are the controlling shareholders and employees. Where this offers commercial or personal advantages, as well as the tax savings, it is difficult to see upon what basis the move could possibly be criticized.

Where the taxpayer orders his or her affairs primarily to avoid or reduce tax, then there is a true case of tax avoidance. Even here, however, the morality of the case depends upon the circumstances. A person with sufficient investment income may stop work in order to avoid paying tax on the extra income. Or, alternatively, he or she may continue to work, but give the investments away to adult children or their families. People who deliberately choose leisure instead of work, or divest themselves of income-producing assets, may be engaged in tax avoidance, but they hardly seem open to moral criticism. They have reduced their taxes, but at the cost of a genuine reduction in income.

Some kinds of tax avoidance are openly countenanced by the law. For example, a person may give to charity, or to a political party, or contribute to a registered retirement savings plan, in order to increase credits or deductions allowed by the Income Tax Act. These credits and deductions are available for the very purpose of encouraging private provision for charitable objects and political parties and private saving for retirement. One can argue about the wisdom of the statute's policy, but one can hardly question the moral right of a taxpayer to do what the statute manifestly approves.

The case which does give rise to controversy is where the taxpayer orders his or her affairs in an artificial way. Here, the taxpayer appears to be in conflict with the general policy of the statute, and is taking advantage of faulty or incomplete legislative language which has been used to give effect to the policy. Thus, a professional person may channel his or her income into a corporation or a trust for no other reason than to reduce his or her tax liability. A person may

---

[1] Chapter 2, Process, above.

take the retained earnings out of a closely-held corporation as a capital gain instead of ordinary income through a complex "dividend-strip". A person may convert income into capital by taking a discount on a loan instead of charging a higher rate of interest. A person may give income-producing property to a spouse and family, knowing that he or she will continue to benefit from the income. A corporation may purchase a defunct company in order to carryover its losses to reduce the purchaser's future profits.[2]

Tax avoidance, in the strong sense of taking advantage of loopholes to avoid the general intent of the statute, is not, of course, subject to any legal penalty. So long as it falls short of evasion, it is by definition legal. For the taxpayer, the only question is one of morality. On the moral question, there is no general agreement. Certainly, tax avoidance is not universally condemned, as witness the famous dictum of Lord Tomlin in the *Duke of Westminster* case: "Every man is entitled if he can to order his affairs so that the tax attaching under the appropriate Acts is less than it otherwise would be".[3] The underlying assumption is that the tax laws are confiscations of private property, interferences with the natural order of the free market, and violations of civil liberty: the oppressed taxpayer is morally entitled to get around the tax laws if it can be done legally.

On the other side of the question, tax avoidance causes a loss of revenue to the government, which presumably shifts the burden onto other taxpayers through the need to maintain tax rates at higher levels than would otherwise be needed. The equities of the situation are further impaired by the fact that, generally speaking, opportunities for tax avoidance are unavailable to those whose income is derived from wages or salary and from whom tax is deducted at source; only those with substantial investment or business income are usually able to profit from tax avoidance. It has even been suggested that widespread tax avoidance may lead to a deterioration of tax morality in that taxpayers who see others avoiding taxes legally and are unable to do the same may feel justified in resorting to illegal methods; this kind of attitude is of course fatal to the system of self-assessment (which does not work in some countries). Finally, it may be said that tax avoidance leads to a substantial expenditure of effort by lawyers, accountants and administrators which is economically unproductive.[4]

---

[2] A difficulty with simple examples is that they have usually been blocked by legislative action. The last two examples are specifically caught by the attribution rules and the loss carryover rules. The first three may well be caught by the general anti-avoidance rule of s. 245, or, depending on the circumstances, by other, more specific rules.

[3] [1936] A.C. 1, 19; the case is described in the text accompanying note 6, below.

[4] The *Report of the Royal Commission on Taxation* (Carter Report), (1966), vol. 3, Appendix A, includes a public-policy analysis of tax avoidance.

22.3 Role of courts

(a)   Duke of Westminster case

In examining the response of the courts to tax avoidance,[5] it is best to start with the *Duke of Westminster* case (1936).[6] This famous case established a set of principles for the United Kingdom (and Canada) that until recently have been profoundly influential. What happened in the case was this. The Duke of Westminster had a number of household servants. Under the British Income Tax Act, the wages of household servants were not deductible for tax purposes (as is true in Canada today). But the Act did allow the deduction of annual payments made in pursuance of a legal obligation other than remuneration of servants. (This is not an allowable deduction under the Canadian Act.) The Duke accordingly entered into deeds of covenant with each of his servants under which he undertook to pay each of them annual sums for a period of seven years. The payments were to be made irrespective of whether any services were performed by the promisee, and were without prejudice to the promisee's entitlement to remuneration if he or she did perform any services to the promisor. However, it was established by evidence that the understanding between the Duke and his servants was that they would rest content with the provision made for them by deed, and would not assert any right to remuneration. In this way, the Duke converted his non-deductible wages obligation into a deductible annuity obligation.

There was no doubt that the deeds were legally effective in that all legal formalities had been carried out. Nor were the deeds shams: the Duke had covenanted to pay the annuities for seven years, and had thereby assumed the risk of having to continue to pay an annuitant who had stopped working for him or who had insisted upon additional remuneration for working for him. Of course, the understanding that the faithful retainers would continue to work for him, and would do so without extra charge, virtually eliminated this risk. But the risk was genuinely assumed, and none of their lordships regarded the deeds as shams. Lord Atkin, the sole dissenter, was the only law lord who found the device unsuccessful in avoiding tax. For Lord Atkin, "the substance of the transaction was that what was being paid was remuneration".[7] But for the other law lords the legal forms were controlling, and the Duke was entitled to deduct the payments.

The *Duke of Westminster* case is usually taken as confirming the following propositions:

---

[5] For full discussion, see Arnold and Wilson, "The General Anti-Avoidance Rule" (1988) 36 *Can. Tax J.* 829 (Part 1), 1123 (Part 2); Krishna, *Tax Avoidance* (1980).

[6] *Inland Revenue Commissioners* v. *Duke of Westminster*, [1936] A.C. 1 (H.L.).

[7] *Id.*, 15.

1. The Income Tax Act should receive a strict or literal interpretation;
2. A transaction is to be judged not by its economic or commercial substance but by its legal form; and
3. A transaction is effective for tax purposes even if it has no business purpose, having been entered into solely to avoid tax.

These three propositions were obviously highly sympathetic to tax avoidance. They cast upon the drafters of tax legislation the burden of finding language that would squarely catch every transaction that ought to be taxable. This forced Parliament to define the rules with great specificity, and to pass amendments adding more and more detail as avoidance techniques emerged and had to be blocked to protect the revenue. The resulting complexity tended to reinforce the courts in their literal approach. The frequency of amendment had the same effect: judicial creativity was suppressed by the knowledge that Parliament could and would act quickly to repair gaps in the Act that a more purposive judicial interpretation might have filled.

(b)   Stubart Investments case

The leading Canadian case on tax avoidance is the decision of the Supreme Court of Canada in *Stubart Investments* v. *The Queen* (1984).[8] A parent company had two subsidiaries. One subsidiary, Stubart Investments Ltd. (Stubart), operated a profitable business, manufacturing food flavourings. The other subsidiary, Grover Cast Stone Co. Ltd. (Grover), operated an unprofitable business, manufacturing concrete products. Because Stubart and Grover were two separate companies, the losses incurred by Grover could not be used to offset the profits earned by Stubart. So long as Grover remained unprofitable, it had no income that would enable it to take advantage of the Income Tax Act's loss carryforward rules, which permit losses accumulated in prior years to be used as a deduction against current income.

Distressed by the prospect of losses going to waste, the parent company devised and executed the following plan for the two subsidiaries: Stubart sold the assets of its profitable food-flavouring business to Grover. Stubart did not actually relinquish the operation of the business, because Grover appointed Stubart to continue to operate the business as Grover's agent. For three years Stubart operated the business as Grover's agent, and at the end of each year Stubart paid over the profits to Grover, the legal owner of the business. Grover reported this income for tax purposes, and used its accumulated losses from the unprofitable concrete business to create a loss carryforward deduction that effectively sheltered the income from tax. Revenue Canada refused to accept that the profits of the food-flavouring business belonged to Grover. The Department therefore reassessed Stubart on the basis that Stubart was required to report as

---

[8] [1984] C.T.C. 294, 84 D.T.C. 6305 (S.C.C.).

its own the income that it had transferred to Grover under the agency arrangement. Stubart appealed from this assessment, and the issue finally reached the Supreme Court of Canada.

The Supreme Court of Canada rejected the position of the Department, and accepted the position of the taxpayer. According to Estey J., who wrote the majority opinion, Stubart's food-flavouring business assets had been legally transferred to Grover; the operation of the business had been conducted by Stubart under a legal agency agreement with Grover; and, under the terms of that agreement, the income of the business belonged in law to Grover. The income was properly reported by Grover, and the loss carryforward provisions of the Act permitted Grover to take advantage of its accumulated losses as current deductions. Nothing in the Act directed or empowered the Department to disregard the legal consequences of the taxpayer's arrangements. Nor did the Act expressly or impliedly impose a business purpose test on tax-avoidance transactions: it was irrelevant that the taxpayers' arrangements had no business purpose other than the avoidance of tax. Therefore, the arrangements were successful in sheltering the food-flavouring business income from tax.

The *Stubart* case was a serious loss to the Department in that an artificial rearrangement of the affairs of two companies was held to be effective to avoid tax. On the other hand, a fair evaluation of the taxpayers' situation would have to acknowledge that the Income Tax Act's loss carryforward rules were arguably too rigid in their insistence that subsidiaries of the same parent were to be treated as separate taxpayers. If the parent corporation had operated the two businesses directly, instead of through subsidiary corporations, there is no doubt that the losses on concrete could have been deducted against the profits on food flavourings. From one point of view, it was the use of subsidiaries that caused the tax problem. But even the use of subsidiaries would not have been a problem if the Act permitted the consolidation of the income and losses of a group of related companies; the Act does not permit consolidation. Thus, the Act was not neutral in its treatment of different forms of business organization, and, as we shall see, lapses from neutrality inevitably provoke avoidance measures by taxpayers. In this case, it was not surprising that companies organized in the "wrong" way would seek to rearrange their affairs so as to take advantage of the tax benefits that would have been available to the companies if they had been organized differently. This is not intended to condone tax avoidance, but simply to place the *Stubart* case in a balanced perspective: the Court was not dealing with axe murderers.

The *Stubart* case was not all bad from the point of view of the Department. Estey J. was at pains to reject the rule of strict interpretation of taxing statutes — the first of the three rules established by the *Duke of Westminster* case. The rule of strict interpretation is examined in the next section of this chapter.

(c) Strict and purposive interpretation

The old rule that tax legislation must be interpreted strictly is perhaps best articulated in a dictum of the House of Lords in 1869:[9]

> . . . as I understand the principle of all fiscal legislation, it is this: if the person sought to be taxed comes within the letter of the law he must be taxed, however great the hardship may appear to the judicial mind to be. On the other hand, if the Crown, seeking to recover the tax, cannot bring the subject within the letter of the law, the subject is free, however apparently within the spirit of the law the case might otherwise appear to be.

On this approach, if the language of the statute is not literally apt to catch the transaction in issue, then the transaction escapes. In other words, where there is doubt or ambiguity in provisions that levy a tax, the interpretation most favourable to the taxpayer should be adopted. While this approach is usually described as strict interpretation, it may be more accurately described as pro-taxpayer interpretation. To be sure, it does lead to a narrow (strict) interpretation of charging provisions in a taxing statute, but it also leads to a wide interpretation of relieving provisions, such as exemptions or deductions.[10]

With other statutes, when there is doubt or ambiguity as to the meaning of a provision, the issue is resolved by consideration of the context in which the provision is found, and the most important element of context is usually the purpose that the statute is designed to achieve. In Canada this "purposive interpretation" has become the dominant approach to taxing statutes as well as to other statutes. Indeed, it is required by the Interpretation Act,[11] s. 12 of which provides as follows:

> 12 Every enactment is deemed remedial, and shall be given such fair, large and liberal construction and interpretation as best ensures the attainment of its objects.

The strict interpretation of taxing statutes is not consistent with the "fair, large and liberal construction" of an enactment or with the concern with "the attainment of its objects" that are stipulated by s. 12 of the Interpretation Act. While examples of strict interpretation can still be found, they are exceptional.

In the *Stubart* case[12] which has just been described, Estey J. for the majority of the Supreme Court of Canada held that "the modern rule" for the interpretation of statutes was that "the words of an Act are to be read in their entire context and in their grammatical and ordinary sense harmoniously with the scheme of the Act, the object of the Act, and the intention of Parliament".[13] This rule applied to the Income Tax Act, no less than to other statutes. The

---

[9] *Partington* v. *A.-G.* (1869), L.R. 4 (H.L.) 100, 122, per Lord Cairns.

[10] E.g., *Johns-Manville Canada* v. *The Queen*, note 17, below (wide interpretation of deduction).

[11] R.S.C. 1985, c. I-21.

[12] Note 8, above.

[13] Note 8, above, 316; 6323.

Income Tax Act, like other statutes, should be interpreted in accordance with the "object and spirit" of its provisions.[14]

In *Corporation Notre-Dame de Bon-Secours* v. *Quebec* (1995),[15] the question arose whether an old-age home was entitled to a full exemption from Quebec's municipal property tax. There was no doubt that 11 per cent of the home, which was a shelter section in which the residents received special care, qualified for the exemption. The question was whether the remaining 89 per cent of the home, which consisted of apartments, also qualified for the exemption. Since the language of the exemption did not provide a clear answer, the Supreme Court of Canada had to settle the question by reference to the purpose of the provision. But what was the purpose of the provision? The purpose of the statute as a whole was to raise revenue. If that was the controlling purpose, then the exemption provision, which reduced the size of the tax base, would have to be narrowly interpreted. Gonthier J., who wrote the opinion of the Court, did not accept this logic. He acknowledged that the primary purpose of a taxing statute was to raise revenue, but he pointed out that a taxing statute "serves other purposes and functions as a tool of economic and social policy"; in this case, the taxing statute also pursued "a secondary policy of exempting social works".[16] In light of this secondary policy, Gonthier J. concluded that the broader interpretation of the exemption was the better one, and he held that the entire home was exempt from tax.

In *Notre-Dame*, the taxpayer succeeded, but the decision was based on the purpose of the statutory provision, not on a presumption that doubt or ambiguity should be resolved in favour of the taxpayer. Gonthier J., following some dicta of Estey J.,[17] held that there was still life in that pro-taxpayer presumption, but that the presumption was a "residual" rule which would apply only in the "exceptional" case where the "ordinary rules of interpretation" left the court with a "reasonable doubt" as to the meaning of a provision.[18] The residual presumption was not relevant in *Notre-Dame*, because Gonthier J. was able to

---

[14] *Id.*, 315; 6322.

[15] [1995] 1 C.T.C. 241, 95 D.T.C. 5017 (S.C.C.).

[16] *Id.*, 250; 5022.

[17] In *Stubart Investments* v. *The Queen*, note 8, above, Estey J. had stated (at 316; 6324) that "the older rule of strict construction of a taxing statute, as modified by the courts in recent years, supra, prevails. . .". This suggestion that the rule of strict construction had not been wholly supplanted seemed inconsistent with the rest of his opinion. Then, in the later case of *Johns-Manville Canada* v. *The Queen*, [1985] 2 C.T.C. 111, 85 D.T.C. 5373 (S.C.C.), in the course of a decision allowing the taxpayer a disputed deduction, Estey J. said (at pp. 126; 5384): ". . . where the taxing statute is not explicit, reasonable uncertainty or factual ambiguity resulting from lack of explicitness in the statute should be resolved in favour of the taxpayer." This pro-taxpayer approach seemed inconsistent with the purposive ("object and spirit") approach, which would often indicate a choice against the taxpayer.

[18] Note 15, above, 251; 5023.

apply the statute to the facts of the case by reference to the purpose of the provision in question. He was not left with a reasonable doubt as to the meaning of the statutory provision. Therefore, he was not called upon to fall back on a presumption in favour of the taxpayer. By emphasizing the "residual" and "exceptional" nature of that presumption, Gonthier J. made clear that the presumption, although not abrogated, should be invoked only in rare cases.

In *Antosko* v. *The Queen* (1994),[19] the Supreme Court of Canada had another occasion to consider the role of a taxing provision's "object and spirit" in determining its meaning. In that case, as an attempt to rehabilitate a failing company, the taxpayer acquired for a nominal consideration from a provincial government agency some debt obligations (a debenture and promissory notes) that had been issued by the company to the agency (which had been lending money to the company). The taxpayer also acquired the shares of the company, and became responsible for running the business. The tax issue arose when the company made interest payments on the debt obligations to the taxpayer. The taxpayer reported the full amount of the interest income for tax purposes, but claimed a deduction for the portion of the interest that had accrued prior to the transfer of the debt obligation from the provincial agency to the taxpayer. The deduction was authorized by the literal language of s. 20(14) of the Income Tax Act, which provided that, on the transfer of a debt obligation, any unpaid interest accrued to the date of the transfer was to be included in the transferor's income, and deducted from the transferee's income. In this case, the transferor, being an agency of the provincial government, was exempt from tax, so that it did not report or pay tax on the interest accrued to the date of transfer.

In *Antosko*, the Minister took the position that it was contrary to the object and spirit of the Act to allow the transferee-taxpayer to deduct the accrued interest in the circumstances of this case, when the transferor was not taxable on the interest. The Supreme Court of Canada rejected the Minister's argument and allowed the taxpayer to take the deduction. Iacobucci J., who wrote for the Court, held that the taxpayer was entitled to rely upon the terms of the statute, which clearly entitled the transferee of a debt obligation to a deduction for the interest accrued to the date of transfer. Even if the deduction was contrary to the object and purpose of s. 20(14) (which was by no means clear), where the words of the statute were "clear and plain", and where the legal and practical effect of the taxpayer's transaction brought the taxpayer within the words of the statute, then the statute had to be applied according to its terms.

With respect, the decision in *Antosko* is sound. It would introduce intolerable uncertainty into the Income Tax Act if clear language in a detailed provision of the Act were to be qualified by unexpressed exceptions derived from

---

[19] [1994] 2 C.T.C. 25, 94 D.T.C. 6314 (S.C.C.).

a court's view of the object and purpose of the provision. As Iacobucci J. said:[20]

> In the absence of evidence that the transaction was a sham or an abuse of the provisions of the Act, it is not the role of the court to determine whether the transaction in question is one which renders the taxpayer deserving of a deduction.

This is not a rejection of purposive interpretation. On the contrary, Iacobucci J. reaffirmed the Court's commitment to purposive interpretation. It is simply a recognition that "object and purpose" can play only a limited role in the interpretation of a statute that is as precise and detailed as the Income Tax Act. When a provision is couched in specific language that admits of no doubt or ambiguity in its application to the facts, then the provision must be applied regardless of its object and purpose.[21]

In *Stubart*, Estey J. made clear that he regarded the replacement of strict interpretation with purposive interpretation ("object and spirit") as a blow to tax avoidance. He said that the reason for using purposive interpretation was to "reduce the attraction of elaborate and intricate tax avoidance plans, and reduce the rewards to those best able to afford the services of the tax technicians".[22] He also said that purposive interpretation would "reduce the action and reaction endlessly produced by complex, specific tax measures aimed at sophisticated business practices, and the inevitable, professionally guided and equally specialized taxpayer reaction".[23] These are admirable sentiments, but the fact is that the Income Tax Act is now drafted in the form of "complex, specific measures", and, as *Antosko* shows, there are severe limitations to the utility of "object and spirit" in interpreting such detailed provisions.

Moreover, as we noticed in the discussion of the *Duke of Westminster* case,[24] strict interpretation was only one of three doctrines that facilitated tax avoidance. The other two were (1) the refusal of the courts to look through the legal form of a tax avoidance transaction to ascertain the commercial substance, and (2) the refusal of the courts to require an independent business purpose as

---

[20] *Id.*, 32; 6320.

[21] *Antosko* may go too far in implying that one can rely on plain meaning *to the exclusion of* legislative purpose. After all, language can never be interpreted independently of its context, and legislative purpose is part of the context. It would seem to follow that consideration of legislative purpose may not only *resolve* patent ambiguity, but may, on occasion, *reveal* ambiguity in apparently plain language: *Pigott Project Management* v. *Land-Rock Resources*, [1996] 1 C.T.C. 395, 403-404, 96 D.T.C. 6245, para. 6248 (S.C.C.) per Cory J. for majority ("even if the ambiguity were not apparent, it is significant that in order to determine the clear and plain meaning of the statute it is always appropriate to consider the 'scheme of the Act, the object of the Act, and the intention of Parliament'.")

[22] Note 8, above, 315; 6322.

[23] *Id.*, 317; 6324.

[24] Note 6, above.

a prerequisite to the effectiveness of a tax-avoidance transaction. So long as these two doctrines remained in place, the door to tax avoidance had not been closed. The result of the *Stubart* case perfectly illustrated the point: an artificial, complex legal scheme, entered into solely for the purpose of tax avoidance, was held to be effective in its tax-avoidance purpose.

Before moving on to consider the doctrines of form and substance and business purpose, we shall attempt to summarize the rules to be derived from the recent interpretation decisions:

1. A taxing statute should be interpreted according to the same rules of statutory interpretation as apply to other statutes (*Stubart, Notre-Dame, Antosko*).

2. Whether a provision of a taxing statute is to be given a strict or a liberal interpretation depends upon the purpose of the provision, not upon whether the outcome favours the taxpayer (*Stubart, Notre-Dame*).

3. In identifying the purpose of a provision of a taxing statute, it should be recognized that, while the purpose of a taxing statute is to raise taxes, the statute may serve other social and economic purposes as well; therefore, exempting provisions are not necessarily to be given a strict interpretation (*Notre-Dame*).

4. Where a provision of a taxing statute is couched in specific language that admits of no doubt or ambiguity in its application to the facts, then the provision must be applied, regardless of its purpose; the purpose of the provision is not to be used to create an unexpressed exception to clear language (*Antosko*).

5. As an exception to propositions 1 and 2 above, in the exceptional case where the application of the foregoing rules leaves the court with a "reasonable doubt" as to the meaning of a provision of a taxing statute, the doubt is to be resolved by a residual presumption in favour of the taxpayer (*Notre-Dame* dictum).

(d)   Form and substance

In the discussion of the *Duke of Westminster* case,[25] we noticed that the success of the Duke's tax avoidance plan depended upon the Court's willingness to characterize the agreements entered into with his servants as annuity contracts rather than employment contracts. The Court's acceptance of the legal form (annuity) rather than the commercial substance (employment) was critical to the success of the plan. Similarly, in the *Stubart* case,[26] the Court accepted the legal forms (sale and agency agreement), although the commercial substance of the arrangement was that Stubart had not divested itself of the business.

---

[25] *Ibid.*

[26] Note 8, above.

The question whether a transaction should be characterized for tax purposes according to its legal form or according to its commercial substance is obviously a different question from whether the Income Tax Act should be given a strict or a purposive interpretation. But the two questions are intimately related. The courts cannot disregard genuine legal forms unless the Act expressly or impliedly directs that result. Under a regime of strict interpretation, the courts are less likely to read the Act as authorizing an inquiry that goes beyond the legal forms than they are under a regime of purposive interpretation. Under a regime of purposive interpretation, the argument that the Act imposes liability on an economic result, as opposed to a legal form, becomes more appealing. However, in most cases, the legal forms must inevitably be controlling. The courts would assume an extraordinary power if, for taxation purposes, they could ignore such basic matters as the obligations of a deed of covenant, the legal and beneficial ownership of property and the separate legal personalities of different companies.

There are, however, some cases where the courts have characterized a transaction by its substance rather than its form. For example, a lump sum payment made by a lessee to a lessor has been characterized as income rather than capital on the basis that its substance was a pre-payment of rent, causing the lessor to agree to (and pay tax on) a lower rate of rent.[27] As another example, when a taxpayer transferred property to another person's wife, and at the same time the other person transferred property to the taxpayer's wife, it was held that the taxpayer had made an indirect transfer to his own wife. Such a transfer attracted the attribution rules, which attribute to the transferor the income from property transferred to the transferor's spouse.[28]

For the most part, however, as noted earlier, the courts will not disregard legal relationships genuinely created. Indeed, tax law would become intolerably uncertain if courts felt unconstrained by the legal form of the taxpayer's arrangements, and felt free to impose tax on a different basis.

(e)   Ineffective transactions

There is an obvious corollary to the general rule that tax is imposed according to the legal relationships or transactions established by the parties. The corollary is that a legal relationship or transaction will not be recognized for tax purposes if that relationship or transaction has not been validly established under the rules of the general law. For example, if a particular tax outcome depends upon the fact that a company or a trust or a partnership has been formed, or a sale of a gift has been made, then it is obviously essential that the taxpayer has complied with the general law of corporations, trusts, partnerships, sales or gifts

---

[27] *Front & Simcoe* v. *M.N.R.*, [1960] C.T.C. 123, 60 D.T.C. 1081 (Ex. Ct.).

[28] *Naiberg* v. *M.N.R.*, [1969] C.T.C. 492, 69 D.T.C. 361 (T.A.B.). The facts were more complicated than related, but the text conveys the essence of the holding.

in order to bring the claimed legal relationship into existence. If under the general law the claimed legal relationship has not been validly established, then tax liability (like any other legal consequence) will depend upon the true legal position. Typically, the problem here is that some essential legal formality has not been carried out, or has not been carried out in time to achieve the desired tax result; for example, a trust may not have been validly created,[29] or may not have been created in time.[30]

Cases where a tax advantage is lost by reason of a failure of legal formality do not rest on any doctrine peculiar to tax law. However, such cases are so common in the tax reports that it is necessary to conclude that the courts tend to scrutinize very closely indeed the formal documentation and other facts which are relied upon to achieve some reduction of tax. A minor defect which in another context might have been dismissed as a sufficient compliance with general law formalities may in the tax context be held to vitiate the transaction.[31]

(f)   Shams

A "sham" will be ignored for tax purposes. A sham was defined in the *Snook* case[32] as:

> . . . acts done or documents executed by the parties to the "sham" which are intended by them to give to third parties or to the court the appearance of creating between the parties legal rights and obligations different from the actual legal rights and obligations (if any) which the parties intend to create.

The *Snook* definition makes clear that a sham always involves an element of deceit. A transaction is not a sham merely because it is artificial, contrived or lacking in an independent business purpose.[33] There is no sham where the legal formalities accurately reflect the true relationship between the parties. In the *Duke of Westminster* case,[34] for example, the deeds of covenant entered into by

---

[29] E.g., *Atinco Paper Products* v. *The Queen*, [1978] C.T.C. 566, 78 D.T.C. 6387 (F.C.A.).

[30] E.g., *Ablan Leon* v. *M.N.R.*, [1976] C.T.C. 506, 76 D.T.C. 6280 (F.C.A.).

[31] In *Stubart Investments* v. *The Queen*, note 8, above, there were some minor technical deficiencies in the formalities associated with the transfer of assets between the sister corporations, but the Supreme Court of Canada held they were insufficient to render the transfer incomplete.

[32] *Snook* v. *London & West Riding Investments*, [1967] 2 Q.B. 786, 802 (C.A.).

[33] From time to time the word "sham" is broadened to include any artificial tax-avoidance transaction: see, e.g., the obiter dictum in *The Queen* v. *Bronfman Trust*, [1987] 1 C.T.C. 117, 129-130, 87 D.T.C. 5059, 5068 (S.C.C.). If this were a merely semantic issue, it would not matter, but the classification of a transaction as a sham carries the legal consequence of invalidity for tax purposes. The broader usage should therefore be avoided. The *Snook* definition, with its requirement of deceit, has been approved by the Supreme Court of Canada in *M.N.R.* v. *Cameron*, [1972] C.T.C. 380, 72 D.T.C. 6325 (S.C.C.) and in the *Stubart* case, notes 35, 36, below.

[34] Note 6, above.

the Duke with his servants were bona fide instruments under which the Duke genuinely undertook an enforceable obligation to pay the annuities. The deeds were not deceptive, and could not be disregarded as shams. In the *Stubart* case,[35] there was a genuine sale of assets and agency agreement between the sister corporations. As Estey J. pointed out, there was no sham, because there was no attempt to create "a false impression" for tax purposes: the "appearance" was "precisely the reality", and fully enforceable obligations were genuinely created. The deceit which is "the heart and core of a sham" was entirely absent.[36]

A sham will be disregarded for tax purposes, and tax will be imposed in accordance with the true facts. If an entire transaction is a sham, the transaction will be completely ineffective. For example, the parties may create false documentation for the sale of an asset when no such sale occurred. (The motive could be to create a capital loss for the pretended vendor.) But if only part of the transaction was a sham, then the transaction will be effective in accordance with the actual rights and liabilities created. For example, there may have been an actual sale of an asset for $1, but the parties inserted a consideration of $150 in the documentation (perhaps, to increase the purchaser's capital cost allowance deduction). In that case, tax liability will flow from the actual consideration of $1.

(g) Business purpose

In the *Duke of Westminster* case,[37] the deeds of covenant that the Duke entered into with his servants were effective for tax purposes despite the fact that they had been brought into existence solely in order to avoid tax. The case thus became authority for the important proposition that there was no business purpose test in English tax jurisprudence. The courts had no power to disregard a transaction for tax purposes simply because the transaction lacked an independent business purpose.

In the United States, there is authority for a business purpose test, which is applied rather unpredictably, but which enables the courts to strike down the most artificial tax-avoidance devices. A common application is to transactions involving a series of steps in which some of the steps were inserted for tax-avoidance reasons. In such a case, the courts can levy tax on the basis of a simpler, more straightforward version of the complex arrangement that was actually carried out.[38]

---

[35] Note 8, above.

[36] *Id.*, 313; 6320-6321.

[37] Note 6, above.

[38] Arnold and Wilson, note 5, above, 859, 880.

In the United Kingdom, a business purpose test has been applied by the House of Lords to a "step transaction". In *Furniss* v. *Dawson* (1984),[39] the House of Lords charged the vendor of property with a capital gain, although the capital gain had actually been received by a company owned and controlled by the vendor that was incorporated in the Isle of Man (a tax haven). Their lordships held that the transaction was to be regarded as a sale and purchase between two United Kingdom parties, which was the commercial reality. The intermediate step of transferring the property to the controlled Isle of Man company (which then sold the property to the true purchaser) had been undertaken solely to divert the capital gain to the Isle of Man and avoid its recognition in the United Kingdom.[40] Their lordships held that this "inserted step", because it had "no business purpose apart from the deferment of tax", was to be disregarded for tax purposes.[41]

The business purpose test of *Furniss* v. *Dawson* has been confined to "step transactions", or "composite transactions", as they are known in the United Kingdom.[42] Even so, the case obviously constitutes a radical change in the approach of the House of Lords to artificial tax avoidance schemes. As Lord Roskill noted, the *Duke of Westminster* case was seriously undermined by *Furniss* v. *Dawson*.[43]

In Canada, there had been occasional cases in which courts had applied a business purpose test in order to defeat artificial tax avoidance schemes, but these cases ran against the general current of authority, which remained faithful to the *Duke of Westminster* case. The issue was fully argued before the Supreme Court of Canada in the *Stubart* case,[44] where counsel for Revenue Canada argued that the transfer of assets between the two subsidiaries should be disregarded for tax purposes on the ground that it lacked any business purpose other than the avoidance of tax. Estey J. for the majority of the Supreme Court of Canada reviewed the American, English and Canadian authorities, and rejected the business purpose test for Canada:[45]

---

[39] [1984] A.C. 474 (H.L.).

[40] The gain would eventually have to be recognized in the United Kingdom, but only when the shares in the Isle of Man company (whose value reflected the capital gain) were sold.

[41] Note 39, above, 527.

[42] *Furniss* v. *Dawson* followed two earlier decisions of the House of Lords, namely, *Inland Revenue Commrs.* v. *Burmah Oil Co.*, [1982] S.T.C. 30 (H.L.) and *Ramsay* v. *Inland Revenue Commrs.*, [1982] A.C. 300. The later case of *Craven* v. *White*, [1989] A.C. 398 confined *Furniss* to step transactions.

[43] Note 39, above, 515 (". . . the ghost of the *Duke of Westminster* and his transaction . . . has haunted the administration of this branch of the law for too long.").

[44] Note 8, above.

[45] *Id.*, 314; 6322.

> I would therefore reject the proposition that a transaction may be disregarded for tax purposes solely on the basis that it was entered into by a taxpayer without an independent or bona fide business purpose.

Wilson J. in her concurring opinion said that the *Duke of Westminster* case was "far too deeply entrenched in our tax law for the courts to reject it" in favour of a business purpose test.[46] Thus, the Supreme Court of Canada could not have been more explicit in its unanimous rejection of the business purpose test. This ruling led to Parliament enacting the general anti-avoidance rule of s. 245, which is the topic of the next section of this chapter.

22.4 General anti-avoidance rule

(a) Origin

The Income Tax Act contains many provisions that are designed to counter tax-avoidance techniques. Some of these are directed at particular practices. For example, the attribution rules of ss. 74.1-75.1 attempt to stop the splitting of income between members of the same family.[47] Others are more general, such as the requirement of s. 67 that expenses are only deductible to the extent that they are "reasonable",[48] or the many provisions that provide special treatment for transactions entered into between parties that are "not at arm's length" (related persons or corporations who may have a common interest in saving tax).[49] Ironically, in *Stubart*,[50] Estey J. relied on the number and variety of these anti-avoidance measures to buttress his conclusion that the Court of its own motion should not create a business purpose test that had not been enacted by Parliament. Since none of the Act's anti-avoidance measures caught the situation in that case, he reasoned that the Court should not assume the power to disregard genuine legal arrangements simply because of their tax-avoidance motivation.

The lesson that the Department of Finance drew from the reasoning in *Stubart* was that the Act ought to include a general anti-avoidance rule, which would cover such a broad range of tax-avoidance activity that an unforeseen device such as that employed in *Stubart* would not fall through the cracks again. Accordingly, the tax reform of 1988 included the enactment of a new s. 245 of the Act, which is a general anti-avoidance rule.

---

[46] *Id.*, 318; 6325.

[47] The attribution rules are examined in ch. 7, Taxation Unit, under heading 7.5, "Attribution Rules", above.

[48] The "reasonable" requirement of s. 67 is examined in ch. 13, Income from Business or Property: Deductions, under heading 13.13, "The 'reasonable' requirement", above. There are other "reasonable" requirements, e.g., ss. 16(1), 103.

[49] E.g., ss. 56(4), 69, 78, 148(7), 212(1)(b); the concept of arm's length is defined in s. 251.

[50] Note 8, above.

(b) Section 245

Section 245 introduces a general anti-avoidance rule to the Act.[51] Section 245 applies to an "avoidance transaction", which is defined in subsection (3) as a transaction that would result in a tax benefit, or a transaction that is part of a series of transactions that would result in a tax benefit, unless the transaction "may reasonably be considered to have been undertaken or arranged primarily for bona fide purposes other than to obtain the tax benefit". A "tax benefit" is defined in subsection (1) as including not only the avoidance or reduction of tax, but also the deferral of tax.

Where a transaction is an avoidance transaction, subsection (2) stipulates that the tax consequences "shall be determined as is reasonable in the circumstances in order to deny [the intended] tax benefit". A draft version of s. 245 (in the 1987 white paper) stipulated that the tax consequences should be designed "ignoring the transaction". This phrase is not in the statutory version, but in most cases no doubt the reasonable tax consequences will be constructed by ignoring the transaction. For example, the deeds of covenant entered into by the Duke in the *Duke of Westminster* case[52] would probably be caught by s. 245, resulting in the payments made to the servants becoming undeductible, as if the deeds did not exist. The sale of assets from the profitable subsidiary to the unprofitable subsidiary in the *Stubart* case[53] would probably be caught by s. 245,[54] resulting in the income being taxed to the profitable subsidiary, as if the sale (and agency arrangement) had never taken place. And the interposition of the Isle of Man company in the sale in *Furniss* v. *Dawson*[55] would probably also be caught by s. 245, resulting in the capital gain being taxed to the original vendor, as if the Isle of Man company had played no role in the series of transactions.

The measurement of the "tax benefit" that s. 245 will deny to the taxpayer when the section applies will in some cases be difficult. Where there were only two ways in which the taxpayer could have arranged his affairs, once the

---

[51] For analysis, see Arnold and Wilson, note 5, above, 1153-1180; Krishna, note 5, above, chs. 4-6. Information Circular 88-2, "General anti-avoidance rule — section 245 of the Income Tax Act" (1988) and Supplement 1 (1990) set out Revenue Canada's views on s. 245 with illustrative examples.

[52] Note 6, above.

[53] Note 8, above.

[54] Information Circular 88-2, note 51, above, para. 8, says that, where a corporation transfers property used in its business to a related corporation to permit the deduction of non-capital losses of the related corporation, the transfer "is consistent with the scheme of the Act and, therefore, subsection 245(2) would not be applied". This could be read as suggesting that the case that caused the enactment of s. 245, namely, *Stubart*, is not covered by s. 245. The Department's example does, however, lack the agency agreement that was present in *Stubart*.

[55] Note 35, above.

taxpayer's actual arrangements have been caught by s. 245, one presumably measures the tax benefit by reference to the (higher) tax cost of the alternative that the taxpayer avoided. But where there were more than two ways in which the taxpayer could have arranged his or her affairs, the court will have to choose one of the options as the basis for measuring the benefit. Does the court always measure the benefit by reference to the most costly option? Or is there some other principle that will supply the benchmark for the valuation of the benefit? The courts have not yet had to consider these questions.

The first case to apply the GAAR provision was *McNichol* v. *Canada* (1997).[56] In that case the provision was applied to a "surplus strip". A surplus strip (or dividend strip) is an arrangement under which the shareholders of a company obtain the benefit of the company's retained earnings without paying the tax that would be payable on a dividend. Whenever capital gains have been more favourably taxed than dividends, a practice of surplus stripping has developed as shareholders try and receive the value of retained earnings in the form of a capital gain. That is what happened in this case. A holding company ("Holdco") owned by four shareholders sold its only asset, which was an office building. After all tax-free distributions had been made to the shareholders, the company was left with cash in the bank of approximately $318,000. Since the company had no business and no other reason for existence, the natural next step would be for the shareholders to wind the company up. However, s. 84(2) of the Act provides that, on the winding-up of a company, the property distributed to shareholders in excess of the paid-up capital is deemed to be a taxable dividend. That provision applied to the entire amount of the company's bank account, and would have forced each of the four shareholders to report and pay tax on a dividend of $79,500. In order to avoid this result, the four shareholders found a purchaser for the shares. The purchaser was an arm's length inactive company, which agreed to purchase all the shares of Holdco for $300,000. The purchasing company had virtually no assets (it had a bank account with $63 in it), but it borrowed the $300,000 from a bank. Then, as soon as the transaction of sale was closed, the purchasing company repaid the loan out of the Holdco bank account, which it then controlled. The purchasing company was left with a profit of $18,000, which was the difference between the value of Holdco's assets and the purchase price.[57] The four shareholders of Holdco each received $75,000, which constituted a capital gain for each of them, but because the lifetime capital gains exemption (since repealed) was then in the Act and available to them, two of the shareholders paid no tax on the gain, and the other two shareholders paid only a small amount.

[56] [1997] 2 C.T.C. 2088, 97 D.T.C. 111 (T.C.C.).

[57] Holdco also had a balance in its refundable dividend tax on hand account, which represented a possible future tax refund.

The Minister assessed the four shareholders on the basis that they had received a dividend on winding-up, invoking s. 245 of the Act. The Tax Court upheld the Minister's assessment. The Court held that the sale of the shares to the inactive company was an "avoidance transaction". The shareholders had the choice of removing the surplus in Holdco by means of either a winding-up dividend or a sale of the shares, and the latter choice was an avoidance transaction. The "tax benefit" to which it gave rise was the difference between the tax payable on receipt of a taxable dividend on the winding up of the company and the tax payable on receipt of a capital gain on the sale of the shares. The sale had not been "arranged primarily for bona fide purposes other than to obtain the tax benefit". The sale had no purpose other than to obtain a tax benefit for the four sellers. It was the anticipation of that tax benefit that enabled them to agree to a price that made the sale attractive to the purchasing company, which was in substance receiving a portion of the tax benefit. Therefore, s. 245 applied, and the Minister was right to assess the shareholders as if they had received a winding-up dividend.[58]

Note that s. 245 goes no further than to nullify the tax benefit sought in the avoidance transaction. No penalty is imposed on the taxpayer by the Act. Of course, the taxpayer will have to pay interest on unpaid tax, and will have wasted the costs, such as the legal and accounting fees, of entering into the avoidance transaction.

(c) Non-tax purpose

The key to the operation of the section is the concept of a non-tax purpose. A transaction is not an avoidance transaction if it was undertaken "primarily" for "bona fide purposes other than to obtain the tax benefit". The section does not use the phrase "business purpose", which was the controlling concept under the 1987 white paper version of s. 245. The main difficulty with the phrase "business purpose", as Arnold and Wilson explain,[59] is that "many legitimate transactions are carried out for non-tax reasons, such as family, personal, or investment reasons, that cannot be characterized as business reasons". The non-tax purpose test is able to accommodate all purposes other than tax avoidance. Nevertheless, the test is really nothing more than "an expanded version of the business purpose test".[60]

The assessment of the purpose of a transaction will not always be easy, but s. 245 provides some guidance. Purpose is expressed in terms of what the

---

[58] *McNichol* was followed in *Equilease* v. *The Queen*, 97 D.T.C. 302 (T.C.C.), where a surplus strip had been used to avoid Canadian withholding tax on the distribution of the assets of a defunct company to its United States shareholder. The surplus strip was held to be ineffective on other grounds, and the GAAR reasoning was not essential to the result.

[59] Note 5, above, 1155.

[60] *Id.*, 1159.

transaction "may reasonably be considered" to have been undertaken or arranged for. This seems to give primacy to the objective facts available to an outside observer, namely, the legal, commercial and tax consequences of the transaction. It should not be necessary to make any finding as to the state of mind of the taxpayer, although no doubt the evidence of the taxpayer as to his or her subjective intention would not be irrelevant. A second point of guidance comes from the word "primarily" in the requirement of a non-tax purpose. This is designed to meet the case where a transaction has both a business (non-tax) purpose and a tax-avoidance purpose. It requires that a finding be made of the primary purpose of the transaction, and if the primary purpose is the business one, the transaction is not an avoidance transaction, and the resulting tax benefit will not be denied by s. 245.

(d)   Misuse or abuse

Subsection 245(4) provides "for greater certainty" that the section does not apply to a transaction that would not result in "a misuse of the provisions of this Act or an abuse having regard to the provisions of this Act". This provision is rather obscure, since the words "misuse" and "abuse" are not defined and do not have clear meanings. The idea seems to be to exclude from s. 245 those transactions that are within the object and spirit of the Act. For example, a taxpayer might contribute to a registered retirement savings plan primarily to obtain the tax benefits of the deduction of the contributions and the tax-sheltered status of the plan's income. Subsection 245(4) forestalls any argument that this transaction, which takes advantage of tax benefits directly bestowed by s. 146 of the Act, could be nullified under s. 245.[61]

In the *McNichol* case, described above,[62] s. 245 was applied to deny a tax benefit to four shareholders of a defunct company who had arranged a sale of the company's shares. The point of the sale was to avoid the tax that would have arisen if they had followed the straightforward course of winding up the company. The sale of the shares gave rise to capital gains in the hands of the shareholders, but the gains were sheltered from tax by the former lifetime exemption for capital gains. The immediate source of the tax benefit in the case was the exemption. It would be hard to argue that simply taking advantage of an exemption deliberately enacted into the Act was a "misuse" of the exemption. However, in this case, the exemption had been used as part of a scheme of surplus-stripping, something that was opposed to a policy of the Act, which was to tax corporate surpluses as dividends. The Court held that this was a misuse of the exemption.

---

[61] IC 88-2, note 51, above, gives other examples that the Department does not regard as a misuse or abuse of the Act.

[62] Note 56, above.

(f)   Discretion

The general anti-avoidance rule is a new development in Canada's income tax law, and the breadth and vagueness of the controlling concepts make its application somewhat unpredictable. It should be noted, however, that the provision does not take the easy route of leaving the issue to the discretion of the Minister. In practice, of course, much will depend upon Revenue Canada's interpretation of s. 245 and the Department's policies with respect to its application. Revenue Canada has established a GAAR committee, comprised of officials from Finance and Justice as well as from Revenue Canada, which is intended to standardize the application of GAAR. The committee reviews all files where GAAR might apply, including requests by taxpayers for advance rulings and referrals from Revenue Canada's audit division, and decides whether or not a GAAR-based ruling or reassessment should be issued by Revenue Canada. Needless to say, the Minister's decisions that emerge from this careful process will not be decisive. The ultimate forum of interpretation remains the courts. The taxpayer can use the objection and appeal process to secure a review by a court of any determination made by the Minister under s. 245, and the court will not be obliged to defer to the Minister's findings of fact or law, or to the Minister's decision as to the tax consequences.

Before 1945, the Income Tax Act was replete with provisions that conferred discretion on the Minister. These provisions attracted much criticism, and by 1948 most of them had been repealed. Since 1948, the Act has reflected a policy that liability to tax should not depend upon governmental discretion. The present position is that the discretions that are to be found in the Act all relate to administrative matters, not to liability. There are no longer any provisions of the Act that make liability to tax turn on the discretion of the Minister.[63]

22.5 Legal ethics

(a)   Roles of tax lawyers

A lawyer (or accountant) in private practice may be retained by a client in any of three different kinds of tax matter: (1) compliance, (2) litigation, or (3) planning.

Compliance is the preparation of the client's income tax return. The lawyer may be instructed to prepare the return, although this task is usually entrusted to an accountant. Or the lawyer may be instructed to provide advice to the client or the client's accountant on a legal issue arising in the preparation of the return.

---

[63] An arguable exception is the power to make remission orders under s. 23 of the Financial Administration Act. This power, which is solely of a relieving kind, is discussed in ch. 2, Process, under heading 2.5(k), "Remission order", above.

Litigation becomes necessary when the client is involved in a dispute with Revenue Canada. Such a dispute will typically start when the Minister issues an assessment that rejects a position taken on the client's income tax return. The lawyer may be instructed to prepare and file an objection to the assessment, to prepare and file appeals to the Tax Court, the Federal Court of Appeal or the Supreme Court of Canada, and to represent the client as counsel at hearings before departmental officials or courts. Accountants as well as lawyers engage in advocacy before departmental officials and in the "informal procedure" of the Tax Court. Only lawyers can appear in the "general procedure" of the Tax Court and in the Federal Court of Appeal and Supreme Court of Canada.

Planning differs from compliance and advocacy in that planning looks to the future rather than the past. The lawyer may be instructed to provide advice on how to structure a proposed transaction so as to minimize the tax liability arising from the transaction, or the lawyer may be instructed to provide more general advice as to the most favourable way to organize and operate a client's business or a client's personal investments. Planning is a field in which accountants as well as lawyers play an important role, but the provision of legal advice on difficult issues and the drafting of legal documents can only be undertaken by lawyers.

(b)   Rules of professional conduct

In performing all three functions, the lawyer is bound by the Rules of Professional Conduct of the provincial bar.[64] Those rules will impose a duty of *competence* on the lawyer, which in some situations will require that the client be referred to a more expert lawyer. These rules will also impose a duty of honesty and candour on the lawyer. The lawyer must not participate in any deceptive or illegal practice, and must not advise the client how to engage in any such practice or how to avoid detection. These rules will also impose a duty of confidentiality on the lawyer. The lawyer must hold in confidence all information about the client's affairs that was acquired as the result of the professional relationship. Confidential information may be disclosed only with the consent of the client or in the rare cases where disclosure is required by law.

These basic rules solve some of the problems that a tax lawyer will encounter, but they leave many others open.[65]

---

[64] E.g., Law Society of Upper Canada, *Rules of Professional Conduct* (1997), Rules 2, 3, 4.

[65] See Vineberg, "The Ethics of Tax Planning" (1969) 9 *U. West. Ont. L.R.* 119; McDonnell and others, "Professional Responsibility in Tax Practice" [1975] *Can. Tax Found. Conf. Rep.* 953; Silver, "Ethical Considerations in giving Tax Opinions" [1994] *Can. Tax Found. Conf. Rep.* 36:1; Smith, "Dealing with Tax Risk in an Opinion" [1994] *Can. Tax Found. Conf. Rep.* 38:1.

(c)   Compliance

In the area of compliance (or return preparation), the lawyer must not mislead the Department either by misstatements or by silence, or permit the client to mislead the Department. But in the course of the preparation of a complex return, there may be judgment calls to be made as to the characterization of a transaction or expenditure which affects the inclusion of an income item or the deductibility of an expense. A lawyer can advise a client to take a position favourable to the client only if there is a reasonable basis in fact or law for that position. If there is no reasonable basis in fact or law for the position, it is unethical for the lawyer to do anything other than advise against the position even if the risk of detection is low. Even if there is a reasonable basis for the client's position, the question arises whether the client ought to be advised to disclose the circumstances of the transaction or expenditure in a rider to the income tax return. There is no agreement among lawyers on this issue, but the better view is surely that any items (or omissions) in a tax return that are debatable should be disclosed and explained in a rider to the return.

In considering ethical issues surrounding compliance, it must be remembered that the integrity of the system depends upon honest self-assessment. The Minister cannot audit more than a tiny proportion of the returns filed, and relies heavily on the information supplied by the taxpayer. In these circumstances, compliance is quite unlike litigation, where each position advanced by a lawyer on behalf of the client is opposed by a lawyer on behalf of an opponent, and ruled upon by a judge. The reality of compliance is that positions taken in a tax return can easily be buried and immunized from any scrutiny short of an (unlikely) audit. In these circumstances, the tax lawyer's ethical duty of honesty and candour requires him or her to counsel full disclosure, including alerting the Minister to debatable items.

In providing a legal opinion as to a legal position to be taken on a return, the lawyer should frankly disclose his or her opinion as to whether the position is likely to be sustained in court if challenged by the Minister; and, if not, whether there is sufficient support for the position (a reasonable basis) to enable it to be asserted at all, but with adequate disclosure to the Minister. There is no reason why lawyers cannot advise taxpayers to resolve honest doubts in their own favour, provided the circumstances are adequately disclosed. But, if there is inadequate disclosure, tax lawyers fail in their duty of candour if they advise the reporting of positions that are not honestly believed to be meritorious.

(d)   Litigation

In litigation, where the lawyer is representing the client in a dispute with the Minister, there do not seem to be any ethical issues that are unique to the tax context. In tax litigation, as in other litigation, the lawyer's duties of honesty and candour require that the lawyer be scrupulous never to mislead his or her opponent or the court by misstating the facts or the law, or by failing to inform the court of a relevant authority. The failure to inform the court of a relevant authority is a breach of legal ethics, even if the authority is adverse to the client and has been overlooked by the opponent's lawyer.

Within these constraints, a lawyer is free to urge on behalf of the client any position that is fairly arguable, even if the lawyer believes that position to be unmeritorious. In the role of an advocate (as opposed to an adviser), the lawyer is not asserting his or her own personal opinion as to the correct legal position, but is simply submitting arguments on behalf of the client. The lawyer leaves to the court the task of evaluating the strengths of the competing arguments, and determining what is the correct legal position.

(e)   Planning

As a planner, the tax lawyer is an adviser and not an advocate. The duties of honesty and candour impose higher standards on the adviser than on the advocate.

No real problem arises with respect to an illegal or deceptive (sham) scheme. Obviously, the lawyer cannot advise the client to engage in illegality or deception, and if the client decides to do so anyway the lawyer must stop acting for the client. It may well be the case that there is only a small risk that the Department will detect and attack the scheme, but that is not a factor that could justify engaging in illegality or deception. If the client decided to play the audit lottery, and take the risk, the lawyer must withdraw his or her representation.

Nor does any ethical issue arise with respect to tax-planned transactions that are within the spirit as well as the letter of the Act. Obviously, the tax lawyer may, indeed must, lend his or her aid to the client who seeks to minimize taxes by means that are contemplated by the Act.

The difficult issue concerns the tax-avoidance scheme that is not a sham and that appears to be permitted by the letter of the Act, but which seems to be contrary to the object and spirit of the Act. In such a case there is a risk that the scheme will be ineffective, either because the provisions of the Act will be interpreted (in accordance with their object and spirit) as not according the claimed tax benefit, or because the general anti-avoidance rule will be invoked by the Minister to nullify the claimed tax benefit. If in the judgment of the lawyer the tax-avoidance scheme if challenged would probably not be upheld by the courts, then it is unethical for the lawyer to advise the client or help the client to implement the scheme, using the argument that the risk of detection and challenge by the Minister is low. If in the judgment of the lawyer the scheme if challenged would probably be upheld by the courts, that is, the transaction is a genuine one that does not fall afoul of the Act, including the general anti-avoidance rule, then it is hard to argue that any norm of professional responsibility is violated if the lawyer accepts the client's instructions to carry out the scheme. The lawyer is representing the taxpayer, not the Minister, and the public-policy reasons for opposing tax avoidance which were outlined earlier in this chapter[66] are not sufficiently specific and powerful to overcome the lawyer's duty to act in the interests of the client.

---

[66] Section 22.2, "Tax avoidance", above.

Index

References are to sections, not pages.

INDEX

References are to sections, not pages.

References are to sections, not pages.

INDEX

References are to sections, not pages.

INDEX

References are to sections, not pages.

INDEX

References are to sections, not pages.

References are to sections, not pages.

References are to sections, not pages.

INDEX

References are to sections, not pages.

CHILD
alimony and maintenance *See* ALIMONY AND MAINTENANCE
attribution of income *See* ATTRIBUTION RULES
child tax benefit, 4.5(d), 7.3, 17.10
definition of, 7.5(c)
family as taxation unit *See* TAXATION UNIT
support *See* ALIMONY AND MAINTENANCE

CHILD CARE EXPENSES
business expense, not a, 11.4
definition of, 3.5(b), 13.6
women, effect on, *See* WOMEN

CLUB DUES
employment benefit *See* EMPLOYMENT INCOME
business expense, not a, *See* BUSINESS INCOME

COLLECTION AGREEMENTS, 1.1

COLLECTION PROCEDURE *See* COMPLIANCE

COMMON-LAW SPOUSE *See* SPOUSE

COMMUTING EXPENSES, 13.3

COMPLIANCE
appeal, 2.5(h)
    deduction for expenses, 17.1
assessment, 2.5(c), 6.3(d)
audit and examination, 2.5(d)-(e)
avoidance of tax *See* AVOIDANCE
burden of proof, 2.5(i)
collection procedures, 2.5
confidentiality, 2.5(l)
E-file, 2.5(a)
evasion, 2.6, 22.1
fairness package, 2.5(k)n
instalments, 6.2(b)
interest, 2.5(c), 6.3(e), 10.10(b)
investigatory powers, 2.6(c)
objection, 2.5(g)
    deduction for expenses, 17.1
payment of tax, 2.5(b), 6.2, 6.3
    liability of transferee, 7.5(j)n
penalties, 2.5(i), 2.6(b), 10.10(c)
prescribed rate of interest *See* interest

INDEX

References are to sections, not pages.

References are to sections, not pages.

INDEX

References are to sections, not pages.

INDEX

References are to sections, not pages.

References are to sections, not pages.

rent, 10.9(b)
stock options, 10.1n, 10.6(a)
supplies, 10.9(b)
travelling expenses, 10.9(b)
union dues, 10.9(b)
definition of employment, 10.4(a)
employee stock option deduction *See* deductions
loan
advance compared *See* advance
home relocation loans *See* deductions
interest-free or low interest *See* benefits
loss of employment, compensation for, 10.8 *See also* RETIRING ALLOWANCE
moving expenses *See* MOVING EXPENSES
office
business compared, 10.4(c)
definition, 10.4(a)
employment compared, 10.4(b)
prizes and awards *See* benefits
received basis, 10.3
reimbursement of expenses, 10.6(e), 10.9(c)
relocation costs *See* MOVING EXPENSES
severance payment *See* loss of employment, compensation for
salary, 10.2, 10.5
unpaid remuneration, 10.4(a)

ENFORCEMENT *See* COMPLIANCE

EQUITY
capital gains taxation, 15.3, 15.4(c)
conversion of deductions to credits, 4.5(c)
definition, 4.3
family as taxation unit, 7.1(b)
horizontal equity, 4.3
imputed income, taxation of, 9.9(d)
neutrality compared, 4.4(b)
progressivity See PROGRESSIVE TAXES
vertical equity, 4.3
world income versus Canadian income, 8.1(b)

ESTATE *See* DEATH, TRUSTS

ESTATE FREEZE, 21.7(c)

ESTATE PLANNING *See* ESTATE FREEZE

References are to sections, not pages.

INDEX

References are to sections, not pages.

INDEX

References are to sections, not pages.

INDEX

References are to sections, not pages.

References are to sections, not pages.

INDEX

References are to sections, not pages.

INDEX

References are to sections, not pages.

References are to sections, not pages.

NEUTRALITY, 4.2, 4.4, 5.3
capital gains taxation, 15.3(b), 15.4(c)
equity compared, 4.4(b)
imputed income, taxation of, 9.9(d)

NON-ARM'S LENGTH *See* NOT AT ARM'S LENGTH

NON-CAPITAL LOSS *See* LOSSES

NON-DEPRECIABLE PROPERTY *See* DEPRECIABLE PROPERTY

NON-RESIDENTS
business income versus property income, 12.1(b)
departure tax *See* DEPARTURE TAX
foreign accrual property income (FAPI), 8.10(b)
rental income (s. 216 election), 8.3n
residence *See* RESIDENCE
s. 217 election, 8.3n
tax liability, 8.3
tax treaties *See* TAX TREATIES
tests for corporations, 8.6
tests for individuals, 8.5

NOT AT ARM'S LENGTH
related persons, 7.5(c), 22.4(a)
significance, 7.5(c), 10.6(a), 22.4(a)

NOTHINGS *See* CAPITAL EXPENDITURES

OBJECTIONS *See* COMPLIANCE

OBJECTIVES
ability to pay *See* EQUITY
balance, 4.2
economic stabilization, 4.2
economic growth, 4.2
equity *See* EQUITY
fairness *See* EQUITY
international competitiveness, 4.2
neutrality *See* NEUTRALITY
progressivity *See* PROGRESSIVE TAXES
revenue, 4.1, 4.2
simplicity, 4.2

OFFICE OR EMPLOYMENT *See* EMPLOYMENT INCOME

INDEX

References are to sections, not pages.

INDEX

References are to sections, not pages.

INDEX

References are to sections, not pages.

INDEX

References are to sections, not pages.

INDEX

References are to sections, not pages.

tax-free transfer to other plans, 17.3
vesting, 17.7(b)n

REGISTERED RETIREMENT INCOME FUNDS (RRIFs), 17.5(g), (h)

REGISTERED RETIREMENT SAVINGS PLANS (RRSPs), 17.5
annuities, 17.5(f)
death of annuitant *See* DEATH
deductible contributions, 17.5(c), 17.5(d), 17.8
    carryforward of unused limit, 17.5(d)
    deadline, 17.5(d)
    earned income, 17.5(c), 17.5(d), 17.8
    phase-in of limits, 17.5(c), 17.8
    refund of premiums, 17.5(d), 17.5(h), 17.8
    retiring allowance, 17.5(d), 17.7
deferred profit sharing plan compared, 17.5(a) *See also* DEFERRED PROFIT SHARING PLANS
definition, 17.5(a)
direct transfers, 17.8
earned income, 17.5(d)
group RRSPs, 17.8
homebuyer's plan, 17.5(e)
included in income at age 71, 17.5(f)
locked-in RRSP, 17.8n
pension adjustment, 17.5(c), 17.5(d)
policy objectives, 17.5(c)
postponement of tax, 17.5(b)
refund of premiums, 17.5(h)
registered pension plan compared, 17.5(a) *See also* REGISTERED PENSION PLANS (RPPs)
registered retirement income funds (RRIFs) *See* REGISTERED RETIREMENT INCOME FUNDS (RRIFs)
self-administered, 17.5(d)
spousal plans, 7.3
    contributions, 17.5(d)
    withdrawals taxable, 17.5(e)
withdrawals taxable, 17.2, 17.5(e)
withholding tax, 17.5(e)

REGRESSIVE TAXES, 5.2(d)

REGULATIONS, 1.3, 2.5

RELATED PERSONS, 7.5(c) *See also* NOT AT ARM'S LENGTH

INDEX

References are to sections, not pages.

RELOCATION COSTS *See* MOVING EXPENSES

RENT *See* PROPERTY INCOME

RENTAL PROPERTY
capital cost allowance restrictions See CAPITAL COST ALLOWANCE
income *See* PROPERTY INCOME

REPLACEMENT PROPERTY *See* CAPITAL GAIN

RESEARCH AND DEVELOPMENT *See* BUSINESS INCOME

RESERVES
deduction, 11.4, 13.9n
for future proceeds *See* CAPITAL GAIN

RESIDENCE, 8.1-8.10
corporations, 8.6
citizenship compared, 8.1(c)
departure tax, 8.9
domicile compared to, 8.1(d)
individuals, 8.5
part-time, 8.2, 8.4, 10.1n
provincial, 8.8
tax havens, 8.10
taxation of non-residents *See* NON-RESIDENTS
treaties, 8.10(c)
trusts, 8.7

RETIREMENT SAVINGS *See* PENSIONS AND RETIREMENT SAVINGS

RETIRING ALLOWANCE, 17.7
deduction for contributions to RRSP, 17.7(b)
definition, 10.8, 17.7(a)
employment income compared, 10.8
tax-free damages compared, 10.8

RETURNS *See* COMPLIANCE

REVENUE CANADA *See* DEPARTMENT OF NATIONAL REVENUE

REVENUES, 4.1

ROLLOVERS
corporation, transfers to, 15.15(a), 15.15(d)
definition, 15.15(a)
farm property and farm corporations, 7.3, 7.5(n), 15.15(a), 15.15(c)

INDEX

References are to sections, not pages.

INDEX

References are to sections, not pages.

INDEX

References are to sections, not pages.

imputed income *See* IMPUTED INCOME
source theory *See* SOURCE THEORY OF INCOME
tax reform 1971, 3.5(b)
tax reform 1988, 3.7(b)
wealth tax *See* WEALTH TAX
windfalls *See* WINDFALLS

TAX CREDITS *See* CREDITS

TAX COURT OF CANADA, 2.5(e), 22.5(h), 22.5(a) *See also* COMPLIANCE

TAX DEFERRAL *See* POSTPONEMENT OF TAX

TAX EXPENDITURES, 4.6
alimony and maintenance, 17.9(b)
benchmark system, 4.6(b)
definition, 4.6(b)
direct expenditures compared, 4.6(a), 4.6(c)
public reporting, 4.6(a)
retirement savings plans, 17.5(c)
workers' compensation, 17.10

TAX PLANNING *See* AVOIDANCE, ESTATE FREEZE, POSTPONEMENT
    OF TAX, TRUSTS

TAX RATES *See* RATES OF TAX

TAX REFORM 1971, 3.5
base broadening, 3.5(b)
capital gains, 3.5(c)
capital losses, 3.5(b)
Carter Commission *See* CARTER COMMISSION REPORT
charitable donations, 3.5(b)
child care expenses, 3.5(b)
dividends, 19.2(c), 19.3(b)
eligible capital expenditures, 14.3
employment income deductions, 3.5(b)
exemptions, 3.5(c)
integration of personal and corporate taxes, 3.5(d)
moving expenses, 3.5(b)
rate structure, 3.5(c), 19.3(b)
unemployment insurance premiums, 3.5(b)
white paper, 3.5(a)

TAX REFORM 1988, 3.7, 4.6(a)
base broadening, 3.7(c)

References are to sections, not pages.

INDEX

References are to sections, not pages.

INDEX

References are to sections, not pages.

WITHHOLDING TAX
employment income, 6.3(a), 10.4(e), 10.10(a), 10.10(c)
non-resident, 8.3, 8.4, 8.10(c)
registered retirement savings plans, 17.5(e)

WOMEN
alimony and maintenance *See* ALIMONY AND MAINTENANCE
attribution rules *See* ATTRIBUTION RULES
disincentives to paid employment family unit of taxation, 7.3(d)
    household labour, taxation of, 9.9(b)
    spousal credit, 7.2(d), 9.9(b)
family *See* FAMILY
incentives to paid employment
    child care expense deduction, 9.9(b)
    income split due to individual unit of taxation, 9.9(b)
spouse *See* SPOUSE

WORKERS' COMPENSATION, 17.10
deduction from taxable income, 10.1n
inclusion in tax base, 9.8, 17.10
tax expenditure, 17.10

YEAR END *See* TAXATION YEAR